Doing Digital Humanities

Digital Humanities is rapidly evolving as a significant approach to/method of teaching, learning and research across the humanities. This is a first-stop book for people interested in getting to grips with digital humanities whether as a student or a professor. The book offers a practical guide to the area as well as offering reflection on the main objectives and processes, including:

- accessible introductions to the basics of DH through to more complex ideas;
- a wide range of topics from feminist DH, digital journal publishing, gaming, text encoding, project management and pedagogy;
- contextualized case studies;
- resources for starting DH such as links, training materials and exercises.

Doing Digital Humanities looks at the practicalities of how digital research and creation can enhance both learning and research, and offers an approachable way into this complex, yet essential topic.

Constance Crompton is Assistant Professor of Digital Humanities at the University of British Columbia – Okanagan Campus, Canada.

Richard J. Lane is a Professor and Principal Investigator of the MeTA Digital Humanities Lab at Vancouver Island University, Canada.

Ray Siemens is the Canada Research Chair in Humanities Computing and Distinguished Professor in the Faculty of Humanities in English and Computer Science at the University of Victoria, Canada.

Doing Digital Humanities

Practice, Training, Research

Edited by
Constance Crompton,
Richard J. Lane and
Ray Siemens

LONDON AND NEW YORK

First published 2016
by Routledge
2 Park Square, Milton Park, Abingdon, Oxon OX14 4RN

and by Routledge
711 Third Avenue, New York, NY 10017

Routledge is an imprint of the Taylor & Francis Group, an informa business

British Library Cataloguing-in-Publication Data
A catalogue record for this book is available from the British Library

Library of Congress Cataloging-in-Publication Data
Names: Crompton, Constance (Constance Louise Kathleen), author. | Lane, Richard J., 1966– author. | Siemens, Raymond George, 1966– author.
Title: Doing digital humanities : practice, training, research/ Constance Crompton, Richard J. Lane and Ray Siemens.
Description: 1st edition. | New York, NY: Routledge, [2016] | Includes bibliographical references and index.
Identifiers: LCCN 2016002745 | ISBN 9781138899438 (hardback: alk. paper) | ISBN 9781138899445 (pbk.: alk. paper) | ISBN 9781315707860 (ebook)
Subjects: LCSH: Humanities—Methodology. | Humanities—Research. | Digital media.
Classification: LCC AZ105 .A35 2014 | DDC 001.301—dc23
LC record available at https://lccn.loc.gov/2016002745

ISBN: 9781138899438 (hbk)
ISBN: 9781138899445 (pbk)
ISBN: 9781315707860 (ebk)

Typeset in Helvetica Neue and Avant Garde
by Florence Production Ltd, Stoodleigh, Devon, UK

Printed and bound in the United States of America
by Edwards Brothers Malloy

Contents

Figures

Tables

Notes on contributors

Jon Bath is Assistant Professor, Art and Art History, and Director of the Humanities and Fine Arts Digital Research Centre at the University of Saskatchewan. He teaches electronic art, digital humanities and the book arts. He is the co-lead of the Modeling and Prototyping team of Implementing New Knowledge Environments (www.inke.ca).

Syd Bauman is an expert in text encoding and XML, with a special interest in the Text Encoding Initiative (TEI). He is the Senior XML Programmer/Analyst for the Women Writers Project, one of the oldest TEI projects in existence. Syd has served as the co-editor of the TEI Guidelines, and on the TEI Technical Council. He occasionally provides XML, TEI and XSLT consulting for DH projects, and often teaches workshops on XML, TEI and XSLT.

Matt Bouchard is a PhD student in the Faculty of Information at the University of Toronto and a researcher with the Semaphore Games Research Cluster. His dissertation work examines player meaning-making in minimalist games. More broadly, Matt is working on video game design, experimental interface design, visualization and implementation advocacy. Professionally, he is an implementation and technology consultant for research groups and businesses.

Susan Brown is Professor of English at the University of Guelph and Visiting Professor at the University of Alberta. Her research addresses interface design, semantic technologies, visualization, infrastructure and both gender and new technologies in Victorian literature. These interests inform *Orlando: Women's Writing in the British Isles from the Beginnings to the Present*, an experiment in digital literary history that she directs and co-edits. She leads the Canadian Writing Research

Collaboratory, an online research environment for literary studies in and about Canada, and is President of the Canadian Society for Digital Humanities/Société canadienne des humanités numériques.

Hélène Cazes is the Director of the Program of Medieval Studies at the University of Victoria. She is also the President of the Canadian Society for Renaissance Studies, Vice-President for the Canadian Society for Renaissance Studies, and Associate Editor for *Renaissance et Réforme/Renaissance and Reformation*. She is the recipient of the Faculty of Humanities Award for Research Excellence for 2013.

Nicole Clouston is a practice-based researcher currently completing her PhD in Visual Art at York University. Nicole uses scientific techniques as artistic medium in her sculptural work creating a new context for engaging the ineffable aspects of scientific knowledge. She has exhibited her work in Victoria, Toronto, and Montreal. Nicole was awarded a SSHRC Canada Graduate Research Scholarship and was the recipient of the Anne Lazare-Mirvish Award. Further information on Nicole and her practice can be found at www.nicoleclouston.com.

Sarah Connell is the project manager for the Women Writers Project at Northeastern University. She is involved with several other projects and initiatives in Northeastern's Digital Scholarship Group, including the Early Caribbean Digital Archive. Her research examines the political work that genre performs in medieval and early modern historical narratives, showing how theories of textual taxonomy enabled writers to negotiate colonial encounters. She is currently developing a text encoding project that applies the theories established in her dissertation, *"No Room in History": Genre and Identity in British and Irish National Histories, 1541–1691*, to an initial set of early historical works.

Robin Davies teaches in the Media Studies Department at Vancouver Island University. He studied Double Bass and Music Technology at McGill's Schulich School of Music. His interests include the utilization of the human voice in aural storytelling, sound design for visual art, the construction and use of software-based musical instruments for live electronic music performance, and helping others embrace technology for use in their creative endeavours. Robin's musical compositions, sound design and remix work can be heard on releases from Six Records, Maple Music, Ad Noiseam, Phoenicia Publishing and Sunchaser Pictures.

Quinn Dombrowski is the Digital Humanities Coordinator in the Research IT group at UC Berkeley. She holds a BA/MA in Slavic Languages and Literatures from the University of Chicago, and an MLIS from the University of Illinois at Urbana–Champaign. Quinn was part of the program staff of Project Bamboo, and co-founded the project directory DHCommons. She has led the DiRT (Digital Research Tools) Directory, formerly Bamboo DiRT, since 2011. Quinn has worked closely with scholars on developing digital humanities projects ranging from an atlas of Bulgarian dialectology and folk culture to a catalogue raisonné for Jan Brueghel.

Maciej Eder is Associate Professor at the Institute of Polish Studies at the Pedagogical University of Kraków, Poland, and at the Institute of Polish Language at the Polish Academy of Sciences. He is interested in European literature of the Renaissance and the Baroque, classical heritage in early modern literature, and scholarly editing.

Katherine Faull is Professor of German and Humanities at Bucknell University in Pennsylvania, USA where she is currently Director of the Program in Comparative Humanities. Trained in the UK and US as a philologist, Katie works increasingly digitally with archival materials from the Moravian church of the eighteenth century. Her textual and geo-spatial mapping work has become an integral part of the National Parks Service's new Indigenous Cultural Landscape interpretive plan for the Susquehanna River.

Julia Flanders is a Professor of Practice in the Department of English at Northeastern University and the Director of the Digital Scholarship Group in the Northeastern University Library. She also directs the Women Writers Project, and serves as editor-in-chief of *Digital Humanities Quarterly* and co-Director of the TEI Archiving, Publishing, and Access Service (TAPAS). Her work focuses on text encoding, humanities data modeling and digital scholarly communication.

Alex Gil is the Digital Scholarship Coordinator for Humanities and History at Columbia University. He specializes in twentieth-century Caribbean literature and digital humanities, with an emphasis on textual studies. He has published in journals in Canada, France and the United States, while sustaining an open and robust online research presence. In 2010–12 he was a fellow at the Scholars' Lab and NINES at the University of Virginia. He now serves as chair of the GO::DH initiative and is actively engaged in several digital humanities projects in New York City and around the world.

Ian Gregory is Professor of Digital Humanities at Lancaster University. A geographer by training, he has worked extensively on using GIS in historical research. Much of this work was initially concerned with quantitative sources; however, more recently he has worked on analysing historical and literary texts in GIS. He is PI on the European Research Council-funded *Spatial Humanities: Texts, GIS, Places* project which is exploring this topic. He has written or edited four books on using GIS in the humanities and published over fifty journal articles or book chapters.

Dene Grigar is Professor and Director of The Creative Media & Digital Culture Program at Washington State University Vancouver whose research focuses on the creation, curation, preservation and criticism of electronic literature. She has authored fourteen media works such as "Curlew" (2014), "A Villager's Tale" (2011), the "24-Hour Micro E-Lit Project" (2009), "When Ghosts Will Die" (2008) and "Fallow Field: A Story in Two Parts" (2005), as well as fifty-two scholarly articles. She also curates exhibits of electronic literature and media art, mounting shows at the Library of Congress and for the International Symposium on Electronic Art and the Modern Language Association, among other venues. With Stuart Moulthrop (University of Wisconsin Milwaukee) she is the recipient of a 2013 NEH Start Up grant for a digital preservation project for early electronic literature that culminated into an open-source, multimedia book for scholars entitled *Pathfinders*, and a book of criticism, entitled *Traversals*.

N. Katherine Hayles is Professor of Literature and Director of Graduate Studies at Duke University, as well as Distinguished Professor Emerita at UCLA. She is author *of How We Think: Digital Media and Contemporary Technogenesis* (Chicago 2012), *Electronic Literature* (Notre Dame 2008), *My Mother Was a Computer* (Chicago 2005), *Writing Machines* (MIT 2002) and *How We Became Posthuman* (Chicago 1999). Her awards include a Guggenheim Fellowship, two NEH Fellowships, a Rockefeller Residential Fellowship at Bellagio, a fellowship at the National Humanities Center, and two Presidential Research Fellowships from the University of California. She has received a Distinguished Scholar Award from the University of Rochester, the Medal of Honor from the University of Helsinki and the Distinguished Scholar Award from the International Association for the Fantastic in the Arts.

David L. Hoover is Professor of English at New York University. Recent publications include the *Digital Literary Studies: Corpus Approaches to Poetry, Prose, and Drama* (2014), with Jonathan Culpeper and Kieran O'Halloran, and "Modes of Composition in Henry James: Dictation, Style, and *What Maisie Knew*," *Henry James Review*, 35(3), 2014: 257–277. Active in digital humanities for more than thirty years, he is currently writing a book on how modes of composition (handwriting, dictation, typing, word-processing) affect authorial style.

J. Matthew Huculak is a Postdoctoral Fellow with the Department of English, The University Library, and the Electronic Textual Cultures Lab at the University of Victoria. He is Co-Founder of the Modernist Versions Project and has taught at DHSI for three years.

Diane Jakacki is the Digital Scholarship Coordinator and Faculty Teaching Associate in Comparative Humanities at Bucknell University, where she explores and institutes new ways in which digital humanities tools and methodologies can be leveraged in research and teaching in a small liberal arts environment. She earned her PhD at the University of Waterloo, and was a Marion L. Brittain Postdoctoral Fellow at the Georgia Institute of Technology. She is an assistant director of DHSI, where she teaches the Digital Pedagogy course. She is also a member of the Map of

Early Modern London's editorial board, the Internet Shakespeare Editions's Pedagogical Advisory Board and the Records of Early English Drama's Digital Advisory Committee, and has published widely on the intersection of digital humanities and early modern studies.

Andy Keenan is a PhD candidate at the University of Toronto's Faculty of Information and Semaphore Games Research Cluster. Andy has experience as a new media and information studies scholar, exploring how users encounter unfamiliar objects and critically evaluating the relationships between audiences and media. His current research looks at player experience in video games with a specific focus on the differences in gameplay practices between expert and novice players.

Christopher P. Long is Dean of the College of Arts and Letters at Michigan State University. His extensive publications in Ancient Greek and contemporary Continental philosophy include three books. His most recent is an enhanced digital book entitled *Socratic and Platonic Political Philosophy: Practicing a Politics of Reading* (Cambridge 2014), the digital platform of which enables readers to engage directly with the author in an online community. He is co-founder of the *Public Philosophy Journal* and he blogs at www.cplong.org. He can be reached on Twitter @cplong.

Elizabeth Losh is an Associate Professor of English and American Studies at William and Mary with a specialization in New Media Ecologies. Before coming to William and Mary, she directed the Culture, Art, and Technology Program at the University of California, San Diego. She is the is the author of *Virtualpolitik: An Electronic History of Government Media-Making in a Time of War, Scandal, Disaster, Miscommunication, and Mistakes* (MIT Press, 2009) and *The War on Learning: Gaining Ground in the Digital University* (MIT Press, 2014). She is the co-author of the comic book textbook *Understanding Rhetoric: A Graphic Guide to Writing* (Bedford/St. Martin's, 2013) with Jonathan Alexander.

Mark A. Mattson is a Scholarly Publishing Associate at The Pennsylvania State University Libraries and Chair of the Penn State Libraries Publishing Board. He is responsible for the daily operations of the Libraries' journal publishing and bibliography publishing programs. Mark's professional interests include scholarly communication studies, open access publishing models, topical web-portal development and publishing, bibliographic database creation and conversion, and information organization and transmission. He is also the creator and curator of the MaBiMaMeth mark-up method. Mark received his MSLS from Clarion University of Pennsylvania.

Aaron Mauro is Assistant Professor of Digital Humanities and English at Penn State Erie, The Behrend College. He is the director of the Penn State Digital Humanities Lab and teaches on topics relating to digital culture, computational text analysis and scholarly communication. His articles on US literature and culture have appeared in *Modern Fiction Studies*, *Mosaic* and *symplokē* among others. He has also published on issues relating to digital humanities in both *Digital Studies* and *Digital Humanities Quarterly*.

Patricia Murrieta-Flores is the Director of the Digital Humanities Research Centre at the University of Chester, UK. Her interest lies in the application of technologies for Humanities research and her primary area of research is the Spatial Humanities and the investigation of different aspects of space, place and time using a range of technologies, including GIS and Corpus Linguistic approaches. She is part of the teams at the ERC and HERA projects "The Past in its Place" and "Deepdead," and she is also a collaborator in the "Spatial Humanities Project" at Lancaster University and the European Cost Action "Reassembling the Republic of Letters."

Michael Nixon is a PhD candidate at the School of Interactive Arts & Technology (Simon Fraser University). His research investigates how computational agents should best experience social relationships and demonstrate their social capabilities in order to participate in narrative experiences. He defended his MSc in 2009, which investigated the use of Delsarte's movement principles for animating believable characters. His other educational background includes a BSc in Computer Science and a diploma in Digital Media Technology from Vancouver Island University.

Élika Ortega is a Postdoctoral Researcher at the Institute for Digital Research in the Humanities at the University of Kansas. Her research focuses on electronic literature, media, intermediality, reading practices, digital humanities and multilingualism in academia. At KU, she has taught Digital Humanities at the graduate and undergraduate levels and co-directed the DH Seminar at the Hall Center for the Humanities between 2015 and 2016. Élika also co-curated the electronic literature exhibit *No Legacy || Literatura electrónica* at the University of California, Berkeley (2016). Her monograph in progress deals with print-digital works of literature from a world literature and comparative media studies perspective. Élika works actively in professional organizations and has been part of the executive committee of Global Outlook::Digital Humanities since 2014, and an executive council officer of the Association for Computers in the Humanities since 2015.

James O'Sullivan (@jamescosullivan) is Digital Humanities Research Associate at the University of Sheffield's Humanities Research Institute. Previous to this he held a faculty position at Pennsylvania State University, and is also currently an Adjunct Professor on the Creative Media & Digital Culture Program at Washington State University, Vancouver. James holds a PhD in Digital Arts & Humanities, as well as advanced degrees in computing, literary and cultural studies. James has been published in a variety of interdisciplinary journals, and in 2014, was shortlisted for the Fortier Prize. James is Chair of the DHSI Colloquium at the University of Victoria, and the founder of New Binary Press. Further information on James and his work can be found at http://josullivan.org.

Phillip R. Polefrone is a PhD Candidate in Columbia University's Department of English and Comparative Literature. His interests include twentieth-century American fiction, the digital humanities, ecocriticism and speculative fiction.

Harvey Quamen is an Associate Professor of English at the University of Alberta. He specializes in science studies, cyberculture, prosopography and Modern and Postmodern literature.

Geoffrey Rockwell is a Professor of Philosophy and Humanities Computing at the University of Alberta, Canada. He has published and presented papers in the area of big data, textual visualization and analysis, computing in the humanities, instructional technology, computer games and multimedia, including a book from Humanities Books, *Defining Dialogue: From Socrates to the Internet* and a forthcoming book from MIT Press, *Hermeneutica: Thinking Through Interpretative Text Analysis*. He is collaborating with Stéfan Sinclair on Voyant Tools (http://voyant-tools.org), a suite of text analysis tools, and leads the TAPoR (http://tapor.ca) project documenting text tools for humanists. He is currently the Director of the Kule Institute for Advanced Study.

Jan Rybicki is Assistant Professor at the Institute of English Studies, Jagiellonian University, Kraków, Poland; he also taught at Rice University, Houston, TX and Kraków's Pedagogical University. His interests include translation, comparative literature and humanities computing, with a particular focus on stylometry and authorship attribution.

Jentery Sayers is Assistant Professor of English, as well as Director of the Maker Lab in the Humanities, at the University of Victoria. His work has appeared in *American Literature*; *e-Media Studies*; *Digital Studies/Le champ numérique*; *The Victorian Review*; *New American Notes Online*; *Literature Compass*; *Computers and Composition Online*; *International Journal of Learning and Media*; *Kairos: Rhetoric, Technology, and Pedagogy*; and *Computational Culture*, among others. He is currently working on four books: *The Digging Condition* (University of Michigan Press), the *Routledge Companion to Media Studies and Digital Humanities* (ed., Routledge), *Making Humanities Matter* (ed., University of Minnesota Press) and *Digital Pedagogy in the Humanities* (ed., with Davis, Gold and Harris, Modern Language Association Books).

Lynne Siemens is an Associate Professor in the School of Public Administration, University of Victoria. Her interests include academic entrepreneurship, collaboration and team work with a focus on understanding methods and processes to facilitate collaborative research across distances, disciplines and organizational boundaries. She has taught workshops in Project Management at University of Victoria's Digital Humanities Summer Institute and University of Leipzig's European Summer School for Culture and Technology. Finally, she is serving as a management advisor for

Implementing New Knowledge Environments (INKE), a Major Collaborative Research Initiative project. Dr Siemens's role includes supporting the development of governance documents, organizational structure and project management.

John Simpson is currently the Digital Humanities Specialist for Compute Canada and is leading development of a national strategy to bring together Arts-based research with High-Performance Computing. He holds a PhD in Philosophy based on research into rational behaviour using agent-based simulations that he wrote himself. Outside of academia he is a manipulator of strings on screens, in hands, and on ukulele and banjo fret boards.

Stéfan Sinclair is Associate Professor of Digital Humanities at McGill University. His primary area of research is in the design, development, usage and theorization of tools for the digital humanities, especially for text analysis and visualization. He has led or contributed significantly to projects such as Voyant Tools, the Text Analysis Portal for Research (TAPoR), the MONK Project, the Simulated Environment for Theatre, the Mandala Browser and BonPatron. He is co-author, with Stan Ruecker and Milena Radzikowska, of *Visual Interface Design for Digital Cultural Heritage* (Ashgate 2011) and with Geoffrey Rockwell, of *Hermeneutica: Thinking Through Interpretative Text Analysis* (MIT 2016).

James Smith received a BS in Physics and Mathematics and an MA in English from Texas A&M University (TAMU). He has over fifteen years' experience developing and managing web applications in academic research and infrastructure environments. At TAMU, he helped pave the way for the development of the Initiative for Digital Humanities, Media, and Culture. As software architect for the Maryland Institute for Technology in the Humanities, he helped develop the Open Annotation data model. James teaches the *RDF and Linked Open Data* workshop at the Digital Humanities Summer Institute. He leads application interface development for external partnerships at Kit Check, Inc.

Jennifer Stertzer is Senior Editor of the Papers of George Washington and Manager of Digital Programs at the Center for Digital Editing, both at the University of Virginia. She also teaches Conceptualizing and Creating Digital Documentary Editions at the Digital Humanities Summer Institute and is on the faculty of the Institute for the Editing of Historical Documents.

Dennis Yi Tenen is Assistant Professor of English and Comparative Literature at Columbia University. A former software engineer at Microsoft and currently a faculty associate at the Berkman Center for Internet and Society at Harvard, he is working to complete a book manuscript called *Plain Text: The Poetics of Human-computer Interaction*, exploring the literary roots of modern computing. His work appears on the pages of *Computational Culture*, *boundary2* and *Modernism/modernity* on topics that range from book piracy to algorithmic composition, unintelligent design and the history of data visualization.

Jacqueline Wernimont is an Assistant Professor of English at Arizona State University, specializing in literary history, feminist digital media, histories of quantification and technologies of commemoration. She is currently a Fellow of the Lincoln Center for Applied Ethics, where she is working on a project on new civil rights that incorporates long histories of data, narrative and justice. She is also at work on two monographs: Writing Early Modern Worlds and How To Do Things with Numbers: Feminist Engagements in Quantopoetic Worlds. She is an active part of the FemTechNet collective.

Markus Wust is the Digital Research and Scholarship Librarian at North Carolina State University Libraries. For three years, he had taught a workshop on Augmented Reality at the Digital Humanities Summer Institute. He holds Master's degrees in German Literature (University of Georgia) as well as Library and Information Studies and Humanities Computing (University of Alberta).

Preface

Communities of practice, the methodological commons, and digital self-determination in the humanities[1]

Ray Siemens

INTRODUCTION: UNDERSTANDING THE *DIGITAL* HUMANITIES, AND BUILDING *IN MEDIAS RES*

No consideration of the larger elements of the digital humanities can be devoid of the sort of profitable, productive navel-gazing in which those in our community engage from time to time. One of the most profitable and most productive enterprises of this sort results from considering elements of the *digital* and those of the *humanities* as they come together, particularly as they do so in a frame provided by the notion of the humanities themselves. Such an approach often begins with a definition, one that rightly notes some key differences between the humanities and other disciplinary groups. Here, we often and rightly consider the humanities as a vibrant set of disciplines and sub-disciplines that has always had good currency and import over time, even though we may not have always called this grouping by the name of the Humanities as we do today – always changing, always reflecting, always looking at the nature of the human experience over time via the representation of that experience in its material manifestations. Here, further, we consider computation or the digital, itself, as a grouping of methods, approaches, technologies, and tools that are themselves dynamically and continually changing. When those outside the humanities and digital humanities typically talk about these two things, they readily accept that computation changes continually, but they often make the assumption that the humanities are staid and fixed, and have always been that way. Nothing, of course, could be further from the truth: each enterprise is dynamic, evolving, and in positive flux. Considering how these two come together is important as well; each brings dynamic perspectives, approaches, methods, and content that are meaningful not only to us as specialists but to the society we serve.

It is the point of intersection of humanities and computation – itself dynamic and changing like the elements it brings together – that provides the most valuable approach to an understanding of what the digital humanities are and where our ideas and our work together fit within the larger frames and contexts the digital humanities and the humanities more generally engage. Preaching to the choir, as they say, this is not a difficult case to make, but when we talk with those outside the humanities and digital humanities about our pursuits we not only need to define what the humanities are, in vibrant terms from whatever perspective(s) we best hold, and need to define what computing is, we also have to assert how the humanities *fit* in a digital age. An especially important context for such discussions is when well-meaning members of communities outside our own will approach us with offers like this: "We love the humanities. We respect what you're doing. Digital humanities is a growing, phenomenal enterprise. We will give you three positions for this . . . but they will be in computer science. [or] But we will be drawing on work done in [say] particle physics." And so on. All wonderful things, to be sure, but what happens with the core and key elements of the *humanities* in the *digital humanities* in such situations?

A larger question here is: How do the humanities fit in a digital age, reflecting and engaging not only its own traditions but, further, those of other disciplines implicated in, drawn in, partnered with, and fully incorporated and embraced by the methods utilized by the digital humanities. Does it do so by situating itself outside the humanities, outside of the very context that makes digital *humanities* different from other computational enterprises? I'd think not; I'd think we'd ideally work to situate it well within the humanities.

In such a place, our process of self-definition takes on a new importance, and an approach beyond one of high-level summation. Here, we might best engage the process of defining the digital humanities much more loosely and generally, ultimately in the forward-looking, open, inclusive vision of what has been termed the *Big Tent*, following the theme of the ADHO gathering at Stanford University, Digital Humanities 2011. In this situation, we talk about building on a tradition that began with textual enumerative and word-counting roots of a previous generation, continued in excellent and sterling work today across all media types and a whole host of approaches that bridge and link the past with the present and look into the future. Here, we talk about remediating old worlds and extant material artifacts, we talk about working with new ones that are created with the technologies we use, and we talk about embracing enlarging scope, privileging diversity within that embrace, and privileging public outreach and engagement. Here, we talk also about founding inclusive networks, bringing us together, encouraging us to collaborate, building method-centered communities of many kinds, and organizing at various levels to achieve common goals. And beyond. The many, many strengths of our community are, I believe, revealed by what this process raises.

Valuable and positively revealing as this process is, following this train of engagement has its challenges too, mostly relating to the specificity and detail excited by the process of definition itself, one that can be fraught even if for all the best reasons. As an exercise in this direction, try defining the scope of digital humanities. Try defining the digital humanities fully. Try defining it accurately, comprehensively. Try defining it in a way that two or three people will agree; then, a group of five or six hundred people. Try defining it in a way where you can situate your own program of research or that of your group in the context of others with whom you share, or are perceived to compete with for, resources; indeed, try talking with your department chair about this. Try defining it enough to be able to situate a group across a department or departments in a faculty, or across faculties. Perhaps most importantly: Try defining it in a way that is ultimately actionable, in a way that you can do something tangible with. There are strategies to do so, to be sure, but they can be fraught. When we do try to define in a way that can lead to action, especially at a local level within an institutional structure, we tend to arrive at institutional- or discipline-specific definitions; these do have some sort of gain in that you can frame digital humanities in the terms of extant structures, but ultimately there's a loss via disciplinarity's constraint in light of current and future growth, narrowing potential collaborative opportunities and limiting the vision of what the intersection points between the humanities and digital could lead to. Conversely, we can choose to ignore disciplinary and institutional structures, adopting the revolutionary approach we find reflected in the several excellent manifestos existing in the area – an approach picked up on in a lot of what some might call the *marketing* of our field – but, in ignoring those structures, we run the risk of losing access to their benefits.

Given this, I ask how can one begin to define all that the digital humanities are in a way that can lead to positive action now, in a way that does not constrain possibility of positive action in future? Truth be told, I am not sure this can be done to the degree of anyone's satisfaction, positive perfectionists that we in our community are, but even so I have had the pleasure of trying to do so, several times, with some wonderful colleagues. One was in the 2004 publication of *The Companion to Digital Humanities*, which I was very pleased to edit with Susan Schreibman and John Unsworth. We felt at the time to be relatively un-revolutionarily in our approach to the volume, working within the field as it then existed to provide an evolving, working definition of the digital humanities across many different types of approaches and focal points, arguing at a very high level from discipline and traditional disciplinary pursuits, to principles, practices, applications, and pragmatics of various kinds. We tried again in 2007, this time myself and Susan Schreibman in the *Companion to Digital Literary Studies*, arguing within the context of literary studies from sub-disciplinary traditions to issues of content and method modeling. This more generalized, multi-perspectived approach worked well. Even though such projects did not lead to a full, accurate, and comprehensive definition of the digital humanities toward action, I believe they led to a not-wholly-disappointing sense that such definition was going to be elusive . . . something best captured as an aside comment by my former dean and administrative sponsor of our Digital Humanities Summer Institute, Andrew Rippin, when he addressed our group in one of its nascent years, noting that something like Wikipedia was an apt and wonderful home for the expanding, changing, in-flux definition of digital humanities, a natural receptor for this confluence of two constantly changing points as they intersect.

Even though a full, accurate, comprehensive, and *fixed* definition of the digital humanities may be elusive, we need at least enough of an understanding of what the digital humanities are to be able to move our initiatives forward, to build further the profitable directions of the digital humanities. Toward this type of understanding, we have several options; I'll note a few of them. One is that we can work with the basis of what we already do and call digital humanities – or humanities computing, or 'les humanités informatique' – but we are not going to be able to move beyond what we already do if we label precisely and definitively in current contexts. Another is that we can take revolutionary steps, but in doing so we run the risk then of throwing the baby out in the bathwater, as they say, and in doing so disconnecting ourselves from a past and a set of institutional structures that are ultimately very valuable to us and, themselves, derive value from our endeavor. Another yet – my clear preference, and one that I see reflected in what many in our community readily do – is working with what we know and building positively towards a future that involves a reflection of the past, embracing the present, and continuing forward openly toward a number of possible futures.

For this approach, we need to switch our typical mode of thinking slightly, moving beyond a focus on *what* it is we do when we get together as digital humanists; we need to think more broadly about also *where*, *how*, and *with whom* it is we do what we do – ultimately considering *who* it is that we are.

CONSIDERING THE COMMUNITY OF PRACTICE AND THE METHODOLOGICAL COMMONS

In this context, and beyond, the notion of the community of practice is a helpful and useful way to think about our community, about *who* we are. My first encounter of that usage in the context of the digital humanities is in connection with the Text Encoding Initiative Consortium, where Julia Flanders and Daniel O'Donnell and a number of others were beginning to describe how the TEI community was evolving, and to situate the core principles of that evolution; conceptually, they were embracing work by Jean Lave and Etienne Wenger. Those core principles were found in and among the set of practices on which the TEI community was based, who was engaged in these practices, where they were engaged in them, and why they engaged in them. As it did for TEI, the notion of the community of practice here offers us a framework to consider and understand *who* we are via *what* it is we do, *where* we do what we do, and *why* we do it in the way that we do it. What is most unique about this frame is how it focuses us on the set of practices we share, who we share the practices with and where, on what we apply them, and to what end we do so. If we are willing to view ourselves from this perspective, through those practices in our community that make us unique and bring us together in that way, we can readily begin a move toward taking action that is less problematic that larger strategies of definition – a move that clarifies our understanding of the sorts of initiatives we might engage in together, that might bring us together, and the shapes that those sorts of initiatives and endeavors might take.

Ultimately, and very happily, the logical end of this view is that, having identified with this community of practice, we find ourselves members of the international Alliance of Digital Humanities Organizations via the constituent organizations that comprise ADHO – for me, that is the Canadian Society of Digital Humanities / Société canadienne des humanités numériques, though I've also had the pleasure of being active in the Association for Computers and the Humanities and other ADHO organizations, and my lab, the Electronic Textual Cultures Lab, is a member of CenterNet. In this context, ADHO itself serves the international structure of our community of practice, via its focus since inception on uniting our constituency as individuals in these larger organizational structures and ultimately providing the sorts of infrastructure and opportunities that bring us together to allow us to do the sorts of things that we all do – even as the communities in which we work at local, regional, national, and extra-national levels change, morph, evolve; even as the technologies change; even as our predilections about the work that we are doing changes; even as the disciplinary homes for many of us change. What sits at the core of any group like ADHO is the members of its community, what is most unique about those who are in the groups that make up ADHO is the set of practices that we all share as we identify with each other as digital humanists of various kinds.

The community of practice, at least in my experience in the digital humanities, has never been divorced from another notion key to what makes us digital humanists: the methodological commons. If what brings us together as a community is our practices, the notion of the methodological commons helps us understand key elements of the work we have done, our work now, and our work as we imagine it in the future – whatever the future might be. The methodological commons has been described, discussed, and envisioned for some time in our community by Harold Short, Willard McCarty, and others, and given good, iterative graphical representation over time; the most used images are "A rough intellectual map for humanities computing," which I include here from online sources (Figure 0.1); a report entitled "Mapping the Field to ALLC" (2002); and a later iteration (Figure 0.2) reflecting further engagement by our community distributed via the *Humanist Discussion Group* (2006).

In these depictions, we see the methodological commons imagined as a detailed series of convergence points between many disciplinary groups and ways/clouds

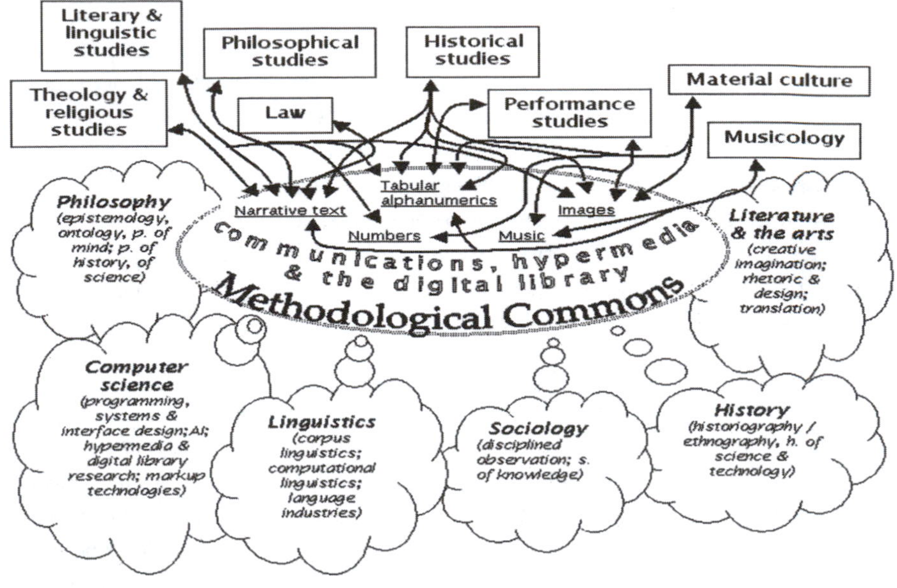

Figure 0.1
A rough intellectual map for humanities computing

Willard McCarty and Harold Short, in "Mapping the field: A report to the ALLC." 2002. Association for Literary and Linguistic Computing.

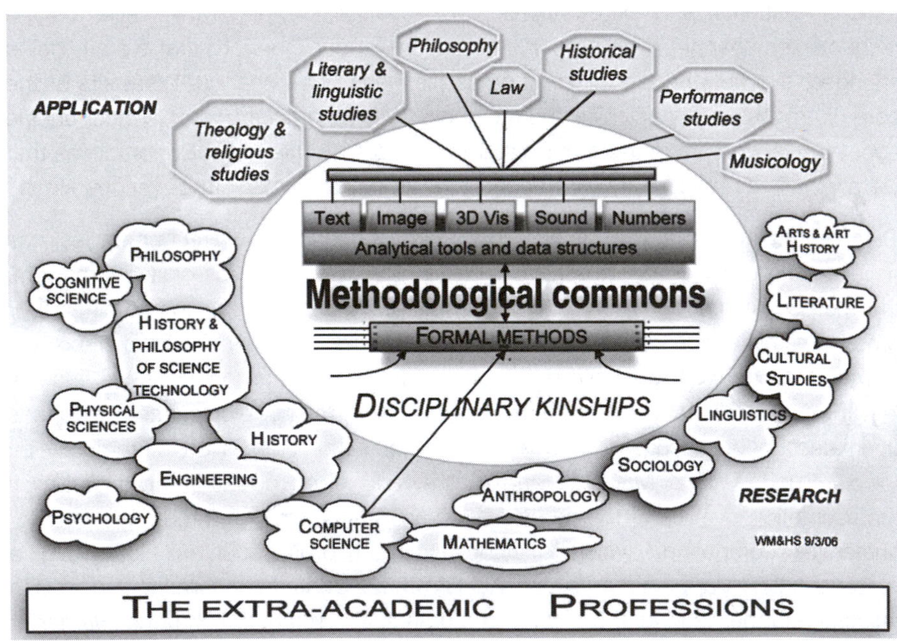

Figure 0.2
An intellectual and disciplinary map of humanities computing

Willard McCarty and Harold Short, via the HUMANIST discussion group. 2006. Alliance of Digital Humanities Organizations.

of knowing, meeting in and among those things central to the practices of our community: data and data structures modeling core materials, and tools modeling formal methods. Largely, the methodological commons focuses on disciplinary and extra-disciplinary interaction around modeled data derived from analog and other sources, and modeled process which we prototype in tools that enact our analytical and other methods on that data. Further, in addition to our content and process modeling, we also work within extant structures to communicate about our work. Using the lens of the methodological commons, we can identify with some accuracy past trends of the activities that brought our community together in the past, that we encounter now, and can imagine being prominent in future.

ENGAGING CORE TRENDS, IN CONTENT AND PROCESS MODELING

In the areas of data and process modeling, the trends we tend to anticipate readily and expectedly are increased data in digital format and increased access to large data in more standard and widely usable formats, as well as an increased familiarity with our tools generally among our colleagues and those beyond the expert communities in which we work and growth in tools that are used across disciplines and amalgamated extra-disciplinary data sets – allowing us to do more than we have ever done before, to explore and test ideas in ways we have never been able to do before. Aligned with this, further, our possibilities for communication are increasing, both in and among those working in our community and communities that exist around the data, and also broadening beyond those specialist communities, broadening beyond disciplinary scope, and extending much further in some cases. These trends, taken together, are in most ways for our community very positive and, at the same time, have potential to challenge us in the best ways possible. For example, in future the pace and scale of our increase in actual data is anticipated to rise at a rate far in excess of past growth, in part via our own incorporation of new methods of data generation, including socially based or crowd methods, and others beyond. At the same time, this significantly increased amount of data can be expected to be met by next-generation tools, themselves iteratively improving, modeling our academic processes – tools that increase the speed of our work across more and larger data sets, tools that are more readily accessible to those outside specialized disciplinary and sub-disciplinary groups, tools that (as we have seen trending in the past, in exemplary instances) are embraced up by members in society at large and put to very good use in contexts beyond those which spawned them. Add to that accelerated communicative patterns of various kinds, like the kind that we enjoy so well in the digital humanities community on Twitter not only with other experts in our community but also experts in other academic communities and, further, into the society at large that we serve.

Taken together, these anticipatable trends point in directions that are potentially very positive, particularly so if we see them as part of our working together towards a better ability to pose new types of questions, with better means of pursuing them, and better ability in our pursuit to reflect our results to experts and to those in the larger society we serve.

Our community will want to be prepared for this. The exact nature of those changes is hard to predict, of course, but if we are flexible in our understanding of what it is we do, how we do it, where we do it, and with whom we do it, we are ready for the positive challenges aligned with these trends that the future holds for us. Foreseeable changes to our data, our tools, and our communication strategies and patterns will alter the way humanities scholarship is done in the next generation at least as much as it has in the past generation, particularly so if these changes put us in considerably closer proximity to, and in contact with, the general public. Some very real and important differences could be realized through these changes in the near future.

Put another way, we might ask: How does our community of practice respond to these sorts of trends? One way is simply to be open about what it is we do, to speak openly about what we do, and to engage in processes that ultimately are productive but may not lead to any sure, fixed answer beyond providing a framework that allows us to take action as we anticipate what comes next – like the way in which we might most productively consider defining the digital humanities.

This is a pivotal moment, not only for the humanities and their connection to society at large but for the role of the digital humanist therein. It is no surprise to us and most of our humanities colleagues that the humanities are becoming increasingly more digital, of course, but what might be less well known outside of our close group is that those who practice the digital humanities are best poised to move us forward in this direction. The question is, how do we begin that movement?

TRAINING AND CURRICULUM DEVELOPMENT, IN CONTEXT

If we accept that we as digital humanists are a community of practice, defined in large part by that which is manifest in the methodological commons, then increased investment by us (and even those we serve) in our practice seems a logical way forward. Certainly this was a conclusion a number of our community reached several years ago, and worked then toward preparing a typology of digital humanities training for Digital Humanities 2010 at King's College London. In this work, we began by considering the least formal types of training, then working from the grassroots, bottom-up, to the most formal types. Among the many informal types of training we looked at, we included things like collegial discussions where one would have a question, know that a colleague down the hall had expertise to answer, and perhaps walk down the hall, knock on the door, and say, "I need your help. Can you show me how to do this?" And that person would quite likely say, in the generous spirit of the digital humanities generally, words like this: "Sure. Watch this. Just do what I do" (indeed, there is a whole training initiative and protocol based on that type of approach). It is hard to count the number of those types of essential interactions, but they happen all the time and form a foundation for us and how we work together; we see it online too. Formalize this sort of approach slightly, and we found we could point to similar types of exchanges, and beyond, in sessions of various kinds where people simply get together and talk on a regular basis over lunch or a drink about the sort of work that they are engaged in. Here, as we continued our work, we very quickly moved from these sorts of exchanges to those involving increasingly more formal consultations, and training events like regional, national, and international skills-based workshops. We then reversed our approach and, looking from the perspective of the most formal types of training, we saw a very different view. We began with more formal curriculum of an accredited kind, initially with dedicated PhD programs, then Masters and Undergraduate programs, DH "inflicted" programs, and occasional curriculum. This done, we consulted with members of our community and asked them about what factors were most important to them in and among what was emerging in our results. Our colleagues suggested that we look at things like institutional and field legitimacy, enrollment numbers, cost of delivery, formality of offering, ease of establishment and implementation, and beyond that toward, also, things like curricular agility with respect to developments in the field – indeed, for a field moving as quickly as ours is, agility is something that is very important to have in any sort of training structures we have.

We ultimately came up with what's best represented in Figure 0.3 (presented at DH 2010), where on the left you see the more formal types of training represented closer to the top, the more informal represented closer to the bottom, and you

<table>
<tr><th></th><th></th><th>Instit'l Legit'cy</th><th>Form'ty</th><th>PP cost Costs</th><th>Approx. #s</th><th>Ease to Impl'mt</th><th>Agility</th></tr>
<tr><td colspan="2">Formal / University Curriculum</td><td>Higher</td><td>Higher</td><td>Higher</td><td>Lower</td><td>Lower</td><td>Lower</td></tr>
<tr><td></td><td>Dedicated PhD programs</td><td>Λ</td><td>Λ</td><td>Λ</td><td>|</td><td>|</td><td>|</td></tr>
<tr><td></td><td>Dedicated Masters programs</td><td>|</td><td>|</td><td>|</td><td>|</td><td>|</td><td>|</td></tr>
<tr><td></td><td>Dedicated U'Grad programs</td><td>|</td><td>|</td><td>|</td><td>|</td><td>|</td><td>|</td></tr>
<tr><td>Current</td><td>Occasional / "inflected" accredited curriculum</td><td>|</td><td>|</td><td>|</td><td>|</td><td>|</td><td>|</td></tr>
<tr><td>Sweet -></td><td>International skills-based workshops</td><td>|</td><td>|</td><td>|</td><td>|</td><td>|</td><td>|</td></tr>
<tr><td>Spot?</td><td>Regional / Nat'l skills-based workshops</td><td>|</td><td>|</td><td>|</td><td>|</td><td>|</td><td>|</td></tr>
<tr><td></td><td>Local skills-based workshops</td><td>|</td><td>|</td><td>|</td><td>|</td><td>|</td><td>|</td></tr>
<tr><td></td><td>Formal consultations, brown-bag sessions</td><td>|</td><td>|</td><td>|</td><td>|</td><td>|</td><td>|</td></tr>
<tr><td></td><td>Collegial discussion, online networking</td><td>|</td><td>|</td><td>|</td><td>V</td><td>V</td><td>V</td></tr>
<tr><td colspan="2">Informal / Peer Networking</td><td>Lower</td><td>Lower</td><td>Lower</td><td>Higher</td><td>Higher</td><td>Higher</td></tr>
</table>

Figure 0.3
Types of training and related factors

find the factors that we associated with these types listed on the right in a legend at the top. In this typology, a dedicated PhD program is reflected as being much higher in terms of institutional legitimacy and formality, and also not surprisingly higher in terms of per-person costs; collegial discussion and online networking, by way of further example, are much higher in terms of the approximate numbers that one can train, ease of implementation, and responsive agility.

Further work focused on identifying positive patterns, ideally those working towards points of most positive intervention, suggesting where we should best consider investment of time and resources. In this, we increasingly came back to a sweet spot, a greatest point of potential impact, that we noted sat somewhere between occasional, inflected curriculum and regional, national skills-based workshops. This was revelatory to us four to five years ago. We had not expected the results of our research to point in this direction. What we had expected, then, were results supporting a "trickle-down" approach, where investment in developing more formal and more legitimized types of training – more PhD programs, more Masters programs – would have the greatest impact and lead to other types of training-related interactions in adjacent ways. What our work suggested instead to us was that a focus on those things in the sweet spot would have the greatest impact, directly and adjacently.

TAKING LOCAL ACTION IN THE INTERNATIONAL DH CONTEXT (DHSI, AND BEYOND)

Given our conclusions, the Digital Humanities Summer Institute – the initiative for which the Zampolli Prize is offered – became one of several intervention points. We took these findings back to members of the DHSI advisory group, constituted in a very informal way about fourteen years ago (we entered our fifteenth year in 2015), and we asked ourselves a number of the same questions related to this investigation. The result was that we decided that we would work with the community to invest more heavily in DHSI and like enterprises. Our discussions, at least initially, focused on the way in which we were operating in relation to other training types in that model our research suggested, focused on issues related to ease of agility and implementation, focused also on the number of members of our community we could work with at any one given time, and also began to explore what we were doing locally at the University of Victoria as it related to the world represented in our community of practice by the constituent organizations of ADHO as well as ADHO itself.

A key strategic response among those at my institution who support DHSI was, further, to agree in principle that we would work the sweet spot upwards, in that we imagined additional investment in DHSI would also be the most ready way to begin development toward a formally accredited curriculum, MA and PhD programs.

This manifest as an additional concern relating to the possibility of blending formally directed and participant-driven curriculum in an accredited framework. Members of our community may know that at DHSI we offer training in basic digital scholarly pragmatics and essential skills, and then we layer offerings requiring additional expertise from that, and, just as importantly, that each year we put out a call for proposals for those who would like to teach the sort of work that they are engaged in and expert in at DHSI. This is how we have, over time, ensured that our community drives the curriculum we offer, and every year we offer as many of those courses as we possibly can – subject to local processes and infrastructure availability. At the same time as continuing development and growth along those lines, we also began looking for ways to work with others, to bring others consciously into our community, to bring them to us locally and to bring us to them locally, to bring them more broadly into the sort of training that we were doing and into our community of practice. In these efforts, we have been very, very lucky in working not only with a number of exemplary members of our community to advise, organize, and offer DHSI each year, but also with a number of generous partners and sponsors – all of whom and which ensure that we continue to operate in this very positive way.

At the same time as our group decided to work with the community to extend DHSI in ways the community felt was appropriate, and pursue in addition a slowly-and-steadily developing accreditation model, we also began working together with other groups who were making similar investments in training toward what was, before 2012, an informal and collegial network of digital humanities institutes. This network was ADHO-proximate, and soon (after a meeting at the DH conference in Hamburg in 2012) started moving toward articulating itself as an international training network, one in which members of this group began considering what is it we do, how we could work together, how we could share our foundational courses, how we could together sustain training at the expert and intermediate levels of our offerings, and how we could ensure that our efforts were distributed temporally and geographically to members of our constituencies who were most engaged in what it is we do. Further points of collaboration and cooperation emerged, having us engaged in many positive ways with each other: working within and among members of the DHSI partner network and well beyond; working not only with institutions and, say, faculties and departments within institutions, but also with research centers within and across institutions; working with large research programs; working with large agencies beyond ADHO, including constituent organizations like the Canadian DH group and also ACH, but also having a pleasure of working with groups like HASTAC, the Modern Language Association, the highly interdisciplinary Canadian Federation of Humanities and Social Sciences, and with our funding agency, the Social Science and Humanities Research Council of Canada. Such mutual benefit in working together also yielded, as we pushed locally for accredited curriculum, the ability for us to articulate that curriculum in a graduate certificate program that draws on the best of what it is we do across *all* the training institutes in our informal network (with possibility of those beyond) by allowing those enrolled in this program to take two of a total of five courses needed to complete the program at institutions outside of Victoria; specifically, we look forward to further partnership here.

Next steps in this vein have been to work toward a more formal ADHO network for digital humanities training which, after several years of formal and informal consultation in this vein, was recognized by ADHO at the 2014 conference in Lausanne. As identified by a questionnaire circulated widely to members of our community as we were engaging in consultation about this, elements of our mandate are already taking shape; these include: coordinating international partnerships; coordinating curriculum across institutes; discussing curricular models; sharing publicity; having a formal summit on DH training; engaging in temporal and geographic coordination so that offerings in the area are available more broadly; and offering advice and peer support – all in a context that I think represents the diversity and many strengths of our community at the CO level and also through SIGs like GO::DH. We hope to initiate this in the coming year.

CONCLUSION: A FOUNDATION FOR DIGITAL SELF-DETERMINATION IN THE HUMANITIES

That's a pretty strong foundation, we feel – one laid by members of our digital humanities community, and one that presents an appropriate response to those concerned with the digital future for the humanities. If we are wondering if the *digital* future for the humanities is something that others suggest to us and perhaps even build for us, this foundation presents a clear response that we're quite readily determining our future for ourselves. Such initiatives result from working with those around us, understanding together what a healthy and open view of the digital humanities can be in the context of the history and interdisciplinarity that it embraces and engages in many ways, ultimately working toward suggesting further points of intervention and action in areas that further define who we are, what we are, what we do, and what brings us together in the places that we do these things.

Through such initiatives, we welcome new members to our community, sharing our community's digital practices within the models pertinent to our field, and at the same time bringing us all closer together in and through those practices even as they evolve, encouraging us to imagine and work toward a future that *we* ultimately shape.

Initiatives such as this provide the methodological foundations for humanities' digital self-determination. In doing so, we "grow our own" and learn to "do our own stunts" (as they say in my part of the world); most importantly, in doing so we ensure that we hold the keys to our own future and the future of the disciplines that we represent in the humanities, determining for ourselves the humanities' digital destiny from an appropriate position of community-shared experience, knowledge, and methodological practice.

NOTE

1 This preface appeared as the Zampolli Prize Lecture, Université de Lausanne, 2 July 2014 at the conference of the international Alliance of Digital Humanities Organizations, *Digital Humanities 2014;* it appears here with permission of *Digital Studies / Le champ numérique*. On behalf of all those involved in and associated with DHSI, I would like to thank everyone in the ADHO community for the honor of the Zampolli Prize and its acknowledgment of the work we all do together. The honorarium associated with the Zampolli Prize has been donated to the DHSI tuition scholarship program for 2015, where it has been matched by several in our partner group – in the ongoing service to our community; funds set aside for the open access publication of this work were donated also to the DHSI tuition scholarship program for 2015.

Acknowledgements

The editors thank all those who have contributed to this volume and the strong community that has produced it – a community that grows with those who engage its contents.

Among DHSI colleagues, the editors would like to thank all members of the Digital Humanities Summer Institute's directorial, advisory, and operational groups over the years, including:

Aaron Mauro, Alyssa Arbuckle, Angel Nieves, Angela Courtney, Angela Norton, Angelsea Saby, Brandy Patterson, Bridget Sweeney, Cara Leitch, Catherine Nygren, Claire Clivaz, Daniel Sondheim, David Cecchetto, Deb Raftus, Diane Jakacki, Elisabeth Burr, Enrico Natale, Greg Fanning, Greg Newton, Harold Short, James Cummings, James O'Sullivan, Jane Kovach, Janet Thomas Simons, Jason Boyd, Jennifer Guiliano, Jentery Sayers, Jon Podracky, Julia Flanders, Karin Armstrong, Kim Shortreed-Webb, Laura Estill, Marc Thoma, Marcus Greenshields, Margaret Hoegg, Mary Galvin, Masahiro Shimoda, Melanie Chernyk, Michael Joyce, Michael Ullyot, Mike Elkink, Neil Fraistat, Nick Morris, Paige Morgan, Patrick Frisby, Paul Arthur, Richard Cunningham, Sarah Kremen-Hicks, Scott Gerrity, Sinisa Trajkovic, and Stewart Arneil.

All instructors and speakers at DHSI through to time of publication:

Aaron May, Adriaan van der Weel, Aimee Knight, Aimée Morrison, Alan Galey, Alan Liu, Alan Stanley, Alec Smecher, Alex Christie, Alex Gil, Allison Benner, Alyssa Arbuckle, Amit Kumar, Andrew Mactavish, Andrew Stauffer, Andy Keenan, Angel Nieves, Arnold Keller, Barbara Bond, Bertrand Gervais, Bill Bowen, Bill Turkel, Boris Capitanu, Brett Oppegaard, Brian Greenspan, Brian Norberg, Brian Owen, Cara Leitch, Catherine

Caws, Cathryn Brandon, Cathy Moran Hajo, Chach Sikes, Chad Gaffield, Christian Vandendorpe, Claire Carlin, Claire Warwick, Constance Crompton, Daniel O'Donnell, Daniel Powell, David Gants, David Hoover, David Robey, Davin Heckman, Dean Irvine, Dene Grigar, Dennis Tennen, Devon Elliott, Diane Jakacki, Dominic Forest, Donald Bruce, Dot Porter, Doug Knox, Edith Law, Edrex Fontanilla, Elizabeth Burr, Elizabeth Grove-White, Elizabeth Losh, Emily Murphy, Erin Kelly, France Martineau, Geoffrey Rockwell, George Dyson, George Tzanetakis, Gerry Derksen, Gerry Watson, Harvey Quamen, Hélène Cazes, Hugh Craig, Iain Higgins, Ian Gregory, Ian Lancashire, Inba Kehoe, Jacque Wernimont, James Cummings, James MacGregor, James Smith, James Sullivan, Jan Rybicki, Janelle Jenstad, Janet Simons, Jason Boyd, Jeff Antoniuk, Jennifer Guiliano, Jennifer Stertzer, Jennifer Whitney, Jennifer Windsor, Jentery Sayers, Jim Andrews, John Barber, John Bonnett, John Lutz, John Maxwell, John Simpson, John Unsworth, John Willinsky, John Yobb, Jon Bath, Jon Martin, Josh Pollock, Juan Pablo Alperin, Julia Flanders, Justin Harrison, Kari Kraus, Karyn Huenemann, Katherine D. Harris, Katherine Walter, Kelley Shanahan, Kevin Kee, Kevin Stranack, Kim Christen, Kim Knight, Kimberly Christen, Laura Estill, Laura Mandell, Lauren Bowman, Lee Zickel, Lisa Charlong, Lisa Snyder, Lisa Surridge, Loretta Auvil, Lorna Hughes, Lynne Siemens, M.D. Coverly, Malte Rehbein, Margaret Conrad, Mark Olsen, Markus Wust, Marshall Soules, Martin Holmes, Mary Elisabeth Leighton, Matt Bouchard, Matt Huculak, Matt Steggle, Matthew Bouchard, Matthew Driscoll, Matthew Hiebert, Matthew L. Jockers, Matthew Kirschenbaum, Meagan Timney, Melissa Dalgleish, Melissa Terras, Michael Ashley, Michael Best, Michael Brundin, Michael Nixon, Michael E. Sinatra, Mihaela Ilovan, Milena Radzikowska, Nancy Ide, Neal Audenaert, Nina Belojevic, Norma Serra, Ollivier Dyens, Orla Murphy, Øyvind Eide, Patrick Finn, Paul Arthur, Peter Liddell, Quinn Dombrowski, R. Darrell Meadows, Raf Alvarado, Rama Hoetzlein, Ray Siemens, Rebecca Niles, Richard Cunningham, Robbyn Lanning, Robert Blake, Robin Davies, Ruth Knechtel, Ruth Tringham, Sandy Baldwin, Scott Gerrity, Scott Weingart, Sebastien Rahtz, Shaun Macpherson, Sheila Petty, Stan Ruecker, Stéfan Sinclair, Stephen Ross, Stewart Arneil, Su Urbanczyk, Susan Brown, Susan Hockey, Susan Schreibman, Syd Bauman, Tanya Clement, Teresa Dobson, Till Grallert, Tim Stinson, Will Luers, Willard McCarty, William Bowen, William J. Turkel, William Winder, and Zailig Pollock.

As well as our institutional, project, and organizational partners and sponsors, those hosting our events: University of Victoria, Vancouver Island University, the Congress of the Social Sciences and Humanities (DHSI@Congress), the conference of the Modern Language Association (DHSI@MLA), Victoria University Wellington, University of Tokyo, UCLA, NYU, Loyola University, American University Beirut, University of Leipzig – and all those in the DH Training Network. See dhsi.org for details of DHSI activities and participants since 2001.

Introduction

Constance Crompton, Richard J. Lane and Ray Siemens

WHAT WE DO WHEN WE DO DH

The Digital Humanities Summer Institute has grown concurrently with the dynamic field of digital humanities. Best defined as the intersection of computational methods and humanities scholarship, with a methodological commitment to thinking and theorizing through making (McCarty; Gold), digital humanities has gained significant momentum during the past quarter century, in keeping with the growing social and cultural importance of computing. The field has reached a certain maturity – at the time of writing the leading journal in the field is fifty years old – and so many digital humanists, both in this volume and in other venues, have offered different origin stories for the digital humanities: from Teena Rochford Smith's *Hamlet* visualizations in the 1880s to Father Roberto Busa's *Index Thomisticus* in the 1950s; from developments in sister disciplines such as Library Science and what we now call "I-Schools," to the Humanities practices of DaVinci and Archimedes (Galey; Hockey; Warwick; Nyhan *et al.*). The discipline is many-faceted and so these multiple origin stories, with their varied inflection, help to elucidate the historical methodologies that explain why we do digital humanities as we do, and how we might consciously shape the discipline to do digital humanities in new ways informed by methodological and theoretical advances in the field. Among other indicators, the growth of the digital humanities is apparent in its increasing integration into curricula, and in its practice by an expanding community of researchers. It is now clear that technology can help further the goals of the Liberal Arts, and *Doing Digital Humanities* offers one community's perspective on how engaging computation can realize those goals.

The personal digital humanities histories of the editors and contributors varies, as explicit attention has not traditionally focused on incorporating technology into the professional activities of the Humanist, leaving most scholars without well-worn paths to becoming digital humanists. Of the various practices in the digital humanities, Constance Crompton arrived through the digital edition creation and text modeling that characterizes encoding using the *Text Encoding Initiative Guidelines* (see Chapters 7 and 14). When she started her graduate studies there were not many digital humanities courses or programs in Canada. Training in the digital humanities had to be pursued outside of the systems of formal academic credit – a worthwhile venture, formal recognition notwithstanding, as the digital techniques she engaged served her scholarship and interests in nineteenth-century literature and culture, queer history, and scholarly editing well. She is currently associate director of the DHSI and an Assistant Professor of Digital Humanities at the University of British Columbia's Okanagan campus, where she directs The Humanist Data Lab.

As a literary theorist, Richard Lane observed the rise of digital humanities with interest during the 1980s and 1990s, before participating in the Digital Humanities Summer Institute in 2005, which he has attended frequently to the present day. Lane's interest in DH coincided with the need to develop the academic side of a burgeoning tech industry in mid-Vancouver Island, which involved planning and helping to launch a digital innovation lab at Vancouver Island University's (VIU) Cowichan Campus, and a digital humanities lab at VIU's Nanaimo Campus, in partnership with Daniel Burgoyne, in the Department of English. The third interconnecting piece in Lane's shift into DH involved supporting British Columbia's Innovation Island Technology Association, and the founding of a tech incubation lab called SquareOne, based in downtown Nanaimo on Vancouver Island. Lane currently co-directs the Critical DH Group (with Emile Fromet de Rosnay), the DH Knowledge Commercialization Group (with Lynne Siemens), and is the Principal Investigator of the MeTA DH Lab.

Ray Siemens arrived in what was then called Humanities Computing in the late 1980s, a computer gamer enrolled in the University of Waterloo English Department's cooperative education program, working with pioneers there like Paul Beam and Neil Randall as an undergraduate research assistant during school term and, during work term, among many assignments at one point in the IBM Toronto Lab, revising the manuals for their TCP / IP (Telecommunications Protocol / Internet Protocol) product. While there was no formal curriculum at that time to speak of, he benefited from an informal and collegial mentorship structure that put him in contact with early DH adopters and leaders, and exemplary projects, at Waterloo, Alberta, Toronto, Oxford, and British Columbia along the way. Just finishing his second term as Canada Research Chair in Humanities Computing at the University of Victoria, Siemens directs the Digital Humanities Summer Institute and the Electronic Textual Cultures Lab.

THE DIGITAL HUMANITIES SUMMER INSTITUTE

This volume comprises chapters by instructors from the Digital Humanities Summer Institute, all of them established or emerging leaders in the field. Since its founding in 2001, the primary goal of the Digital Humanities Summer Institute has been to develop and sustain a community of practice in the confluence of computing and humanities activities. The DHSI originated as a collection of early-career scholars who wished to build a supportive community of practice around computational applications in the arts and humanities, growing from an *ad hoc* event – something akin to what we might now call an unconference – that drew between twenty and thirty people. By 2015, it had developed into an institute drawing 750 participants with an involved international collegiate of approximately 3,000 alumni. The gathering offers colleagues from multiple disciplines and professions (in the public and private sectors), as well as engaged members of the public, a place to gather, learn, and share in the context of a focused humanities-intensive environment. DHSI also provides a space for individuals to reflect upon, and connect over new digital media, multimedia, image, and text-based computing technologies. Through workshops, colloquia, and networking events, participants meet to share their research, interests, and expertise across traditionally divergent lines of knowledge creation.

This volume is our attempt to extend the core mission and mandate of DHSI in textual form. Whether or not you have attended the DHSI, through reading this book please count yourself as a member of the community. Long-time DHSI instructors have written the chapters offered here. Whether you are well versed in the digital humanities and are looking to expand your skills and engagements in new directions, or are new to the digital humanities and would like a practical overview of the field to see how digital humanities methods might inform your work, help you evaluate colleagues' digital humanities work from a position of knowledge, or assist you in the development of skills that span across disciplines, this volume is intended for you. In *Doing Digital Humanities* you will find an overview of core competencies aimed at helping research teams make informed decisions about suitable collaborators, skills development, and project workflow; guidance for individuals, collaborative teams, administrators, and academic managers who support digital humanities researchers; contextualized case studies of digital humanities scholarship; and resources for starting digital humanities projects, including links to further readings, training materials, exercises, and resources.

DOING DIGITAL HUMANITIES

The four sections of this volume frame the theoretical, conceptual, technical, and institutional contexts that make up digital humanities practice. The Foundations chapters introduce the theoretical precepts of digital humanities, with a specific focus on the particularities of the discipline that have been forged at the intersection of histories of race, language, gender, access, method, and scholarly practice. Together, the chapters outline how digital humanists might best interrogate these histories in the interest of an equitable discipline. In "Thinking-through the history of computer-assisted text analysis," Geoffrey Rockwell and Stéfan Sinclair argue for method archaeology, the replication of historical methods, not to verify the findings as one would in using the scientific method, but to better understand the historical practices and contexts on which our contemporary humanities knowledge builds. This understanding will help readers see the contextually specific construction of knowledge and help them respond to Rockwell and Sinclair's call for humanists to think more critically about the links between histories of race, languages, gender, and the construction of computing in the Humanities. In "Global outlooks in digital humanities," Alex Gil and Élika Ortega introduce the multilingual context of Global Outlook DH, a Special Interest Group (SIG) of the Alliance of Digital Humanities Organizations (ADHO), with a particular focus on minimal computing best practice. In "Problems with white feminism," Jacqueline Wernimont and Elizabeth Losh question the persistent privileging of whiteness in the digital humanities despite our sister disciplines' intersectional work on race, class, gender, sexuality, ability, and age in the context of digital scholarship. Wernimont and Losh offer practical strategies for white and racialized digital humanists to engage in intersectional scholarship for a more equitable and sustainable DH. Susan Brown expands on sustainable practice in "Towards best practices in collaborative online knowledge production." Focusing on metadata standards, collaboration best practice, and sustainable workflows, she addresses the particularities of scholarly culture in shaping the long-term and short-term engagement with communities inside and outside the academy. In "Understanding the pre-digital book," Hélène Cazes and J. Matthew Huculak focus on the material object – the book – as preserved in the institutional space known as Special Collections; Cazes and Huculak argue that the dichotomy between the physical and the digital needs to be rejected, turning instead to a continuum of "inscriptions" on a myriad of surfaces and media. Providing "a methodology, workflow, and template" for a DH course on the pre-digital book, the chapter is wide-ranging and engaged in the humanistic passion for literary texts pre- or post-digital in a way that is, in their words, "neither nostalgic nor reactionary."

Part 2, "Core concepts and skills," offers practical introductions to digital humanities methods. In "Critical computing in the humanities," Phillip R. Polefrone, John Simpson, and Dennis Yi Tenen introduce critical computing principles that can both guide and demystify computing best practice, followed by digital humanities core competencies, and concluding with an introduction to the command line, programming, and plain text editing. Moving from plain text, to text that contains computationally tractable editorial interventions, Julia Flanders, Syd Bauman, and Sarah Connell explain best practices for creating rich digital text models. In "Text encoding," they introduce TEI, the language of the Text Encoding Initiative, and outline how to create robust, sustainable, and sharable models of primary texts and secondary scholarship through interpretive markup and formal data modeling. Working with plain text, Jan Rybicki, Maciej Eder, and David L. Hoover introduce stylometry, the statistical analysis of stylistic variation. Harvey Quamen and Jon Bath also address best practices for formalizing humanities data. In "Databases," they introduce the history of databases and how to model humanities content in database form in a way that lets scholars ask questions of research material that cannot be asked of (or answered by) plain text or tables. Ian Gregory and Patricia Murrieta-Flores provide a comprehensive overview and in-depth introduction to GIS in "Geographical information systems as a tool for exploring the spatial humanities." Starting with the history of GIS and its eventual shift into humanities GIS, spatial humanities, and deep mapping, the chapter examines techniques, importing data, exploring and manipulating data, spatial analysis, and cartography and interactive mapping. Challenges that are unique to humanistic research are tackled rigorously throughout the chapter. Moving from text-based scholarship to multimedia, Robin Davies and Michael Nixon introduce digitalization fundamentals, outlining how to use project goals and dissemination needs to guide the digitization of analog media. The section concludes with "Electronic literature and digital humanities" by Dene Grigar, which reflects on a pair of texts, "Electronic literature: what is it?" by N. Katherine Hayles and "Electronic literature: where is it?" by Dene Grigar, which together introduce the foundations of born-digital literature.

Central to the digital humanities is the core humanities practice of, as Stan Ruecker has argued, enriching and augmenting cultural artifacts through interpretation and analysis. As the Creation, Remediation, and Curation chapters make clear, much of this important work relies on remediation and curation in the process of creating new digital resources. In "Foundations for digital editing, with focus on the documentary tradition," Jennifer Stertzer illustrates the continuity between analog and digital textual editing. Attending to the processes by which TEI-encoded editions are produced, Julia Flanders, Syd Bauman, and Sarah Connell introduce Extensible Stylesheet Language for Transformations (XSLT), a key scripting language for transforming TEI-encoded documents (as well as other XML-encoded materials) into new formats for visualization, analysis, and display. Outlining the value of linked data in "Working with the Semantic Web," James Smith recommends best practices for linking to primary and secondary sources and authorities, in ways that position digital work in a larger scholarly context. Exploring the advantages of open-source extensible web-based content management systems, Quinn Dombrowski also provides a rich introduction to "Drupal and other content management systems." The focus on audience and functionality enables readers to comprehend the decision-making needed to choose a CMS before embarking on a major web-based project; Dombrowski also examines the benefits of using Drupal, providing a wealth of detailed information for new Drupal adopters. In "Augmented reality," Markus Wust introduces AR and virtual reality as a fertile ground for representing real-world objects in a digital context. Moving further into the material world, Nicole Clouston and Jentery Sayers introduce digital fabrication in a scholarly context. Finally, drawing on ludic studies, Matt Bouchard and Andy Keenan take a self-reflexive approach to agile game prototyping in "From theory to experience to making to breaking." Contextualized in the theories and practice of games studies and play studies, the prototype game "Root of Play" serves as a case study that illustrates how to teach iterative design in a dynamic pedagogic situation.

The chapters in the concluding Part 4, "Administration, dissemination, and teaching," address the larger institutional and administrative structures that shape contemporary humanities scholarship. The demands of transdisciplinary collaboration that digital humanists encounter when embarking on team-based research are the subject of Lynne Siemens' "Project management and the digital humanist." Based on extensive experience gained from developing and refining the project management course at the DHSI, Siemens provides not only a detailed guide to the topic, but also foregrounds and articulates the practicalities of applying business models to humanistic research planning and successful project management. In "Doing DH in the classroom," Diane Jakacki and Katherine Faull reflect on best practices for sharing the pleasure of DH research and creation with undergraduate students. While DH has historically been the purview of graduate programs, Jakacki and Faull's case study shows how undergraduate DH can improve students' digital literacy, research skills, and historical engagement. In "Digital liberal arts and project-based pedagogies," Aaron Mauro outlines how to introduce project-based learning into the liberal arts curriculum in a way that lets students actively participate in digital humanities research. Moving from outreach via community-engaged curriculum design to outreach via the web, in "Dissemination as cultivation" O'Sullivan, Long, and Mattson offer case studies of social media use for public engagement and what they call *thick collegiality*, two cornerstones of dissemination and collaborative community building that are often left out of traditional scholarship metrics. Engagement with the digital humanities, like engagement with any discipline, rewards learning and practice. We offer the chapters that follow in support of your humanities-related goals whether they be skill acquisition and development, co-creation and dissemination of new tools and research, collaboration and broad community building, or more.

REFERENCES

Galey, Alan. *The Shakespearean Archive*. Cambridge: Cambridge University Press, 2014. Print.

Gold, Matthew K. "The Digital Humanities Moment." *Debates in the Digital Humanities*. Minneapolis: University of Minnesota Press, 2012 ix–xv. Print.

Hockey, Meredith. "The History of Humanities Computing." *Companion to Digital Humanities*. Hardcover. Oxford: Blackwell, 2004.

McCarty, Willard. "What is Humanities Computing? Toward a Definition of the Field." http://ilex.cc.kcl.ac.uk/wlm/essays/what/.

Nyhan, Julianne, Andrew Flinn, and Anne Welsh. "Oral History and the Hidden Histories Project: Towards Histories of Computing in the Humanities." *Digital Scholarship in the Humanities* 30.1 (2015): 71–85. Web. 10 June 2015.

Warwick, Claire. "The End of the Beginning: Building, Supporting and Sustaining Digital Humanities Institutions." Digital Humanities Summer Institute, Victoria. 2015.

Part 1

Foundations

CHAPTER 1

Thinking-through the history of computer-assisted text analysis[1]

Geoffrey Rockwell and Stéfan Sinclair

In 1887 the polymath T. C. Mendenhall published an article in *Science* titled "The Characteristic Curves of Composition," which is one of the earliest examples of quantitative stylistics but also presents one of the first text visualizations. Mendenhall thought that different authors would have distinctive curves of word length frequencies that could help with authorship attribution, much like a spectroscope could be used to identify elements. In Figure 1.1 you see an example of the characteristic curve of *Oliver Twist*. Mendenhall counted the length in characters of each of the first 1,000 words and then graphed the number of words of each length. Thus one can see that there are just under fifty words of one letter length in the first one thousand words.

Mendenhall's paper led to a commission to use his technique to show that Bacon was really the author of Shakespeare's plays (Mendenhall 1901). A wealthy Bostonian, Augustus Hemingway, paid for the tedious work of two women who counted word lengths only to show that no, Bacon's prose didn't have the curve characteristic of Shakespeare's drama. As Joanne Wagner shows in "Characteristic Curves and Counting Machines: Assessing Style at the Turn of the Century" (1990), mechanistic research processes were as attractive then as they are now. At the time, rhetoric and stylistics were trying to establish themselves as scientific disciplines.

It is not surprising that others have been inspired by or experimented with Mendenhall's quantitative approach using computers. Anthony Kenny starts his *The Computation of Style* (1982) not with Father Busa, who is traditionally considered the founding pioneer of humanities computing, but by discussing how Mendenhall and pre-computing contemporaries proposed and tried different stylistic tests, developing a field that then benefited from the availability of electronic computers

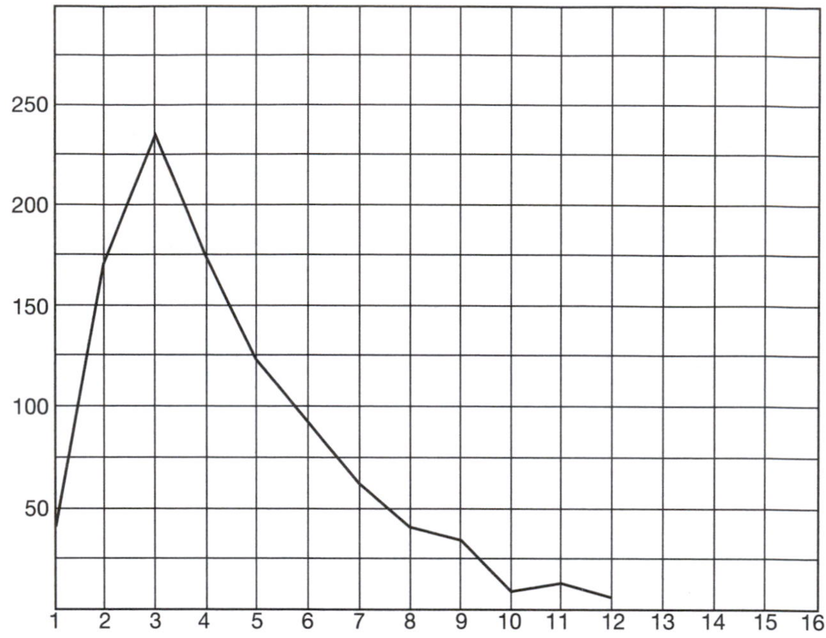

Figure 1.1
First 1,000 words in *Oliver Twist*. The vertical (y) axis indicates the number of words and the horizontal (x) axis indicates the number of letters in each word.

Mendenhall, 1887

after WWII. With the computer it became possible not only to do the statistics faster, but also to gather the statistics automatically from electronic texts. With the dramatic increase of available e-texts quantitative studies have exploded, and some have even returned to Mendenhall. As recently as 2009, Marlowe fan Daryl Pinsken in a blog essay replicated Mendenhall's technique using a computer to show that while Bacon may not look like Shakespeare, Marlowe does.

And that is what this chapter is about – the replication of text analysis techniques as a way of thinking-through the history and possibilities for computer-assisted text analysis. This chapter proposes replication as one way of doing the history of computing that thinks *through* computing rather than only about computing. We will illustrate our proposal by discussing the replication of two studies, that of Mendenhall and another early analytical method by John B. Smith on Joyce. These two experiments are in turn replicated as interactive IPython notebooks that you can use to try replication (we will explain IPython notebooks later in this article; see the appendix for links to the notebooks).

HISTORICAL REPLICATION

One way to understand the history of analytical methods in the digital humanities is to try to replicate them. Historical replication is not the same as scientific reproducibility. Reproducibility is about guaranteeing results by testing them in order to advance science. Historical replication is a way of understanding outcomes, practices, and context of historical works by deliberately following through the activities of research. As such it is a "re-ply" or folding back to engage practices of the past as relevant today and not simply of historical note. It is one of many ways to conjure up the context of historical moments to aid understanding, a fundamental humanistic impulse.

To replicate, or fold back, is more than just an adjustment of direction or a turning. It is to enter into a dialogical relationship with the work of the past. It is to reply to the past by recreating the original study or practice, an impossible act, given that what is past is past. It doesn't do this to pass judgment so much as to treat the past as interlocutor. Obviously the past can't speak, which is why we replicate it or reanimate the practices, taking them seriously as we do. What we get are monsters, like Frankenstein's monster, stitched together from what is at hand.

Replication is important to method, because the way method brings truth to bear on new work is through the replication of a process to new matters. The process is known through re-application, or it might be more accurate to say it is negotiated through replication. In the scientific use of established methods, there is a knowing that comes from reusing methods that have community engagement. Replication, as we imagine it, does not apply established methods to new matters, but seeks to recover, understand, and reflect on past methods by trying them. The analytical methods of Mendenhall and other historical figures are no longer used in the digital humanities, which is why this is also a way of practicing media archaeology, though it might be more accurate to describe this as method archaeology (Zielinski 2008).

We propose a replication as an interpretative practice that can serve heuristic and epistemological purposes that extend our horizons of understanding. Heuristic, because replication is a way of experimenting with old methods made new in a way that can lead to unexpected insights into the everyday practices of computing, both as they were practiced then, and as they could be practiced today. It is as we may think. Heuristic also because such replications, if documented properly, are a way of sharing research tactics so that they can become a subject of further discussion, experimentation, and recombination; a dialog with the future.

Replication serves epistemological purposes because it allows us to better imagine the mix of concepts and methods that constituted knowing at the time rather than impose our paradigms of knowing. We view this as an experimental extension to Ian Hacking's historical ontology (2002), which builds on Foucault's archaeology of ideas. The idea is to understand the concepts, practices, and things of a time as they were understood then, as a way of expanding our understanding. Replication thus can contribute to the genealogy of things such as methods, games, and software where their use (application) is what is important. It is thus in a hermeneutical tradition of the humanities where we treat past ideas and practices as if capable of being understood as vital today rather than as merely historical.

What makes replication particularly relevant is that we can consider it a research practice of the digital humanities. In the spirit of interpreting things by following hints for interpretation from the phenomenon itself, we need to be sensitive to the discussions of method in computing tools for humanists, or at least in the documentation surrounding these tools. These discussions of method hint at replication as they describe methods one could use. They are rarely complete or unambiguous, as we will see, but they do describe implementation as a potential activity of digital humanists. To go further, they describe digital practices as *the* activity of the computing humanist.

REPLICATING MENDENHALL

What does this activity of replication practice? The next two sections of this chapter will walk through what was learned from two replications. Let's first return to Mendenhall's "Characteristic Curve." Our first observation is not about the method itself so much as the agenda of the method. Mendenhall's very project strikes us today as an unusual choice of way of knowing about texts through quantification. Why this fascination with authorship and style? And it isn't just Mendenhall. Up until the 1980s, stylistics was what many textual scholars did with computers to texts. One reason for the interest in authorship is that it was an important task in the humanities, going back to the likes of Valla and the attempts by Italian Renaissance humanists to recover a classical textual heritage. If concern with authorship now seems the purview of forensics, it is because of the work of humanists stabilizing the archive. Now we use computers and quantification not to continue the traditional work of humanists, but to extend it and ask new questions.

A second observation has to do with the technology of the day. Today we take interactive visualizations for granted, which makes iterative interpretative practices easier. Before the personal workstation (be it a terminal or computer) the humanist used computers in a batch mode, which privileged different types of practices. Batch work calls for a formalization of the entire (and expensive) process imagined – a practice very different from the throw-the-text-at-a-data-wall-and-see-what-sticks approach possible with powerful modern interactive tools.

It shouldn't therefore surprise us that stylistics was also presented by Mendenhall and successors as a way to bring the scientific reliability of mechanistic processes to the study of rhetoric. Mendenhall compared his visualizations to the curves produced by the spectrographic analysis of materials. It wasn't just scientific method that was brought to stylistics; Mendenhall also brought the rhetoric of visualization as evidence.

That said, one thing we did not do in our efforts to replicate was to actually count words by hand. Instead we treated Mendenhall as being at the beginning of a tradition of quantitative stylistics that saw fulfillment in automation. Replicating Mendenhall on computer can seem like a way of appropriating his work to computing, and that is also one of the points we want to make about the history of computing – it stretches back beyond the development of electronic computers. If you want to understand the computing humanities you need to understand the importance of stylistics, especially in the early decades of humanities computing. If you want to understand stylistics you need to understand the methods that were developed before the advent of the computer and then how the computer automated these mechanistic methods. The same is true of the other major use of computers in the humanities in the decades after WWII: concording. These liminal practices connect computing to the humanities.

If we consider Mendenhall as being a founder of quantitative stylistics, it changes our founding story for humanities computing.[2] The cosmology story of humanities computing usually starts with Father Busa's mid-twentieth-century efforts to produce a computerized concordance of the works of Thomas Acquinas,[3] but Mendenhall and others predate Busa by half a century.

> Mendenhall's version of "the style is the man," however, was more severe. Rather than style being the result of the choices of a human agent, choices that were made repeatedly and thus constituted personality, personality was "inescapably" revealed in style. Style became the tell-tale signifier of character, and since style could not be changed, the implication was that character could not either. (Wagner 1990, 40–41)

A third point to be made about Mendenhall is one Joanne Wagner points out: that one of the assumptions behind stylistics as practiced by Mendenhall is that style is character in the strong sense that it is "the man," and further, that an author typically can't alter their fundamental characteristics consciously. There are all sorts of problems with the assumptions about the human character of stylistics, starting with the problem of the stability and unconscious nature of style when it can be measured. In fact we get a different curve when we plot all of *Oliver Twist* as opposed to just the first 1,000 words as Mendenhall did. Even more problematic is drawing inferences from stylistic differences. Stylistics, and for that matter any type of computer-assisted analysis, produces measures that still need to be interpreted. What does it mean if an author has a different curve, or uses two-letter words more often? It would probably be more accurate to think of stylistics as being about discourse, not people; or as Sedelow put in 1969, "characterizing the language usage of any writer or speaker" (1969, 1).

The final point, and one that anyone who has done programming in text analysis knows, is that it is remarkably hard to formally describe a word. In our notebook we used the Natural Language Toolkit (NLTK) for Python and its method for recognizing words in a text (tokenization), like so many of the decisions as to what are the boundaries for a word, what to do with hyphens and apostrophes, and what to do with abbreviations, are hidden. Tokenizing into words is, nonetheless, a fundamental step in almost all text analysis processes. It is a step that is language-specific. In English, text analysis benefits from the correlation between words as concepts and the orthographic words or strings that we can use computers to separate. Mendenhall doesn't say if they had to think about what a word really is, but writing analytical code for historical replication gives one pause when such an apparently simple thing gets slippery.

SMITH AND IMAGERY

The second study we replicated is from John B. Smith's "Image and Imagery in Joyce's *Portrait*" (1973). Smith's article is a gem of a paper that uses text analysis to test an aesthetic theory drawn from the novel back on the novel itself. Smith takes a theory about what makes a work of art (like a novel) from *A Portrait of the Artist as a Young Man* and then formalizes it so it can be used to interpret the *Portrait* with a computer. Smith's paper, unlike Mendenhall's paper, is not a work of quantitative stylistics, but a hermeneutical use of computing. Smith draws his theory of interpretation from that being interpreted and applies it back. Smith was a pioneer in developing and theorizing interactive analytical tools meant for interpretative use; in the 1970s he developed the RATS utilities (1972), in 1978 he published a theory of "Computer Criticism," and in the 1980s he developed ARRAS, an influential interactive tool for interpretative text analysis (1984).

In terms of process, what Smith did in "Image and Imagery" was to use a custom dictionary of some 1,300 terms with emotional valence to track and visualize image intensity through the novel. He divided the text into 500-word chunks, approximately the number of words on a page, as he puts it. Then he had the computer count the number of imagery words from his dictionary in each chunk, weighting some words as more significant, and graphing the results. In Figure 1.2 you see the published graph that he uses to then reinterpret the novel.

Replicating Smith's work proved much harder than Mendenhall's; the method included more steps. First of all we had to reconstitute Smith's dictionary of words with emotional valence. Fortunately Smith is still alive and we had been in contact as we are archiving his work.[4] He pointed us to an appendix to his book on Joyce titled *Imagery and the Mind of Stephen Dedalus* (1980), which we digital scanned and converted to text (OCRed), and then corrected in order to recreate his method.

However, even with the list, we weren't getting the same graph. In particular, we weren't getting a dramatic spike near the end of Book I at the pandybat incident. There are a number of reasons why we might, in good faith, not get the same result as Smith did. Our edition is different, the chunk boundaries could be different,

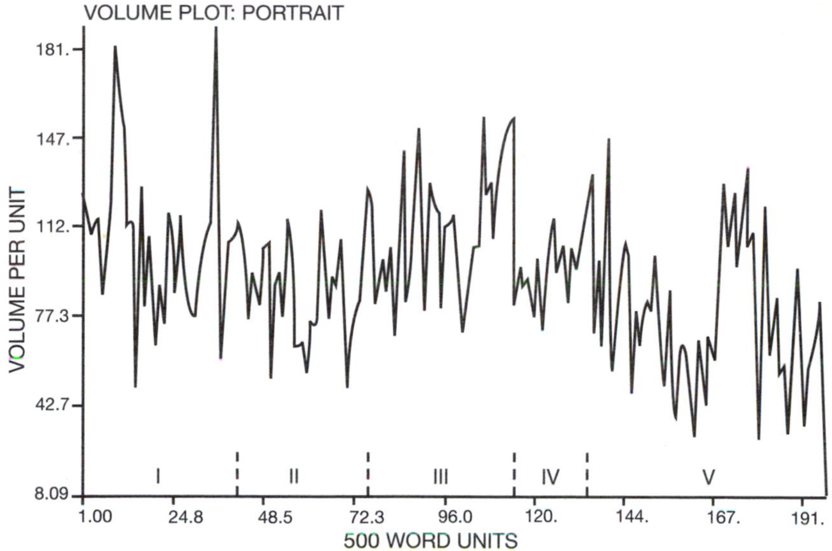

Figure 1.2
Plot of volume of emotional words

Smith, 1973

and while we know Smith weighted some words he thought important, we don't know which ones. In conversation with Smith we suspect that the weighting of selected words that Smith knew were important probably explains the difference. He was interpreting Joyce, we were interpreting Smith. The shape and success of historical replications may in some cases depend on coincidences and conveniences, such as an historical interlocutor who can provide guidance – we are acutely aware of the contingencies of our approach. Each replication is a deformation (McGann 2001).

Should replication have as its goal complete and faithful re-enactment? Should we have counted words by hand when replicating Mendenhall rather than use the computer? Should we strive to use exactly the same instruments or is the idea to recover a sense of the project and its way of knowing?

We found that replication helped us understand the human details in the method. You don't realize how fiddly and dependent on undocumented or undocumentable decisions these methods (and results) are until you try them. Smith's method is hermeneutical; it comes from an interpretation of the text, it formalizes it, and it then returns a visualization for further interpretation. He doesn't make scientific claims about computer-assisted study – it is more a praxis of iteration of which our replication could be seen as yet another iteration. It is thinking-through that involves computing, just as this is.

NOTEBOOKS AND LITERARY PROGRAMMING

As mentioned above, our replications have been implemented as interactive notebooks that can be edited and run on other texts. We first implemented them in Mathematica notebooks (www.wolfram.com/mathematica/) and then IPython notebooks as IPython is open-source software (Pérez and Granger 2007). In Figure 1.3 you can see both the code that can be executed in our notebook and the resulting visualizations that recreate the graphs in Mendenhall's article. Mathematica and IPython provide mature literate programming environments where we can mix discussion of the replicated method with the code that replicates the method. The notebooks can be read or users can run the code on their own texts from the notebook if they wish to try the method.

Literate programming was first described by Donald Knuth in 1984 as an alternative to structured programming. Literate programming emphasizes the primacy of thinking-through in a "literate" or human-readable fashion what a program should do. As Knuth put it, "Instead of imagining that our main task is to instruct a computer what to do, let us concentrate rather on explaining to human beings what we want a computer to do" (Knuth 1984, 1).

Mathematica, first released in 1988, is an environment for interactive computation that successfully implemented Knuth's "notebook" model. It is now widely emulated in environments for data science such as IPython (http://ipython.org/). We propose

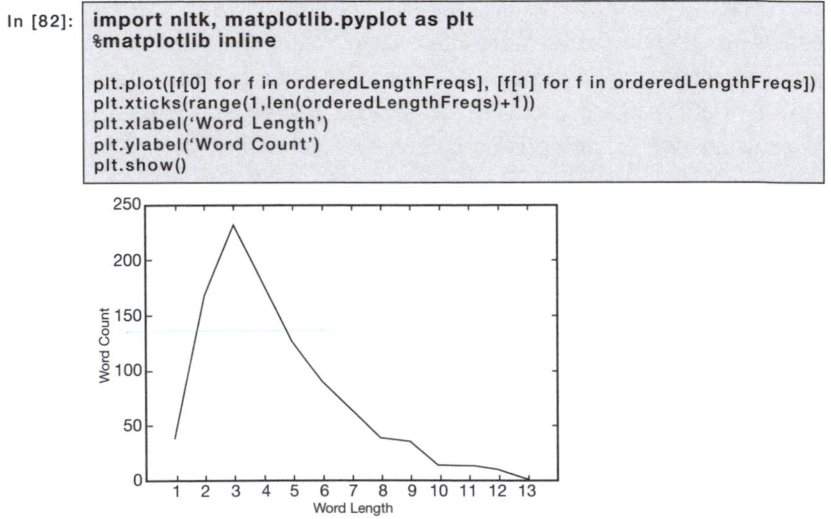
In [82]:
import nltk, matplotlib.pyplot as plt
%matplotlib inline
plt.plot([f[0] for f in orderedLengthFreqs], [f[1] for f in orderedLengthFreqs])
plt.xticks(range(1,len(orderedLengthFreqs)+1))
plt.xlabel('Word Length')
plt.ylabel('Word Count')
plt.show()
250
200
150
100
50
0
Word Count
1 2 3 4 5 6 7 8 9 10 11 12 13
Word Length

Figure 1.3
Screenshot from Mendenhall's Characteristic Curve notebook

literate notebooks as suited for publishing methods and replication of methods for humanities scholars. We aren't the only ones to use literate notebooks this way. Matthew Wilkens, for example, links an essay he gave at the MLA on "Literary Attention Lag" (2015) to both the data and an IPython notebook with the code used (http://nbviewer.ipython.org/gist/wilkens/ed8b6eaa35497d2cd491).

Literate programming is particularly suited to humanities computing as it privileges human reading and experimentation, which in turn encourages understanding of methods through experimentation. These replications are therefore also experiments towards what Willard McCarty calls a Methods Commons for the sharing of methods and code. The Text Mining the Novel project (http://novel-tm.ca/) of which we are a part is adapting the Text Analysis Portal for Research (http://tapor.ca) and linking it to a Methods Commons (http://methodi.ca) for precisely this purpose – the sharing and interpretation of method. It is not enough to tell people about insights from thinking-through computing; we need to show them how computing was practiced and let others experiment with our processes. We replicated Mendenhall and Smith, and through our notebooks others can replicate our replication. The goal is to facilitate the sort of ongoing reinvention of wheels that keeps the humanities alive.

CONCLUSION: DOING THE HISTORY OF TEXT ANALYSIS

Obviously, replication is only one way of doing the history of computing in the humanities. Martin Campell-Kelly in his important 2003 book on the history of the software industry identifies other ways of doing the history of software. We adapt them and extend them here to the digital humanities. Some other practices include:

- Doing the *historiography* so that we know what materials are available to study the history of software, and so that we have a better sense of what is missing. Given that many of the actors such as John B. Smith and Sally Sedelow are still alive and have personal archives, we actually have the opportunity to backfill some of what is missing. Julianne Nyhan, for example, has being doing oral history in the Hidden Histories project (Nyhan *et al.* 2012).
- Developing *archives*, especially of the ephemera of computing projects in the humanities. Much of the history is not in published work, but in project materials, tools, manuals, e-texts, institutes, grant proposals, conferences, demos, and so on. More than most disciplines, the new knowledge is not shared through peer-reviewed publications but in various formats on the web. A "culture of stewardship" that preserves research data has been called for in documents such as "Capitalizing on Big Data: Toward a Policy Framework for Advancing Digital Scholarship in Canada" (TC3+ 2013). In

our case, this should not only include the research archives developed *by* digital humanists, but also archives of the practices of the digital humanities. We also need to recognize that archiving such materials with adequate documentation is not a trivial task (Rockwell *et al.* 2014).[5]

- Exploring *periodization* that is based on inflections points in the history. Are there periods or epochs that reflect changes in technology or the academy? Can periodization help us understand the history of computing and humanities computing? Campbell-Kelly (2003) does this in his history of software. In our book *Hermeneutica* (Rockwell and Sinclair 2016), we propose that the digital humanities changed with the advent of the web as both a subject for DH work and a means of disseminating DH work. We would go further and tentatively suggest that there are other inflection points when the field of text analysis changed with the availability of, for example, personal computers in the early 1980s and large datasets such as Google Books more recently.
- Understanding the dynamic between the *public discourse around computing*, the technologies promoted by industry and how computing was being discussed in the academy. In parallel to exploring periods and inflection points that correlate with other changes, we should look at the public and academic discourse around computing (Gouglas *et al.* 2013). To what extent was humanities computing influenced by, or in reaction to, anxieties about automation? We speculate that humanities computing was uncritically caught up in the general spirit of playful experimentation with these new devices that swept many disciplines, but that needs to be documented.
- *Thinking critically* about the histories of race, languages, gender, and computing in the humanities. As Tara McPherson puts it, "Why Are the Digital Humanities So White?" (2012) or, to paraphrase Domenico Fiormonte (2012), why is DH so English? McPherson's essay raises questions about how intertwined the history of computing and race are, while Fiormonte questions the dominance of Anglophones and English as the lingua franca of DH work. A history of the field needs to confront such questions. We should not use computing as a way to retreat from difficult questions, but think-through thick histories woven from many perspectives.

Wagner at the end of her article jumps to Stanley Fish's critique (1980) of Louis Milic and stylistics in "What is Stylistics and Why Are They Saying Such Terrible Things About It?" Milic was one of the most important computing humanists doing stylistics in the 1960s and 1970s. He wrote a seminal essay, "The Next Step" (Milic 1966), for the very first issue of *Computing and the Humanities* in which he bemoans the use of computers simply to automate traditional practices such as concording and calls for innovative uses. Fish's insulting critique effectively silenced stylistics and delayed serious consideration of how computing might provide innovative research practices outside what was then the narrow field of humanities computing. Who wants to do something others are saying terrible things about? But, as Fish recognizes in his blog essays about the digital humanities at the MLA, a "rough beast has slouched into the neighborhood threatening to upset everyone's applecart" (Fish 2011), and that beast is the digital humanities. Among other practices the digital humanities are reintroducing is the big data version of stylistics now called "distant reading" or "macroanalysis" (Moretti 2007; Jockers 2013). Digital humanists are sharing their experiments again, trying quantitative methods, and drawing critical attention. No doubt terrible things will be said . . . again, and such terrible things are also part of the history. We need to put the hype, enthusiasms, and terrible things people say into historical perspective. We need to resist thinking that the digital humanities and discontents are so new any more. With an historical awareness, reaching back to Mendenhall, of quantitative discourse analysis comes a maturity of discipline. Ironically, the digital humanities have a history of being considered new (over and over), which denies the critical distance history can offer. It is time to do better – we should do the digital humanities in the spirit of how we do all humanities work, with a look over our shoulders at the thinking of those that came before. We should think-through history too.

APPENDIX: IPYTHON NOTEBOOKS

We have prepared two IPython notebooks that illustrate this:

- Mendenhall's Characteristic Curve: https://github.com/sgsinclair/epistemologica/blob/master/Mendenhall-CharacteristicCurve.ipynb
- John B. Smith and Imagery: https://github.com/sgsinclair/epistemologica/blob/master/Smith-Imagery.ipynb

NOTES

1 A version of this chapter was given as a paper at the joint CSDH-SCHN and ACH conference in Ottawa, June 2015.

2 We should note that Mendenhall was not the *first* quantitative stylistician. He himself mentions getting the idea from a remark "somewhere" by Augustus DeMorgan. Wagner (1990) documents some of Mendenhall's contemporaries who critiqued his methods and suggested others.

3 See Susan Hockey's (2004) "History of Humanities Computing" for a more detailed account of Busa and other post-WWII pioneers.

4 See the John B. Smith Archive that was deposited at the University of Alberta Education and Research Archive at: http://hdl.handle.net/10402/era.41201.

5 In fact, we believe that creating and documenting research data should be considered scholarly activity.

REFERENCES

Campbell-Kelly, M. (2003). From Airline Reservations to Sonic the Hedgehog: A History of the Software Industry. Cambridge, MA, MIT Press.

Fiormonte, D. (2012). "Towards a Cultural Critique of the Digital Humanities." Historical Social Research 37(3): 59–76.

Fish, S. (1980). "What is Stylistics and Why Are They Saying Such Terrible Things About It?" Is There a Text in This Class? The Authority of Interpretive Communities. Cambridge, MA, Harvard: 68–96.

Fish, S. (2011). "The Old Order Changeth." New York Times, Opinionator blog at http://opinionator.blogs.nytimes.com/2011/12/26/the-old-order-changeth/.

Gouglas, S., G. Rockwell, V. Smith, S. Hoosein, and H. Quamen (2013). "Before the Beginning: The Formation of Humanities Computing as a Discipline in Canada." Digital Studies / Le champ numérique 3(1).

Hacking, I. (2002). Historical Ontology. Cambridge, MA, Harvard University Press.

Hockey, S. (2004). "The History of Humanities Computing." A Companion to Digital Humanities. Ed. S. Schreibman, R. Siemens, J. Unsworth. Online at http://bit.ly/1qdbU8X.

Jockers, M. L. (2013). Macroanalysis: Digital Methods and Literary History. Urbana, IL, University of Illinois Press.

Kenny, A. (1982). The Computation of Style. Oxford, Oxford.

Knuth, D. E. (1984). "Literate Programming." The Computer Journal 27(2): 97–111.

McGann, J. (2001) Rethinking Textuality. Online report at www2.iath.virginia.edu/jjm2f/old/jj2000aweb.html.

McPherson, T. (2012). "Why Are the Digital Humanities So White? or Thinking the Histories of Race and Computation." Debates in the Digital Humanities. Ed. M. K. Gold. Online at http://dhdebates.gc.cuny.edu/debates/text/29.

Mendenhall, T. C. (1887). "The Characteristic Curves of Composition." Science 9(214): 237–249.

Mendenhall, T. C. (1901). "A Mechanical Solution of a Literary Problem." The Popular Science Monthly LX(7): 97–105.

Milic, L. (1966). "The Next Step." Computers and the Humanities 1(1): 3–6.

Moretti, F. (2007). Graphs, Maps, Trees: Abstract Models for Literary History. London, Verso.

Nyhan, J., A. Finn and A. Welsh (2012). "A Short Introduction to the Hidden Histories Project and Interviews." Digital Humanities Quarterly 6(3). Online at www.digitalhumanities.org/dhq/vol/6/3/000130/000130.html.

Pérez, F. and B. E. Granger (2007). "IPython: A System for Interactive Scientific Computing." Computing in Science and Engineering 9(3): 21–29. IPython is at http://ipython.org.

Pinsken, D. (28 February 2009). "On Mendenhall and Compelling Evidence of Marlowe Authorship by Daryl Pinsken." The Marlowe-Shakespeare Connection Blog at http://marlowe-shakespeare.blogspot.ca/2009/02/on-mendenhall-and-compelling-evidence.html.

Rockwell, G., S. Day, J. Yu, and M. Engel (2014) "Burying Dead Projects: Depositing the Globalization Compendium." Digital Humanities Quarterly 8(2). Online at http://digitalhumanities.org/dhq/vol/8/2/000179/000179.html.

Rockwell, G. and S. Sinclair (2016). Hermeneutica: The Rhetoric of Text Analysis. Cambridge, MA, MIT Press.

Sedelow, S. Y. (1969). Automated Language Analysis: 1968–1969. Chapel Hill, NC, University of North Carolina. Research Report for Office of Naval Research.

Smith, J. B. (1972). “RATS: A Middle-Level Text Utility System.” Computers and the Humanities 6(8): 277–283.

Smith, J. B. (1973). “Image and Imagery in Joyce’s *Portrait*: A Computer-Assisted Analysis.” Directions in Literary Criticism: Contemporary Approaches to Literature. Ed. S. Weintraub and P. Young. University Park, PA, The Pennsylvania State University Press: 220–227.

Smith, J. B. (1978). “Computer Criticism.” STYLE XII(4): 326–356.

Smith, J. B. (1980). Imagery and the Mind of Stephen Dedalus: A Computer-Assisted Study of Joyce’s *A Portrait of the Artist as a Young Man*. Lewisburg, PA, Bucknell University Press.

Smith, J. B. (1984). “A New Environment for Literary Analysis.” Perspectives in Computing 4(2/3): 20–31.

TC3+ (2013). Capitalizing on Big Data: Toward a Policy Framework for Advancing Digital Scholarship in Canada. Consultation Document from Tri-Council (SSHRC, NSERC, and CIHR) and others at www.sshrc-crsh.gc.ca/about-au_sujet/publications/digital_scholarship_consultation_e.pdf.

Wagner, J. (1990). “Characteristic Curves and Counting Machines: Assessing Style at the Turn of the Century.” Rhetoric Society Quarterly 20(1): 39–48.

Wilkens, M. (2015). “Literary Attention Lag.” Blog post at http://mattwilkens.com/2015/01/13/literary-attention-lag/.

Zielinski, S. (2008). Deep Time of the Media: Toward an Archaeology of Hearing and Seeing by Technical Means. Cambridge, MA, MIT Press.

CHAPTER 2

Global outlooks in digital humanities

Multilingual practices and minimal computing

Alex Gil and Élika Ortega

The expansion and consolidation of the field of digital humanities has brought with it an awareness of the international scope of the field and a previously unseen internationalization of inquiry interests, academic and otherwise cultural specificities and practices, infrastructural availability, languages, and others. Several of these issues were first addressed by the pioneer work of Alan Liu (2012) and Tara McPherson (2012), among others. The depth of cultural diversity suggested by them, however, proved to be a truly global phenomenon, though quite an uneven one. The impact that the digital turn has had in the past few decades opens the door for exciting international collaborative ties but in order to achieve that, this unevenness must not only be recognized but also tackled. In this landscape, DH now has the sense of a migratory community in a state of becoming, constantly being reshaped. Known and largely valued by its collaborative culture and commitment to openness, DH as a community now faces the task and challenge of bridging this growing diversity. Many factors affect the formation of communication and collaboration networks across different DH communities, many of them determined by the geopolitical, economic, and cultural divides of the world we live in. Among them, the design of infrastructure and the translation of languages can provide spaces of self-reflexive engagement capable of lowering barriers in communication and collaboration.

Global Outlook::Digital Humanities (GO::DH) is a Special Interest Group (SIG) of the Alliance of Digital Humanities Organizations (ADHO) founded in 2013. Its purpose is to help break down barriers that hinder communication and collaboration among researchers and students of the digital arts, humanities, and cultural heritage sectors across political, economic, and regional boundaries (GO::DH "About"). Since it was founded, GO::DH has worked to implement tools and strategies capable of bridging the gaps among digital humanities (DH) practices and communities around the world. The SIG's base conceptualization is that around the world DH communities have much to learn from each other; there is not just a global "expert" North and a global "apprentice" South. As Isabel Galina stated in her DH2013 keynote address, "We can all learn and benefit from each other and collaboration should work in both directions" (par. 22). Through our work we seek to move away from the unproductive dichotomy of center and periphery, and underscore the position that DH – or any other field – is essentially evaluated best regionally or locally. In this chapter, we summarize two years of work and acknowledge that even though only two of us are listed as authors, none of our projects, initiatives, and ideas would have taken place if not for the tireless involvement of many. Furthermore, due to the immediate relevance of much of the group's work, many of our writing outputs have appeared informally in our collective or personal websites and blogs. Here, we borrow from and actualize those pieces in an effort to gather our thoughts in a cohesive manner and share them as far and wide as possible.

GO::DH ORIGINS AND ETHOS

The origins of GO::DH lie in the acknowledgment that DH is and has been widely practiced around the world in manners that had not been properly recognized until recently. As pointed out by Dan O'Donnell, studies such as Melissa Terras' "Quantifying Digital Humanities" (2011) implied that beyond the thin band of centers (as defined by members of centerNet) across the Northern Hemisphere and in Australia, New Zealand, and South Africa, the rest of the world was "empty spaces" in the geography of DH. Further, even when digital work in the humanities was being conducted by researchers, teachers, and scholars in the "blank areas," it remained largely invisible to researchers in the "global North" associated with the largest international digital humanities societies and organizations. A similar situation was outlined in Marin Dacos' response to Terras, "La Stratégie du Sauna Finlandais" (published in 2013 with data collected in 2012). In his survey, Dacos investigated, at an individual scale, the potential diversity of the field that had been overlooked until then and showed "*une très grande diversité linguistique et géographique, l'existence d'un hors-monde qui n'a pas vu l'enquête ou n'y a pas prêté attention, la marginalité de l'anglais comme première langue, mais sa domination comme second idiome*" (par. 1). A diversity that, even when intuited, needed to be acknowledged, examined, and incorporated into the history and scope of the field.

The results of these works showed a literal disconnect between researchers in mid- and low-income economic regions and those appearing prominently on the maps, often found in high-income regions. As O'Donnell noted, the researchers were simply not part of the same digital, academic, and social networks (par. 3). Although DH aims to be a highly international and collaborative endeavor, by 2013 it remained the case that our internationalization and collaborative activity had been primarily conducted on an East–West basis among a relatively small number of generally contiguous, high-income economies (see also Fiormonte 2012; Galina 2013). Since then, the more that those working in high-income economies have learned about DH outside of these areas, the more evident it is that we need to continue to stretch and reformulate our definitions, genealogies, and concepts, and rethink the many scales at which humanistic engagement with computers is practiced.

In human terms, as Alex Gil explained in "The (Digital) Library of Babel," GO::DH was born out of:

> a series of conversations at DH2012, Hamburg, among several scholars from North America, Europe and Asia, on the difficulties of making connections with mainland China. By this point, centerNet had already made enormous strides in connecting centers across the constituent members of ADHO, but they had found some difficulties connecting outside of that tent. (par. 12)

Shortly afterwards, Gil elaborates, GO::DH began taking shape during INKE's Birds-of-a-Feather gathering in December of 2012, in Havana:

> In earlier conversations, the group was dangerously imagined as an advocacy group encouraging ADHO members to seek out scholars on the empty hinterlands of Melissa Terras' map in order to provide assistance to them. During the fortuitous debates in Havana, however, GO::DH started molding its current ethos for transnational collaboration based on a different gambit: to go global – we would look for intersections within existing practices and networks, rather than replicate or over-valorize the already established models. In doing so, we aimed to transform the we, to redraw the map, and to reconfigure the conversations. Our we is now a function of our intersections around the world. (par. 13)

Thus, GO::DH is not an outreach or aid program. The group's initiatives have worked within the divides and limitations imposed by the world we live in, though always trying to stretch them as much as possible. Instead, GO::DH aims to facilitate communication and establish strategies of exchange in DH capable of showing that all around the world we have much to learn from one another. Aside from theorizing about the cultural, economic, social, and academic factors affecting the visibility, communication, and collaborations of DH work around the world, our approach to breaking down these barriers has been one of praxis. The organization develops complementary strengths, interests, abilities, and experiences of its membership through special projects, events, activities, and publicity (Priego and O'Donnell 2013; Priego and Gil 2013). Some of our core activities are discovery, community-building, research, and advocacy. We take steps to foster collaboration and cooperation across regions and economies; we coordinate research on and in support of the use of technology in areas across the globe; and advocate for a local-based to global perspective. The "accents" of DH, as Roopika Risam has called them, "decenter a hegemonic definition or expectation of digital humanities scholarly practice, give us a framework to move beyond the tedious task of defining digital humanities and to fully appreciate both the affordances and challenges of 'doing' digital humanities around the world" (par. 30).

Although much is left to be done, the work of GO::DH has already begun to evidence the rich variety of DH practices around the world as well as their subtle differences, and has shown the need to engage with what they can teach us about the global through the local. In 2013 the "Rewriting Wikipedia Project" sought "to increase the number of and improve existing entries on marginalized peoples and cultures" ("Rewriting Wikipedia Project"). That same year, the "GO::DH Essay Prize" focused on "aspects of the national, regional, or international practice of the Digital Humanities" ("Essay Prize"). The open and ongoing "Translation Commons" aims to "encourage multilingual community collaboration in the digital humanities" ("Translation Commons"). During the SIG's second year, in 2014, "Around DH in 80 Days" was launched: "a multi-institutional, interdisciplinary Digital Humanities collaboration seeking to introduce new and veteran audiences to the *global* field of DH scholarly practice by bringing together current DH projects [instead of centers] from around the world" (Around DH "About"). Similarly, during the DH2014 conference in Lausanne, Switzerland, the "DH Whisperer" campaign invited conference attendees to engage in community translation exercises (ADHO "GO::DH and MLMC"). Even though all of these initiatives have gained prominence within a small period of time, their impact branches out and continues to shape new and ongoing projects. In the following pages, we narrow our focus to discuss two particular approaches the SIG has taken towards promoting multilingualism as the basis of global dialogues and minimal computing practices within DH.

COMMUNITY TRANSLATION: MULTILINGUALISM IN DH

The explosion in the number of DH practitioners, funding programs, curricula, and publications in the English-speaking academy has, in many ways, rendered English as the lingua franca of the field. As shown by Dacos, this trend has been further exacerbated by the fact that English is the second language of most DH practitioners (par. 11). While the strength DH has enjoyed in English-speaking academia has had positive outcomes for all practitioners, it is also true that its domination has overshadowed work done in other languages and communities. We see the circulation of work done in a variety of languages as a springboard to move ideas around the world, to enrich our pool of sources and approaches, to further the already existing diversity in the field, and to expand our sense of what DH does.

The domination of English in academic circles is in no way exclusive to DH and is rooted in global geopolitical developments. For example, in "Absolute English,"

Michael D. Gordin argues that the process of English gaining dominance in scientific discourse is closely tied to recent historical and political developments such as the end of World War II and the Cold War. Gordin also reflects upon the common assumption that contemporary science "advances at such a staggering rate precisely because we have focused on 'the science' and not on superficialities such as language" (par. 3). This point, he continues:

> is much easier to sustain if the speaker grew up speaking English, but the majority of scientists working today are actually not native English speakers. When you consider the time spent by them on language-learning, the English-language conquest is not more efficient than polyglot science – it is just differently inefficient. There's still a lot of language-learning and translation going on, it's just not happening in the United Kingdom, or Australia, or the United States. The bump under the rug has been moved, not smoothed out. (par. 4)

As humanists, DH practitioners can hardly be assumed to dismiss language as a superficial element in our scholarship. Cultural specificities, distinct modes of thinking and arguing, and the development of local vocabularies to address the issues concerning us locally and globally must be maintained. Even if it seems at odds with an idea of self-determination, communication and exchanges among the growing number of DH communities must also be facilitated.

As a vehicle to further cultural exchanges, multilingualism in DH work is promising yet challenging. Ways to ensure horizontal communication between diverse linguistic DH communities are elusive and cannot rely solely on the allegedly globally available realm of the Web. Multilingualism must be a community endeavor. Conversations about cultural and linguistic awareness have been, expectedly, very different in tone, objective, and impact. "These tensions", Domenico Fiormonte states, "originate from profound global changes in the production and diffusion of knowledge, which are challenging the instruments and hierarchies of traditional forms of evaluation (peer review, impact factor, etc.), and demanding new forms of governance for shared and participatory knowledge" ("Global Perspective" 3). A multitude of factors such as those outlined by Fiormonte have caused debates on multilingualism to move, migrate, and metamorphose as distinct communities have found their niche of practice and created their vocabularies, and as notions of center and periphery are challenged and, sometimes, even reconfigured (Clavert 2013; Dacos 2013). Furthermore, as David Golumbia rightly points out in "Postcolonial Studies, Digital Humanities, and the Politics of Language," there is an entire new layer of complexity if we think about non-imperial or minority languages (par. 2).

Within the major DH organizations, fundamental efforts had been initiated before 2008 when the protocol for the Standing Committee on Multilingualism and Multiculturalism (MLMC) was approved by ADHO. Currently, the MLMC is charged with "developing and promoting policies in ADHO and its constituent organizations that will help them to become more linguistically and culturally inclusive in general terms, and especially in the areas where linguistic and cultural matters play a role" (ADHO "Revised Protocol"). MLMC's tasks are relevant to the bulk of ADHO work, including its protocols, websites, conference, publications, CFPs, and reviewing processes. The work from the MLMC has led to important practices, including the translation of the ADHO annual international conference CFP into as many as twenty languages, the possibility of giving papers in the official languages of the organization, and others. Although MLMC has taken steps in the right direction, as Martin Grandjean showed in "Le Rêve Du Multilinguisme Dans La Science: L'exemple (malheureux) Du Colloque #DH2014," it has not always been as successful as might have been intended or hoped for (par. 10). The complexity and sensitivity of the issue of multilingualism touch on the large-scale problems of economic inequality, colonial history, and political disagreements that have shaped the world we live in and, by extension, the landscape in which we work.

GO::DH has initiated a handful of ongoing ("Translation Commons") and *ad hoc* ("DH Whisperers") projects aiming to bridge problems of miscommunication across languages and academic cultures, beginning with a local self-determination of what constitutes DH work and where its value resides. Our objectives have focused on valuing the character of the community, showcasing its multilingual and multicultural wealth, raising awareness about the different academic cultures and norms, and proposing ways to ensure local–global work is reviewed in a culture- and language-sensitive manner.

Following the GO::DH way, the development of a Translation Toolkit seeks to open the work of fostering local–global communication to members in the DH community. Recently, "DH Whisperers," the Toolkit's immediate background, constituted an informal approach to enabling the community to help in matters of translation. The project had a simple dynamic: those attendees who were willing to help out translating to/from any language being used at the DH2014 conference, formally and informally, could ask GO::DH members for a badge to identify them as whisperers, write down in it the languages they could help out in, and then wear it for the rest of the conference ready to use their linguistic skills as needed (Ortega par. 5). Through this project GO::DH members were able to grasp two aspects of multilingualism that distinguish the DH community: first, a really great linguistic variety that included to various degrees speakers of at least Arabic, Catalan, Dutch, English, French, Galician, German, Greek, Hindi, Italian, Japanese, Norwegian, Polish, Portuguese, Russian, Spanish, and Swedish; and second, the enormous pool of community volunteers interested in actively learning about work from around the world and participating in the translation efforts.

The lessons learned during this spontaneous and informal experience reveal the need to expand and spread similar practices and approaches to facilitate further diversity within DH. Although it is undeniable that English serves as a lingua franca in DH, we believe that the Translation Toolkit will help all of us take a critical stance towards that assumption, foster the inclusion of the growing linguistically and otherwise diverse community, and facilitate the spread of DH work globally. As a living project, the Translation Toolkit is available on the Web where it continues to be enriched with the community's contributions. Its fundamental approach, "whispering" or community translation, follows the principle that there is no right or single approach to translation and multilingualism, and embraces the principle that all strategies might work at particular times and circumstances.

As the global DH community continues to expand and take different shapes, it is our hope that the toolkit will gather strategies applicable to several aspects in DH work, from conference talks to informal and formal publications, websites, etc. Nevertheless, we are well aware that translation efforts and logistics are as complex as the problem they address. Therefore, an important part of making translation and multilingual practices a community effort is the ready availability of the tools used to support it. With this in mind, most of our strategies incorporate a familiar set of tools with minimal technical requirements, which are freely available online and can travel to locations with limited connectivity, and which most DHers are likely to use already. Community translation practices require a bit of extra work from everyone involved. However, it is one of the objectives of this chapter to highlight the relevance of these extra efforts and emphasize how crucial they are for the consolidation of a truly global DH community. At GO::DH we strongly believe that the more people willing to engage in these practices, the easier they will become to implement, and more resources will become available.

MINIMAL COMPUTING

Minimal computing as a conceptual provocation has been around GO::DH since the formative days of INKE's Birds-of-a-Feather gathering in Havana ("Havana Gathering"). As a result of the then extant embargo, some peculiar academic and popular minimal computing practices had developed in Cuba: USB parties to share document libraries, email chains as forms of publication, SMS hacks, and much more. Since our colleagues in Cuba have formed an integral part of the GO::DH network, these concerns never went away, and have now come to inform much of what we do. More recently, a new working group was formed around minimal computing, and we have launched an early version of an *informational site* for us to share thought pieces and resources around minimal computing.

In general, we can say that minimal computing is the application of *minimalist principles to computing*. In reality, though, minimal computing is in the eye of the beholder. A Raspberry Pi could be understood as an example of a minimalist piece of hardware because the creators reduced computing components to what they saw as a bare minimum to achieve simple tasks. The learning curve for using one, though, can be threatening to beginners, and therefore requires more than minimum effort.

On a user interface, on the other hand, eliminating clutter (unnecessary buttons, distracting design, etc.) can also be understood to be part of a minimalist approach, making it easier for users to engage and also lighter on browsers. Google's success, for example, may be owed to the reduction of the search function to one box. In order to achieve this feat, though, we estimate that Google uses an enormous amount of code and data in the back end, needing enormous computing power to run.

Here, we prefer to (un-)define minimal computing around the question "What do we need?" If we do so, our orientations vis-à-vis ease of use, ease of creation, increased access, and reductions in computing – and by extension, electricity – become clearer. Designer and theorist Ernesto Oroza, writing on what he terms Cuba's "Architecture of Necessity," can be helpful here:

> I am using **Architecture of necessity** term as a metaphor. On the one hand it can be read as a descriptive term, austere in its rhetorical value, almost obvious. On the other hand, the term enunciates an architecture that is its self-diagram, and this image becomes structural and programmatic. I believe that architecture should be that. The home must be a structure of agreements. *A factual connection between needs, materials, technology, urban regulations and social conditions.* (par. 3)

The architecture of need that Oroza describes grows out of the long-term incapacity of government infrastructures or bureaucracies to regulate against urgency; an attitude of disobedience against wholeness or finished products; a cleverness that can make-do with available materials; and a constant care for our social surroundings. This set of conditions, different depending on the locality, apply to many sectors of DH (and the humanities at large) not simply as analogy, but as lived experience. Minimal computing for us considers a digital scholarly practice that approaches its own self-diagram along these lines.

The we in "what do we need?" are the scholars *qua* scholars around the world: librarians, professors, students, cultural workers, independent or affiliated to institutions. Needless to say, workers in the humanities have many diverse needs, so we focus here on what we consider the most important shared one: the renewal, dissemination, and preservation of the scholarly record. We take for granted the intersections of our work with the human record writ large, and the pressing work of scholarly critique of (present) culture, our teaching, and the public humanities.

Our first answers to the question, then, come from an acknowledgment of the hybrid and global future we see being shaped for the scholarly record: parts digital, parts analog. In this new media environment we continue to protect, study, and renew the analog, as we attempt to harness the new media in smart, ethical, and sustainable ways. For several reasons, this implies learning how to produce, disseminate, and preserve digital scholarship ourselves, *without the help we can't get*, even as we fight to build the infrastructures we need at the intersection of, with, and beyond institutional libraries and schools. To reiterate, our minimal computing does not stand in as a universal call, but rather as a localizable space for new questions and practices, an injunction to constantly repeat the question, "what do we need?"

Most scholars need to write and make public. That is one of our core activities, and yet, the writing done today using proprietary tools such as Microsoft Word, often required by editors, creates a disconnect between scholars and the socio-technical mechanisms that are needed to go from the file formats generated by these proprietary applications to a relatively accessible record. As Dennis Yi Tenen and Grant Wythoff put it in "Sustainable Authorship in Plain Text using Pandoc and Markdown,"

> More than causing personal frustration, this reliance on proprietary tools and formats has long-term negative implications for the academic community. In such an environment, journals must outsource typesetting, alienating authors from the material contexts of publication and adding further unnecessary barriers to the unfettered circulation of knowledge. (par. 5)

The culture of "user friendly" interfaces that has helped popularize computers for almost three decades now, and which underlines the dominant role of .docx, .pdf, and .epub files today, has also led to some basic misunderstandings of what computers can and should do. In the case of writing, the expectation that you should get what you see continues to distance producers from their tools. As with any human tool, we need to understand computers a bit more intimately if we're going to use them with any degree of critical awareness, and in order to avoid falling into what Matthew Kirschenbaum dubs the "haptic fallacy," or "the belief that electronic objects are immaterial simply because we cannot reach out and touch them" (par. 13). In our case, this need comes with some urgency because what has remained invisible or grossly misunderstood to producers of scholarship in certain parts of the world are the material conditions of their own knowledge production – digital and analog – with noxious effects for labor and ecological practices.

In "Sustainable Authorship," Tenen and Wythoff recommend a workflow that goes from the creation of a text to the generation of different file formats for web and print that involves open technology that is relatively easy to learn, to share, and to preserve. Minimal computing of the Wythoff and Tenen variety represents then a return to basics that opens up the possibility of understanding small, but more complete "technological stacks" in order to reconnect producers of scholarship to the tools they use. In their case, minimal computing reconciles minimal knowledge with the production of a minimal artifact, without creating necessary friction for the readers. The learning curve may seem steep, though, for a large number of scholars, despite the reassurances and encouragement of those who consider them minimal. Again, we must ask, "what do we need?" Scholars don't strictly "need" to use the minimal approach recommended by Tenen and Wythoff (as in, they are not required to use it by those who promise to take care of the rest). And yet if we do, we are on our way to fulfilling the need to write and publish in sustainable and ethical ways.

Another consequence of reconnecting with our knowledge production is an increased awareness of the cost of scholarly and human memory on the molecular arrangement of the planet. As Stefán Sinclair and others reported on Twitter, in a recent talk at the #CSDHACH2015 conference in Ottawa, Wendy Chun prompted the audience to "*print it out and delete it*," citing the ecological cost of storage for digital preservation. Minimal computing shares these concerns, prodding a creative practice that seeks to reduce our impact while achieving our needs. "Print it out and delete it" is a radical answer. We, of course, are concerned about the whole tree, not just the root. The alternative futures implied by Chun's call include a minimal computing practice where we open up scholarly artifacts for dissemination for a window of time, say one year, and then we intentionally shut them down after interested parties have had a chance to "print." The resulting impact on the consumption and distribution of paper and other materials would clearly lead to other problems. This is precisely why minimal computing cannot be a set of decisive answers focusing exclusively on the digital, but rather a set of tentative answers and provocations around the hybrid analog/digital ecologies of the world to come. In this sense, we align our efforts with a long durée ahead of us marked by an eclectic making-do, as Bethany Nowviskie prompts in her DH2014 Lausanne keynote, "Digital Humanities in the Anthropocene."

A reason dear to us at GO::DH is access. If we believe that we should have a robust scholarly record available to scholars everywhere through that global library we call the Internet, we eventually must agree that the burden of cost should be lifted from the reader, but more à propos, that the interfaces that we use to distribute our work do not overburden the systems and bandwidth available to our colleagues around the world. Our first experiment in this regard was, appropriately, the "Around DH in 80 Days" project.

Around DH launched on 21 June 2014, highlighting a different DH project from around the world every day for the next eighty days. The final list was curated from a larger crowdsourced list by a team of editors representing the many regions of the world. Early work on Around DH was done on the Scalar platform by Ryan Cordell's "Doing Digital Humanities" course at Northeastern University. While Scalar is an excellent platform for multimedia-rich work, we chose to build the final version of the project on Jekyll, a static site generator. Jekyll – and systems like it – work by generating a full site in HTML/CSS as a folder of files that we can copy onto a server, obviating the need for databases or AJAX. The static files enormously reduce the speed the site loads on browsers, and are easy to print. We hoped that minimizing load speeds would make the site more accessible in low bandwidths around the world. As a bonus, duplicating a static site can be done simply by copying the files, therefore increasing the chances of survival. Even the map on the site was rendered as SVG from a data store in the back end, making it part of the HTML of the final product. The aesthetics of the site reflect this approach. We used the default theme provided by Jekyll, with some small tweaks, making the reading experience simple as well. The overall result is a site that does what it sets out to do without unnecessary bloat.

In the coming years, we hope to curate a larger conversation around minimal computing on our minimal computing site. The site itself is deployed in Jekyll, leveraging the publishing capacity of Github pages, which allows us to tap into Github servers around the world. The site will welcome thought pieces and links to resources by members of the GO::DH community. In a similar vein, we are planning an informational site for the Translation Toolkit outlined above.

AFTERTHOUGHT

As a group that bases the majority of its work on collective praxis, it is challenging to try to arrive at conclusions. As can be seen from these pages, the work of GO::DH is exploratory and an ongoing process. In agreement with the SIG's objectives, multilingualism and community translation, and minimal computing, are two of our approaches contributing to the formation of a truly global DH community. These two scholarly practices seek to bring into DH an awareness of the different practices and local conditions. They also seek to highlight how purposeful and self-reflexive uses of tools can help lower barriers of communication. Furthermore, we hope to inspire others to rely on their communities to design and implement strategies and exercises that nurture their field.

REFERENCES

ADHO. "GO::DH and MLMC Partner on Initiative for Multi-Lingual Participation." N.p. Web. 20 May 2015. (http://adho.org/announcements/2014/godh-and-mcml-partner-initiative-multi-lingual-participation).

ADHO. "Revised Protocol for the Standing Committee on Multi-lingualism & Multi-culturalism." N.p. Web. 20 May 2015. (http://adho.org/administration/multi-lingualism-multi-culturalism/revised-protocol-standing-committee-multi).

Around DH. N.p. Web. 20 May 2015. (http://arounddh.org).

Around DH. "About." N.p. Web. 20 May 2015. (http://arounddh.org/about).

Clavert, Frédéric. "The Digital Humanities Multicultural Revolution Did Not Happen Yet." *L'histoire contemporaine à l'ère numérique*. N.p., 26 April 2013. Web. 20 February 2015. (http://histnum.hypotheses.org/1546).

Dacos, Marin. "La Stratégie Du Sauna Finlandais." *Blogo Numericus*. N.p., 1 June 2013. Web. 19 February 2015. (http://bn.hypotheses.org/11138).

Fiormonte, Domenico. "Digital Humanities from a Global Perspective." *Laboratorio dell'ISPF* XI – 2014 (2014). N.p. *mEDRA*. Web. 20 February 2015.

Fiormonte, Domenico. "Towards a Cultural Critique of the Digital Humanities." *Historical Social Research / Historische Sozialforschung* 37.3 (141) (2012): 59–76. Print.

Galina, Isabel. "Is There Anybody Out There? Building a Global Digital Humanities Community." *Humanidades Digitales*. N.p., 19 July 2013. Web. 19 February 2015. (http://humanidadesdigitales.net/blog/2013/07/19/is-there-anybody-out-there-building-a-global-digital-humanities-community/).

Gil, Alex. "The (Digital) Library of Babel | @elotroalex@elotroalex." N.p., 7 June 2014. Web. 19 February 2015. (http://elotroalex.webfactional.com/digital-library-babel/).

Global Outlook::Digital Humanities. "About." *Global Outlook::Digital Humanities*. N.p., n.d. Web. 19 February 2015. (www.globaloutlookdh.org/about).

Global Outlook::Digital Humanities. "GO::DH Essay Prize." *Global Outlook::Digital Humanities*. N.p., n.d. Web. 19 February 2015. (www.globaloutlookdh.org/global-outlookdigital-humanities-global-digital-humanities-essay-prize/).

Global Outlook::Digital Humanities. "Rewriting Wikipedia Project." *Global Outlook::Digital Humanities*. N.p., n.d. Web. 19 February 2015. (www.globaloutlookdh.org/the-rewriting-wikipedia-project/).

Global Outlook::Digital Humanities. "Translation Commons." *Global Outlook::Digital Humanities*. N.p., n.d. Web. 19 February 2015. (www.globaloutlookdh.org/translation-commons/).

Golumbia, David. "Postcolonial Studies, Digital Humanities, and the Politics of Language." *uncomputing*. N.p., 31 May 2013. Web. 20 February 2015. (www.uncomputing.org/?p=241).

Gordin, Michael D. "Absolute English. How Did Science Come to Speak Only English?" *Aeon Magazine*. N.p., 4 February 2015. Web. 19 February 2015. (http://aeon.co/magazine/science/how-did-science-come-to-speak-only-english/).

Grandjean, Martin. "Le Rêve Du Multilinguisme Dans La Science: L'exemple (malheureux) Du Colloque #DH2014." *Martin Grandjean*. N.p., 27 June 2014. Web. 19 February 2015. (www.martingrandjean.ch/multilinguisme-dans-la-science-dh2014/).

INKE – Implementing New Knowledge Environments. 2012. "Havana Gathering 2012." Web. 19 February 2015. (http://inke.ca/projects/inke-conference-2012-havana/).

Kirschenbaum, Matthew. "Materiality and Matter and Stuff: What Electronic Texts Are Made Of." *ebr*. 1 October 2001. Web. 20 May 2015. (www.electronicbookreview.com/thread/electropoetics/sited).

Liu, Alan. "What is Cultural Criticism in the Digital Humanities?" In *Debates in the Digital Humanities*, University of Minnesota Press, 2012. Print. 490–509.

McPherson, Tara. "Why are the Digital Humanities so White?" In *Debates in the Digital Humanities*, University of Minnesota Press, 2012. Print. 139–160.

Nowviskie, Bethany. "Digital Humanities in the Anthropocene." *Bethany Nowviskie*. N.p., 10 July 2014. Web. 20 May 2015. (http://nowviskie.org/2014/anthropocene).

O'Donnell, Dan. "In a Rich Man's World: Global DH?" *dpod blog*. N.p., 2 November 2012. Web. 19 February 2015. (http://dpod.kakelbont.ca/2012/11/02/in-a-rich-mans-world-global-dh/).

Oroza, Ernesto. "Architecture of Necessity". N.p. Web. 20 May 2015. (http://architectureofnecessity.com/).

Ortega, Élika. "Whispering/Translating during DH2014: Five Things We Learned | Readers of Fiction." *Readers of Fiction*. N.p., 21 July 2014. Web. 3 November 2014. (http://lectoresdeficcion.blogs.cultureplex.ca/2014/07/21/dhwhisperer/).

Priego, Ernesto, and Alex Gil. "Global Perspectives: Interview with Alex Gil." *4Humanities*. Web. 19 February 2015. (http://4humanities.org/2013/01/interview-with-alex-gil/).

Priego, Ernesto, and Daniel Paul O'Donnell. 2013. "Bringing Diversity of Experience Together: An Interview with Daniel O'Donnell." *4Humanities*. May. Web. 19 February 2015. (http://4humanities.org/2013/05/interview-daniel-o-donnell/).

Risam, Roopika. "Across Two (Imperial) Cultures." *Roopika Risam*. N.p. 31 May 2015. Web. 6 June 2015. (http://roopikarisam.com/2015/05/31/across-two-imperial-cultures-2/).

Tenen, Dennis, and Grant Wythoff. "Sustainable Authorship in Plain Text using Pandoc and Markdown." *The Programming Historian*. N.p., 10 March 2014. Web. 20 May 2015. (http://programminghistorian.org/lessons/sustainable-authorship-in-plain-text-using-pandoc-and-markdown).

Terras, Melissa. "Quantifying Digital Humanities." *Melissa Terras' Blog*. (http://melissaterras.blogspot.ca/2012/01/infographic-quanitifying-digital.html).

CHAPTER 3

Problems with white feminism

Intersectionality and digital humanities

Jacqueline Wernimont and Elizabeth Losh

Feminist digital humanities, in so far as we can say that such a thing exists, has a problem, which can be summarized in one word: whiteness.[1] The scholars listed in tables of contents, conference programs, and websites of professional organizations are notably lacking diversity when it comes to racial representation. Even the most "recognized" feminist scholars of race in the digital humanities still tend to be white. This is not a problem unique to feminist digital humanities theory or practice; the field and the academy in general mirror what we see in the sub-fields or areas. That said, we can and should do better.

In some ways it is not surprising that the overlapping zones of feminist theory and praxis and digital humanities scholarship have inherited the same problems that have vexed feminist work since at least the middle of the twentieth century. On the other hand, given that people very often cite work from the 1970s onward as central to the field, it was reasonable to hope that the insights of the civil rights movement and third wave feminisms (to say nothing of fourth wave) would have been integral to humanists' engagements with digital media, tools, and methods. At this point in time, digital humanists should already be mindful of how the path dependencies of platforms and infrastructures are raced as well as gendered. Nevertheless, even in attempts to address inequities, DH scholars have unintentionally deployed analogies that further entrench exclusionary paradigms, as is the case with the many suggestions that digital humanities is a field like carpentry or computer science.[2] Such analogies are often efforts to suggest a crafty openness – one that eschews the elitism of academic theory – that also perpetuate a logic that has excluded women (tacit or "thing" knowledge has long been gendered) and people of color. Carpentry and computer science have pernicious histories of excluding people of color by maintaining gatekeeping with unions and associations and through the definition of skilled labor itself, tendencies that digital humanities seems to be replicating.

Some of this is a historiographic problem. Rather than merely focusing on contemporary debates between active digital humanities scholars, more fundamental questions need to be asked about how we understand key terms and specifically what we mean by "users," "access," "responsibility," and "defaults." For example, do digital humanities scholars tend to assume that the typical user is affluent enough to own a desktop or laptop computer and is therefore not dependent on public computing in schools or libraries with strict rules about limiting time at terminals on which censoring software is pre-installed? Does the rhetoric of making and breaking suppose that home computing is an individual, rather than familial experience, such that tinkering and taking apart carries little risk of damaging family member access? If the user has a platform for personal computing available on a cell phone, what is being assumed about this person's access to network coverage, affordable data, and the robust hardware and software of the latest devices? Do white digital humanists understand "terms of use" agreements as relatively neutral, although those who have suffered from a long legacy of unjust medical experimentation, real estate covenants, and appropriation of intellectual property may justifiably have more suspicion of fine print? In encouraging users to explore corpora in databases, is the dominant subjective position rewarded, even if alternative narratives are uncovered?

This definitional work deserves a grounding in a richer history of rules and regulation, the design of architectures and environments, and the terms of participation. After all, algorithmic culture predates computational culture by centuries. Scholars such as Alondra Nelson, Mel Chen, Chikako Takeshita, Anita Say Chan, Kelli Moore, and many others are interrogating the norms, centers, and standards of technocultural formations. Unfortunately, feminist science and technology studies (STS) and feminist human–computer interaction (HCI) often suffer from similar problems with perpetuating white privilege in the academy, and STS and HCI have the added burden of their inheritances of ethnographic methodologies from the cultures of colonization. Nonetheless, this work requires grappling with a history in which technologies and the entanglements of race, gender, class, nation, age, and disability have always been mutually constitutive.

Beth Coleman has famously asserted that race may function as a technology, which, like the technologies embedded in consumer electronics, may be black-boxed from view and prohibited from rewiring and reconfiguration. Although introducing the theme of technological determinism might not be appropriate for moving discussion forward, there are definitely ways that race functions as more than merely performance, as the recent controversy about Rachel Dolezal assuming a black identity to head an NAACP chapter and teach Africana studies indicates. In understanding the ways that the technological properties of race may be occluded, Fox Harrell notes that the quantification bias of databases tends to reinforce stereotypes, as in the case of game characters with certain racial signifiers becoming associated with default statistics that mark them as possessing attributes of strength, speed, criminality, and sensuality and lacking those of intelligence, skilled labor, and leadership.

By emphasizing "identity, agency, relationship, community, and power" in its definitional documents, Internet studies tends to devote more time and attention to issues of race than the digital humanities. However, a disciplinary reorientation toward Internet studies might not be either possible or desirable for digital humanists. First, organizations such as the Association for Internet Researchers often exclude humanities scholars from professional opportunities for presentation and publication by requiring explicit attention to methodology (and a formulaic methods section) and adherence to the conventions of reproducible science and informed consent that are unfamiliar to scholars of literature, media, history, or philosophy. Second, many who are theorizing digital culture find inadequacies in designating "identity" and "community" as such central categories, because the implicit celebration of human desire and agency – both individually and collectively – masks issues about inequality, infrastructure, and design[3] and ventriloquizes for a subaltern that cannot really speak, in Gayatri Spivak's terms.

As a case in point, it is useful to examine how *Undercurrents*, an online forum for discussion about interrelationships among race, gender, technology, and globalization, attempted to challenge the version of "net critique" that was being promulgated by the *Nettime* mailing list.[4] From the outset, *Undercurrents* sought to surface "hidden" or "unspoken questions about the racial politics of net.culture, new media, and cyberfeminism." Particularly powerful was the originators' connection between digital culture and postcolonialism: "We believe that electronic communication and postcolonial migration are parallel forces that jointly affect who we are as human collectivities and how we live regardless of whether we ourselves are migrants." Linking whiteness and the spatializing rhetorics of cyberculture, the *Undercurrents* manifesto observes that:

> contemporary cybertheory, which cyberfeminism also partakes of, maintains a storehouse of tactics that suppress racial issues and thus tacitly invest in whiteness as the universal identity that underpins net.culture. These tactics don't have to be conscious to be effective – on the contrary they work best when they are internalized as normative.

Similar undercurrents within digital humanities communities surfaced with Jamie Skye Bianco's "This Digital Humanities Which is Not One," Tara McPherson's "Why is the Digital Humanities So White?" and "U.S. Operating Systems at Mid-Century," all three of which appeared in print in 2012. A decade after the *Undercurrents* list was initiated, it seemed that very little progress had been made with respect to our understandings of intersectionality and digital practices in scholarly discourse. But of course, progress narratives are themselves suspect within feminist theory and the reality is that at any given moment we may be co-present in networked publics with feminists who identify with second, third, or fourth wave feminist theory and/or practice. Echoing Bianco, who cites Luce Irigaray, we could note the multiplicity of *this feminism which is not one*, and is perhaps better marked as *feminisms*. If we follow Bianco, this would give us plural feminisms *and* plural digital humanities and we might well ask if this is an additive or multiplicative relationship. Are we simply proliferating types of feminist digital humanities to the point where the phrase "feminist digital humanities" explodes the minute it is uttered like a radically unstable isotope?

At the moment we may not have an answer to that question, but we do want to join the chorus of voices raising the problem and we want to talk about the ways in which this has shaped our work. We are both white feminists with relatively secure professional positions within the US academy who have benefitted from systems that protect us from forces of appropriation and precarity. Our experiences are necessarily impacted by these positions and it is our responsibility to use some of that privilege to critique the problem of whiteness within feminist digital humanities. As Mikki Kendall, the originator of use of the #SolidarityIsForWhiteWomen hashtag asserts, "I really think that it's on white women to talk to white women in feminism about race."

The lack of a common feminist groundwork means that we very often need to return to a kind of Feminisms 101 opening for courses on digital humanities, ensuring that the insights of scholars such as Kimberlé Crenshaw, who developed the working definition of intersectionality, are alive for all in the room. Similarly, we find ourselves doing consciousness-raising work about hashtag feminism, Black Twitter, and efforts to facilitate trans-inclusive discussions that acknowledge and credit the informational labor of others. When we teach the MEALS acronym to focus attention on the ways that technology is always **m**aterial, **e**mbodied, **a**ffective, involves **l**abor, and is **s**ituated, we very often find that we also need to unpack that 's' in order to understand how race, class, gender, sexuality, ability, and age are all at work in the particularities of lived experience.

This is critical work, in the sense that it is simultaneously central to our work and functions as critique-in-practice. If we are to find areas for either tactical or strategic collaboration as feminist digital scholars, we have to do the work of exploring assumptions about default positions, understanding what we mean when we say "we," and recognizing that "the personal is political" means differently for different people. Twenty-first-century communication and computational technologies are unevenly distributed, have differential impacts, and participate in polyvalent histories of oppression. If we do not want to be complicit in the oppressive conditions created by our tools, our theories, and our institutional structures, then we are obligated to do something about them.

INNOVATION INEQUALITY

In addition to finding it useful to situate our work in long histories of feminist debate and deliberation, we both utilize historical perspective to understand the ways that our technologies are crafted and operate. This suggests to us a need to understand how innovation inequality, or the differential impacts of uneven distribution of innovation, shapes lives and lived experiences.[5] An early example might be the printing press, which was largely unavailable as a means of publication outside of elite networks in the sixteenth and seventeenth centuries, limiting women's ability to communicate their ideas to large audiences and exacerbating a devalorization of practices such as midwifery.[6] For a more contemporary example, consider the shift from landlines and public phone booths to cellular phone technologies. As market saturation proceeds, the economic value of operating and maintaining corner phone booths declines precipitously and even becomes associated with urban criminality.

Such innovation-driven change has different lived consequences for those who can afford to participate in mobile technology culture and those who cannot. How does one access emergency services, for example, without a cell phone? Not only are certain affordances harder to access, but newer innovation-dependent affordances such as health tracking are unevenly distributed. As certain technologies appear to become ubiquitous, assumptions that everyone is a so-called digital native and has ready access to the latest technologies effectively oppress and marginalize those who have neither the knowledge nor the devices. As Susan Cozzens and Dhanaraj Thanur observe, "technology flows . . . create social and economic boundaries such that certain technologies stop diffusing between and within countries, thereby creating innovation inequality."[7] We are living in a moment with both digital divides and ever-widening participation gaps, and intersectionality is one of our best tools for seeing these challenges.

In addition to problematizing innovation inequality that excludes many parties from participation, we are also interested in revealing how people of color *actively participate* and *have actively participated throughout history* in the larger supply chain of computational media. Often this requires challenging the dominant narrative of digital culture, which tends to lionize the programmer, inventor, and planner as the heroes of technology in new media origin stories. As the research of Craig Watkins indicates, communities of color are actually often early adopters, particularly when it comes to new uses for mobile technologies and social platforms. Stereotypical digital divide narratives elide existing capacity, local expertise, and the power dynamics of white-based education. Digital humanities scholars often want to overlook the invisible labor of people of color who not only extract the rare earth minerals and assemble the hardware components of twenty-first-century devices, but also digitize books and documents, correct optical character recognition errors, clean up metadata, staff call centers, and perform physical maintenance on servers, routers, cables, and dishes.

Even as we recognize those whose labor makes the tools themselves available, we do well to recognize women of color and trans and queer scholars already working within areas that might well fit as "digital humanities" work. Too often work in Tumblr or hashtag activism on Twitter, like Jessica Marie Johnson's and Kidada Williams' *African Diaspora Ph.D.* or Marcia Chatelain's #FergusonSyllabus, are placed outside of DH research proper.[8] For reasons that deserve more unpacking than we can do here, intellectual collaborative work by women of color, which is transforming pedagogy and research, has not yet been embraced by the broader field of DH.[9] Similarly, Simone Browne's powerful work on black identity, surveillance, and sousveillance strike us as necessary interventions into white-dominated conversations about the surveillance society and the ways in which machine learning and HCI are always shot through with conscious and unconscious bias. Google's Photo app mislabeling a black man and woman as gorillas is just the latest example of algorithmic bias[10] and points to the urgency of the work of Browne and others. It is worth noting that much of Browne's work appears in venues dedicated to cultural studies and new media studies.[11] Similarly, the transformational work of queer OS theorists and performers such as Zach Blas and Micha Cárdenas tend to find ready homes in media and performance studies but may be relatively unknown in conventional digital humanities venues. Given the long history of DH's engagement with performance and deformance through the work of Lisa Samuels, George McGann, and Mark Sample, we wonder why we have not yet seen work like Browne's, Blas', and Cardneas' foregrounded in the same ways.

ORIGINS

Intellectual genealogies may be partially responsible for these kinds of occlusions and erasures. As Lauren Klein's "Digital Origin Stories" observes, it often looks as though DH began either in technological/military developments such as the Electronic Numerical Integrator and Computer project (ENIAC), or with Father Roberto Busa's *Index Thomisticus*. Beginnings in firing tables for long-range ballistic weapons and/or a database of nearly eleven million words in medieval Latin lead to particular kinds of presents. Radiating out from the military–industrial context of ENIAC is what Tara McPherson's "U.S. Operating Systems at Mid-Century" has identified as the partitioning, modular logic of segregation and computational development.[12] From Busa's work scholars often craft a genealogy through bibliographic and textual studies, privileging the work of archive and edition development. Take for example Matthew Kirschenbaum's genealogy in which "humanities computing," the Association for Computers and the Humanities, the Association for Literary and Linguistic Computing, and the National Endowment for the Humanities' Office of Digital Humanities converge to establish DH as a field that holds work in/on hypertext and digital editions at the core.[13]

Klein and McPherson's work on origin narratives highlights the ways in which DH partakes of cultures that are dominated by patriarchal, often violent and/or repressive structures – military on the one hand, ecclesiastic on the other. As Klein notes, "the history of digital humanities is also, necessarily, a history of gender, labor, and empire." This is a particularly resonate point given Scott Weingart's annual "Acceptances to Digital Humanities" blog series.[14] Reporting on work he and Nickoal Eichmann are doing together, Weingart made the following observation: "if your first name isn't a standard name on the US Census or Social Security database, you're much less likely to get accepted to a Digital Humanities conference." What's more, his analysis suggests that topics that are traditionally feminized, such as "drama, poetry, art history, cultural studies, GLAM, and institutional support and DH infrastructure," are far less likely to be accepted for the annual conference.[15] Efforts such as Global Outlook DH, the Digital Diversity Timeline, and Amy Earhart's "The Diverse History of Digital Humanities" are designed to highlight the diverse histories and presents within DH and to further delve into the socio-political contexts of those emergent practices.[16]

Part of this work is an effort to decentralize North American and British digital humanities as "the DH." As Padmini Ray Murray observed at the 2015 Digital Diversity event, "my DH is not your DH," reminding her largely North American audience that the technical, social, and intellectual assumptions of US-based digital humanities are not universal. Murray completed her observation, "and there is joy in that," articulating that difference and distance need not mean a fracturing or fractiousness within global digital humanities engagements. Her rhetorical move, which has been repeatedly cited on Twitter and within other talks in 2015, functions as a crucial reminder that digital humanities practices are contingent and situated – they depend upon the contexts in which they operate even as practitioners work to build bridges across differences.

Part of what is at stake here is the recognition that the situatedness of computational culture is constantly under erasure with the idea of global "net-citizens." As mobile phones become increasingly important platforms for digital activity, for example, the assumption that smartphones and access to 4G networks represent a norm is only possible from very particular, privileged contexts. Alex Gil's work on minimal computing is a helpful reminder that DH under dictatorship is different;[17] likewise Angel Nieves' observation that having constant electrical power creates different conditions of possibility for digital cultural work.[18] As Pryia Kurian *et al.* note, utopian fantasies that Internet organizing and activism will elide race, class, sexuality, and other nodes of oppression miss the ways in which online technologies are "powerless" to address access gaps. What's worse, assumptions about universal access and privilege leave some feminists "unable to relate to the needs of some of the most oppressed and deprived sections of the citizenry."[19] Even in spaces where regular access to tools and Internet service can be assumed, feminist scholars observe that the push to mobile devices shapes how we interact with, and understand the importance of, public schools, museums, and libraries as cultural resource sites that have historically served underrepresented constituencies.

Hearkening back to Kendall's suggestion that it is "on white women to talk to white women about race," we note that it is also on white women and men to recognize that being a member of an "underrepresented group" results in extra labor burdens and extra risks. As Kendall suggests, it isn't the person of color's responsibility to talk about race in order to educate those who benefit from white privilege. Academics of color doing digital work often need to do a second shift beyond the regular duties of research, teaching, and service to handle institutional and associational repair work that is not of their making, and those doing work in the digital humanities are already expected to be twice as productive by building dossiers in both print and digital formats.

For those scholars of color who identify with queer, disabled, or working-class communities, there is often a third or fourth shift as well. Rather than facilitating the burnout of the most precarious in our communities in the name of inclusion and learning, we would do well to shift the burden onto those whose privilege allows them to carry it most lightly. Worse, perhaps, than the additional labor burden is the risk of appropriation; take for example the now infamous Black Twitter study led by University of Southern California PhD candidate Dayna Chatman, who is an African-American woman. When news of the USC/Annenberg study broke in a story on the Annenberg Innovation Lab website, the initial story indicated that three white men were leading the study, minimizing, if not outright effacing Chatman's central role as the lead and originator of the project.[20] As Chatman writes, her work is designed to highlight "how Black people actually consume, interpret, and deal with [racist/sexist] representation"; it demonstrates active meaning-making by Black digital authors rather than passive consumption.[21] It is a particularly cruel irony but not particularly surprising that her own active meaning-making was initially elided.

IT IDENTITIES

Of course, even as we invoke "the user" in discussions of access, we observe that the singular notion of a "user" presents a problematic category. Whether the user is imagined as expert or naive, IT discourses tend to reinforce a rhetoric of disintermediation, integrity, and self-sufficiency in which inputs and outputs are closely tied to a fluent symbiosis of human and machine. Even if the interface invariably both displays and filters simultaneously, as in the case of a screen that both screens and screens out, the user is presented as an independent entity capable of decision-making, which might be part of why the metaphor of navigation is so central to HCI. Even when cognition is presented as both embodied and distributed (Hutchins, Suchman) and digital spaces are seen as non-Cartesian (Munster, Presner), the model of the user exploring data reinforces a figure/ground relation of colonization, personal computing as manifest destiny, and "my" applications, devices, and databases.

In contrast, feminists attend to the roles of cyborgs, intermediaries, negotiators, translators, go-betweens, and other hybrid entities in computational media. But perhaps more needs to be done to see those hybrid entities in shades other than white. In addition to needing to do more on/with race, as George H. Williams observes, "while professionals working in educational technology and commercial web design have made significant progress in meeting the needs of [disabled] users, the humanities scholars creating digital projects too often fail to take these needs into account."[22] Williams' observation that "digital knowledge tools that assume everyone approaches information with the same abilities and using the same methods risk excluding a large percentage of people" might be taken more broadly as a new manifesto for the field, one that dispenses with colonialist, ableist, and racist paradigms in which human–computer interaction retains its status as embodied, situated, and contingent and therefore, decidedly non-universal.

As digital humanists, we need to move from a focus on populating the archive to a focus on animating the archive to get beyond a politics of minimal representation. For example, the Schomberg Center for Black Cultural Research at the New York City Public Library describes itself as "the largest of collection of artifacts that recognize the social, cultural and artistic accomplishments of LGBTQ people in the black community." This is a laudable project, but very little of the collection is available online, and most of the curation is handled by paid professionals, although the center does maintain an active blog. How could members of communities of color become invested in potential digital humanities projects? As Ellen Rooney observes, twenty-first-century feminisms need to do more than just be "additive."[23]

Jentery Sayers and others have also pointed out that there is also a distinct ocular bias in the digital humanities, and many of the best-funded projects manifest a tendency to privilege archives of digital files for reading or viewing rather than for listening, which excludes and devalues certain forms of cultural production. Although *Provoke! Digital Sound Studies* is intended to address this gap and speak to this need to develop an auditory digital humanities that includes the contributions of sound studies and critical race scholars, it has an all-white editorial team.[24] In contrast, what would it mean to have the members of the Crunk Feminist Collective identified as digital humanists in their work curating and commenting upon vernacular archives of hip hop culture in which no rights have been cleared? Their DH platforms of choice rely on "building blog communities" rather than designated platforms for multimedia scholarship such as Scalar, their participation model emphasizes "scholar-activists" and even those outside the academy, and their public statements often take positions of political advocacy, which is expressly forbidden in many DH grants.[25]

Furthermore, white feminists too often uncritically accept class differences between manual work and knowledge work that are inevitably marked by race as well. Curtis Marez has attempted to disrupt this binary by showing how agricultural laborers with the United Farm Workers were early adopters of new media technologies in the campaigns of Cesar Chavez, and Alex Rivera and Ricardo Dominguez have explored forms of Latino futurism that complement a rich body of work in Afro-futurism that renarrates the story of the digital divide.

DIGITAL PROFILES AND RESPONSIBILITY

While corporate and higher education approaches to computational culture differ, there is a disturbing trend to blur the boundaries as Google becomes the go-to platform for university emails and the educational technology communities become increasingly focused on quantification and "student experience optimization." Globally, corporate efforts are underway to harvest the "data shed," or large-scale quotidian output of data, of a broad range of people. This is perhaps most obvious with the rise of "self-tracking" devices such as the FitBit and Jawbone, through which people of means can track daily activities and compare their data profiles with peers around the world. Despite emancipatory claims on behalf of such devices, they reposition health care and wellness as the responsibility of the device owner and leave large swathes of people and activities outside the range of what is countable. Amelia Abreau writes of the "moments when I realize that my own life has started to veer outside of the grid of what is valued and made visible by data and quantification."[26] Drawing from Abreau's observations, white feminists would do well to think hard about how many people's lives are never within that grid. At the same time, the quantifying and tracking are not limited to those who opt in; corporations and governments are able to gather large-scale data using census, banking, and health data of those who have little to no digital life of their own. As white feminists we might experience this harvesting of our data differently from feminists of color, who see their own data used not only for tracking of consumer preferences but for punitive purposes, such as denying loans or government benefits or surveilling family members at risk of incarceration. Moreover, being a data producer is not the same thing as having permission to possess active agency and facility with digital tools, particularly when the right to purge or revise inaccurate information in one's personal record tends to be another domain of white privilege.

As Seeta Peña Gangadharan notes, "data profiling, which in general terms involves sorting through data, discovering patterns and relationships within this data, and making predictive determinations of behavior" has become a major part of digital life. She observes that the technological innovations in this area have transformed and facilitated "the ability of state and corporate actors to use data profiles for persuasive, coercive ends," making racial profiling, redlining, and medical profiling urgent issues for anyone studying contemporary digital culture.[27] It is clear that what the commercial sector calls "algorithmic optimization" and targeting can exacerbate historical injustices, such as redlining and its new manifestation reverse-redlining, which limited Black and Latino families' access to loans and, therefore, their mobility and financial security, in order to preserve white housing enclaves. While housing policy and practices can seem remote to the concerns of feminist digital humanities, we would argue that understanding the racialized stakes of quantified culture is essential even in those spaces where it seems we are "just" counting words.

CONCLUSION: DIGITAL LIVES

We began this piece by observing that feminist digital humanities too often misses the important intersectionality of our global digital cultures and their histories of participation with a broader range of technocultural practices. Rather than worry that radical multiplicity leads to fractiousness, we embrace the difficulties of dissensus and difference and want the focus to be on defining much more basic terms than "digital humanities" as a field. As white feminists who take responsibility both for our privileges and for the work of disrupting the monolithic narratives of egalitarianism and oppression emphasized in white feminism, we work to educate ourselves and our colleagues on issues of race, class, sexuality, ability, and more. We also are aware that sometimes our greatest contribution can be our absence, or our silence, in being effective allies, rather than assume that we can speak for people of color, who may also identify as queer or trans, or appropriate the robust digital humanities activities that might not always be recognized as scholarly. Many times we are most effective when we create space and then get out of the way, particularly when addressing the issue of online harassment, which also tends to be invisible in digital humanities discourses. We work in solidarity with feminists with different experiences, desired outcomes, and avenues for imagining political, social, and personal possibilities. We're relatively certain that there isn't a single right answer, or that we at least don't know it. What we can do is help to insist that we and the many manifestations of digital humanities do better.

NOTES

1 Two important pioneering works engage directly with this issue: Bailey, Moya Z., "All the Digital Humanists Are White, All the Nerds Are Men, but Some of Us Are Brave," *Journal of Digital Humanities* 1.1 (2011), http://journalofdigitalhumanities.org/1-1/all-the-digital-humanists-are-white-all-the-nerds-are-men-but-some-of-us-are-brave-by-moya-z-bailey/ and Risam, Roopika "Beyond the Margins: Intersectionality and the Digital Humanities," *Digital Humanities Quarterly* 9.2 (2015) www.digitalhumanities.org/dhq/vol/9/2/000208/000208.html

2 For example, see Stephen Ramsay, "DH and CS," http://stephenramsay.us/2013/04/30/dh-and-cs/ and Geoffrey Rockwell, "Inclusion in the Digital Humanities" www.philosophi.ca/pmwiki.php/Main/InclusionInTheDigitalHumanities

3 See the Facebook conversation initiated by Andre Brock on 20 May 2015 and synthesized by Charles Ess.

4 *Undercurrents* was launched in 2002 by Irina Aristahrkova, Maria Fernandez, Coco Fusco, and Faith Wilding https://mailman.thing.net/mailman/listinfo/undercurrents

5 As a phrase, "innovation inequality" is new, but the idea that technologies are adopted and adoptable in differential ways is not. See Susan Cozzens and Djanaraj Thakur (eds), *Innovation and Inequality: Emerging Technologies in an Unequal World* (Edward Elgar, 2014).

6 For more, see Helen King's *Midwifery, Obstetrics and the Rise of Gynaecology: The Uses of a Sixteenth-Century Compendium* (Ashgate, 2007).

7 Cozzens and Thakur, "Introduction," *Innovation and Inequality: Emerging Technologies in an Unequal World* (Edward Elgar, 2014).

8 See for example Marcia Chatelain's piece on the hashtag/syllabus "How to Teach Kids About What's Happening in Ferguson," *The Atlantic Online*,

www.theatlantic.com/education/archive/2014/08/how-to-teach-kids-about-whats-happening-in-ferguson/379049/. For Johnson's work on #adph see her tumblr: http://africandiasporaphd.tumblr.com/

9 See Scott Weingart's analysis of conference acceptances in his "Irregular ScotBot" blog, particularly the Acceptances to DH series, www.scottbot.net/HIAL/

10 Richard Nieva, "Google Apologizes for Algorithm Mistakenly Calling Black People Gorillas," www.cnet.com/news/google-apologizes-for-algorithm-mistakenly-calling-black-people-gorillas/ accessed 4 July 2015.

11 See for example: Simone Browne, "'Everybody's Got a Little Light Under the Sun': Black Luminosity and the Visual Culture of Surveillance." *Cultural Studies* (2012) and "Digital Epidermalization: Race, Identity and Biometrics." *Critical Sociology* 36.1: 131–150. (2010).

12 Tara McPherson, "U.S. Operating Systems at Mid-Century," in *Race After the Internet*, ed. by Lisa Nakamura and Peter Chow-White (MIT, 2012).

13 Matthew Kirschenbaum, "What is Digital Humanities and What's it Doing in English Departments?," in *Debates in Digital Humanities*, ed. Matt K. Gold. http://dhdebates.gc.cuny.edu/debates/text/38

14 www.scottbot.net/HIAL/?p=41327

15 Ibid; also note the ways this falls in line with the findings of Bird *et al.* regarding the proportion of "institutional housekeeping" done by female academics in "Creating Status of Women Reports: Institutional Housekeeping as 'Women's Work'." Sharon Bird; Jacquelyn Litt; Yong Wang *NWSA Journal*; Spring 2004; 16, 1; Women's Interest Module pg. 194.

16 www.globaloutlookdh.org/ http://cwrc.ca/digitaldiversity2015/ http://dhhistory.blogspot.com/

17 http://xpmethod.plaintext.in/strains/minimal-computing.html

18 www.researchgate.net/profile/Angel_Nieves

19 Rawwida Baksh and Wendy Harcourt (eds), *The Oxford Handbook of Transnational Feminist Movements* (Oxford University Press, 2015), p 875.

20 www.annenberglab.com/projects/dsail-black-twitter-project; see also Chatman's response to the initial story https://dchatman3.wordpress.com/2014/09/04/in-reply-my-reflections-on-comments-about-our-research-on-black-twitter/

21 Ibid.

22 George H. Williams, "Disability, Universal Design, and Digital Humanities," in *Debates in Digital Humanities*, Matt K. Gold, ed. http://dhdebates.gc.cuny.edu/debates/text/44 accessed 4 July 2015.

23 Ellen Rooney, *Companion to Feminist Literary Theory* (Cambridge University Press).

24 http://soundboxproject.com/about.html

25 www.crunkfeministcollective.com/about/

26 Ameila Abreau, "Quantify Everything, a Dream of a Feminist Data Future," *ModelViewCulture*, https://modelviewculture.com/pieces/quantify-everything-a-dream-of-a-feminist-data-future

26 Seeta Peña Gangadharan, "Digital Inclusion and Data Profiling," *First Monday*, Volume 17, Number 5–7, May 2012. http://journals.uic.edu/ojs/index.php/fm/article/view/3821/3199 doi:10.5210/fm.v17i5.3821

CHAPTER 4

Towards best practices in collaborative online knowledge production

Susan Brown

This chapter focuses on the affordances web technologies offer for sharing the processes of scholarly production on an unprecedented scale. The Web has been writeable from its earliest days, thanks to the basic database functions of Create, Read, Update, and Delete, although early on the ability to do so required some technical knowledge. What is commonly called "Web 2.0" was not so much a shift in technology but the application of existing technologies to make it very easy for people to write, which is to say publish, to the Web, with the result that vast numbers of people began to participate in knowledge creation online, whether in the form of wikis, blogs, or social media.

Increasingly, scholars are creating Web materials to disseminate their work. However, despite the demonstration by Wikipedia, now the world's largest information resource, of the power of shared knowledge creation, collaboration in the humanities lags behind that in the social and natural sciences (Larivière *et al.*) and the digital humanities (Spiro). Even in the digital humanities, people, tools and expertise, and projects are isolated (Davis and Dombrowski), with the result that many scholars see the isolation of resources as one of the major impediments to effective research online (Bulger *et al.*). The status of citation as a bedrock of scholarly practice indicates the extent to which knowledge production has always been collaborative. However, in this context, collaborative practices are inflected by multiple factors associated with the transition from print to digital media, including differences in the way authority operates, the easy reproducibility of content, the apparently endless possibilities for inter-relation, major shifts in modes of reading and analysis, the flood of digital content that shifts us into an attention economy, challenges of long-term curation and sustainability, and the wealth of possible forms of digital scholarly publication in an age of incunabula. New streams of networked language challenge us, in ways we now only partially comprehend, with their massive shareability and mashable dynamic forms, to devise new forms of research collectivity that will help to overcome the isolation both of research resources and of researchers working in a digital environment.

This chapter therefore addresses key principles that should inform considerations of tools and environments for collaborative scholarship, along with significant features of workspaces and work processes that help translate those principles into active components of projects. It works with an understanding of "best" practices as those that lead to superior scholarship, the definition of which is contested in many ways. For the purposes of this essay, the criteria include not only better control over scholarly processes involving more than one contributor, but also better suitability for preservation, interoperability, and reuse, and a greater ability to meet ethical and professional obligations associated with working in groups. Although it eschews discussion of any particular collaborative platform, except occasionally by way of example, the perspective here emerges from two decades of experience with the Orlando Project (Brown *et al.*), an ongoing born-digital literary history project that has involved well over a hundred contributors, with many hands involved over time in producing component entries, and from developing the Canadian Writing Research Collaboratory (CWRC), an online environment for digital literary studies (Brown, "Scaling").[1]

Establishing and coordinating collaborative relationships is a complex activity that takes time and effort. Despite our aspirations, research billed as collaborative may not turn out to be as rewarding for all those involved as it was intended to be (Fong *et al.*). The early stages of a project offer the opportunity to start to establish the terms of a collaboration through meetings and frequent communication among prospective members, grant-writing, a project charter, and the production of a data management plan (Ruecker and Radzikowska; Siemens; Spiro). All of these will facilitate thinking through the collaborative aspects of a project at an early formative stage, and regular evaluation of collaborative work can help keep the collaborations on track. Face-to-face contact at key points has been shown to be crucial for certain types of close collaboration (Siemens), although crowdsourcing and citizen science initiatives have proven that it is possible to bring people together effectively for collaboration without any personal interaction (*Transcribe Bentham*; *Old Weather*). For projects involving students or identified collaborators who require training, in-person training programs are highly desirable supplements to providing project documentation or training materials online. Grouping participants in cohorts (even cohorts of two) so they can learn together, ideally with support from more experienced project members, and move from foundational to more advanced contributions, can be very effective.

The focus here is less on coordinating collaborative relationships and more on the potential for leveraging standards and systems to enable collaborative scholarship online. That does not mean sidestepping the human element in collaboration, but rather addressing it differently. We need to retain in our consideration and design of computational systems the sophisticated understanding of human subject formation and engagement with technology that has emerged from the humanities. The language used here thus largely eschews the alienating vocabulary from the field of human–computer interaction (HCI) with its emphasis on discrete tasks, efficiencies, and "usability" narrowly conceived (Drucker), in order to focus on the processes of collaborative scholarship and the relationship of those processes to the specific features and affordances of technical systems. However, because that vocabulary is ubiquitous in discussions and technical documentation of software, it is occasionally invoked for clarity.

COORDINATING CONTRIBUTORS

Collaboration is pervasive in digital humanities for numerous reasons (Price; Spiro). Most pertinent here are the ability to draw on varied skills sets and different disciplinary frameworks, to involve people with different levels of expertise including for pedagogical and mentoring purposes, to scale up research by involving a larger number of people than is usual in humanities research (potentially including citizen scholars from beyond academia), and to allow contributors to work asynchronously and across distances. All of this requires coordinating people's activities. This can be done, and is often done too in smaller projects, in an *ad hoc* fashion using lists or spreadsheets that are updated manually, but within an extensive project involving large numbers of contributors this is not very sustainable, so many systems for supporting collaborative work provide ways to coordinate people's activities.

For instance, a project may involve systems administrators and programmers who need access to the entire system, project leaders or managers who may not need root access but will require access to all the materials, editors who need to be able to access materials to edit and approve them for publication, and contributors who are involved at an early stage but don't need access beyond their own work or beyond a certain stage of production. How granularly access is controlled has a great deal to do with system capabilities, how many people are involved and their levels of technical expertise, how clearly roles and responsibilities are defined, and the degree of trust involved. More sophisticated systems will not only allow different types of access and permissible actions to be assigned to different individuals, but will allow each individual to be assigned a role (user role). Their role then determines what materials a person can access and how (user permissions). Systems that can handle assigning multiple roles to the same person in relation to different subsets of materials, and that can control who does what at what stage of a particular workflow, are ideal for large projects, since they allow for maximum flexibility. However, systems that simply provide the ability to control who can do what across an entire set of materials are the norm, and many projects rely on human trust and management to ensure, for instance, that items that have been approved and published are not modified by research assistants without review by an editor. Projects whose activities extend across large numbers of contributors, perhaps including citizen scientists or crowdsourcing, often have to set up specialized workflows to process these types of contributions (Rockwell; Causer *et al.*). The technical requirements for coordinating contributors thus depend hugely on the nature of the work, its anticipated scale, and the relationships among contributors.

Platforms, however, only work with people. Effective computational systems are deeply rooted in communities. As John Seely Brown and Paul Duguid argue, most systems work through "a combination of technological frailty and social resourcefulness," with the informal human interactions of the latter compensating for the former (77). The functionality of any particular computational system, whether it is a loosely linked combination of tools or an integrated platform offering multiple tools within a single interface, can only enable and not replace human interactions of support and empowerment. The language of "project management" may be alienating in its reliance on a business model, but the practice of coordinating people's work requires focus and substantial time. On smaller projects, this can sometimes be done by lead researchers, or by experienced assistants guided by more experienced researchers. Larger projects, particularly ones involving software development, require a rare combination of technical knowledge and humanities training with the ability to track complex development paths. In both cases, dedicated project management software, or often a combination of tools for various purposes, can be very helpful to facilitate such activities as: intra-project communications; tracking of to-dos, work tickets, and bugs; tracking individuals' work or overall project progress (through tools such as hour tracking or Gantt charts); and facilitating the sharing and storage of organizational documents (as opposed to research materials). Two things to bear in mind in considering the bewildering array of available tools are: the more that a system builds on or integrates with tools that people already use (such as email), the more likely it is to gain broad uptake; and a powerful system with a steep learning curve requires at least one dedicated person to maintain it and keep the information up to date, and is unlikely to be adopted by people who are not using it on a daily basis.

DATA FORMATS AND METADATA STANDARDS

Research data is incredibly various. Christof Schöch surveys the complexity of "data" in the humanities, and Christine Borgman situates it in the context of digital scholarship (*Scholarship*). The form in which a project's materials – the basic stuff, or data, and metadata that describes that stuff – is stored might seem removed from matters of collaboration. Yet interoperability – the ability to share data, to allow it to be used for multiple purposes by different programs and within different environments, and to meet the diverse research interests of collaborators – is deeply dependent upon such banal matters as data and metadata standards (Besser; Foulonneau and Riley). Moreover, if digital scholarship is to engage in that centuries-long form of collaboration represented by citation practices, it needs to do its best to ensure that it can be preserved for reference and reuse. As Abby Smith Rumsey argues:

> Digital preservation begins at the time of creation, well before the digitized material comes to rest in a preservation repository, where it will be managed by professional archivists throughout its life cycle. Choosing which formats to use, deciding how to name and manage files, performing routine backup and migration – these are all critical preservation actions that individuals and organizations must take to help ensure that their content will be preserved. (2003, 5)

Standards for both the formats in which datasets are stored and the metadata used to describe them are crucial to providing digital research materials with the best prospect of long-term accessibility and reusability by the research community. With respect to data longevity, some of the most fundamental principles include using open rather than proprietary formats; storing data in a format that separates them wherever possible from formatting or presentation-oriented code; using shared and ideally open repositories rather than storing materials in an *ad hoc* way; and ensuring that the repository is a managed environment with robust, off-site backup and data curation built into it. The gold standard for long-term preservation is to assign Persistent URLs (PURLS) or Digital Object Identifiers (DOIs) so that datasets can be more easily indexed, retrieved, and cited.

Online sources can provide an excellent start to understanding the choices to be made with respect to data formats, management, and curation; these currently include "An Introduction to Humanities Data Curation" by Julia Flanders and Trevor Muñoz, "The NINCH Guide to Good Practice in the Digital Representation and Management of Cultural Heritage Materials" (NINCH), and the Force 11 "Joint Declaration of Data Citation Principles." Researchers should also seek up-to-date advice on best practices and local resources for their particular types of materials from other digital scholars, data specialists, or digital librarians familiar with their particular field. The disciplinary and methodological diversity in the humanities gives rise to a wide array of types of research outputs, ranging from textual files, still images, sound and moving image files, geospatial data, and myriad types of databases, not to mention combinations of these in interactive media including websites, electronic literature, and video games. There is no single solution.

Moreover, considering "the situated, partial, and constitutive character of knowledge production," what is generally discussed as "data" is properly understood as "capta", that is, "taken and constructed" rather than "recorded and observed" (Drucker Abstract; para 3). Precisely because no data are "raw" (Gitelman), understanding the implications of specific data format and metadata standards matters. Standards change, and they are also legion, as indicated by Jenn Riley's infographic and associated glossary of 105 cultural heritage metadata standards and their relation to community, domain, function, and purpose (Riley and Becker, Figure 4.1).

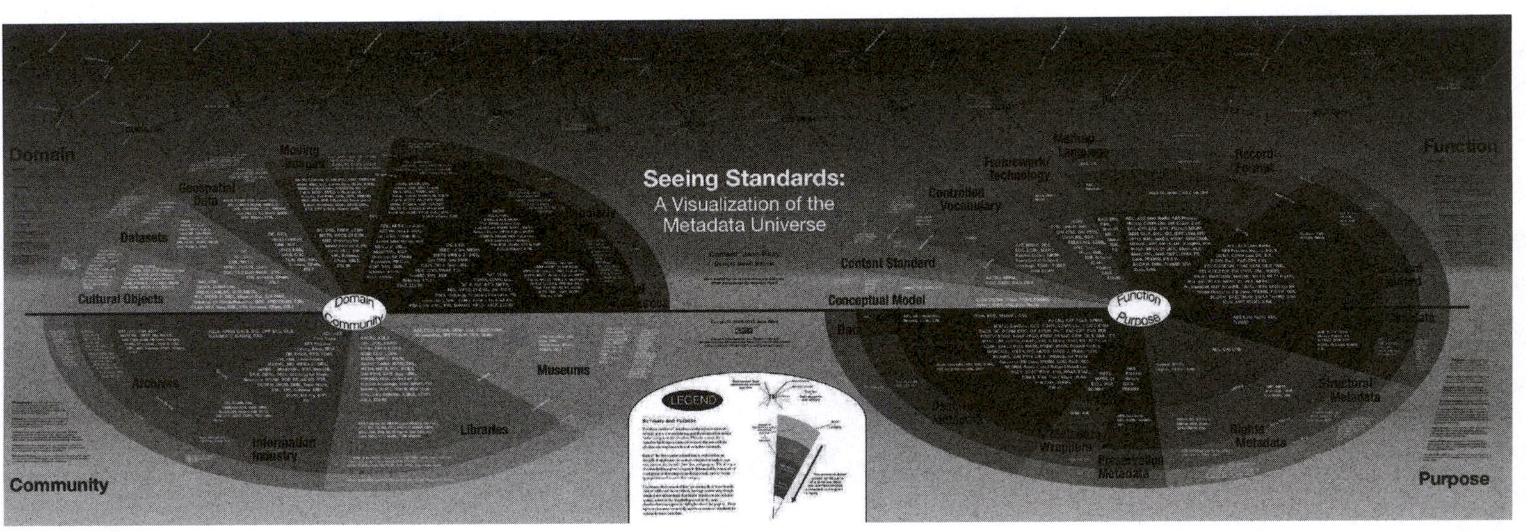

Figure 4.1
Jenn Riley, "Seeing Standards: A Visualization of the Metadata Universe"

Devin Becker, Designer

Metadata standards, by embedding categories that organize knowledge and shape our understanding of the world, are a highly political form of infrastructure, and their implications need to be considered carefully (Bowker and Star). Some standards make it impossible to represent the complexity of certain fundamental concepts (Brown and Simpson, "Curious"), and, as Christine Borgman has argued, "Interoperability allows some data and stakeholders in and keeps others out" (*Big Data*, 47).

There is an "inherent tension" between diversity and standardization, and we are at a moment in the development of information systems where multiple efforts are underway to explore the extent to which it is possible to "capture the cultural diversity of knowledge resources while still incorporating sufficient systematic information to enable effective retrieval" (Boast *et al.*, 397). Nevertheless, the overwhelming tendency of digital projects is to devise bespoke categories or vocabularies that emerge from particular researchers' views of their data. This kind of emergent knowledge organization reflects the expert or community of experts that produces it, but impedes collaboration by making it very difficult for researchers or projects to combine their data, or for other researchers to build upon it. It also works against the collaborative potential of all digital information by making it harder to locate relevant information within larger systems (Bair and Carlson). The Semantic Web is one of several attempts to negotiate the tension between specificity and the need to create cross-walks between different vocabularies and conceptual frameworks (Berners-Lee *et al.*; Lassila *et al.*), but it is too early to determine its value for humanities research. This framework has been proposed as the basis for a new kind of collaborative scientific platform (Di Franzo *et al.*).

There is, moreover, the crucial matter of how well data and metadata formats support the tracking of provenance. As Julia Flanders and Trevor Muñoz argue,

> The curation of research data – raw and abstracted material created as part of research processes and which may be used again as the input to further research – carries with it the burden of capturing and preserving not only the data itself, but information about the methods by which it was produced. (para 3)

As discussed below in the context of workflow, digital research materials and products need to refer not only to the information sources on which a particular assertion is based or the source from which a particular component of a dataset is derived, but who made the assertion or how the information was obtained, and where in the chain of other actions related to the resource that action occurred. This is crucial because knowledge is sociotechnical (Borgman, *Scholarship*, 228) and situated: "Knowledge claims are of a time and of a place" whereas information objects are prone to operate and be perceived as fixed and "timeless abstractions" (Boast *et al.*, 400).

INTERFACE

Interfaces, the graphical and haptic means by which researchers interact with computational systems, are perhaps the single most influential factor in the adoption of software, the point at which the situatedness of both knowledge and researchers comes home to roost. Interfaces, both experimental ones that trouble how information is usually designed for us (Galey and Ruecker) and normalized ones that form part of our daily information infrastructure, make arguments about the meaning of what they present. They have a massive impact on how we engage with knowledge, hailing us as subjects and interpellating us through categories such as race, gender, and disciplinary formations within the complex apparatuses of the knowledge economy. Even the interfaces of editing environments differ quite significantly in the kind of activity that they invite (Brown, "Remediating"), and trying to bring researchers into complex interfaces of collaborative work environments can be very challenging given the "ideology of ease" (Dilger).

The LAIRAH project found that 30–35 percent of digital resources go unused, due to poorly designed interfaces, inadequate communication of a site's purpose, and lack of documentation (Warwick *et al.*). For projects involved in tool development, these findings should bring home the desirability of involving information and graphical user interface (GUI) designers early. LAIRAH found that the adoption rate for new tools is slow, and even where they are adopted, they are often used according to old paradigms rather than spawning new ones: it is therefore key to provide easy on-ramps for users. Since we learn and understand according to what we already know, paradigm shifts are hampered by the extent to which interfaces are either adopted wholesale from other domains, or adapted within the humanities on shoestring budgets without adequate regard for design. This has major implications for collaborative research environments:

> The participatory environment of the creation of cultural materials calls for analysis and display of the co-dependent relation between communities of thought and their expression. We have yet to engage seriously with modeling environments that support cultural difference, rather than register it, often in static and even monolithic ways, on standard platforms developed by dominant industry players. **If the platforms set the terms of cultural production then whose worldview and ideologies will they embody and structure into the creation of knowledge?** (Burdick *et al.*, 91)

Developing new literacies in scholarly collaboration through new affordances, and making tools that truly suit the scholarship, is a highly experimental, iterative, long-term process, but one whose urgency is clear. Projects that work in tool and interface development are active at the rockface of new forms of knowledge production, and we need the outcomes of their design thinking, community engagement, and testing to push forward this work. In the meantime, it behooves us all to think carefully on the interfaces of available tools and platforms beyond their obvious affordances, for they will help to shape the collaborations for which they are used.

TOOLS AND WORKFLOWS

Scholars who collaborate in humanities research participate in a vast array of activities: entering existing materials to transform it into "data"; the more or less manual processes that are variously termed cleaning, munging, or wrangling data; entering or managing metadata; organizing, structuring, or relating materials; transcribing, authoring, editing, analyzing, and visualizing; not to mention coding tools to do these and other things to suit particular needs. Larger projects often engage in software development. However, many projects must choose among existing tools for collaborative work, and there are numerous sometimes conflicting factors to consider.

Mainstream tools have the major advantage of familiarity, and they are increasingly designed with collaboration in mind. For collaboration on a small scale aimed at preparing materials towards final appearance in print, for example, they may be perfectly adequate. The challenges of switching to the use of new tools should not be underestimated, and even quite simple, well-established collaborative authoring environments such as wikis can be hard to learn. Researchers thus need to be convinced of the advantages of switching work environments in order to make the time investment in switching. However, there can be real advantages to doing so, such as the ability to work in or export to standard formats, or the ability to associate items, such as data and metadata, in systematic ways. Projects looking to process materials computationally or to deliver them in sophisticated digital environments as opposed to print surrogates should look beyond office productivity tools.

The degree of integration of tools and the kinds of interfaces they offer is a significant consideration. Using a plethora of different tools can make learning a workflow much harder than performing several actions within a single environment, although scholars are tremendously adaptable given sufficient reason. Likewise, despite the growing technical literacy of humanities scholars, many are uncomfortable working at the command line or having to modify code in order to manipulate or analyze their materials. While the question of whether one has to be able to code or build in order to consider oneself to work in digital humanities remains controversial (Ramsay; Posner; Sample), it is undoubtedly the case that many involved in using digital tools for collaborative scholarship – including a growing number of scholars who have no aspirations to engage in digital humanities *per se* – are much more comfortable working within graphical user interfaces (GUIs), particularly ones that offer a number of affordances. Hence the popularity of content management systems (CMS), which range from quite specialized ones such as web-based blogging platforms to very flexible and extensible ones such as Drupal. Such systems can help to coordinate collaborators, including assigning roles; allow scholars to organize their data and metadata; allow for editing of materials, prevent inadvertent overwriting of documents, and retain versions in case it is necessary to examine or revert to them; support the formatting and publishing of materials on the Web; provide indexing, search, and retrieval, and so on. The degree of expertise required to run different systems varies widely, so one has to bear in mind the amount of ongoing technical or programming support available, but such systems should be evaluated carefully for the extent to which they support working with appropriate standards for the field of inquiry, such as the Extensible Markup Language (XML) format for text.

Complementing more mainstream options are scholarly tools and platforms that have been developed with the needs of humanities researchers, and humanities standards, in mind. To mention just a few, these range from, at one end of the spectrum, quite focused solutions such as the Zotero bibliographic software management tool that can run as a plug-in in both a browser and a word processor, bridging the world of web resources and writing environments, but built on open principles so that its application programming interfaces (APIs) allow it to be hooked up and integrated with other environments, as well supporting extensions of its functionality for unforeseen uses (Cohen). At the other end of the spectrum are platforms such as DARIAH, TextGrid, or CWRC, which aim to support a wider range of activities in integrated environments in order to achieve interoperability and foster best practices across quite a wide range of projects. Although such tools and systems are built by researchers for researchers, there are often disadvantages to consider. Smaller open-source tools, even ones that are quite fully developed, often lack documentation and support, which can make them harder to use, more challenging for fixing bugs or contributing improvements back to the code, and harder to maintain, so projects adopting them may require technical expertise long after the startup phase. It can be helpful in such situations to try to find an organizational partner, such as a research library, digital humanities centre, or technical division that has expertise in the platform. In addition, open-source software often cannot be sustained, so it can quickly go stale and break unless significant resources are available for its upkeep. It is wise to research how recently the code has been updated and how it is being maintained. A major consideration is the level of support available for a particular system. Technical support is unlikely to be as available for free or open-source software systems; their proponents are generally people who are happy digging around in user forums to try to find solutions to problems, or larger projects with dedicated technical personnel.

Where tools will operate and who will operate them are important questions. Because problems specific to particular hardware and software combinations can be hard to isolate, collaborative groups that are geographically distributed may want to consider web-based tools as opposed to those that run on individuals' personal computers. Web tools obviate the need for installation, patches, and upgrades, and ensure that everyone is using the same individual version of the software at any given time. So, for instance, some analysis and visualization tools, such as the Voyant suite (Sinclair and Rockwell), are web-based and make it very easy to input data. By contrast, more flexible and powerful tools, such as the R, D3 or Mallet packages, require command-line comfort or basic coding skills plus familiarity with how to transform data to conform to the software. Shifting from the PC environment to a mainframe high-performance computer environment in order to speed up work on large sets of materials can require still another skill set to move the data to the processing and run it in batches. Ideally, a few people involved in a larger project will catch the processing bug and learn to use these systems, but the majority of scholars in the humanities much prefer a well-designed, stable, documented GUI on the Web.

Coordinating workflow is a component of collaborative scholarly work on which research quality depends but which in many platforms is weak. Digital objects may have to move through a variety of stages such as ingestion; metadata creation, derivation, or enhancement; transformation; the production of derivative versions; content creation, correction, or revision; editorial oversight; and peer review, before they reach the point of publication. Nor are workflows linear; they often involve iterative loops back to earlier stages, even post-publication, since digital objects are not fixed and therefore are continually susceptible to revision and update as the state of knowledge changes (Borgman, *Scholarship*, 232; Brown and Simpson, "Changing"). In an environment involving numerous collaborators, then, tracking this process of continual change is a major concern. Again, there is no single solution to suit all. The header element in a document conforming to the Text Encoding Initiative guidelines, for instance, provides a means of storing the metadata for a digital text within the file for the text itself, so as to keep the relevant information together. This metadata can include elements that record with considerable granularity the actions of those who have been responsible for producing the text, or in other words a record of the workflow associated with it (TEI Consortium). Binary objects such as images, audio, or visual files cannot incorporate such workflow metadata directly, and ideally should be stored in repositories that keep links between such files and the metadata related to them, often by bundling them together into a composite object. Keeping workflow information in a totally separate environment such as a spreadsheet is far from ideal, since it is hard to leverage that information to sort or process the related materials, and increases the risk that work and the record of it will get out of sync.

Even when workflow information is stored with or closely linked to an object, it often takes considerable effort and programming time to be able to do much with that information. Unfortunately, many projects fall back on tracking work manually, since the available tools for managing workflow are often difficult to integrate with other systems, lack features needed by humanities researchers, and are costly to customize or extend even when open-source. Being able to sort a set of results, produce reports, or extract subsets of materials based on workflow status is highly desirable in a collaborative environment. Interfaces designed to visualize the state and stage in the

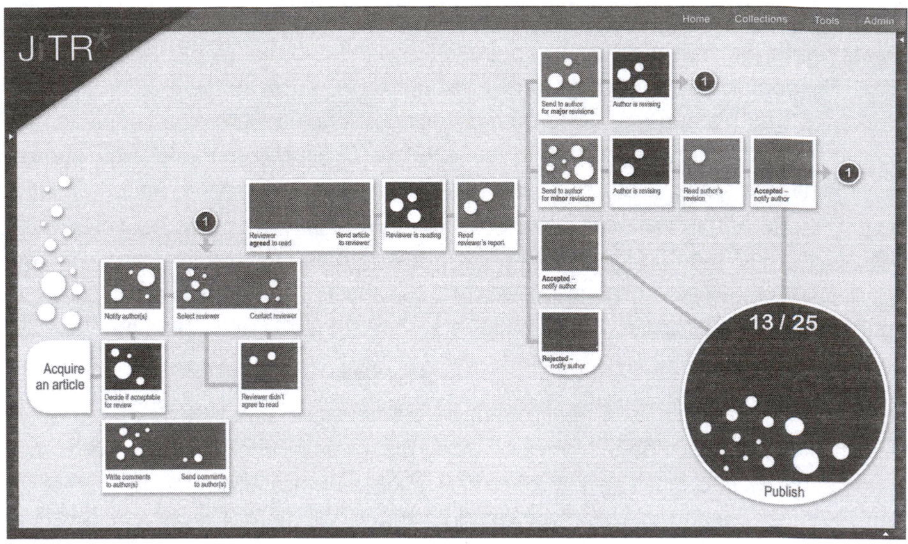

Figure 4.2
Workflow interface prototype by Luciano Frizzera

See Ruecker *et al.* ("Visual")

workflow process of all objects in a collection, to allow entry of status updates, and to allow researchers to modify the objects themselves would support advanced collaborative workflows (Figure 4.2).

COMMONS, CREDIT, AND COLLABORATIVE KNOWLEDGE CIRCUITS

Collaboration enables scaling up through shared labour. It participates in the potentiality of what Michael Hardt and Antonio Negri term "multitude," which they characterize as producing a "spiral, expansive relationship," a "dual relationship between production and the common – the common that is produced and is also productive – [that] is key to understanding all social and economic activity" in the current, digital age (197). This larger context should make those engaged in research collaboration the more attentive to matters of labour and credit, particularly given the extent to which digital humanities endeavours are imbricated within higher education systems that are in the process of casualizing academic labour within a shift towards neo-liberalism (Slaughter and Rhoades).

One of the arts of successful collaboration is trying to figure out, given the various stakes and roles and subject positions, what is rewarding to each contributor within the specific context. Among the many that are relevant, credit is perhaps most closely linked to the concerns with data, metadata, and platforms that have been outlined here. The need to acknowledge more fully the contributions of all participants in a collaborative relationship (Nowviskie; Fair Cite) can be addressed in part by aiming for best practices in role assignment and workflow management as outlined here. Granular information about the extent and nature of contributions, when tracked carefully, can provide the means of acknowledging in a more precise and compelling fashion the contributions of individuals either to a single digital scholarly artifact, or to an entire collection (Figure 4.3a–b).

A study of virtual research environments conducted by the Joint Information Systems Committee (Carusi and Reimer) stresses broad community engagement and user-driven development as keys to the success of online collaborative environments across a number of disciplines. Such factors are as relevant to small and strategic collaborative projects as large ones. Indeed, this chapter has hopefully demonstrated that participation in best practices, even when working alone, is tantamount to collaborating with the entire scholarly community, present and future. Technologies for interoperability across data types and domains, such as the Semantic Web, hold out the potential for global, multilingual collaboration from

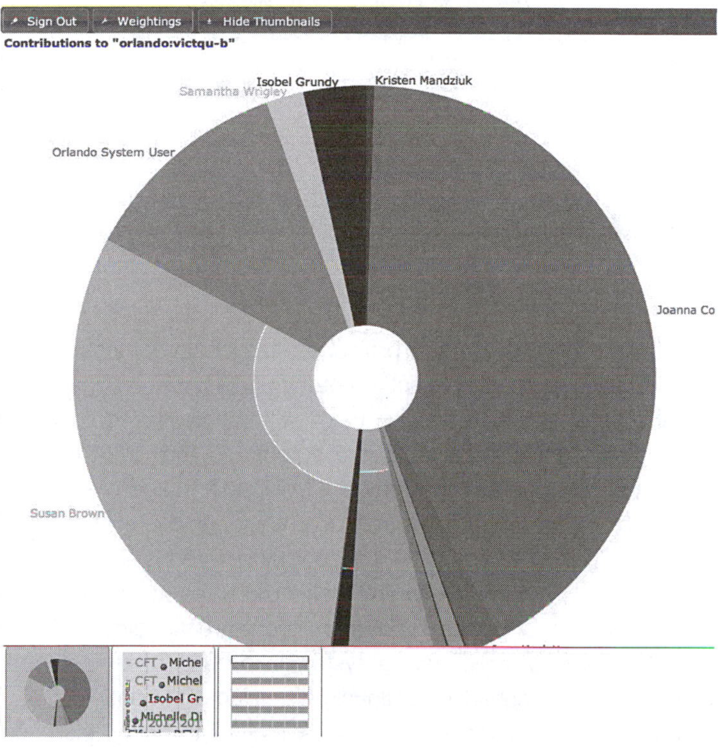

Figure 4.3a
CWRC Credit Visualization prototype: a researcher's contribution to a single document.

Draws on Arazy *et al.*

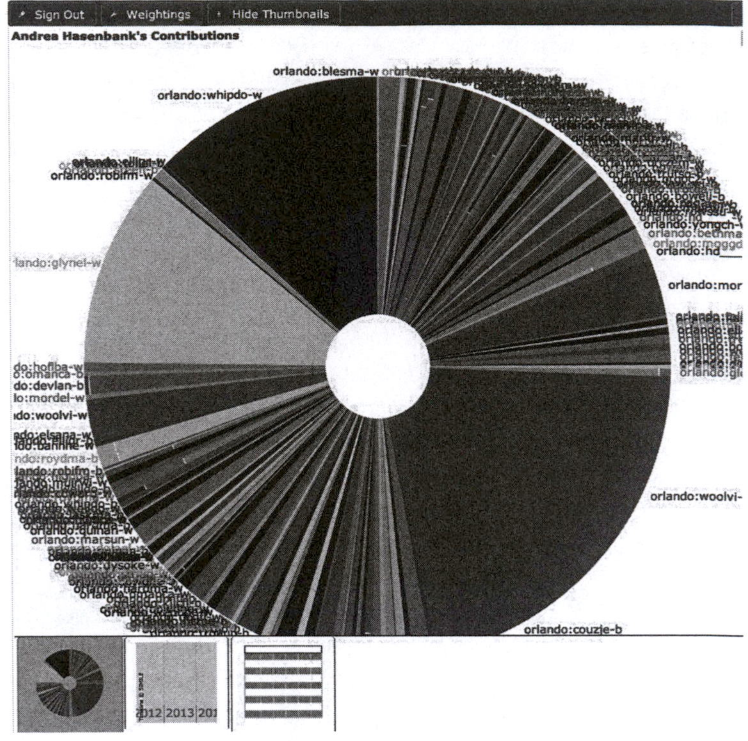

Figure 4.3b
CWRC Credit Visualization prototype: a researcher's contribution to a collection.

Draws on Arazy *et al.*

diverse contributors. Glimpses of this project are evident in, for instance, the Social Networks and Archival Contexts project's prototype tools, which aggregate materials from numerous archives and combine them with contextual data to enrich the experience of them. Because the links are automated, however, it also contains laughable mismatches, such as the use of a Wikipedia image of John Sykes, the rock guitarist of Thin Lizzy fame, to illustrate an entry for an overseer on a nineteenth-century plantation owned by Henry Hull a century before his birth ("John Sykes"). As Laura Mandell has argued, there are major problems in the use of dirty data for data mining; she launched the TypeWright tool to rectify dirty OCR. This is the next, necessary phase for collaborative systems: to build in such feedback loops to allow user expertise to enhance continually the value of dynamic digital materials. If we can bring such collaborative knowledge circuits into being, then ecosystems made up of individual and team researchers, citizen scholars, publishers, libraries, and memory institutions, supported by robust scholarly communities and collaborative infrastructures, have the potential to scale up online knowledge production exponentially, with results we can only glimpse in current experiments in search, retrieval, data mining, and visualization.

No existing system supports best practices in all of the components of collaborative scholarship outlined here, and best practices themselves are both context-dependent and regularly evolving, so it is unlikely that any "one size fits all" solution will present itself given the diversity of humanities research endeavours. Moreover, technical affordances cannot compensate for a lack of human care and attention to processes and relationships. Strong collaborative relationships take time to build and maintain, and there is a complex and challenging interplay of scholarly culture with technological tools that is at work in any attempt to forge a scholarly community within a digital environment. Nevertheless, considering from the outset what aspects of the collaborative relationship matter most to a project, being cognizant of best practices, and choosing carefully among the many available standards, collaborative tools, and working environments, can help a group cohere and define its goals, enable those involved to work effectively together, and position a project well for as-yet-unforeseen collaborations with other people and projects. There is no question that working towards best practices in collaborative digital scholarship, like collaboration itself, generally takes more planning, more effort, more time, and involves greater cost than adopting more immediately pragmatic strategies. However, it holds out the rewards both of enabling work that could not be accomplished otherwise and, by fostering more interoperable knowledge production, of contributing to and participating in a collaborative knowledge ecosystem of breathtaking scope and potential.

NOTE

1 I am indebted here to my many collaborators in both of these projects, and in particular those within CWRC with whom I have worked particularly closely on training and collaborative workflow processes and with whom I have taught courses and workshops on the CWRC platform: Jeffery Antoniuk, Michael Brundin, Karyn Huenemann, and Mihaela Ilovan. Many thanks to Abi Lemak for help in the preparation of the references. I would also like to acknowledge my colleagues on the Implementing New Knowledge Environments project with whom I have thought much about collaboration. I am grateful to the Social Sciences and Humanities Research Council and the Canada Foundation for Innovation for funding these related projects.

REFERENCES

Arazy, Ofer, Eleni Stroulia, Stan Ruecker, Cristina Arias, Carlos Fiorentino, Veselin Ganev, and Timothy Yau. "Recognizing Contributions in Wikis: Authorship Categories, Algorithms, and Visualizations." *Journal of the American Society for Information Science and Technology* 61.6 (2010): 1166–1179.

Bair, Sheila, and Sharon Carlson. "Where Keywords Fail: Using Metadata to Facilitate Digital Humanities Scholarship." *Journal of Library Metadata* 8.3 (2008): 249–62. University Libraries Faculty and Staff Publications, Paper 12. Western Michigan University, 1 January 2008. http://scholarworks.wmich.edu/cgi/viewcontent.cgi?article=1012&context=library_pubs.

Berners-Lee, Tim, James Hendler, and Ora Lassila. "The Semantic Web." *Scientific American* 284.5 (2001): 28–37.

Besser, Howard. *The Past, Present, and Future of Digital Libraries*. Oxford: Blackwell, 2004.

Boast, Robin, Michael Bravo, and Ramesh Srinivasan. "Return to Babel: Emergent Diversity, Digital Resources, and Local Knowledge." *The Information Society* 23.5 (2007): 395–403. doi:10.1080/01972240701575635

Borgman, Christine L. *Big Data, Little Data, No Data: Scholarship in the Networked World*. Cambridge, MA: MIT Press, 2015.

Borgman, Christine L. *Scholarship in the Digital Age*. Cambridge, MA: MIT Press, 2007.

Bowker, Geoffrey, and Susan Leigh Star. *Sorting Things Out: Classification and Its Consequences*. Cambridge, MA: MIT Press, 2000.

Brown, John Seely, and Paul Duguid. *The Social Life of Information*. Cambridge, MA: Harvard Business Press, 2002.

Brown, Susan, Patricia Clements, and Isobel Grundy. *The Orlando Project*. 2006–2015. www.artsrn.ualberta.ca/orlando/.

Brown, Susan. "Remediating the Editor." *Interdisciplinary Science Reviews* 40.1 (2015): 78–94.

Brown, Susan. "Scaling Up Collaboration Online: Toward a Collaboratory for Research on Canadian Writing." *International Journal of Canadian Studies* 48 (2014): 233–251.

Brown, Susan, John Simpson, the INKE Research Group, and CWRC Project Team. "The Changing Culture of Humanities Scholarship: Iteration, Recursion, and Versions in Scholarly Collaboration Environments." *Scholarly and Research Communication* 5.4 (2014).

Brown, Susan, and John Simpson. "The Curious Identity of Michael Field and its Implications for Humanities Research with the Semantic Web." *IEEE Big Humanities Data* (2013): 77–85.

Bulger, Monica, Eric Meyer, Grace De la Flor, Melissa Terras, Sally Wyatt, Marina Jirotka, Katherine Eccles, and Christine McCarthy Madsen. "Reinventing Research? Information Practices in the Humanities." *Information Practices in the Humanities. A Research Information Network Report* (2011).

Burdick, Anne, Johanna Drucker, Peter Lunenfeld, Todd Presner, and Jeffrey Schnapp. *Digital_Humanities*. Cambridge, MA: MIT Press, 2012.

Carusi, Annamaria, and Torsten Reimer. "Virtual Research Environment Collaborative Landscape." *Joint Information Systems Committee* (2010). www.jisc.ac.uk/publications/reports/2010/vrelandscapestudy.aspx.

Causer, Tim, Justin Tonra, and Valerie Wallace. "Transcription Maximized; Expense Minimized? Crowdsourcing and Editing *The Collected Works of Jeremy Bentham*." *Literary and Linguistic Computing* 27.2 (2012): 119–137. doi:10.1093/llc/fqs004.

Cohen, Daniel J. "Creating Scholarly Tools and Resources for the Digital Ecosystem: Building Connections in the Zotero Project." *First Monday* 13.8 (2008).

Data Citation Synthesis Group: Joint Declaration of Data Citation Principles. Ed. M. Martone. San Diego, CA: FORCE 11, 2014. www.force11.org/datacitation.

Davis, Rebecca, and Quinn Dombrowski. "Divided and Conquered: How Multivarious Isolation Is Suppressing Digital Humanities Scholarship," Washington, DC: *National Institute for Technology in Liberal Education*, Spring 2011. web.archive.org/web/20130927214037/www.nitle.org/live/files/36-divided-and-conquered.

Di Franzo, Dominic, John S. Erickson, Marie Joan Kristine T. Gloria, Joanne S. Luciano, Deborah L. McGuinness, and James Hendler. "The Web Observatory Extension: Facilitating Web Science Collaboration Through Semantic Markup." *Proceedings of the Companion Publication of the 23rd International Conference on World Wide Web Companion*. International World Wide Web Conferences Steering Committee, 2014.

Dilger, Bradley. "The Ideology of Ease." *Journal of Electronic Publishing* 6.1 (2000).

Drucker, Johanna. "Humanities Approaches to Graphical Display." *Digital Humanities Quarterly* 5.1 (2011): 1–21.

Fair Cite. https://faircite.wordpress.com/

Flanders, Julia, and Trevor Muñoz. "An Introduction to Humanities Data Curation." *Digital Humanities Data Curation*. 2011. http://guide.dhcuration.org/intro/.

Fong, Deanna, Katrina Anderson, Lindsey Bannister, Janey Dodd, Lindsey Seatter, and Michelle Levy. "Students in the Digital Humanities: Rhetoric, Reality and Representation." University of Victoria, DHSI Colloquium 2014.

Foulonneau, Muriel, and Jenn Riley. *Metadata for Digital Resources: Implementation, Systems Design and Interoperability*. Oxford: Chandos, 2008.

Galey, Alan, and Stan Ruecker. "How a Prototype Argues." *Literary and Linguistic Computing* 25.4 (2010): 405–424. doi:10.1093/llc/fqq021

Gitelman, Lisa, ed. *Raw Data is an Oxymoron*. Cambridge, MA: MIT Press, 2013.

Hardt, Michael, and Antonio Negri. *Multitude: War and Democracy in the Age of Empire*. New York, NY: Penguin Group, 2005.

"John Sykes, 1959-." Social Networks and Archival Contexts Prototype Research Tool. http://socialarchive.iath.virginia.edu/ark:/99166/w6db95w4.

Larivière, Vincent, Yves Gingras, and Éric Archambault. "Canadian Collaboration Networks: A Comparative Analysis of the Natural Sciences, Social Sciences and the Humanities." *Scientometrics* 68.3 (2006): 519–533.

Lassila, Ora, Frank van Harmelen, Ian Horrocks, James Hendler, and Deborah L. McGuinness. "The Semantic Web and Its Languages." *Intelligent Systems and their Applications, IEEE* 15.6 (2000): 67–73.

Mandell, Laura. *Breaking the Book: Print Humanities in the Digital Age*. Oxford: Wiley Blackwell, 2015.

National Initiative for a Networked Cultural Heritage (NINCH). *The NINCH Guide to Good Practice in the Digital Representation and Management of Cultural Heritage Materials*. National Initiative for a Networked Cultural Heritage, 2002. www.nyu.edu/its/pubs/pdfs/NINCH_Guide_to_Good_Practice.pdf.

Nowviskie, Bethany. "Evaluating Collaborative Digital Scholarship (or, Where Credit is Due)." *Journal of Digital Humanities* 1.4 (2012): 16–30.

Old Weather. www.oldweather.org

Posner, Miriam. "Think Talk Make Do: Power and the Digital Humanities." *Journal of Digital Humanities* 1.2 (2012).

Price, Kenneth M. "Collaborative Work and the Conditions for American Literary Scholarship in a Digital Age." *The American Literature Scholar in the Digital*

Age. Ed. Amy E. Earhart and Andrew W. Jewell. University of Michigan Press, 2011. 9–27.

Ramsay, Stephen. "On Building." *Defining Digital Humanities: A Reader*. Eds. Melissa Terras, Julianna Nyhan, and Edward Vanhoutte. Farnham, Surrey: Ashgate, 2011. 243–45.

Riley, Jenn, and David Becker. "Seeing Standards: A Visualization of the Metadata Universe." Indiana University Libraries. 2010. www.dlib.indiana.edu/~jenlrile/metadatamap/.

Rockwell, Geoffrey. "Crowdsourcing the Humanities: Social Research and Collaboration." *Collaborative Research in the Digital Humanities*. Ed. Marilyn Deegan and Willard McCarty. Farnham, Surrey: Ashgate, 2012. 135–154.

Ruecker, Stan, and Milena Radzikowska. "The Iterative Design of a Project Charter for Interdisciplinary Research." *Proceedings of the 7th ACM Conference on Designing Interactive Systems*. Cape Town, South Africa: ACM, 2008.

Ruecker, Stan, Luciano Frizzera, Milena Radzikowska, Geoff Roeder, Ernesto Pena, Teresa Dobson, Geoffrey Rockwell, Susan Brown, The INKE Research Group. "Visual Workflow Interfaces for Editorial Processes." *Literary and Linguistic Computing* 28.4 (2013): 615–628.

Sample, Mark. "The Digital Humanities Is Not About Building, It's About Sharing." *Defining Digital Humanities: A Reader*. Eds. Melissa Terras, Julianna Nyhan, and Edward Vanhoutte. Farnham, Surrey: Ashgate, 2011. 255–258.

Schöch, Christof. "Big? Smart? Clean? Messy? Data in the Humanities." *Journal* of Digital Humanities 2.3 (2013): 2–13. http://journalofdigitalhumanities.org/2-3/big-smart-clean-messy-data-in-the-humanities/.

Siemens, Lynne. "It's a Team if You Use 'Reply All:' An Exploration of Research Teams in Digital Humanities Environments." *Literary and Linguistic Computing* (2009): 225–233. doi:10.1093/llc/fqp009

Sinclair, Stéfan, and Geoffrey Rockwell. *Voyant Tools*. 2015. www.voyant-tools.org/.

Slaughter, Sheila, and Gary Rhoades. "The Neo-liberal University." *New Labor Forum* (2000): 73–79.

Smith Rumsey, Abby. "Creating Value and Impact in the Digital Age Through Translational Humanities." *Council on Library and Information Resources*. 2013. www.clir.org/pubs/ruminations/03smithrumsey www.clir.org/pubs/ruminations/03smithrumsey/report.pdf.

Spiro, Lisa. "Computing and Communicating Knowledge: Collaborative Approaches to Digital Humanities Projects." *Collaborative Approaches to the Digital in English Studies*. Ed. Laura McGrath. Computers and Composition Digital Press, an imprint of Utah State University Press, 2011. Book URL: http://ccdigitalpress.org/cad/index2.html. Chapter URL: http://ccdigitalpress.org/cad/Ch2_Spiro.pdf.

TEI Consortium. "2. The TEI Header." *TEI: Guidelines for Electronic Text Encoding and Interchange*. P5. Version 2.9.1. Text Encoding Initiative, 2007. www.tei-c.org/release/doc/tei-p5-doc/en/html/HD.html.

Transcribe Bentham. 2015. http://blogs.ucl.ac.uk/transcribe-bentham/.

Warwick, Claire, Melissa Terras, Paul Huntington, and Nikoleta Pappa. "If You Build It Will They Come? The LAIRAH Study: Quantifying the Use of Online Resources in the Arts and Humanities Through Statistical Analysis of User Log Data." *Literary and Linguistic Computing* 23.1 (2008): 85–102. doi:10.1093/llc/fqm045

CHAPTER 5

Understanding the pre-digital book

"Every contact leaves a trace"[1]

Hélène Cazes and J. Matthew Huculak

There is a recent spate of publications theorizing Special Collections (SC) departments in the twenty-first-century university library, particularly in how they "are inextricably linked with the very future of the higher education and how successfully it responds to the challenges of the 21st century."[2] Rather than being inaccessible spaces where rare material is guarded and kept away from the public, SC is being theorized as a space of community engagement that "articulates the goals of the library" as well as the university at large; a place for "enhancing undergraduate pedagogy"[3] (Mitchell *et al.*); and as a place where researchers can explore how the text was "shaped by the ways in which it was initially embodied in its historical moment."[4] For the Digital Humanities Summer Institute, SC is a collaborative space of hands-on training and theoretical engagements with material objects for the foundational course, "Understanding the Pre-Digital Book."

The course is not meant to be a throwback to the Fredson Bowers days of "pure scholarship" through descriptive bibliography with "ideal" texts;[5] rather, it is an acknowledgment that many students might not be familiar with the terminologies relating to the physical study of books, which is necessary when marking them up using the Textual Encoding Initiative (TEI), or even when theorizing how to represent a material object in digital form. The course should bridge the gap between the art of descriptive bibliography and digital remediation – when such gaps exist – and provide a lexicon for describing one's experience with a text. Students are asked to see books as unique manifestations of social relations – what is commonly referred to in textual studies as the "sociology of texts";[6] the course should introduce students to basic terms in order to describe those relations.

For those starting their journeys in digital humanities, it might seem all too natural to differentiate between *digital* texts produced on computers and text that appears in a *physical* form on paper or parchment; however, it is a false dichotomy to separate one inscription technology from another – as media theorist Matthew Kirschenbaum shows: every contact leaves a trace, whether that contact be ink on paper or a spindle on a magnetic platter.[7] Yet, a dual problem has arisen within the DH and media studies communities: First, textual studies have not been given enough credit "as among the most sophisticated branches of media studies we have evolved"; and second, "textual critics have tended to treat the computer mainly as a platform-independent venue for studying the artifacts of other media." [8] In short, the digital does not replace the old; it simply creates newer problems within a larger history of inscription technologies. Because SC have traditionally been the repositories of such media shifts in the university library, it is a productive space to examine inscriptions ranging from Byzantine clay tablets to e-literature on early personal computers. The Pre-Digital Book course assumes that bibliography is a good place to start in media inquiry.

When Hélène Cazes first proposed "Understanding the Pre-Digital Book," she argued that to understand the "post-digital book," students should be given the opportunity to engage with the "pre-digital book" in order to locate themselves within a larger tradition of bibliography and textual studies, which "has furnished us with some of the best accounts we have of texts and textual phenomena."[9] And the home of such phenomena has traditionally been in SC – one of the few places in the library where librarians, students, and other researchers gather to preserve, study, and theorize cultural objects in our community. It is a place where the overlapping of disciplines and institutional boundaries naturally occurs. But how can such a space be utilized for intense DH institutes? Is there a place for collaborative endeavours between the librarians, archivists, faculty, and students? These are the practical concerns and questions one must address when embarking on collaborative adventures. But because the University of Victoria is home to the Electronic Textual Cultures Lab (ETCL) and the Digital Humanities Summer Institute (DHSI), both under the leadership of Ray Siemens, there is an air of collaboration and enthusiasm to try new models of scholarship in our community. These models are easily adaptable to other institutions with an eye towards collaborative learning.

This chapter attempts to provide members of the DH community a methodology, workflow, and template – one that has worked successfully here at the DHSI – for running a "Foundations" course in Special Collections. This chapter is divided into three parts: First, the question "Why the Pre-digital book course in the first place?" is answered; second, a workflow and basic syllabus for running the course in the library are provided; third, issues of working with librarians and archivists in the library are explored.

WHY THE PRE-DIGITAL BOOK? A PRE-HISTORY OF THE COURSE BY HÉLÈNE CAZES

Books change – and ways for talking about books change too. These transformations do not follow the same scholarly fashions or paces. *Bibliography*, meaning books written about books, can never – and never could – be summarized as merely a description or analysis of an intellectual and material production called a "book." The terms of bibliography have shifted and branched off over time: bibliology, history of the book, library science, new bibliography, catalogues, inventories, histories, and now information science or information technologies, etc. The ways of compiling methodologies and bibliographies are as diverse in perspective as are the many cultures that have attempted to theorize the thresholds between reception and circulation of texts – for to theorize a text is much more than mere description: it is a way a culture chooses to acknowledge a perceived transmitted heritage; it is a way of making a textually mediated cultural tradition. These ways, of making traditions, change too.

The digital revolution not only changed the way tradition was done, but also the ways we talked about tradition and about its orientations. Or so it seems. Suddenly, "potentiality" appeared to be a sure promise, and, potentially, anyone everywhere could access anything. Digital humanities – new technologies, and new knowledge of these technologies – were suddenly needed for this new world of books; books that were not just books, but real *potential* books: virtual libraries, virtual texts, virtual catalogues. And, suddenly, there were new ways of finding one's way in these libraries: search engines with simplified interfaces, chunks of texts that could be interrogated in one click, questions that sprang from new promises of responses and . . . a world where reading rooms could remain empty for days. Meanwhile, libraries provided computers and training, alongside books and other media (films, tapes, CD-ROMs, etc.). Of course, it did not happen in a blink of the eye, but this is how it felt: the 1990s and 2000s had turned over what we thought was bibliography, in all its varieties.

Book lovers, avid readers, curious minds have not disappeared: no, research and writing had become even more personal, but away from communal spaces, albeit open to all (or so it seemed, at first). Numbers changed, too, with the new information technology: machines could read vast quantities of texts – much more than someone trained in speed-reading could ever accomplish in a lifetime; readerships now included potential groups who would not otherwise have access to material. Value and authority could no longer be validated by sheer expertise, institutional recognition, or granted acceptance: it had to be legitimized according to new criteria: legibility, circulation, consensus. *Wikipedia* is the proud symbol of this reversal between numbers (files accessed, audiences, bytes) and former markers of quality (literary canon, selective transmission, scholarship).

What an adventure! I was fortunate to be at the University of Victoria, where the digital humanities (and their well-known Digital Humanities Summer Institute) flourish; marvelling at the world of open texts and open communities that lay in connected computers, I felt like a young Gargantua discovering Paris libraries in Rabelais' *Pantagruel*: a huge, infinite feast of treats, free, and for all. Renaissance humanists claimed, reclaimed, and continued the editing of classical works handed down by the tradition: this is the meaning of the Re-naissance, a new birth on sound, philological ground; it is intended for everyone, leading to discoveries, freedom, and progress through knowledge and through the questioning of authorities. More than a set of disciplines, humanities were taken as an attitude towards cultural transmission, and book culture was the road to authentic learning and sharing. Cities of books and manuscripts, public and university libraries were established, not as shrines, but as marketplaces for the exchange and collection of ideas, debates, and records.

The universe of digital humanities runs fast and welcomes all researchers, students, readers, to its race. The creation of a pre-digital course, within the Digital Humanities Summer Institute, in 2012, did not intend to put the brakes on swift inquiry. On the contrary, set in the library, the course was conceived as a complement to the training courses in text encoding, data collecting, media inclusion, web design, etc.

Book culture is now a forum in which to rethink the former disciplines of History of the Book and Bibliography, which have new supports and new techniques with the new technologies. It seemed relevant – almost urgent – to include this reflection in the dialogues and developments about texts and learning in the era of digital production. Indeed, when a search engine can almost instantly provide responses that would have required months of browsing through catalogues, reviews, and specialized bibliography in the past, the digitization programs and the data collections promise a world where this "research step" can be skipped: interrogations, if correctly formulated in the right place, could yield reliable and fast "results." Why, then, propose to sit in the reading room of the special collections, looking at catalogues, abbreviations found in printed index cards – long discarded, medieval manuscripts already digitized and posted online, ancient books already available on Google Books (for most of them), maps no longer accurate, and obsolete printed bibliographies?

The intention for the course was neither nostalgic nor reactionary. The phrase Pre-Digital Humanities was coined to recall the number-less quality of bibliography: the slow examination, mediated by scholarship, of a textual object. In the race to digitizing, encoding and spreading heritage objects, in order to make them both available and accessible, online collections have favoured quantity and speed. It went so fast that the slow examination of criteria or expertise was discarded as secondary: numerically speaking, errors would anyway be negligible in comparison with the exploitable data.

But the transformation of books, manuscripts, maps, archives and other textual artifacts into digital objects, necessarily, involved a displacement of values and perceptions: a virtual library is not the reproduction of a real library through another medium: it is a different type of library, altogether. Thus, websites, databases, virtual books or sets of photographs cannot be considered as exact equivalents of their sources: the reproduction, even if it is an old-fashioned facsimile, is already secondary. The primary sources, then, are paradoxically more rare, more difficult to consult, and more difficult to understand in the digital world: they require physical travel, passes to precious collections, skills for handling fragile material, but more importantly, they require the curiosity and will to enquire about their location, condition, and contents.

The digital virtuality defined two kinds of contact with the texts and their witnesses: a seemingly immediate digital access, in which the instantaneity of screen view is mistaken for an absence of mediation and the potentiality of consultation creates an illusion of universal legibility; a physical access, more restricted (by space, time, credentials, etc.), mediated by the request at a library counter, but truly immediate once the object is on the table.

The course "Understanding the Pre-Digital Book" was designed to address these changes of perspectives on the book. Ideally faithful to the original, the digital copy remains a copy and scholars need tools to assess how the copy was made, and for which purpose? Which criteria of selection, of the source and, within the source, of what was deemed worth digitizing? Who is the intended audience? Upstream and downstream, the pre-digital humanities aim to accompany the digital humanities but also the ante-digital humanities (produced before the age of computers and connections): a link between diverse representations and acquisitions of knowledge, they are a perpetual neologism, whose definition is constantly in progress.

The course is primarily a confrontation of primary sources in the presence of their digital reproductions. The simple juxtaposition of objects is a learning and teaching tool: colours, weight, formats, smells, all sensory perceptions are reduced to the screen by scope and definition. But other elements appear in the real encounter with a volume that were, often purposely, discarded from the digital product: stains, notes, inserts, doodles, etc. A Victorian book might still carry the soot stains from the thumb of a reader. The original primary sources are also fragile, precious, difficult to handle. The consultation of the original object brings back, then, the thick and deep layers of history: the history of the object in how it was made, the history of its provenances and displacements, the history of its owners and readers, but also the history – for it takes time – of its examination. Held in a collection, browsed by an individual, the pre-digital item is never a copy; *it is always unique*. Variations, specific conditions, even errors in the making, are telling signs of a book's story, whereas variations in the code or deterioration of a file lead to the absence of a digital object and remain untold stories forever. Secondary sources of all sorts, bibliographies, descriptions, and commentaries record, with codes and a history of their own, the ongoing story leading to the moment of a book's "autopsy," or the consultation by a reader.

The pre-digital approach, rooted in descriptive bibliography, does not stand still in the comparison of what is lost and what is kept from an original in the digital transition: in constant movement, it appraises which categories are relevant for describing the experience, real and virtual, of a specific book, manuscript, or record. Students are asked to enter into that experiential and imaginative space to ask themselves, what is relevant in describing my experience of this object? The dimensions of the real experience cannot be reproduced – only described; dimensions for the virtual experience are ours to create, though. The process does not look back, in order to restore a paradise lost with the advent of the Internet, but looks forward to a dialogue regarding the transition: what to translate? How? For whom? Hence, the syllabus enounces:

> Pre-digital discourse is linked with bibliography and bibliology – understood as means to write and read meaningful accompaniments to the digital object – but also with options and intentions for the digital project itself. Its contents vary with the locutor, with the situation of communication, and with the readers. Its generic definition varies as well: from caption, catalogue entry, and bibliographical reference, to analytical description or research paper.

Ideally, the pre-digital discourse opens a dialogue with post-digital continuations: comments, questions, complements, corrections, etc.

Pre-digital discourse, thus, is not to be mistaken for "bibliography," although some tools, notions, and references are being borrowed for this set of disciplines.

"Vertical and horizontal" bibliographies have existed since lists of books were first compiled: Required readings, Useful titles, Catalogues, Inventories, Descriptions, etc. Pre-digital assessment and writing make use of bibliographical notices, lists, and descriptions. But it builds its own categories. In the pre-digital zone, references and entries come in handy, both from bibliographies (lists of books or titles) and bibliology (description and analysis of the materiality of a book).

Conceived as a workshop in order to allow direct and personal contact by students with the holdings of our library, the course alternates basic elements of bibliography/bibliology and new questionings on digital objects and collections. The proposed readings are a situation and a compilation of material for these questions, not a set of notions and words to be memorized and used without examination. Holdings from the Special Collections – or from personal collections – are described and pre-digitized by students, who share their ideas in class and on the blog. The group acts as a model-community for the circulation of information and research, becoming the first audience of the digital projects envisioned. Similarly, the class alternates lectures, given by several instructors, and hands-on sessions. This organization emphasizes the collective and collaborative nature of the cultural transmission. The students, working in small groups, choose themes and projects: instructors, present at all times, provide methodological guidance and punctual support. A blog, public, constantly in progress, records online the discoveries and proposals from students: predigitalbooks.wordpress.com

Students repeatedly report their surprise at the course. Were they expecting that notions of book history and bibliography would be boring? Often more knowledgeable than the instructors for programs and codes, many of them had never held in their (clean) hands a medieval parchment or a Renaissance folio. For the instructor looking at the intent students, carefully holding the items while silently examining them, it appears that the presential encounter of library sources is a new experience for most people in the class, generating both fascination and some kind of shyness. A quick how-to-handle-precious-objects usually breaks the spell and allows students to feel allowed to touch and manipulate the holdings, although a diffuse sense of reverence and ownership remains perceptible at these occasions: students speak of "their" manuscript or "their" book, and take a long time in their examination, out of scrupulous care and out of pleasure. Less iconic holdings, such as scientific prints, Victorian serials or poetry volumes, brought a similar wonder. This, I call the pre-digital miracle: it is an irreducible part of the experience, grounded in the real unbound world of libraries. Where does this emotion come from? Why is it so easily shared and felt? Undoubtedly, this accounts too for the success of the course.

In the era of the born digital, websites, programs, pdf files, etc. are examined as objects in transition and inscribed in history and carrying the depth of transmission through generations. In order to carve out a space for printed books within the spectrum of pre-and-post digital inscription technologies, a neologism was needed to describe the focus of the course. The term "pre-digital" fitted our needs since it addresses the following set of inquiries:

Pre-digital (or predigital). Adjective. Neologism 2011. Definition in progress. *Describes a textual object in regards with its possible or realized digitization. Implies a series of questions on the nature of the object to be digitized and on the planned readings of the object in its digitized format, such as:*

- What is the present environment of the object?
- What are the past environments for this object?
- Who are the creators (author(s), scribe(s), editor(s), printer(s), publisher(s), bookseller(s), commentator(s) . . .) of the object as it reaches the hands of the digitizer?
- What is the intended digital environment for this object? Is the change of medium part of a larger project (digitization of a collection, of different states of the same title, of the printer's works, of an author's works, of someone's library, of a reference library, of a genre) or centred on the one pre-digital book (as a unique artifact with its unique destiny)?

- Which information is it important to transmit during the process?
- Will a notice be attached to the object?
- How will the notice attached to the object convey information on its history, its materiality, its meanings?
- Which parts of the object have priority for the final form: text, image, ownerships, provenance, craftsmanship, annotations, all of these, none of these?

Tradition, the act of preserving and transmitting cultural heritage as well the act of receiving and acquiring this heritage, does not stop with print culture: in the digital environment, new tradition-making is taking place online in blogs, open access journals, and project management software – or any tool someone working in new knowledge environments might make use of. Pre-digital humanities are a study and a part of this process in that the precursors to these new environments, for better or worse, model how we think of the digital (we "scroll" down a webpage, for example). Focusing on the transitional moment of transfer to another medium, they build our understanding of digital humanities: in this context, history is neither a material nor a discipline; it is the dimension of this very transition, which opens to the previous transmissions and transformations.

Awareness of the multiple perspectives and layers of the pre-digital items ensures the freedom of the digital world, which is necessarily built on assumptions and reductions (as is anything that is built): when one recognizes categories and choices, one is able to form a judgment and to propose alternatives. A digital reproduction or description of an object, or a tool pertaining to the accessibility of either an item or a collection, contains a part of interpretation that makes possible the analysis of the original and the determination of a purpose for the digital object. Direct access to the source (item or collection) opens the possibility of assessing the interpretative process and its choices. For instance, the question of format was often addressed: diversity of sizes in the pre-digital world, identical consultation screen for all the digital objects. Does the presence of a ruler suffice to create an experience of "smallness" for Thumb Bibles or "greatness" for elephant folios? How can a measure be described in terms of effect? More importantly, the consultation, without the mediation of digital images, software or introductive descriptions, brings the awareness of digitizing, designing and accessibility choices to the pre-digital source. Only the potentiality of this confrontation of the source and the confidence to be able to assess the mediating process can ensure a clear appreciation of the interpretative choices, of the purposes of a digital project, and of the relevance of these decisions. In this sense, the knowledge of the original format is part of the freedom of the user. A part of the Summer Institute and of the Certificate in Digital Humanities, the workshop has no program other than this freedom.

AWARENESS OF THE MECHANISM

Descriptive bibliography is a way of drawing awareness to the mechanisms of the book, but we also do not want students to lose sight of the freedom they have in imagining new ways of representing textual objects online – which itself is also another medium through which one can represent text. A driving principle of the course is that remediation has occurred throughout textual history: the digital is part of a spectrum of remediation. However, at remedial moments, the gaps between versions of a thing allow us to question the properties of both things; in this sense, the pre-digital course is concerned with issues surrounding the digitization of objects. The primary question, once students choose an object to work with, is, "what is distinctive about this object and how might it be represented digitally?" This, in turn, gives rise to more questions: How might the digital inform the book object, and how might the book object teach us about digital representation across disciplines in digital scholarship? These are questions that are practiced in DH centres around the world.[10]

COLLABORATION IN SPECIAL COLLECTIONS

Collaboration is at the heart of DH and the pre-digital book classroom, since the course draws upon the expertise of multiple disciplines, literary eras, and institutional spaces. It provides an opportunity for leaders to work one-on-one with librarians and archivists as well as colleagues from across the institution. *Since this course requires the participation of multiple stakeholders within a community, it provides an opportunity to model collaboration among departments, institutions, or faculties*. At UVic, the library is a partner in DHSI, and as such, is a strong supporter of our teaching initiatives. The library provides the SC classroom for our use during the entire week in which classes can freely – and securely – use the treasures at the institution for research.

The course also draws upon the local experience of our colleagues. The week is divided up roughly into four main textual eras (which can adapted to an institution's local holdings): the manuscript era, the early printing era, the machine printing era, and the electronic era, and each "era" is taught by a different faculty member or librarian. In order to maintain a sense of continuity, members are encouraged to see themselves as participating in a seminar – where the conversations and relationships started on the first day provide the continuity for the rest of the week.

ACTIVITIES FOR FIVE DAYS

There are a number of ways to successfully run the Pre-Digital Book course, but the following methodology has worked well at the DHSI Summer Institute.

Before the course begins: planning a successful week

The description for the course from the DHSI website is as follows:

> This course is aimed at those – whether or not they have a digital humanities project in mind – who wish to learn more about "book culture" in history and contexts from the medieval through modern periods. Each class session will combine intensive lectures with individual and small group hands-on work with items from UVic's special collections to focus on the circumstances of production and reception of textual objects over time. By providing an overview of textual creation, transmission, and conservation, this course will offer digital humanists an introduction to the methodologies and reference tools (historical, codicological, and contemporary) necessary to understand a book in its original contexts and thus to make informed encoding decisions for the digital era. We will explore the technological shifts that made textual culture possible (quill, ink, paper, lithography, etc.) so that we can locate our current textual moment within a larger technological history.
>
> We will also discuss toolkits (ideological and software-based) that will enable us to analyze and describe archival materials, facsimiles, and editions in a variety of ways so that we can make informed decisions when producing digital surrogates of archival material. Students will learn about the process of textual creation in both pre-and-post digital eras and will produce a critical apparatus/prototype/plan/bibliography of a digital surrogate by week's end.[11]

Some students come with a project and object in mind, while others will rely on an institution's instructional holdings (and thus, organizers should pre-select, with the Special Collections librarian, which items can freely circulate in class). Course assignments that take into account the diverse material interests of the students will need to be designed. Since DHSI is meant to encourage conversations outside of the classroom, organizers shouldn't burden the class with too many tasks outside of the classroom. A nice balance can be achieved by having the students create a short descriptive bibliography along with a digital prototype of their object on a course WordPress site. There is great value in giving an opportunity to prototype an idea during the week, and it provides an occasion to ask questions and collaborate among class members.

Since the course is about collaboration, the "leader" of the class contacts colleagues about ten months in advance in order to receive teaching commitments and determine who will be teaching on what day so that any potential scheduling conflicts can be avoided. We prefer to have five teachers on hand who can teach the following areas: manuscript culture, paper and ink making, hand-press culture, machine printing, e-literature, and other "modern" forms, such as comics. In the past, the teachers would commit to spending the entire week teaching together; however, for some, this might be too much of a time commitment, so we now ask teachers to commit to two days of participation: once on orientation day, where we have a "roundtable seminar," and one day for teaching. The "leader" of the course is the constant through the week as the facilitator – and as a lecturer when appropriate.

Day one

The morning of day one of the Pre-Digital Book provides a snappy introduction to the week's theory, as well as Special Collections as a whole, including instructions on handling rare material ranging from Byzantine clay tablets to photographs to floppy disks – for example, when is it appropriate to wear white gloves and when is it not? For some students, this is the first time they have ever been in Special Collections and Archives, so it is a good idea to give an introduction to the library unit. Our Special Collections librarian, Heather Dean, has been generous in dedicating time to the course since she has a pedagogical priority of using the collections for experiential learning. It is also a great way for the library to highlight its strengths for an international audience.

Students who do not bring a particular object in mind to study are asked to choose something from our SC to interrogate during the week. We provide material ranging from manuscripts to modern personal letters; these items should be vetted, with a librarian, in advance, so two months' planning time is recommended. We generally fill three library book carts with material.

Day one also provides an opportunity to introduce students to the tradition of descriptive and analytical bibliography – pointing out its strengths and weaknesses. I love to show Bowers' definition of the discipline:

> The purpose, then, of the physical description of the book is twofold: to serve as a basis for the analysis of the method of publication, which has a direct bearing on the relations and transmissions of texts; to provide sufficient evidence for readers to identify books in their possession as being members of the precise state, issue, impression, and edition of the "ideal copy" listed, or as being unrecorded variants requiring further bibliographical investigation.[12]

This offers a launching pad to discuss an overview of the history and lexicon of "ideal copies," authorship, and textual transmission. The course is not meant to be a comprehensive rare book school that will certify a student in bibliography. It is a new book school that introduces students to concepts of prototyping, experimentation, remediation, and hands-on experience. These are tasks that can be accomplished in a week.

The afternoon of day one is set up as an open-discussion seminar in which we invite the teachers and various members of our community who are involved with digital projects to discuss issues and answer questions about what it means to digitize an object.[13] This is an important moment for team building within the classroom since it gives students an opportunity to share their work and war stories in an open, supportive forum. This initial roundtable sets the tone for the rest of the week and should not be skipped.

The day ends with students spending thirty minutes writing their first blog post in which they talk about the reasons why they want to study a particular object.

Readings for day one

Belanger, Terry. "Descriptive Bibliography." *The Bibliographical Society of America*. N.p., n.d. Web. 28 September 2015.

Bowers, Fredson. *Principles of Bibliographical Description*. New York: Russell & Russell, 1962. Print.

Mak, Bonnie. "Introduction." *How the Page Matters*. Toronto: University of Toronto Press, 2012. 3–8. Print.

Manoff, Marlene. "Theories of the Archive from Across the Disciplines." *Portal: Libraries and the Academy* 4.1 (2004): 9–25. *Project MUSE*. Web. 20 April 2015.

Day two

The second day starts with an introduction to non-machine-repeatable material: old manuscripts, scrolls, a book of hours, clay tablets, or papyrus. The *pièce de résistance* for this day in our collections is a genealogical roll (Shelf Mark: Ms.Brown.Lat.1; Location: 5A/08, Acc. 1989–069, Item #6), which unfurls to a length of 21 feet.[14] Students are asked to physically engage with the scroll by touching the vellum and noting inconsistencies in the skin (where the scroll was glued together, where hair follicles were not scraped as well as other parts of the document, etc.). Students are given a history of ink production[15] – particularly the red ink – and surface-preparing techniques.

We then examine facsimiles of ancient manuscripts and ask what type of information is lost in the remediated facsimile edition of an ancient mss. When these two items are juxtaposed, the jump from print to digital is not as jarring since the class can clearly see information loss in terms of the skin of the document, the quality, texture, and depth of the original item, when reproduced on modern paper or new vellum. The instructor of this section, Dr Iain Higgins, likes to point out that bibliographers missed a lot of information when engaging in their "pure" art when describing manuscripts.

If an institution has black lights on hand, they may be used to encourage students to look for palimpsests or other "hidden" ink/items/stains on manuscripts; it is a fruitful exercise to turn off the lights and see if there are texts beneath the texts in the classroom. By the end of the day, students realize that remediation is not a product of the digital era; rather, it has been a part of textual culture from its beginning – including the scraping of skins to remove one text in order to print another. The digital is merely part of a spectrum of remediation through time. The day ends with students committing to an object of study for the week and blogging about their experiences.

Readings for day two

Bischoff, Bernhard. *Latin Palaeography: Antiquity and the Middle Ages*. Cambridge: Cambridge University Press, 1990. Print.

Day three

After being introduced to the technologies of early manuscript culture, day three commences discussions about the era of mechanical printing. This is where descriptive bibliography is most useful in the course, as students learn the "mechanics" of book production, ranging from page layout, signatures, catchwords, headlines, and laid paper. M. J. Pearce's *Workbook of Analytical and Descriptive Bibliography* offers a concise booklet for deciphering the type, engravings, ornaments, and page layouts for describing the make-up of incunabula, as well as an easy-to-navigate template for writing descriptive bibliography.

Students are encouraged to do this traditional descriptive work while also looking for idiosyncratic marks that make the book object unique. Does it have fingerprint smudges? In one case, a fly (dated by a member of our biology department as being hundreds of years old) was found flattened between two pages. What does this tell us about the history of this book? How might one – or should one – represent that insect in remediated versions of the book?

The day ends with students creating a short descriptive bibliography for the course's WordPress site.

Readings for day three

van der Weel, Adriaan van der. "The Order of the Book." *Changing Our Textual Minds: Towards a Digital Order of Knowledge*. Manchester University Press, 2012. Print.

Day four

Day four is by far our most popular day according to student feedback. Drs. Mary Elizabeth Leighton and Lisa Surridge, experts in Victorian printing, run a linocut workshop using a kit[16] available at many art stores (the class is asked to wear old clothes). Leighton and Surridge first introduce students to the techniques of Victorian printing, including woodcuts, lithography, and copperplates. Students learn how to identify the different types of illustration by looking at books and periodicals in our collections. The class then moves to a "lab" (outside of Special Collections), where they cut their own linocut blocks and print them to paper. This type of experiential learning allows students to see how difficult it is to coax detail out of blocks of linoleum. And, everyone gets to go home with a copy (or copies) of their own original artwork. It is always a pleasure to see members of the course discover latent creative talent in the lab.

What students realize is that there is a depth to illustration that is difficult to remediate in digitization (how does one describe the individual cut, depth, and angle of an illustration? How does one identify a copper illustration versus a steel one?)

Readings for day four

Gascoigne, Bamber. *How to Identify Prints: A Complete Guide to Manual and Mechanical Processes from Woodcut to Ink Jet*. Thames and Hudson, 1986. Print.

Day five

Day five can be a wildcard for class discussion and teaching, drawing on the expertise of various members of the community. A librarian in our community happens to be a comic book aficionado and gives a presentation on the comic form. Our SC librarian gives a presentation on the preservation of e-literature. A member from our local gallery talks about issues of digitizing objects such as World War I prisoner of war name-tags. A member of the TEI community might discuss the transition from book to screen and issues of markup in textual representation. Here students learn that issues of digitization move beyond the book and into the cultural matrix of objects that make up a history of collections.

The afternoon is dedicated to students who give presentations on their own work during the week. Depending on the class size, a leader may have to allot more time starting in the morning.

Readings for day five

Miller, Peter N. "How Objects Speak." *The Chronicle of Higher Education*, 11 August 2014. *The Chronicle of Higher Education*. Web. 20 April 2015.
Retrieved from http://chronicle.com/article/How-Objects-Speak/148177/

The take home: mediation

By the end of the week students should feel comfortable recognizing the mediated environments of texts: be it through the material substrate of print or through the "collections policies" of an institution. To study text is to study mediation. It is to ask questions about what is lost and gained in remedial moments such as our own. Although the course may provide a foundation for proper markup, it also challenges potential DH practitioners to think about the objects of their study both inside and outside of tools of transmission. It may be that this course engenders questions that lead to new tool development in order to capture information that other tools ignore. Or, it may teach that any transmission environment is bound by limitations: whether that be the colour of ink available or the hierarchical structure of a markup language.

Ultimately, students will leave the class with a half-page descriptive bibliography, a "prototype" and short daily logs on the course website, and a linocut print they made during the workshop.

WORKING IN THE LIBRARY: LIBRARIANS AND ARCHIVISTS AND OTHER COLLABORATORS

Collaboration can be hard, especially in institutional settings, primarily because many of us carry disciplinary lexicons and assumptions that do not necessarily carry over to other departments or divisions within the university community. An example of this dynamic is found in Marlene Manoff's examination of the word "archive" across the disciplines.[17] What may seem like such a simple word is shot through with theoretical and methodological assumptions: to the literature scholar, the archive is generally approached through Derrida; but to an archivist, it is an actual physical, institutional space in which she works. "The Pre-Digital Book" course gives librarians, archivists, students, and faculty an opportunity to explore the ways in which the objects of study that make up both the metaphorical and physical archive operate within the context of the local culture and discourse community. Lynne Siemens' Project Management course is a good place to learn about methods of collaborating in small and large groups. Do see the Pre-Digital Book course as an opportunity to build community across an institution – and do make sure to allot enough time to let conversations unfold.

OTHER THINGS TO CONSIDER

- If teaching in the library, classrooms might need to be booked up to a year in advance.
- An instructor from the English department might get credit for teaching at DHSI as part of the service rubric of tenure and promotion. Other members of the community might not get credit for volunteering. Thus, it is good to explore these institutional issues for determining time commitments and expectations for the course.

This work is extremely rewarding and, at least at the University of Victoria, has opened up new avenues for collaboration during the year. The Special Collections classroom is now being used for three regular English courses, and a regular reading group has formed, sponsored by the Electronic Textual Cultures Lab, that brings librarians, staff, students, and researchers together to discuss intra-institutional collaboration. Just as every contact leaves a trace, so does every fruitful collaboration.

NOTES

1 Kirschenbaum 2008.
2 Bengtson 2001.
3 Mitchell *et al.* 2012.
4 Jenstad and Kelly 2015.
5 Bowers, *Principles* 1962.
6 A term used by D.F. McKenzie to describe the social networks and actors that go into the making of a book.
7 Kirschenbaum 2008.
8 Ibid., 16.
9 Ibid., 16.
10 McCarthy *et al.* 2012.
11 Huculak and Cazes 2015.
12 Bowers, *Principles* 23.
13 For example, in 2015 Dr Janelle Jenstad of the Map of Early Modern London project, Dr Alison Chapman, Editor of the Database of Victorian Periodical Poetry, and Matt Huculak of the Modernist Versions Project fielded questions and provided contexts for the reasons behind their teams' work.
14 Dr Adrienne Boyarin's undergraduate students describe items in SC for online description: www.uvic.ca/library/locations/home/spcoll/collections/medieval/ms-brown-lat-1.php
15 Ted Bishop's *The Social Life of Ink* is a great primer.
16 Speedball Linocut Kit.
17 Manoff 2004.

REFERENCES

Bahde, Anne, Heather Smedberg, Mattie Taormina, and Ebooks Corporation, eds. *Using Primary Sources: Hands-on Instructional Exercises*. Santa Barbara, CA: Libraries Unlimited, 2014.

Belanger, Terry. "Descriptive Bibliography." *The Bibliographical Society of America*. Accessed 28 September 2015. http://bibsocamer.org/publications/bibliography-defined/.

Bengtson, Jonathan B. "Reinventing the Treasure Room: The Role of Special Collections Librarianship in the 21st Century." In *Advances in Librarianship*, 25:187–207. Advances in Librarianship 25. Emerald Group, 2001.

"Bibliography Defined." *The Bibliographical Society of America*. Accessed 20 August 2015. http://bibsocamer.org/publications/bibliography-defined/.

Bischoff, Bernhard. "The External Characteristics of the Written Heritage." In *Latin Palaeography: Antiquity and the Middle Ages*, 20–37. Cambridge: Cambridge University Press, 1990. www.cambridge.org/us/academic/subjects/literature/anglo-saxon-and-medieval-literature/latin-palaeography-antiquity-and-middle-ages.

Bowers, Fredson. "Introduction." In *Principles of Bibliographical Description*, 3–18. Winchester, UK: Oak Knoll Press, 1995.

Bowers, Fredson. *Principles of Bibliographical Description*. New York: Russell & Russell, 1962.

Chartier, Roger. "'Preface' & 'Epilgoue.'" In *The Order of Books*, vii–xi and 89–91. Palo Alto, CA: Stanford University Press, 1994.

Conway, Paul. "Preservation in the Age of Google: Digitization, Digital Preservation, and Dilemmas." *The Library Quarterly: Information, Community, Policy* 80, no. 1 (1 January 2010): 61–79. doi:10.1086/648463.

Dooley, Jackie. "Ten Commandments for Special Collections Librarians in the Digital Age." *RBM: A Journal of Rare Books, Manuscripts and Cultural Heritage* 10, no. 1 (20 March 2009): 51–60. http://rbm.acrl.org/content/10/1/51.

Drucker, Johanna. "Theory as Praxis: The Poetics of Electronic Textuality." *Modernism/modernity* 9, no. 4 (2002): 683–691. doi:10.1353/mod.2002.0069.

English, James F. "Everywhere and Nowhere: The Sociology of Literature After 'the Sociology of Literature'." *New Literary History* 41, no. 2 (2010): v–xxiii. doi:10.1353/nlh.2010.0005.

Gascoigne, Bamber. *How to Identify Prints: A Complete Guide to Manual and Mechanical Processes from Woodcut to Ink Jet*. London: Thames and Hudson, 1986.

Huculak, J. Matthew, and Hélène Cazes. "Course Offerings." *Digital Humanities Summer Institute*, September 2015. http://dhsi.org/courses.php.

Jenstad, Janelle, and Erin E. Kelly. "A Curatorial Model for Teaching Renaissance Book History in Canada." *Renaissance and Reformation / Renaissance et Réforme* 37, no. 4 (30 April 2015): 81–100. http://jps.library.utoronto.ca/index.php/renref/article/view/22641.

Kirschenbaum, Matthew G. *Mechanisms: New Media and the Forensic Imagination*. Cambridge, MA: MIT Press, 2008.

Mak, Bonnie. "Introduction." In *How the Page Matters*, 3–8. Toronto: University of Toronto Press, 2012.

Manoff, Marlene. "Theories of the Archive from Across the Disciplines." *Portal: Libraries and the Academy* 4, no. 1 (2004): 9–25. doi:10.1353/pla.2004.0015.

McCarthy, Elizabeth, Anne Welsh, and Sarah Wheale. "Early Modern Oxford Bindings in Twenty-first Century Markup." *Library Review* 61, no. 8/9 (31 August 2012): 561–576. doi:10.1108/00242531211292079.

Miller, Peter N. "How Objects Speak." *The Chronicle of Higher Education*, 11 August 2014. http://chronicle.com/article/How-Objects-Speak/148177/.

Mitchell, Eleanor, Peggy Seiden, and Suzy Taraba, eds. *Past or Portal? Enhancing Undergraduate Learning Through Special Collections and Archives*. Chicago: Association of College and Research Libraries, 2012.

Pearce, M. J. *A Workbook of Analytical & Descriptive Bibliography*. London: C. Bingley, 1970.

Prescott, Andrew. "An Electric Current of the Imagination: What the Digital Humanities Are and What They Might Become." *Journal of Digital Humanities*, 26 June 2012. http://journalofdigitalhumanities.org/1-2/an-electric-current-of-the-imagination-by-andrew-prescott/.

Rimmer, Jon, Claire Warwick, Ann Blandford, Jeremy Gow, and George Buchanan. "An Examination of the Physical and the Digital Qualities of Humanities Research." *Information Processing & Management* 44, no. 3 (May 2008): 1374–1392. doi:10.1016/j.ipm.2007.09.001.

Schreibman, Susan, Ray Siemens, and John Unsworth. *Companion to Digital Humanities* (Blackwell Companions to Literature and Culture). Hardcover. Oxford: Blackwell, 2004. www.digitalhumanities.org/companion/.

Vandegrift, Micah, and Stewart Varner. "Evolving in Common: Creating Mutually Supportive Relationships Between Libraries and the Digital Humanities." *Journal of Library Administration* 53, no. 1 (1 January 2013): 67–78. doi:10.1080/01930826.2013.756699.

van der Weel, Adriaan van der. *Changing Our Textual Minds: Towards a Digital Order of Knowledge*. Manchester: Manchester University Press, 2012.

FURTHER READING

Bowers, Fredson. *Principles of Bibliographical Description*. New York: Russell & Russell, 1962. Print.

Pearce, M. J. *A Workbook of Analytical & Descriptive Bibliography*. London: C. Bingley, 1970. Print.

Part 2

Core concepts and skills

CHAPTER 6

Critical computing in the humanities

Phillip R. Polefrone, John Simpson and Dennis Yi Tenen

We write this chapter as a general reflection on teaching computing fundamentals in the humanities context, and more specifically in the wake of teaching *Computing Foundations for Human(s|ists)* at the Digital Humanities Summer Institute (DHSI), University of Victoria and *Computing in Context* at Columbia University.[1] These courses were intended for humanities researchers with no previous programming experience who wanted to learn how programs work by writing a few simple, useful programs of their own.[2] The syllabus was designed to foster "digital literacy" and foundational skills that can support further self-guided exploration.

To these ends, topics covered in our classes included working with files and folders, advanced searching through large collections of texts, algorithmic thinking, data manipulation, and text analysis. The tools we use are few and simple: the command line interface included in most modern computers, the ubiquitous and powerful Python programming language, and a text editor. By the end of the course, our students worked on their own and in small groups to create a small web scraper, an "essay grader," a comma-separated value file manipulator, and a program that evaluates poetry based on its measure of similarity to Byron.

Our aim in this chapter is not to recapitulate the experience of teaching, but to reveal some of the core principles that went into making the courses: to talk about the rationale behind our teaching philosophy, and, more broadly, to suggest an approach to teaching programming in the humanities.

We will elaborate on the above principles in three sections. "Critical computing principles" describes the ideas behind our approach to computation, which is premised on extending rather than replacing long-standing critical practices of humanistic inquiry. In the second section, "Digital humanities core," these ideas lead us to a list of core skills for the practicing digital humanist. These are meant to be neither totalizing nor exhaustive. Rather, we outline several necessary prerequisites needed to advance the great variety of work in the field. We conclude with a section that details the "Three locations of computing," which orient the reader to three significant sites of computation: the command line, the text editor, and the programming language interpreter.

Ultimately, the essay gives our unified take on the skills and competencies required to advance research in the digital humanities and computational culture studies. The outlined program should be used as a guideline, not dogma. We hope it contributes to the broader conversation about curricular development, certification, and student and faculty training.

CRITICAL COMPUTING PRINCIPLES

Computational methodologies can complement the rich history of research in the humanities. But to take hold, quantitative approaches to the study of culture must align with extant ideals and practices. Inspired by a number of initiatives advancing a similar philosophy, we refer to this approach as "critical computing."[3] The following seven propositions will connect technological preferences with values intrinsic to humanistic inquiry:

1. Demystify everyday computation.
2. Use few, free, small, universal, and powerful tools that you can alter and understand.
3. Privilege simplicity and human legibility over complexity and machine efficiency.
4. Invest in technologies that align with the values of our community.
5. Identify research objectives prior to selecting the appropriate tools and methodologies.
6. Divide big problems into small, modular components.
7. Be "lazy" by automating mundane tasks, but do it right by commenting your code, taking notes, and sharing with others.

Demystify everyday computation

Contemporary computational devices are a foundation of daily life. They are involved in everything from financial markets, to archival research, to the way many keep in touch with friends and family. Yet for those without technical training, the inner workings of these devices remain a source of mystery and, consequently, frustration.

Recognizing this, our courses target the underlying structure of tools that many rely on for their daily computation, teaching our students how these tools work (and not just how to use them). Beyond the principles of programming, we want our students to understand the basics of networking, system administration, and project management. By revealing the innards of opaque computational "black boxes," we hope to empower our students to take control of their everyday digital practice.

The most universal daily computing task of the humanities, regardless of research interest, is writing. For this reason, we structure our early classes by creating small "experiments" that address our students' own writing habits. Such exercises might include a lab session in which students analyze their own documents for commonly overused "weasel words," for example.[4] Working with one's own documents introduces important technical concepts such as "relative" and "absolute" paths, file formats, character encoding, and small shell utilities such as `grep` (used to search through text files), `wc` (word count), or `sed` (stream editor for text transformation). These concepts can later be extended into more advanced techniques in data manipulation or natural language processing. Short text-manipulation exercises form the students' first programs, performing tasks such as "safely rename all the files in this folder according to such-and-such rule," or "keep a daily log of my writing progress."

Use few, free, small, universal, and powerful tools that you can alter and understand

Researchers, librarians, students, and faculty are faced with a bewildering array of software choices. In deciding whether to invest time and resources into learning a new tool or methodology, we are inspired by the free software movement in general and the Unix operating system philosophy in particular. The Unix philosophy of computing prioritizes small, modular pieces of software that "do one thing well" (McIlroy *et al.*). Such software can then be chained together with other small but powerful tools to achieve complex results. Free software, besides being cost-effective ("free as in beer"), also makes the tool itself available to inspection, interpretation, revision, and ultimately critique. Transparency and the ability to modify code to suit one's own needs is what makes code "free as in speech" (Stallman). Above all, we seek out universal tools that we can understand and, where needed, customize to fit our own particular applications. These tools can be applied in diverse contexts such as library infrastructure, web design, data science, and the production of critical editions.

When thinking of what to teach or where to invest our time, we look for "bootstrapping" effects that come from using powerful, universally available, and extensible software. In other words, we privilege skills and concepts that will have the highest impact in the long run by transferring to the greatest number of contexts or tasks. The command line, for example, is useful at first to manage files. It later becomes an important resource for data gathering, cleanup, and analysis. Learning about relative and absolute paths locally makes it easier to understand networking protocols and uniform resource locators (URLs). Familiarity with the command line leads to the ability to administer servers remotely and to encrypt one's communications – skills needed for journalists, activists, librarians, and scholars alike.

Privilege simplicity and human legibility over complexity and machine efficiency

Whenever possible we privilege simplicity and human legibility over complexity and machine performance. The tools and file formats that we use in our research and archival efforts have serious implications for the long-term accessibility of academic knowledge. The ubiquitous use of Microsoft Word and Adobe Acrobat file formats, for example, makes it difficult to publish, store, and gather insight even from our own published work. As humanists begin to adopt the use of complex tools and databases, needless complexity becomes even more of a barrier to knowledge sharing.

Simplicity should not be confused with simple-mindedness. As with clarity in writing, clarity in computation comes from painstaking mastery of method and technique. Such mastery is fundamentally difficult, but it is to be preferred to shortcuts that sacrifice clarity for illusory "ease" of use. The student just entering the field of digital humanities and computational culture studies faces the choice of learning to program machines universally, or learning multiple, fragmentary, and non-standardized tools that have limited salience outside of the classroom. The proliferation of tools that obscure fundamental concepts in order to avoid "scaring" beginners adds complexity in the long run. Opaque tools disfranchise an audience otherwise eager to take on new intellectual challenges. Their use prevents us from communicating with other computationally minded disciplines and from competing meaningfully in the wider job market.

Invest in technologies that align with the values of our community

The non-transparent nature of many popular file tools and file storage formats extracts a heavy toll on our community. Each tool that we add to our "tool chain" increases the cognitive burden of training, support, and peer review.

It may be appealing at first to hide computational internals behind "user-friendly" visual interfaces. Yet these interfaces do not share a common visual language; the labor of learning one interface therefore does not not transfer well across other software platforms. Our colleagues in computer science sometimes worry that introducing command line interfaces and raw coding environments may alienate humanists. We believe that limited, "dumbed-down" interfaces do even more harm, further mystifying computing to an audience that already feels removed from everyday material contexts of knowledge production. In building foundations, we want our students to spend their time well: to learn tools and skills that can support a wide variety of activity in diverse cultural settings. The extra care we take in explaining the reasoning behind our technological choices can motivate students through any initial difficulties of learning how to code "the hard way," without shortcuts or artificial limitations.

In considering new tools and methodologies, humanists who rarely work with truly large datasets would do well to weigh the risk of rapid obsolescence against any hypothetical gains in speed or performance offered by closed systems such as a new note-taking platform, database system, or proprietary text editor.[5] When selecting a tool or a data format for storage, we ask: Does it need special software to render? How long has it been around? Does the community that supports it align with our values? Our choice of the Python programming language, for example, was guided by the fact that Python encodes simplicity and human readability into its technical specifications.[6] It has broad support from the scientific computing community and in the private sector. It is administered by a non-profit organization, which has articulated a clear diversity statement, has elected a trans woman to its board of directors in 2015, and routinely sponsors efforts, such as PyLadies and PyCaribbean. Such efforts increase participation from publics traditionally underrepresented in the technology sector.[7]

Identify research objectives prior to selecting the appropriate tools and methodologies

Because the tools that we teach are universal, we are able to better tailor our courses to the diverse needs of our students. In formulating their research objectives, beginners often make the mistake of starting with the tool. In this way, someone may describe their interests as "using topic modeling on a corpus of nineteenth-century literature." To this we reply: To what ends? Clearly articulated research objectives suggest appropriate tools and methodologies and not the other way around. Thus the question of "genre formation in the nineteenth century," for example, might lead to the use of topic modeling, while the study of narrative would perhaps be better served by other means, such as event detection or automatic plot summarization. Our goal therefore is to give the students a glimpse of a rich and variegated toolkit that could help advance a variety of research objectives.

Divide big problems into small, modular components

Our goals in the classroom go beyond the instrumental. The ability to automate machines is merely a side effect of algorithmic, analytical thinking. To learn to think like a programmer is useful in many contexts: it involves dividing big, complex, and seemingly intractable problems into small, modular, solvable components. Writing a grant proposal, for example, a book, or a dissertation may initially seem like a daunting and onerous task. Progress can be made once it is divided into small discrete steps, as though it were a recipe for making a cake (an exercise we use in the classroom). Our coding exercises therefore often begin by having our students describe their research objectives, step by step, in language natural to them and to their task.

Be "lazy" by automating mundane tasks, but do it right by commenting your code, taking notes, and sharing with others

Pseudocode in plain English becomes the basis for well-documented programs and readable code. Modular and well-documented code does a service to the community: it is a pleasure to maintain and it communicates the purpose of the program clearly. It teaches others just as it allows them to further adapt the codebase to suit their own needs and to further share and to remix.

Good programmers are *lazy in the right way*. After doing a task more than a few times, a programmer's intuition will be to automate the task. For example, we often use the `rsync` command to back up our documents; however, after a few months of running it manually, we can delegate that task to the built-in scheduler called `cron`. Similar strategies can be used to improve bibliographic management, manuscript preparation, and research and editorial workflows.[8]

Doing things badly or in a haphazard fashion accumulates technological, intellectual, and eventually an ethical debt owed to ourselves and to our peers. Code comments (or the lack of them) are a common site of egregious laziness: it is easy to skip documenting your code or to document it insufficiently. When the code works, one might say, why bother? However, a piece of code that makes perfect sense today may seem impenetrable tomorrow. Without comments, code becomes difficult to alter and maintain. For these reasons we advise our students against simply cutting and pasting code snippets from our (or anyone else's) tutorials. We want them to think independently, to annotate, and to review their notes. In the broader academic context, lazy practices are unethical because they "bank" against the labor of others in the future. They make research more difficult to share and to replicate.

DIGITAL HUMANITIES CORE

Programming can involve long stretches of frustration ("Why does this not work?") punctuated by the short bursts of elation that come with accomplishing something difficult ("It works!"). Rather than allowing students to view their initial lack of results as failures, we attempt to channel feelings of hindrance into a discipline of problem-solving and discovery. The "difficulty" of coding can be made more productive when related to the analogous and more familiar challenges associated with archival research, academic writing, and foreign language acquisition. Understood in this broader context, coding constitutes a small but foundational part of a larger, variegated academic skill set.

Depending on one's research interests and career path, a DH practitioner will need to acquire a subset of the following core skills (with examples of particular technologies in parenthesis):

- Text markup (plain text, *Markdown*, *Pandoc*, *TEI*);
- Command line interface proficiency (*Bash*, pipes, regular expressions);
- Content management (*Jekyll*, *WordPress*);
- Version control (*Git*);
- Programming language (*Python*, *R*, *JavaScript*);
- Networking (cloud computing, Virtual Private Networks);
- Security (Pretty Good Privacy, Secure Socket Shell);
- System administration (*Linux*, *Apache*, *MySql*);
- Project management (*GitHub Issues*, *BaseCamp*);
- Design (data visualization, typography, user experience);
- Probability, statistics, and algorithms.

We do not mean for this list to represent a comprehensive statement about computation in the humanities. Rather, we would argue that most projects, however large or small, employ at least *some* aspects from the above "dream list." The ubiquity of these modular components is what classifies them as "core" or "foundational" competencies. Few people, *including* computer scientists and software engineers, would claim mastery over the full range of skills we have delineated above. Rather, individual practitioners are likely to develop proficiency in one or several areas of expertise. An expert in digital publishing, for example, will have drastically different requirements from someone interested in geographic information systems or computational methods.

Critical computing in the humanities begins with text. Whatever our home discipline, we are all involved in the reading and writing of texts. Text gives us intrinsic motivation to explore our own computer environments: to understand how documents are produced and where they reside physically within the machine. Learning to author documents in a *text markup* language such as HTML or Markdown naturally leads to more advanced topics such as the basics of operating systems, file system hierarchy standards, and version control. For many of these competencies, familiarity with the *command line* is a prerequisite. Using the command line for mundane but necessary academic skills such as regular file backup can familiarize students with foundational concepts such as relative and absolute file paths or the distinction between plain text and binary formats. Familiarity with Bash and regular expressions extends competency on the command line to text manipulation methods.

The core principle of demystifying everyday computation leads to the topics of *content management* and *version control* early in the curriculum. Although not a simple subject, version control comes naturally to a community used to thinking about drafts, manuscripts, and revisions. Increasingly, version control systems also serve as content management systems used to host websites, share data, and publish. For example, the editors of *The Programming Historian* use GitHub, a version control system, to publish and to distribute their journal. The team behind *Project GITenberg* "leverages the power of the Git version control system and the collaborative potential of Github to make books more open."[9] As of 2015, *GITenberg* hosts more than 43,000 books (Hellman *et al.*). Using a similar model to create personal academic profiles, compile image galleries, or edit critical editions, our students learn while experimenting with aspects of academic production directly relevant to their careers. Furthermore, version control systems improve the quality of academic collaboration. Git and similar tools act as powerful research notebooks. They encourage all researchers involved to keep meticulous notes, which make it possible to document the flow of ideas and labor and to attribute work fairly. For these reasons we encourage the use of version control early and expect such systems to play an increasing role in academic evaluation.

A *programming language* occupies a central place in computational practice. All forms of digitality pass through some form of encoding and automation. Only a small step separates text manipulation at the command line using simple shell scripts from more advanced research-oriented programming languages such as *Python*, *R*, and *Haskell*. We often "trick" our students into programming by automating simple tasks such as word counting and file management at the command line. Thus small tasks such as "create a directory," "move a file," and "count all words in this directory" can eventually grow into text analysis.

Because the Internet plays such a key role in transforming academic practice, knowing the basics of *networking* and network *security* – infrastructure, routing, packet switching, protocols, and encryption – is also key to pursuing higher-level goals such as preserving free speech online, protecting a journalist's sources, or bypassing censorship filters, particularly in places where politics and geography impinge on intellectual freedom. The care and maintenance of personal document archives – research papers, article drafts, and book manuscripts – naturally leads into server management. The server is where many of the skills learned earlier come to fruition. Running websites requires a long "stack" of technological components. Advanced *system administration* technologies "in the stack" such as the Apache HTTP server, MySQL relational database management system, and the PHP programming language are difficult (if not impossible) to master without prior knowledge of the command line, networking, and programming fundamentals.

No project is complete without some sense of planning and organization. *Project management* is an important part of computation in the private sector, and it is an increasingly formalized part of software engineering. Projects succeed and fail by the measure of their ability to coordinate action across differences in time, temperament, and geography. When teaching programming, we ask our students to start with "scoping" their projects in plain English first, then to transform these technical specifications into pseudocode, which finally serves as the basis for program design and architecture. We ask our students to submit these documents along with code and we consider them an essential part of the project's output. In addition to getting better results, attention to project management prepares our students for working in groups outside of academia.

Because computational projects in the digital humanities often involve the creation of public-facing tools and archives, they necessarily overlap with the disciplines of *design*, such as data visualization, graphical user interfaces, and user experience design. Johanna Drucker has been a powerful voice in urging our community to encounter design both in practice and as an object of study.[10] The disciplines of human–computer interaction and human factor engineering hold exciting possibilities for a productive collaboration between schools of engineering and the humanities.

Finally, programming fundamentally involves a measure of *probabilistic reasoning, statistical methods,* and *algorithmic thinking*. Without logic there can be no computation. Ultimately, the art of programming involves the ability to think algorithmically, to atomize complexity into discrete programmable steps, to formalize intuition, and to build models. Logic and statistical reasoning underlie every word cloud, every topic model, and every network visualization tool. Critical computing practice, like critical thought, requires access to deep structure. Those who aspire to become active and equal participants in the formation of computational knowledge (rather than mere passive recipients of tools and methodologies developed elsewhere) must at some point confront the established standards for training required for quantitative work in any field.

An intensive, week-long class, like the one that we teach at DHSI, can begin to address only a small portion of the skills required to run a successful project in the digital humanities. A diverse team of practitioners with complementary expertise will likely comprise any given digital humanities project. For this reason, in our teaching, we concentrate on the following "three locations of computing," which support nearly all aspects of specialization represented above. Some familiarity with a text editor, the command line, and a programming language improves general digital literacy, useful to the librarian, the information scientist, and the computational humanist alike.

THREE LOCATIONS OF COMPUTING

We often begin our courses by outlining the above "big picture" principles, challenges, and considerations. Like learning a foreign language, programming takes time and patience to master. As is the case with any difficult skill, motivation to observe "best practices" correlates to chances of long-term success. Developing the intellectual motivations to stick with the program is therefore one of our paramount goals. For this reason, we strive to address common "frustration points" of everyday computing. In our experience, even simple tasks such as downloading an online file can be rife with anxiety for many students: *Where did that file go? How do I find it again? What type of file is it? Is it safe to open it?* Modern operating systems of this sort conceal from the average user the details needed to make informed decisions. Practitioners interested in fields of information science, critical software studies, platform studies, video game studies, or media archeology must learn to extend their inquiry beyond the available surfaces.

Our task as instructors is to reveal the hidden mechanics of computation. Moments of apprehension can be turned into opportunities for discovery. Students, university faculty, and librarians naturally approach documents, file systems, and datasets as matters of critical importance. Such artifacts preserve much precious intellectual labor. In our experience, students respond enthusiastically to the mission of reclaiming these material contexts of their daily intellectual production.

As suggested by the metaphor of the software development "environment," a site of computation denotes an interface through which humans engage with machines. A "site" is also a conceptual space, containing a logic or a grammar of interaction. We find three such sites in searching for the universal grounds of general digital literacy: the command line, the language interpreter, and the text editor.

Command line interface

Because all interaction with the machine on the level of the operating system is in some sense an operation of files, the aspiring coder must develop a firm grasp of the file system topography. Despite its retro appearances, the modern command line offers an intuitive, text-based, "call and response" style of interaction with the file system consistent across a remarkable variety of platforms, from mobile phones to supercomputers, using the "terminal" or terminal emulator.[11] Everything from downloading a sample corpus, to writing a research paper, to debugging code eventually leads to the command line. We therefore embrace it from the beginning of the course.

The command line is one way among several to communicate with a machine. On the level of hardware, the machine "speaks" in binary code. It "interprets" or translates English language-like commands (in a language called Unix Shell)[12] into binary code. When deleting a file, for example, one instructs the machine to `rm filename.txt` instead of dragging and dropping it into the trash folder, as one would using a graphical user interface. Note that "dropping into the trash folder" offers a visual metaphor for the underlying bitwise operations. The terminal command transforms the metaphor into the more exact command, `rm`, which stands for "remove." Similarly, to direct the computer to move a file, we would use the `mv` or "move" command. Unlike their visual and metaphorical counterparts, the shell commands contain many advanced options, not amenable to visual metaphor.

The `man` command accesses the manual. Thus, `man mv` displays the manual pages for the move command.

Furthermore, because shell commands are in themselves a type of programming language, they can be chained together to produce a "script," or short program. The script can then be used to automate system administration of data analysis tasks. To give the reader an example of a command line script, we will briefly examine the following lines of code, which ultimately give us a frequency count for each word in Herman Melville's *Moby Dick*. Download the plain text version of the novel from Project Gutenberg and save as `moby.txt` to follow along.

We encourage the reader to follow along with these exercises by opening their terminal window and using the `man` command to learn about each of the steps involved. For example, `man grep` will show the manual pages for the `grep` utility. More detailed explanations of each step can be found online at the publisher's site.

```
# find the whale
grep "whale" moby.txt

# substitute whale for chicken globally
cat moby.txt | sed 's/whale/chicken/g' > chicken.txt

# see what happened to the whales
grep "chicken" chicken.txt

# remove punctuation.
cat moby.txt | tr -d "[:punct:]" > moby-nopunct.txt

# check if it worked
tail moby-nopunct.txt

# translate all upper case into lower
cat moby-nopunct.txt | tr '[:upper:]' '[:lower:]'
     > moby-clean.txt
tail moby-clean.txt

# sort by word frequency
cat moby-clean.txt | sed 's/[[:space:]]/\'$'\n/g'
     | sort | uniq -c | sort -gr -k1 > word-
     count.txt
head word-count.txt
```

We include the above examples to give the reader a compelling example of possibilities at the command line. The online exercises accompanying the present volume will give detailed explanation of the commands involved. For now, note that shell scripting encourages the "data flow" style of text processing. Vertical lines (|) and angle brackets (>) allow us to chain the commands into a system of pipes and redirects, passing the text output of one operation on to the next one. Once saved to disk, these small scripts can be used to perform text transformations and frequency counts on any file.

Learning the command line is not just a matter of interacting with files. With time it becomes possible to use commands such as `wc` and `sed` to perform sophisticated data cleaning and text analysis operations. The above exercise also introduces the difference between relative and absolute file paths (`documents/book/*.txt vs. /usr/documents/book/*.txt`). It contains the basics of regular expressions (`[ a-z]`). Finally, the exercise can lead to the basics of remote server management, debugging, networking, security, and encryption.

Python

The second of our foundational sites of computing is the Python interpreter. Where the command line "translates" from shell into machine code, the *Python* interpreter translates from the *Python* language. *Shell* is a domain-specific command language, designed specifically to interact with the operating system. It traces its roots to the late 1970s, and this longevity makes it stable and ubiquitous. *Python*, on the other hand, was introduced in the early '90s and became popular in the early 2000s (Lutz). Unlike *Shell*, it is a general-purpose, high-level programming language. Like *Shell*, it privileges human readability, which fits with our principles.

We chose *Python* among other excellent choices (such as *R* and *Haskell*) for several reasons. First, *Python* is popular. According to the TIOBE language popularity index, *Python* holds roughly 3.6 per cent of the market, trailing only behind *Java* and C-family languages (*C*, *C++*, *C#*), all of which are significantly more difficult to learn and more complicated to implement. Although detailed statistics by field are not

Table 6.1 Common uses of Python and Shell programming languages

When to use Shell	When to use Python
Automate daily tasks	Data science
Manage files & folders	App development
Remote server administration	Natural language processing
Data munging[1]	Data visualization
Quick & dirty text manipulation	Web scraping Corpus analysis Everything else

[1]Data munging is a recursive computer acronym that stands for "Mung Until No Good," referring to a series of discrete and potentially destructive data transformation steps (Raymond).

available, we infer that in the domain of scientific computing and data science *Python* holds the majority share of the market. This is important, because it means that learning *Python* is a good investment of time. It can lead to jobs inside and outside of academia. Projects using *Python* will find collaborators more easily than those using a less popular language.

Python's popularity has an important side-effect. Being a general-purpose language, it has been adapted into a wide variety of contexts, from machine learning to web application development. The *Python* community packages common design patterns for any given application into ready-made "building blocks." In aggregate, such building blocks comprise domain-specific software libraries, widely available for reuse. *Python* is consequently composed of much more than the packages that are bundled in a fresh installation of the interpreter: it also includes the rich variety of software libraries and toolkits with which it interacts. For example, the Natural Language Toolkit contains libraries that perform many common tasks needed for text analysis.

Let us translate the same code we used to explore Melville's *Moby Dick* in *Shell* into *Python*. As before, feel free to follow along online or on your machine. Do not worry if you do not understand all the code yet. In our class, we cover this material over the course of a week. For now, the examples here should give the reader a general feel for *Python* programming: grammar, logic, and control structures. (Note: This example uses Python 3. Installations of Python 2.x should omit parentheses for `print` commands.)

Let's begin by finding all the whales and substituting them for chicken, just for fun:

```
# open file and read contents into a list of lines
# mimics the shell behavior in the previous example
with open('moby.txt', 'r') as f:
  lines = f.read().splitlines()
```

Unlike *Shell*, *Python* is an object-oriented language. Just as everything in the Unix world is a file, everything in the *Python* world is an object. Objects have methods associated with them. You can imagine an object of the type "dog," for example, to have methods such as "sit" and "fetch." And an object of the type "cat" to have methods such as "hide" and "hunt." Methods often return other objects. Thus we may expect the method `dog.fetch()` to return an object of the type `toy`. Note that the parentheses help differentiate the method from the object itself: one is a verb, the other a noun.

But the built-in *Python* objects are limited to just a few primitive types such as string, integer, and list. The type of data manipulation we show here depends on knowing what type of object we are working with at all times. When we first open `moby.txt` we "stuff" it into an object of type *file* that we call, arbitrarily, `f`. File objects have useful methods such as `read()` which returns an object of type *string*. Strings have the helpful ability to arrange themselves into lines, which are delineated by hidden newline characters. `splitlines()` uses this feature of the string to return a *list* of strings, which we can assign to an arbitrarily named variable `lines`. Because `splitlines()` returns lists, Python attempts to do the right thing by making the `lines` variable of the type *list*.

To check the type of an object we can run `type(lines)`. `print(lines)` will show the contents of our list container. Let us now try to replace all whales with chickens, just for fun:

```
# replace whale for chicken in every line and
print results
for line in lines:
  if 'whale' in line:
    print(line.replace('whale', 'chicken'))
```

Note that although we have not explained control structures such as `for` and `if`, their use is pretty intuitive. The Pythonic for `line in lines` is not too far from the English "for every line in lines." The next line says to do something if the word "whale" is in the line. Where `lines` is a *list*, each individual member of the list is an object of type *string*. Like dogs and cats, strings can do things, as they have methods attached to them. The method `replace()` works as expected. Unlike self-contained methods like `splitlines()`, the `replace()` method takes two arguments: first, the word to be replaced, and second, the replacement word. Such details can be found in the Python documentation and become more familiar with time.

In conclusion, we come to an operation central to any computational text analysis. To count the unique words as we did before, we need to divide up each line into words. We can then get rid of punctuation, make everything lower case to avoid duplication, and create a list of all words found in the novel. The list of all words is commonly referred to as "tokens" where the list of unique words gives us the "types." The type–token distinction is incredibly useful in stylistic analysis, for example. It can be used to build more complex models about the quality of writing, for example, or about the age range of the intended audience. We expect sophisticated prose by adults to exhibit a high token-to-type ratio. Children's literature uses a more limited vocabulary that repeats more often, giving us a lower ratio value.

```
from string import punctuation
from collections import Counter

tokens = []

# split each line into a list of words
# remove punctuation and make each word lowercase
# append "cleaned" words to the list "tokens"
```

```
for line in lines:
  for word in line.split():
    tokens.append(word.strip(punctuation).lower())

# display 100 most common types
types = Counter(tokens)
types.most_common(100)
```

Conveniently for us, *Python* strings have the method `split()`. First we import some helpful libraries that contain some of the logic that we need to perform our operations. Then we declare an empty list and give it an arbitrary name, `tokens`. We then iterate over each line, and after that over each word in the line. Once the word has been stripped of punctuation (another neat trick given to us by the built-in *Python* functionality) and converted to lower case, we append it to our list of words. The only thing that remains is to count unique word types with `Counter()`, the second method we imported, and to print the most common words in the novel using the available `most_common()` method. Note that even without any preparation, the logic of the code above is readily apparent. Python's built-in functions sound like English. They are easy to read and therefore easy to share and maintain.

The above code could be written in a more concise way. We opted for code that is more verbose but also far more expressive. The reader can perhaps already tell that while *Python* is wordier, it offers many more built-in features than *Shell*. This would be even more apparent if we were working with images or binary formats instead of plain text files. For a quick count of words in a novel, we may initially opt to use the Unix shell. As our models and logic grow more complex, though, we are likely to begin writing in *Python*.

Text editor

The humble text editor is the third and possibly most important site of computing in the digital humanities. In addition to supporting programming, the text editor mediates our research and publication practices. For this reason, we ask our students to re-evaluate their relationship with tools such as Microsoft Word and Google Docs. These often fail to meet our community's criteria for usability and they do not align well with humanistic values. At the very least, to write code we need a *plain text* editor that does not add any hidden formatting characters to our code. We also need an editor that we can modify and extend without being hampered by proprietary licenses or restrictions. Many text editors meet these criteria. Among them are *Atom*, *Emacs*, *Leafpad*, *Notepad++*, and *Vim*.

Where command prompts and *Python* interpreters allow for an "interactive," back-and-forth dialog style of programming that happens in real time, the text editor gives a measure of permanence to the conversation. When working with datasets, we often begin with exploratory data analysis at the command line or an interactive

Python interpreter to familiarize ourselves with the data and form intuitions about its explanatory potential. Once those intuitions are formed, we can move to writing and debugging code in the text editor. The code helps describe our formal models. It lets us test our intuitions against the dataset as a whole. The Python interpreter and the Shell remain open in the background. We will use them to manage our files and to test snippets of code. But the text editor is where we can begin to think algorithmically. It is where our projects gain a more permanent shape.

About halfway through the session, the students are ready to formulate a project of their own. Rather than using prepackaged exercises, we encourage our students to formulate small research projects related to their own work or interests. In our last class, a group of librarians built a program to copy selected metadata from one `.csv` file to another while checking for errors in data formatting (such as an improperly formatted date, for example). Another group built an automatic essay grader. Yet another analyzed poetry for its similarity to Byron. A fourth group wrote a script that automates the download of a film script corpus.

All of these projects begin with a set of step-by-step instructions in English. Thus, a simple essay grader may be expressed as follows:

```
# Open and read a file.

# Calculate variation of sentence lengths.

# Assign a score based on variation.

# Calculate a measure of linguistic variety.

# Assign a vocabulary score.

# Find common spelling mistakes and "weasel words."

# Average the scores to come up with a total grade.
```

Once formalized, we can begin to convert the logic from the English language pseudocode into *Python*, expanding and filling in the code under the comments.

Using this process, students work alone or in groups to define the scope of their program. Even at this stage we can begin a critical discussion about the models implicit in the proposed program. For example, does the above logic for an essay "grader" accurately capture what we mean by "writing well" or "writing poorly"? Is it enough to reduce notions of value to "a measure of linguistic variety"? What can we do to make our model more robust and to make it better correspond to our native intuitions about literary value? In another recent course at Columbia University, students building an automatic essay-grader had to explain and defend the basis of their grading criteria. In doing so, they confronted their own implicit criteria for good writing and initiated a spirited debate about algorithmic judgments of clarity and style. Some students rewarded rich vocabularies. Others looked for variation in sentence and paragraph length. In this way, we use the algorithm to challenge intuitions about academic writing and literary value..

When the scope and logic of the program have been determined, we work with individual groups to help translate the English-language heuristic into workable *Python* code. Inevitably, the programs grow more sophisticated. In the above example, students used published work to test their grading algorithm. It was interesting to see how Ernest Hemingway fared against David Foster Wallace, for example. In a longer course, we might have introduced supervised learning techniques to classify essays for quality based on similarity to work that has already been evaluated. The difficulty of any specific project may be tailored to the length of the course and to the level of individual expertise. During such free-form "laboratory" sessions we encourage students to help each other and to share expertise with their peers.

The command line, the *Python* interpreter, and the text editor provide the foundations of critical computing in the humanities. We do not expect all of our students to become programmers. But at the very least, they become exposed to a powerful problem-solving method and to operating system internals used widely in all aspects of computation, from sending email to writing papers.[13]

NOTES

1 "Human(s|ists)" is actually a regular expression, a way to search text for specified patterns. In this case it picks out anything starting with "Human" and ending in *either* "s" or "ists". So, it acts as a stand-in for both "Humans" and "Humanists."

2 An archived version of the DHSI course can be accessed at web.archive.org/web/20150614161609/https://github.com/denten-workshops/dhsi-coding-fundamentals/blob/master/README.md

3 We are not the first nor the only instructors to think about digital pedagogy this way, nor are we the only ones to be offering a course based on these principles. *Software Carpentry*, for example, has been advocating a similar approach since its inception. Similarly, the *Programming Historian* is "an online, open access, peer-reviewed suite of tutorials that help humanists learn a wide range of digital tools, techniques, and workflows to facilitate their research." See also Harrell.

4 Weasel words are words that sound very meaningful, but diminish instead of adding to the impact of persuasive writing. The "very" in the previous sentence, for example, is a weasel word.

5 Unix philosophy privileges inputs and outputs in plain text format, which can be used to store everything from personal notes, to article drafts, to huge datasets of metadata. Unix provides many powerful utilities that work with plain text. The notion of human readability is encoded at the operating system level.

6 Python Enhancement Proposal 20 reads: "Simple is better than complex. Complex is better than complicated. Sparse is better than dense. Readability counts."

7 See Python Software Foundation ("Diversity"), Python Software Foundation ("PSF Board Resolutions"), and Python Software Foundation ("Python Software Foundation") for further detail on the Python Software Foundation and its initiatives.

8 The public GitHub code repository of W. Caleb McDaniel, a historian at Rice University, is exemplary in this regard (McDaniel).

9 The name *Project GITenberg* is a playful nod to *Project Gutenberg* (www.gutenberg.org/), a website that has been influential in the sharing out of copyright works online but which does not make edits done to its resources transparent.

10 See, for example, her work with Emily McVarish on *Graphic Design History* (Drucker and McVarish).

11 While some platforms default to a text-based command line (the "terminal"), most modern graphical machines use a "terminal emulator" to achieve the same results: Windows, Mac, and Linux systems either have built-in terminal emulators or support many third-party applications that serve the same function.

12 See S. R. Bourne's overview for more detail on the Unix shell (Bourne).

13 A detailed history of author contributions can be found on our GitHub page at https://github.com/denten-workshops/dhsi-coding-fundamentals/commits/master/book-chapter/main.md

REFERENCES AND FURTHER READING

Bird, Steven, and Ewan Klein. *Natural Language Processing with Python*. 1st edition. Cambridge, MA: O'Reilly Media, 2009. Print.

Bourne, S. R. "UNIX Time-Sharing System: The UNIX Shell." *Bell System Technical Journal* 57.6 (1978): 1971–1990. Web. 7 November 2015.

Chacon, Scott. *Pro Git*. 2nd edition. 2014 edition. Apress, 2014. Print.

Dawney, Allen. *Think Python: How to Think Like a Computer Scientist*. 2nd edition. O'Reilly Media, 2015. Print.

Drucker, Johanna, and Emily McVarish. *Graphic Design History*. 2nd edition. Boston: Pearson, 2012. Print.

Harrell, D. Fox. "Toward a Theory of Critical Computing: The Case of Social Identity Representation in Digital Media Applications." *CTHEORY* 0.0 (2015): n. pag. Web. 9 September 2015.

Hellman, Eric, Raymond Yee, and Seth Woodworth. "Project GITenberg." 2012. Web. 10 November 2015.

Janssens, Jeroen. *Data Science at the Command Line: Facing the Future with Time-Tested Tools*. 1st edition. O'Reilly Media, 2014. Print.

Kernighan, Brian W. *D Is for Digital: What a Well-Informed Person Should Know About Computers and Communications*. CreateSpace Independent Publishing Platform, 2011. Print.

Lutz, Mark. *Programming Python*. Sebastopol, CA: O'Reilly, 1996. Web. Nutshell Handbook.

Manning, Christopher D., and Hinrich Schütze. *Foundations of Statistical Natural Language Processing*. Cambridge, MA: MIT Press, 1999. Print.

McDaniel, W. Caleb. "Wcaleb (W. Caleb McDaniel)." *GitHub* November 2015. Web. 10 November 2015.

McIlroy, M.D., E.N. Pinson, and B.A. Tague. "UNIX Time-Sharing System: Foreword." *Bell System Technical Journal* 57.6 (1978): 1899–1904. Web.

Nelson, Theodor H. *Computer Lib: You Can and Must Understand Computers Now*. 1st edition. Nelson, 1974. Print.

Petzold, Charles. *Code: The Hidden Language of Computer Hardware and Software*. 1st edition. Microsoft Press, 2000. Print.

Python Software Foundation. "Diversity." *Python.org* 2015. Web. 9 November 2015.

Python Software Foundation. "PSF Board Resolutions." *Python.org* October 2015. Web. 10 November 2015.

Python Software Foundation. "Python Software Foundation." *Python.org* 2001. Web. 9 November 2015.

Raymond, Eric S. "Mung." *The Jargon File* 2004. Web. 15 June 2015. http://web.archive.org/web/20150615165058/http://www.catb.org/jargon/html/M/mung.html

Stallman, Richard. "Why Open Source Misses the Point of Free Software." 2007. Web. 11 September 2015.

CHAPTER 7

Text encoding

Julia Flanders, Syd Bauman and Sarah Connell

INTRODUCTION

At its heart, text encoding is a process of creating a digital model of a textual source using markup: codes that live in the transcription of the text and identify its structure and content. For instance:

```
<l>Behold <name type="personification">America</name>,
  <del seq="2" resp="#editorC"><add seq="1"
  resp="#editorC">the sights thou lovest</add></del></l>
<l><del seq="3" resp="#smith">The w</del> thy endless
  workshops see</l>
```

The simple content of this passage, if transcribed directly, would be difficult to make sense of:

> Behold America, the sights thou lovest, The w thy endless workshops see

To this string of words and letters, the markup adds important human knowledge: that the text in question is two lines of a poem; that “America” here is used as a kind of personification rather than a simple place name; that certain words were added and deleted (and the order in which that happened); and that a specific editor takes responsibility for specific parts of the interpretation.

This process is analytical, strategic, and interpretive. It is analytical, in identifying a set of components into which the text can meaningfully be broken and whose relationship can be represented through the markup. In this example, the analysis engages with the text as a literary and manuscript object, but ignores (for instance) its linguistic properties, which could equally have been included in the model. Markup is strategic, in that text encoding is always aimed (deliberately or by default) at some intellectual or practical goal; the choices we make in analyzing and representing the text in this way are best made with an awareness of our own aims and motivations. And markup is interpretive, in that the act of encoding will always take place through a connection between an observing individual and a source object. The resulting interpretation may be highly idiosyncratic, or it may be widely shared and uncontroversial; we can move our encoding in the latter direction through training, documentation, and prior agreement. But it is worth remembering that these efforts produce shared interpretations rather than something that escapes interpretation altogether. The editorial team performing this markup could presumably agree upon and document a set of criteria that would enable them to produce an internally consistent edition, while the scholarly community as a whole might still disagree about whether Whitman's prose-like poems (and this one in particular) are "poetry."

In the modern world of digital scholarship, text encoding serves a number of important functions. Text markup systems first emerged in the 1980s as a way to manage and publish large-scale documents (such as airplane service manuals), following the principle that formatting and layout could be handled by stylesheets based on the informational content of the markup. The encoded document might indicate the presence of headings with a `<head>` element, and the stylesheet might format those headings in different ways depending on the kind of output required.[1] This "single-source" approach to publication, in which structure and formatting are clearly separated, is still central to digital humanities data design. Text markup also plays an important role in supporting data curation, since it can enable very explicit documentation and since it permits a strong degree of transparency in transcriptional and editorial methods (as in the use of the `@resp` attribute in the example above). The most commonly used markup language in digital humanities, the *Text Encoding Initiative Guidelines*,[2] has the additional advantage of being a community standard and of being built using XML, which is an international standard, thus minimizing many of the risks of digital obsolescence. Finally, text markup also serves an important role in digital humanities research. As we have seen, the act of creating a digital model of this kind represents a strong statement concerning the source material being modeled, and constitutes a kind of theory of the text. The evolution of these models, and of our modeling approaches, is an important part of the digital humanities research agenda, and for anyone creating a digital edition or collection using text markup, the creation of a good encoding practice constitutes a significant research effort.

There are many thousands of markup languages in the world, and even within the domain of digital humanities there are many XML languages of relevance. In this chapter, we will be focusing intensively on the *TEI Guidelines*. The TEI is central to digital humanities practice, where it occupies a distinctive niche. It is focused on representing research materials – especially primary sources like historical and literary documents, archival materials, and other forms of textual data – and it also provides ways of representing the editorial and critical processes humanists use to prepare these materials for research and circulation. The TEI can be used to create digital editions, teaching anthologies, research corpora, full-text thematic research collections, digital archives, and many other forms of publication.[3] Despite its unique role in digital humanities, the TEI also demonstrates a set of core principles that can be extended to most other text encoding languages, and thus serves as a useful pedagogical starting point for those who are interested in markup as a domain.

TECHNICAL ORIENTATION: UNDERSTANDING XML

To understand text encoding and the TEI, it is first necessary to understand XML and how it works. Essentially, XML is a metalanguage that provides a set of rules for creating documents that are intelligible both to humans and to computers (rules such as "element start tags begin with a less-than sign"). The TEI, then, is a language for representing textual data that is expressed using the rules of XML.

The basics of XML: nesting, elements, and attributes

In XML, the various bits of a document that the encoder finds interesting are indicated as such using *elements*. An element has three core constituent parts: the *start tag*, the *end tag*, and the *content*, which is whatever lies between the start tag and the end tag. So, given the example:

```
<name>America</name>
```

`<name>America</name>` is an element; `<name>` is the start tag, `</name>` is the end tag, and `America` is the content. We call the entire construct a "name element." The content of an element may be text, other elements, some combination of the two, or nothing at all.[4]

Because elements can nest inside other elements, XML allows us to model a document's hierarchical structure quite naturally. For example, the *Lord of the Rings* trilogy comprises three parts, each part comprises two books, each book consists of a sequence of chapters, and each chapter is made up of paragraphs.

```
<part>
  <identifier>The Fellowship of the Ring</identifier>
  <book>
    <identifier>Book I</identifier>
    <chapter>
      <identifier>A Long-Expected Party</identifier>
      <para>When Mr. Bilbo Baggins of . . .
      <para>Bilbo was very rich and . . .
```

Thus, elements can be thought of as the "building blocks" of a model of a text. It is useful to recognize that because elements nest inside other elements, the structure of an XML document can be imagined as a set of boxes, in which each box may contain other boxes – just as Book I of *Fellowship* contains the chapter titled "A Long-Expected Party," which contains paragraphs, which contain text, including things like character names, and so on. It is also important to recognize that the structure of an XML document can also be thought of as a *tree*. These trees are much like family trees, usually drawn with the single root element at the top. Unlike a family tree, however, each element in an XML tree has only one parent (except for the root element, which has none).

With the tree view in mind, the relationships between elements can be described familially: we can use concepts such as "child," "parent," "grandchild," "sibling," and "descendant." For example, in Figure 7.1, `<author>`, `<title>`, and `<imprint>` are all children of `<citation>`.

Because the name of an element is used to describe its role in the structure of the document, we may think of elements as the "nouns" of encoding. But, we may want to express more information than what is conveyed merely by the name of an element. Just as we can express more information about nouns by using

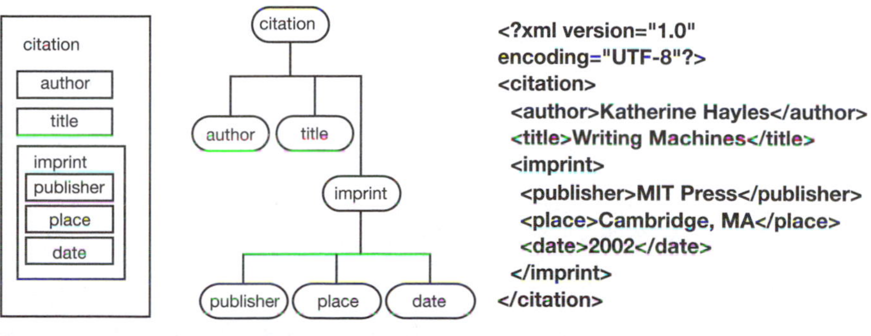

Figure 7.1
The same XML citation data visualized in three ways: as a set of nested boxes, as a tree, and as XML encoding

adjectives, we can add more information to an XML element using *attributes*. Attributes behave like adjectives, but are more precise because they give more information about what they describe. The *name* of the attribute indicates which aspect of the element it describes – for instance, its type, or its size, or its color – while the *attribute value* gives a specific descriptor within that category of information. Compare, for example, "the orange truck" with `<truck color ="orange">` or `<truck cargo="oranges">`.

Attributes must follow a few rules: they may only occur in a start tag or empty-element tag, they must always be preceded by whitespace, and the value must always be surrounded by a pair of matching single or double straight quotation marks. The name of an attribute, which must be unique among the attributes of a particular instance of an element, follows the same rules as the name of an element: it must start with a letter, and can contain only letters, digits, underscores, dots, and hyphens.[5] The value of an attribute may not contain a less-than sign (U+003C, "<"), lest it be confused with the beginning of a tag, nor an occurrence of whichever quotation mark is used to delimit it.

The rules of XML: well-formedness and validity

In order to be processed as an XML document, a file has to follow an important set of basic rules. Files that follow these rules are *well-formed XML*, and those that do not follow the rules are not XML. These rules can be summarized quite simply:

- All delimiters (angle brackets, quotation marks, etc.) must be used properly.
- There must be a single root element containing the entire XML document.
- Elements must all nest neatly inside one another, without overlapping.

That last rule deserves further explanation. In XML, an *element* can contain another *element*, but it cannot contain only part of another element. That is, if the start-tag of element B is inside element A, then the end-tag of element B must also be inside element A. Thus:

```
<A>. . .<B>. . .</B>. . .</A>
```

is correct, but

```
<A>. . .<B>. . .</A>. . .</B>
```

is not XML.

But how does one know which elements and attributes to use? Each particular encoding language, such as TEI, DocBook, EAD, or MusicML, has a set of elements and attributes to choose from, and a set of rules about which can go where. For example, in TEI an `<l>` (metrical line) can go inside an `<lg>` (group of metrical lines), but an <lg> cannot go inside an <l>. And a <pb> (page break) or <note> can go almost anywhere, including in the middle of a <w> (word). This set of rules can be referred to as the document's *grammar*, and is formally expressed in a file called a *schema*. A file that obeys the grammar expressed in a schema is said to be *valid* against that schema.

Both validity and well-formedness are important, but their impact on encoding varies. While it is difficult to overstate the necessity of keeping an encoded file well-formed, the benefits of validity depend on circumstance.

Pointing and linking

It is very common in XML documents in general, and TEI documents in particular, to want to express a relationship between two parts of a document, or between parts of separate documents. We experience this every day on the World Wide Web, where a common *link* expresses the relationship "you might want to go here," and is typically instantiated with the behavior that the browser follows the link if you click on it. But links can be used to express more precise relationships as well: for example, "this note is annotation of that sentence," or "this poem is a translation of that poem."

In order to say "that sentence" or "that poem," we need to be able to identify the element that contains that sentence or poem. XML provides a special attribute, `@xml:id`,[6] exactly for this purpose: to uniquely identify a specific occurrence of an element. Once we have placed an `@xml:id` (whose value must follow the rules for element and attribute names, and additionally must be unique across all `@xml:id` values in the entire document) on a particular instance of an element, we can point to that identifier using a URI.[7] Thus we can establish a "pointing" gesture from one element to another. As we'll see later, the semantics of what that pointing gesture means depends on the context. For example, the pointer associated with a <note> element links to the spot or passage being annotated. The pointer associated with a `@facs` attribute of a <pb> element typically points to a JPEG image of the page that is transcribed immediately following the <pb>.

You have now learned the essentials of XML, which apply to all XML languages:

- Elements are delimited by tags.
- Tags are delimited by angle brackets, with a slash distinguishing the end-tag.
- There must be one and only one outermost or "root" element.
- Attributes, which must be preceded by whitespace, are expressed as name="value" (or name='value') in the start tag or empty-element tag only.
- Elements may not overlap: each one must end inside the same element in which it started.

- XML documents *must* be well-formed (that is, they must follow the rules above).
- XML documents may further follow the rules of a given encoding language, such as TEI, and thus be valid with respect to that language.
- An element may bear an `@xml:id` attribute, which may be used to refer to it.

While there are some details[8] we have not addressed, this section has covered the vast majority of XML that the typical humanities project will need to understand.

THE BASICS OF ENCODING WITH TEI

Now that we've established how XML languages work in general, learning the *TEI Guidelines* is a matter of mastering its vocabulary and grammar, and understanding how the TEI thinks about representing documents. The TEI is a very extensive XML language containing over 550 elements, so our goal here is to explain the kinds of things the TEI can do, on the assumption that you can look up the details you need in the *TEI Guidelines* themselves. As we've already noted, the TEI is designed to represent historical, cultural, and literary documents for a predominantly scholarly audience. Here are some key features of the TEI that support this goal:

- extensive *metadata*, contained within the TEI header, which provides documentation of the textual source and the editorial and technical methods involved in the encoding;
- elements to represent the *large-scale architecture* of documents: major sections and their subdivisions, front and back matter;
- elements representing the *smaller-scale structural components* of the document, which contribute to our understanding of the document's genre and meaning: headings, stage directions, quotations, dictionary entries, narrative dialogue, bibliographic references, and the like;
- mechanisms for representing *linkages* between different places in the document, or between different XML structures: for instance, to represent footnotes, cross-references, translations, glossaries, and similar kinds of information;
- elements representing *references to named entities* (such as people, places, texts, and organizations) and other features of the document's content, such as dates or contextual references; closely related to these are elements for capturing information about these named entities (in prosopographies, gazetteers, and the like);
- elements representing the *rhetorical texture* of the document, including emphasis, irony, and dialect usage;

- elements representing the *physical characteristics* of the document, including pagination, damage, and arrangement of the text on the physical page;
- elements representing the *genesis* of the document, including authoring, revision, and annotation;
- elements representing the *editorial or transcriptional process* itself, including indications of where the text is difficult to read, where the editors disagree on the transcription, or where the editors have made emendations to the text.

Most of these features are not required, but instead reflect options that we may or may not find appropriate depending on our project's goals. At a minimum, the TEI expects that we want to create a representation of our document that accounts for its basic structures, contains an accurate transcription of its content, and expresses our significant editorial interventions explicitly.

Let's step through a simple example. Here is a contrived example of some source text:

> **Chapter 4: The Manor House**
>
> Charles hadn't visited the manor house since Easter, 1955, and now he remembered why.
>
> "Hullo", he called out as he walked up the drive, and then, as if to himself, "To be or not to be?, to walk or not to walk . . . oh, *hang* it all!" His meditation on Hamlet was interrupted as he collided with a peacock. "Sacré bleu!" he exclaimed with irritation, his sang-froid completely deserting him. It was going to be a long week. His catalog of irritations included:
>
> 1. The weather
> 2. The peacocks
> 3. His meagre grasp of French

It has some basic features common to many prose documents: a heading, a few paragraphs, a list (containing three items), and various embedded phrases that are visually or conceptually distinct from their surroundings (names, quotations, dialogue, foreign words). It's worth noting right away that some document structure is already being expressed in this source text, using typography and layout; however, the structure here is intended to be legible by humans. Part of what we're doing in our XML markup is to translate this typographical markup into a form that the computer can understand. Here is a simple TEI encoding of this passage:

```
<div>
  <head>Chapter 4: The Manor House</head>
  <p><name>Charles</name> hadn't visited the manor
  house since <date>Easter, 1955</date>,
  and now he remembered why.</p>
  <p><said>Hullo</said>, he called out as he walked up the
  drive, and then, as if to himself, <said><quote>To be or
  not to be?</quote>, to walk or not to walk...oh,
  <emph>hang</emph> it all!</said> His meditation on
  Hamlet was interrupted as he collided with a peacock.
  <said>Sacré bleu!</said> he exclaimed with
  irritation, his <foreign>sang-froid</foreign>
  completely deserting him. It was going to be a long week.
  His catalog of irritations included:
  <list>
    <item>1. The weather</item>
    <item>2. The peacocks</item>
    <item>3. His meagre grasp of French</item>
  </list>
  </p>
</div>
```

The elements above are simple and intuitive; indeed, at this level, the TEI's approach to documents is similar to other encoding languages, including HTML. We can already see several levels of structure from our initial inventory:

- large-scale elements that represent major document divisions:
  - `div`: basic structural chunking, can nest recursively inside itself;
- mid-level structural elements that can go inside a major division, and that contain words and phrase-level elements:
  - `head`: a heading, i.e. the title for the current chapter, section, poem, etc;
  - `p`: a paragraph;
  - `list`, `item`: a list composed of items;
  - `said`: direct speech or thought;
  - `quote`: material quoted from another text;
- small-scale elements that represent individual words and phrases, focused on content features, and rhetorical texture:
  - `name`: a proper noun;
  - `date`: a phrase indicating a date;

- emph: a linguistically emphasized phrase;
- foreign: a word or phrase in a foreign language.

A few things are worth noting here about the encoding process. First, in some cases it involves taking information that is expressed through typography (e.g. the quotation marks in the source) and expressing it through markup instead (the <said> and <quote> elements). In the process, we are gaining semantic specificity: our analytical processes can now distinguish clearly between material that is "spoken" and material that comes from another textual source (such as Shakespeare), where before we had to infer that information unreliably from the quotation marks. This explicitness can be extremely valuable for data analysis, but it also carries a cost: both the encoding of particular elements and the processing of them is more work. Each project needs to examine those costs and benefits to ascertain whether or not such encoding is worthwhile.

Let's take the same example, and add some further layers of complexity:

```
<div type="chapter" xml:lang="en" n="4">
  <head>The Manor House</head>
  <p><name type="person" ref="#charles">Charles</name> hadn't
  visited the manor house since <date when="1955-04-10">
  Easter, 1955</date>, and now he remembered why.</p>
  <p><said>Hullo</said>, he called out as he walked up the
  drive, and then, as if to himself, <said><quote
  source="#hamlet">To  be or not to be?</quote>, to walk
  or not to walk...oh, <emph rend="italic">hang</emph> it
  all!</said> His meditation on Hamlet was interrupted
  as he collided with a peacock. <said xml:lang="fr">
  Sacré bleu!</said> he exclaimed with irritation,
  his <foreign xml:lang="fr">sang-froid</foreign> completely
  deserting him. It was going to be a long week. His catalog
  of irritations included:
  <list>
    <item n="1">The weather</item>
    <item n="2">The peacocks</item>
    <item n="3">His meagre grasp of French</item>
  </list>
  </p>
</div>
```

```
<div type="editorial">
    <listPerson>
        <person xml:id="charles" role="fictional" sex="m">
            <persName>
                <surname>Higginbotham</surname>
                <forename>Charles</forename>
            </persName>
        </person>
    </listPerson>
</div>
```

Structurally, this encoding is almost identical to the first example, but it expresses a greater level of analytical complexity. For one thing, information has been added to it that reflects the editorial consciousness at work. The `@xml:lang` attribute tells us what language the different parts of the document are in.[9] The `@n` attribute gives us a way of representing order, and the `@when` attribute allows us to provide an accurate, machine-readable representation of the date (which in this example would otherwise be very difficult to process automatically). The `@type` attribute enables us to characterize an element more precisely: for instance, to say that our structural division is a "chapter" and that "Charles" is the name of a person. Another addition is a set of attributes which provide linkages to sources of information outside the transcription itself: the `@source` attribute gives us a link to a bibliographic citation for the source of the quotation (allowing us to document that this is a quotation from *Hamlet*), and the `@ref` attribute gives us a link to an entry in our list of characters (allowing us to provide additional information about characters in the novel, such as their sex, race, country of origin, and so forth).

As noted above, this analytical encoding may entail a kind of transformation of textual content into data: for instance, in the above encoding, we have interpreted the printed words "Chapter 4:" to indicate that this is the fourth chapter, and we have represented that information using the `@n` attribute. But, further, our encoding discards the original documentary evidence (the words "Chapter 4") in favor of a purely "data-like" representation. Although document-centric and data-centric approaches are not mutually exclusive – we could easily retain both forms of information – they represent different encoding approaches which may be appropriate in different kinds of projects. The data-centric approach affords a better computational purchase on the data, whereas the document-centric approach is better suited to cases where the document's individual variations and idiosyncrasies are of primary scholarly value.

This example has also focused on a very simple textual genre: a prose narrative. The TEI also includes provision for a vast array of other document types and genres, including: poetry, drama, dictionaries, oral histories, linguistic corpora, scholarly editions, and many others. These are outside the scope of this chapter, but you can explore the *TEI Guidelines* to learn more.

So far we have been concentrating our attention on a single document section; now we can step back and put this markup into the context of the overall TEI document structure. A TEI document includes, at a minimum:

- a <TEI> element which encloses the entire document;
- a <teiHeader> element, which contains the metadata for the document, including bibliographic information about the electronic file and its source, details of the editing and transcription methods, documentation of the file's systems of information organization (such as classification systems and controlled vocabularies), and a log listing revisions to the encoded document;
- an element containing a representation of the source document or whatever material constitutes the content of the TEI document.

The TEI provides three different ways of representing a source document, each of which can stand alone or can be combined with the others. The most familiar and most commonly used is the <text> element, which contains a transcription of the source document using markup of the kind we have been examining: a representation of the document as an intellectual artifact reflecting concepts of genre and textual structure. Within <text>, a <body> element is required (containing the body of the text, using markup of the kind we have already covered above); the optional <front> and <back> elements represent the front and back matter of the source and are structured in a manner similar to <body>. We can also represent a transcription of the source using an entirely different markup approach: one that focuses on the physical organization of the document into "surfaces" consisting of "zones" of writing that contain individual lines of text. The TEI <sourceDoc> element takes this approach and is intended primarily for manuscript documents and for situations where the editor does not wish to make inferences about genre, textual structure, or other aspects of writerly intention, but simply wishes to record an inscription on a surface. The final option is the TEI <facsimile> element, which represents the document as a set of images, and provides mechanisms for coordinating these images with a transcription (recorded as either <text> or <sourceDoc>). Detailed coverage of <sourceDoc> and <facsimile> is beyond the scope of this chapter, but they are covered comprehensively in the *TEI Guidelines*. The overall potential architecture of a TEI document is as follows:

```
<TEI>
  <teiHeader> metadata </teiHeader>
  <sourceDoc> the document represented as a set of surfaces and
    zones </sourceDoc>
  <facsimile> the document represented as a set of
    images </facsimile>
```

```
    <text> the document represented as an intellectual structure
      <front> optional front matter </front>
      <body> main body of the transcribed text </body>
      <back> optional back matter </back>
    </text>
  </TEI>
```

Finally, to complete our view of a TEI document we need to zoom back even further. TEI documents operate within an ecology that may include other TEI files, XML files in other languages, schemas, and stylesheets.

USING THE TEI

As discussed above, text encoding is an analytical, strategic, and interpretive process that enables the encoder to make explicit claims about the structure, appearance, content, and editorial history of documents. Text encoding is also work – that is, using the TEI entails completing a set of processes, including transcription and markup, error checking and proofreading, schema customization, and publication. The TEI provides an idea about how documents work: implementing the TEI by encoding one or more documents means projecting a set of actions through time. For this reason, it is important to plan for all of the tasks involved in text encoding and to budget time and resources accordingly. The following section will unpack the various activities that are part of text encoding and offer suggestions for how you can tackle them strategically.

Transcription and markup

The process of creating a TEI file includes two strands of activity: acquiring the contents of the text and representing the text's structures through markup. These might not happen concurrently and there are different options available for each. To acquire the text itself, many researchers prefer to transcribe the text by hand, but one can also generate a transcription using optical character recognition (OCR), or find a prior transcription (e.g. from a source like Project Gutenberg), or work with a vendor who specializes in transcription services. Similarly, although many scholars prefer to do the actual TEI markup by hand as part of the transcription process, the markup can also be added afterwards (either by hand or using semi-automated methods). Combining transcription and markup can bring out textual nuances by slowing the process down and making encoding an activity that occurs during typing, rather than reading, the source text. However, a combined transcription and markup process also requires that the encoder balance multiple tasks, which can prove challenging when the texts or the encoding standards – or both – are complex. If resources allow, it can be helpful to perform multiple encoding passes; for example, a project might want to capture the basic structural information about its texts – divisions, paragraphs, verse groups, and so on – in a first pass and then add more detailed and contextual encoding at a later stage.

Error checking

Texts and text encoding both have the potential to be quite complex. Consistency and accuracy are huge challenges for any text encoding project, and they increase with the number of people involved and with the detail of the encoding. However, proofing practices that combine automated error checking with hand proofing can help to ensure that published files are largely consistent and free of errors. Knowing your texts and your encoding will help in planning for error checking; you will want to be aware of the places where your encoding is vulnerable to inconsistencies and where consistency matters most.

The simplest kinds of encoding errors are errors of invalidity and ill-formedness: cases where the XML markup is simply broken or inconsistent with a project's standards. The easiest way to deal with such errors is to prevent them before they occur. Effective XML editing software will constrain encoding so that poorly formed or invalid markup is identified immediately and can be fixed promptly. XML software, however, can only prevent errors involving violations of the rules established in the schema. Encoding errors that involve using the wrong element – as long as that element does not violate those rules – will not be caught. Because humanities texts are so complex, the TEI schema is necessarily complex as well, and there are typically a fairly large number of elements that are valid in any given context. If a passage of verse is encoded as prose or a place name is encoded as a personal name, the XML software has no way of noticing the error. In the section below, we discuss XML tools that can check for very specific kinds of errors and inconsistencies and are not constrained by the XML schema.

Hand proofreading an XML-encoded document is slightly more complex than proofreading an ordinary transcription, because it requires checking both the transcription and the encoding. For example, a text may read "*Arthur* rode down the windingg lane to *London*." Hand proofreading can confirm that the content of the transcription is correct (for example, that the first word should be "Arthur" and not "Uther") and that the encoding follows project standards. In this case, a proofreader might check that the right elements are used (perhaps `<persName>` for "Arthur" and `<placeName>` for "London"), that other details of the encoding are correct (that the italicization of names and the typographical error "windingg" are encoded according to project standards), and that the markup itself is entered correctly (for example, making sure that the period is not entered inside of the `<placeName>` element). Because this requires looking for a wide range of potential issues, two proofreading passes – one in which the XML itself is proofread, and a second pass using a formatted output – helps in locating errors in encoding and transcription. In both cases, comparing the text against the source copy, line by line, is the most effective (though undoubtedly time-consuming) way of finding and fixing errors.

Schema development and management

The *TEI Guidelines* are a very comprehensive treatment of a very large subject: the encoding and representation of humanities texts in digital form. The *Guidelines* thus cover far more than any individual encoding project is likely to need, and for this reason they are designed so that they can be customized. This customization process permits encoding projects to eliminate unneeded elements, constrain attributes and structure more closely, and add new elements for features the TEI does not include.

Customization is a key part of TEI usage. Practically, it is easier to work with an encoding language that contains only the elements and attributes you are actually going to use. Customization also permits projects to describe their data in a way that more precisely matches their goals and interests, by using project-specific descriptive terms rather than the generic ones provided by the unmodified TEI Guidelines. A customized schema can also ensure a higher degree of consistency in encoding, by making certain features required or by constraining their content more tightly. Finally, customization expresses the project's encoding choices explicitly and formally, which can be very helpful when sharing data with other projects or when working with a programmer or interface designer. Before creating a new customization it can be helpful to examine existing customizations for similar materials, to see how others have approached the same modeling problems.

Creating a TEI customization file is much like encoding any other TEI document. Customization files can be authored in any XML editor; all you need to know is what elements are used to describe the kinds of features (inclusion and omission of elements, changes to attribute values, etc.) that such a document contains. The TEI also provides a simpler approach to customization, via a web tool called "Roma." Roma provides a web interface through which users can select modules, elements, and attributes to be included in the custom schema, create controlled value lists for attributes, and make other more advanced changes. Roma can also be used to generate custom schemas and reference documentation, and to modify customizations developed by another project.

Strategic planning for encoding projects

For any text encoding project larger than a single text, some initial planning is essential to make informed decisions about how much and what kinds of information to capture. This initial planning should include some analysis of the goals and constraints of the project itself and some analysis of the documents that the project will encode. You will want to plan out:

- the level of detail at which the project will be representing its texts;
- how the encoding and transcription should be accomplished, whether by hand or by an automated process, and by whom;
- details of transcription and editorial methods, such as the project's approach to modernization and regularization of the text, how to treat errors, how to treat textual variants, and how to represent graphical and material aspects of the text;
- how much additional information to record concerning the text's contents: for instance, glosses for unfamiliar words, biographical information about persons mentioned in the text, and information about historical context;
- the needs and expectations of your audience, which will impact decisions such as whether to regularize archaic spellings, or how much time to invest in encoding contextual information.

Because encoding usually represents a considerable investment in time, it is important to have (and to document) clear goals and plans at the outset, while recognizing that these will likely need to be modified as the project develops.

Tools and technologies

The work processes described above all entail careful inspection and manipulation of XML data, and while most of them can in principle be accomplished without specialized tools, they are all easier when you have the right tools available. For the process of creating TEI data, an XML-aware editor is almost essential: it checks for and in many cases prevents well-formedness errors (such as omitted tags or delimiters) and can make it much easier to see and control the structure of your XML file. Many XML editors are also schema-aware, so they can validate your document against the TEI schema you're using and also prompt you with appropriate elements as part of the transcription and encoding process. The result is much greater accuracy in your initial encoding pass, with fewer errors to correct (and assistance in finding those that remain).

XML editors take advantage of several XML-related technologies which interact with the XML structure in different ways. XPath is a query language that lets us identify and select specific parts of the XML tree: for instance, all `<name>` elements appearing within `<l>` elements. Using XPath within an XML editor, we can perform complex searches to identify possible inconsistencies in our encoding – if you wonder whether you ever did use `<name>` inside a stage direction, you can easily find out. Building on XPath, Schematron is a validation language that enables you to write XPath queries that check for the presence or absence of specific features in your encoding, and generate reports summarizing the results. This method is extremely useful for enforcing consistency, particularly if you are working with a large collaborative team.

Another important genre of XML tool is, of course, tools for publishing XML. Many of these rely on the core technology of XSLT, which is a programming language for transforming and manipulating XML data, widely used to convert TEI data into other formats such as HTML or JSON for web display (see Chapter 14). Some XML publishing tools can be used on your own computer and are simple enough to require no configuration; TEI Boilerplate is an easy-to-use and customizable tool for displaying TEI data in a web browser. Other XML publishing tools are suitable for publishing larger projects: examples include the Extensible Text Framework, eXist, BaseX, and MarkLogic. Such tools vary widely in functionality and cost; what they have in common is the ability to ingest and index large numbers of TEI files, and to support the creation of user interfaces that permit searching, browsing, and reading. For those who are not able to create such publications on their own, there also exist public frameworks for publishing TEI data, including the TEI Archiving, Publishing, and Access Service (TAPAS), and TextGrid.

Clearly the world of TEI is a large one, and steadily expanding; this chapter has done no more than provide a brief overview and an entry point. Whether you become an expert encoder with a large-scale project of your own, or simply become a more critical user of other people's data, the TEI is a central tool of digital humanities and a fascinating topic in its own right.

NOTES

1 DeRose, Steven, David Durand, Elli Mylonas, and Allen Renear. "What is Text, Really?" *Journal of Computing in Higher Education* 1.2 (Winter 1990), pp 3–26.

2 TEI Consortium, eds. *TEI P5: Text Encoding Initiative Guidelines for Electronic Text Encoding and Interchange*. TEI Consortium. www.tei-c.org/Guidelines/P5/. Full references to all standards and resources mentioned hereafter are included in the section on "Further Reading and Reference" at the end of this chapter.

3 See online for more details on other XML formats.

4 In that last case (no content at all), XML allows a short cut indicator. Instead of writing "<anchor></anchor>" you may write "<anchor/>". XML does not care which you use, and in some sense, cannot even tell the difference. The short form is called an "empty-element tag."

5 Element and attribute names may also include a namespace prefix, delimited by a colon, indicating the XML language in which they appear. For example, the "xml" prefix in the @xml:lang attribute indicates that this attribute is defined in the XML specification. Note as well that "letter" is not restricted to the 26 letters of the standard English alphabet, but can be almost any letter in any language. So, e.g. <参照文字列3> is valid, but <modelRef 3d= "www.example.edu/wireframes/3D"> is not (because the attribute name must start with a letter, not a digit).

6 The at-sign (U+0040, "@") is commonly used to indicate "this is the name of an attribute"; it is not itself part of the attribute name.

7 A Uniform Resource Identifier; for our purposes here, these are the same as URLs, or Uniform Resource Locators. A URL typically looks like "http://www.example.edu/project/document.xml#place". In such a construct, the part before the number sign (U+0023, "#") indicates which file is being referred to; the part after the number sign indicates which particular part of the file is being referred to. In this example the specific element being referred to is the one that has an @xml:id with value "place". If the part to the left of the number sign is missing, the default is to look in the same file in which the URI occurs.

8 For example, see the online resources accompanying this chapter for information on special characters and comments in XML.

9 The value of @xml:lang is constructed using a specific system. See www.w3.org/International/articles/language-tags/ for details. A list of existing language codes is available at www.iana.org/assignments/language-subtag-registry/language-subtag-registry.

FURTHER READING AND REFERENCE

Standards:

- Unicode (http://unicode.org): a standard for the representation of text character across languages and platforms. See in particular the Unicode code charts: http://unicode.org/charts/.
- XML (http://w3.org/XML/): the Extensible Markup Language. The current version of the specification is at http://w3.org/TR/xml/ and also provides some useful background on the origin and goals of XML. David Birnbaum's "What is XML and why should humanists care?" offers a good introduction to XML for beginners (http://dh.obdurodon.org/what-is-xml.xhtml).
- Namespaces in XML (http://w3.org/TR/xml-names11/): a specification that allows the use of elements from different XML languages in the same XML document.
- XPath: http://w3.org/TR/xpath-30/.
- TEI Guidelines: http://tei-c.org/release/doc/tei-p5-doc/en/html/index.html.

Resources for learning and using the TEI:

- TEI by Example (http://teibyexample.org): a site for learning TEI that includes tutorials, examples, and interactive exercises.
- Women Writers Project TEI workshop materials (http://wwp.northeastern.edu/outreach/resources.html): tutorials, slides, lecture notes, handouts, and examples for introductory and advanced TEI.
- TEI Boilerplate (http://teiboilerplate.org): an easy-to-use tool for publishing TEI directly in a web browser; supports user-created styles.
- TEI Simple (https://github.com/TEIC/TEI-Simple#readme): a subset of the TEI tagset that includes a formally defined set of rules for processing the text.
- TAPAS (http://tapasproject.org): a public framework for publishing and archiving TEI data, free to TEI members.

- TextGrid: http://textgrid.de (English-language version at https://textgrid.de/en/). A set of repository-based tools for creating and publishing TEI-based digital editions.
- Versioning Machine (http://v-machine.org): a framework for comparing and publishing multiple versions of TEI-encoded documents.
- Roma (http://tei-c.org/Roma/): a web-based tool for creating customized TEI schemas and documentation.
- OxGarage (http://tei-c.org/oxgarage/): a set of web-based tools for converting data to and from TEI.
- The TEI website (http://tei-c.org/index.xml) and wiki (wiki.tei-c.org/index.php/Main_Page) have lots of useful information, sample customizations, XSLT programs that projects have made available, a list of projects that use TEI, and, of course, the Guidelines themselves.

CHAPTER 8

Computational stylistics and text analysis

Jan Rybicki, Maciej Eder and David L. Hoover

INTRODUCTION

Computational stylistics and text analysis have a long, rich history. In retrospect, because of the nature of texts and the capabilities of computers, it seems quite predictable that they would be among the first applications of computers to the humanities. Many religious, literary, and historical texts are highly valued cultural achievements, and some of them have been analyzed for hundreds or even thousands of years. They also contain large numbers of highly significant and meaningful words and other textual features. Thus it seems natural that scholars should have moved quickly to enhance and augment their own description, characterization, and analysis of these rich cultural documents by harnessing the power of computers to store, search, count, and compare textual features. The rapid growth of the power of computers and the rapid increase in the availability of electronic versions of texts have revolutionized the scope and the kinds of analysis that can be performed. At their core, however, computational stylistics and text analysis have remained true to their origins, and continue to use the power of the computer to improve our understanding of texts.

"Computational stylistics" seems a relatively transparent phrase, but it may be useful to pick it apart a bit. First, "computational" obviously and correctly implies the use of computers, but it leaves unexpressed the rather wide range of ways they can be used. Simple text searches, concordances, and textual manipulation and selection could be counted as computational, but most practitioners would reserve the term in this context for some kind of statistical analysis, ranging from t-tests, to principal components analysis and cluster analysis, to delta analysis, data mining of various kinds, support vector machines, topic modeling, and even neural networks. Most of these analytic methods have their origins in the closely related field of authorship attribution, and, given that many of them focus on stylistic differences, the two fields are sometimes difficult to distinguish (Craig 1999). The process of distinguishing authors emphasizes the importance of differences and similarities, and almost all of the analytic methods applied to texts are focused on detecting these differences and similarities.

Style

Style, the subject matter of "stylistics" is, most broadly, simply a way of doing something. In the simplest case, it is an author's way of writing. In practice, however, the focus is on the effects of an author's style on his or her texts. In one recent formulation, "Style is a property of texts constituted by an ensemble of formal features which can be observed quantitatively or qualitatively" (Herrmann, van Dalen-Oskan, and Schöch 2015: 44). It is widely assumed, though unprovable, that the features that constitute each author's style form a unique stylistic fingerprint, so that, if the correct features are chosen, any two authors can be distinguished from each other. Considered as a property of texts, style can also be extended to apply to what can loosely be called genres (the Gothic novel, epic poetry, satire, narrative, drama), literary-historical periods (Victorian, Romantic), chronological divisions within an author's career (early and late Henry James), or to variations within a single text (the "voices" of different characters or narrators, for example), among many other possibilities.

Style is chiefly linguistic, though in some cases graphological features, the layout or arrangement of text, and even the physical characteristics of a text may contribute to a style. In addition to the obviously linguistic elements of style, such as vocabulary, grammar, morphology, phonology, and figures of speech, most practitioners would include broader characteristics, such as world view, theme, and tone, as potential elements for analysis (for an excellent checklist of stylistic features, see Leech and Short 2007: 61ff). Style is also patterned and distributed. Local and unique stylistic features can be important, but a recognizable style normally involves some kind of repetition, consistency, or pattern.

Stylistics

Stylistics is essentially comparative, even if the comparison is not always explicit. Almost all statements about a style imply a comparison; for example, even the seemingly simple statement that Faulkner's style is marked by long sentences implies a contrast with the lengths of the sentences of other authors. Long compared to what? Although the question of what norm is appropriate for the comparison remains vexed, the widespread availability of electronic texts and corpora of texts has made defensible choices and the creation of specialized corpora to use as norms easier to make. Pattern, distribution, and comparison obviously invite a computational approach. Indeed, computation analysis is the only practical way to analyze extremely frequent textual characteristics, or to study unreadably large collections of texts.

Despite the variety of stylistic features, it is fair to say that the overwhelming majority of computational stylistic analyses have involved words, though word n-grams (sequences of words) have recently become increasingly popular features to analyze. Not only are words (and n-grams) easily identifiable and countable, compared to figures of speech, themes, or syntactic patterns, they are also much more frequent than most other textual characteristics and are obviously, though not unproblematically, meaningful (unlike, for example, sequences of letters or parts of speech). A "word" seems an intuitively simpler concept than it is in practice, and various decisions about how to identify and count the words of a text are defensible under different circumstances. For the purposes of computational stylistics, a word (type) is normally defined as any unique sequence of alphanumeric characters that is not interrupted by a space, or by any punctuation mark except the apostrophe or hyphen. (A *type* is a unique form, while a *token* is an individual occurrence of a type: the previous sentence contains two tokens of the type "or".) Unfortunately, this definition does not distinguish homographic forms such as the noun and verb meanings of *desert*, but experience has shown that computational stylistics is robust enough that the resulting errors in counting do not seriously distort analysis.

Text analysis

Text analysis is a close relative of computational stylistics, but with a wider range and a heavier emphasis on analysis. While computational stylistics has focused almost exclusively on literary texts, text analysis has been applied to many other kinds of texts, from political speeches to blogs, from historical documents to tweets, from legal documents to the sacred texts of religions, from letters to philosophical treatises, from poetry to programming. Perhaps the most obvious further difference between computational stylistics and text analysis is that the latter is more likely to focus on meaning and content. Nevertheless, almost all of the methods of text analysis have also been applied to questions of literature, authorship, and style.

It would be an exercise of folly to attempt an introduction here to data mining, topic modeling, sentiment analysis, semantic analysis, neural networks, part-of-speech analysis, word-frequency analysis, and to the wide range of statistical analysis techniques that have been applied to the dozens of different textual features that have been analyzed. Instead, it seems more useful to approach computational stylistics and text analysis by focusing on problems at three different scales: microanalysis, middle-distance analysis, and macroanalysis or distant reading.

The first analysis on the micro scale is an authorship problem involving a collaboratively written text, *The World's Desire* by H. Rider Haggard and Andrew Lang, using a popular recent technique called Rolling Delta. This is followed by an analysis of the voices of the six narrators in Virginia Woolf's *The Waves*. Middle-distance analysis is represented by a modification of John Burrows's Zeta (Burrows

2006) that examines the vocabulary of more than 350 high-stakes exit essays written by American high school students. Macroanalysis is demonstrated by turning to the chronological signal visible in much larger corpora: in this case, in 1,000 English novels from Swift (Jonathan) to James (E. L.).

MICROANALYSIS, OR ZOOMING INTO A SINGLE TEXT

Empirical investigations in the field of computational stylistics and text analysis are, as noted above, almost exclusively focused on comparison: to reliably describe a given text's statistical characteristics, in a vast majority of cases one compares the text to other texts collected in a comparison corpus. From this perspective, a single text, perceived in a context of similar or not-so-similar texts, becomes a monadic entity *per se*. Even if such a text is further divided into smaller samples (see, e.g. Kestemont, Moens, and Deploige 2015), the main goal of finding relations between discrete textual entities (works) continues to be the main focus.

This approach assumes that a (literary) work is a monolith, which is not always true: an epistolary novel might consist of multiple stylistic registers, a Menippean satire might combine sections of epic poetry, tragedy, and philosophical prose, a collaboratively written work might contain two or more independent authorial voices, and so forth. In such cases, capturing an average stylistic profile from the text in its entirety is certainly not the optimal scenario. Arguably, much more can be observed when such a text is divided into segments and treated independently. One of the possible applications of this approach is discussed below, where Virginia Woolf's *The Waves* is dissected according to particular characters' voices; another application involves chunking the input text into consecutive samples, or equal-size blocks of *n* words (tokens), which are then measured as independent, yet sequentially ordered, samples.

The World's Desire

Pioneering work in sequential stylometry was presented in a study on the authorship of Walewein (van Dalen-Oskam and van Zundert 2007), in a comparison of three disputed English prose texts (Burrows 2010), and in a study of *The Tutor's Story*, written collaboratively by Kingsley and Malet (Hoover 2012). The sequential methodology evolved into the Rolling Delta method (Rybicki, Hoover, and Kestemont 2014), later extended and generalized as Rolling Classify (Eder 2015a). This method will be used here to assess the nature of collaboration between Henry Rider Haggard and Andrew Lang on *The World's Desire*, first published in 1890.

Background

Henry Rider Haggard (1856–1925) is the author of several adventure novels, among which the bestsellers *She* (1887) and *King Solomon's Mines* (1885) attracted a good deal of attention. Andrew Lang (1844–1912), a poet, novelist, literary critic, and folklore scholar, earned his fame as a translator of Homeric poems. *The World's Desire*, a classic fantasy novel written collaboratively by the duo, not particularly long (*ca*. 85,000 words), is a story of the hero Odysseus, who returns home to Ithaca after his journey: instead of finding his home at peace, however, he is involved in several new adventures. The plot of the novel as well as its mythological background was set by Lang, while Haggard contributed his imagination and style. From the correspondence of the two writers, we know that Haggard had written a first draft, entitled *The Song of the Bow*, which was later reworked by Lang. Haggard then took over and wrote a great share of the text. In Haggard's own words:

> Roughly the history of this tale . . . is that Lang and I discussed it. Then I wrote a part of it, which part he altered or rewrote. Next in his casual manner he lost the whole MS. for a year or so; then it was unexpectedly found, and encouraged thereby I went on and wrote the rest. . . . The MS. contains fifty-three sheets at the beginning written or re-written by Lang, and about 130 sheets in my writing, together with various addenda. (Haggard 1926)

It is assumed that Haggard actually wrote most of the novel except the first four chapters, which were written entirely by Lang. Working on the first drafts of the novels, the two authors were aware of stylistic differences between them. Haggard quotes Lang's letter, which confirms his habit of depreciating his own work:

> Nov. 27th. The typewritten "Song of the Bow" has come. The Prologue I wrote is better out. It is very odd to see how your part (though not your *chef d'oeuvre*) is readable, and how mine – isn't. (Haggard 1926)

The two authors in The World's Desire

The work by Haggard and Lang seems to be a perfect case study of mixed authorship of a single text. To tell its authorial voices apart, the Rolling Classify was applied. First, the goal was to compile a reference corpus containing authorial profiles of both Haggard and Lang. Out of an extensive list of Haggard's works, ten novels and two collections of short stories were selected to train a Haggardian profile: *Cetywayo and His White Neighbours* (1882), *Allan's Wife and Other Tales* (1887), *Allan Quatermain* (1888), *Colonel Quaritch, V.C.* (1888), *Cleopatra* (1889), *Beatrice* (1893), *Black Heart and White Heart* (1900), *Ayesha: The Return of She* (1905), *Benita* (1906), *The Yellow God* (1908), *Child of Storm* (1913), *Allan and the Holy Flower* (1915). When it comes to Lang, a similar selection of twelve novels and short stories collections was compiled: *Much Darker Days* (1884), *In the Wrong Paradise and Other Stories* (1886), *He* (1887), *The Gold of Fairnilee* (1888), *Prince Prigio* (1889), *The Green Fairy Book* (1892), *Prince Ricardo of Pantouflia* (1893), *The Disentanglers* (1902), *The Crimson Fairy Book* (1903), *The Brown Fairy Book* (1904), *The Olive Fairy Book* (1906), *The Lilac Fairy Book* (1910).

The above representative text samples are used to train a model using one of the supervised classification techniques, namely, support vector machines. The testing procedure starts with chunking *The World's Desire* into consecutive samples, or equal-size blocks of 5,000 words, with an overlap of 4,500 words, to achieve a dense sampling rate. Next, the support vector machine classifier is applied sequentially to the particular samples, which are checked against the training set, in order to identify the most similar authorial profile. The final stage of the analysis involves a graphical representation of stylistic changes throughout the chunked text. To this end, horizontal stripes are used, which are colored according to the assigned class.

In Figure 8.1, the results of the Rolling Classify technique applied to *The World's Desire*, using 100 MFWs, are shown. One can easily observe a stylistic takeover in the first part of the text. The break point takes place in the middle of the sixth chapter. Also, some sections by Lang seem to appear in the central part of the novel. However, these evaporate when a different MFW stratum is tested.

In Figure 8.2, one can observe the behavior of *The World's Desire* when 500 MFWs are analyzed. This time, Haggard's signal shows up for a short moment in the first chapters of the novel. The picture is once more slightly different when 1,000 MFWs are taken into consideration (Figure 8.3). It is quite clear that for very long vectors of frequent words, the distinction between two authorial voices in the sixth chapter is the only takeover that can be observed.

Comparison of Figures 8.1–8.3 leads to the conclusion that the mixed authorship has the form of a sudden takeover rather than a mixture of interwoven authorial voices. However, it is much more difficult to explain the apparent takeovers that appear in different segments of the novel depending on the input parameters of the model. This observation is confirmed by a series of similar tests using different classifiers and different style-markers, such as the most frequent word 2-grams (word pairs). At this point, one of the most difficult problems of text classification

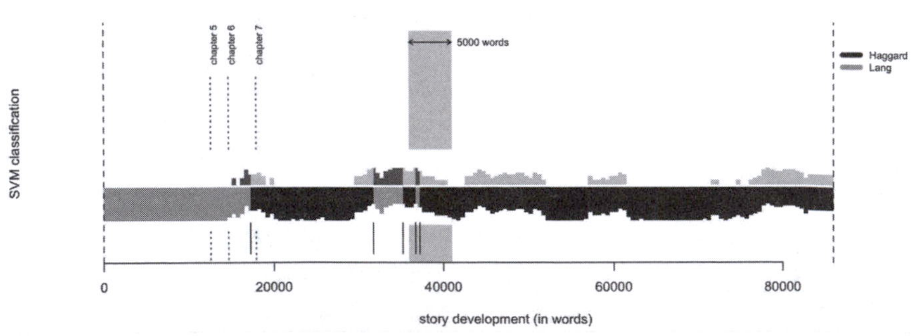

Figure 8.1
Sequential analysis of *The World's Desire* by Haggard and Lang: Rolling SVM and 100 MFWs

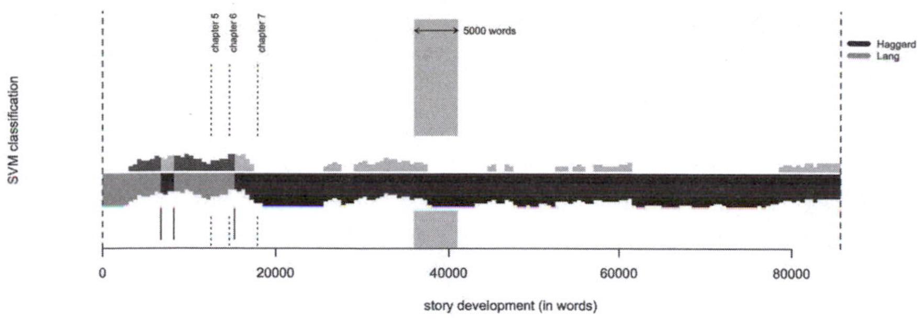

Figure 8.2
Sequential analysis of *The World's Desire* by Haggard and Lang: Rolling SVM and 500 MFWs

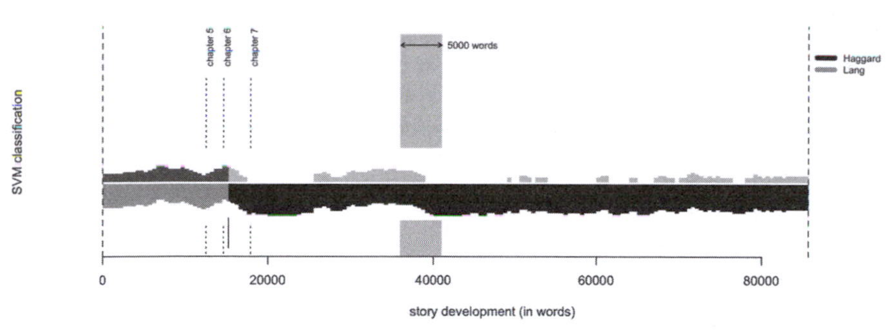

Figure 8.3
Sequential analysis of *The World's Desire* by Haggard and Lang: Rolling SVM and 1,000 MFWs

arises, namely, the distinction between an actual signal and wrong decisions of the classifier (also referred to as false positives). Since this problem goes far beyond the scope of this chapter, it will not be discussed in detail. However, an intuitive and relatively simple way of filtering out the false positives is to perform a series of similar yet not identical tests, in which the parameters of the model (e.g. the number of MFWs) are modified. Patterns that appear despite differences in MFWs tested seem to suggest the existence of a signal, while any ephemeral clutter in the results might simply mean false positives. If this rule-of-thumb is true, *The World's Desire* has one takeover only, which falls in the middle of the sixth chapter.

Virginia Woolf's character voices

The Waves, Virginia Woolf's most experimental novel, consists of alternating soliloquies or monologues by three male and three female characters, from childhood through middle age, each clearly indicated by a simple speech-reporting phrase such as "said Bernard" or "said Jinny." Woolf's technique has invited considerable critical comment about what axes of difference or unity characterize the novel, as Stephen Ramsay has noted:

> Are Woolf's individuated characters to be understood as six sides of an individual consciousness (six modalities of an idealized Modernist self?), or are we meant to read against the fiction of unity that Woolf has created by having each of these modalities assume the same stylistic voice? (2011: 10)

Ramsay's claim that it would be a mistake to treat the question of whether the six voices are the same or different as one that can be answered has been disputed (Hoover, forthcoming; see also Hoover 2014 and Plasek and Hoover 2014). However, it seems worthwhile to leave the polemic aside, here, and look a bit more closely at the voices. (For a thorough recent discussion of the various views about the similarities and differences among the voices in *The Waves*, see Balossi, 2014: chapters 1–2.)

Distinguishing the six voices

Testing the similarities and differences among the six voices is not as simple as it might seem. Because they are so obviously different from the monologues, it seems prudent first to eliminate the sections of third-person narration that begin each chapter and to remove all quotations from other characters from the monologues, so as to analyze only each character's voice (as does Burrows 1987: 191, 205–207). More problematically, the lengths of the six monologues vary from Susan's 6,067 words to Bernard's 32,664. The final chapter of the novel, which is all in Bernard's voice, begins "Now to sum up," showing that it is likely to be quite different from the rest of the novel. This chapter has been excluded from the analysis, as it was in three previous analyses of the novel (Burrows 1987: 206; Ramsay 2011; Balossi 2014: 84). Unfortunately, this still leaves the numbers of words by each character quite unbalanced: Bernard, 16,460; Jinny, 6,281; Louis, 8,694; Neville, 9,958; Rhoda, 8,401; Susan, 6,067. To give each character the same weight, each monologue has been reduced to the length of Susan's. Simply taking the first 6,067 words of each, however, would mean that only Susan's whole life would be represented, so the lines of each monologue were randomized and each was cut to 6,067 words. After creating a word frequency list based on the six equal parts, a series of cluster analyses was performed, based on the 100, 200, . . . 1,000 most frequent words of this list on the six equal parts and all the remaining text in sections of about 3,000 words. All the analyses correctly group all of the sections by a single character except the one based on the 500 most frequent words; a representative analysis based on the 900 most frequent words is shown in the cluster analysis in Figure 8.4.[1] A similar analysis, along with others based on word 2-grams (sequences of two words) and words selected on the basis of consistent occurrence rather than high frequency, also clearly distinguish the six voices in *The Waves* (see Hoover,

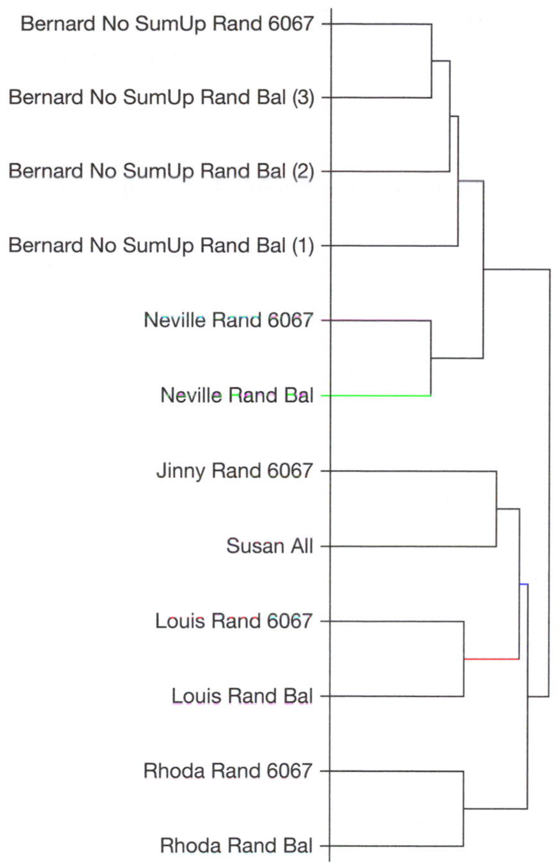

Figure 8.4
Randomized 6,067-Word Sections of *The Waves* – 900 MFWs

forthcoming, for details). In spite of the fact that these six voices are all obviously versions of Woolf's voice, they are much easier to distinguish than are sections of texts by some pairs of authors.

Age and gender and the six voices

Given how distinctive the six voices are when analyzed with the lines randomly organized, it may be surprising that, at the same time, Woolf also manages to distinguish the young voices from the older ones. In chapter one, the six are young children and in chapter two they go off to boarding schools. By chapter three they are entering college, and at the end of the novel the five surviving characters are middle-aged. A cluster analysis based on the 500 MFWs of the first and second chapters is shown in Figure 8.5. Note that only Bernard's part, at 1,598 words, is longer than 1,000 words, Jinny's is only 405 words, and Neville's only 505; most analysts would consider these too short for reliable analysis. Nonetheless, all six of the first chapters cluster separately from those from the second (sections from the second chapter that are longer than 2,000 words have been divided into one section of 1,000 words and a second section consisting of the remainder). The two sections by Bernard and Neville (though not Louis) also cluster together, and the sections of chapter two by the three female characters cluster separately from those of the male characters, suggesting that, at least when they are children, Woolf has also created a gender split in their language. Cutting these chapters into

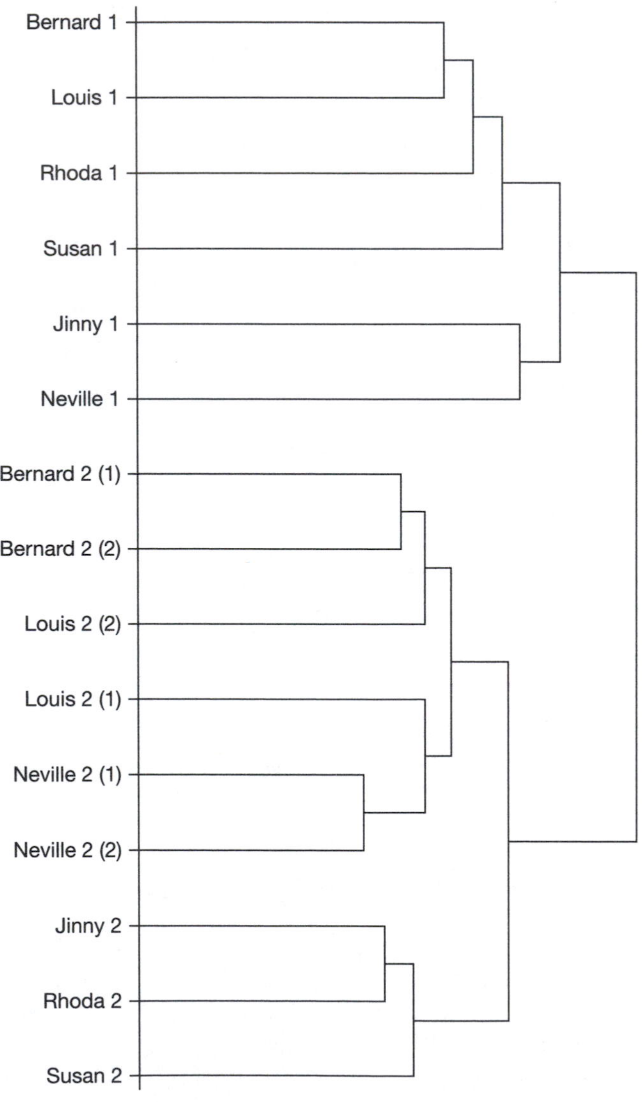

Figure 8.5
Chapters One and Two of *The Waves*, 500 MFWs

still smaller sections (405–799 words) shows just how carefully Woolf has distinguished the voices in her novel. As Figure 8.6, based on the 700 MFWs, shows, only the second half of Rhoda's chapter one fails to cluster with the rest of the chapter one sections at the top of the graph, and the sections of Rhoda, Jinny, and Susan from chapter two cluster together, though those of Bernard, Neville, and Louis cluster only partially. What is extraordinary here is how well these

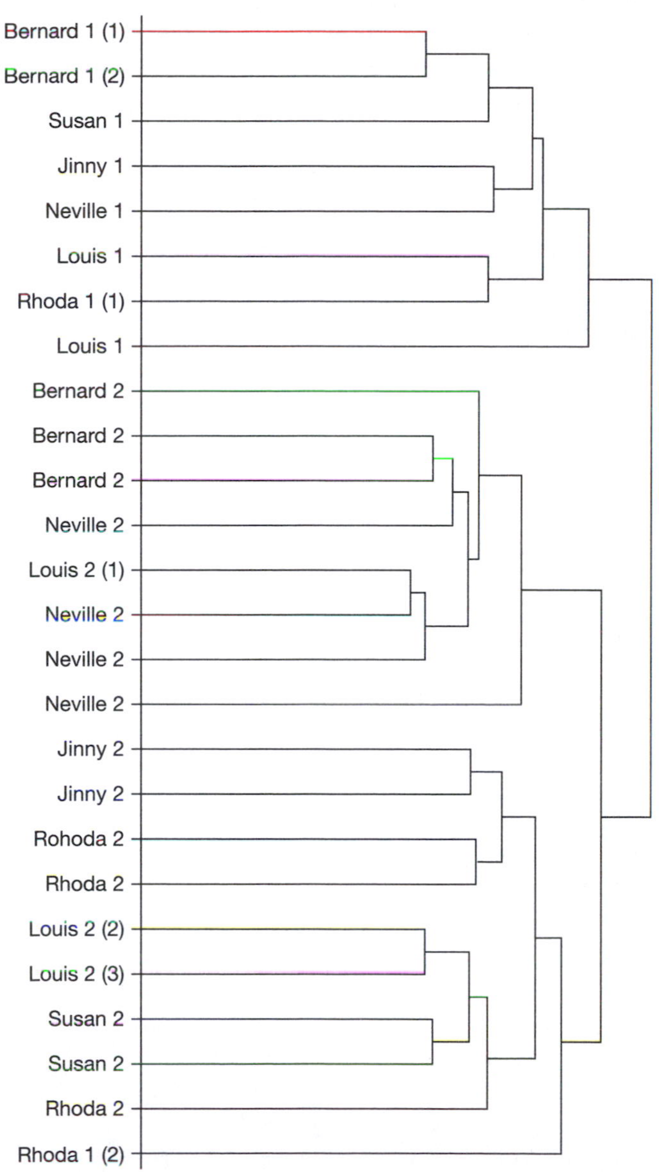

Figure 8.6
Chapters One and Two of *The Waves*, 700 MFWs (sections of 405–799 words)

very short sections group together both by age and by character, and, except for two of the sections by Louis, also by gender. (For a more detailed analysis of the younger and older voices, based on very different methods, see Balossi 2014: chapter 6 and Appendix E; for a discussion of the strengths of authorship, genre, gender, and other signals in texts, see Jockers 2013: chapter 6).

One more analysis will show that Woolf also distinguishes the voices of her characters as boarding school students in chapter two from their voices as adults in chapter eight. As Figure 8.7 shows, with the exception of Bernard's monologue from chapter eight, all of the monologues from chapter two cluster separately from those of chapter eight. An examination of the monologues from chapter two suggests that, even at a young age, Bernard's style is more mature and complex than those of the other characters. Although the gender separation of chapter two naturally reappears here, it disappears entirely in the monologues from chapter eight (looking back at Figure 8.4 shows that the randomized parts also fail to group by gender).

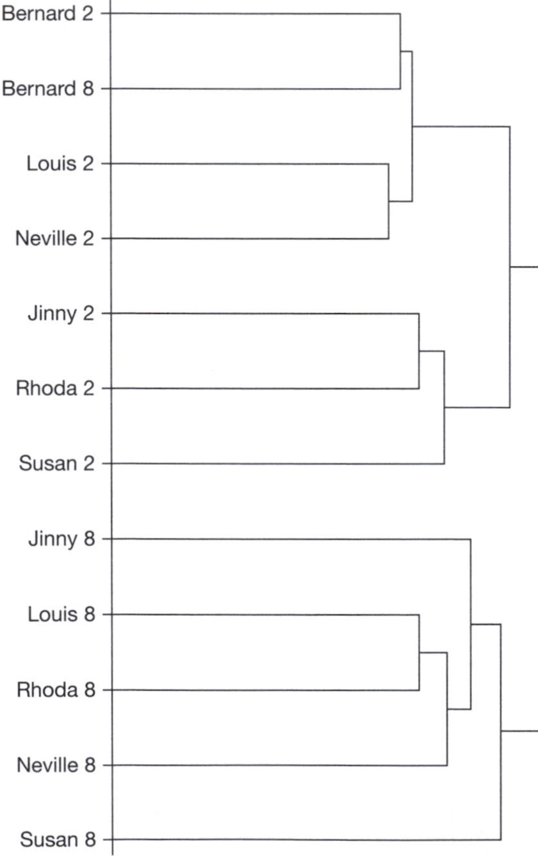

Figure 8.7
Chapters One and Two of *The Waves*, 700 MFWs (sections of 405–799 Words)

Obviously, there is no space here for any approach to a full investigation, but these results show convincingly that the methods of computational stylistics can be valuable for exploratory studies, not least by suggesting productive new possibilities for further analysis and discussion.

MIDDLE-DISTANCE ANALYSIS: HIGH-STAKES WRITING EXAMS

Consider now a middle-sized group of very different texts: high-stakes exit-level writing exams. Although these texts lack any significant intrinsic value of their own, the tools of computational stylistics and text analysis can still produce revealing and worthwhile results. The texts to be analyzed here are a set of 366 essays written by North American high school students in the context of state-wide exit-level writing exams, administered in the final year of high school. These essays were collected and analyzed in a study of the idea of voice in writing assessment (Jeffrey 2010). The essays are not ideal for computational text analysis because they are quite short, averaging only about 430 words and ranging from 128 to 1,307 words (only 21 are shorter than 200 or longer than 800 words). They also come from 39 states, and are responses to many different prompts that call for writing in a variety of genres; for example, analytic, narrative, argumentative, explanatory, and informative. If analyzing texts can achieve interesting results under these unfavorable conditions, we can expect excellent performance on longer texts under more favorable conditions.

Methodology

The method demonstrated here is a variant of Burrows's Zeta (Burrows 2006; Hoover 2007), as modified by Craig and Kinney (2010) and further modified in wide-spectrum analysis (Hoover 2013). The method is especially useful for characterizing the vocabularies of any pair of authors, genres, texts, or indeed any pair of text collections that can be divided unambiguously into two classes. Here, the first comparison will be between low-scoring and high-scoring passing exams (failing exams tend to be very short and defective). Although there are undoubtedly differences of many kinds between the two groups, here we concentrate on what kinds of consistent vocabulary differences, if any, exist between the low-scoring and high-scoring essays.

Wide-spectrum analysis, unlike most methods of text analysis, is based on consistency of use rather than frequency, and its calculation is simple and straightforward. For example, assume there are 200 texts, approximately the same length, by two authors, 100 by each author. Assume further that the word "eyes" is present in 62 (0.62) of the texts by the first author and absent from 92 (0.92) of the texts by the second author. These percentages are added together to yield a distinctiveness score for "eyes" of 0.62 + 0.92 = 1.54. Although distinctiveness scores can range from two (100 per cent presence plus 100 per cent avoidance) to zero (0 per cent presence plus 0 per cent absence), in practice scores above 1.5 are strongly characteristic of the first author and those with distinctiveness scores below 0.5 strongly characteristic of the second author. Note that quite different distributions can produce similar distinctiveness scores. For example, a word that is present in 77 per cent of the texts by one author and absent from 77 per cent of texts by the other would also have a distinctiveness score of 1.54.

Because of the wide range of sizes in the essays to be analyzed and the variety in prompts and genres, all the low-scoring essays have been combined into one text and all the high-scoring essays into another text and then the lines of each combined text have been sorted in random order. The final 14,000 words of each randomized text have been reserved for testing, leaving the rest of the texts for training purposes. Finally, to avoid basing the analysis on topical words, or words that are frequent because of specific prompts used in states with large numbers of essays, the word list has been manually culled by removing proper names (names of states and character names from text-based prompts, for example) and other topical words. The randomized training and testing texts were then cut into blocks of 2,000 words and analyzed in the wide-spectrum spreadsheet, which automates the process of comparing the two main sets of texts, calculates a distinctiveness score for all the words, and sorts those above a neutral score of one from high to low and those below one from low to high. The sheet also collects the most distinctive words for each group in order of distinctiveness, graphs the results, and prepares them for further graphing.

Vocabulary and the evaluation of high school writing

The results of the analysis described above are presented in Figure 8.8. The horizontal axis in Figure 8.8 indicates the percentage of the word types in each section that are characteristic of the training sections of the high-scoring exams and the vertical axis shows the percentage of the word types in each section that are characteristic of the training sections of the low-scoring exams. (A word type is defined here as a unique spelling; each 2,000-word section typically contains only about 700–800 types because many common words are repeated.) For example, for the high-scoring training section at the bottom right of the graph, only about 23 per cent of the 820 different types are characteristic of low-scoring exams, while almost 53 per cent are characteristic of high-scoring exams. It is easy to see that this method does an excellent job of categorizing the sections that were held out for testing, in spite of the fact that the test sections had no part in creating the word lists on which Figure 8.8 is based. All fourteen of the high-scoring and low-scoring sections are much closer to the appropriate training texts than to the opposite ones. (Tested sections do not usually fall within the clusters of training texts because they contain many words that are not in the training sets, so that the percentages of types that are characteristic of each group are lower than for the training texts.)

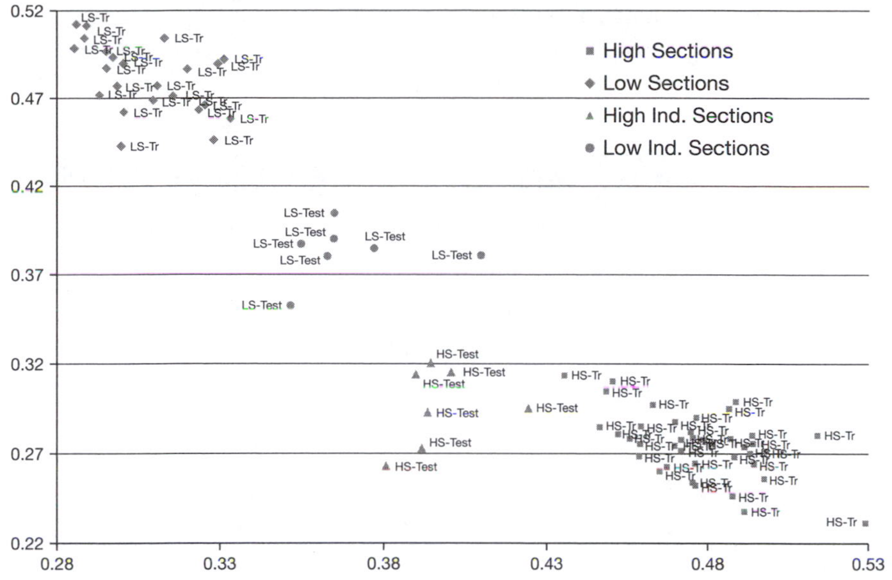

Figure 8.8
High- and low-scoring essays

Although wide-spectrum analysis does an excellent job of categorizing the test texts here, its real value is in characterizing the texts themselves. Below are the fifty most distinctive words for the two groups, unlabeled so that readers can try their hand at identifying which list is characteristic of the high-scoring essays and which is characteristic of the low-scoring ones.

> big, lot, might, makes, stop, maybe, talking, major, example, picture, conclusion, older, sometimes, I'm, try, bad, tell, trouble, hurt, harder, anywhere, got, end, give, remember, problems, affect, car, understand, times, goes, cars, younger, basketball, nice, anything, wouldn't, saying, public, everybody, kids, decision, weather, doing, mom, teen, extending, normally, technique, someone

> completely, must, eyes, desire, physical, constantly, individual, far, stress, mind, precious, human, light, involved, simply, rather, understanding, fit, build, led, ever, reader, air, changes, beginning, red, responsibility, order, nothing, began, increase, eventually, future, views, clock, merely, which, college, true, difficult, actually, science, once, learning, one's, ability, walk, although, various, aware

Most readers correctly identify the first list as words characteristic of the low-scoring essays and the second list as words characteristic of the high-scoring essays. There is no space for a full analysis of the differences in the lists, but two important dimensions are formality and specificity (see Jeffrey 2010 and Jeffrey, Hoover, and

Han 2013 for more details). The low-scoring essays use a much more casual and informal vocabulary, most noticeable in *big*, *lot*, *I'm*, *bad*, *got*, *wouldn't*, *kids*, and *mom*, while the high-scoring essays use more formal words such as *desire*, *physical*, *individual*, *precious*, *responsibility*, *science*, *one's*, and *various*. The low-scoring essays also tend to use vague and unspecific vocabulary such as *lot*, *sometimes*, *bad*, *anywhere*, *affect*, *nice*, *anything*, *everybody*, *doing*, *someone*, while the high-scoring essays tend to be more specific, using words such as *completely*, *constantly*, *stress*, *human*, *build*, *increase*, *difficult*, and *learning*.

An examination of the 1,000 most distinctive words for each group confirms these trends. For example, the first list above contains two contractions and the second none, and there are just three contractions among the 1,000 most distinctive high-scoring words, compared to twenty-two among the 1,000 most distinctive low-scoring words. Along with *anywhere*, *anything*, *sometimes*, and *someone* in the list above are *somebody*, *someday*, *someone's*, *something*, *sometime*, *whenever*, and *whatever* among the 1,000 most distinctive. The nouns in the two lists are also revealing:

Low-scoring nouns:

> lot, example, picture, conclusion, trouble, end, problems, car, times, cars, basketball, kids, decision, weather, mom, teen, technique

High-scoring nouns:

> eyes, desire, individual, stress, mind, light, understanding, reader, air, changes, beginning, responsibility, order, future, views, clock, college, science, ability

It isn't *hard* to *use* a *lot* of *nice* low-scoring *examples* to *give* a *picture* of *kids* who *at times* have *problems*, *athletes* who *really love cars*, *watching television*, and *playing sports such as basketball*, and *want* to *talk* about the *weather* (words that are among the 1,000 most distinctive low-scoring words are in italics).

However, the high-scoring words *present* a *well-rounded individual*, a *reader* with a *passion* for *learning* and a *desire* for *future responsibility* who is *admired* by her *teachers*, *almost all* of *whom acknowledge* her *leadership potential* and her *deep understanding* of *literature* (words that are among the 1,000 most distinctive high-scoring words are in italics).

This kind of analysis provides a great deal of interesting evidence about what the exam graders value and do not value, though it would be dangerous and irresponsible to imagine that the two passages above fairly characterize the two groups of students. While there is no space here to pursue the analysis further, it should be clear that such evidence can be very profitably used in discussing and evaluating the process of high-stakes writing tests and their implications for education.

MASSIVE TEXT ANALYSIS OF 1,000 NOVELS

It seems that any quantitative analysis worth its salt should yield significant chronological differences in a 1,000-novel corpus that extends from the times of Jonathan Swift to those of E. L. James, especially if it is based on such simple linguistic features as word frequencies. There is an obvious expectation of linguistic difference between the former's and the latter's images of, say, bondage in, respectively, *Gulliver's Travels into Several Remote Nations of the World* and *Fifty Shades of Grey*:

> I had the fortune to break the strings, and wrench out the pegs that fastened my left arm to the ground, for, by lifting it up to my face, I discovered the methods they had taken to bind me, and at the same time with a violent pull, which gave me excessive pain, I a little loosened the strings that tied down my hair on the left side, so that I was just able to turn my head about two inches.
>
> His deft fingers skim my back occasionally as they work down my hair, and each casual touch is like a sweet, electric shock against my skin. He fastens the end with a hair tie, then gently tugs the braid so that I'm forced to step back flush against him. He pulls again to the side so that I angle my head, giving him easier access to my neck.

Or is there? While no machine is needed to learn and discover the difference between the two texts, most of the differences between the two depictions – apart from what was then and what is now acceptable in print – seem to concern syntax rather than lexis: "I a little loosened the strings" sounds eighteenth century, not twenty-first; but the narrator of *Shades*, had it been part of the game, would probably have said "I loosened the strings a little," and the words and their frequencies would have remained unaffected. And yet Figure 8.9 shows the two texts at two different extremities in a network visualization of nearest-neighbor links between texts based on cluster-analyzed delta distances between them based in turn on most-frequent word frequencies (Eder 2015b). While the texts by the two authors are bound by the strongest signal known to stylometry, that of authorship, the authorial groups for both groups clearly order according to general chronology.

More importantly, not only those two texts behave this way. Whatever is between and around their data points follows suit, and the entire network exhibits a very Morettian evolution of grayscale from black to light gray, from left to right, and from early to late. There are departures from a purely linear sequence, of course, and some authors move and/or evolve vertically rather than horizontally; but the overall phenomenon is unmistakable. But then this has already been noted a long time ago with other methods, different statistical tools, and other corpora (not to reach too far back, cf. Brainerd 1980; Burrows 1994; Opas 1996). It is perhaps more significant that, against the background of this great evolution, local evolutions in chronology can be observed in some authors – those, obviously, who are represented

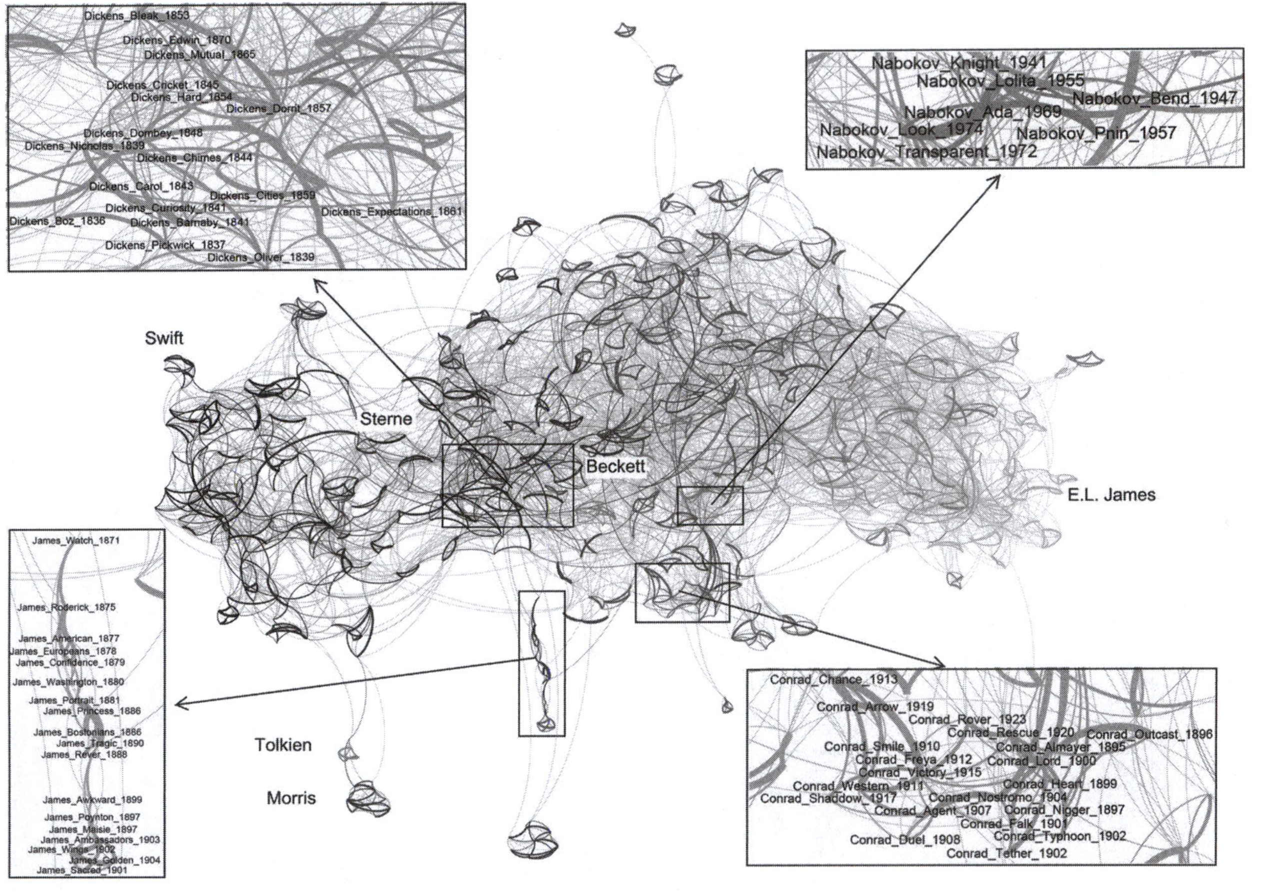

Figure 8.9
Network visualization of 1,000 English novels published between 1704 and 2013

by more texts in this corpus than either J. Swift or E. L. James. The latter's more august last-name-sake, Henry, has already been shown to evolve in the context of his own work (Hoover 2007); but here, too, the chronological sequence of his works in Figure 8.9 is almost perfect. Dickens evolves as well: while less linearly, his evolution seems to follow the general left-to-right trend. By contrast, Joseph Conrad's evolution seems to go against the grain: it is almost as if the Polish-born writer evolved his English towards a more "traditional" usage of most frequent words.

When the two evolutionary phenomena – that of an English literature more or less smoothly moving in a single direction with time, and of a similar movement within a single author – are put together, the picture becomes, perhaps paradoxically, less clear. When one compares the scale of the evolution of Henry James with that of the entire corpus, the former seems to be blown out of proportion. Obviously, there is no direct reflection of any quantitative distance between the texts, and the distances themselves are the combined results of the balanced forces of the gravitational pull of the networking algorithm; still, if the entire "stylistic drift" were to be blamed on historical-linguistic factors alone, that proportion would probably be better maintained. Perhaps most significantly, whatever it is that a network analysis of this kind represents, it seems to accord quite well with combined literary and linguistic expectations. In simpler language, this network makes a lot of sense.

It would then seem that, in this context, the real interest of a network graph like the one in Figure 8.9 is not where it agrees with literary history, but where it does not. The anomaly of counter-chronological Conrad has already been mentioned, but another Slavic ESL user, Nabokov, behaves in exactly the same way. Lawrence Sterne's *Sentimental Journey* and *Tristram Shandy* have been unseasonably removed to the right; this seems to illustrate quite well the very experimental nature of the latter work that culminated in Shklovsky calling its author "a radical revolutionary as far as *form* (emphasis added) is concerned" (Shklovsky 1990: 147). By contrast, Beckett's trilogy leans left, and it has been called "archaic" by Harold Bloom (1988: 9). Nearby lies the magical land of Narnia, but that is even easier to explain as a throwback to archaized, or mediaevalized, fantasy. The other famous fantast, Tolkien, departs from the flow altogether as one of the outsiders; hanging on to the main body of the English novel network by the threads of his links to the historical romances of Bulwer-Lytton, he gravitates towards the poetic romances of William Morris – and that, too, seems to make a lot of sense.

CONCLUSIONS

The presentation of the above examples – the examples being necessarily simple and the presentation necessarily short – is intended to show how the tools and methods of computational stylistics can be used in the study of literature by any interested scholar who takes the trouble of learning the comparatively simple and comparatively user-friendly software. The authors have hoped to show that while computational stylistics sails into uncharted waters by becoming a partner in what Moretti has called distant reading (2015) and what Jockers has called macroanalysis (2013), there is much it can do to help in the traditional study of texts, whether it sticks to its earliest application in authorship attribution; whether it produces an image of literary history; or whether it helps to tell good student essays from bad.

It is interesting to see how the three levels of computational text analyses, the micro, the medium, and the macro, can produce results that create an added value at different levels of literary study. It is a very traditional task for scholars of literature to discern who wrote which part of a text; here, the computational stylist provides support – or correction – to what has been established on the basis of such obvious sources as the correspondence and the reminiscences of Haggard and Lang. It should be remembered that the importance of their *The World's Desire* in the body of popular fiction of their time can probably equal the recent media frenzy about the authorship of Harper Lee's *Go Set a Watchman* and *To Kill a Mockingbird*.

It is safe to assume, faced with the results of the study of *The Waves*, that Virginia Woolf did not count the words she used to create the idiolects of her six "voices"; but the final outcome is as if she did with the sole purpose of diversifying her characters' voices. Any critic who wants to claim that the six monologues are all in the same style must explain how that claim can be reconciled with this diversity. The most significant added value of this analysis to the existing body of academic criticism on Woolf, however, is in fact nothing less than a heightened appreciation of the writer's genius: she has been able to produce character styles so distinctive that the differences between them are discernible through quantitative analysis; and that she has diversified them by age and by gender.

In the much more down-to-earth material of the high-school essays, quantitative textual analysis produces results that are interesting for other reasons. Rather than providing an additional method of dealing with a large body of papers to be graded, it seems like a direct indication to students and teachers alike how to write essays; and this sort of investigation fits well into recent psycho- and sociolinguistic approaches exemplified by James Pennebaker's *The Secret Life of Pronouns* (2011).

One of the oldest tasks of literary studies, classification and systematics of authors, is well served by macroanalysis of the kind presented by the last example in this short survey. The history of literature has been trying to put authors in groups and periods and tendencies without the possibility of reading them all; stylometric software reads books differently than humans, but at least it "reads" more of them than any single human – and it can graph the results of this "reading" according to much less impressionistic criteria than those criticized – and perhaps also those adopted – by such specialists on the function and the task of criticism as T.S. Eliot or Terry Eagleton. But it must be understood that computational stylistics has no quarrel with the Eliots and the Eagletons. Instead, when a computational stylist meets an open-minded traditional literary scholar, the twain come up with a new quality in textual analysis on any of the three scales discussed and exemplified in this chapter. Computational stylistics aims not at replacing Bloom with Burrows; it makes much more sense to bring them together for the benefit of our knowledge of literature, our potential in reading and understanding texts – and our appreciation of both the literary tradition and the individual literary talent.

NOTE

1 Cluster analysis is an exploratory method of analysis that is often used in authorship studies. It compares the similarities and differences among the frequencies of all the words being analyzed in all the texts. The texts that use the words in the most similar way are grouped together in such a way that the more similar two texts are, the closer to the left of the graph they join together. In Figure 8.4, the two most similar sections are the top two by Bernard (the vertical proximity of sections such as Neville Rand Bal and Jinny Rand at 6,067 is not meaningful).

REFERENCES

Balossi, Giuseppina. 2014. A Corpus Linguistic Approach to Literary Language and Characterization: Virginia Woolf's *The Waves*. Amsterdam: Johns Benjamins.

Bloom, Harold. 1988. Samuel Beckett's Molloy, Malone Dies, The Unnamable. New York: Chelsea House.

Brainerd, Barron. 1980. "The Chronology of Shakespeare's Plays: A Statistical Study." Computers and the Humanities 14: 221–230.

Burrows, John F. 2010. "Never Say Always Again: Reflections on the Numbers Game." In Text and Genre in Reconstruction: Effects of Digitalization on Ideas, Behaviours, Products and Institutions, ed. Willard McCarty, 13–35. Cambridge: Open Book Publishers.

Burrows, John F. 2006. "All the Way Through: Testing for Authorship in Different Frequency Strata." Literary and Linguistic Computing 22(1): 27–47.

Burrows, John F. 1994. "Tiptoeing into the Infinite: Testing for Evidence of National Differences in the Language of English Narrative." Research in Humanities Computing 2: 1–33.

Burrows, John F. 1987. Computation into Criticism. Oxford: Clarendon Press.

Craig, Hugh. 1999. "Authorial Attribution and Computational Stylistics: If You Can Tell Authors Apart, Have You Learned Anything about Them?" Literary and Linguistic Computing 14(1): 103–113.

Craig, Hugh, and Arthur Kinney, eds. 2010. Shakespeare, Computers, and the Mystery of Authorship. Cambridge: Cambridge University Press.

Eder, Maciej. 2015a. "Rolling Stylometry." Digital Scholarship in the Humanities 30, advance access published 7 April 2015, doi:10.1093/llc/fqv010.

Eder, Maciej. 2015b. "Visualization in Stylometry: Cluster Analysis Using Networks." Digital Scholarship in the Humanities 30, advance access published 1 December 2015, doi:10.1093/llc/fqv061.

Haggard, Rider. 1926. The Days of My Life: An Autobiography. London: Longmans, Green and Co.

Herrmann, J. Berenike, Karina van Dalen-Oskam, and Christof Schöch. 2015. "Revisiting Style, a Key Concept in Literary Studies." Journal of Literary Theory 9(1): 25–52.

Hoover, David L. Forthcoming. "Argument, Evidence, and the Limits of Digital Literary Studies." In Matthew Gold, ed., Debates in the Digital Humanities.

Hoover, David L. 2014. "Making Waves: Algorithmic Criticism Revisited. DH2014, University of Lausanne and Ecole Polytechnique Fédérale de Lausanne, 8–12 July.

Hoover, David L. 2013. "The Full-Spectrum Text-Analysis Spreadsheet." Digital Humanities 2013, Lincoln, NE: Center for Digital Research in the Humanities, University of Nebraska, 226–229.

Hoover, David L. 2012. "The Tutor's Story: A Case Study of Mixed Authorship." English Studies 93(3): 324–339.

Hoover, David L. 2007. "Corpus Stylistics, Stylometry, and the Styles of Henry James." Style 41(2): 174–203.

Jeffrey, Jill. 2010. "Voice, Genre, and Intentionality: An Integrated Methods Study of Voice Criteria Examined in the Context Of Large Scale-writing Assessment." Diss. English Education. New York University.

Jeffrey, Jill, David L. Hoover, and Mihye Han. 2013. "Lexical Variation in Highly and Poorly Rated U.S. Secondary Students' Writing: Implications for the Common Core Writing Standards." AERA 2013 Annual Meeting, San Francisco.

Jockers, Matthew L. 2013. Macroanalysis: Digital Methods and Literary History. Urbana-Champaigne: University of Illinois Press.

Kestemont, Mike, Sara Moens, and Jeroen Deploige. 2015. "Collaborative Authorship in the Twelfth Century: A Stylometric Study of Hildegard of Bingen and Guibert of Gembloux." Digital Scholarship in the Humanities 30(2): 199–224.

Leech, Geoffrey, and Michael Short. 2007. Style in Fiction. 2nd edition. London: Addison-Wesley.

Moretti, Franco. 2015. Distant Reading. London: Verso.

Opas, Lisa Lena. 1996. "A Multi-Dimensional Analysis of Style in Samuel Beckett's Prose Works." Research in Humanities Computing 4: 81–114.

Pennebaker, James. 2011. The Secret Life of Pronouns: What Our Words Say About Us. New York: Bloomsbury Press.

Plasek, Aaron, and David L. Hoover. 2014. "Starting the Conversation: Literary Studies, Algorithmic Opacity, and Computer-Assisted Literary Insight." DH2014, University of Lausanne and Ecole Polytechnique Fédérale de Lausanne, 8–12 July.

Ramsay, Stephen. 2011. Reading Machines: Toward an Algorithmic Criticism. Urbana: University of Illinois Press.

Rybicki, Jan, David L. Hoover, and Mike Kestemont. 2014. "Collaborative Authorship: Conrad, Ford, and Rolling Delta." Literary and Linguistic Computing 29: 422–431.

Shklovsky, Victor. 1990. Theory of Prose. Elmwood Park: Dalkey Archive Press.

van Dalen-Oskam, Karina, and Joris van Zundert. 2007. "Delta for Middle Dutch – Author and Copyist Distinction in Walewein." Literary and Linguistic Computing 22 (3): 345–362.

CHAPTER 9

Databases

Harvey Quamen and Jon Bath

WHY DATABASES?

In popular parlance, databases are nothing more than big repositories of information. In reality, though, they can be important avenues through which we engage our research projects. A database, according to our definition, is a rigorously organized set of data whose informational patterns help us to maximize the number of possible questions we can ask of it. If you just need to archive some information, for example, a database probably is not what you need. If you just want to alphabetize a list of people or to sort a list of authors by birth date, a database probably is not what you need. A simple spreadsheet can easily handle those cases. But if you are embarking upon a project in which you will be actively engaging with your data, pushing its limits, and asking challenging questions of it – finding patterns, seeing changing dynamics over time, locating anomalies, looking for missing information – then you will need a database.

The one factor that separates a database from a spreadsheet or a plain text document is a query language, which is the major interface mechanism through which we communicate with the database. Becoming fluent in your chosen database's query language should be a central goal as you begin your database voyage. The query language not only allows us to add, modify, and delete data, the query language is the means through which we ask questions of that data. Your ability to ask research questions of your data can be no more sophisticated than your fluency allows. A word processor's "find" function might be sufficient to tell you which of your project's authors were born in 1882, but you will need a query language to ask a more sophisticated question such as, "Give me a list of UK writers born geographically north of Hull who wrote for periodical magazines, published a novel before age thirty, moved to London, succumbed to drug or alcohol abuse, and died before they were fifty. And give that to me on a map organized by British county."

In this chapter we will give a brief overview of various types of databases and their history, with a particular focus on relational databases. We will then discuss data modelling, the process through which you organize your data and its internal relationships in order to maximize the types of questions you can ask of it. We work through this design process for a hypothetical research project, and, finally, introduce Structured Query Language (SQL), the means by which you interact with relational databases. Should your interest be piqued, we invite you to refer to this chapter's supplementary online materials, which contain instructions on downloading and installing MySQL, on working from the command line on your particular operating system, and on performing some extra tutorial exercises that go beyond our discussion in this chapter.

TYPES OF DATABASES

The oldest and most robust databases are so-called "relational databases," and they are the topic of this chapter. You can think of them as a series of interconnected spreadsheets. Each sheet – called a table in database lingo – usually contains information on a real-world entity such as People or Books or Songs or Birds or Rock Concerts or Places. Those tables are then tied together via relationships: Bob Smith (a Person) saw a black-billed magpie (a Bird) in Greenwood Park (a Location). William Shakespeare (a Person) wrote *Julius Caesar* (a Play) which was performed at the Globe Theatre (a Venue). U2 (a Band) played "Where the Streets Have No Name" (a Song) at their 360° Tour performance (an Event) in Wembley Stadium (a Venue).

That pattern of data organization is based on data storage theories published in 1970 by IBM scientist E. F. Codd (Codd 1970). By the 1980s, a query language called *Structured Query Language* (or "SQL," alternately pronounced as "ess-que-ell" or "sequel") was developed in order to manage those patterns of data. Today, the query language of most relational databases is some dialect of SQL, which, by design, looks quite a lot like English. We will see more of it in a moment.

In the 1980s and 1990s, companies such as Oracle and Microsoft wrote commercial database software that built upon Codd's ideas, and in the mid-1990s Monty Widenius, David Axmark, and Allan Larsson wrote an open-source database package and gave it away for free. They called it MySQL, and its release was one of the major drivers of the Web 2.0 movement. MySQL powered, and in many cases continues to be the back-end for, many of the early web apps such as Facebook, Wikipedia, YouTube, the Internet Movie Database, and WordPress blogs. Since it is both free and of professional-caliber, it is a great place to start, and many projects never need to use anything else.

Relational databases make many data management tasks incredibly easy, and for that reason they are a solid technology for digital humanists. However, there are some sophisticated data patterns that challenge what SQL does well, and other database technologies have been developed to handle those kinds of data structures. One example is a "graph database." Graph databases such as Neo4j are very good at data structures that look like social networks: multiple points, or nodes, that are connected to each other with lines called edges. For example, think of people on Facebook, each of whom is a point joined to other people through "friend" edges. Franco Moretti's visualization of the character relationships in *Hamlet* is another example of a network graph (Moretti 2011). Computer scientists and mathematicians call those structures "graphs." Neo4j, for example, stores its data natively as a graph rather than as a series of tables and it uses a customized query language called "Cypher," which is based on SQL, to query these graphs.

There are some people who have developed an active antipathy to all things SQL. The growing "NoSQL" movement (an acronym which at first meant "no SQL at all," but has recently been modified to mean "not only SQL") has developed databases that forgo query languages altogether. Databases such as CouchDB and MongoDB are noSQL databases. These databases require users to search and manipulate the data using programming languages instead of SQL. NoSQL users must have a working knowledge of a programming language (such as JavaScript) in order to use these kinds of databases effectively.

We are agnostic – we believe that DH practitioners should choose the database that best fits their project. But in our classes we have seen that DHers do well by first learning relational databases and SQL before they graduate to other types of databases. Once you are familiar with the strengths and weaknesses of relational databases, you will be in a stronger position to evaluate your database needs in future projects.

KEY CONCEPTS OF DATA MODELLING

Relational databases work – and work well – because they structure unwieldy data into highly organized patterns that are effectively and easily examined by a query language. As we have already mentioned, the main component of a relational database is the table. A table looks like a spreadsheet in that it is comprised of rows and columns (more commonly called fields). A database typically contains many tables, but each table contains information about only one specific "entity" drawn from your particular data domain: people or books or cars or periodicals or animals or events. Each row in a table is a record, and the various fields in each record contain information about one particular instance of that table. In the respective columns in a table of authors, for example, we might learn that William Shakespeare was born in 1564, died in 1616, and was English. The same table might tell us that Virginia Woolf was born in 1882, died in 1941, and was also English (Table 9.1).

Table 9.1 Sample output from an "author" database table

id	first	last	birth	death	nationality
1	William	Shakespeare	1564-04-23	1616-04-23	English
2	John	Fletcher	1579-12-20	1625-08-29	English
3	Virginia	Woolf	1882-01-25	1941-03-28	English
4	Emily	Dickinson	1830-12-10	1886-05-15	American
5	Hart	Crane	1899-07-21	1932-04-27	American

Other tables might tell us about different entities: a table about artistic works might tell us that *Hamlet* was a play first performed (we think) in 1600 and *To the Lighthouse* was a novel published in 1927 (Table 9.2). Notice that only one piece of information is stored in each field. In the following sections on relationships and data normalization we discuss why this atomization of data is an important step in maximizing the flexibility of your database and thus increasing the number of potential questions your database can be used to answer.

Typically, we give each record in an entity table its own unique identifier. In Tables 9.1 and 9.2 above, we've stored that identifier in a column called "id." A unique identifier like this – called a *key*, or more specifically in this case, a *primary key* – might look like a series of numbers or letters or both, but a primary key's job is to identify uniquely one particular row in that table. Both William Shakespeare and Virginia Woolf will have their own unique primary keys within our table of people. A primary key is the means by which we can distinguish one Bob Smith from another Bob Smith – although those two people have the same name, they will have different primary keys and so can always be disambiguated in the database. Sometimes those keys are public knowledge – as is the case, for example, with your employee number or your student number. Canadian Social Insurance numbers and American Social Security numbers fit into that category. But sometimes these keys are completely internal to the database itself and have no external meaning; often the value of these keys is simply an accident of the order in which items were entered into the database.

Table 9.2 Sample output from a "work" database table

id	title	year
1	Hamlet	1600
2	The Two Noble Kinsmen	1634
3	To the Lighthouse	1927
4	The Waves	1931
5	Poems	1890
6	The Bridge	1930

Entity tables are characterized, then, by a few qualities: (1) each *table* contains information on one type of entity; (2) each *row* or *record* contains information on one particular instance of that entity; (3) each *field* contains information about that instance's attributes; and (4) each row will have an identifier called a *primary key* that uniquely identifies it.

RELATIONSHIPS

In addition to entity tables, there are other tables that manage various relationships between entities, and these are called junction tables (or sometimes relationship tables or mapping tables). We might construct an "authorship" table, for example, that tells us that the person William Shakespeare is the author of texts called *Hamlet* and *The Two Noble Kinsmen*. Or that Virginia Woolf happens to be the author of texts called *Mrs. Dalloway* and *The Waves*. The junction table "authorship" manages a relationship between two other tables called "person" and "text." The mechanism by which the database handles this relationship is the copying and storage of only the primary keys of the entities to which we refer. In the junction table, the keys are really pointing to records in other tables and so keys copied here into a relationship table are called foreign keys. In Table 9.3, we learn that Person 1 wrote Text 1, which was a Play Production, and Person 3 wrote Work 4, which was a Book Publication.

This pattern is the heart and soul of a relational database: we manage relationships between entities by following these primary-key-to-foreign-key links. For many people who are just learning database concepts, it is this step that is often the most counter-intuitive because it seems like a lot of extra work to refer to three different tables simply to understand who wrote which texts. Our humanistic training has taught us to "hoard" data – we like to bring it all together in one tiny, compact place so that everything is visible at exactly the same time. For many humanists, a spreadsheet might seem more natural.

Table 9.3 Sample output from a junction table connecting authors with works

```
+-----------+---------+-----------------+
| person_id | text_id | type            |
+-----------+---------+-----------------+
|         1 |       1 | Play Production |
|         1 |       2 | Book Publication |
|         2 |       2 | Book Publication |
|         3 |       3 | Book Publication |
|         3 |       4 | Book Publication |
|         4 |       5 | Book Publication |
|         5 |       6 | Book Publication |
+-----------+---------+-----------------+
```

In fact, though, we can aggregate all that information into one place by writing a database query, which we will do shortly when we discuss SQL. But unlike documents or spreadsheets, databases encourage us to push our data farther apart – that is, to treat the various entities as being independent from one another. Bringing everything closer together often means that we are no longer able to distinguish the constitutive properties of, say, "people" from the constitutive properties of "texts." Moreover, by separating the data into tables that each describe discrete entities, we ensure that information does not get duplicated in various parts of the database. The name "William Shakespeare" occurs once and only once in our database (in record #1 in the "person" table). The title *The Waves* also occurs once and only once in our database (in record #4 in the "text" table). Data duplication – the kind you almost always see in spreadsheets – leads inevitably and inextricably to error. Copying primary keys into another table as foreign keys is how databases maintain data correctness and integrity.

This multiple table structure also allows the database to avoid another problem inherent with the spreadsheet: what do you do in cases when you need to store multiple values for a single field? For example, what if a text has two authors, as when William Shakespeare and John Fletcher collaborated on *The Two Noble Kinsmen*? Traditionally in a spreadsheet you would add another column for second author, but this solution is only valid until you come across texts that have three authors – as when John Fletcher collaborated with Francis Beaumont and Philip Massinger on plays such as *The Coxcomb* and *Thierry and Theodoret*. As a result, projects having poor data design often end up making arbitrary decisions such as "a book can have only two authors." Or, alternatively, they decide to store all the authors in a single field as a list, thereby making it extremely difficult later to separate the works of a specific individual.

The relational database structure eliminates this problem because it stores each relationship, such as that between author and text, as a separate row in the junction table. Consequently, the problematic case of multiple authors does not require any structural change to our tables. It merely means adding more rows to the "authorship" table. In our case, we can see from the repetition of the foreign keys in the "person_id" column that "one person can author many texts." In Table 9.4, for example, subsequent rows from the table show us that Person #3 (Virginia Woolf) wrote both *To the Lighthouse* (Text #3) and *The Waves* (Text #4).

Table 9.4 Sample output from a junction table connecting one author with two works

```
+-----------+---------+------------------+
| person_id | text_id | type             |
+-----------+---------+------------------+
|         3 |       3 | Book Publication |
|         3 |       4 | Book Publication |
+-----------+---------+------------------+
```

Table 9.5 Sample output from a junction table connecting two authors with one work

```
+-----------+---------+------------------+
| person_id | text_id | type             |
+-----------+---------+------------------+
|         1 |       2 | Book Publication |
|         2 |       2 | Book Publication |
+-----------+---------+------------------+
```

And, conversely, we can say that "one text can be written by many authors." In Table 9.5, we see that *The Two Noble Kinsmen* (Text #2) was written by both Person 1 (William Shakespeare) and Person 2 (John Fletcher).

The notion that "one person may write many texts" is an example of a "one-to-many" relationship, perhaps the most common type of relationship that you will see in your database career.

DIAGRAMMING DATA RELATIONSHIPS

Database designers depict these relationships using many different iconographies, but here is a common one that we use in our classes. Each box in Figure 9.1 represents a database table (listing columns and their respective data types), and the lines between them represent the type of relationships that those entities share.

A line like the one shown in Figure 9.2 represents the "one-to-many" relationship. The "crow's foot" or "trident" side of the line represents the concept "many," and the straight end of the line represents the concept "one."

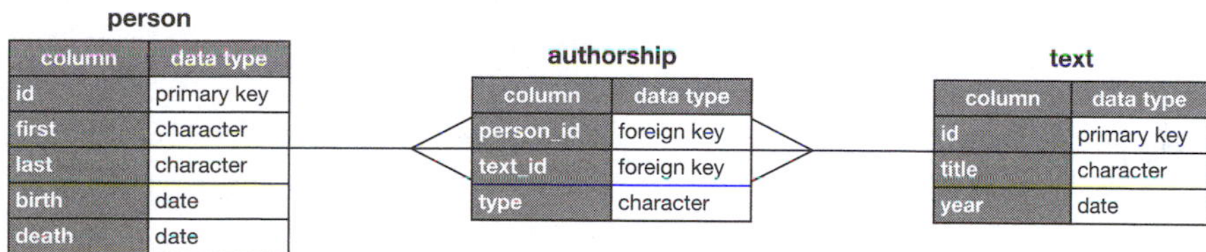

Figure 9.1
Example of a database diagram

Figure 9.2
Iconogaphy for a "one-to-many" database relationship

The relationship iconography is read left-to-right as "one thing on the left can be related to many things on the right," and is read right-to-left as "each thing on the right can be related to only one thing on the left." Notice, too, that we store the foreign key on the "trident" side of the relationship. The iconography of the three-table structure above tells us visually that the "authorship" table will contain two foreign keys because it has two "trident" line endings. It also tells us that one "person" can have many rows in the "authorship" table, and that each row in the "authorship" table maps to only one "person." If a "text" has multiple authors, that "text" will be represented by multiple rows in the "authorship" table.

In the humanities, we love the idiosyncratic messiness and unique complexity of our research topics. Despite the unwieldiness of our data, however, databases really map only three kinds of relationships: *one-to-one*, *one-to-many*, and *many-to-many*. We have just seen two classic examples of one-to-many relationships: one author can have many texts and one text can have many authors. Additionally, though, we might say that the "person" and "text" tables have a many-to-many relationship: many authors write many texts and many texts are written by many authors. Were we to diagram that relationship, it might look like Figure 9.3.

Remember that because we store the foreign key on the trident side of the line, we are now led into a problem. We need somehow to store multiple foreign keys from the "text" table in each row of the "person" table. That means either adding columns or putting lists of data into each field – both bad ideas. And we have the same problem in the opposite direction: in order to store the possibility of multiple authors per text, we need to store multiple foreign keys from the "person" table in the "text" table. That also means either adding columns or jamming lists of keys into one field.

Resolving this dilemma is what tempts many data designers to declare via divine fiat that "any book can have at most two authors" or that "each text will be listed with only a primary author." As we have already discussed, those decisions are poor ones because they misrepresent the actual data and limit the potential questions you can ask of your data. The correct solution is the three-table version expressed

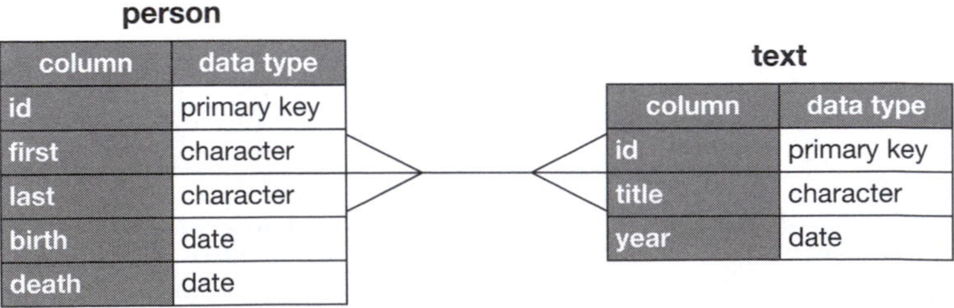

Figure 9.3
A "many-to-many" database relationship

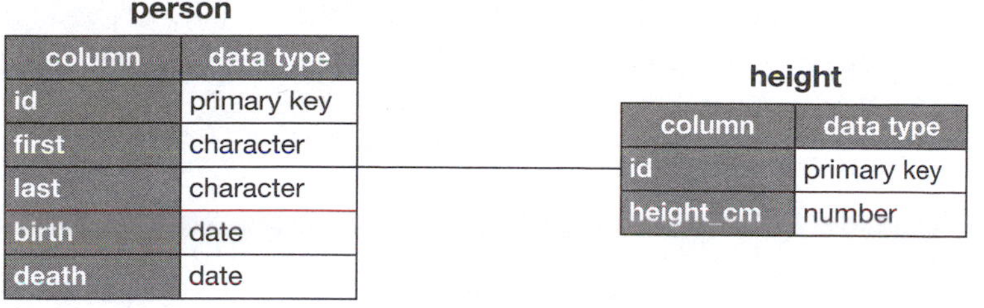

Figure 9.4
A "one-to-one" database relationship

in Figure 9.1. The "authorship" table can adroitly handle texts having one, two, ten, or even a hundred authors. The number does not matter. A prolific writer such as Lope de Vega – with about 3,000 sonnets and 500 plays – will not challenge our database structure in the slightest. Nor will, for example, Wikipedia entries that have hundreds of contributors.

Resolving a many-to-many relationship, then, results in two one-to-many relationships stored in a junction table. Junction tables are the database's way of taming unwieldy data into manageable patterns.

One-to-one relationships exist, too. For example, on a driver's license, a person has one height, one weight, and one eye colour. If we were to diagram a one-to-one relationship between "person" and "height," it might look like the diagram shown in Figure 9.4. Notice that the ends of the line have no tridents. Read left-to-right it says, "each person has one height" and right-to-left it reads as "each height has one person."

More often, though, a database designer would characterize height and weight not as separate entities but rather as characteristics (or attributes) of a person. They would become columns rather than distinct tables. When one-to-one relationships are as closely allied as height and weight are to person, the best decision is to combine them on the same table. The general rule, then, is to condense one-to-one relationships into the same table. Sometimes, though, it makes sense to keep the two endpoints of a one-to-one relationship separate. For example, there are only a relatively small number of eye colours, so it might make sense to keep a separate table of eye colours and then use foreign keys to link them to people. Working through this example you realize it is really a one-to-many relationship: many people have the same eye colour.

DATABASE DESIGN PROCESS

To design your database, begin by writing out a short prose paragraph about your project. Include the kinds of information you think you will need to store and think about how you will want to use that data. What kinds of questions will you ask? How will other users engage with your data? Can you collect all your data now or will you be doing that in phases?

Let's work through an example:

> My project tracks film and television adaptations of Jane Austen novels. For each adaptation, I'd like to log the title, year, director, and the actors who played the roles of the main characters. I would like to find out the most and least popular novels to adapt and to see in which decades Austen has been the most popular.

Circle all the major nouns in your paragraph. Those are great candidates for entity tables. Determine the salient properties or characteristics of each entity. You might think of those as adjectives, but do not get bogged down by the grammar.

In our case, there are five major entities: "novel," "character," "role," "adaptation," and "person." Those entities have attributes, of course: both novels and adaptations have titles (after all, the title of the adaptation might not match that of the novel). Characters have names and belong to a particular novel (which we will model as a foreign key attribute). And because we are logging both actors and directors, it makes sense to create a generic "person" table rather than separate tables for actors and directors. We can log those IDs as foreign keys whenever we need to reference a particular person. The location of the foreign key will tell us whether they are acting or directing. We will avoid data duplication in case anyone has ever both directed and acted in an Austen adaptation. Our data design looks like Figure 9.5.

Notice that "role" is a very important junction table. In some sense, it is the heart and soul of both our database and our entire research project. It maps relationships between the characters of the novels, the actors who play them, and the various adaptations in which they appear. Every role can be uniquely identified with those three pieces of information. Consequently, the "role" table contains three foreign key columns. We could choose to store more there, of course: perhaps a photo or film clip of the character, the salary the actor earned, links to reviews, etc.

Notice, too, that the "novel" and "literary_character" tables work together as a pair. They share a one-to-many relationship: each novel has many characters (reading left-to-right) and each character belongs to one novel (reading right-to-left). Other one-to-many relationships in this database include person-to-role (each person can play many roles, but each role is played by only one person) and adaptation-to-role (each adaptation contains many roles, but each role belongs to only one adaptation).

To summarize our design process:

1 *Entities* become *tables* in the database. Entities are often nouns and may range from the concrete (baseball cards, pets, contracts) to the abstract (concepts, ideals, imaginary friends).

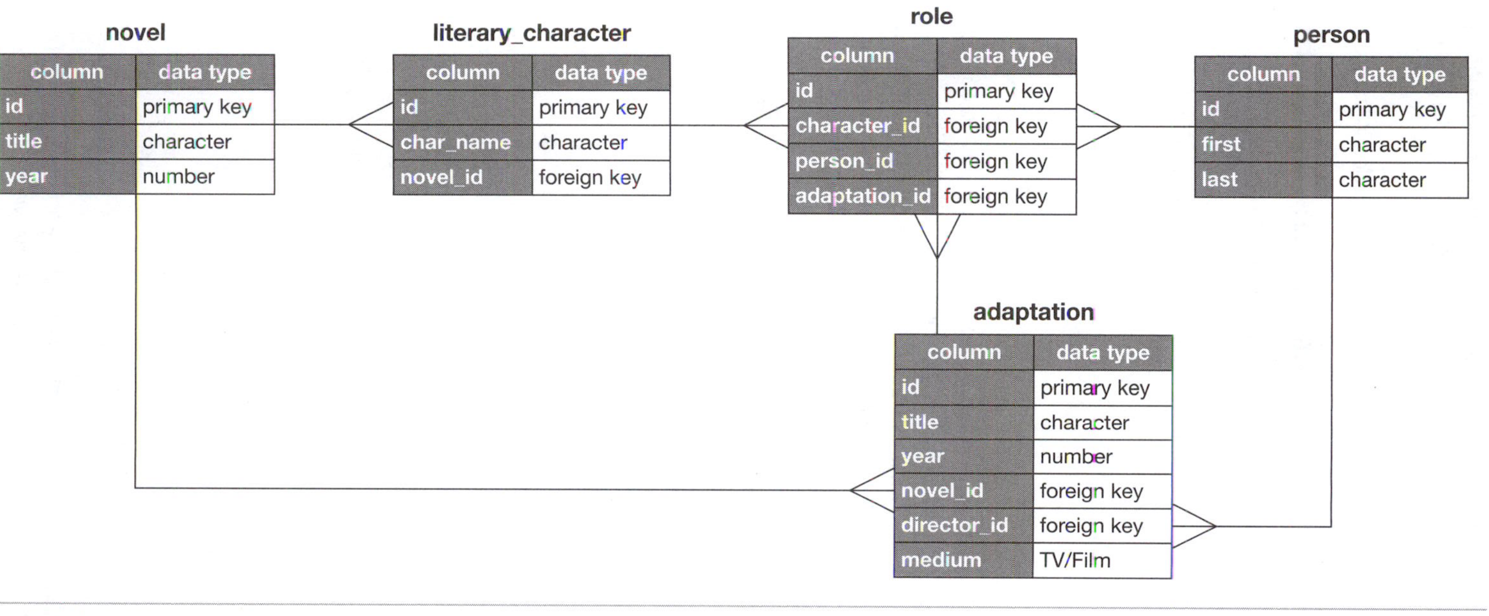

Figure 9.5
Design diagram for Jane Austen film adaptation database

2. An entity's *attributes* (or *qualities* or *properties* or *identifiers*) become *columns* in its table. Attributes may be adjectives (colour, size), but may also be nouns (names, titles).
3. Entities should be assigned unique identifiers called *primary keys*, which help to identify uniquely each instance in the table. If your project does not already have a primary key strategy in place, just allow the database to assign an infinitely increasing sequence of numbers.
4. *Relationships* map out how the entities interact with, or connect to, one another. The relationships may be more tightly or loosely bound, but in the end there are only three kinds: one-to-one, one-to-many, and many-to-many. Relationships are defined by copying an entity's primary key into another table (where it is called a *foreign key*).

A note of design advice: databases are not always taxonomies. They can classify things, of course, but the idea behind database design is not necessarily to figure out the hierarchy of increasingly bigger or more abstract categories into which your data fit. Both bicycles and automobiles are objects with wheels, for example. But rather than puzzling out the ontological status of non-motorized two-wheeled vehicles versus motorized four-wheeled vehicles, figure out instead the relationships that these objects share with the other entities in your project; i.e. what vehicles are owned by which people. Remember, these databases are called relational for a reason.

QUERY LANGUAGE: SQL

We interact with the database using a query language called Structured Query Language (or SQL). Through SQL, we can put data into the database, modify data when we need to, delete data when we wish, and – most importantly – ask questions of our data. SQL looks like English and is constructed as a series of clauses whose particular grammatical pattern makes sense to the MySQL database package.

SQL has many verbs and commands. We will start with the four big data-manipulating verbs:

SELECT asks a question of the database.

INSERT puts data into the database.

UPDATE modifies data already in the database.

DELETE erases data in the database.

SELECT is perhaps the most commonly used verb, and the one we use whenever we want to ask a question of the database. It is the verb on which we will focus for the rest of this chapter (you can see more verbs and SQL examples in the online supplementary materials). **SELECT** always returns to us an answer, even if the answer is "none." The pattern of the **SELECT** verb is always the same:

> **SELECT** a column or list of columns
>
> **FROM** a table or list of tables
>
> **WHERE** certain criteria are met;

Notice three things: (1) queries always end with a semi-colon; (2) queries can optionally span across multiple lines; and (3) certain keywords are traditionally capitalized. Words reserved for MySQL's use cannot become the names of tables or columns. We typically capitalize those reserved words and then use lowercase for the names of tables and columns. MySQL will not give you an error if you use lowercase for reserved words, but good capitalization will help you learn SQL more quickly. Table names and column names are, however, case sensitive, so you will need to capitalize those consistently the way you did when you created the table.

The Jane Austen database is included in this chapter's online supplementary materials. If you wish, follow the instructions there to install MySQL, load this database, and follow along.

We type our SQL command after the typical MySQL command-line prompt (**mysql>**). Let us see the contents of the "novel" table (Table 9.6; in what follows, we have typed the query in bold).

We are asking MySQL to select (or extract) everything from the "novel" table and to present the results to us. Here, the * wildcard character stands in for "everything" – and, in this case, MySQL interprets "*" to mean "all columns." Since this query has no **WHERE** clause, we are not eliminating any rows from the output because MySQL has been given no criteria by which a row could be excluded. Consequently, this query returns all rows and all columns from the table.

Table 9.6 Sample output from SQL query showing everything from the "novel" table

```
mysql> SELECT * FROM novel;
+----+-----------------------+------+
| id | title                 | year |
+----+-----------------------+------+
|  1 | Sense and Sensibility | 1811 |
|  2 | Pride and Prejudice   | 1813 |
|  3 | Mansfield Park        | 1814 |
|  4 | Emma                  | 1815 |
|  5 | Northanger Abbey      | 1818 |
|  6 | Persuasion            | 1818 |
+----+-----------------------+------+
6 rows in set (0.00 sec)
```

A **WHERE** clause can be added at the end of the query to select only those results that match certain criteria. For example, if we wanted to see which novels were published in 1815 (Table 9.7):

Table 9.7 Sample output from SQL query showing everything published in 1815 from the "novel" table

```
mysql> SELECT *
    -> FROM novel
    -> WHERE year = 1815;
+----+-------+------+
| id | title | year |
+----+-------+------+
|  4 | Emma  | 1815 |
+----+-------+------+
1 row in set (0.01 sec)
```

Again, the * wildcard in this context translates to "all columns," but we could extract only certain columns if we wished by specifying them in the **SELECT** clause (Table 9.8):

Table 9.8 Sample output from SQL query showing all titles from the "novel" table

```
mysql> SELECT title FROM novel;
+-----------------------+
| title                 |
+-----------------------+
| Sense and Sensibility |
| Pride and Prejudice   |
| Mansfield Park        |
| Emma                  |
| Northanger Abbey      |
| Persuasion            |
+-----------------------+
6 rows in set (0.01 sec)
```

We can learn about the contents of the other tables the same way (Table 9.9):

Table 9.9 Sample output from SQL query showing everything from the "person" table

```
mysql> SELECT * FROM person;
+----+---------------+-------------+
| id | first         | last        |
+----+---------------+-------------+
|  1 | John          | Alexander   |
|  2 | Aishwarya Rai | Bachchan    |
|  3 | Alan          | Badel       |
|  4 | Howard        | Baker       |
|  5 | Celia         | Bannerman   |
|  6 | Michael       | Barry       |
|  7 | Kate          | Beckinsale  |
... etc ...
```

Notice that both the "novel" and "person" tables have an "id" column in which we store each row's primary key. Those keys have no public meaning outside our database, but here they help to insure data integrity because we can use them elsewhere as foreign keys. We can see the same primary key structure at work in the "adaptation" table (Table 9.10):

Table 9.10 Sample output from SQL query showing everything from the "adaptation" table

```
mysql> SELECT * FROM adaptation;
+----+-------------------------+------+--------+----------+-------------+
| id | title                   | year | medium | novel_id | director_id |
+----+-------------------------+------+--------+----------+-------------+
|  1 | Sense and Sensibility   | 1971 | TV     |        1 |          33 |
|  2 | Sense and Sensibility   | 1981 | TV     |        1 |           8 |
|  3 | Sense and Sensibility   | 1995 | Film   |        1 |          46 |
|  4 | Sense and Sensibility   | 2008 | TV     |        1 |           1 |
|  5 | Pride and Prejudice     | 1938 | NULL   |        2 |        NULL |
|  6 | Pride and Prejudice     | 1940 | Film   |        2 |          47 |
|  7 | Pride and Prejudice     | 1952 | TV     |        2 |          50 |
|  8 | Orgoglio e pregiudizio  | 1957 | TV     |        2 |          16 |
|  9 | Pride and Prejudice     | 1958 | TV     |        2 |        NULL |
... etc ...
```

Here, however, we can see that "adaptation" also has some foreign keys: the "novel_id" column stores a key from the "novel" table and "director_id" stores a key from the "person" table. There are also a few NULL values. NULL in a database means "no value." In this case, it means we were uncertain of a few things. Rather than guess, we simply allow the field to remain NULL.

MULTIPLE-TABLE QUERIES

Single-table queries are relatively straightforward, but the real power of the database lies in multiple-table queries. After all, unless we have very good memories, we cannot easily tell which novel has primary key #2 or which person has primary key #50. Queries can reconcile those foreign-to-primary-key relationships. Writing a multiple-table query (sometimes called a "join" by database experts) is best accomplished by following a systematic process:

1. List all the tables you will need.
2. List all the columns you will need (and preface them with a dot).
3. Draw boxes around the particular fields you want to **SELECT**.
4. Draw lines between primary/foreign key combinations.
5. Append any relevant **WHERE** criteria.
6. Write the query.

Here, for example, is a diagram that selects all the titles and years of adaptations of *Pride and Prejudice* (Figure 9.6):

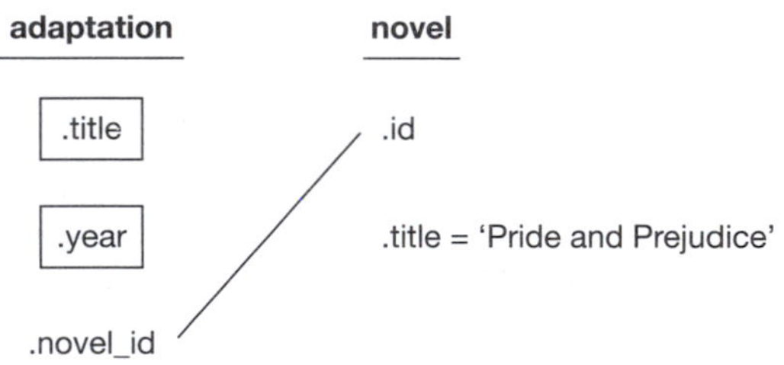

Figure 9.6
Diagram for devising a multi-table SQL query

We want to **SELECT** the "title" and "year" from rows in the "adaptation" table in which the "novel_id" foreign key matches the primary key of the novel *Pride and Prejudice*. Notice that we do not have to know in advance the primary key value of *Pride and Prejudice*; we will let the database find that for us. The novel's title is a more intuitive value for humanists to grasp and we will use that information to shape our query.

When we write this query, we will use a standard nomenclature: the **table.column** syntax. That syntax always works in any query, but we rarely use it in single-table queries because there is no ambiguity about the location of particular columns. Here, however, both "novel" and "adaptation" have columns called "year" and "title" so we need to be more precise. In SQL (Table 9.11):

Table 9.11 Sample output from SQL joining the "adaptation" and "novel" tables

```
mysql> SELECT adaptation.title, adaptation.year
    -> FROM adaptation, novel
    -> WHERE adaptation.novel_id = novel.id
    -> AND novel.title = 'Pride and Prejudice';
+-------------------------+------+
| title                   | year |
+-------------------------+------+
| Pride and Prejudice     | 1938 |
| Pride and Prejudice     | 1940 |
| Pride and Prejudice     | 1952 |
| Orgoglio e pregiudizio  | 1957 |
| Pride and Prejudice     | 1958 |
| De vier dochters Bennet | 1961 |
| Pride and Prejudice     | 1967 |
| Pride and Prejudice     | 1980 |
| Pride and Prejudice     | 1995 |
| Bridget Jones's Diary   | 2001 |
| Bride & Prejudice       | 2004 |
| Pride & Prejudice       | 2005 |
+-------------------------+------+
12 rows in set (0.00 sec)
```

Notice that we must list in the **FROM** clause all the tables we are using, even if we are not **SELECT**ing any columns from that table. Here, MySQL needs to be told to reference the **novel** table even though the final result (determined by the **SELECT** clause) will display no information from that table. Metaphorically, the various tables are like islands and the primary/foreign key combinations are bridges from one island to the next. The **FROM** clause needs to list every island that MySQL will land on as it moves from table to table searching for relevant data. We need only one path from island to island. Some new database designers want to map every table to every other table with foreign key columns, but that is not necessary. As long as we can find one path through the table landscape that gives us what we want, we can extract any column from any table.

CONCLUSION

Managing increasingly large datasets effectively and asking sophisticated questions of that data are the main reasons why digital humanists are turning to databases as they shape and develop their research projects. Designing the database and wrangling your project's data into it can teach you quite a lot about your research project. Once your data are in a database you can use SQL to discover trends, patterns, biases, tendencies, and even anomalies in your data. In this chapter we've just scratched the surface as to the types of questions you can ask of a database, and we invite you to look at the online resources for further examples of how you can use databases and SQL to explore your data.

REFERENCES

Codd, E. F. "A Relational Model of Data for Large Shared Data Banks." *Communications of the ACM* 13.6 (June 1970): 377–387. PDF.

"Jane Austen in Popular Culture." Wikipedia. https://en.wikipedia.org/wiki/Jane_Austen_in_popular_culture. Web.

Moretti, Franco. "Network Theory, Plot Analysis." *New Left Review* 68 (March–April 2011): 80–102. PDF.

CHAPTER 10

Digitization fundamentals

Robin Davies and Michael Nixon

INTRODUCTION

What constitutes a digital humanities (DH) project? First, there is material to be digitized, including various manuscripts, images, and audio/video recordings. This material may be fragile or rare and require special handling, and there may be medium-specific artifacts that need digitizing as well (e.g. marginalia, dates on the backs of photos). Some of these can be considered essential elements, while others are recorded as metadata, and stored in a subsidiary format. Next, digitized material will often be incorporated into a processing or analysis system. There are a wide variety of these, ranging from tools for text analysis to visualization to dynamic programmatic transformation, and they tend to allow what Moretti calls distant reading (Moretti). Finally, some combination of the initial plainly digitized materials and their new dynamic formats need to be published, typically on the Web.

Given this broad description of the DH project, it's easy to see how the field continues to grow and draw attention as a means for scholarly engagement. Kathleen Fitzpatrick states:

> For me [DH] has to do with the work that gets done at the crossroads of digital media and traditional humanistic study. . . . On the one hand, it's bringing the tools and techniques of digital media to bear on traditional humanistic questions. But it's also bringing humanistic modes of inquiry to bear on digital media. (Lopez *et al.*)

As we think about the nature of DH in relation to new analytical tools, it is also useful to draw attention to David Berry's concept of three "waves." He identifies the first wave as one occupied with acts of digitization and structuring material for classification and access (Berry). The second starts to draw on new methods of interpretation and interaction, especially for interrogating "born-digital" work. Finally, he suggests a third wave may lie ahead of us, bringing with it shifts in knowing, a "way of thinking about how medial changes produce epistemic changes" (Berry 4). This helps clarify the scope of DH projects and the developing nature of what constitutes a contribution to the field.

In this chapter, we will focus on several kinds of tools, leveraging foundational digitization practices for transferring humanities data into a digital medium, and modeling it for sustainable computational research. In particular, we will take a scenario-based approach to reveal important foundational considerations behind the choices researchers make as they work through a DH project involving the digitization of artifacts.

The three scenarios that we will be describing are: *creating a digital edition*, *distributing oral histories*, and *coordinating access to music notation*. First, we will look at how to provide access to scholarly, edited texts that have been digitized, with reference to the Internet Shakespeare Editions (ISE, http://internetshakespeare.uvic.ca/). Next, we will look at challenges digitizing audio files and related material, with reference to the Memorial University of Newfoundland Folklore and Language Archive (MUNFLA, www.mun.ca/folklore/munfla/). Lastly, we will examine a scenario where researchers have to innovate in their use of file formats for multimedia data. There we will look at the Single Interface for Music Score Searching and Analysis project (SIMSSA, http://simssa.ca).

We will use the lenses of *Goal*, *Process*, and *Sharing* to examine these projects. *Goal* allows us to focus on ensuring that hidden priorities and constraints of technology are a good match to the practitioner's motivations and intended contribution. *Process* takes us to the core practice of converting analog materials into a digital format, while reminding us of implicit trade-offs; it points at commonly adopted best practices. Finally, *Sharing* increases awareness of the complete digitization life cycle to further the goals of preservation and publication. This helps us consider how dissemination can best be accomplished.

CREATING A DIGITAL EDITION

In this section, we will discuss some critical issues involved in digitizing text. Earlier, we noted Berry's observation that the first wave of DH projects is primarily concerned with providing digital access to material, and one of the mainstays of this is the digital edition. Such editions clearly highlight the importance of considering your goal, however. Patrick Sahle provides a working definition of a scholarly edition as "the critical representation of historical documents" (Sahle), including both representation by data *and* by media. Notably, he also points out that if an edition is to be scholarly it must go beyond being simply a digital facsimile. The notion of a requisite different paradigm is useful, and helps connect to the values highlighted in Berry's second wave; new modes of access and even "reading" are facilitated.

Thus, it is important to understand how you might leverage the existing infrastructure of digital tools for textual analysis, and what requirements such interoperability might impose on your digitization process. You will need to decide how your digitized materials can be used with students to facilitate teaching, or by researchers conducting various kinds of scholarly work. By looking around at existing tools, you could determine whether you're reasonably able to produce digital material appropriate for use with them. While we all are likely to want to support a broad range of uses, it's also valuable to decide on a reasonable scope to avoid continually increasing the amount of work to be undertaken. So, if you are planning to create a digital scholarly edition, you will find yourself concerned with a range of possible technical operations and a need to make choices about all of them. Always reflect back on your goal to determine whether the addition of a particular element is actually desirable.

An example of such a possibility is an early consideration that you will need to make: whether to have the original text transcribed. Transcription is a laborious process that will have to be managed for quality control – as an example, the UK 1911 Census project had a goal of 98.5 percent accuracy due to the complexities of deciphering the many handwriting samples involved ("About Census"). However, transcription will directly produce "born-digital" text for your use.

You might choose direct digital imaging using a scanner or digital camera. This could be the case when there are details unique to a particular manuscript that you wish to capture as images, such as those the US National Archives and Records Administration (NARA) considers to determine if an artifact merits preservation: aesthetic or artistic quality, unique physical features, details for establishing authenticity, and serving as an important exemplar of the work (National Archives and Records Administration). These digital images can be integrated with text to allow researchers to spot any details that would otherwise elude textual description.

Recommending digital imaging hardware is outside the scope of this chapter, and it is increasingly the case that contemporary equipment is broadly capable, so instead determine the kind and quality of images that can be produced, and compare them to relevant minimum standards. Additionally, don't overlook the power of what can be accomplished with existing hardware in constrained scenarios, such as using a digital camera (perhaps even a mobile device in certain cases!) to capture works incompatible with a flatbed scanner.

Essential is a high-quality digital master image that represents all significant information from the source document. Creating this master image is important for the goals of preservation and access, and can prove economical in the long run. It aids preservation by serving – accompanied by appropriate documentation and metadata – as a surrogate sufficiently detailed to eliminate the need to view the original. This does imply careful archival storage of the digital image, allowing for retrieval, quality monitoring, and support for the foreseeable range of future applications. The master image takes on increased value to the degree that the one you're making can be considered the canonical or most reliable archive version, although it is critical for your personal project regardless.

There are a few technical details relevant to the Process stage worth covering here. These include pixels and resolution, bit depth, and file formats. Digital images consist of a grid of small squares, known as picture elements (pixels). These are mapped to the display device. Resolution refers to the level of detail of an image: it is measured in pixels for computers and digital cameras; in pixels per inch (ppi) for scanners; in dots per inch (dpi) for printers. Bit depth refers to the number of available tones or colours for each pixel, with a higher number providing a larger palette. For example, 8-bit colour has a range of 256 colours since that is the maximum size of the integer that can be stored to represent it.

There have been many file formats created to manage picture information, but we will only mention the most relevant. RAW is a format you may find on your digital camera, and really stands for a variety of proprietary formats that contain all available image sensor data. While these files should generally be retained, images must be converted to a universally understood format before sharing. TIFF is flexible and platform-independent with broad support by numerous image-processing applications. Master images should be archived in this format. The PNG format is a compressible, free open-source successor to the GIF format and supports true colour. Their compression does not discard information: it is *lossless*. PNG is recommended as a presentation format for images. Finally, the JPEG format is ideal for sharing photos online due to its excellent compressibility. However, it is *lossy*, and will irretrievably compromise information and image quality. JPEG files should be treated as essentially read-only and produced from higher-quality images for sharing on the web as an alternative to PNG files.

Following on this information, here is a general overview of best practices for digital conversion. Digital cameras should capture 24-bit colour depth (1 bit for black & white text) TIFF (or optionally RAW) files. Flatbed scanners should capture 24-bit colour (1-bit monochrome for text, 8-bit Greyscale for shaded print), 600+ ppi TIFF files. These recommendations, along with more regarding slides and photographs, are contained in the online *Capture your Collections guide* (Canadian Heritage Information Network). Various other institutions (e.g. NARA, the Library of Congress) establish their own best practices (Cornell University Library/Research Department), which include variations such as 8-bit gray colour depth at 300 dpi for capturing images of text, and maximum resolutions such as a maximum width of 3,000 pixels for photos.

Once you have captured the master image of your texts, you must now turn that digital image into text. The Optical Character Recognition (OCR) process takes digital images and attempts to recognize typographic details in them. While the free software that came with your scanner often suffices for capturing images, you may find it doesn't provide OCR capability or lacks features such as training to improve recognition accuracy on a corpus. We have had success on projects with software such as Adobe Acrobat Pro, Abbyy FineReader, and even the basic free-ocr.com. Before performing OCR, ensure that master images of text are high-contrast and not skewed; both properties can be managed to a degree in photo editing software, although ensuring good source images directly is best.

However, an OCR system can make only educated guesses about what printed materials are trying to represent. Rose Holley discusses this:

> True accuracy, i.e. whether a character is actually correct, can only be determined by an independent arbiter, a human. This can be done by proof-reading articles or pages, or by manually re-keying the entire article or page and comparing the output to the OCR output. These methods are very time consuming. (Holley)

Therefore, one should ensure that one's chosen OCR system is both accurate and capable of showing uncertain text in a reasonable way.

Once reliable digital text has been obtained, it can be put to a number of uses. The ISE follows a standard approach. The text was transferred to an XML file and marked up with appropriate elements based on the Text Encoding Initiative (TEI) standard. Then, HTML files are procedurally produced using the XSLT process on the original XML files (Siemens *et al.*).

Michael Best describes how the ISE take advantage of various Web technologies, by enabling users to choose a desired level of annotation, language, and ultimately how each work will be accessed (Best 31). Readers can read linearly or by searching text or annotation using automated tools; they can also read a variety of integrated essays, from performance histories to the editor's own critical viewpoint. Best also explores possibilities such as using animated graphics to switch between alternate meanings of an archaic word, as in the case of the weyard/wayward/weird women in *Macbeth* (Best 33).

DISTRIBUTING ORAL HISTORIES

The Memorial University of Newfoundland Folklore and Language Archive (MUNFLA) serves here as a point of departure for discussing the digitization part of the Process stage, using the audio medium as an example. "The archive comprises extensive collections of Newfoundland and Labrador folksongs and music . . ., folk narratives of many kinds, oral history, folk customs, beliefs and practices, childlore and descriptions of material culture" (MUNFLA). A large portion of this archive is analog audio media, which will need to be digitized to enable easy access. While this process can happen on demand, it is time-consuming; a well-tended, fully digital collection would be more portable and durable than fragile and decaying analog tape. Since MUNFLA's inception, digitization has occurred in phases, funding permitting, "to preserve the materials and to make them more widely available to researchers." Digitizing "involves struggling with technical parameters (levels of resolution for both pictures and sound files that give as clear a sound or image as possible with as low a bit rate as possible)" (Inkpen).

An audio analog to digital converter (ADC) is the hardware responsible for digitization, and the ADC deserves some attention here; it produces, at the *sampling rate*, a series of pulses that are shaped/modulated by the microphone's electric signal (Figure 10.1). In a computer, the end result of the ADC process is typically Waveform Audio File format (WAVE) or Audio Interchange File Format (AIFF) content.

CD-quality audio – still a benchmark, even as the recording industry leaves that format behind – uses a sampling rate of 44.1 kHz. This means that the audio waveform is sampled 44,100 times per second, permitting the signal to contain frequencies up to 20 kHz, the theoretical upper-end of the range of human hearing. Readers interested in the origin of the 44.1 kHz rate should consult Michael Unser's discussion of the Nyquist–Shannon sampling theorem (Unser).

Using progressively lower sampling rates, to reduce the amount of data stored in the digital facsimile, will remove higher frequencies from the audio signal. Subjectively, these higher frequencies are often described as the bright or crisp parts of an audio signal, and their presence helps with intelligibility and clarity. Signals missing these high frequencies can sound dull or muffled, and it is harder to separate the different sound sources in the audio. In an effort to more faithfully represent the analog waveform, the recording industry often makes use of higher sampling rates – such as 48 kHz, 96 kHz, or 192 kHz – the merits of which are fiercely debated.

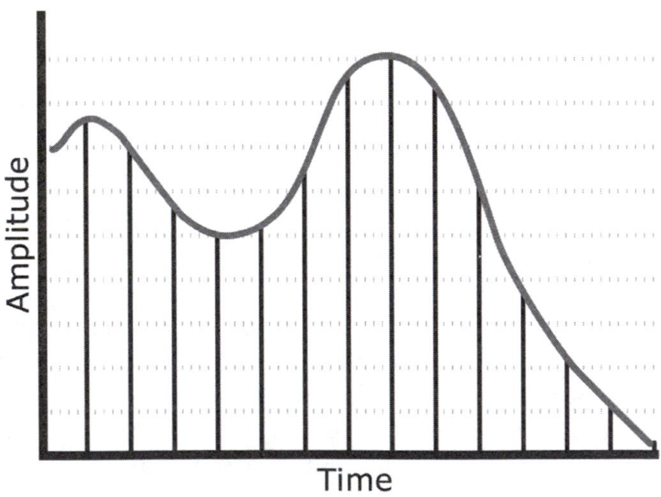

Figure 10.1
Sound as a series of sampled pulses

GRAMMY audio engineering winner Andrew Scheps, for example, acknowledges "diminishing returns . . . building audio hardware" to deal with higher sampling rates (Scheps 15:53).

The *bit depth* determines the possible *value* of each sample. The CD uses 16-bit audio, meaning the sample can be set to one of 2^{16}, or 65,536 possible values. Bit depth is directly connected to the way the volume of a signal is measured. Part of the appeal of an analog system is that quantities change smoothly over a range of possible values; digital systems can be jarringly jagged. Consider an example from daily life: a light switch – digital in nature – provides only two states, on or off, whereas a rheostat – analog in nature – facilitates a gradual, conceivably unnoticeable, change in light level. Thus, reducing the bit depth of a digital signal brings what is already approximation closer and closer to dichotomy.

While it may be permissible for the ADC to omit elements of the analog signal when making a digital facsimile, the conversion process must not introduce digital artifacts that misrepresent the analog original. Two examples of this kind of misrepresentation are (1) aliasing, which happens when the sample rate is insufficient to capture high frequency detail in a signal (Figure 10.2), and the ADC makes an erroneous approximation, and (2) quantization distortion, which introduces errors in a digital signal resulting from simplifications made measuring the loudness of the audio signal (Figure 10.3).

To understand further the concept of aliasing, consider this visual example. If a wheel is spinning clockwise at a speed of one revolution every ten seconds, and a camera documenting the wheel's revolution shoots one frame every nine seconds, someone viewing the resulting sequence of frames would say the wheel is actually turning counter-clockwise. In this case, the camera's samples provide an incorrect record of what is happening in the real world.

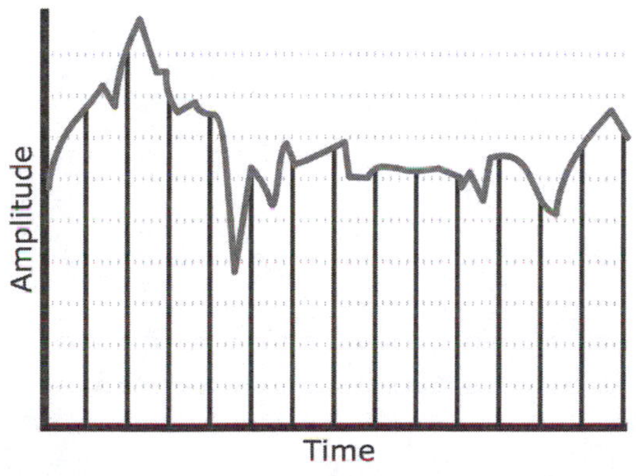

Figure 10.2
Aliasing

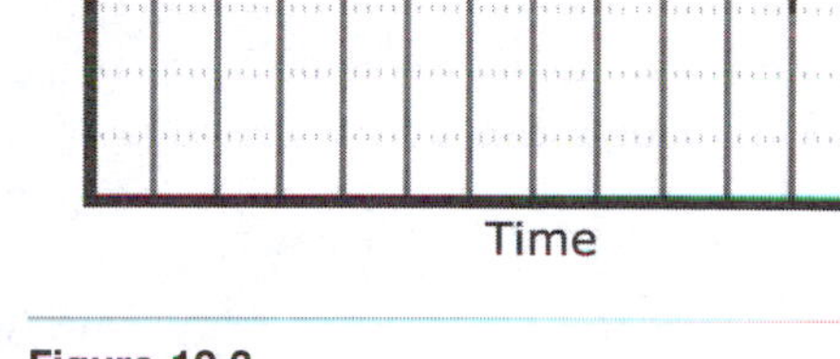

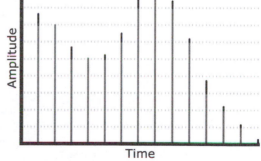

Figure 10.3
Quantization distortion

In photography, a camera records the amount of red, green, or blue light reaching a specific location on a sensing chip. As discussed earlier, if a camera uses eight bits to represent the amount of red light, there are only 256 possible values for red; the camera must then choose the closest colour match for each pixel. These choices, known as quantizations, introduce errors: distortions of reality. Therefore, when digitizing, variables such as sampling rate and bit depth should be set as high as is possible and necessary. The digital result is then faithful to the analog content, and contains sufficiently detailed data to facilitate prescribed analyses.

The Moving Picture Experts Group 1 or 2, Layer III format (MP3), popularized by portable music players and made notorious by online file sharing disputes, is the *de facto* standard for digital music distribution. The biggest advantage of an MP3 over the archive WAVE is its relatively small size. MP3 files can be one-tenth or one-twelfth the size of their archive sources. A smaller file size means fewer data have to be stored and streamed online, and facilitates the lower bit rate desired by distributors such as MUNFLA. Most listeners will not perceive any difference between a WAVE and its MP3 counterpart, but clearly significant changes have been made to the data. The MP3's COmpression and DECompression (codec) system, which encodes and decodes audio data to achieve this reduction, capitalizes on the characteristics of human hearing to achieve efficient lossy compression.

Jonathan Sterne has written extensively on the topic of perceptual encoding, and points to telephony research at the root of the MP3 format: "There was something to be gained by employing the ear, and specifically its perceptual limitations as outlined in the theory of masking and critical bands, as the basis for digital sound reproduction in limited-bandwidth environments" (Sterne 112). Briefly, however, let us consider three ways a codec could eliminate some data.

First, in a stereo recording there are two separate channels of audio information meant for playback on a device with two speakers. However, a great deal of what we hear from television and radio has exactly the same content on both channels. Consider a CD recording of an audiobook: it must have two channels, to conform to the CD specification, but the performer's voice is actually recorded in mono, so exactly the same information is stored on both channels. One easy method, then, to simplify in a lossy version, is to eliminate that redundant information, and simply re-duplicate it on playback. Another option for oral histories would be to make a blanket conversion of content to mono, assuming nothing important is conveyed by the signal being stereo. Some applications, such as Hollywood blockbuster surround sound, may require more than two channels, and even a simple oral history recording might contain useful ambient sound captured in stereo.

A second area of opportunity for producing lossy audio lies in masking. Audio from the real world fights for our ears' attention. The sound of a passing ambulance's siren will mask (drown out) a quiet conversation happening on the sidewalk. Although a microphone will notice small changes in sound pressure created by the latter sound, a lossy compressor can safely remove any record of those changes, as the human ear won't notice.

Third, our ears are more sensitive to some frequencies, which should be championed, and some frequencies do not need to be included at all, such as those outside the range of human hearing. A codec can remove very high- and low-frequency sounds, particularly if other material is masking those sounds. In these ways, the codec's algorithms calculate whether a particular sound will be audible and relevant to the listener; if not, it will be removed from the audio file.

Thus content captured into a WAVE file during acquisition is simplified for delivery. Distribution of content, in the Sharing stage, will likely see MUNFLA employing MP3 files, or those produced to a standard such as the Advanced Audio Codec (AAC) or Ogg Vorbis (OGG), which feature similar kinds of perceptual-based data economizations. These files will likely be distributed via a web-based system, easing the burden on archivists making CD copies of digital audio content for individuals.

Copyright is an additional Sharing consideration. The archive's website states: "All copies made by MUNFLA are for user research and private study. Permission for use of archival materials is for single use only" (MUNFLA). Making users aware of their rights can help to ensure compliance as a goodwill measure. Offering a license that provides more specificity about usage rights is even better, and the Creative Commons licensing system ("About Us") is an excellent example of a flexible method for enabling this process.

A good template for controlling access to content for research purposes is the website Freesound.org, which exists to share user-generated audio content, although users must register a free account. The Freesound team is proud of its tracking capabilities: "All the data about downloads, ratings and comments is available with corresponding timestamps since 2005" (Font *et al.* 412). Similarly, in an effort to make users somewhat responsible for their use of the archive content, MUNFLA could automatically respond to each request with a custom download link that doesn't expire and inherently maintains a record of any data access.

Finally, the content owner may also take steps to thwart digital piracy by either directly or indirectly prohibiting copying. A full discussion of Digital Rights/Restrictions Management (DRM)-enabled formats and associated issues is beyond the scope of this chapter, but archives such as MUNFLA may wish to take steps to prevent unauthorized duplication. Consider the strategy of the Pragmatic Bookshelf publishing imprint (pragprog.com): ebooks purchased from the site are DRM-free, meaning the content can be freely copied and reformatted. However, PDFs purchased from the site sport a custom-watermarked footnote on every single page. This footnote contains the words "Prepared exclusively for" followed by the downloader's name, in an effort to avoid sharing between people, as opposed to copying for a single person's use in multiple contexts. A watermark of this nature may be an acceptable feature of text-based material online or off, and even video media. However, aural watermarking poses numerous challenges. Listeners do not want the audio quality to be affected by extraneous noises, tones, or advertisements, and a watermark could also hinder analysis via digital tools. One designer describes an algorithm's non-intrusive function: "With default parameters, the proposed watermarking algorithm demonstrates practically undistinguishable (sic) watermarking which is transparent to an average listener with audio equipment of any quality on majority of audio content" (Radzishevsky).

COORDINATING ACCESS TO MUSIC NOTATION

DH projects of any size, particularly when collaborative in nature, need to make decisions about file formats to ensure data's portability throughout the project lifecycle, and longevity once the work is complete. Choosing appropriate formats is essential early in the Process stage, for content acquisition, and later in the Sharing stage, for content delivery.

This section will examine the capture and storage of musical notation, specifically addressing translation of musical scores from physical objects through scanning, and the resulting data's representation in a digital file format. While choice of file format is a consideration in any project, printed music is chosen here as a medium with a less-established digitization practice.

In some cases, a well-known file format may be appropriate, such as a TIFF (acquisition) and JPEG (delivery) solution for photographs, or a WAVE (acquisition) and MP3 (delivery) solution for oral histories.

Other projects' goals may require custom, less prevalent formats to make data accessible as intended. SIMSSA provides such an example: SIMSSA's goal "is to teach computers to recognize the musical symbols in these images and assemble the data on a single website, making it a comprehensive search and analysis system for online musical scores" (Fujinaga *et al.* 100). Though the researchers of SIMSSA "have chosen the MEI (Music Encoding Initiative) format" (102), a very recent (2013) standard, to hold musical data, they also note certain aspects of the music recognition and storage process will require "an avenue of research that has never before been explored" (102). Let us consider the data on which SIMSSA plans to operate.

Early composers and transcribers of musical performances considered the many facets of musical data – pitch, duration, dynamics, timbre – and determined which components of music were essential to record, in an effort to store the music, making it transportable and shareable. Thomas Forrest Kelly shows that frequently a storage format is a product of its time, developed to meet current goals, not necessarily future demands:

> It's not that the system is inefficient (although for some purposes it is); it's just that it developed over time with specific music in mind. As music changed, the musical notation changed too, but not by completely reinventing itself.

> Instead certain aspects of the existing system were developed or given new significance as people wanted to record additional aspects of music. (Kelly 4)

In this way the format itself becomes a kludge; the original structure is stretched and repurposed to accommodate additional data. Modern digital formats for a variety of media exhibit the same kind of purpose-specific mutation. For example, the various versions of Hypertext Markup Language (HTML) document users' desires to eschew standards and make a format capable of new, perhaps exciting things. Ben Henick writes:

> The virtues of interoperability do not, however, harmonize easily with the hot desire for bells, whistles, and pretty things often felt by artists and marketers. [Web] Browser vendors cannot ignore the imperative to innovate, and the market usually works on a shorter life cycle than the standards acceptance process. (Henick 43)

Audio, too, has only some consistency; the manner in which music is stored in an MP3 file is very clearly defined by a number of standards. However, the completely unstandardized structure of meta ID3 tags – housing genre, artist, ratings, and other data – appended to MP3 files shows how software such as Apple's iTunes can leverage and extend an existing, "informal standard" (Nilsson).

It is sensible, then, that creators and users of digital content would aim to streamline the storage of content for easy distribution. One entertainment software giant had this kind of forethought, creating the Interchange File Format (IFF): "By proposing a standard format structure, Electronic Arts wanted to avoid a situation where hordes of programmers would wantonly create whatever file formats were most expedient for their specific applications" (Wallace 24). Similarly, the history of computing is full of examples where a company created a format to address a current need and it gained enough popular usage to remain the *de facto* standard. The aforementioned AIFF is one example of how the IFF concept can produce files accessible to software from the past, present, and future (Morrison). On the consumer side of file formats, it's important to understand how comprehensive and inclusive the design process was, in order to choose a format that's most likely to stay relevant and usable for a long time.

Returning to SIMSSA, and its goal of a "single interface" for many users, it is clear why the project requires the interoperability of the MEI format. The MEI aims for longevity in addition to the affordances of digital exploration. "Because of its emphasis on comprehensibility and software independence, the data format defined by the schema may also serve an archival function" ("Music Encoding Initiative").

Fundamentally, MEI stores musical information as text, which separates the data from their presentation. MEI uses XML as a foundation, leveraging its combination of elements and attributes. Thus, it doesn't matter what form of written notation was employed originally to store a note on paper; the digital translation is something like this:

```
<note pname="c" oct="4" dur="4" />
```

In the above example, a quarter-note C in the fourth octave is created.

Needless to say, it is hard to imagine performing music from this markup kind of score. However outdated and inefficient conventional music notation is, Kelly reminds us we "still use their system, and it allows us to record sound for the future even today, a millennium later" (Kelly 4). Though Medieval notation systems been able to stand the test of time, they are clearly not easily deciphered by modern computers at the centre of big data initiatives.

When scanning text documents, OCR converts a sequence of glyphs to a digital representation. Printed musical information carries with it the same kinds of visual challenges as text in this regard: ink and paper quality will often affect the interpretation, and the software will have a harder time dealing with the inconsistent marks made by hand as opposed to press. Holley suggests a number of best practices to deal with these challenges; for example: "Obtain best source possible (marked, mouldy, faded source, characters not in sharp focus or skewed on page negatively affects identification of characters)" (Holley).

But music, though it may contain text, has a much wider variety of symbols, and potential arrangements of those symbols. Optical music recognition (OMR) software thus extends greatly the OCR groundwork. "Since existing OMR software is less reliable and less comprehensive than OCR software, our first challenge is to develop reliable OMR software that can process many forms of music notation" (Fujinaga *et al.* 100).

An important aid in this challenge of training machines lies in the possibility of collaborative computing, whereby users knowledgeable about content take part in the digitization process, most notably verification of recognition systems' accuracy. Adopting this strategy, users of SIMSSA "will correct the OMR for music sources they care about" (100), which reminds us a dataset is only as comprehensive as interested parties' investments.

Though it hasn't yet been created, a tool accessible via the Web will be part of SIMSSA's Sharing stage, allowing users to interact with existing data and provide data of their own. In addition, users could choose to render MEI documents from the SIMSSA archive in other formats. For example, the Portable Document Format (PDF) – introduced in 1993 by Adobe Systems Incorporated – would be sensible for users wanting to choose a musical font and generate conventional notation to view on screen or in print. If computers or other hardware is used for automated performance of MEI content, a Musical Instrument Digital Interface (MIDI) file – introduced by a collective of industry forces in 1983 (Chadabe) – could be employed.

Researchers wanting to do custom analysis of musical data could develop tools to manipulate the MEI content directly.

CONCLUSION

In this chapter, we proposed a three-stage model for thinking about projects: Goal, Process, and Sharing. Thinking and working iteratively through these allows consideration of important Goals and how they will inform other stages of the project. For example, Sharing images via website implies that multiple kinds of files will be created during the Process stage: archive-quality files (acquisition), plus lower-resolution files (delivery). We also explored the idea that DH encompasses a wide range of work, and showed how contemporary DH projects span the three waves envisioned by David Berry, by looking at issues involved in creating a digital edition, distributing oral histories, and coordinating access to music notation.

REFERENCES

"About Census." *1911 Census*. N.p., n.d. Web. 17 June 2015.

"About Us." *Creative Commons Canada*. N.p., n.d. Web. 23 June 2015.

Berry, David M. "The Computational Turn: Thinking about the Digital Humanities." *Culture Machine* 12.0 (2011): 1–22. Print.

Best, Michael. "Standing in Rich Place: Electrifying the Multiple-Text Edition Or, Every Text Is Multiple." *College Literature* 36.1 (2009): 26–36. *Project MUSE*. Web. 4 June 2015.

Canadian Heritage Information Network. "Capture Your Collections 2012: Small Museum Version – Fundamentals." *Canadian Heritage Information Network*. N.p., n.d. Web. 19 June 2015.

Chadabe, Joel. "The Electronic Century Part IV: The Seeds of the Future." N.p., n.d. Web. 12 June 2015.

Cornell University Library/Research Department. "Table: Representative Institutional Requirements for Conversion." *Moving Theory into Practice: Digital Imaging Tutorial*. N.p., 2002. Web. 19 June 2015.

Font, F., G. Roma, and X. Serra. "Freesound Technical Demo." Barcelona, Spain: ACM Press, 2013. 411–412. Web.

Fujinaga, Ichiro, Andrew Hankinson, and Julie E. Cumming. "Introduction to SIMSSA (Single Interface for Music Score Searching and Analysis)." London, UK: ACM Press, 2014. 100–102. Web. 27 May 2015.

Henick, Ben. *HTML & CSS: The Good Parts*. Sebastopol: O'Reilly Media, 2010. Print.

Holley, Rose. "How Good Can It Get? Analysing and Improving OCR Accuracy in Large Scale Historic Newspaper Digitisation Programs." *D-Lib Magazine* 15.3/4 (2009): n. pag. *CrossRef*. Web. 27 May 2015.

Inkpen, Deborah. "MUNFLA: Digitizing the Past." *Gazette* 22 January 2004: 9. Print.

Kelly, Thomas Forrest. *Capturing Music: The Story of Notation*. New York: W. W. Norton, 2015. Print.

Lopez, Andrew, Fred Rowland, and Kathleen Fitzpatrick. "On Scholarly Communication and the Digital Humanities: An Interview with Kathleen Fitzpatrick." *In the Library with the Lead Pipe* (2015): n. pag. www.inthelibrarywiththeleadpipe.org. Web. 29 May 2015.

Moretti, Franco. *Graphs, Maps, Trees: Abstract Models for a Literary History*. London: Verso, 2007. *Google Scholar*. Web. 30 May 2015.

Morrison, Jerry. "EA IFF 85 Standard for Interchange Format Files." 1985. Web. 27 May 2015.

"Music Encoding Initiative." N.p., n.d. Web. 11 June 2015.

National Archives and Records Administration. "Intrinsic Value In Archival Material." *National Archives*. N.p., 1999. Web.

Nilsson, Martin. "History – ID3.org." 8 October 2012. Web. 27 May 2015.

Radzishevsky, Alex. "AudioWatermarking.info – AWT2 Product Details." N.p., n.d. Web. 14 June 2015.

Sahle, Patrick. "Virtual Library Digital Scholarly Editing." text. *A Catalog of Digital Scholarly Editions*. N.p., 2011. Web. 17 June 2015.

Siemens, Ray *et al.* "Underpinnings of the Social Edition." *Online Humanities Scholarship: The Shape of Things to Come*. Ed. Jerome McGann *et al.* Houston: Rice University Press, 2010. 50. *Google Scholar*. Web. 24 June 2015.

Sterne, Jonathan. *MP3: The Meaning of a Format*. Durham, NC: Duke University Press, 2012. Print.

Unser, Michael. "Sampling – 50 Years After Shannon." *Proceedings of the IEEE* 88.4 (2000): 569–587. Web.

Wallace, Louis R. "IFF: The Standard of Sharing." *Amiga World* (1987): 23–30. Print.

CHAPTER 11

Geographical information systems as a tool for exploring the spatial humanities

Ian Gregory and Patricia Murrieta-Flores

INTRODUCTION

Geography, location and place have traditionally been under-studied by the humanities. This is not because of a lack of interest in them, or because of a failure to acknowledge their importance, but instead because these are difficult concepts to handle effectively. Mental maps of places mentioned in a source are notoriously hazy even to a reader who knows the area well. Manually attempting to map these places on paper is a time-consuming and unsatisfactory process resulting in a map that would frequently be an end-point of the research: reliant on decisions taken early in the investigation process, too inflexible to revise and suitable only for reproducing poorly in a monograph reliant on grey-scale publishing on a small page.

Geographical technologies including geographical information systems (GIS) and virtual globes such as Google Earth have the potential to break down these barriers and are leading to the development of a new field termed *spatial humanities*. A GIS is frequently thought of as a mapping system; however, as will be described in more detail below, it is perhaps better thought of as a database management system for data that can be associated with locations. Once a GIS database has been created, the map becomes central to the research process, allowing the researcher to ask questions in which location is central: 'how is this distributed across the study area?', 'why is this found here and not there?', 'what else is found at places this is found?' and so on. As the research is undertaken a wide range of maps and other visualizations will be created and refined, with the map being an integral part of the research process. At the end of the process the researcher can choose which maps to publish. Grey-scale and colour versions of maps can easily be produced and maps can also be published electronically with interactive functionality that enables users/readers to explore them in more detail. Thus, the role of maps in disseminating the author's message can be separated from their role as a research tool that enables the author to develop and refine their message.

This is not to say that the new world of spatial humanities is problem free. As will be discussed in more detail below, there are a number of problems remaining, including the time that it takes to create a GIS database, the complexity of GIS software, and issues around the fact that GIS was developed to handle quantitative sources in the Earth and social sciences using very different paradigms from those found in the humanities. Nevertheless, we are at a point where these technologies will allow early adopters to create a step change in the way that location is explored in the humanities, which, in turn, will lead to new understanding about geographical knowledge across the full range of disciplines that make up the humanities. This chapter introduces GIS as a tool for research within the humanities; a range of other publications are available for readers who are interested in the approaches that it offers to the field or case study examples of how humanities researchers are applying the technology.[1]

DEFINITIONS AND TERMINOLOGY

As with many technologies, GIS comes with a range of terminology with overlapping definitions. *Geographical information* is effectively any data set that refers to specific locations on the Earth's surface where we are interested in the differences between locations. A *geographical information system* is frequently thought of as a software system that enables spatial information to be stored, manipulated, queried, analysed and visualized.[2] As such, a GIS combines the ability of a database to explore thematic questions associated with *what* is in the database, with the abilities of a mapping system to explore spatial questions associated with *where* features are located. The two main commercial GIS software packages are ArcGIS, which dominates the academic market, and MapInfo.[3] Recently, free open-source software, including Quantum GIS (QGIS), Grass and gvSIG, have begun to rival these products.[4] *Geographical information science* (GISc) is a broader field concerned with how geographical information can best be studied.[5] Within GISc geographical information is the source material, GIS is the technology to analyse it, and GISc is the intellectual context in which this work take place.

GIS has its roots in the Earth sciences in the 1960s where it was developed to monitor subjects such as land-use. It spread into human geography in the 1980s where it was particularly used to analyse quantitative sources such as census data. The adoption of GIS in the humanities started with archaeology in the early 1980s with the rapid rise of its use both for cultural resource management and as a research tool. By the 1990s, the development of research methods for spatial analysis in the field was already widely practised.[6] In the 1990s, historians started to use GIS. This occurred largely independently to developments in archaeology, with the primary emphasis being on quantitative sources such as demographic or environmental data.[7] Despite its narrow focus, this approach was successful enough to create its own sub-field, *historical GIS*.[8] Through the 2000s, the use of GIS in history spread into new areas and the emphasis increasingly shifted from technology and methods to applied research. In history, this led to historical GIS being increasingly re-branded as *spatial history*, reflecting the increasing importance of historical research questions and downplaying the technology. The advent of digital humanities in the early 2000s increased interest in using GIS with more traditional humanities sources, particularly texts, and also images, virtual landscapes and historical maps. This has led to fields known as both *humanities GIS* and *spatial humanities*.[9] There has also been a move to develop *deep mapping*, a paradigm that attempts to move the use of geographical information away from GIS.[10]

THE BASIC TECHNOLOGY

GIS is based around a crude but effective model in which the features on the Earth's surface are represented within a computer. As was stated above, to represent geographical information we need thematic information about *what* there is and spatial information about *where* it is located. This involves having two types of data linked together within the software. On the one hand there is what GIS software terms *attribute data*, which is 'data' as most users would understand it in that it might be a table of statistics, a digital text or corpus, or a collection of images. Within GIS software each item of attribute data needs to be linked to a coordinate-based location, referred to as *spatial data*. There are only really four types of spatial data: *points*, *lines*, *polygons* (which represent areas) and *pixels*. With tabular attribute data, every row in the table will have a corresponding item of spatial data; with a collection of images, each image is likely to have its own spatial data, probably a point derived from the image's metadata. When the attribute data are unstructured texts such as corpora, these usually need to be converted into tabular form as described in more detail below. The combination of spatial and attribute data within a GIS is usually referred to as a *layer*. A layer is the GIS equivalent of a table in a database in that it is the basic structure used to store the information associated with one theme. The difference between a table and a layer is that a layer consists of both spatial and attribute data.

Depending on the type of spatial data used, GIS data can be classified into two main types: *vector* and *raster*. Vector data consist of points, lines or polygons and are used to represent discrete features such as historical sites (which can be points or polygons depending on the scale), transport networks (lines) or towns and cities (which can again be points or polygons). Raster data use pixels to represent continuous surfaces, of which the topography of the terrain is the most common. Each pixel represents a small area of the Earth's surface and has a height or other value associated with it. The user is unlikely to be interested in the values associated with one individual pixel; instead it is the way that multiple pixels represent a continuously varying landscape that is of interest.

Whatever the format of spatial data, coordinates are centrally important to the ability of GIS to represent, integrate and analyse data. All coordinates should be in a real-world coordinate system. This means using either latitude and longitude or a map projection. Latitude and longitude locate any point on the Earth's surface using the angle north or south of the equator and east or west of the Greenwich meridian. A map projection converts from degrees on a globe to a regular grid suitable for display on a computer screen or piece of paper. Usually the projection has an origin (whose coordinates are 0,0) at an arbitrary point and coordinates are expressed in metres or other units east or west (x) and north or south (y) of this location. Examples of projections include Universal Transverse Mercator (UTM) and British National Grid. Projections are complicated, as moving from a globe to a flat surface inevitably distorts one or more of angles, distances, areas and shapes.[11] From a GIS perspective, the important point is that as long as spatial data use real-world coordinates the computer can both calculate measurements such as the distances between points, the length of lines and the area of polygons, and can also integrate any data sets that use the same coordinate system. Good GIS software is able to convert from one coordinate system to another.

Figure 11.1 shows an example of how this structure can be used to represent a source. Using techniques described below, a corpus of 1.5 million words of writing about the English Lake District was converted into a point layer such that each place-name from the text is represented by a point. The points shown in Figure 11.1a represent place-names that occur within the same sentence as the word 'beautiful'. The spatial data thus indicate locations that writers within the corpus are associating with 'beautiful', the attribute data (Figure 11.1b) give more information on this such as the author that the reference was taken from, the date it was written, the genre that author was writing in, and so on. As the spatial data are projected using British National Grid they can be combined with a variety of other layers on the same projection, which, in this case, provide context, including a line layer showing main roads and a polygon layer showing the major lakes. The final layer is a raster surface representing heights.

GETTING SOURCES INTO GIS

The process of adding spatial data to a source or database is known as *geo-referencing*. In the sciences and social sciences this stage of database creation was often the most time-consuming part of a GIS project because many quantitative

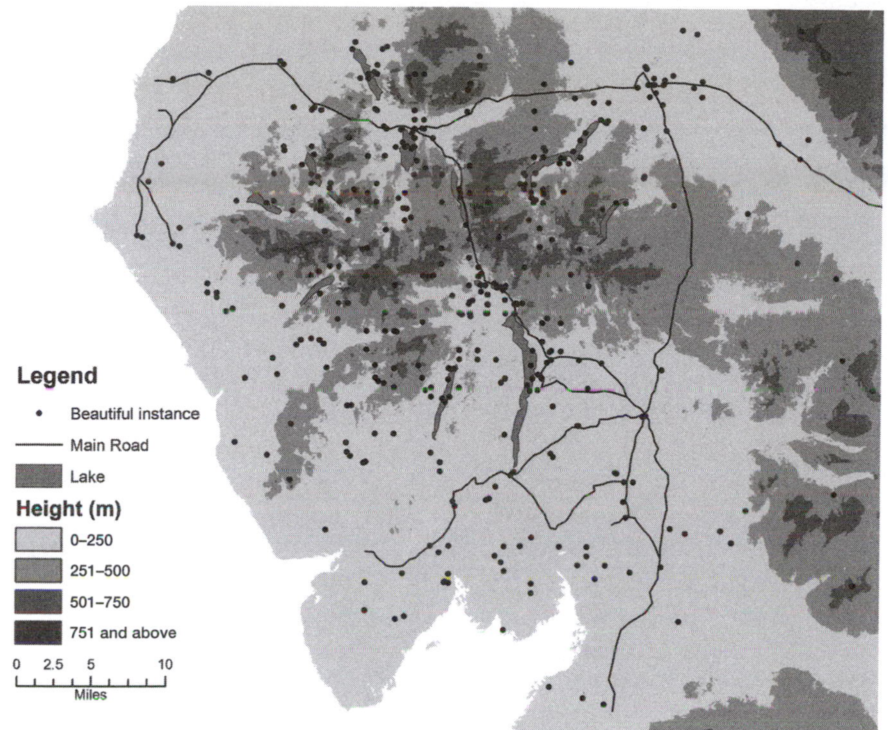

a. Spatial data

Place-name	Search-term	Author	Date	Genre
Wyburn	Beautiful	Joseph Budworth	1792	Travelogue
Helvellyn	Beautiful	William Wilberforce	1779	Journal
Deepdale Beck	Beautiful	Edward Baines	1829	Guide
Glenridding	Beautiful	M. J. B. Baddeley	1900	Guide

b. A fragment of the attribute data of the 'beautiful' layer

Figure 11.1
Layers in GIS. The English Lake District showing: a point layer of places described in the corpus as 'beautiful', a line layer of main roads, a polygon layer of the major lakes, and a raster surface representing height.

sources require polygon boundaries to be digitized, which, as will be described below, is a slow and time-consuming process. In the humanities, however, this is frequently less of a problem. Humanities sources are often best represented using points, and these are relatively quick and easy to read into GIS form. The easiest way to create a point layer is to start with a table that includes coordinates in two of the columns (one for eastings or longitudes, and one for northings or latitudes).

Place-name	Author	Date
Sca Fell	S.T. Coleridge	1802
Helvellyn	W. Wordsworth	1822
Great Gable	E. Baines	1829

a. Source table

Place-name	Latitude	Longitude
Fairfield	54.4973	-2.9922
Great Gable	54.4836	-3.2118
Helvellyn	54.5304	-3.0123
Sca Fell	54.4558	-3.2133
Skiddaw	54.6551	-3.1394

b. Gazetteer

Place-name	Author	Date	Standard place-name	Latitude	Longitude
Sca Fell	S.T. Coleridge	1802	Sca Fell	54.4558	-3.2133
Helvellyn	W. Wordsworth	1822	Helvellyn	54.5304	-3.0123
Great Gable	E. Baines	1829	Great Gable	54.4836	-3.2118

c. Joined table

Figure 11.2
Using a gazetteer to join coordinates to a table. The joined table (c) has had coordinates added from the gazetteer through the use of a relational join that matches identical place-names. An additional field, standard place-name has been added to allow spellings from the source to be matched with those on the gazetteer.

Object-level metadata often takes this form. Converting such a table into a GIS layer is trivial, requiring only a few mouse clicks. The software simply uses the coordinates to create the spatial data, which provides the information required to convert the table into a layer.

Where a table contains place-names without coordinates, the required coordinates can often be found using a *gazetteer*, which, in its simplest form, is a database table that lists place-names and gives coordinates for them.[12] An increasing number of gazetteers are freely available over the Internet.[13] Gazetteers can be used to provide coordinates for place-names through the use of a relational join, a database operation in which two tables are effectively joined together using a common field. An example of this is shown in Figure 11.2. As a relational join will only join exact matches, work is often required to standardize the spellings on the input table to match those on the gazetteer. It is good practice to keep the original spellings as well as the standardized versions found in the gazetteer. A user will also usually have to find locations for place-names that are not found in the gazetteer – Google Maps or paper maps may be appropriate for doing this – and may have to disambiguate place-names that may refer to different places such as, for example, 'London', which may be in England or Ontario. Despite these issues, given a good gazetteer and a relatively clean set of place-names, this process is quick and effective. Once coordinates have been found we effectively have a table with coordinates that can be converted into a GIS layer as described above.

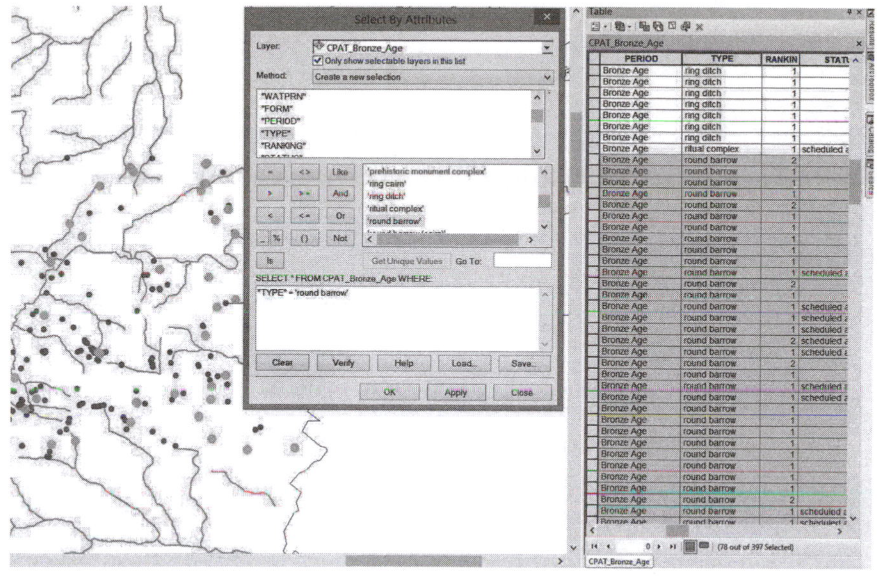

Figure 11.3
Selection by attributes in ArcMap. Using as an example a layer with archaeological information, we carried out a query selecting by attribute all those records in the 'CPAT Bronze Age' layer that correspond to the 'TYPE' 'Round Barrow'. The results show these records highlighted both in the attribute table and the mapped spatial data.

Where place-names occur in an unstructured text such as a corpus, georeferencing is more difficult because the place-names must be identified in the text. This can be done manually but this is only feasible for relatively small corpora. To automate this process, progress has been made in *geoparsing*, which involves first automatically identifying place-names in the corpus using natural language processing (NLP) and subsequently matching these to a gazetteer.[14] XML tags that identify the place-names and include their coordinates as attributes are added to the text. The text then needs to be converted to tabular form, which usually involves extracting the tagged place-names and some of the text that surrounds them and converting them into a table where each instance of a place-name forms a row.[15] Thus, there is currently no way of completely georeferencing a corpus without converting it into tabular form and thus losing some of the structure of the text.

Digitizing lines and polygons is much slower and more time-consuming than creating points. Typically this is done is by first scanning and georeferencing the map from which the features will be taken, as described below. Digitizing lines is then done by clicking the mouse along the line to capture its shape. Polygons are created by digitizing one or more lines to completely enclose an area. Where two polygons share a boundary, for example the boundary between two administrative units, this usually only needs to be digitized once, with the software being able to work out which polygon is to its left and right.

The data sources above all create vector data. A user may also want to georeference images such as historical maps, in which case it will create a raster image. Taking a historical map as an example, the first stage is to scan or photograph the map, creating a bitmap image such as a JPEG or TIFF. This can then be read into GIS software and is georeferenced by giving the software the real-world coordinates of four or more known points on the image, such as the four corners. The software uses these to georeference the entire image.

EXPLORING AND MANIPULATING DATA IN GIS

One of the most powerful capabilities of GIS is its ability to query its data in different ways. Searching the database can be done based on spatial criteria, attribute criteria, or combinations of both. Queries based on these criteria are common in humanities research. For instance, in Figure 11.3, an archaeologist who is working with a layer of prehistoric evidence from the national monument record might want to identify all of the Bronze Age round barrows recorded. An *attribute query* is done to select features based on values stored in the attribute data table. In this case, the researcher would select all the features that have the attribute 'Bronze Age' in the field called 'Period', and the attribute 'Round barrow' in the field called 'Class'. This selection is often done using Structured Query Language (SQL). The results of the query will be presented in both tabular and map form.

There are also many instances in which the scholar might want to look for information based on spatial criteria. Simple *spatial queries* are implemented simply by clicking the spatial data on the map to display the attributes associated to it. Spatial queries can also be done in more sophisticated ways to find out the relationships between features on different layers. One way of doing this is through an *overlay* operation. For example, a historian working with a WWII data set might want to:

- identify all of the concentration camps within modern-day Poland using a layer of camp locations and a layer of modern country boundaries;
- find all the factories destroyed within 1 km of a particular river using a layer of factories (including an attribute that flags whether it was destroyed) and a layer of rivers.

In both of these cases the overlay operation combines the spatial and attribute data from the two layers. The second case involves an extra step involving another GIS technique called *buffering* in which polygons are created that enclose the areas within a set distance of the features on a layer, such as within one kilometre of rivers (represented using lines) or ten miles of towns (represented using points).

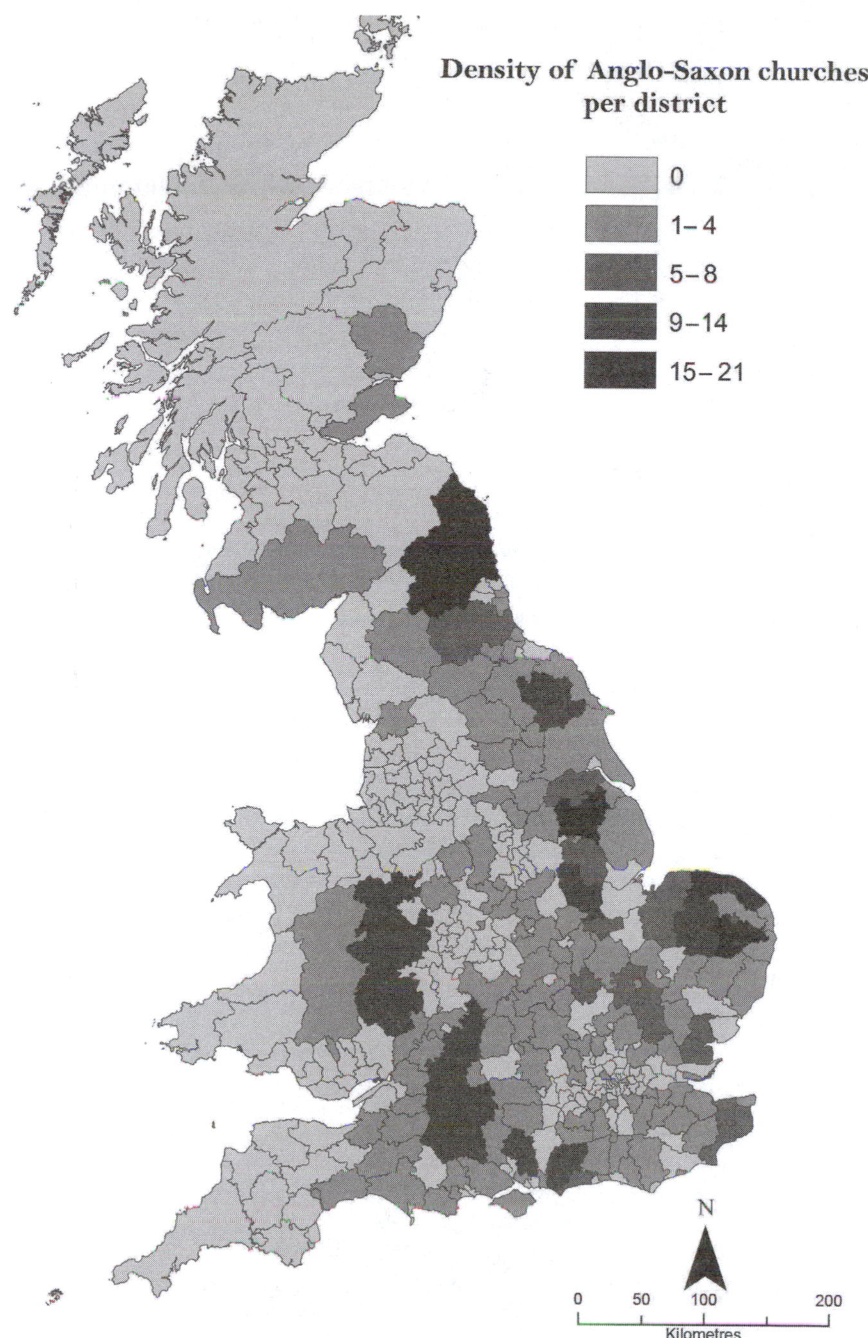

Figure 11.4
Density of Anglo-Saxon churches per district. The map was produced using an overlay between a polygon layer (districts) and a point layer (Anglo-Saxon churches), which returned a count of points that fall within each polygon.

Using these types of query, questions such as the following can be posed:

- What percentage of the total concentration camps were located in each country?
- What proportion of bombed factories were located near German cities?

Figure 11.4 shows an example of the results of an overlay. The map has been created by taking a point layer showing the locations of Anglo-Saxon churches in Britain. This has been overlaid with a polygon layer of modern administrative districts to allocate each church to a district. The total number of churches in each district has then been calculated and the results mapped.

SPATIAL ANALYSIS

The fact that GIS data combine spatial and attribute data opens up the potential to develop forms of analysis that explicitly include location. These techniques are referred to as *spatial analysis* and can be defined as a 'subset of analytic techniques whose results depend on the locations of the objects of analysis'.[16] These techniques can be statistically complex but do not need to be. They typically aim to identify and summarize spatial patterns within one layer, or the relationships between two or more layers in ways that go beyond simple querying or map overlay.[17] Spatial analysis thus explores *what* happens *where* and can be used either to explore data or to test particular hypotheses.

We might want to know, exploring a WWI dataset, whether soldiers from particular regiments came from specific neighbourhoods. Using a point layer representing the soldiers' addresses we can ask: does this point layer exhibit any spatial pattern? If so, what form does it takes? The answer to this will usually be that it is clustered in particular locations, that it is regularly distributed, or that the distribution appears random. Importantly, spatial analysis will allow us to identify how confident we are that the pattern is not random. If the pattern is not random, this would allow us to investigate further the reasons for the pattern by adding additional data. For instance, we might use census data to investigate whether clusters of recruitment are found in areas with particular social or economic characteristics.

Spatial analysis can be combined with textual analysis techniques such as corpus linguistics to create geographical text analysis. This allows us to ask questions such as which locations does the corpus concentrate on, what themes does the text associate with particular locations, and what geography do particular words or themes within the text follow?[18]

These are only a few examples of the spatial explorations that can be carried out. There are many kinds of questions in the humanities that involve exploring spatial relationships, and there are numerous techniques, methods and models to explore them. Other methods include: visibility, cost surface, and network analyses.[19] These approaches allow the researcher to investigate issues such as: the role of visibility in the construction of medieval castles or the location of memorial monuments; the role of routes of communication in historical travel writing, or migration during prehistoric times; the centrality of markets in historical commercial enterprises, or the distribution of a particular good, among many others. In addition, although not widely implemented in the humanities yet, *geosimulation* is a promising approach.[20] Agent-based modelling, for instance, can be used in the exploration of the influence of different variables in the outcome of historical battles, or possibly, the dispersion or adoption of an idea or concept.

CARTOGRAPHY AND INTERACTIVE MAPPING

GIS provides powerful cartographic functionality that allows the results of an analysis to be presented to a user/reader; however, cartographic design principles need to be understood in order to create meaningful maps from a database.[21] Among the most important are legibility, visual contrast, hierarchical organization and balance. A good map should be easy to read and understand, have good visual contrast on the elements presented, and include elements such as a legend, scale bar and north arrow. When creating a map, the author should attempt to follow two rules: first, the map should be a stand-alone product that can be understood without referring to any accompanying text, and second, the basic message of the map should be understandable within ten seconds of the user/reader looking at it.

Traditional maps present what the author feels is important to the reader. An alternative approach is to present data to the user and allow them to explore it themselves. A range of related technologies, in particular virtual globes such as Google Earth[22] and Internet mapping technologies such as Google Maps and Bing Maps,[23] can be used in partnership with GIS, but are primarily designed to be effective at presenting geographical information over the Internet in a readily usable form. To achieve this, they usually have user-friendly mapping capabilities but limited database functionality, friendly user interfaces and a soft learning curve. Almost all standard GIS packages allow the conversion of their proprietary file formats into Keyhole Markup Language (KML – an XML notation developed for the creation of geographic annotation and visualization in Google Earth), allowing GIS data to be shared in a way that is accessible to non-experts.

Humanities sources as varied as twentieth-century census data, the history of cities and historical photographs have also been placed on the Internet with custom-written interfaces.[24] These sites all use location to structure their data such that users can query them based on location. They differ from traditional maps in that rather than presenting a message to a reader, the user has to develop their own argument by repeatedly querying the sources the site contains.

CONCLUSIONS

GIS is a tool that allows the researcher to represent his/her source in a way that combines the thematic with the spatial and thus allows questions to be asked about what is found where. The basic data model used by GIS, combining attribute and spatial data, is crude but nevertheless effective in that it allows researchers to ask questions in which location is important, to integrate different data sets based on where the features they contain are found, to analyse data in ways that are explicitly geographical, and to present the results of the analysis through maps and other forms of visualization.

There are also limitations with GIS. The GIS data model is centred around the idea that the source under study can be represented in tabular form. While this is fine for sources such as statistics and collections of images, it is clearly less than ideal for texts. Nevertheless, texts can be incorporated into GIS format using the idea that each place-name becomes a row of data in a table. A second limitation is that each item of attribute data can only be associated with a single location. This is fine for most features but is problematic for sources associated with flows such as trades or migrations that have a start and end point and perhaps a route in between. A more fundamental criticism of GIS is that it prioritizes space but has only limited functionality to manage time. This is a valid critique but it is important to realize that the human brain is very poor at conceptualizing space and time simultaneously, and that to understand one it is usually necessary to simplify the other. Another valid critique of GIS is that it insists on precise locations for spatial data and is poor at representing uncertainty in this. This is valid, and interpreting spatial patterns requires careful thought about the accuracy, or otherwise, of the locations used.

There are also practical limitations with GIS associated with the investment in time required. Both learning to use GIS software and transforming data into GIS form can be very time-consuming. If the data contain place-names that can be relatively easily georeferenced to points using a gazetteer, then georeferencing the data is manageable. Subjects where good gazetteers do not exist, or where lines or polygons need to be digitized, need to be approached with care.

Despite these limitations, we are in the early stages of a step change in the way that geography, location and place are researched within the humanities, enabled by the opportunities that GIS offers within the digital humanities. For those prepared to invest the time – and with the confidence to think innovatively about new approaches to sources and research questions – there are many opportunities to be taken and many rewards to be had.

The research leading to these results has received funding from the European Research Council (ERC) under the European Union's Seventh Framework Programme (FP7/2007-2013) / ERC grant "Spatial Humanities: Texts, GIS, places" (agreement number 283850).

NOTES

1 For how GIS and spatial approaches fit into the humanities see, in particular, Bodenhamer *et al.* 2010. For a review of case studies see: Gregory 2014; and chapters in Knowles 2008.
2 Gregory and Ell 2007.
3 See: www.esri.com and www.mapinfo.com, respectively.
4 See: www.qgis.org, http://grass.osgeo.org and www.gvsig.com, respectively.
5 Goodchild 1992.
6 Aldenderfer and Maschner 1996.
7 See, for example, Cunfer 2005; Donahue 2004; Gordon 2008; Gregory 2008.
8 Gregory and Healey 2007.
9 Gregory and Geddes 2014.
10 Bodenhamer 2015.
11 Robinson *et al.* 1995, chap 5.
12 Southall *et al.* 2011.
13 See, for example, the Geonames gazetteer www.geonames.org and the Getty Thesaurus of Geographical Names www.getty.edu/research/tools/vocabularies/tgn. Tools are also available that will use a gazetteer to automatically add coordinates to a list of place-names or addresses, such as www.findlatitudeandlongitude.com/batch-geocode and http://sandbox.idre.ucla.edu/geocoder.
14 Grover *et al.* 2010; Gregory, Donaldson *et al.* 2015.
15 Gregory, Cooper *et al.* 2015; Gregory and Donaldson in press.
16 Goodchild 1996.
17 Wheatley and Gillings 2000.
18 See, for example: Murrieta-Flores *et al.* 2015; and Gregory and Hardie 2011.
19 Chang 2009, chaps 13, 14 and 17. See also: Lee and Stucky 1999; Howey 2007; and Jang 2012.
20 Benenson and Torrens 2004.
21 Dent *et al.* 2009; Dorling and Fairburn 1997; MacEachren 1995; Robinson *et al.* 1995.
22 See: www.google.com/earth.
23 See: www.google.com/maps and www.bing.com/maps, respectively.
24 Examples include: Social Explorer (www.socialexplorer.org); Vision of Britain through Time (www.visionofbritain.org); the Map of Early Modern London (https://mapoflondon.uvic.ca); Locating London's Past (www.locatinglondon.org) and Enchanting the Desert (web.stanford.edu/group/spatialhistory/cgi-bin/site/project.php?id=1061).

REFERENCES

M. Aldenderfer and H.D.G. Maschner *Anthropology, Space, and Geographic Information Systems* (Oxford: Oxford University Press, 1996)

I. Benenson and P.M. Torrens *Geosimulation: Automata-based modelling of urban phenomena* (Chichester: John Wiley, 2004)

D.J. Bodenhamer 'Narrating space and place' in *Spatial Narratives and Deep Maps*, ed. by D.J. Bodenhamer, J. Corrigan and T.M. Harris (Bloomington, IN: Indiana University Press, 2015), pp. 7–27

D.J. Bodenhamer, J. Corrigan and T.M. Harris *The Spatial Humanities: GIS and the future of humanities scholarship* (Bloomington, IN: Indiana University Press, 2010)

K-T Chang *Introduction to Geographic Information Systems* (Boston, MA: McGraw-Hill, 2009)

G. Cunfer *On the Great Plains: Agriculture and environment* (College Station, TX: Texas A&M University Press, 2005)

B.D. Dent, J. Torguson and T. Hodler *Cartography: Thematic Map Design, 6th edition* (Boston, MA: WCB-McGraw-Hill, 2009)

B. Donahue *The Great Meadow: Farmers and the land in colonial Concord* (New Haven, CT: University of Yale Press, 2004)

D. Dorling and D. Fairburn *Mapping: Ways of representing the world* (Harlow: Longman, 1997)

M.F. Goodchild 'Geographical Information Science' *International Journal of Geographical Information Systems*, 6 (1992), pp. 31–45

M.F. Goodchild 'Geographic information systems and spatial analysis in the social sciences' in *Anthropology, Space, and Geographic Information Systems*, ed. by M. Aldenerfer and H.D.G. Maschner (New York: Oxford University Press, 1996), pp. 241–250

C. Gordon *Mapping Decline: St. Louis and the fate of the American city* (Philadelphia: University of Pennsylvania Press, 2008)

I.N. Gregory 'Different places, different stories: Infant mortality decline in England & Wales, 1851–1911' *Annals of the Association of American Geographers*, 98 (2008), pp. 773–794

I.N. Gregory 'From Historical GIS to Spatial Humanities: An evolving literature' in *Toward Spatial Humanities: Historical GIS and spatial history*, ed. by I.N. Gregory and A. Geddes (Bloomington, IN: Indiana University Press, 2014), pp. 186–202

I. Gregory, D. Cooper, A. Hardie and P. Rayson 'Spatializing and analysing digital texts: Corpora, GIS and places' in *Spatial Narratives and Deep Maps*, ed. by D.J. Bodenhamer, J. Corrigan and T.M. Harris (Bloomington, IN: Indiana University Press, 2015), pp. 150–178

I. Gregory and C. Donaldson 'Using geographical technologies to understand Lake District literature' in *Literary Mapping in the Digital Age*, ed. by D. Cooper, C.D. Donaldson and P. Murrieta-Flores (Aldershot: Ashgate, in press)

I.N. Gregory, C. Donaldson, P. Murrieta-Flores and P. Rayson 'Geoparsing, GIS and textual analysis: Current developments in Spatial Humanities research' *International Journal of Humanities and Arts Computing*, 9 (2015), pp. 1–14

I.N. Gregory and P.S. Ell *Historical GIS: Technologies, methodologies, scholarship* (Cambridge: Cambridge University Press, 2007)

I.N. Gregory and A. Geddes 'From Historical GIS to Spatial Humanities: Deepening scholarship and broadening technology' in *Toward Spatial Humanities: Historical GIS and spatial history*, ed. by I.N. Gregory and A. Geddes (Bloomington, IN: Indiana University Press, 2014), pp. ix–xix

I. Gregory and A. Hardie 'Visual GISting: Bringing together corpus linguistics and Geographical Information Systems' *Literary and Linguistic Computing*, 26 (2011), pp. 297–314

I.N. Gregory and R.G. Healey 'Historical GIS: Structuring, mapping and analysing geographies of the past' *Progress in Human Geography*, 31 (2007), pp. 638–653

C. Grover, R. Tobin, K. Byrne, M. Woollard, J. Reid, S. Dunn and J. Ball 'Use of the Edinburgh geoparser for georeferencing digitized historical collections' *Philosophical Transactions of the Royal Society A*, 368 (2010), pp. 3875–3889

M.C. Howey 'Using multi-criteria cost surface analysis to explore past regional landscapes: A case study of ritual activity and social interaction in Michigan, AD 1200–1600' *Journal of Archaeological Science*, 34 (2007), pp. 1830–1846

M-H. Jang 'Three-dimensional visualization of an emotional map with geographical information systems: A case study of historical and cultural heritage in the Yeongsan River Basin, Korea' *International Journal of Geographical Information Science*, 26 (2012), pp. 1393–1413

A.K. Knowles *Placing History: How GIS is changing historical scholarship* (Redlands, CA: ESRI, 2008)

J. Lee and D. Stucky 'On applying viewshed analysis for determining least-cost paths on Digital Elevation Models' *International Journal of Geographical Information Science*, 12 (1999), pp. 891–905

A.M. MacEachren *How Maps Work: Representation, visualisation and design* (London: Guildford Press, 1995)

P. Murrieta-Flores, A. Baron, I. Gregory, A. Hardie and P. Rayson 'Automatically analyzing large texts in a GIS environment: The Registrar General's reports and cholera in the 19th century' *Transactions in GIS*, 19 (2015), pp. 296–320

A.H. Robinson, J.L. Morrison, P.C. Muehrcke, A.J. Kimerling and S.C. Guptill *Elements of Cartography, 6th edition* (Chichester: John Wiley & Sons, 1995)

H. Southall, R. Mostern and M.L. Berman 'On historical gazetteers' *International Journal of Humanities and Arts Computing*, 5 (2011), pp. 127–145

D. Wheatley and M. Gillings *Spatial Technology and Archaeology: The archaeological applications of GIS* (London: Taylor & Francis, 2000)

FURTHER READING

For those wishing to know more about current research using GIS in the digital humanities, an annotated bibliography is provided by I.N. Gregory 'From Historical GIS to Spatial Humanities: An evolving literature' in *Toward Spatial Humanities: Historical GIS and spatial history*, ed. by I.N. Gregory and A. Geddes (Bloomington, IN: Indiana University Press, 2014), pp. 186–202. See also many of the works cited in this chapter.
Online lists of useful resources include:

- The Historical GIS Research Network (www.hgis.org.uk), which includes listings of both publications and online resources.

- The GeoHumanities Special Interest Group of the Alliance of Digital Humanities Organizations (http://geohumanities.org), which includes an online list of Humanities GIS projects and a GeoDiRT (Digital Research Tools) listing.
- The *Humanities GIS Zotero Library* (www.zotero.org/groups/humanitiesgis).
- The University of Saskatchewan's HGIS Lab provides both an online bibliography and a page of links (www.hgis.usask.ca).

For those wishing to learn to use GIS, a useful starting point is the lessons provided by the *Geospatial Historian* site (https://geospatialhistorian.wordpress.com), which also includes more pages of links to projects and resources. A more generic set of training materials, focused on the QGIS package, is available from www.qgistutorials.com, or, for a wider range of software, see www.gistutor.com.

CHAPTER 12

Electronic literature and digital humanities

Opportunities for practice, scholarship and teaching

Dene Grigar

The two essays in this section provide foundational information about the emergent literary form, electronic literature or "e-lit." Also referred to as born-digital literature, e-lit differs from digitalized print-based works, such as Emily Dickinson's poetry made available for distribution on the web, in that it involves "works with important literary aspects that take advantage of the capabilities and contexts provided by the stand-alone or networked computer" ("ELO," What Is E-Lit?") and other types of computing devices. It is expressed in a variety of forms including hypertextual literature, net art, bots, netprov, codework, and interactive fiction, to name a few examples. While works of this type have been around for decades and influenced by European avant-garde artist movements, such as Dada (Funkhouser 2007, 32–35), e-lit is a fairly new field of study, coming of age in the late 1990s due to the work undertaken by organizations such as the Electronic Literature Organization (ELO) and the Electronic Poetry Center in the United States; Electronic Literature as a Model of Creativity and Innovation in Practice (ELMCIP) in Europe; the Hermeneia Research Group in Spain; and NT2 (Le Laboratoire De Recherches Sur Les Oeuvres Hypermédiatiques) in Canada, among others, and supported by agencies such as the National Endowment for the Humanities (NEH), the Rockefeller Foundation, and Ford Foundation. While its practices can reflect, in varying degrees, visual, sonic, time-based and performative art; creative writing; and computing, its deep connection to literature offers digital humanities scholars a compelling avenue of exploration and opportunities for practice, scholarship, and teaching.

The most influential theorist of electronic literature is noted scholar N. Katherine Hayles whose essay, "Electronic literature: what is it?," is reprinted in this section. Hayles' early support of e-lit was seen in her two NEH Summer Seminars (1995,

2001), where she explored "literature in transition" and gave birth to a host of scholars and artists working in DH and e-lit today, including Tara McPherson, Kathleen Fitzpatrick, Rita Raley, Joseph Tabbi, Stephanie Strickland, Marjorie Luesebrink, and Diana Slattery. I was fortunate to participate in the 2001 seminar and experienced firsthand the support provided to scholars and artists and her commitment to growing the field. Following the second NEH seminar, Hayles moved the ELO from its first home in Chicago, where Executive Director Scott Rettberg resided, to UCLA where she served on the English Department faculty. She hosted the 2002 State of the Arts Symposium at the university, an event that laid the groundwork for symposia and conferences that have done much to raise awareness of this literary art form. More recently she led the development of collections of papers by prominent e-lit artists – Judy Malloy, Stephanie Strickland, and Robert Kendall – at Duke University's David M. Rubenstein Rare Book and Manuscript Library. Hayles now teaches in the Literature Program at Duke University.

Hayles' essay, published originally on the ELO's website in 2007 and expanded for her book, *Electronic Literature: New Horizons for the Literary* (Notre Dame University Press, 2008), provides a survey of the "state of electronic literature" as it existed in the mid-2000s and remains today one of the seminal works of the field. She describes e-lit as "'digital born,' a first-generation digital object created on a computer and (usually) meant to be read on a computer" (Hayles). Today we expand this description to include works such as Erik Loyer's *Strange Rain*, Jody Zellen's "Spine Sonnets," and Jason Edward Lewis' *P.o.E.M.M.*, produced for access on mobile devices. In the nine years following the publication of the essay, scholarship by Jill Walker Rettberg, Belinda Barnet, Alice Bell, Leonardo Flores, Matthew Kirschenbaum, Jessica Pressman, Lori Emerson, and Noah Wardrip-Fruin, among others, has added to our knowledge of the form. A suggested list of readings by these and other scholars follows this essay.

The second essay included in this volume, "Electronic Literature: Where Is It?," was published in 2008 by the *Electronic Book Review* as a response to an essay written by journalist Andrew Gallix, entitled "Is E-Literature Just One Big Anti-Climax?" I had previously been interviewed by Gallix for his essay and was surprised, upon reading it, that he had misquoted me and made the claim that e-lit was "dead" (Gallix). My essay lays out four major misconceptions found in his argument. In doing so, it was intended to work in conjunction with Hayles' essay by issuing a call to action to "bring elit to the classroom, to help promote it in the contemporary literary scene, and support artists who produce it so that it can foster and bolster literary sensibilities and literacies of future generations" (Grigar).

Since the publication of my essay, e-lit has been featured in exhibits at the Library of Congress (2013), at three annual meetings of the Modern Language Association (2012, 2013, 2014), the Digital Humanities Summer Institute (2014), and the International Society on Electronic Art (2015); plans are currently underway by the ELO to develop K-12 curricula for teaching e-lit in schools, and e-lit is now more commonly addressed in higher education classrooms than it previously had been when Gallix published his polemic; the ELO's digital preservation of early e-lit efforts has continued and has been funded by the NEH; international efforts to make databases accessible to the public have been successful; and conferences and festivals featuring e-lit have taken place in Paris, Bergen, NYC, and other cities in Europe, the US and beyond.

REFERENCES

Barnet, Belinda. *Memory Machines: The Evolution of Hypertext*. London: Anthem Press, 2013.

Bell, Alice. *The Possible Worlds of Hypertext Fiction*. New York: Palgrave Macmillan, 2010.

Emerson, Lori. *Reading Writing Interfaces: From the Digital to the Bookbound*. Minneapolis: University of Minnesota Press, 2014.

Funkhouser, C. T. *Prehistoric Digital Poetry: An Archaeology of Forms, 1959–1995*. Tuscaloosa: University Alabama Press, 2007.

Hayles, N. Katherine. *Electronic Literature: New Horizons of the Literary*. South Bend, IN: Notre Dame University Press, 2008.

Kirschenbaum, Matthew. *Mechanisms: New Media and the Forensic Imagination*. Cambridge, MA: The MIT Press, 2008.

Pressman, Jessica, Mark Marino, and Jeremy Douglass. *Reading Project: A Collaborative Analysis of William Poundstone's Project for Tachistoscope {Bottomless Pit}*. Iowa City: University of Iowa Press, 2015.

Rettberg, Scott. "Developing an Identity for the Field of Electronic Literature: Reflections on the Electronic Literature Organization Archives." *Dichtung Digital* 41. September 2012. www.dichtung-digital.org/2012/41/rettberg/rettberg.htm (accessed 7 November 2015).

Walker Rettberg, Jill. "Electronic Literature Seen from a Distance: The Beginnings of a Field." *Dichtung Digital*. 41 5. September 2012. www.dichtung-digital.org/2012/41/walker-rettberg/walker-rettberg.htm (accessed 12 July 2015).

Wardrip-Fruin, Noah. "Christopher Strachey: The First Digital Artist?" *Grand Text Auto*. 1 August 2005. https://grandtextauto.soe.ucsc.edu/2005/08/01/christopher-strachey-first-digital-artist/ (accessed 14 August 2015).

Wardrip-Fruin, Noah. *Expressive Processing: Digital Fictions, Computer Games, and Software Studies*. Cambridge, MA: The MIT Press, 2009.

Collections of artistic works

Anthology of European Electronic Literature. ELMCIP. http://anthology.elmcip.net (accessed 7 November 2015)

Electronic Literature Collection 1. Electronic Literature Organization. http://collection.eliterature.org/1/ (accessed 7 November 2015).

Electronic Literature Collection 2. Electronic Literature Organization. http://collection.eliterature.org/2/ (accessed 7 November 2015).

Electronic Literature Collection 3. Electronic Literature Organization.

Flores, Leonardo. *I ♥ E-Poetry*. http://iloveepoetry.com (accessed 7 November 2015).

FURTHER READING

Berens, Kathi Inman. "Judy Malloy's Seat at the (Database) Table: A Feminist Reception History of Early Hypertext Literature." *Literary & Linguistic Computing* 29.3 (2014): 340–348.

Cayley, John. "Weapons Of The Deconstructive Masses: Whatever the *Electronic* in *Electronic Literature* May or May Not Mean." *Hyperrhiz* (Summer 2009). http://hyperrhiz.io/hyperrhiz06/essays/weapons-of-the-deconstructive-masses.html (accessed 14 August 2015).

Ensslin, Astrid. *Canonizing Hypertext: Explorations and Constructions*. London: Bloomsbury Press, 2007.

Ensslin, Astrid. *Literary Gaming*. Cambridge, MA: The MIT Press, 2014.

Funkhouser, C. T. *New Directions in Digital Poetry*. New York, NY: Continuum Press, 2012.

Grigar, Dene. "The Present [Future] of Electronic Literature." *Transdisciplinary Digital Art: Sound, Vision and the New Screen*. Ed. Randy Adams, Steve Gibson and Stefan Muller. Heidelberg, Germany: Springer-Verlag Publications, 2008. 127–142.

Grigar, Dene. "Curating Electronic Literature as Critical and Scholarly Practice." *Digital Humanities Quarterly* (8.4) 2015.

Grigar, Dene. "Electronic Literature: Where Is It?" *Electronic Book Review*. Translated into Italian and reprinted at *Group Giada*. 2015. www.gruppogiada.it/dene-grigar-la-elit-dove-e/ (accessed 28 November 2015).

Grigar, Dene and Stuart Moulthrop. *Pathfinders: Documenting the Experience of Early Digital Literature*. 1 June 2015. http://scalar.usc.edu/works/pathfinders (accessed 17 July 2015).

Hayles, N. Katherine. "Flickering Connectivities in Shelley Jackson's *Patchwork Girl*: The Importance of Media-Specific Analysis." *Postmodern Culture* 10.2 (2000). http://pmc.iath.virginia.edu/text-only/issue.100/10.2hayles.txt (accessed 15 August 2015).

Hayles, N. Katherine. *Writing Machines*. Cambridge, MA: The MIT Press, 2002.

Hayles, N. Katherine. "Print is Flat, Code is Deep: The Importance of Media-Specific Analysis." *Poetics Today* 25.1 (2004): 67–90.

Moulthrop, Stuart. "For Thee: A Response to Alice Bell's *Possible Worlds of Hypertext Fiction*." *Electronic Book Review*, 01–21–2011. www.electronicbookreview.com/thread/electropoetics/networked (accessed 15 August 2015).

Salter, Anastasia. *What Is Your Quest?: From Adventure Games to Interactive Books*. Iowa City: University of Iowa Press, 2014.

Sample, Mark. "House of Leaves of Grass." *Fugitivetexts*. http://fugitivetexts.net/houseleavesgrass/ (accessed 14 August 2015).

CHAPTER 12A

Electronic literature

What is it?

N. Katherine Hayles

A CONTEXT FOR ELECTRONIC LITERATURE

> The Scriptorium was in turmoil. Brother Paul, the precentor in charge, had detected a murmur from the back row and, furious that the rule of silence was being compromised, strode down the aisle just in time to see Brother Jacob tuck something under his robe. When he demanded to see it, Brother Jacob shamefacedly produced a codex, but not one that the antiquarii of this monastery had copied – or of any monastery, for this Psalter was printed. Shocked as much by the sight of the mechanical type as Brother Jacob's transgression, Brother Paul so far forgot himself that he too broke the silence, thundering that if books could be produced by fast, cheap and mechanical means, their value as precious artifacts would be compromised. Moreover, if any Thomas, Richard or Harold could find his way into print, would not writing itself be compromised and become commonplace scribbling? And how would the spread of cheap printed materials affect the culture of the Word, bringing scribbling into every hut and hovel whose occupants had hitherto relied on priests to interpret writing for them? The questions hung in the air; none dared imagine what answers the passing of time would bring.

This fanciful scenario is meant to suggest that the place of writing is again in turmoil, roiled now not by the invention of print books but the emergence of electronic literature. Just as the history of print literature is deeply bound up with the evolution of book technology as it built on wave after wave of technical innovations, so the history of electronic literature is entwined with the evolution of digital computers as they shrank from the room-sized IBM 1401 machine on which I first learned to program (sporting all of 4K memory) to the networked machine on my desktop, thousands of times more powerful and able to access massive amounts of information from around the globe. The questions that troubled the Scriptorium are remarkably similar to issues debated today within literary communities. Is electronic literature really literature at all? Will the dissemination mechanisms of the Internet and World Wide Web, by opening publication to everyone, result in a flood of worthless drivel? Is literary quality possible in digital media, or is electronic literature demonstrably inferior to the print canon? What large-scale social and cultural changes are bound up with the spread of digital culture, and what do they portend for the future of writing?[1]

These questions cannot be answered without first considering the contexts that give them meaning and significance, and that implies a wide-ranging exploration of what electronic literature is, how it overlaps and diverges from print, what signifying strategies characterize it, and how these strategies are interpreted by users as they go in search of meaning. In brief, one cannot begin to answer the questions unless one has first thoroughly explored and understood the specificities of digital media. To see electronic literature only through the lens of print is, in a significant sense, not to see it at all. This essay aims to provide (some of) the context that will open the field of inquiry so that electronic literature can be understood as both partaking of literary tradition and introducing crucial transformations that redefine what literature is.

Electronic literature, generally considered to exclude print literature that has been digitized, is by contrast "digital born," a first-generation digital object created on a computer and (usually) meant to be read on a computer. The Electronic Literature Organization, whose mission is to "promote the writing, publishing, and reading of literature in electronic media," convened a committee headed by Noah Wardrip-Fruin, himself a creator and critic of electronic literature, to come up with a definition appropriate to this new field. The committee's choice was framed to include both work performed in digital media and work created on a computer but published in print (as, for example, was Brian Kim Stefans's computer-generated poem "Stops and Rebels"). The committee's formulation: "work with an important literary aspect that takes advantage of the capabilities and contexts provided by the stand-alone or networked computer."

As the committee points out, this definition raises questions about which capabilities and contexts of the computer are significant, directing attention not only toward the changing nature of computers but also the new and different ways in which the literary community mobilizes these capabilities. The definition is also slightly tautological, in that it assumes pre-existing knowledge of what constitutes an "important literary aspect." Although tautology is usually regarded by definition writers with all the gusto evoked by rat poison, in this case the tautology seems appropriate, for electronic literature arrives on the scene after five hundred years of print literature (and, of course, even longer manuscript and oral traditions). Readers come to digital work with expectations formed by print, including extensive and deep tacit knowledge of letter forms, print conventions, and print literary modes. Of necessity, electronic literature must build on these expectations even as it modifies and transforms them. At the same time, because electronic literature is normally created and performed within a context of networked and programmable media, it is also informed by the powerhouses of contemporary culture, particularly computer games, films, animations, digital arts, graphic design, and electronic visual culture. In this sense electronic literature is a "hopeful monster" (as geneticists call adaptive mutations) composed of parts taken from diverse traditions that may not always fit neatly together. Hybrid by nature, it comprises a trading zone (as Peter Galison calls it in a different context) in which different vocabularies, expertises, and expectations come together to see what might come from their intercourse.[2] Electronic literature tests the boundaries of the literary and challenges us to re-think our assumptions of what literature can do and be.

GENRES OF ELECTRONIC LITERATURE

In the contemporary era, both print and electronic texts are deeply interpenetrated by code. Digital technologies are now so thoroughly integrated with commercial printing processes that print is more properly considered a particular output form of electronic text than an entirely separate medium. Nevertheless, electronic text remains distinct from print in that it literally cannot be accessed until it is performed by properly executed code. The immediacy of code to the text's performance is fundamental to understanding electronic literature, especially to appreciating its specificity as a literary and technical production. Major genres in the canon of electronic literature emerge not only from different ways in which the user experiences them but also from the structure and specificity of the underlying code. Not surprisingly, then, some genres have come to be known by the software used to create and perform them.

The varieties of electronic literature are richly diverse, spanning all the types associated with print literature and adding some genres unique to networked and programmable media. Readers with only a slight familiarity with the field, however, will probably identify it first with hypertext fiction characterized by linking structures, such as Michael Joyce's *afternoon: a story*,[3] Stuart Moulthrop's *Victory Garden*,[4] and Shelley Jackson's *Patchwork Girl*.[5] These works are written in Storyspace, the hypertext authoring program first created by Michael Joyce, Jay David Bolter, and John B. Smith and then licensed to Mark Bernstein of Eastgate Systems, who has improved, extended, and maintained it. So important was this software, especially to the early development of the field, that works created in it have come to be known as the Storyspace school. Intended as stand-alone objects, Storyspace works are usually distributed as CDs (earlier as disks) for Macintosh or PC platforms and, more recently, in cross-platform versions. Along with Macintosh's Hypercard, it was the program of choice for many major writers of electronic literature in the late 1980s and 1990s. As the World Wide Web developed, new authoring programs and methods of dissemination became available. The limitations of Storyspace as a Web authoring program are significant (for example, it has a very limited palette of colors and cannot handle sound files that will play on the Web). Although Storyspace continues to be used to produce interesting new works, it has consequently been eclipsed as the primary Web authoring tool for electronic literature.

With the movement to the Web, the nature of electronic literature changed as well. Whereas early works tended to be blocks of text (traditionally called lexia)[6] with limited graphics, animation, colors, and sound, later works make much fuller use of the multi-modal capabilities of the Web; while the hypertext link is considered the distinguishing feature of the earlier works, later works use a wide variety of navigation schemes and interface metaphors that tend to de-emphasize the link as such. In my keynote speech at the 2002 Electronic Literature Symposium at UCLA, these distinctions led me to call the early works "first-generation" and the later ones "second-generation," with the break coming around 1995.[7] To avoid the implication that first-generation works are somehow superseded by later aesthetics, it may be more appropriate to call the early works "classical," analogous to the periodization of early films.[8] Shelley Jackson's important and impressive *Patchwork Girl* can stand as an appropriate culminating work for the classical period. The later period might be called contemporary or postmodern (at least until it too appears to reach some kind of culmination and a new phase appears).

As the varieties of electronic literature expanded, hypertext fictions also mutated into a range of hybrid forms, including narratives that emerge from a collection of data repositories such as M. D. Coverley's *Califia* and her new work *Egypt: The Book of Going Forth by Day*[9]; the picaresque hypertext *The Unknown* by Dirk Stratton, Scott Rettberg, and William Gillespie, reminiscent in its aesthetic of excess to Kerouac's *On the Road*[10]; Michael Joyce's elegantly choreographed Storyspace work, *Twelve Blue*, disseminated on the Web through the Eastgate Hypertext Reading Room[11]; Caitlin Fisher's *These Waves of Girls*, including sound, spoken text, animated text, graphics, and other functionalities in a networked linking structure[12]; Stuart Moulthrop's multimodal work *Reagan Library*, featuring QuickTime movies with random text generation[13]; *The Jew's Daughter* by Judd Morrissey in collaboration with Lori Talley, with its novel interface of a single screen of text in which some passages are replaced as the reader mouses over them[14]; Talan Memmott's brilliantly designed and programmed *Lexia to Perplexia*[15]; and Richard Holeton's parodic *Frequently Asked Questions about Hypertext*, which in Nabokovian fashion evolves a narrative from supposed annotations to a poem[16], along with a host of others. To describe these and similar works, David Ciccoricco introduces the useful term "network fiction," defining it as digital fiction that "makes use of hypertext technology in order to create emergent and recombinatory narratives."[17]

Interactive fiction (IF) differs from the works mentioned above in having stronger game elements.[18] The demarcation between electronic literature and computer games is far from clear; many games have narrative components, while many works of electronic literature have game elements. (As a pair of mirror phrases in

Moulthrop's *Reagan Library* puts it, "This is not a game" and "This is not not a game.") Nevertheless, there is a general difference in emphasis between the two forms. Paraphrasing Markku Eskelinen's elegant formulation, we may say that with games the user interprets in order to configure, whereas in works whose primary interest is narrative, the user configures in order to interpret.[19] Since interactive fiction cannot proceed without input from the user, Nick Monfort in *Twisty Little Passages: An Approach to Interactive Fiction*, the first book-length scholarly study of IF, prefers the term "interactor."[20] In this pioneering study, Montfort characterizes the essential elements of the form as consisting of a parser (the computer program that understands and replies to the interactor's inputs) and a simulated world within which the action takes place. The interactor controls a player character by issuing commands. Instructions to the program, for example asking it to quit, are called directives. The program issues replies (when the output refers to the player character) and reports (responses directed to the interactor, asking for example if she is sure she wants to quit).

Alternating gameplay with novelistic components, interactive fictions expand the repertoire of the literary through a variety of techniques, including visual displays, graphics, animations, and clever modifications of traditional literary devices. In Emily Short's *Savoir-Faire*, for example, solving many of the IF puzzles requires the user to make a leap of inference from one device to another that resembles it in function; for example, if a door and box are properly linked, opening the box also opens the door, which otherwise will not yield.[21] Such moves resemble the operation of literary metaphor, although here the commonality is routed not through verbal comparison of two objects but rather functional similarities combined with the player character's actions – a kind of embodied metaphor, if you will. In subtle ways, IF can also engage in self-referential commentary and critique. In Jon Ingold's *All Roads*, the player character is a teleporting assassin, William DeLosa, over whom the interactor discovers she has minimal control.[22] The allusion evoked by the title ("all roads lead to Rome") suggests that the imperial power here is the author's power to determine what the interactor will experience. The player character's vocation can thus be interpreted to imply that the meta-textual object of assassination is the illusion that hypertext is synonymous with democracy and user empowerment.

Donna Leishman spins a variant of interactive fictions in her work, where the visual interface invites game-like play but without the reward structure built into most interactive fictions. Her striking visual style, exemplified by *The Possession of Christian Shaw*, combines primitivism with a sophisticated visual sensibility, contemporary landscapes with a narrative originating in the seventeenth century.[23] Rather than striving to progress by solving various puzzles and mysteries, the interactor discovers that the goal is not reaching the end (although there is a final screen providing historical context for the visual narrative) but rather the journey itself. The literariness (as distinct from the gaming aspect) is instantiated in the work's dynamics, which are structured to project the interactor inside the troubled interior world of Christian Shaw. With no clear demarcation between Christian's perceptions and exterior events, the work deconstructs the boundary between subjective perception and verifiable fact.

While works such as *The Possession of Christian Shaw* use perspective to create the impression of a three-dimensional space, the image itself does not incorporate the possibility of mobile interactivity along the Z-axis. The exploration of the Z-axis as an additional dimension for text display, behavior, and manipulation has catalyzed innovative work by artists such as David Knoebel, Ted Warnell, Aya Karpinska, Charles Baldwin, Dan Waber, and John Cayley. In a special issue of *The Iowa Review Web* guest-edited by Rita Raley,[24] these artists comment on their work and the transformative impact of the Z-axis. One need only recall Edward Abbott's *Flatland* to imagine how, as text leaps from the flat plane of the page to the interactive space of the screen, new possibilities emerge.[25] One kind of strategy, evident in Ted Warnell's intricately programmed JavaScript work, *TLT vs. LL*, is to move from the word as the unit of signification to the letter. The letters are taken from email correspondence with Thomas Lowe Taylor and Lewis Lacook (the sources for TLT and LL), with the "versus" indicating contestations translated in the work from the level of semantic content to dynamic interplay between visual forms. In "Artist's Statement: Ted Warnell," he comments that the breakthrough for him was thinking of the "versus" as "taking the form of 'rising' (coming to top/front) rather than 'pushing' (as if it were) from left/right."[26] Consequently, the emphasis shifts to a dynamic surface in which rising and sinking motions give the effect of three dimensions as the layered letter forms shift, move, and reposition themselves relative to other letters, creating a mesmerizing, constantly mutating dance of competing and cooperating visual shapes.[27] David Knoebel's exquisitely choreographed "Heart Pole," from his collection "Click Poetry," features a circular globe of words, with two rings spinning at ninety degrees from one another, "moment to moment" and "mind absorbing." A longer narrative sequence, imaged as a plane undulating in space, can be manipulated by clicking and dragging. The narrative, focalized through the memories of a third-person male persona, recalls the moment between waking and sleeping when the narrator's mother is singing him to sleep with a song composed of his day's activities. But like the slippery plane that shifts in and out of legibility as it twists and turns, this moment of intimacy is irrevocably lost to time, forming the "heart pole" that registers both its evocation and the on-goingness that condemns even the most deeply-seated experiences to loss.[28]

The next move is to go from imaging three dimensions interactively on the screen to immersion in actual three-dimensional spaces. As computers have moved out of the desktop and into the environment, other varieties of electronic literature have emerged. Whereas in the 1990s email novels were popular, the last decade has seen the rise of forms dependent on mobile technologies, from short fiction delivered serially over cell phones to location-specific narratives keyed to GPS technologies, often called locative narratives. In Janet Cardiff's *The Missing Voice (Case Study B)* (1996), for example, the user heard a CD played on a Walkman keyed to locations in London's inner city, tracing a route that takes about forty-five minutes to complete; *Her Long Black Hair* was specific to New York City's Central Park and included photographs as well as audio narratives.[29] Blast Theory's *Uncle Roy All Around You* combined a game-like search for Uncle Roy, delivered over PDAs, with participants searching for a postcard hidden at a specific location.[30] Meanwhile, online observers could track participants and try to help or confuse them, thus mixing virtual reality with actual movements through urban spaces.

The complements to site-specific mobile works, which foreground the user's ability to integrate real-world locations with virtual narratives, are site-specific installations in which the locale is stationary, such as a CAVE virtual reality projection room or gallery site. In their specificity and lack of portability such works are reminiscent of digital art works, although in their emphasis on literary texts and narrative constructions, they can easily be seen as a species of electronic literature. Like the boundary between computer games and electronic literature, the demarcation between digital art and electronic literature is shifty at best, often more a matter of the critical traditions from which the works are discussed than anything intrinsic to the works themselves.[31]

Pioneering the CAVE as a site for interactive literature is the creative writing program at Brown University spearheaded by Robert Coover, himself an internationally known writer of experimental literature. At the invitation of Coover, a number of writers have come to Brown to create works for the CAVE, including John Cayley, Talan Memmott, Noah Wardrip-Fruin, and William Gillespie. Works produced there include Cayley's *Torus* (2005) in collaboration with Dmitri Lemmerman, Memmott's *"E_cephalopedia//novellex"* (2002), Noah Wardrip-Fruin's *Screen* with Josh Carroll, Robert Coover, Shawn Greenlee, and Andrew McClain (2003)[32], and William Gillespie's *Word Museum* with programming by Jason Rodriguez and David Dao.[33] Performed in a three-dimensional space in which the user wears virtual reality goggles and manipulates a wand, these works enact literature not as a durably imprinted page but as a full-body experience that includes haptic, kinetic, proprioceptive, and dimensional perceptions.[34] The enhanced sensory range that these works address is not without cost. CAVE equipment, costing upward of a million dollars and depending on an array of powerful networked computers and other equipment, is typically found only in Research 1 universities and other elite research sites. Because of the high initial investment and continuing programming and maintenance costs, it is usually funded by grants to scientists. Of the few institutions that have this high-tech resource, even fewer are willing to allocate precious time and computational resources to creative writers. Literature created for this kind of environment will therefore likely be experienced in its full implementation only by relatively few users (although some idea of the works can be gained from the QuickTime documentation that Cayley and others have created for their CAVE pieces), thus sacrificing the portability, low cost, robust durability, and mass distribution that made print literature a transformative social and cultural force.[35] Nevertheless, as conceptual art pushing the boundary of what literature can be, this kind of coterie electronic literature has an impact beyond the technology's limitations. Moreover, the Brown programming team has recently developed a spatial hypertext authoring system that allows authors to create and edit their works using a representation of the CAVE on their laptops, with capabilities to link text, images, 3-D photographs and videos, and 3-models.[36] This development could potentially be used not only to create but also to view CAVE works. Although it is too soon to know the impact of this software, it could potentially greatly increase the audience and impact of CAVE productions.

Like the CAVE productions, interactive dramas are also site-specific, performed with live audiences in gallery spaces in combination with present and/or remote actors. Often the dramas proceed with a general script outlining the characters and the initiating action (sometimes the final outcome will also be specified), leaving the actors to improvise the intervening action and plot events. In a variation on this procedure, M. D. Coverley coordinated *M is for Nottingham* as a trAce project in July, 2002. Writers, including Coverley and Kate Pullinger, joined in collaborative writing at a Web site preceding the Incubation 2 Conference in Nottingham, riffing on the murder mystery genre to create a story revolving around the "death" of the book. During the conference the denouement was acted out by volunteers in costume, thus adding a component of live dramatic production. At SIGGRAPH 2006, *Unheimlich*, a collaborative telematic performance created by Paul Sermon, Steven Dixon, Mathias Fucs, and Andrea Zapp, was performed, mixing audience volunteers (among them the media artist Bill Seaman) placed against a bluescreen background on which were projected images of actors improvising at a remote location.[37] Mixing the virtual and the real within a loose dramatic framework, *Unheimlich* created a borderland that encouraged playful innovation and improvisational collaboration.

Interactive drama can also be performed online. Michael Mateas and Andrew Stern's *Façade* (2005) has a graphical interface and is programmed in a language they devised called ABL (A Behavior Language), which structures the action into "beats."[38] The drama situates the user as a dinner guest of a couple, Grace and Trip, celebrating their tenth wedding anniversary. Although the couple appears prosperous and happy, in *Who's Afraid of Virginia Woolf* fashion, cracks soon develop in the façade. The user can intervene in various ways, but all paths lead to an explosion at the end, a programming choice that maintains intact the Aristotelian plot shape of a beginning, middle, and end.

How to maintain such conventional narrative devices as rising tension, conflict, and denouement in interactive forms where the user determines sequence continues to pose formidable problems for writers of electronic literature, especially narrative fiction. Janet Murray's entertaining and insightful *Hamlet on the Holodeck: The Future of Narrative in Cyberspace* was one of the first critical studies to explore this issue in depth, surveying a wide variety of forms, including hypertext fiction, computer games, and interactive drama. With her usual acuity, she accurately diagnoses both sides of the question. "Giving the audience access to the raw materials of creation runs the risk of undermining the narrative experience," she writes, while still acknowledging that "calling attention to the process of creation can also enhance the narrative involvement by inviting readers/viewers to imagine themselves in the place of the creator."[39] Marie-Laure Ryan, in *Avatars of Story*,[40] pioneers a transmedial approach to narrative that seeks to construct a comprehensive framework for narrative in all media, consisting of simulative, emergent, and participatory models. She further constructs a taxonomy for narratives specifically in New Media that takes into account textual architecture and the actions and positions of the user, which she types as three binaries describing interactivity: internal/external, exploratory/ontological, and external/exploratory. Like Murray, she notes the tension between the top-down approach to narrative in which the narrator spins a story, and the bottom-up model of interactivity where the user chooses how the story will be told.

The response to this tension in electronic literature has been a burst of innovation and experimentation, with solutions ranging from the guard fields of classic Storyspace works (in which certain conditions must be met before a user can access a given lexia) to the Aristotelian constraints of *Façade*. Even where multiple reading pathways exist, many interactive works still guide the user to a clear sense of conclusion and resolution, such as Deena Larsen's *Disappearing Rain*[41] and M. D. Coverley's *Califia*. Nevertheless, the constraints and possibilities of the medium have encouraged many writers to turn to non-narrative forms or to experiment with forms in which narratives are combined with randomizing algorithms.

An important spokesperson for these approaches is Loss Pequeño Glazier, a poet and critic who has established the Electronic Poetry Center, which along with Kenneth Goldsmith's Ubuweb is one of the premier online sites for electronic poetry on the Web.[42] In his book *Digital Poetics: Hypertext, Visual-Kinetic Text and Writing in Programmable Media*, Glazier argues that electronic literature is best understood as a continuation of experimental print literature.[43] In his view, the medium lends itself to experimental practice, especially to forms that disrupt traditional notions of stable subjectivities and ego-centered discourses. Although he under-estimates the ways in which narrative forms can also be disruptive, he nevertheless makes a strong case for electronic literature as an experimental practice grounded in the materiality of the medium. Moreover, he practices what he preaches. For example, his *White-Faced Bromeliads on 20 Hectares*[44] uses JavaScript to investigate literary variants, with new text generated every ten seconds. The procedure disrupts narrative poetic lines with disjunctive juxtapositions that derail the line midway through, resulting in suggestive couplings and a sense of dynamic interplay between the prescripted lines and the operations of the algorithm. The combination of English and Spanish vocabularies and the gorgeous images from Latin American locations further suggest compelling connections between the spread of networked and programmable media and the transnational politics in which other languages contest and cooperate with English's hegemonic position in programming languages and, arguably, in digital art as well.

Generative art, whereby an algorithm is used either to generate texts according to a randomized scheme or to scramble and rearrange pre-existing texts, is currently one of the most innovative and robust categories of electronic literature.[45] Philippe Bootz has powerfully theorized generative texts, along with other varieties of electronic literature, in his functional model, which makes clear distinctions between the writer's field, the text's field, and the reader's field, pointing out several important implications inherent in the separation between these fields, including the fact that electronic literature introduces temporal and logical divisions between the writer and reader different from those enforced by print.[46] Bootz also usefully points out that in a European context, hypertext has not been the dominant mode but rather textual generators and animated works, citing particularly the group of writers associated with ALAMO (Atelier de Littérature Assistee par le Mathematique et les Ordinateurs, or Workshop of Literature Assisted by Mathematics and Computers), which includes among others Jean-Pierre Balpe, and the group with which he is associated, LAIRE (Lecture, Art, Innovation, Recherche, Écriture, or Reading, Art, Innovation, Research, Writing).[47] Bootz has pioneered many seminal works of generative and animated literature dating from the 1980's, including recently *La série des U (The Set of U)*[48], an elegant poem with text, pictures, and programming by Bootz and music by Marcel Frémiot. The work generates a different text-that-is-seen (texte-à-voir) each time it is played through subtle variations in the timing at which the textual elements appear and the relation between the verbal text and the sonic component, which is not directly synchronized with the words but nevertheless gives the serendipitous impression of coordination through programmed meta-rules.

American explorations of generative text include Noah Wardrip-Fruin's *Regime Change* and *News Reader*, created in collaboration with David Durand, Brion Moss, and Elaine Froehlich, works that Wardrip-Fruin calls "textual instruments" (a designation to which we will return). Both pieces begin with news stories (for *Regime Change*, President Bush's claim that Saddam Hussein had been killed, and for *News Reader*, the headlined stories in Yahoo.com), then employ the n-gram technique pioneered by Claude Shannon to find similar strings in the source and target documents, using them as bridges to splice together the two texts.[49] Naming such works "instruments" implies that one can learn to play them, gaining expertise as experience yields an intuitive understanding of how the algorithm works. Other randomizing algorithms are used by Jim Andrews in works such as *On Lionel Kearns*,[50] which splices extracts from the poems of Canadian writer Lionel Kearns to create scrambled texts, accompanied by amusing and effective visualizations that function as interpretations of Kearns' work. As Andrews, Kearns, and Wardrip-Fruin acknowledge, these works are indebted to William Burroughs's notion of the "cut-up" and "fold-in." They cite as theoretical precedent Burroughs's idea that randomization is a way to break the hold of the viral word and liberate resistances latent in language by freeing it from linear syntax and coherent narrative.[51] Other notable instances of randomizing works are Jim Andrews's *Stir Fry Texts*, in which collaborators used Andrews's "Stir Fry" algorithm to randomize their texts[52]; *When*

You Reach Kyoto, a visual/verbal collaboration by Geniwate and Brian Kim Stefans[53]; Millie Niss and Martha Deed's *Oulipoems*[54]; and Patrick-Henri Burgaud's *Jean-Pierre Balpe ou les Lettres Dérangées*, a tribute to poet and software developer Jean-Pierre Balpe (a pioneer in text generation algorithms) in which the work performs as a textual instrument that the user can manipulate.[55] If tenacious (and lucky), the user will find the "deranged" letters becoming coherent at the end, where "this is not the end" appears across Balpe's bibliography.

Just as the twentieth century saw an explosion of interest in the book as a medium, with an impressive canon of artists' books and other experimental practices exploring the potential of the book as an artistic and literary venue, so electronic literature has seen a growing body of work that interrogates networked and programmable media as the material basis for artistic innovation and creation. "Code work," a phrase associated with such writers as Alan Sondheim, MEZ (Mary Ann Breeze), and Talan Memmott and critics such as Florian Cramer, Rita Raley, and Matthew Fuller, names a linguistic practice in which English (or some other natural language) is hybridized with programming expressions to create a creole evocative for human readers, especially those familiar with the denotations of programming languages. "Code work" in its purest form is machine-readable and executable, such as Perl poems that literally have two addressees, humans and intelligent machines. More typical are creoles using "broken code," code that cannot actually be executed but that uses programming punctuation and expressions to evoke connotations appropriate to the linguistic signifiers.[56] Replete with puns, neologisms, and other creative play, such work enacts a trading zone in which human-only language and machine-readable code are performed as interpenetrating linguistic realms, thus making visible on the screenic surface a condition intrinsic to all electronic textuality, namely the intermediating dynamics between human-only languages and machine-readable code.[57] By implication, such works also reference the complex hybridization now underway between human cognition and the very different and yet interlinked cognitions of intelligent machines, a condition that Talan Memmott has brilliantly evoked in *Lexia to Perplexia* with neologisms such as "remotional" and "I-terminal ."

The conjunction of language with code has stimulated experiments in the formation and collaboration of different kinds of languages. Diane Reed Slattery, Daniel J. O'Neil, and Bill Brubaker's *The Glide Project* enacts the visual language of Glide, which can be seen and performed as gestures in a dance but cannot be spoken because the semicircular shapes comprising it have no verbal equivalents, only clusters of denotations, functioning in this respect somewhat like ideographic languages.[58] Other experiments traversing the borderland between gestural and verbal languages have been performed by Sha Xin Wei and collaborators in *TGarden*,[59] where virtual reality technologies are used to record the movements of dancers as they attempt to create new gestural vocabularies, a topic brilliantly explored by Carrie Noland in "Digital Gestures" analyzing digital works that evoke embodied gestures.[60] Such experiments in multiple and interrelated semiotic systems are both enabled by and reflective of the underlying fact that behaviors, actions, sounds, words, and images are all encoded as bits and ultimately as voltage differences. Another kind of interrogation of the conjunction between code and language has been explored by John Cayley through procedures that he calls "transliteral morphing," algorithms that transform source texts into target words letter by letter, a strategy that emphasizes the discreteness of alphabetic languages and its similarities to the discreteness of digital code.[61] In *riverIsland*, Cayley uses transliteral morphing to juxtapose different translations of Chinese poems, comparing and contrasting the discreteness of alphabetic languages with the more analogue forms of Chinese morphographic language systems.[62]

The multimodality of digital art works challenges writers, users, and critics to bring together diverse expertise and interpretive traditions to understand fully the aesthetic strategies and possibilities of electronic literature. Some writers, for example Thom Swiss, prefer to find graphic artists as collaborators. Others, such as Stephanie Strickland in her elegantly choreographed and playfully imagined hypertextual poem "The Ballad of Sand and Harry Soot," incorporate images by artists, including in this case the beautiful mechanized sand sculptures of Jean Pierre Hebert and Bruce Shapiro.[63] Still others who think of themselves as primarily graphic artists and programmers write texts to incorporate into their works; I would put Jason Nelson's playful and imaginative net art into this category, including his haunting *Dreamaphage*, with its bizarre narratives and childlike yet somehow ominous graphics.[64] Still others who come to digital media from backgrounds as print writers, such as M. D. Coverley, are on steep upward learning curves in which their visual and graphic sensibilities are rapidly becoming as accomplished as their verbal expertise (compare, for example, the design qualities of *Califia* with the stunning graphic design of *Egypt: The Book of Coming Forth by Day*). From a critical point of view, works that appear in both print and electronic instantiations, such as Stephanie Strickland's innovative poetry book *V: Wave Son.nets/Losing l'Una* and the Web work *V:Vniverse*, programmed in Director in collaboration with Cynthia Lawson, illustrate that when a work is reconceived to take advantage of the behavioral, visual, and/or sonic capabilities of the Web, the result is not just a Web "version" but an entirely different artistic production that should be evaluated in its own terms with a critical approach fully attentive to the specificity of the medium.[65] Moreover, in a few cases where the print and digital forms are conceptualized as one work distributed over two instantiations, as is the case with *V*, possibilities for emergent meanings multiply exponentially through the differences, overlaps, and convergences of the instantiations compared with one another. Other notable works that have appeared in different media instantiations include Lance Olsen's *10:01*, first published as a print hypertext and then transformed into a Web work in collaboration with Tim Guthrie,[66] and Geoff Ryman's *253*, which made the opposite transition from Web hypertext to print book.[67]

As such works make vividly clear, the computational media intrinsic to electronic textuality have necessitated new kinds of critical practice, a shift from literacy to what Gregory L. Ulmer calls "electracy."[68] The tendency of readers immersed in print is to focus first on the screenic text, employing strategies that have evolved over centuries through complex interactions between writers, readers, publishers, editors, booksellers, and other stakeholders in the print medium. For readers who do not themselves program in computational media, the seduction of reading the screen as a page is especially seductive. Although they are of course aware that the screen is not the same as print, the full implications of this difference for critical interpretation are far from obvious. Moreover, the shift from print to programmable media is further complicated by the fact that compositional practices themselves continue to evolve as the technology changes at a dizzying pace.

Among the critical voices exploring the new territories of networked and programmable media are many practitioner-critics whose astute observations have moved the field forward, including among others John Cayley, Loss Pequeño Glazier, Alan Sondheim, Brian Kim Stefans, and Stephanie Strickland.[69] Among those who work on the critical interpretation of electronic media, Ian Bogost, Wendy Hui Kyong Chun, Florian Cramer, Matthew Fuller, Mark B. N. Hansen, Matthew Kirschenbaum, Adalaide Morris, and Rita Raley deserve special mention for their insistence on the specificity of networked and programmable media.[70] At the same time, these critics also build bridges between digital art, literature, and games on the one hand, and traditional critical practice and philosophical writing on the other. In my view the optimal response requires both of these moves at once – recognizing the specificity of new media without abandoning the rich resources of traditional modes of understanding language, signification, and embodied interactions with texts.

Exemplifying this kind of critical practice is Matthew Kirschenbaum's *Mechanisms: New Media and Forensic Textuality*. Drawing an analogy with the scrutiny that bibliographers and textual critics lavish on print texts, Kirschenbaum argues that close examination of electronic objects is necessary fully to comprehend the implications of working with digital media. And look closely he does, all the way down to microscopic images of bit patterns on the disk substrate. He parses the materiality of digital media as consisting of two interrelated and interacting aspects: forensic materiality and formal materiality. Whereas forensic materiality is grounded in the physical properties of the hardware – how the computer writes and reads bit patterns, which in turn correlate to voltage differences – formal materiality consists of the "procedural friction or perceived difference . . . as the user shifts from one set of software logics to another" (27, ms). Using the important distinction that Espen J. Aarseth drew in *Cybertext: Perspectives on Ergodic Literature*[71] between scriptons ("strings as they appear to readers") and textons ("strings as they exist in the text") (62), Kirschenbaum pioneers in *Mechanisms* a methodology that connects the deep print-reading strategies already in effect with scriptons (letters on the page, in this instance) to the textons (here the code generating the screenic surface). He thus opens the way for a mode of criticism that recognizes the specificity of networked and programmable media without sacrificing the interpretive strategies evolved with and through print.

Stephanie Strickland, an award-winning print poet who has created significant work in digital media, has a keen sense both of literary tradition and of how criticism needs to change to accommodate digital media. In "Writing the Virtual: Eleven Dimensions of E-Poetry,"[72] she focuses on the ways in which E-poetry achieves dynamism, leading her to coin the neologism "poietics" (from "poetry" and "poiēsis," the Greek word for "making"). With succinct brilliance and a wide spectrum of examples, she emphasizes thematic emergences, such as the emphasis on ruins; new processes of user psychology, such as the "intense attachment" users experience at sites of interaction; and new configurations of physical parameters, such as the manifestation of time as "active, stratigraphic, and topologic," leading to the conclusion that time is "written multiply"[1]. Recombinant flux using computational writing engines and generators is part of this dynamism, reflecting a desire, she argues, to create works that instantiate in their operations the incredibly swift operations of code and the deterministic and yet aleatory operations of digital networks.

The intermixture of code and language on which recombinant flux depends is situated within a more general set of practices in which human thinking and machine execution collaborate to produce literary works that reference both cognitive modes. Any work that uses algorithmic randomizers to generate text relies to a greater or lesser extent on the surprising and occasionally witty juxtapositions created by these techniques. It should be noted that algorithmic procedures are not unique to networked and programmable media. Before personal computers became as ubiquitous as dust mites, writers in print media were using a variety of techniques to achieve similar results, as Florian Cramer points out in *Words Made Flesh: Code, Culture, Imagination*. Jim Rosenberg's *Diagram* series poems, for example, in which the user can manipulate shapes representing grammatical relationships such as verbs and conjunctions, were implemented first on paper and only later in computer code.[73] Other works using algorithmic procedures in print media include Raymond Queneau's *Cent mille milliards de poémes*, John Cage's mesostics, and Jackson Mac Low's *The Virginia Woolf Poems*.[74]

Brian Kim Stefans implicitly references this tradition when he published his computer poem "Stops and Rebels" in his print collection of essays, *Fashionable Noise: On Digital Poetics*, along with extensive annotations available only in the print version.[75] In these annotations, which amount to a hyperlinked essay, he meditates on the conjunction of human and machine cognition. He anthropomorphizes the computer program that generated the poem by calling it the "Demon." The Demon, he notes, is involved in a two-way collaboration: between the programmer who works with the limitations and possibilities of a computer language to create the program, and between the user and the computer when the computer poem is read and interpreted. Both collaborations invoke and enact the creative (mis)understandings and (mis)prisings that emerge from the overlaps and disjunctions between humans as meaning-seeking animals and intelligent machines for whom meaning has no meaning. This dimension of randomized electronic works makes them distinctively different from print works associated with algorithmic operations. A given work may, of course, ignore this specificity in its explicit textual content. Nevertheless, the conditions in which a work is created, produced, disseminated, and performed *always* mark it in distinctive ways that provide openings for critical interrogation and media-specific analysis, as Matthew Kirschenbaum decisively demonstrates in *Mechanisms: New Media and Forensic Textuality*.

The collaboration between the creative imagination of the (human) writer and the constraints and possibilities of software is the topic of Ian Bogost's *Unit Operations: An Approach to Videogame Criticism*, in which he develops an extended analogy between the unit operations of object-oriented programming and a literary approach that explores the open, flexible, and reconfigurable systems that emerge from the relations between units.[76] In a sense, literary criticism has long regarded print works as enacting these kinds of systems, infinitely reconfigurable as critical attention shifts focus from one kind of textual parsing to another. By re-describing traditional interpretations as "unit operations," Bogost is able to explore similarities between them and object-oriented programming, thus building a framework in which video games (his central focus), print literature, electronic literature, and computer programming can be seen as related and interpenetrating domains.

As Bogost's approach suggests, taking programming languages and practices into account can open productive approaches to electronic literature, as well as other digital and non-digital forms. The influence of software is especially obvious in the genre of the Flash poem, characterized by sequential screens that typically progress with minimal or no user intervention. (There are, however, exceptions to this practice, notably the Flash poem "Errand Upon Which We Came,"[77] a collaboration between Stephanie Strickland and M. D. Coverley in which the authors include on principle possibilities for user intervention and choice.) Brian Kim Stefans's "The Dreamlife of Letters,"[78] although highly unusual in its stunning virtuosity, is in this sense more typical. Asked to respond to a theoretically dense piece by Rachel Blau DuPlessis, Stefans liberated the words from their original context by alphabetizing them and parsing them into 36 groups. He then choreographed the groups with different behaviors in a tour de force of animation and visualization. The eleven-minute Flash work playfully brings out, in Concrete fashion, the implications and connotations of the sexually laden language of the original, as well as new implications that emerge from the juxtapositions created by the alphabetized text. As the letters and words dance, stretch, collapse, fall, conjoin, separate, seduce, and swirl, it is as though the morphemes and phonemes of language have themselves acquired an eroticized graphic imagination, a collective unconscious capable of feeling and expressing desire – that is to say, of dreaming. Robert Kendall's "Faith," although 180 degrees athwart from "The Dreamlife of Letters" in sensibility and theme, like Stefans' visual poem uses the computer's multimodal capabilities to create a work in which color, animation, music, and timed sequence collaborate with the verbal text to create signification.[79] The work proceeds in five stages (four of which are distinctly color-coded in orange, red, burgundy, and black/gray respectively), layering letters and words onto previously existing ones to create new meanings. For example, the orange "logic" from the first stage is interpolated in the second stage into "I edge/ logic/ out," with the new letters appearing in red; in the third stage, "edge" transforms into "hedge," with the new letter appearing in burgundy. As the words change position and become interpolated into new texts, they retain a hint of their previous significations through the colors that link them to their earlier appearances. The effect creates a palimpsest that visually performs the vacillations the lyric voice verbally articulates as it oscillates between logic and faith.

Young-hae Chang Heavy Industries (YHCHI), a Seoul-based collaboration between Young-hae Chang and Marc Voge, follows a different aesthetic strategy in creating Flash works where the emphasis falls mainly on the text, music, and timed sequence, with animation and color playing subsidiary roles. In "Dakota," for example, black text on a white background proceeds in rhythmic syncopation to the jazz music of Art Blakey, evoking both a Kerouac-like road trip and Ezra Pound's first two *Cantos*.[80] Jessica Pressman classifies this work as "digital modernism," a phrase describing electronic works that emphasize their connection with modernist print texts.[81] In YHCHI's "Nippon," a similar aesthetic strategy is used to narrate the story of a Japanese woman who entertains salarymen in an after-hours bar, with Japanese ideograms in red and English in black appearing on the successive screens, choreographed to a Japanese folk song by R. Taki.[82] The interplay here is especially complex, emerging not only from the rich ambiguities of each language in itself but also from the overlaps, tensions, and divergences between the two languages. In addition, the timed sequence rarely corresponds to a comfortable reading speed, either lingering too long or flashing by too quickly, so that the user is constantly aware of straining to decode the text. While alluding to print predecessors, this time-based work also performs its difference from a codex book in its rhythmic pace synchronized to the music tempo and operating outside the user's control.

Hypertext fiction, network fiction, interactive fiction, locative narratives, installation pieces, "codework," generative art, and the Flash poem are by no means an exhaustive inventory of the forms of electronic literature, but they are sufficient to illustrate the diversity of the field, the complex relations that emerge between print and electronic literature, and the wide spectrum of aesthetic strategies that digital literature employs. Having been a widely visible presence only for some two decades (although its predecessors stretch back at least to the computer poems of the early 1960s, and far beyond this in the print tradition), electronic literature has already produced many works of high literary merit that deserve and demand the close attention and rigorous scrutiny critics have long practiced with print literature. Such close critical attention requires new modes of analysis and new ways of teaching, interpreting, and playing. Most crucial, perhaps, is the necessity to "think digital," that is, to attend to the specificity of networked and programmable media while still drawing on the rich traditions of print literature and criticism.

ELECTRONIC LITERATURE IS NOT PRINT

Paying attention to the ways in which electronic literature both continues and disrupts print conventions is a neat trick, and the criticism is littered with those who have fallen prey to Scylla or Charybdis, ballyhooing its novelty or failing to see the genuine differences that make it distinctive from print. After a generation of spirited debate it is now possible to see the landscape more clearly, in part because we are able to build on the path-breaking work of those who came before. Early hypertext theorists, notably George Landow and Jay David Bolter,[83] stressed the importance of the hyperlink as electronic literature's distinguishing feature, extrapolating from the reader's ability to choose which link to follow to make extravagant claims about hypertext as a liberatory mode that would dramatically transform reading and writing and, by implication, settings where these activities are important, such as the literature classroom. Given the major works of electronic literature that then loomed large, particularly Michael Joyce's *afternoon: a story* and Stuart Moulthrop's *Victory Garden*, this emphasis was understandable, for these works consist mainly of screens of text with very limited graphics, no animation, and no sound.

One problem with identifying the hyperlink as electronic literature's distinguishing characteristic was that print texts had long also employed analogous technology in such apparati as footnotes, endnotes, cross-reference, and so on, undermining the claim that the technology was completely novel. Perhaps a more serious problem, however, was the association of the hyperlink with the empowerment of the reader/user. As a number of critics have pointed out, notably Espen J. Aarseth, the reader/user can only follow the links that the author has already scripted.[84] Moreover, in a work such as *afternoon: a story*, looping structures are employed from which there is no escape once the reader has fallen into them, short of closing the program and beginning again. Compared to the flexibility offered by the codex, which offers the reader complete freedom to skip around, go backwards as well as forwards, and open the book wherever she pleases, the looping structures of electronic hypertexts and the resulting repetition forced on the reader/user make these works by comparison more rather than less coercive. As Aarseth astutely observed, the vaulted freedom supposedly bestowed by interactivity "is a purely ideological term, projecting an unfocused fantasy rather than a concept of any analytical substance" (51).

A corollary to the emphasis on multiple reading paths was the connection Landow and Bolter forged between deconstruction and electronic literature. In the heady days when deconstruction was seen as a bold strike against foundational premises, hypertext was positioned as the commonsense implementation of the inherent instabilities in signification exposed by deconstructive analysis. Hypertext, Bolter wrote in his seminal book *Writing Space*, takes "the sting out of deconstruction."[85] In conflating hypertext with the difficult and productive aporias of deconstructive analysis, these theorists failed to do justice either to the nuanced operations of works performed in electronic media or to the complexities of deconstructive philosophy. Nevertheless, both theorists have made important contributions, and their books remain landmarks in the field. Moreover, both have significantly revised their earlier work to take into account the rapidly changing technology and additional insights it catalyzed. In the second edition of *Writing Space*, subtitled *Computers, Hypertext and the Remediation of Print*, Bolter incorporates insights from the important work he co-authored with Richard Grusin, *Remediation: Understanding New Media*, which posits and extensively illustrates the recursive dynamic between immediacy and hypermediation in New Media.[86] Landow similarly has twice revised his original text, considerably expanding his insights and adding new material to take account of the Web in *Hypertext 2.0: The Convergence of Contemporary Critical Theory and Technology* and globalization in *Hypertext 3.0: Critical Theory and New Media in an Era of Globalization*.[87]

The shortcomings of importing theoretical assumptions developed in the context of print into analyses of electronic media were vividly brought to light by Espen J. Aarseth's important book *Cybertext: Perspectives on Ergodic Literature*. Rather than circumscribe electronic literature within print assumptions, Aarseth swept the board clean by positing a new category of "ergodic literature," texts in which "nontrivial effort is required to allow the reader to traverse the text" (1). Making a different analytical cut through textual groupings that included computer games, print literature, and electronic hypertexts, among others, Aarseth established a grid comprised of eight different operators, many of which have purchase mostly with electronic texts rather than print. The grid yields a total of 576 different positions on which a variety of different kinds of texts can be located.[88] Although the method has limitations, notably that it is blind to content and relatively indifferent to the specificity of media, it has the tremendous virtue of demonstrating that electronic texts cannot simply be shoved into the same tent with print without taking into account their different modes of operation. These innovations have justifiably made *Cybertext* a foundational work for the study of computer games and a seminal text for thinking about electronic literature.[89] Markku Eskelinen's work, particularly "Six Problems in Search of a Solution: The challenge of cybertext theory and ludology to literary theory," further challenges traditional narratology as an adequate model for understanding ergodic textuality, making clear the need to develop frameworks that can adequately take into account the expanded opportunities for textual innovations in digital media. Proposing variations on Gérard Genette's narratological categories, Eskelinen demonstrates, through a wide variety of ingenious suggestions for narrative possibilities that differ in temporal availability, intertextuality, linking structures, etc., how Aarseth's ergodic typology can be used to expand narratology so it would be more useful for ergodic works in general, including digital works.[90]

Similar ground-clearing was undertaken by Lev Manovich in his influential *The Language of New Media*.[91] Although his emphasis is primarily on cinema rather than electronic literature, his "five principles of new media" have helped to define the distinctiveness of new media forms in contrast to print and other electronic media such as broadband television.[92] Four of the five follow in straightforward fashion, respectively, from the binary basis for digital computers (numerical representation), object-oriented programming (modularity and variability), and networked architectures with sensors and actuators (automation). The deepest and most provocative for electronic literature is the fifth principle of "transcoding," by which Manovich means the importation of ideas, artifacts, and presuppositions from the "cultural layer" to the "computer layer" (46). Although it is too simplistic to posit these "layers" as distinct phenomena (because they are in constant interaction and recursive feedback with one another), the idea of transcoding nevertheless makes the crucial point that computation has become a powerful means by which preconscious assumptions move from such traditional cultural transmission vehicles as political rhetoric, religious and other rituals, gestures and postures, literary narratives, historical accounts, and other purveyors of ideology into the material operations of computational devices. This is such an important insight that, although space does not allow me to develop it fully here, I will return to it later to indicate briefly some of the ways in which it is being explored.[93]

With these ground-clearing arguments, new opportunities became available to rethink the specificities of print and electronic literature and to explore their commonalities without collapsing one into the other. Loss Pequeño Glazier's *Digital Poetics*, cited earlier, argues that the materiality of practice is crucial both to experimental print literature and to innovative electronic work. As he and others have argued, notably Matthew Kirschenbaum, John Cayley, and Matthew Fuller, code must be considered as much a part of the "text" of electronic literature as the screenic surface. Web pages, for example, rely on HTML, XML, or similar markup languages to be properly formatted. Alexander Galloway in *Protocol* puts the case succinctly: "*Code is the only language that is executable*" (emphasis in original).[94] Unlike a print book, electronic text literally cannot be accessed without running the code. Critics and scholars of digital art and literature should therefore properly consider the source code to be part of the work, a position underscored by authors who embed in the code information or interpretive comments crucial to understanding the work.

Jerome McGann, whose work on the Rossetti Archive[95] and contributions to the Institute of Advanced Technology in the Humanities (IATH) at the University of Virginia have made him a leading figure in the field, turns this perspective on its head in *Radiant Textuality: Literature after the World Wide Web* by arguing that print texts also use markup language, for example, paragraphing, italics, indentation, line breaks and so forth.[96] Although this point somewhat muddies the waters in that it conflates operations performed by the reader with those performed by the computer, it nevertheless establishes common ground between scholars interested in bibliographic and textual criticism of print works and those oriented to close examination of digital texts. Also contributing to building bridges between digital protocols and close reading practices is the *The Ivanhoe Game*, a joint project of Johanna Drucker and Jerome McGann, now being developed at Speculative Computing Laboratory at the University of Virginia.[97] Part literary criticism, part creative play, and part computer game, *The Ivanhoe Game* invites participants to use textual evidence from a given literary text to imagine creative interpolations and extrapolations, facilitated through a computer interface.[98] Noah Wardrip-Fruin and David Durand follow similar lines of inquiry in *Cardplay*, a program that uses virtual playing cards to create the script of a play. Similar projects are Mark Bernstein's *Card Shark* and *Thespis*, systems to create hypertext narrative using AI techniques.[99] As with *Regime Change* and *News Reader* discussed earlier, Wardrip-Fruin and Durand call these programs "textual instruments," likening them both to computer games and musical instruments.

Complementing studies focusing on the materiality of digital media are analyses that consider the embodied cultural, social, and ideological contexts in which computation takes place. Although a full account of this body of work is beyond the scope of this discussion, a few seminal studies should be noted. Mark Hansen, focusing more on digital arts than electronic literature, makes powerful arguments for the role of the embodied perceiver as not only a necessary site for the reception of digital art work but as a crucial aspect foregrounded by works that literally do not make sense without taking embodiment into account.[100] Working the opposite side of the street, so to speak, is Friedrich A. Kittler's emphasis on the genealogy of technology as a formative force in its own right.[101] Kittler's controversial opening line in the "Preface" to *Gramophone, Film, Typewriter*, "Media determine our situation," although not unproblematic, suggests the larger contours within which electronic literature can be seen as a cultural force helping to shape subjectivity in an era when networked and programmable media are catalyzing cultural, political, and economic changes with unprecedented speed.[102] Writing on New Media poetics, Adalaide Morris aptly discusses this aspect of digital literature by commenting that it articulates for us what we already in some sense know.[103] To this I would add that it creates practices that help us know more about the implications of our contemporary situation. Much as the novel both gave voice to and helped to create the liberal humanist subject in the seventeenth and eighteenth centuries, so contemporary electronic literature is both reflecting and enacting a new kind of subjectivity characterized by distributed cognition, networked agency that includes human and non-human actors, and fluid boundaries dispersed over actual and virtual locations.

Located within the humanities by tradition and academic practice, electronic literature also has close affinities with the digital arts, computer games, and other forms associated with networked and programmable media. It is also deeply entwined with the powerful commercial interests of software companies, computer manufacturers, and other purveyors of apparatus associated with networked and programmable media. How and in what ways it should engage with these commercial interests is discussed in Alan Liu's magisterial work, *The Laws of Cool: Knowledge Work and the Culture of Information*.[104] Liu urges a coalition between the "cool" –

designers, graphic artists, programmers, and other workers within the knowledge industry – and the traditional humanities, suggesting that both camps possess assets essential to cope with the complexities of the commercial interests that currently determine many aspects of how people live their everyday lives in developed societies. Whereas the traditional humanities specialize in articulating and preserving a deep knowledge of the past and engage in a broad spectrum of cultural analyses, the “cool” bring to the table expert knowledge about networked and programmable media and intuitive understandings of contemporary digital practices. Electronic literature, requiring diverse orientations and rewarding both contemporary and traditional perspectives, is one of the sites that can catalyze these kinds of coalitions. Realizing this broader possibility requires that we understand electronic literature not only as an artistic practice (though it is that, of course), but also as a site for negotiations between diverse constituencies and different kinds of expertise.

Among these constituencies are theorists and researchers interested in the larger effects of network culture. Of the very large number of studies that have appeared in recent years, I will mention two to illustrate the kinds of scholarship that should rightly fall within the domain of electronic literature. First is Alexander Galloway and Eugene Thacker’s *The Exploit*, a work that builds on Gilles Deleuze’s notion of the control society[105] and Michael Hardt and Antonio Negri’s *Empire* and *Multitude*[106] to argue that the materiality, rhetorical force, and structure of the network provide the basis for new kinds of political power and oppression while also opening possibilities for new modes of theoretical analysis and political resistance.[107] Complementing their study is Rita Raley’s *Tactical Media*, a brilliant analysis of a systemic shift from strategy to tactics in contemporary political resistance as enacted by a diverse group of artistic computer games, online art works, and art installations. Adrian Mackenzie’s *Cutting Code: Software as Sociality* studies software as collaborative social practice and cultural process.[108] Analyzing a range of technical practices from Unix operating systems to extreme programming, *Cutting Code* explores how social forms, subjectivities, materialities and power relations entwine in the creation, marketing, and use of software.

Mackenzie’s work serves as a salutary reminder that just as one cannot understand the evolution of print literature without taking into account such phenomena as the law cases that established legal precedent for copyright and the booksellers and publishers who helped promulgate the ideology of the creative genius authoring the great work of literature (for their own purposes, of course), so electronic literature is evolving within complex social and economic networks that include the development of commercial software, the competing philosophy of open-source freeware and shareware, the economics and geopolitical terrain of the Internet and World Wide Web, and a host of other factors that directly influence how electronic literature is created and stored, sold or given away, preserved or allowed to decline into obsolescence.

PRESERVATION, ARCHIVING, AND DISSEMINATION

Over the centuries, print literature has developed mechanisms for its preservation and archiving, including libraries and librarians, conservators, and preservationists. Unfortunately, no such mechanisms exist for electronic literature. The situation is exacerbated by the fluid nature of digital media; whereas books printed on good-quality paper can endure for centuries, electronic literature routinely becomes unplayable (and hence unreadable) after a decade or even less. The problem exists at both the software and hardware levels. Commercial programs can become obsolete or migrate to new versions incompatible with older ones, and new operating systems (or altogether new machines) can appear on which older works will not play. With a foreshortened canon limited to a few years and without the opportunity to build the kinds of traditions associated with print literature, electronic literature would be doomed to the realm of ephemera, severely hampered in its development and the influence it can wield.

The Electronic Literature Organization has taken a proactive approach to this crucial problem with the Preservation, Archiving and Dissemination Initiative (PAD). Part of that initiative is realized in the *Electronic Literature Collection* Volume 1, co-edited by me and Nick Montfort, Scott Rettberg, and Stephanie Strickland. Featuring sixty works of recent electronic literature, some of which are only available in the *ELC*, the *ELC* includes a brief description of each work, a note by the author(s), and a keyword index. Available for free downloading at the Electronic Literature Organization site (http://collection.eliterature.org), it offers the literary works through a Creative Commons license that allows them to be freely disseminated, so long as they are not altered. Collecting innovative, high-quality work is an important step forward in opening electronic literature up to a wider audience and moving it into the classroom. (I am frequently asked by colleagues how they can find "the good stuff" among the immense flood of works available on the Web; now there is an easy – albeit still very partial – answer to that question.) It is anticipated that the *ELC* will continue on a biennial basis, with each subsequent volume compiled by an editorial collective that will take responsibility for soliciting important works and making them available in accessible cross-platform formats.

Another part of the PAD initiative is this essay, intended as a general introduction that can serve to orient newcomers to the field. By attempting to give a recognizable shape to this fast-moving and diverse community of artists, writers, designers, programmers, and critics and the works they create and interpret, I hope this essay will also interest specialists who may be familiar with one or more areas of electronic literature but not necessarily with the field as a whole. This essay is the final component of a triad of critical works commissioned by the Electronic Literature Organization as part of the PAD initiative, joining two white papers published at the ELO site, "Acid-Free Bits" by Nick Montfort and Noah Wardrip-Fruin,[109] and "Born-Again Bits" by Alan Liu, David Durand, Nick Montfort, Merrilee Proffitt, Liam

R. E. Quin, Jean-Hughes Rety, and Noah Wardrip-Fruin.[110] Whereas this essay focuses on surveying the fieldand thus on dissemination), the two white papers are centrally concerned with preserving and archiving electronic literature.

"Acid-Free Bits" offers advice to authors to help them "find ways to create long-lasting elit, ways that fit their practice and goals" (3). The recommendations include preferring open systems to closed systems, choosing community-directed systems over corporate-driven systems, adhering to good programming practices by supplying comments and consolidating code, and preferring plain-text to binary formats and cross-platform options to single-system options. Since electronic literature does not have the economic clout to convince commercial developers to insure its continuing viability on their platforms, it is simply good sense to prefer open systems to closed. Likewise, plain-text formats will remain human-readable while binary formats will not, and cross-platform options increase the availability of works to interested audiences. These commonsense recommendations make available to writers and authors issues they can consider at the beginning of projects, before substantial time and resources are invested in options that may prove damaging to long-term preservation and costly to change, once the work has been implemented.

More encompassing, and even more visionary, is the proposal in "Born-Again Bits" for the "X-Literature Initiative." The basic premise is that XML (Extensible Markup Language) will continue to be the most robust and widespread form of Web markup language into the foreseeable future. Working from this assumption, the proposal envisions a set of practices and tools that will enable older electronic literature to be migrated to XML for preservation, facilitate XML-compliant authoring, insure the inclusion of appropriate metadata to allow works properly to be identified and archived, develop tools for the easy reading, annotating, and teaching of electronic literature, and provide authors with applications for creating electronic literature in X-Lit formats. The scope here is breathtaking, and if even a portion of the proposal can be successfully implemented, the contribution to the preservation, dissemination, and archiving of electronic literature will be immense.

The "X-Literature Initiative" makes startlingly clear that the formation we know as "literature" is a complex web of activities that includes much more than conventional images of writing and reading. Also involved are technologies, cultural and economic mechanisms, habits and predispositions, networks of producers and consumers, professional societies and their funding possibilities, canons and anthologies designed to promote and facilitate teaching and learning activities, and a host of other factors. All of these undergo significant transformation with the movement into digital media. Exploring and understanding the full implications of what the transition from page to screen entails must necessarily be a community effort, a momentous task that calls for enlightened thinking, visionary planning, and deep critical consideration. It is in these wide and capacious senses that electronic literature challenges us to re-think what literature can do and be.

NOTES

1 Among many manifestations of these questions, I single out one as particularly telling, a high-profile panel discussion in Paris, organized by the French government, to debate the following topic: "The Internet: A Threat to Culture?." Panelists include representatives from Virgin Records and AOL and the Director of the Bibliothéque Nationale de France, October 2006.

2 See for example Peter L. Galison, *Image and Logic: A Material Culture of Microphysics* (Chicago: University of Chicago, 1997), pp. 47, 55.

3 Michael Joyce, *afternoon: a story* (Watertown MA: Eastgate Systems, 1990). An earlier version was circulated in 1987; see Matthew Kirschenbaum, "Save As: Michael Joyce's *afternoons*," *Mechanisms: New Media and Forensic Textuality* (Cambridge: MIT Press, 2007) for a detailed account of all the different versions and editions.

4 Stuart Moulthrop, *Victory Garden* (Watertown MA: Eastgate Systems, 1995).

5 Shelley Jackson, *Patchwork Girl* (Watertown: Eastgate Systems, 1995).

6 George P. Landow popularized the term "lexia" in *Hypertext: The Convergence of Contemporary Critical Theory and Technology* (Baltimore: The Johns Hopkins University Press, 1991). Terry Harpold in *Exfoliations* (Minneapolis: University of Minnesota Press, 2007) objects to the term, arguing that in its original source, Roland Barthes's *S/Z*, it denoted textual divisions that the reader made as part of her interpretive work. The term is now so well-established, however, that it seems difficult to change. Moreover, terms frequently change meanings when they migrate across fields, disciplines, and media.

7 N. Katherine Hayles, "Deeper into the Machine: Learning to Speak Digital," *Computers and Composition* 19 (2002): 371–386; reprinted in revised form with images in *Culture Machine* 5 (February 2003) http://culturemachine.tees.ac.uk/frm_f1.htm and in *State of the Arts: The Proceedings of the Electronic Literature Organization's 2002 State of the Arts Symposium*, edited by Scott Rettberg (Los Angeles: Electronic Literature Organization), pp. 13–38.

8 David Ciccoricco, in *Reading Network Fiction* (Tuscaloosa: University of Alabama Press, 2007), takes issue with the first and second generation characterization, arguing that the use of images is a matter of degree rather than an absolute break. My distinction, however, was concerned not only with the increased visuality of post-1995 works but also the introduction of sound and other multimodalities, as well as the movement away from a link-lexia structure into more sophisticated and varied navigational interfaces. The major factor in precipitating the shift, of course, was the huge expansion of the World Wide Web after the introduction of the Netscape and other robust and user-friendly browsers. In any construction of periods, there will always be areas of overlap and remediation, but it nevertheless seems clear that a major shift took place around 1995.

9 M. D. Coverley, *Califia* (Watertown: Eastgate Systems, 2000); *Egypt: The Book of Going Forth by Day* (Newport Beach: Horizon Insight, 2006).

10 Scott Rettberg, William Gillespie, and Dirk Stratton, *The Unknown* (1998) www.unknownhypertext.com.

11 Michael Joyce, *Twelve Blue*, *Electronic Literature Collection 1*, eds N. Katherine Hayles, Nick Montfort, Scott Rettberg, and Stephanie Strickland (Maryland: Electronic Literature Organization, 2006) http:collection.eliterature.org (hereafter noted as *ELC* 1). When works are also available at other locations, these will be listed second; for *Twelve Blue* (Eastgate Hypertext Reading Room, 1996) www.eastgate.com/TwelveBlue/Twelve_Blue.html.

12 Caitlin Fisher, *These Waves of Girls* (2001) www.yorku.ca/caitlin/waves/.

13 Stuart Moulthrop, *Reagan Library* (1999) http://iat.ubalt.edu/moulthrop/hypertexts/rl/pages/intro.htm.

14 Judd Morrissey in collaboration with Lori Talley, *The Jew's Daughter*, *ELC* 1 and (2000) www.thejewsdaughter.com.

15 Talan Memmott, *Lexia to Perplexia* (2000) www.uiowa.edu/~iareview/tirweb/hypermedia/talan_memmott/index.html.

16 Richard Holeton, *Frequently Asked Questions about "Hypertext," ELC* 1.

17 David Ciccoricco, *Reading Network Fiction*, "Introduction," p. 7 ms.

18 An interesting illustration of the difference between narrative and game is provided by Natalie Bookchin's, "The Intruder," in which she makes computer games from Jorge Luis Borges's fiction www.calarts.edu/~bookchin/intruder/.

19 Markku Eskelinen, "Six Problems in Search of a Solution: The Challenge of Cybertext Theory and Ludology to Literary Theory," *dichtung-digital* (2004) www.dichtung-digital.com/2004/3-Eskelinen.htm.

20 Nick Montfort, *Twisty Little Passages* (Cambridge: MIT Press, 2003), pp. vii–xi.

21 Emily Short, *Savoir-Faire* (2002) ELC 1.

22 Jon Ingold, *All Roads*, *ELC* 1 and (2001) www.ingold.fsnet.co.uk/if.htm.

23 Donna Leishman, *The Possession of Christian Shaw*, *ELC* 1 and (2003) www.6amhoover.com/xxx/start.htm.

24 *The Iowa Review Web* 8.3 (September 2006) www.uiowa.edu/~iareview/main pages/new/september06/sept06_txt.html.

25 The move is, however, not without caveats. Aya Karpinska comments that "a screen is a screen. It's not space," anticipating that her future work will move into actual space through mobile technologies, Rita Raley, "An Interview with Aya Karpinska on 'mar puro'" www.uiowa.edu/~iareview/main pages/new/september06/karpinska/karpinska_intervew.html. Dan Waber comments that "I think the word and the letter have been three dimensional in many ways for a very long time. As long as there has been language there has been a way of looking at its materiality, and that way of looking at it adds a dimension automagically," Rita Raley, "An Interview with Dan Waber on 'five by five'" www.uiowa.edu/~iareview/mainpages/new/september06/wabere/waber_interview.html.

26 "Artist's Statement: Ted Warnell" www.uiowa.edu/~iareview/mainpages/new/september06/warnell/warnell.html.

27 Ted Warnell, *TLT vs. LL* (2006) www.uiowa.edu/~iareview/mainpages/new/september06/warnell/11x8.5.html.

28 David Knoebel, "Heart Pole" http://home.ptd.net/~clkpoet/htpl/index.html.

29 Janet Cardiff, *The Missing Voice (Case Study B)* (1999); print book edition (London: Artangel, 1999); for a description, see www.artfocus.com/Janet Cardiff.html; *Her Long Black Hair* (2005) www.publicartfund.org/pafweb/projects/05/cardiff/cardiff-05.html.

30 Blast Theory, *Uncle Roy All Around You* (premiered London, 2003) www.blasttheory.co.uk/bt/work_uncleroy.html.

31 Joan Campàs in "The Frontiers between Digital Literature and Net.art" finds several areas of convergence, including emphasis on process, information and algorithm, "new perceptual situations, hybridization and simulation, the artistic and literary objectivization of the concept of the Net" and "software as work of art and as a text," among others, *dichtung-digital* 3 (2004): 12 www.dichtung-digital.com/2004/3-Campas.htm. She also has trenchant observations about how electronic literature is more often browsed than read; although, recently, in what we might call the second generation of hypertext criticism as practiced by such critics as David Ciccoricco, Terry Harpold, Matthew Kirschenbaum, and Jessica Pressman, electronic literature *is* read, and read very closely.

32 For a description of *Screen*, see Josh Carroll, Robert Coover, Shawn Greenlee, Andrew McClain, and Noah Wardrip-Fruin www.uiowa.edu/~iareview/mainpages/tirwebhome.htm.

33 William Gillespie, with programming by Jason Rodriguez and David Dao, *Word Museum*; see documentation, www.uiowa.edu/~iareview/mainpages/new/september06/gillespie/wordmuseum.html.

34 Rita Raley discussed *Torus* in the broader context of digital works using haptic and proprioceptive stimuli in "Reading Spaces," Modern Language Association Convention, Washington DC, 28 December 2005.

35 See John Cayley's website www.shadoof.net/in for a download of *lens* in a QuickTime maquette; the piece was originally designed for the CAVE.

36 Information from Robert Coover in an email dated 25 September 2006.

37 Paul Sermon, Steven Dixon, Mathias Fucs, and Andrea Zapp, *Unheimlich* (2006) http://creativetechnology.salford.ac.uk/unheimlich/.

38 Michael Mateas, *Façade* (2005) www.interactivestory.net/.

39 Janet Murray, *Hamlet on the Holodeck: The Future of Narrative in Cyberspace* (Cambridge: MIT Press, 1998), p. 40.

40 Marie-Laure Ryan, *Avatars of Story* (Minneapolis: University of Minnesota Press, 2006).

41 Deena Larsen, *Disappearing Rain* (2001) www.deenalarsen.net/rain/.

42 Electronic Poetry Center http://epc.buffalo.edu/; Ubuweb www.ubu.com/.

43 Loss Pequeño Glazier, *Digital Poetics: Hypertext, Visual-Kinetic Text and Writing in Programmable Media* (Tuscaloosa: University of Alabama, 2001).

44 Loss Pequeño Glazier, *White-Faced Bromeliads on 20 Hectares*, *ELC* 1 http://epc.buffalo.edu/authors/glazier/java/costa1/00.html.

45 Generative art is, of course, a major category of digital arts generally. For example, Bill Seaman's ambitious installation work, *The World Generator* (1996), used images, sound, and spoken text to create a recombinant poetics that created emergent and synergistic combinations of all these modalities http://digitalmedia.risd.edu/billseaman/poeticTexts.php.

46 Philippe Bootz, "The Functional Point of View: New Artistic Forms for Programmed Literary Works," *Leonardo* 32.4 (1999): 307–316. See also the earlier article "Poetic Machinations," *Visible Language* 30.2 (1996): 118–137, and the later "Reader/Readers," p0es1s: *Ästhetik Digitaler Poesie/The Aesthetics of Digital Poetry*, edited by Friedrich W. Block, Christiane Heiback, and Karin Wenz (Berlin: Hatje Cantz Books, 2004), pp. 93–122, which gives a further elaboration and refinement of the functional model.

In "Digital Poetry: From Cybertext to Programmed Forms," *Leonardo Electronic Almanac* 14.05/06 (2006) http://leoalmanac.org/journal/lea_v14_n05–06/pbootz.asp, he slightly shifts terminology to technotexts and intermedia, with a focus on a procedural model of communication.

47 Philippe Bootz discusses the web-based literary journal created by LAIRE in "*Alire*: A Relentless Literary Investigation," *Electronic Book Review* (15 March 1999) www.electronicbookreview.com/thread/wuc/Parisian.

48 Philippe Bootz, *La série des U*, *ELC* 1; *Alire* 12 (2004).

49 Noah Wardrip-Fruin with Brion Moss and Elaine Froehlich, *Regime Change and News Reader* http://hyperfiction.org/rcnr/.

50 Jim Andrews, *On Lionel Kearns*, *ELC* 1 and www.vispo.com/kearns/index.htm.

51 William S. Burroughs and his partner in crime, Brion Gysin, wrote extensively about the technique and philosophy of the cut-up that Burroughs pioneered in *Naked Lunch*, among other works. For more information and algorithms allowing you to cut up your own texts, see www.reitzes.com/cutup.html.

52 Jim Andrews and collaborators, *Stir Fry Texts* www.vispo.com/StirFryTexts/.

53 Geniwate and Brian Kim Stefans, *When You Reach Kyoto* (2002) www.idaspoetics.com.au/generative/generative.html.

54 Millie Niss with Martha Deed, *Oulipoems*, *ELC* 1 and (2004) www.uiowa.edu/~iareview/tirweb/feature/sept04/oulipoems/.

55 Patrick-Henri Burgaud, *Jean-Pierre Balpe ou les Lettres Dérangées*, *ELC* 1 (2005).

56 John Cayley has a trenchant criticism of "code work" in "The Code is not the Text (unless it is the Text)," *Electronic Book Review* (2002) www.electronicbookreview.com/thread/electropoetics/literal.

57 For a fuller explanation of intermediating dynamics between language and code, see N. Katherine Hayles, "Making: Language and Code," *My Mother Was a Computer: Digital Subjects and Literary Texts* (Chicago: University of Chicago Press, 2005), pp. 15–88.

58 Diane Reed Slattery, Daniel J. O'Neil and Bill Brubaker, *The Glide Project* www.academy.rpi.edu/glide/portal.html. Slattery is also the author of *The Maze Game* (Kingston NY: Deep Listening Publications, 2003), a print novel that gives the backstory of the development, politics, and cultural significance of the Glide language.

59 Sha Xin Wei, *TGarden* http://f0.am/tgarden/; see also Sha Xin Wei and Maja Kuzmanovic, "Performing Publicly in Responsive Space: Agora, Piazza, Festival and Street," Worlds in Transition: Technoscience, EASST Conference: Citizenship and Culture In the 21st Century (September 2000), Vienna, Austria www.univie.ac.at/Wissenschaftstheorie/conference2000.

60 Carrie Noland, "Digital Gestures," *New Media Poetics: Contexts, Technotexts, and Theories*, eds Adalaide Morris and Thomas Swiss (Cambridge: MIT Press, 2006), pp. 217–244.

61 John Cayley, "Literal Art: Neither Lines nor Pixels but Letters," *First Person: New Media as Story, Performance, and Game*, eds Noah Wardrip-Fruin and Pat Harrigan (Cambridge: MIT Press, 2004), pp. 208–217; see also John Cayley, "Literal Art" www.electronicbookreview.com/thread/firstperson/programmatology.

62 John Cayley, www.shadoof.net/in/.

63 Stephanie Strickland, with technical implementation by Janet Holmes (1999), "The Ballad of Sand and Harry Soot" www.wordcircuits.com/gallery/sandsoot/frame.html. The poem appeared first in print as the winner of the Boston Review's Second Annual Poetry contest.

64 Jason Nelson, *Dreamaphage*, version 1 (2003) and version 2 (2004), *ELC* 1 and www.secrettechnology.com/dreamaphage/opening.html.

65 Stephanie Strickland, *V: WaveSon.nets/Losing l'Una* (New York: Penguin, 2002); Stephanie Strickland with Cynthia Lawson, *V: Vniverse* www.vniverse.com/.

66 Lance Olsen, *10:01* (Portland: Chiasmus Press, 2005). Lance Olsen with Tim Guthrie, *10:01*, *ELC* 1.

67 Geoff Ryman, *253: The Print Remix* (London: St. Martin's Press, 1998); the Web version is at www.ryman-novel.com.

68 Gregory L. Ulmer, *Internet Invention: From Literacy to Electracy* (New York: Longman, 2002).

69 Alan Sondheim's writings are represented in a collection of texts made over a ten-year period in "Internet Text, 1994 [Through Feb. 2, 2006]," *ELC* 1; Brian Kim Stefans, *Fashionable Noise: On Digital Poetics* (Berkeley: Atelos Press, 2003); Stephanie Strickland, "Writing the Virtual: Eleven Dimensions of E-Poetry," *Leonardo Electronic Almanac* 14:05/06 (2006) http://leo almanac.org/journal/vol_14/lea_v14_n05–06/sstrickland.asp and "Dali Clocks: Time Dimensions of Hypermedia," *Electronic Book Review II* (2000) www.altx.com/ebr/ebr11/11str.htm.

70 Ian Bogost, *Unit Operations: An Approach to Videogame Criticism* (Cambridge: MIT Press, 2006); Wendy Hui Kyong Chun, *Control and Freedom: Power and Paranoia in the Age of Fiber Optics* (Cambridge: MIT Press, 2006); Florian Cramer, *Words Made Flesh: Code, Culture, Imagination* (Rotterdam: Piet Zwart Institute) http://pzwart.wdka.hro.nl/mdr/research/fcramer/wordsmadeflesh/); Matthew Fuller, *Behind the Blip: Essays on the Culture of Software* (New York: Autonomedia, 2003); Mark B. N. Hansen, *New Philosophy for New Media* (Cambridge: MIT Press, 2004); Matthew Kirschenbaum, *Mechanisms: New Media and Forensic Textuality* (Cambridge: MIT Press, 2006); Adalaide Morris, "New Media Poetics: As We May Think/How to Write," *New Media Poetics*, eds Adalaide Morris and Thomas Swiss (Cambridge: MIT Press, 2006), pp. 1–46; Rita Raley, Tactical Media (Minneapolis: University of Minnesota Press, 2007).

71 Espen J. Aarseth, *Cybertext: Perspectives on Ergodic Literature* (Baltimore: The Johns Hopkins University Press, 1997).

72 Stephanie Strickland, "Writing the Virtual: Eleven Dimensions of E-Poetry," *Leonardo Electronic Almanac* 14:05/06 (2006) http://leoalmanac.org/journal/vol_14/lea_v14_n05–06/sstrickland.asp.

73 Jim Rosenberg, *Diagram Series 6: 6.4 and 6.10*, *ELC* 1; see also *Diagram Poems* www.well.com/user/jer/diags.html.

74 Raymond Queneau, *Cent mille milliards de poèmes* (Paris: Gallimard, 1961); John Cage, *M: Writings '67–'72* (Middletown: Wesleyan University Press, 1973); Jackson Mac Low, *The Virginia Woolf Poems* (Providence RI: Burning Deck, 1985).

75 Brian Kim Stefans, *Fashionable Noise: On Digital Poetics* (Berkeley: Atelos Press, 2003).

76 Ian Bogost, *Unit Operations: An Approach to Videogame Criticism* (Cambridge: MIT Press, 2006), especially p. 4.
77 Stephanie Strickland and M. D. Coverley, "Errand Upon Which We Came" www.thebluemoon.com/coverley/errand/home.htm.
78 Brian Kim Stefans, "The Dreamlife of Letters," (1999) www.chbooks.com/archives/online_books/dreamlife_of_letters/.
79 Robert Kendall, "Faith," *ELC* 1; also *Cauldron and Net*, 4 (Autumn 2002) www.studiocleo.com/cauldron/volume4/confluence/kendall/title_page.htm.
80 Young-hae Chang Heavy Industries, "Dakota" www.yhchang.com/DAKOTA.html.
81 Jessica Pressman, *Digital Modernism: Making It New in New Media*, PhD dissertation (2007: Los Angeles, University of California, Los Angeles).
82 Young-Hae Chang Heavy Industries, "Nippon" www.yhchang.com/DAKOTA.html.
83 Jay David Bolter, *Writing Space: The Computer, Hypertext, and the History of Writing* (New York: Lawrence Erlbaum Associates, 1991); George P. Landow, *Hypertext: The Convergence of Contemporary Critical Theory and Technology* (Baltimore: The Johns Hopkins University Press, 1991).
84 Aarseth, *Cybertext*, pp. 77, 89 and *passim*.
85 Jay David Bolter, *Writing Space: The Computer, Hypertext, and the History of Writing*, p. 147.
86 Richard Grusin and Jay David Bolter, *Remediation: Understanding New Media* (Cambridge: MIT Press, 2000).
87 George P. Landow, *Hypertext 2.0: The Convergence of Contemporary Critical Theory and Technology* (Baltimore: The Johns Hopkins University Press, 1997) and *Hypertext 3.0: Critical Theory and New Media in an Era of Globalization* (Baltimore: The Johns Hopkins University Press, 2006).
88 Espen J. Aarseth, "Textonomy: A Typology of Textual Communication," *Cybertext*, pp. 59–75.
89 Espen J. Aarseth has also taken a leading role in establishing game studies as an academic discipline, being one of the founders of the field and of the leading journal in the field, *The International Journal of Game Studies*.
90 Markku Eskelinen, "Six Problems in Search of a Solution: The challenge of cybertext theory and ludology to literary theory," *dichtung-digital* (March 2004) www.dichtung-digital.com/index.
91 Lev Manovich, *The Language of New Media* (Cambridge: MIT Press, 2000).
92 Manovich, *The Language of New Media*, pp. 27–46.
93 For an example, see N. Katherine Hayles, "Traumas of Code," *Critical Inquiry* 33.1 (Autumn 2006): 136–157.
94 Alexander Galloway, *Protocol: How Control Exists after Decentralization* (Cambridge: MIT Press, 2004), p. 165.
95 Jerome J. McGann, *The Complete Writings and Pictures of Dante Gabriel Rossetti: A Hypermedia Archive* www.rossettiarchive.org/.
96 Jerome McGann, *Radiant Textuality: Literature after the World Wide Web* (New York and London: Palgrave Macmillan, 2001).
97 For information on the computerized version of *The Ivanhoe Game*, see www.patacriticism.org/ivanhoe/; for information on the Speculative Computing Laboratory, see www.speculativecomputing.org/.
98 See Johanna Drucker, *The Ivanhoe Game*.

99 Noah Wardrip-Fruin and David Durand, "*Cardplay*, a New Textual Instrument," Association for Computers and the Humanities and Association for Literary and Linguistic Computing (ACH/ALLC), University of Victoria, Victoria, BC, Canada (15–18 June 2005) http://mustard.tapor.uvic.ca:8080/cocoon/ach_abstracts/proof/paper_175_durand.pdf; Mark Bernstein, "Card Shark and Thespis: Exotic tools for hypertext narrative," *Proceedings of the Twelfth ACM Conference on Hypertext and Hypermedia*, Aarhus, Denmark (New York: 2001), pp. 41–50.

100 Mark B. Hansen, *New Philosophy for New Media* (Cambridge: MIT Press, 2004).

101 Friedrich A. Kittler, *Discourse Networks 1800/1900* (Stanford: Stanford University Press, 1992); Friedrich A. Kittler, *Literature Media Information Systems*, ed. by John Johnston (New York: Routledge, 1997).

102 Friedrich A. Kittler, "Preface," *Gramophone, Film, Typewriter* (Stanford: Stanford University Press, 1999), p. xxxix.

103 Adalaide Morris, "New Media Poetics: As We May Think/How to Write," *New Media Poetics: Contexts, Technotexts, and Theories*, pp. 1–46.

104 Alan Liu, *The Laws of Cool: Knowledge Work and the Culture of Information* (Chicago: University of Chicago Press, 2004).

105 Especially pertinent to their discussion is Gilles Deleuze, "Postscript on Societies of Control," *October* 59 (Winter 1992): 3–7.

106 Michael Hardt and Antonio Negri, *Empire* (Cambridge: Harvard University Press, 2001); *Multitude: War and Democracy in the Age of Empire* (New York: Penguin, 2005).

107 Alexander Galloway and Eugene Thacker, *The Exploit* (Minneapolis: University of Minnesota Press, 2007).

108 Adrian Mackenzie, *Cutting Code: Software as Sociality* (London: Peter Lang, 2006).

109 Nick Montfort and Noah Wardrip-Fruin, "Acid-Free Bits," Electronic Literature Organization (14 June 2004) http://eliterature.org/pad/afb.html.

110 Alan Liu, David Durand, Nick Montfort, Merrilee Proffitt, Liam R E. Quin, Jean-Hughes Rety, and Noah Wardrip-Fruin, "Born-Again Bits" (30 September 2004) http://eliterature.org/pad/bab.html.

Original Publication details

Source: The Electronic Literature Organization

Edition: V.1.0 January 2, 2007

URL: https://eliterature.org/pad/elp.html

CHAPTER 12B

Electronic literature

Where is it?

Dene Grigar

> 7. University presidents, provosts, and humanities deans should support the development and use of digital information and technology in the humanities. ("*Reinvigorating the Humanities: Enhancing Research and Education on Campus and Beyond*," Association of American Universities, 2004)

INTRODUCTION

This recommendation concerning the use of digital information and technology in the humanities is among 10 such suggestions put forth by the Association of American Universities as a way to *"reinvigorat[e] the Humanities"*. Interestingly, it appears before the recommendation for "sustaining . . . book publishing" and below the suggestion to "emphasize to . . . the broader community the fundamental importance of the humanities" (iv), suggesting, perhaps, an emphasis on digital texts as a way for the humanities to attract the growing number of technology-savvy students and supporters.

The humanities needs invigorating. A 2002 publication by the MLA Ad Hoc Committee on the Professionalization of PhDs entitled *"Professionalization in Perspective"* reports that new PhDs in language and literature have a 50 per cent chance of landing a tenure-track job, and a 2003 report published by the ADE Ad Hoc Committee on the English Major, simply but broadly entitled, *"The Undergraduate English Major,"* discusses the dwindling number of English majors in the US. While many factors are blamed for the demise of the humanities – a recent essay by Mark Bauerlein argues that theory *"damaged the Humanities"* –

no suggestion for rehabilitating it can be as controversial as making "digital information and technology" its savior.

The notion that there should be a direct correlation between the dynamic and fast-paced digital world that we all find ourselves living in today and the fixed and plodding realm of academe born out of a structure built during the Middle Ages may seem odd, particularly to those who actually read the 158-page AAU document four years ago. But to those of us who have long worked in digital media, particularly in the intersection between digital technology and literature in the area of electronic literature (what we refer to as "elit"), such a concept requires no thought. It is, for us, a *no-brainer*.

But if this is the case, and this document that AAU members from the 60 top-tier universities in the country were commissioned to produce over four years ago is, indeed, a tome carrying much weight and gravity for academics in the US, then where is the evidence that the humanities is taking the suggestions to heart and embracing digital media? Where, outside of the composition classroom and language labs, is digital technology being utilized, for example? Most importantly for readers of Electronic Book Review (ebr; www.electronicbookreview.com/) who cut their teeth on Michael Joyce's "afternoon: a story," or are seduced into electronic literature by the narratives of video games, where in academe is electronic literature promoted? In 2007, N. Katherine Hayles asked, *"Elit: What Is It?"*, now it is time to ask, "elit: *where* is it?"

It is this question that concerns my essay. It is one I have often asked myself through the years, first as a graduate student in the early 1990s studying in an interdisciplinary humanities program where I developed a fascination for hypertext literature, to my first academic position – a twelve-year period in an English and Rhetoric Department where I authored my first elit work – to a position now directing an interdisciplinary digital media program where I teach electronic literature and produce 3D lit in a motion-tracking lab. I ask it again because it was the subject of an exchange I had in the fall of 2008 with a French writer, Andrew Gallix, who asked me why the excitement for digital writing had died down and if I thought electronic literature had been absorbed by contemporary art. The end result of Gallix's exploration was an essay published in the *Guardian*, entitled *"Is e-literature just one big anti-climax?"* It serves as an effective example of the kind of misperceptions surrounding the growth and development of experimental literature and foregrounds a discussion of elit's place in the academy – and popular culture.

In brief, the author reports that elit, as it came to us from the heady days of hypertext circa the 1990s, is "already dead" and has not yielded any "fiction that is utterly compelling." To be honest, his claims that elit has been unsuccessful because we cannot "curl up in bed with a hypertext" and because the forms emerging from intermedial art "have less and less to do with literature" speak to a not-so-subtle bias toward traditional print-based forms and a lack of understanding of how the medium works. Many of the views that emerged in the "comment" section of his essay echoed Gallix's stance and, in some cases, went further in arguing that technology had no business in the creation of literary writing. A French writer and British readers would not necessarily be familiar with an arcane American position paper from the AAU arguing for the need for technology in the humanities, nor should they be, but after reading his audience's responses, one couldn't help but wonder how we can ever expect attitudes regarding digital-born literature to change in the staid atmosphere of the traditional English classroom if those in the mainstream public – particularly a public eagerly blogging at an online newspaper site – cannot.

We can identify four major misperceptions regarding elit stemming from Gallix's article: (1) reading patterns differ between print-based literature and elit, (2) elit is no longer literary, (3) elit is produced by artists or supported by academics at a lower rate than in previous periods, and (4) elit's existence can only be discerned through its presence in popular culture. This essay analyzes each of these misperceptions and issues a call to action.

READING PATTERNS

Perhaps one way of getting to the heart of the questions Gallix poses is to think about the role of reading and literature in contemporary culture. A 2007 study undertaken by the National Foundation for Educational Research (NFER), for example, shows that reading remains steady among children ages nine to eleven but that interest has shifted away from traditional print-based forms of writing toward comic books. Poetry especially has lost favor among this group. Also enlightening is the report from the National Endowment for the Arts, entitled *"Reading at Risk: A Survey of Literary Reading in America,"* which shows that literary reading – which we can glean from the study is defined as traditional print-based literature – has declined among US adults at a rate of 14 per cent over 1992–2002. Paralleling this trend is the overall decline in reading in general. Another study undertaken by the NEA in 2007, entitled *"To Read or Not To Read: A Question of National Consequence,"* for example, shows that people of all ages spend well over ten times the amount of time watching TV than reading. Taken in this light, Gallix should actually have been asking about the death of all literature rather than singling out only electronic.

Despite these troubling trends, it is doubtful that anyone looking at these data would conclude from them that print literature is dead, nor should the data be interpreted in this way. *Research* shows that even though reading has dropped in popularity, book sales have remained steady. True, revenue was down slightly in the first quarter of 2008, but offsetting losses are increased sales of mass market books, paperbacks, and e-books, among others. This information does not even take into account that reading is needed to get by in everyday life, from browsing the Internet to answering a text message, and goes far beyond the act of engaging with print literature.

Though this suggestion may set up a misleading comparison (not to mention that moving from Internet "if" – "potential" – to "when" oversteps the mark). Clearly, video games are gaining what we can understand as literary sophistication, in particular those described by Juul as "coherent world" games. But there's no reason to think that this sort of literary game is on course to subsume the non-literary variety (for lack of a better binary pair).

Likewise, we should not conclude that elit is dead. Because elit genres that emerged early on, such as hypertext fiction, hypertext poetry, interactive fiction, and those that have come about due to improved broadband capabilities, such as video poems, animated fiction, and so on, are disseminated differently from print-based literature, a dollar for dollar comparison between elit and print-based literature is not easily made. Many works of elit, for example, are delivered through publishing houses such as Eastgate Systems, but many more are accessed free from the Internet. We can, however, look at data concerning sales and popularity of video games, considered by some, such as Henry Jenkins, to be a hybrid narrative form that has not yet achieved literary quality but could in the future become a "serious art form in [its] own right" (Vitka) to get a sense of elit's potential for reaching large audiences. Nielsen's Trend Index, for example, reports that the number one role-playing game in the US, World of Warcraft, engaged players at an average of 546 minutes per week in 2008; a look at the amount of time players engaged in all top ten games shows a total time of interaction of thirty-six hours per week. Paralleling this information is the fact that in 2008 game consoles could be found in 40 per cent of American households. This growing trend resulted in $18.8 billion in annual sales in 2007 alone and meant that the most popular after-dinner activity for families during the 2008 holiday season would be playing video games together (Male 14).

In sum, current patterns in reading show that reading print-based literature has dropped in popularity and will continue to do so despite the modest rise in sales of books. As yet, video games are not perceived as elit and have, according to some, not achieved literary quality on par with books, but they do have the potential to do so; when they do, elit may very well overtake print-based literature in popularity.

LITERARY QUALITY OF ELIT

The second misperception Gallix's essay hints at is that electronic writing has lost its literariness, a flaw that has contributed to its demise. Where are those wonderful works from the 1990s by Kathy Acker and William Gibson that "push[ed] the envelope on papyrus" (Gallix)? In this very "late age of print" (Bolter 2), impacted as we are by the moving images of YouTube, the social interaction of Facebook and MySpace, and the kinesthetic physicality of Wii, this point is an odd one, the refrain of the *ubi sunt* lurking in this sentiment misplaced. The insinuation that the elit produced today is somehow lesser in literary quality than works such as Joyce's "afternoon: a story" and Shelley Jackson's *Patchwork Girl*, which preceded the ubiquity of the

Web and improved broadband technology, does not hold water when one considers works such as Stephanie Strickland's "slippingglimpse" and Kate Pullinger's "Inanimate Alice," which both utilize the strengths offered by the electronic medium to produce art. True, the hybridity of the forms and technological innovation that artists bring to their work results in a high level of experimentation that may at first obfuscate literary content and resist all attempts at categorizing and classifying it.

Epistemology in Western culture has been predicated on our ability to name things in order to know them. If Mark Amerika is right and we are, indeed, "witnessing the emergence of a 'digitally-processed intermedia art' in which literature and all the other arts are being 'remixed into yet other forms still not fully developed'" (Gallix), then engaging in such works would surely flummox even the most experienced reader of elit, for missing would be those neat cognitive structures – those "abstract containers" – where we place similar objects for the purpose of making sense of them (Lakoff 6). Even if we reject old classical models of categorization based on an objectivist construction of knowledge and built on the erroneous notion of disembodiment and, instead, embrace an experiential model that holds that "thought fundamentally grows out of embodiment" (xv), we still face challenges in understanding hybrid, experimental works such as elit. For knowledge, from this perspective, is gleaned from "the way people interact with objects" (51); therefore, without learned patterns of activity, what Espen Aarseth hints at when he alludes to trivial activity (94), then we literally may not be able to suss out what a thing truly is. If we try to compare the experience we have with elit, which differs so vastly from work to work, to the predictable physical interaction we have with a book, then rolling a cursor over an image, as one does with Donna Leishman's "Red Riding Hood," breathing into a headset, as one does with Kate Pullinger's "The Breathing Wall," or pointing at words projected on the wall of a room as one does with Noah Wardrip-Fruin's "Screen" place elit outside the category of fiction or poetry no matter how much writing appears on the screen for each. We are essentially fooled into thinking that what we are reading isn't literary because the differences in the sensory modalities used to interact with these works are so different from print-based literature. This is not to say that as we continue to deploy hearing and movement along with vision when interacting with objects and begin to accept not just the cinematic but also the literary quality in the movement of objects, we will not gain the conceptual framework for recognizing the literariness of elit. The more ubiquitous computing becomes, the more we interact with media in electronic environments, the more we experience electronic writing, the easier it will be to expand our sensibility about literature created and distributed in media beyond print.

PRODUCTION AND SUPPORT OF ELIT

The key to helping others to understand that elit is literary, then, is to offer experiences with it in the same place that we help others understand print literature: in the classroom. But if you look around the American academy today, you will see that traditional literature departments are dominated by cultural studies, great books, and linguistics programs. Growing in importance are programs in digital humanities; however, these programs are generally separate from English departments, and their focus is placed not so much on the production of native-born digital writing (i.e. elit) as it is on preserving and presenting analog-based literary works for digital contexts (i.e. Emily Dickinson's poetry on the web). Writing programs also constitute a pervasive area of academic study that sometimes emphasize literature, depending on the program, and are expressed as composition studies, rhetoric, creative writing, and technical and professional writing. Here too the teaching of elit is not common.

Additionally, English departments that rely on teacher training in secondary education for their bread and butter also neglect teaching elit because, frankly, the demands of testing and classroom instruction leave little room for non-conventional content. I speak from personal experience in this regard: One of the service projects I undertook in my first English faculty position was to oversee teacher education, a position I held for six years. During that time, I took the teacher exam in order to better understand the skills and knowledge that were expected of my students and visited English departments at the area high schools in order to know better the content students were expected to deliver. The teacher exam, for example, focused only on methods for delivery of traditional literary content. William Shakespeare's *Romeo and Juliet*, Toni Morrison's *Beloved*, F. Scott Fitzgerald's *The Great Gatsby* represent the kind of works students needed to know in order to pass the exam and gain employment in schools. When one of my students arrived at her first teaching position without having read Nathaniel Hawthorne's *The Scarlet Letter*, a representative from her department complained bitterly to me about it and called into question the credibility of my department's educational goals. The state education agency left little wiggle room at any level of literature instruction for the exploration of new content after the introduction of the No Child Left Behind initiative adopted when George W. Bush was elected our governor. Emphasis on basic skills and a shared cultural heritage made it impossible to slip in a work by a Deena Larsen or a Diana Slattery and, at the same time, cover what was already an overloaded curriculum bent on teaching the standardized test. Added to this challenge was the fact that English courses were taught in traditional classrooms with no access to computers. Even if I managed to teach my methods course in a lab, once my students arrived in their own classrooms after graduation they would find themselves without access to computers or an overhead projection system that would have allowed them to show a work to their students. If assigned a work of elit, secondary-level students would have found it necessary to visit the resource center in order to access works. Sadly, the situation has not improved in the years since I left this position.

Recognizing the link between teaching and promoting a love of literature, the National Council of Teachers of English issued a position statement in 2006 entitled, "*Resolution on the Essential Roles and Values of Literature in the Curriculum*."

In that paper, the organization lays out four recommendations for accomplishing that goal, one of which is to promote "a wide range of high-quality literature representing diverse experiences and perspectives . . . in all content areas, including reading instruction." While the idea that NCTE would actually suggest expanding its vision so that electronic literary works could be taught in the classroom, all excitement is tempered when we realize that the statement is in reaction to a decline in reading *books* ("*Book Sales*") and that the general aim of the resolution is to promote the love of *print* literature.

Elit may also not be read in mainstream literature classes because it cannot appear in the conventional print-based anthologies used so frequently in literature courses. Even those textbooks that offer companion websites with additional online material for instruction fail to include any truly digital-born works and offer instead print-based works digitalized for delivery electronically. Instructors relying on such resources who do not seek out additional readings promote the established canon, solely constructed on print-based works.

Ironically, the field of digital media, where many of us gravitate to if we leave English, has likewise ignored elit. For the most part, digital media theory has been dominated by scholars and critics trained in formalistic theories of cinema and visual art. Lev Manovitch uses Russian formalism, for example, as his lens for formulating views of "new" media, while Oliver Grau focuses his attention on Italian Futurism. What chance does an emergent form with literature in its name have when faced with such a strong art history perspective? Likewise, Stephen Wilson devotes little attention in his 900+-page book *Information Arts* to early hypertext work, with no mention of more contemporary elit pieces. That "net art" became the name of choice for some working in the area of web-based elit should come as no surprise under these circumstances, since the term "literature" in the name of elit may have limited its inclusion in media art festivals, exhibitions, and art scholarship. So, the irony is that the electronic aspect of elit creates suspicion for traditional English departments, just as the notion of literature does not fit well for the visual or media arts.

Despite this unsettled position in academe, thousands of elit works are collected by such groups as the Electronic Literature Organization, Hermeneia, and trAce Online Writing Centre; discussed at conferences such as the Visionary Landscapes: The Electronic Literature Organization 2008 Conference, Interrupt, and the Electronic Literature in Europe; and featured in publications such as ebr, Drunken Boat, and The Iowa Review Web. While this level of artistic and scholarly activity is not doing much to change the views toward elit in traditional English departments or visual arts programs with a digital media strand, it fuels faculty positions at top research institutions wanting to stay at the forefront of experimentation – not ironically at many of the same top-tier institutions belonging to AAU. Brown University and the University of Baltimore, for example, have long shown interest in studying and producing elit: the former, thanks to Robert Coover and more recently to John Cayley; and the latter, to Stuart Moulthrop and Nancy Kaplan. Other English departments, such as those at Duke University and Yale University, have shown commitment to elit by hiring noted theorists Kate Hayles and Jessica Pressman, respectively. Georgia Tech has long been the home for Janet Murray and Jay David Bolter. Likewise, MIT's Writing and Humanistic Studies has artist-theorist Nick Montfort on faculty, and The MIT Media Lab has recently announced two new tenure-track positions that include a focus on digital storytelling. So, the issue is not that elit is not taught in the academy, but rather that it has not yet become an organized field of study anywhere save cutting-edge institutions. So, in reality, unless it is an English department where a Kate Hayles or Joe Tabbi works, a Digital Humanities Program where a Matthew Kirshenbaum teaches, or a Writing program where a Nick Montfort is on faculty, Michael Joyce's work will not receive the same level of attention that James Joyce's does.

Finally, resistance to technology in the production of literature is real and goes beyond practical problems relating to access, skills, economic opportunity, or democratic divides (Mossberger xi–xv). It generates from deeply held views of the proper relationship between humans and machines, of what constitutes the good, the beautiful, and the true, and of the nature of art. This resistance, indeed, is expressed by many in Gallix's audience and explains in part why elit has not yet become part of popular culture.

One particular reader of Gallix's essay who signed in as "anytimefrances" wrote:

> i think it will be a sad day for literature when it goes completely e-text. my feeling is that people won't feel the same sort of 'obligation' to read as they have in the past. i saw the Sony reader for the first time just the other day in W/stones and though it looks, apart from the smallness of the "page" easy enough to read i found myself having an unpleasant sense of its being "gnick" – a word we used to use for anything suave and technical. it really is inescapable that one is mediated through technological chips and that sure effects one's emotional capacity to respond.

Rather than recognizing that reading any kind of literature has dropped in popularity, or that writing, pen and paper, the computer, alphabet, pencils, and so on all constitute technology, anytimefrances holds to the belief that it is the technological quality of elit that makes it unpalatable to readers and kills our "emotional" connection to a work of art. Taking on the misperception presented by anytimefrances and others responding to the blog, elit artist Rob Kendall facetiously comments:

> Now let us give a moment's pause to consider the oldest tragedy of artistic trespass, the original sin of literary endeavor. The day when poetry departed the sonorous lips of the bards to become embalmed in marks on clay tablets, something in literature died forever. Writing was the medium of accountants and bureaucrats, unfit for the lofty flights of poesy. Our noble art was irreversibly debased when it violated the boundary protecting art from commerce.

What Kendall suggests is that technology is more obvious in elit works than in traditional literature, so comfortable with inscription and print-based technologies we have become. This view is echoed in Hayles' discussion of "printcentric" bias found in views toward literature (*Writing Machines* 20). Resistance to elit essentially parallels that which generally occurs when literature is touched by changing modes of production. Plato's famous diatribe against writing in the Phaedrus written well over two thousand years ago is a case in point. Generations after us may not be bothered by the pixilated screen, audio, moving text, or the physical interaction required by the works they experience, but those fixed resolutely on the written word like their literature silent and static.

PRESENCE IN POPULAR CULTURE

But not being mainstreamed does not mean elit does not exist or that if it did exist at one time, it is now dead. One of the biggest misperceptions regarding elit's presence found in Gallix's essay is the idea that in order for something to have presence, it must be in the limelight, as if fame (or infamy) is proof of one's existence. In a world where a one-minute video on YouTube can, indeed, turn an unknown singer into a household name or we measure our worth by the number of "Friends" we have in our Facebook pages, perhaps Gallix has a point: Elit as an art form is not featured in *Entertainment Weekly* and so has not yet registered in mainstream culture. But then writing by Robert Pinsky hasn't either, and it doesn't mean that people are not producing poetry anymore. It just means that Pinsky's work is found elsewhere, outside of the consciousness of those who feed on *People* or find solace in the *Star*.

The notion of the "shock of the new" does play a role in elit's earlier, high-profile image which Gallix alluded to in his question. Robert Coover's 1992 essay for the *New York Times*, "The End of Books," highlights that heady period when elit was a new phenomenon. Yet even an argument that claims that because elit is no longer the new darling of the press, it no longer exists, falls flat when we consider that publicity surrounding J. K. Rowling grew quiet after the publication of her seventh Harry Potter novel. Would anyone agree that this silence meant that she is no longer writing or that people are no longer reading her books? I somehow doubt it. Being a sensation is not a measure of worth or value; it just means that one is, for a moment in time, a sensation.

Yes, the article did kick up some controversy, reigniting the long-standing, romantic debate that technology is bad and writing (seen as "not" technology, despite the fact that it is) is good. Ironically, the article brought elit a renewed sense of notoriety in the essay's five-day run in the press and spurred many of us to re-engage in a debate about its worth. But it is not fifteen minutes of fame on a blog that is needed to grow the field but long-term, purposeful action to promote and educate people about it. I, for one, would like to see elit mainstreamed in the academy beyond those universities interested in experimental art, for what we teach in our classrooms can go a long way in shaping future reading audiences. So, I ended my "comments" on the *Guardian* blog by "challeng[ing readers] who have not yet read a work of elit to experience" it. The rationale for this action is that if each one of us who claims to admire works of electronic literature took the time to teach it in our classes, either as an entire course about the art form or alongside works of print-based literature promoted in the traditional literary canon, we could develop an audience to appreciate, understand, and critique elit, much in the same way many of us aim to educate students about Shakespeare, Morrison, or Fitzgerald. Showing students literary works that incorporate digital technology seamlessly and meaningfully, such as Dan Waber's "Strings" and Nick Montfort's "ad verbum," can help to reach a growing audience of potentially technology-savvy, young supporters. This is a concept with which Hayles is quite familiar and it underpins the website that accompanies her book, *Electronic Literature: New Horizons for the Literary*, where in the "Resources" section she provides course syllabi for teaching elit.

RETHINKING LITERACIES: A CALL TO ACTION

The solution, then, to making the public more aware of elit lies in rethinking our notion of literacy. It involves technological literacy that is not simply seen as "a complex set of socially and culturally situated values, practices, and skills involved in operating linguistically within the context of electronic environments, including reading, writing, and communicating" (Selfe 11), but one that extends to visual, sonic, kinetic, and kinesthetic modalities, allowing us to "situate knowledges" to offer "a more adequate, richer, better account of the world" (Selfe 146–148). Such an approach would mean that art forms that include a literary component could be used to promote literacy. Hayles suggests such an approach when she writes that "[l]iteracy for this purpose . . . [is] define[ed] as creative artworks that interrogate the histories, contexts, and productions of literature, including as well the verbal art of literature proper" (Hayles, EL, 4).

While many articles and books focus on the use of art to teach literacy to young audiences, little work on the subject of literacy theorizes about how electronic literary art impacts definitions of literacy or perspectives regarding literacy practices. Cynthia Selfe's seminal text on technological literacy, *Technology and Literacy in the Twenty-First Century* (1999), for example, calls upon government officials, educators, business and industry leaders, and parents to work for change, omitting artists in her call to action. Similarly, textbooks that address visual or media literacy emerging with the rise of web-based technologies, such as Lee Odell and Susan Katz's *Writing in a Visual Age* (2006) and W. James Potter's *Media Literacy* (2008), focus on analyses of written and visual elements of commercial and news sites. Neither suggests approaches for discussing other modes of literacy made possible by digital technology or provides insight into the way art can be a catalyst for changing and evolving notions of technological literacy.

Gallix's essay and the anti-technology comments it spurred has become for me a metaphor for all that is flawed in our perception about the relationship between technology and writing, from the level of what we write, to that of how we write, to finally the way in which we disseminate our writing. I think about a work such as Stephanie Strickland's *True North*, which was produced at first as an analog book of poetry that she later reconceptualized as a hypertextually linked body of poems. Anyone reading the electronic version would have a very difficult time making the argument that it is of lesser quality than the book, because both contain the *exact same words*. The only difference between the two versions is the medium in which she expresses her thoughts. Yet the argument used to deny the worth of digital objects by those leaning toward literary orthodoxy would automatically discount the electronic iteration of *True North* just for the simple reason that it is not print. The truth of the matter is that if indeed students spend 10 times more of their energy with fingers on a keyboard instead of a nose in a book, then it stands to reason that we should rethink our notion of literacy and advocate elit as not only viable but also a compelling art form for teaching all aspects of reading, writing, and communicating.

FINAL REMARKS: ELIT IS STILL HERE

Elit is not dead, nor is it dying. Authors are still producing it. Online publications are still featuring it. Conferences are still held about it. As Scott Rettberg pointed out in his comments at the *Guardian* blog, "there are more writers working in the field than there were a decade ago, there have been more books written and published about the various forms of electronic literature including at least five in the last two years." What is true, however, is that English as an academic field that has for years developed future reading audiences for literature is struggling for survival, while enrollment in digital media programs is surging. This real-life scenario means that the AAU may be on to something: Incorporating technology into our classes may be one potent method for saving the humanities. And if elit conferences and publications show us anything, it also means that electronic literature, that hybrid, hard-to-define, ever-shifting emergent genre of literature that nettles the traditionalists and crosses too many disciplinary borders to find a safe haven in academe, just may, in the end, be the way to keep the literary arts alive. So, as Montfort and Moulthrop at *Grand Text Auto* both suggest in their response to Gallix's essay, rather than focus our attention on the tired old question, is elit dead?, isn't our time better spent finding ways to bring elit to the classroom, to help promote it in the contemporary literary scene, and to support artists who produce it so that it can foster and bolster literary sensibilities and literacies of future generations?

REFERENCES

Aarseth, Espen. *Cybertext: Perspectives on Ergotic* Literature. Baltimore, MD: The Johns Hopkins University Press, 1997.

Bauerlein, Mark. "How Theory Damaged the Humanities." *The Chronicle Review* 31 July 2008. Retrieved: 25 October 2008.

Bolter, Jay David. *Writing Space: The Computer, Hypertext, and the History of Writing*. Hillsdale, NJ: Lawrence Erlbaum, 1991.

"Book Sales in Decline as U.S. Economy Contracts." 13 July 2008. Book *Publishing News*. 24 December 2008.

Electronic Literature Organization. 25 October 2008.

Electronic Literature in Europe. 24 December 2008.

Gallix, Andrew. "Is e-literature just one big anti-climax?." Guardian: Books Blog 24 September 2008. Retrieved: 25 October 2008.

Grau, Oliver. *MediaArtHistories*. Cambridge, MA: The MIT Press, 2007.

Hayles, N. Katherine. "Elit: What Is It?" *Electronic Literature Organization*. 2007. Retrieved: 25 October 2008.

Hayles, N. Katherine. *Electronic Literature: New Horizons for the Literary*. Notre Dame, IN: The University of Notre Dame Press, 2008.

Hayles, N. Katherine. *Writing Machines*. Cambridge, MA: The MIT Press, 2002.

Interrupt 2008. Brown University. 17–19 October 2008.

Lakoff, George. *Women, Fire, and Dangerous Things: What Categories Reveal about the Mind*. Chicago, IL: The University of Chicago Press, 1987.

Male, Sharon. "How America Got Game." *Parade Magazine* 30 November 2008: 14.

Manovitch, Lev. *The Language of New Media*. Cambridge, MA: The MIT Press, 2001.

Mossberger, Karen, Caroline J. Tolbert, and Mary Stansbury. *Virtual Inequality: Beyond the Digital Divide*. Washington, DC: Georgetown University Press, 2003.

Odell, Lee and Susan M. Katz. *Writing in a Visual Age*. Boston, MA: Bedford/St. Martin's Press, 2006.

Potter, W. James. *Media Literacy*. Los Angeles, CA: Sage, 2008.

"Professionalization in Perspective." MLA Ad Hoc Committee on the Professionalization of PhDs. *Profession* 24 (2002) : 187–210. Retrieved: 25 October 2008. The Modern Language Association. www.mla.org/Resources/Career/Career-Resources/Career-and-Job-Market-Information/Professionalization-in-Perspective

"Reinvigorating the Humanities: Enhancing Research and Education on Campus and Beyond." Association of American Universities. 22 April 2004. Retrieved: 25 October 2008. www.aau.edu/workarea/downloadasset.aspx?id=6808

"Resolution on the Essential Roles and Values of Literature in the Curriculum." 2006 NCTE Position Statement. National Council of Teachers of English. 24 December 2008. www.ncte.org/positions/statements/valueofliterature

Schramm, Margaret, J. Lawrence Mitchell, Delores Stephens, and David Laurence. "The Undergraduate English Major." ADE Ad Hoc Committee on the English Major. The Modern Language Association. Retrieved: 25 October 2008. https://ade.mla.org/bulletin/article/ade.134.68

Selfe, Cynthia L. *Technology and Literacy in the Twenty-First Century: The Importance of Paying Attention*. Carbondale, IL: Southern Illinois University Press, 1999.

Strickland, Stephanie. *True North*. Watertown, MA: Eastgate Systems, 1997.

Strickland, Stephanie. *True North*. Notre Dame, IN: University of Notre Dame Press, 1997.

"Video Games." October 2008. Nielsen's Trend Index. 24 December 2008.

Visionary Landscapes: The Electronic Literature Organization 2008 Conference. Washington State University Vancouver. 29 May–1 June 2008.

Vitka, William. "Once Upon A Time: Will Video Games Ever Have Their Moby Dick or Citizen Kane?" 24 March 2008. CBS News. 24 December 2008.

Wilson, Stephen. *Information Arts: Intersections of Art, Science, and Technology*. Cambridge, MA: The MIT Press, 2002.

Original Publication details

Source: Electronic Book Review

Date: 2008-12-28

URL: www.electronicbookreview.com/thread/technocapitalism/invigorating

Part 3

Creation, remediation and curation

CHAPTER 13

Foundations for digital editing, with focus on the documentary tradition

Jennifer Stertzer

Digital editing has come to represent an expansive range of approaches, procedures, and goals for what, at present, is synonymous with a web-based delivery of edited content. This, despite the fact that production workflows may be performed with online tools or by using local machine-installed software. Though this definition focuses on the medium of access, and how it has changed from print to digital, the scholarly editor's responsibilities have remained unchanged; those engaged in editing historical and literary materials both seek to make objects accessible and to provide contextualization for their interpretation.[1] The goal of this chapter is to examine the elements of editorial decision-making and tool-assisted processes that make remediated content accessible and contextualized in digital formats. It is to explore different methods by which editors formulate strategies that suit variable aggregation of materials. It is to consider the continually developing arrays of presentation/publication software and storage systems available to support historical editing in digital media. To this end, this chapter will discuss the steps of the editorial process: (1) edition conceptualization, (2) development of a content management strategy, (3) selection of materials, (4) transcription, (5) organization, (6) annotation and index creation – and how these steps are shaped and influenced by digital tools, platforms, and edition development.[2]

The idea of an edition has long provided editors working with historical documents an intellectual and tangible framework. Before the rise of digital publication, documentary editing projects produced print, and in some cases, microform editions.[3] Like their digital derivatives and successors, these early editions encompassed a variety of approaches: some were comprehensive, others selective; some documents were arranged chronologically or topically while others were divided into series; some editors focused on individuals, others on organizations, or themes. Decisions regarding methodology were made after carefully reviewing the available source materials, imagining what questions users would bring to the edition, and balancing both within the confines of available resources. Regardless of approach, editions were created to make documents and content accessible: transcriptions made hard-to-decipher text readable, annotations provided contextualization and aided in understanding, indexes allowed users to search for both explicit text as well as indirect references, concepts, themes, and ideas. Users of these print editions, however, had a limited number of ways to access, browse, and search these editions. The print medium confined these editions to linear presentation. Users experienced the documents in ways that were both pre-conceived and intentional, a result that was more or less unavoidable given the inflexibility of the print medium.

Though the advent of digital publication has alleviated issues of rigidity, it has not made the intellectually rigorous work of the editor any easier – or as is sometimes hinted at – unnecessary.[4] In fact, quite the opposite is true. In addition to the long list of editorial tasks, editors now must also consider, learn, develop, and implement digital tools, systems, and publication platforms. Furthermore, the same technologies that allow editors to develop new ways of making both the content and context more accessible require editors to re-imagine ways in which people will want to use the edition and respond in creative and innovative ways.

CONCEPTUALIZING THE EDITION

One of the first questions an editor must address is what kind of edition to create. All subsequent editorial decisions will be greatly influenced by this decision; simply put, in order to figure out *how* to get there, you need to know *where* you're going. There are numerous formats and types of editions currently in use: electronic edition, eBook, digital edition, legacy edition conversion, a combination of two or more, not to mention projects, databases, archives, and thematic research collections. These types reflect content, technology, methodology, and approach. They also illustrate an evolution of the field and the ways we describe our work and publications. But because there is not a shared vocabulary, meaning can be ambiguous and limiting. Kenneth Price, in his article "Edition, Project, Database, Archive, Thematic Research Collection: What's in a Name?", asks "how do the conceptions inherent in these choices of language frame and perhaps limit what we attempt?" (Price 1).[5] Over the years, editors have grappled with definitions. In 2002, the Association for Documentary Editing's Committee on Electronic Standards asserted that:

> simply rendering a text in electronic form does not constitute an electronic edition . . . [the ADE-CES] defines an electronic edition as primary source material prepared with 1) rigorous attention to the text, (2) explanatory annotation and 3) an explanation of the editorial practices used on the texts.[6]

Less than ten years later "electronic edition" was redefined; in 2010 at the Institute for the Editing of Historical Documents,[7] online and electronic editions were defined as anything accessible via the computer, generally via the Web. Digital editions, however, were defined as online editions that made distinctive use of the digital medium, bringing to bear the powerful organization, search, and display features of digital tools and platforms; the distinction between electronic and digital editions being a continuum, not a binary opposition. At present, the Modern Language Association's Committee on Scholarly Editions (CSE) has created a white paper, "Considering the Scholarly Edition in the Digital Age," tackling the questions of what a "(digital) scholarly edition" is and how the "CSE, through its practices and guideline, encourage excellence in (digital) scholarly editing." The white paper includes a list of minimal conditions for scholarly editions as well as additional stipulations for digital scholarly editions, but also acknowledges the continual evolution of the field and the need to fairly evaluate nuances found in editions. The solution is for editions to "include a statement of purpose that the reviewer can measure against" in order to determine the appropriateness and effectiveness of methods.[8] This is critically important, as a project's materials, workflows, editorial methods, and publication goals could be significantly different from other projects.

The rise of available technologies and platforms had a clear impact on the definition's evolution, but the definition also reflected a change in how editors thought about their different editions. It is important to note that many documentary projects entered the world of digital editing through the conversion of legacy volumes. In these cases, a digital edition was a version, or form, of an originally print publication; first came the print edition, then a "digital" one. Digital editions of previously published print editions were purposely designed to look, function, and feel like the print version. Tables of content, annotation, and indexes remained unchanged. At the same time, a few projects ventured into new frontiers and were born-digital, such as the Dolley Madison Digital Edition. These groundbreaking projects forced editors to consider what constitutes a digital edition. Is "digital edition" solely a term to describe text-based electronic scholarship, or should it imply and encompass a project's goals, source materials, methodology, standards, and publication(s)? This chapter will assume the latter; a digital, especially a born-digital, edition is not simply making texts, images, maps (or audio and video files, for that matter) *available*. Rather, the goal should not only be to make all materials that comprise our editions visually and physically *accessible*, but *intellectually accessible*: editions should aim to reach a broad audience; provide accurate and understandable primary source materials; supply context for those materials; and engage with the audience.

Practically speaking, there are several features and challenges that editors must keep in mind when conceptualizing the edition. These can be grouped into two categories: development/workflow – or how an editor works and what types of features are developed for the edition; and user experience – or how users will be able to interact and engage with the edition. In the development/workflow environment such features include: space to include large quantities of source and editorial materials; ability to create multiple interfaces; browse/search/analysis options; inclusion of/linking to related materials; integration of text and graphics; and flexibility, including the ability to make corrections, updates, and additions, and provide downloadable data. Some development and workflow challenges include: decisions about what to include/exclude; learning curve for workflow/publication technologies; editor could potentially need both subject matter and technological expertise; and edition might need to migrate to more current forms of technology. In terms of user experience, features include: less controlled environment; variety of browse/search/analysis options; ability to interact with materials in multiple ways; and increased accessibility. Challenges include: reliance on specific technology to view; most likely not linear like a book, user will need to learn how to navigate; and balance between too little and too much content – do not want to overwhelm or disappoint.

CONTENT MANAGEMENT AND ACCESSIBILITY

Having an early understanding of the project's scope is critical. Identifying the materials to be collected, deciding how comprehensive the edition will be, and finally thinking about how the edition will be made accessible to users should be addressed in the beginning.

Control

Regardless of the project's scope, most editors will need to locate, collect, and organize their materials. Several tools are available to aid in this process, from simple spreadsheets to more sophisticated platforms, such as content management systems or databases. Whatever the chosen technology, it is important to systematically collect and consistently catalog the materials being assembled. Editors need to collect and catalog not only the materials they plan on including in the edition; they must include and manage ancillary, supporting, and secondary resources as well. Carefully designing a system of intellectual and physical control over the collected materials ensures efficiency and organization and will make the subsequent editorial steps easier to manage. Some initial questions to consider when evaluating technological options include: What types of information should be collected about the materials? Will this information be used solely for organizational purposes, as metadata, or for developing into an online resource? Does there need to be a place to store image files of the materials within the control system? Most editors will want to develop a database to serve as a content management system. Proprietary applications such as Microsoft Access and FileMaker Pro are options; consider Drupal if managing and publishing content in the same system is desired or required.[9] When structuring the database, it is helpful to think about output.

What information needs to be separated into its own field? What fields are necessary to sort documents by? What kinds of printouts or reports on the documents might be helpful? Is a standardized metadata system desirable? Involvement in this process is crucial, as it is an intellectual exercise of identifying and organizing important content, and editors should be involved with designing and building the database or drafting specifications for a developer.

It is sensible to start by considering what types of information (document and metadata) to create and collect. While this list is far from exhaustive, it provides a starting point to begin thinking about the materials:

1. Identification/accession number. This should be unique to the object.
2. The object's date or date range. Consider also creating a place to house date notes to record issues regarding circa, speculative dating, missing dates, and partial dates.
3. Name of correspondents, author(s), recipient(s), or creator(s). Or if, e.g. legal or financial document, how to structure associated names.
4. Title, either assigned or supplied.
5. Location information: repository (including online sources), private owner, dealer, or printed source.
6. Length of the document: number of pages, images, or objects.
7. Document type. Identify the kind of document, such as letter, newspaper article, invitation, ledger, etc.
8. Document's version. Editors working with materials that survive in multiple versions should develop a system for coding these variations.[10]
9. Notes on editorial substance. Does the document contain an unknown hand, enclosure not found, in one hand but signed in another?
10. Notes on document's physical appearance and structure. Is the document damaged, torn, or missing part of a page? What is the size of the document? Is it a single document or part of a larger collection, such as a journal, book, or ledger?
11. Subject information. Financial, legal, correspondence, diary, military, or some combination of two or more. Could even create subcategories for these types.
12. Document notes. Similar to the date notes field, this is a place to store any additional information about the item for future reference. These notes can be used and viewed only by the editor or shared with the user/reader.

Whenever possible, create and implement taxonomy lists; standardizing information will make searching easier and could aid in repurposing this content for other applications.

Selection

The next step in the editorial process involves selection: what objects should be considered, how should they be evaluated, and how to choose between objects that cover similar topics. In designing the selection policy, first tackle large-scale issues:

1. How inclusive will the edition be? Selective, comprehensive?
2. Will the edition be based on a topic, theme, or individual's life?
3. Will the edition be limited to correspondence, diaries, speeches, articles, or other formats? If the edition is thematic, what boundaries will there be on selection? Limit by archive, chronology, or types of objects?
4. Will it be based on a single archival collection or document (such as a diary), or will objects from multiple repositories be included?
5. If editing correspondence, will letters both to and from the subject be included? What about third-party correspondence?
6. Does the edition have start and stop dates?
7. What is the desired number of documents? Will the edition be bound by resource limitations, time limits, or space?
8. Will portions or excerpts of documents, whole documents, or both, be included?

Once parameters for the materials to include in the edition have been determined, evaluate the content of the documents: determine the themes to cover and rate the documents accordingly; determine whether a representative sample of various topics covered in the archive should be included; identify well-known documents/correspondents that need to be included; and determine whether only unpublished materials will be included. After the editor has identified objects to consider for possible inclusion and evaluated the types of content contained within, a selection policy that reflects the decisions made can be designed.

Transcription

Transcription is the key component of documentary editions and the first obligation of the editor is to get the transcription right. It makes challenging, difficult-to-read primary sources legible for users and is one of the steps in making content accessible. In digital editions, transcriptions also provide the basis for text searches and interpretative tools, such as textual analysis and data visualizations. Some decisions concerning transcription relate to the editor's rationale for the edition. Transcription policies, procedures, and practices, however, are mostly determined by the methodological approach: typographic, diplomatic, expanded, and regularized, or clear text. The transcription approach will determine how to handle issues of formatting, including placement of elements such as dateline, salutation, signature, and postscripts, and whether to retain line breaks and pagination, and presentation of text. Decisions regarding treatment of abbreviations, contractions, punctuation, upper and lower case characters, symbols, shorthand, and code also need to be addressed and must be regularized by the transcription policy.[11] While some techniques overlap, the four primary methodological frameworks provide distinct approaches to standardization and emendation:

1. Typographic. Attempts to duplicate the appearance of the source text as much as possible, within the limits of technology.
2. Diplomatic. Symbols or abbreviations are used to indicate textual details such as interlineations and cancellations. Some formatting, such as placement of routine elements, is standardized. Missing information is supplied; editor also supplies words unintentionally omitted by author. Corrections and emendations are not made silently; if it cannot be described with symbols, a footnote is used for explanation.
3. Expanded. Certain classes of corrections and standardizations are made silently and explained only in editorial policy. Abbreviations, contractions, character styles, and punctuation also standardized.
4. Regularized/Clear text. Texts contain neither critical symbols nor footnote numbers to indicate that emendations have been made or some detail has been omitted. Instead, these are reported in tables whose citations are keyed to pages and lines.[12]

It's obvious that editors have developed unique and descriptive ways of editing and publishing complex primary sources in print format to try to represent the original.[13] Digital publication platforms, however, allow for easy incorporation of images of the source materials, and encoding and database solutions make it possible to display multiple transcription views.[14] These options could potentially affect the way editors approach transcription – is it necessary to spend lots of time formatting documents when an image can be presented alongside the transcription? When considering how faithful to be to the original text, it is helpful to keep in mind the intended audience, design of the edition, and search and display plans. Document type should also influence this decision, as authorial spacing and formatting might be important to capture (e.g. financial documents, reports, and accounts). Ultimately, editors will always struggle with the balancing act of making documents accessible and making transcriptions accurate representations of the original. Regardless of the chosen method, it is of utmost importance to develop guidelines and rules, rigorously follow them, and make available to users.

Organization

Organization options in print editions are limited – tables of content lay out the overarching organizational model for the edition, which is primarily chronological, followed by transcriptions and annotations, and finally an index. But how to organize a digital edition? Are tables of content necessary or just carry-overs from the world of print? There are a variety of options for organizing objects into a digital edition. Divisions, or rationales for grouping objects, can result organically from decisions made during the selection process. Organizing objects thematically or chronologically, or dividing based on format (document type, version) or location (archive, repository), are all perfectly acceptable ways to shape an edition, making it possible for the user to choose any of these options to approach the edition. But it is helpful to remember that this arrangement will likely be a user's initial experience; digital tools and platforms can allow users to search, browse, and assemble materials in ways that suit their interests. So while it is important to craft the default layout carefully, providing options for alternative navigation and assemblage will ensure the edition is broadly accessible.

Next, think about the ways in which users will want to access the content: chronologically, by author/recipient, title, format, index/taxonomy terms, repository/collection, location, document type, and/or version. Creating digital editions that can be explored systematically and extensively like this requires structured metadata. Metadata, or data that describes other data, is essential when working with diverse materials. Abbreviations, shorthand, inconsistent spellings and terminology can be made reliably searchable and browsable if the metadata is both congruous and thorough. The process of managing metadata is similar to that of cataloging objects – create a system to identify content that will benefit from metadata, develop a controlled vocabulary, and consistently apply.

Annotation

Editors have a variety of techniques with which to make objects intellectually accessible. In addition to capturing metadata, as discussed above, editors can supply annotations, tag content, and develop indexes and taxonomy lists. In the context of digital editions, annotations are broadly conceived: introductions, headnotes, source notes, endnotes and footnotes, biographical and geographical directories, timelines and chronologies, maps and gazetteers, family trees, photographs and illustrations, glossaries, visualizations, essays, metadata, and taxonomy lists. All types, however, should serve the same purpose: annotation is added to make materials more understandable, provide context, and add value. When designing annotation, keep in mind the nature of the materials and the needs/interests of the audience. There are several elements to consider when developing annotation guidelines: first, who will use the edition – scholars, students, the general public; second, what are the objects like – do they detail events or topics that might be unfamiliar to most people, do they cover topics that are not commonly known, and do they require specialized knowledge to be understood; third, in what context will they be read, as a stand-alone resource or used in conjunction with other resources; and finally, how selective is the edition – a highly selective edition needs to provide more context, alerting users to and/or summarizing documents not included in the edition as well as pointing to related materials.

Traditionally, editions provided readers with enough annotation to understand the texts: people, places, organizations, and events were identified; summaries of preceding and proceeding histories added; and source notes containing additional information about the original manuscript followed its transcription. A digital edition should include this type of annotation; digital platforms make it easier, though, to repurpose and reuse this content. Common digital tools and platforms – XML, Drupal, Omeka, WordPress – offer a variety of technical strategies and options to integrate stand-alone as well as shared annotations. The documents, content, annotation policy, and desired search/browse/query features will help shape these decisions. For example, events described in the documents might need stand-alone annotation in order to provide specific contextualization. However, the editor might also want to create an "id." for that event so that every time the "it" is mentioned in a casual way, a user can refer to a single explication. In addition to decisions regarding what and how to annotate, editors will also need to decide where and how annotations will display. Digital tools and platforms currently in use provide a variety of display options: document-centered notes that stay with the document, sidebars, links, pop-ups, hierarchical taxonomy lists, etc. Display decisions will also be made considering the same questions listed above in conjunction with the capabilities of the digital tools and platforms in use.[15]

Indexing

Indexes also help make content accessible and understandable. While it might seem like a relic of the print edition, thinking in terms of an index's hierarchical structure and its economy of words dovetails nicely with building effective taxonomy lists and tagging schemas. An index is a systematic arrangement of entries designed to enable users to locate information within an edition. Structurally hierarchical, the top-level entry headings list people, places, events, and major subjects within an edition, usually presented alphabetically and subdivided into logical subentries. An index should be considerably more than an outline and considerably less than a concordance of words and phrases. In short, a good index makes the content accessible. As with annotation and tagging, it is helpful to keep several things in mind when developing indexing guidelines. First, entries and subentries should reflect the nature of the materials in the edition and should be phrased to serve the needs of the edition's audience. Editions of financial, legal, scientific, or other specialized topics might use technical phrasing. Also think about what types of questions users will ask of the material's contents – who, what, when? – and consider what terms users will intuitively search. Also think of ways to point users in directions they might not have considered. Finally, when an edition focuses on a single person, organization, topic, or event, entries under that heading need to be broken down into intelligible subentries. Don't just make a list of references; use descriptive subentries to help users easily find information.

It is also incredibly helpful to keep the index's design in mind during the editorial process. Start with what subjects, places, themes, and people are important in the edition, and develop and manage a list, preferably in the content management system/database. Next, consider how the content is related and where cross-references can be effectively used. Making connections between related documents, subjects, people, and places is enormously helpful to the user. Within the platform, maintain a preliminary annotated index linking mentions with entry. Keeping track of where a person is mentioned and associating that reference with a well-formed index entry will help avoid confusion in the end – which John Smith is it? As with other steps in the editorial workflow, develop a statement of method and make it available to users, explaining how and what has been indexed. And last, but certainly not least, be consistent! Planning is key and worth every minute spent.

CONCLUSION

Though digital editing has presented hurdles for editors, the process of tackling these challenges has provided us with a unique and exciting opportunity – an opportunity to think creatively about access and develop innovative solutions for achieving our goals. While editors will still need to develop editorial processes, procedures, and methodologies, digital tools and platforms provide opportunities to also develop interactive and engaging digital editions. Our digital editions can now reflect content management strategies, selection decisions, transcription displays, organization schemas, and annotation/index design. We are no longer just making documents and content available – we are making these things accessible.

NOTES

1 As the title implies, this chapter focuses on documentary editing, specifically the editing of historical documents. While the conceptual and methodological approaches covered are applicable to digital editions generally, there are several works that address the concerns and issues related to textual studies and literary editing specifically, including Susan Schreibman's "Digital Scholarly Editing," Martha Nell Smith's "Electronic Scholarly Editing," and Kenneth Price's "Electronic Scholarly Editions."

2 There are two works that go into great depth examining the field and practice of documentary editing: Michael Stevens and Steven Burg, *Editing Historical Documents: A Handbook of Practice*, and Mary-Jo Kline and Susan Perdue, *A Guide to Documentary Editing*.

3 Kline and Perdue explain that microforms can contain "images of the source's target, the source itself, [or] the editorial transcription" and "are accompanied by a separate finding aid containing not only an index to the documents but also statements of editorial method and historical introductions analogous to those required of book editions."

4 The advent of crowdsourcing and the demand for rough, unchecked transcriptions have caused some to question whether further editorial work is necessary. But just making a transcription available online does not make the content accessible. While transcriptions are an important component of digital editions, annotations, indexes, metadata, and content organizations – the building blocks of searches, queries, browse options, and views – make the content truly accessible and understandable.

5 See Price for an expanded discussion of these definitions.

6 For a full definition, see "Minimum Standards for Electronic Editions".

7 The Institute for the Editing of Historical Documents provides instruction in the principles of the field and insight into the realities of documentary editing.

8 Committee on Scholarly Editions, Modern Language Association. "Considering the Scholarly Edition in the Digital Age: A White Paper of the Modern Language Association's Committee on Scholarly Editions." Web. 4 November 2015. https://scholarlyeditions.commons.mla.org/2015/09/02/cse-white-paper/

9 Decisions regarding technology will be greatly influenced by who will publish the edition. A university press might require XML files, while there are a variety of options when self-publishing.

10 For example, see "Symbols and Terms Designating Documents," Hoth and Ebel xxvii.

11 For transcription policy examples, see "Editorial Apparatus," Hoth and Ebel xxv–xxvi.

12 For examples of methodological approaches, see "The Conventions of Textual Treatment" in Kline and Perdue.

13 Most editors regularize the appearance of parts of the document, such as standard locations for date, place, salutation, and signature; regularized paragraph indents, addition of missing terminal punctuation; regularizing capitalization at the start of sentences, etc.

14 Making use of images can present challenges. Issues of copyright, cost of use, and file size must be taken into consideration.

15 See Dombrowski's "Choosing a Platform for your Project Website" and McCarthy and Grant's "Choosing Content Management Technologies."

REFERENCES AND FURTHER READING

Dombrowski, Quinn. "Choosing a Platform for Your Project Website." Web. 1 April 2016. http://digitalhumanities.berkeley.edu/blog/13/12/04/choosing-platform-your-project-website

Hajo, Cathy Moran. "Minimum Standards for Electronic Editions." Association for Documentary Editing. Web. 2 October 2015. www.documentaryediting.org/wordpress/?page_id=508

Hoth, David R., and Carol S. Ebel, eds. *The Papers of George Washington*, Presidential Series, Volume 16. Charlottesville: University of Virginia, 2011. Print.

Kline, Mary-Jo, and Susan H. Perdue. *A Guide to Documentary Editing*. Web. 29 October 2015. http://gde.upress.virginia.edu

McCarthy, Kate, and Rebecca Grant. "Choosing Content Management Technologies." Web. 1 April 2016. http://dri.ie/sites/default/files/files/choosing-cms-technologies-2014.pdf

Price, Kenneth M. "Edition, Project, Database, Archive, Thematic Research Collection: What's In a Name?" *DHQ: Digital Humanities Quarterly*. Summer 2009 3:3. Web. 2 October 2015. http://digitalcommons.unl.edu/cgi/viewcontent.cgi?article=1068&context=englishfacpubs

Price, Kenneth M. "Electronic Scholarly Editions." *Blackwell Companion to Digital Literary Study*, ed. Susan Schreibman and Ray Siemens. Oxford: Wiley-Blackwell, 2008. Web. 3 November 2015. www.digitalhumanities.org/companion/view?docId=blackwell/9781405148641/9781405148641.xml&chunk.id=ss1-6-5&toc.depth=1&toc.id=ss1-6-5&brand=9781405148641_brand

Schreibman, Susan. "Digital Scholarly Editing." *Literary Studies in the Digital Age: An Evolving Anthology*, ed. Kenneth M. Price and Ray Siemens. Modern Language Association, 2013. Web. 3 November 2015. https://dlsanthology.commons.mla.org/digital-scholarly-editing/

Smith, Martha Nell. "Electronic Scholarly Editing." *A Companion to Digital Humanities*, ed. Susan Schreibman, Ray Siemens and John Unsworth. Blackwell, 2004. *Blackwell Reference Online*. Web. 3 November 2015. www.blackwellreference.com/subscriber/tocnode.html?id=g9781405103213_chunk_g978140510321325

Stevens, Michael E., and Steven B. Burg. *Editing Historical Documents: A Handbook of Practice*. Walnut Creek, CA: AltaMira Press, 1997. Print.

CHAPTER 14

XSLT

Transforming our XML data

Julia Flanders, Syd Bauman and Sarah Connell

INTRODUCTION: WHAT IS XSLT?

XSLT, the Extensible Stylesheet Language for Transformations, is a tool for transforming XML, and together they are a crucial technology for the digital humanities. Because of XML's status as a standard and its excellent archival qualities, it is often used in digital humanities to represent high-quality research materials such as primary source collections and digital editions, using languages such as TEI and EAD. XSLT serves to convert XML data from one XML language into another: for instance, converting data from EAD to XHTML, or transforming TEI header metadata into MARCXML. But it can also be used to convert XML into non-XML plain-text formats, such as RTF, tab-delimited data, or JSON. As a result, XSLT is an essential tool for transforming data from archival formats into specific output formats as required by specific tools, as those arise: for instance, KML for Google maps, JSON or SVG for visualizations, HTML for the Web, metadata formats for a repository. Furthermore, XSLT permits us to treat our data as essentially fungible and malleable over time. At one point we may wish to express our data as a customized form of TEI; at another, we may wish to convert them to a format used by our collaborators. With XSLT, we can accomplish these transformations straightforwardly; as long as our data are well modeled in the first place, we do not need to anticipate their future uses in detail.

As we know, XML represents data as a tree structure (for more information about XML, please see Chapter 7 in this volume). So one way of understanding this transformation process is to think about it as a way of mapping one tree structure onto another. XSLT is a language for expressing such a mapping, and an XSLT processor takes an XML file as its input, performs a conversion based on the mapping, and creates as its output a new document representing the new tree structure. (In cases where the output format is something other than XML, we can think of it as a tree with a single node.)

Expressed this way, XSLT looks simple. As with so many things, the devil is in the details – and there are many details. Our goal in this chapter is not to teach XSLT in detail – which would require more space than we have – but to explain how it works, describe the major concepts you need in order to understand it, and discuss the kinds of tasks it is good for. If XSLT is a tool you need to use, we hope this chapter will be a good first step in learning it.

HOW XSLT WORKS: TWO SIMPLE EXAMPLES

Let's take a very simple example: a poem encoded in rudimentary TEI. For purposes of this example, we'll ignore the TEI header and other complexities and focus on the poem itself:

```
<lg>
  <head>Trees</head>
  <l>I think that I shall never see</l>
  <l>A poem as lovely as a tree</l>
  <byline>Joyce Kilmer</byline>
</lg>
```

Let's imagine that we'd like to convert this XML document into HTML, to put it on a web site. Our desired HTML encoding (again, very rudimentary) might look something like this:

```
<html>
  <head><title>A Sample Poem</title></head>
  <body>
    <h2>Trees</h2>
    <p>I think that I shall never see</p>
    <p>A poem as lovely as a tree</p>
    <p style="text-indent:50px">Joyce Kilmer</p>
  </body>
</html>
```

These two documents are superficially quite different: for one thing, HTML doesn't have an element specifically for representing poetry, so we might use the HTML <p> element instead. (We'll return later to the problem of how we distinguish the HTML <p> element from the TEI <p> element; for now, let's just note that from an XML perspective they are entirely different.) HTML also doesn't have anything similar to the TEI <byline> element, so we can use <p> again for that, but we might like to distinguish this line from the lines of the poem itself, perhaps by indentation. Similarly, the enclosing elements in the two examples (<lg>, <html>, <body>, and so forth) are different in the two languages, and our HTML output in this example has some additional layers that the TEI input lacks. However, from another perspective the two examples are deeply similar: in both cases, the poem is modeled as consisting of four major components: the title, the two lines, and the byline. The fact that TEI and HTML group these components together differently, and give them different levels of semantic precision, is less important for our conversion than the fact that both examples cut the text up into the same kinds of pieces.

Now let's look at how an XSLT stylesheet represents the mapping between these two structures. You can imagine an XSLT stylesheet as a set of rules (called "templates") that say "if you find this thing, turn it into this other thing." For instance, in our simple example, an XSLT stylesheet to convert our TEI input into our HTML output might have templates expressing the following transformation rules (Figure 14.1):

- If there is a <byline>, turn it into an HTML <p> element with a @style attribute carrying a 50-pixel indentation.
- If there is a <head> element, turn it into an HTML <h2> element.
- If there is an <l> element, turn it into an HTML <p> element.
- If there is an <lg> element, turn it into an HTML document with a <head> and a <body> element inside, and put the rest of the input content inside the <body>.

It is worth noting that some of the output (e.g. "Joyce Kilmer") is copied from the input document, and some of the output (e.g. "A Sample Poem") is generated by the XSLT almost irrespective of the input. This is always the case – that some of the output (ranging from none to all) is copied from the input, and some (ranging from none to all) is generated by the XSLT. It is also worth noting that XSLT is an XML language and so its syntax may look familiar to those who have worked with other XML languages such as the TEI. For more on the basic rules and concepts of XML, see Chapter 7 in this volume.

Let's now express one of those templates using XSLT itself:

```
<!-- If there is an <lg> element, turn it into an HTML
     document with a <head> and a <body> element inside, and
     put the rest of the input content inside the <body>. -->
<xsl:template match="lg">
```

```
  <html>
    <head>
      <title>A Sample Poem</title>
    </head>
    <body><xsl:apply-templates/></body>
  </html>
</xsl:template>
```

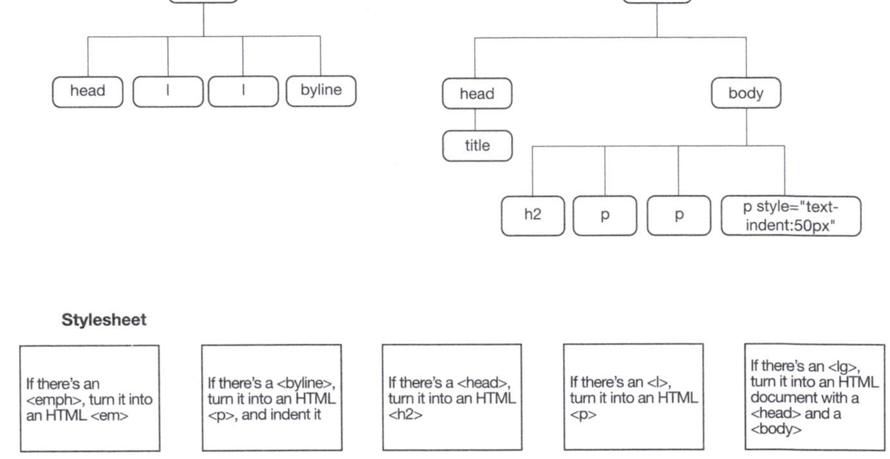

Figure 14.1
Schematic of transforming a TEI poem to XHTML

Although this code is unfamiliar, it's not impenetrable: based on our understanding of XSLT thus far, we can read through and figure out what is happening here. The outer <xsl:template> element is ready to be used if it "matches" an <lg> element in our input document. In that case, the enclosed HTML code (including some boilerplate content) is written into our output. And inside the <body> element in that output, there's an instruction to "apply templates" – that is, to continue to apply the templates of our XSLT code to the structure of our input document. Here is a second code sample:

```
<!-- If there is a <head> element, turn it into an HTML <h2>
    element. -->
  <xsl:template match="head">
    <h2><xsl:apply-templates/></h2>
  </xsl:template>
```

This one is even simpler than the first: the <xsl:template> "matches" the <head> element in our input document (or "input tree"). When there is a <head>

element present in the input, the result is an <h2> element in the output. And, inside that <h2> element, we are again told to "apply templates." We'll explore what this means in more detail in a moment. Here is the full stylesheet, much of which you should now be able to read for yourself based on these examples:

```
<?xml version="1.0" encoding="UTF-8"?>
<xsl:stylesheet xmlns:xsl="http://www.w3.org/1999/XSL/Transform"
 xmlns="http://www.w3.org/1999/xhtml"
 xpath-default-namespace="http://www.tei-c.org/ns/Examples"
 version="2.0">
 <!-- If there is an <lg> element, turn it into an HTML
      document with a <head> and a <body> element inside, and
      put the rest of the input content inside the <body>. -->
 <xsl:template match="lg">
   <html>
     <head>
       <title>A Sample Poem</title>
     </head>
     <body><xsl:apply-templates/></body>
   </html>
 </xsl:template>

 <!-- If there is a <head> element, turn it into an HTML <h2>
      element. -->
 <xsl:template match="head">
   <h2><xsl:apply-templates/></h2>
 </xsl:template>

 <!-- If there is an <l> element, turn it into an HTML <p>
      element. -->
 <xsl:template match="l">
   <p><xsl:apply-templates/></p>
 </xsl:template>

 <!-- If there is a <byline>, turn it into an HTML <p> element
      with a @style attribute carrying a 50-pixel indentation. -->
 <xsl:template match="byline">
   <p style="text-indent:50px;"><xsl:apply-templates/></p>
 </xsl:template>
</xsl:stylesheet>
```

At this point, we now have an input tree (our tiny TEI document), and an XSLT stylesheet that tells us how the input tree will be transformed. The next step would be to run the input document through that stylesheet and perform the transformation. What actually happens during this process? Understanding the XSLT processor's "thought process" can help us understand the logic of XSLT itself, so we'll take a moment and unpack that in some detail here.

When we run an XSLT transformation, the XSLT processor works by taking the input tree structure, piece by piece, and applying transformation rules to each piece, or "node."[1] In fact, the processor works its way down the input tree, branch by branch, starting at the "root" node, then taking each of its children in turn, as shown in Figure 14.2.

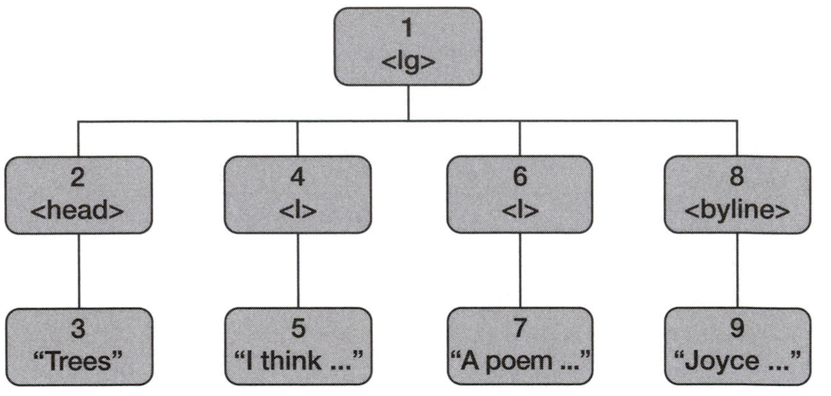

Figure 14.2
Node processing order

At each node, the processor stops and asks "does the stylesheet have a template that does something with this node?" If so, it does what the template tells it to do. Then it looks for a sign from the stylesheet that it's permitted to continue processing, and if it gets the go-ahead, it returns to the input tree and tackles the next node. The process continues until the processor reaches the last node of the input tree, or until it fails to receive the go-ahead that permits it to continue processing. We'll see in a moment what that go-ahead looks like.

As we can see, the first node the processor will encounter in our input tree is the `<lg>` element,[2] and the XSLT stylesheet does contain a template for that element:

```
<xsl:template match="lg">
  <html>
    <head>
      <title>A short test document</title>
    </head>
    <body><xsl:apply-templates/></body>
  </html>
</xsl:template>
```

The @match attribute tells us what input node this template is intended to handle: in this case, the TEI <lg> element. And the content of the <xsl:template> element tells us what code will be created in the output tree. We can immediately see something interesting here: the output tree code is actually the skeleton of an HTML file. In other words, this template (the first one to be processed) will create the basic structure of the output tree, and populate it with some required elements: the HTML <head>, <title>, and <body> elements – basically a template of an HTML document. And the <xsl:apply-templates> element at the heart of the output is that crucial "go-ahead" signal that tells the processor "OK, go back to the input tree and process the next node in the processing order," which in this case is the first child of the current <lg> element, i.e. the <head> element.[3] So at the end of this first step in the process, we have the rudiments of our output tree, and we have been given permission to continue on and populate that tree with additional content, derived from processing more of the input tree.

When it's sent back to the input tree, the processor looks at the next node, <head>, and asks: does the stylesheet contain a template to handle a TEI <head> element? It does, and it tells us to create an HTML <h2> element, and then gives us the go-ahead to continue back and process more of the input tree:

```
<xsl:template match="head">
  <h2><xsl:apply-templates/></h2>
</xsl:template>
```

Back at the input tree, the next node in order is the content of the <head> element, so the processor fetches that content and puts it into the output tree as well:

```
<html>
  <head><title>A Sample Poem</title></head>
  <body>
    <h2>Trees</h2>
  </body>
</html>
```

At this point, we seem to have reached a dead end: we've explored one whole branch of the input tree (the `<head>` element and its contents). But remember that our "go-ahead" in that first template – the `<xsl:apply-templates/>` inside the `<xsl:template match="lg">` – told us to process *all* of the children of the `<lg>` element. So that go-ahead is still in effect: when we finish working our way down the first branch of the input tree (the first child of the `<lg>` and its descendants), we go back to the job of processing the children of `<lg>`, and start working on the next branch: in this case, the second child of the `<lg>` element, which is the first line of the poem itself. Our stylesheet contains a template to handle the TEI `<l>` element:

```
<xsl:template match="l">
  <p>
    <xsl:apply-templates/>
  </p>
</xsl:template>
```

So the processor will use that template to create an HTML `<p>` element in the output tree, and populate it with the first line of the poem:

```
<html>
  <head><title>A Sample Poem</title></head>
  <body>
    <h2>Trees</h2>
    <p>I think that I shall never see</p>
  </body>
</html>
```

When the processor tackles the second line of the poem, it will use that same template again.

We've now established a cycle: take the next node in the input tree, find a template that matches it, use the template to create appropriate content in the output tree, and then proceed to the next node. This cycle continues as the processor works its way through the remaining lines of the poem, and then the closing `<byline>` element; it finally concludes when the processor runs out of elements in the input tree to process.

Let's pause here for a moment and emphasize a few points. First, note that the "go-ahead" received in the very first step holds the key to the entire process. That `<xsl:apply-templates>` within the template for the top-most element (i.e. the TEI `<lg>` element) is what enables the processor to keep going back to the input tree after it exhausts each branch. In this simple stylesheet, there's only one such choke-point, but in a more complex stylesheet there might be several critical "apply-templates" instructions that effectually control access to entire segments of the input tree. So, if you notice that pieces of your input tree are being ignored by the processor, it may be because the `<xsl:apply-templates>` that controls that branch of the input tree is not getting executed, or is not working.

Second, it's important to remember that for stylesheets like this, it is the structure of the *input tree* that determines how the XSLT stylesheet gets used. For example, if the input poem had the `<byline>` between the `<title>` and the first `<l>`, then the output would have the `<p style="text-indent:50px;">` with the content "Joyce Kilmer" between the `<h2>` heading and the `<p>` with content "I think that I shall never see." Because the input tree is XML, it is not processed from top to bottom, but in "tree order." If instead of thinking of XML as a tree structure, we think of it as a set of nesting boxes, we could imagine the processing working from the outside in.

Third, because the input tree determines how the stylesheet is used, it's important to remember that the XSLT processor only looks for templates that match *existing elements in the input tree*; templates for other elements never get used. So our stylesheet might include a template to handle the TEI `<name>` element, but our poem sample doesn't include this element, so that template would be ignored by the XSLT processor. This is good news, with a caveat: it's good news because it means that we can write stylesheets to handle a wide variety of documents containing different combinations of elements. The unused templates don't do any harm; they just wait patiently until they are needed. The caveat is that we need to be aware that just because we included some content in our stylesheet doesn't mean that it will appear in our output document. For instance, we might have some boilerplate metadata in a template that matches the `<profileDesc>` element in our TEI header. But if our input document doesn't have a `<profileDesc>`, none of that boilerplate will be included in the output document.

Finally, we need to consider the opposite situation: what happens when there is an element to be processed in the input document for which there is no template? In this situation, XSLT provides a "built-in" template that will be used. The built-in templates are very simple, and sometimes do exactly what you want. They provide the following behavior:

- for an *element*, process that element's children (i.e. as if `<xsl:apply-templates/>` were the only instruction);
- for *text*, copy the text into the output;[4]
- for anything else (*attribute*, *comment*, *processing instruction*), do nothing; in particular, do not put anything into the output.

So a stylesheet that has no templates at all (and thus will necessarily only use the built-in templates) will produce as output all of the content of the input XML document (including whitespace) without any elements or attributes. Note that this output is definitionally ill-formed XML, since it fails the "one and only one outermost element" rule of well-formedness.

It's also worth noting that there is some information lost in this transformation – for example, the HTML does not preserve the markup indicating that these are poetic lines – and that information loss is a common (though not inevitable) part of the transformation process. However, we also gain a great deal from the ability to transmute our data from one format to another: in particular, from the ability to store data in an information-rich format such as TEI and transform it into specific functional formats as needed for output. The ability to produce KML, JSON, RTF, and the many other formats noted above from a single TEI document, for example, is an extraordinarily powerful one.

We're now ready to consider a second example. For our first example, we've been working with a case where the structure of the output tree closely mirrors that of the input tree: both have their content in the same order and the transformation consisted chiefly of changing the names of the XML elements being used. But we can also use XSLT in ways that rearrange our input data much more dramatically, or use it much more selectively. For example, we could write a stylesheet that puts the individual lines of the poem into cells in an HTML table and sorts them into alphabetical order, or we could write a stylesheet that suppresses the poem's content altogether and shows only the author's name, repeated hundreds of times.

What about working with XML documents that are not "documents" in the usual sense, but are structured more like databases, with repeating regular data elements such as bibliographic citations, gazetteers, or biographical records? These kinds of data call out for transformations that would let us summarize the data and work selectively with their individual components. Let's consider another simple example, this time a set of data about people, represented as a TEI personography:

```
<TEI xmlns="http://www.tei-c.org/ns/1.0">
  <teiHeader>
    <fileDesc>
      <titleStmt>
        <title>A tiny prosopography</title>
        <author>Julia Flanders</author>
      </titleStmt>
      <publicationStmt>
       <publisher>Routledge</publisher>
        <availability>
          <licence target="http://creativecommons.org/licenses/
            by/3.0/">
            This work is licensed under a Creative Commons
            Attribution 3.0 Unported License, and should be
            attributed to the <ref target="http://www.wwp.neu.
            edu/">Women Writers Project</ref>.
          </licence>
        </availability>
```

```
      </publicationStmt>
      <sourceDesc>
        <p>Born digital.</p>
      </sourceDesc>
    </fileDesc>
  </teiHeader>
  <text>
    <body>
      <listPerson>
        <person role="author">
          <persName>
             <surname>Cavendish</surname>
             <forename>Margaret</forename>
          </persName>
          <birth when="1623"/>
          <death when="1673-12-15"/>
        </person>
        <person role="ruler">
          <persName>
            <surname>Stuart</surname>
            <forename>Charles</forename>
          </persName>
          <birth when="1600-11-19"/>
          <death when="1649-01-30"/>
        </person>
        <person role="author">
          <persName>
            <surname>Herrick</surname>
            <forename>Robert</forename>
          </persName>
          <birth when="1591-08-24"/>
          <death when="1674-10-15"/>
        </person>
        <person role="ruler">
          <persName>
            <surname>Tudor</surname>
            <forename>Elizabeth</forename>
          </persName>
          <birth when="1533-09-07"/>
          <death when="1603-03-24"/>
        </person>
      </listPerson>
    </body>
  </text>
</TEI>
```

Imagine that this is a tiny segment of a much longer file, including the names and birth/death dates of hundreds of people who are classified as either "authors" or "rulers." There are several things we can imagine doing with this kind of data. For instance, we might sort them out into two separate groups based on the value of the `@role` attribute. Then, within each list, we might display a selection of data from each person's record, in a consistent format. Here is a sample stylesheet that does both of these things:

```
<xsl:stylesheet version="2.0"
    xmlns:xsl="http://www.w3.org/1999/XSL/Transform"
    xpath-default-namespace="http://www.tei-c.org/ns/1.0"
    xmlns="http://www.w3.org/1999/xhtml">

  <xsl:template match="TEI">
    <html>
      <head>
        <title>Persons!</title>
      </head>
      <body>
        <div>
          <h1>Authors</h1>
          <ol>
            <xsl:apply-templates select=
              "/TEI/text/body/listPerson/person[ @role='author'] "/>
          </ol>
        </div>
        <div>
          <h1>Rulers</h1>
          <ol>
            <xsl:apply-templates select=
              "/TEI/text/body/listPerson/person[ @role='ruler'] "/>
          </ol>
        </div>
      </body>
    </html>
  </xsl:template>

  <xsl:template match="person">
    <li>
      <xsl:value-of select="persName/surname"/>
      <xsl:text> (</xsl:text>
      <xsl:value-of select="birth/@when"/>
      <xsl:text> - </xsl:text>
```

```
      <xsl:value-of select="death/@when"/>
      <xsl:text>)</xsl:text>
      <br/>
    </li>
  </xsl:template>

</xsl:stylesheet>
```

If we imagine our XSLT processor working its way through this example, we can see that it has some things in common with the earlier example: the processor will go to the top node of the input tree (in this case, the <TEI> element) and then look to the stylesheet to see whether there is a matching template. As before, the matching template establishes the skeleton of the output tree, in the form of a simple HTML document containing some boilerplate content and the outer shells of two ordered lists (the HTML <ol> elements). However, at this point we see something new: instead of the unadorned <xsl:apply-templates> of our earlier example, the "go-ahead" in this case tells the processor something more specific. Rather than saying "go back to the input tree and process the children of the current input node," it says "go back to the input tree, select a specific set of nodes, and process only those." The specific nodes are identified here using a mechanism called XPath (to be addressed in more detail later on), which allows us to navigate within the XML tree and select nodes based on their location within the tree, the attributes they carry, and other properties. In this case, the nodes being selected for the first list are all of the <person> elements that carry a @role attribute with the value of "author" that appear within a <listPerson> that is nested within a <body> that is nested within a <text> that is nested within the <TEI> element. The nodes to be included in the second list are very similar, except that instead of a @role of "author", they must carry a @role of "ruler".

Once the processor has identified those nodes, it then can look for a template in the stylesheet that is intended to handle them, and indeed such a template exists. Here again, we see something new: instead of simply putting all of the content into the output tree, this template does something more selective: the <xsl:value-of> element tells the processor to select specific nodes from within the <person> element, again using XPath.

In the first case, the selected node is an XML element: the stylesheet asks for all of the <surname> elements that are children of <persName> elements that are children of the current <person> element. Since there is only one such element, its value is returned.[5] In the other two cases, the selected node is the value of an attribute: the @when attribute from the <birth> and <death> elements within <person>. In other words, the stylesheet is reaching carefully into the input tree and pulling out specific pieces of information to place in the output tree, and ignoring the rest of the input tree altogether. When the process is done, our output tree will look like this:

```
<?xml version="1.0" encoding="UTF-8"?>
<html xmlns="http://www.w3.org/1999/xhtml">
  <head>
    <meta http-equiv="Content-Type"
          content="text/html; charset=UTF-8" />
    <title>Persons!</title>
  </head>
  <body>
    <div>
      <h1>Authors</h1>
      <ol>
        <li>Cavendish (1623 - 1673-12-15)<br /></li>
        <li>Herrick (1591-08-24 - 1674-10-15)<br /></li>
      </ol>
    </div>
    <div>
      <h1>Rulers</h1>
      <ol>
        <li>Stuart (1600-11-19 - 1649-01-30)<br /></li>
        <li>Tudor (1533-09-07 - 1603-03-24)<br /></li>
      </ol>
    </div>
  </body>
</html>
```

These two examples offer a very brief and simple view of the kinds of things XSLT can do, and an illustration of the underlying logic that animates the XSLT processor. They represent only a tiny sampling of XSLT's capabilities: XSLT is a full-fledged programming language containing functions for a huge variety of powerful data manipulations. But these examples may serve as a starting point to help you determine whether XSLT is a useful tool for you to learn, and to help get you started if you want to learn more. In what follows, we'll cover some further important concepts that are at the heart of XSLT, and then step back to consider XSLT in a larger context.

CRUCIAL FEATURES: XPATH AND NAMESPACES

XPath

As we have seen, an XSLT stylesheet does its work by identifying nodes in the input document and manipulating or transforming them to create an output document. The ability to identify a specific node, or a set of nodes, in an XML document is perhaps the most important and powerful aspect of the entire undertaking. The method by which we accomplish this is XPath, a query language for selecting nodes in an XML document. XPath provides a way to navigate within the XML document's tree structure, and to say things such as "select the third child of my parent <quote> element" or "select all of the <persName> elements that have a @ref attribute." Some of XPath's concepts and notations will be familiar to anyone who has written file paths in an HTML document: the slashes that denote child directories are directly analogous to XPath's mechanism for representing child elements. The following expression means "the <persName> elements that are children of a <quote> that is itself the child of a <div> that is itself a child of the current node":

```
div/quote/persName
```

Other XPath notations may be familiar to those who work with CSS; the following expression means "the <div> element children of the current node that carry a @type attribute with the value 'chapter'":

```
div[ @type="chapter"]
```

XPath also makes use of a wildcard notation. For instance, the following expression means "all the child elements of the current node that have a @type attribute whose value is 'chapter'":

```
*[ @type="chapter"]
```

Full details of XPath, including a crib sheet, are included in the online materials that accompany this chapter.

Namespaces

XSLT operates in a polyglot XML world: indeed, its entire purpose is to translate between XML languages. But how do we know what XML language we are actually using in any given XML document? If we look back to our first example, the HTML output tree contains several elements (<head>, <body>, <p>, <title>) that will be familiar to users of the TEI Guidelines, and might even be mistaken for TEI elements:

```
<html>
  <head><title>A Sample Poem</title></head>
  <body>
    <h2>Trees</h2>
    <p>I think that I shall never see</p>
    <p>A poem as lovely as a tree</p>
    <p style="text-indent:50px">Joyce Kilmer</p>
  </body>
</html>
```

And yet these elements mean something quite different, depending on whether they are HTML elements or TEI elements: for instance, in TEI the `<head>` element denotes the heading for a section of the document, whereas in HTML it is used to enclose the file metadata. How can we tell the difference – and more importantly, how can our stylesheets and other programs tell the difference? Namespaces are the solution, the mechanism by which we identify the XML languages we are using and distinguish them from one another.

Basically, each XML element has a 2-part name: the *namespace*, which says what language the element is from, and its *local name*, such as “p” or “head” or “sourceDesc.” The namespace part is expressed as a string that looks like a URI. For example, “http://www.tei-c.org/ns/1.0” (the TEI) or “http://www.w3.org/2000/svg” (Scalable Vector Graphics). At its most basic, the namespace is specified for each occurrence of each element by declaring it with a namespace declaration. For example, `<head xmlns="http://www.w3.org/1999/xhtml">` indicates an HTML `<head>` element.[6]

But specifying the namespace in full on each and every element gets very annoying very quickly. So XML provides a shortcut: a namespace can be bound to a *prefix*, and then the prefix can be used instead. We have already taken full advantage of namespace prefixes. The `<xsl:template>` element has a local name of “template,” in whatever namespace is associated with the “xsl” prefix (in this case “http://www.w3.org/1999/XSL/Transform”).

In the full XSLT code sample we examined earlier, several namespaces were declared, including the namespace for XSLT itself, the namespace for XHTML (used for the elements in the output tree), and the XPath default namespace, which is the namespace for the tree in which XPath needs to navigate in order to select portions of the input tree (in this case, TEI) (Figure 14.3).

A more complete explanation of namespaces is provided in the online materials accompanying this chapter.

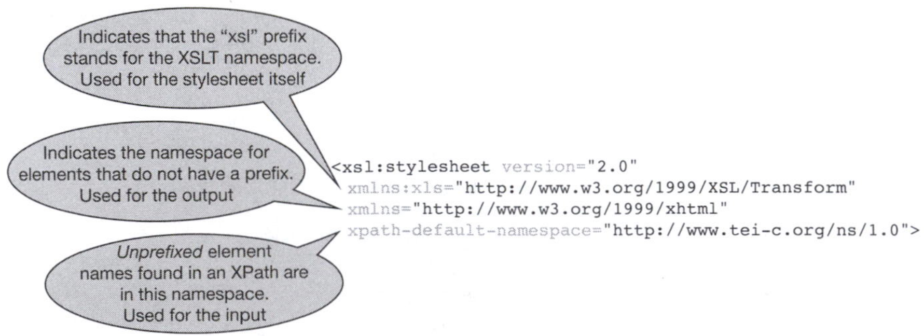

Figure 14.3
Sample namespace declarations

USING XSLT

Now that you understand the internal logic of XSLT and what it is useful for, you're in a position to decide whether it is something you want to learn more thoroughly. If it is, there are additional materials available online at the website that accompanies this book, as well as a list of resources for further study. It may be helpful to conclude this discussion with a few notes on the use of XSLT in a digital humanities context.

As we've now seen, XSLT is a very distinctive kind of programming language. For our purposes, its most important property is that it understands XML as a tree structure. What this means is that instead of treating an XML document as a sequence of characters (angle brackets, spaces, and so forth), it treats it as a set of informational nodes (elements, attributes, content), and it performs its operations on these nodes. As a result, it can ignore the accidental details of the XML file, such as spacing or the order in which attributes appear, making it much more accurate and powerful as an XML manipulation tool than something like Perl or regular expressions. Perhaps most importantly of all, its XML output will always be well balanced (cleanly nested, with all start- and end-tags and required delimiters in place). Because it "thinks" in XML, it can act intelligently in an XML environment.

XSLT can be put into action in several different contexts. We can author and run XSLT stylesheets using an XML editor such as Oxygen, and during the learning process this kind of environment can make it easy to test and debug our stylesheets. Detailed instructions for writing and using XSLT stylesheets are included in the online materials that accompany this chapter. A finished XSLT stylesheet can be built into a web-publishing work flow (for instance, using a pipelining system such as XProc or Cocoon) that runs on a web server, and it can also be embedded in a web page and executed by the user's own browser software. For large-scale data conversion tasks, XSLT stylesheets can also be run from the command line or built into other conversion processes. XSLT processing software (needed to execute the stylesheet) is now built into many content management systems such as Drupal, permitting those systems to handle XML data. XSLT also sits at the heart of many of the XML publishing frameworks that are commonly used in digital humanities projects, such as XTF and eXist.

After reading this chapter, which has barely scratched the surface of XSLT's capabilities, you may be wondering how much XSLT you want and need to learn, and what kinds of things you can realistically do with these skills. We have focused here on the basic concepts of XSLT with the goal of making them seem as straightforward and comprehensible as possible, and our hope is that many readers will in fact feel motivated and empowered to learn more. For users of XML, there is a great deal one can usefully do with fairly simple XSLT: converting files from TEI into HTML, making global updates to one's encoding, extracting data for visualizations. Building larger-scale systems, such as a full-featured XML publication using a tool like XTF, requires significantly greater expertise and effort. After a week-long workshop, a novice can build satisfying XSLT tools for personal use in a few days or weeks, but full-scale publications require weeks to months of development by someone who uses XSLT regularly and expertly. The novice can become that expert, but only through sustained study and practice. If your research or employment involves regular work with XML, and if you have found the material in this chapter intuitive, then mastering XSLT may be a very worthwhile investment of time – and a very enjoyable one. But even when used in a purely exploratory way, XSLT offers deeper insight into the logic of XML, and in that spirit is well worth experimenting with.

NOTES

1 XML documents contain multiple types of nodes – these include the document node, element nodes, text nodes, attribute nodes, comment nodes, processing instruction nodes, and namespace nodes.

2 This is not entirely true. The built-in template for processing the document node (sometimes called the "root" node) gets processed first. But it has no effect on our output, so it is easier to ignore it for now.

3 This is not entirely true. Yes, the <xsl:apply-templates/> instruction means "go process my children," but the children of an element include not just its child elements, but also any text, comments, or processing instructions inside the element. In this particular case there is a whitespace-only text node before the <head> child element. It will actually get processed before the <head> element. This has little to no effect on our output, and makes conceptualizing the process harder, so it is reasonable to ignore this detail when first learning XSLT.

4 Later we will see that this is the equivalent of having <xsl:value-of select="."/> as the only instruction.

5 The value of an element is the concatenation of all its text node descendants. Often this is exactly what you want. Sometimes it's not.

6 Namespace declarations look very much like attributes, but don't behave quite the same way.

CHAPTER 15

Working with the Semantic Web

James Smith

The Semantic Web and linked data are computational applications of existing scholarly practices: linking to primary and secondary sources, signaling trusted vocabularies and authorities, and positioning a work in a larger conversation. The World Wide Web Consortium (W3C)[1] has been instrumental in developing the recommendations that enable these practices in a computational context. Before diving into these practices in the context of the Semantic Web and linked data, I want to consider what they look like in a scholarly text.

The following sentence is simple and to the point: "The new sovereign has achieved self-determination." In the absence of conflicts between connotation and denotation, between what writers mean to say and what readers perceive, this might be enough. But which "new sovereign?" What "self-determination?"

When writing for the World Wide Web, such as in a blog post, I can link to primary or secondary material positioning my use of these phrases in a historical context. For example, I might link to an edition of a work of literature published by Project Gutenberg (www.gutenberg.org/) if I want to provide open access to a classic text without depending on a particular scholarly treatment of that text, or, if writing for a popular audience, to a Wikipedia entry giving the background on a topic (e.g. https://en.wikipedia.org/wiki/Project_Gutenberg). I might not reference Wikipedia to justify a statement in a scholarly context, but it can provide a reasonably accurate introduction for many topics.[2] These links are ways through which the reader can explore new material or reassure themselves that they and the writer share a common understanding of the topic at hand.

When writing for a medium that doesn't have the same affordances as the World Wide Web for linking, we must resort to what might appear to be cruder methods.

We can't expect the reader to put down our text to follow a reference; to do so might mean traveling to a nearby library. Instead, we use intra-textual references and exposition as a crude form of hyperlinking to explain our meaning.

In his first chapter of *Distant Reading*, Franco Moretti fills out the sentence above to disambiguate his meaning:[3]

> The new sovereign – *ab-solutus*, untied, freed from the ethics-political bonds of the feudal tradition – has achieved what Hegel will call "self-determination": he can decide freely, and thus posit himself as the new source of historical movement: as in the *Trauerspiel*, and *Gorboduc*, and *Lear*, where everything indeed begins with his decisions; as in Racine, or *La Vida es Sueno*.

Moretti expands on what he means by "new sovereign" by recalling the change in understanding of what it meant to be "sovereign" as Europe emerged from feudalism, traditionally demarcated in part by the Peace of Westphalia in 1648.[4] He "links" to Hegel's definition of "self-determination" and describes his understanding of Hegel so that the reader doesn't need to follow the "link."

More than this, Moretti is saying that he "trusts" Hegel's vocabulary, but without comment on how strong that trust might be or if it is a positive trust or a negative trust (i.e. mistrust). If he didn't want to bring Hegel's work into the milieux, he wouldn't have referenced him the way he does here. The reader familiar with Hegel will more easily understand what Moretti is saying even without further explicit references. It might be slight in this particular example, but there's an alignment (or misalignment if Moretti is mistrusting Hegel) in the language of Moretti and Hagel that is not accidental. We might say that Moretti's writing is "informed" by Hegel. It's also "informed" by *Lear* and all the other literature he references.

As we read a text, we bring to mind all the material we have encountered before. In the above passage, Morretti mentions several works of literature in the hope that we will have read at least one. Our cultural authorities might differ in our writing, but we still provide a range of references in the hope that the reader will know at least one. It is critical that the scholar read far and wide in their career: the greater the shared background, the more efficient the communication.

This act of making as many connections as possible between the text and what we already know is the essence of a close reading. Experts exercise this close reading regardless of their area of expertise. The main differences from subject to subject involve the implied material the writer expects the reader to have at hand and how they make links. The above example from Moretti illustrates how this happens in textual scholarship, one of the defining fields of digital humanities.

I don't have room in this chapter to explore all of the richness of the Semantic Web, linked data, and information representation. I won't dive into defining vocabularies (collections of well-defined properties that I'll explore later in this chapter), writing code, or running computer services. Rather, I will explore how to create computational connections that mimic the connections we already make in our writing: namely, how to describe shareable, semantically meaningful data, how to signal our choice of authorities in describing our work, and how to reference existing bodies of information in order to help the reader develop a deeper understanding and insight into our work and its place in the scholarly community.

STRUCTURING INFORMATION

Just as a scholarly treatise tries to convey information with which we can mentally compute, sets of information, or *datasets*, share information with which we can digitally compute. Before I can show how we can link, signal vocabularies, and position computational information within a community, I need to show how we can structure information beyond just sharing a table in a Microsoft Word™ document.

When we hear the word "data," we tend to imagine numbers upon numbers, a tabulation of measurements such as "3 years" or "100 people." Data are just information, however that information is used. The bibliographic description of a book, the text of a novel, and the labeling of that text with parts of speech are all data.

I pulled an older and less common volume from my shelves to serve as a data source (see Figure 15.1). Examples of data in the figure are "1954," "Bâle," "COURS D'INTERLINGUA EN VINGT LEÇONS," and "Phil.André Schild." Of course, these pieces of information aren't found without some context. They are all on the front cover of a book, so we can assume that they relate to the book. Based on publishing

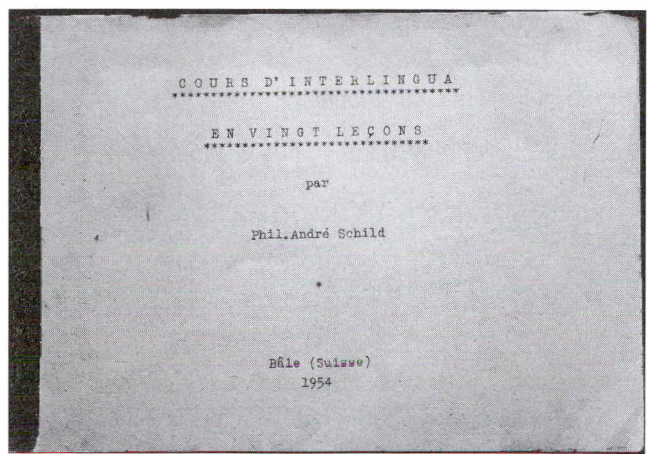

C O U R S D' I N T E R L I N G U A
****

E N V I N G T L E Ç O N S
****

par

Phil.André Schild

*

Bâle (Suisse)
1954

Figure 15.1
Title page of *Cours D'Interlingua en Vingt Leçons*

conventions, the "1954" is likely the date of publication, "Bâle" is likely the (French) name of the city of publication, and "Phil.André Schild" is likely the author.

I can rewrite all of this as phrases: the book has a title of *COURS D'INTERLINGUA EN VINGT LEÇONS*; the book has a publication date of 1954; the book was published in "Bâle, Suisse" (French); the book was written by Phil.André Schild.

My syntax might appear strained, but let's look at how I've constructed the phrases by placing them in Table 15.1. I'll bracket phrases indicating a topic or property with guillemets because they stand for semantically defined concepts. Values are quantifiable and literal, so they do not have guillemets. For now, think of the guillemets as handwaving.

On its face, this kind of table seems to allow me to show any quantifiable data, but if I expand the value column to hold more than just quantities, namely subjects, then I can make connections between things. For example, I can say that «the book» «was written by» «the author» and that «the book» «was published in» «the place of publication». The subject is «the book», but the values are other subjects: «the author» and «the place of publication». This allows me to link together two different subjects as illustrated in Figure 15.2.

Figure 15.2 is a graphical representation of what is called a *graph* in computer science: a set of *vertices* (topics and values) connected by *edges* (properties). A graph can have many representations. I chose a graphical one for this figure, but I can also represent the graph as a list of connections:

- «The book» «has a title of» "COURS D'INTERLINGUA EN VINGT LEÇONS."
- «The book» «has a publication date of» 1954.
- «The book» «was published at» «the place of publication».

Table 15.1 Information gathered from Figure 15.1

Subject	**Property**	**Value**
«the book»	«*has a* title *of*»	COURS D'INTERLINGUA EN VINGT LEÇONS
«the book»	«*has a* publication date *of*»	1954
«the place of publication»	«*has a* city name *of*»	Bâle (in French)
«the place of publication»	«*has a* country name *of*»	Suisse (in French)
«the author»	«*has a* title *of*»	Phil. (in French)
«the author»	«*has a* given name *of*»	André
«the author»	«*has a* surname *of*»	Schild

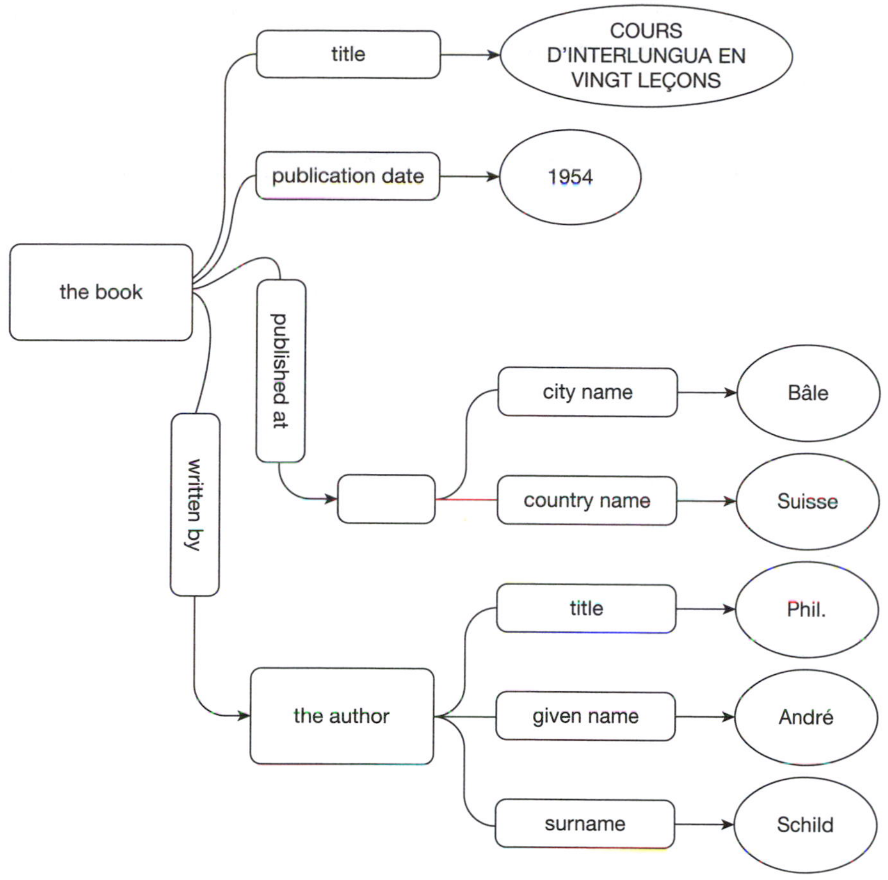

Figure 15.2
Some properties of «the book»

- «The book» «was written by» «the author».
- «The place of publication» «has a city name of» "Bâle" (in French).
- «The place of publication» «has a country name of» "Suisse" (in French).
- «The author» «has a title of» "Phil." (in French).
- «The author» «has a given name of» "André."
- «The author» «has a surname of» "Schild."

Or we could compact the list of statements into a stylized paragraph:

> «The book» «has a title of» "COURS D'INTERLUNGUA EN VINGT LEÇONS"; «has a publication date of» 1954; «was published at» «the place of publication»; «was written by» «the author». «The place of publication» «has a city name of»

> "Bâle" (in French); «has a country name of» "Suisse" (in French). «The author» «has a title of» "Phil." (in French); «has a given name of» "André"; «has a surname of» "Schild."

Up to this point, I've done some handwaving with my subjects and properties, but that won't work if I want to share this information. What do I mean by «the book» or «the author»? In the opening section, I described how scholars disambiguate by referencing a use in a specific context or by calling to mind definitions from outside their work: "The new sovereign – ***ab-solutus*, untied, freed from the ethics-political bonds of the feudal tradition** – has achieved . . ." (emphasis added). I could create a text description of each topic in a document describing my data. Many examples around the web show how to do this,[5] but in each case, someone must write additional software that can apply the intended semantics to the data.

Using only lists of associated subjects, properties, and values, I can represent any relatable information. The details are beyond the scope of this chapter, but it boils down to being the fact that any graph can be described by listing all of the ways edges connect vertices (the properties are the edges and subjects and values are the vertices).

REPRESENTING INFORMATION

In its simplest form, linked data are data with hyperlinks. Just as we can articulate our intended connotations in text with links to definitions or background material, we can use links in data to reference a particular connotation of a datum. Which Paris do we mean when we say that an event "happened in Paris"? We might feel that there's always enough context to know which "Paris" is meant. The "Paris" of the 1820s is not the "Paris" of the 1940s, and the "Paris" of France is not the "Paris" of Texas. We would never mistake one for the other.

It might be sufficient to say that an army numbered in the thousands, rather than give a precise number, because the significance is in the magnitude (thousands rather than hundreds), or the relative magnitude (one side had twice the number of soldiers as the other side), and not the number itself. We might be comfortable with this vagueness in data while retaining a preciseness in the textual narrative surrounding those data. The text drives the interpretation of the details in the data.

Those with a computational background that supersedes their humanities background might do the reverse: require great precision in the data, even in describing the lack of precision, while maintaining a lack of precision in the surrounding textual narrative. Anything that is not clear in the narrative will be made clear by a careful study of the data and methods. Data and methods enable the interpretation/interpolation of details in any accompanying text.

Scholarly work in the digital humanities seems to fall on one side or the other: humanities-centered narrative with some vague computational description, or solid computational description with some imprecise narrative. In both cases, the reader must use the computational to inform the narrative and the narrative to inform the computational. When all we have is text, we must enforce self-consistency entirely within the text. When combining computation with text, we can use each to reenforce and inform the other.

In order to explain what I mean by «the book», I could use a hyperlink for the Library of Congress Control Number, `<http://lccn.loc.gov/58045006>`, as if I were linking in a blog to a broadly informative definition of the thing I'm talking about. I can also use some hyperlinks defined by DBPedia,[6] Dublin Core,[7] and Schema.org.[8] Using hyperlinks, I can rewrite my paragraph:

> «http://lccn.loc.gov/58045006» «http://purl.org/dc/elements/1.1/title» "COURS D'INTERLINGUA EN VINGT LEÇONS"; «http://purl.org/_dc/elements/1.1/date» 1954; «http://purl.org/dc/elements/1.1/_publisher» «http://dbpedia.org/_resource/Basel»; «http://schema.org/_author» «http://dbpedia.org/_resource/André_Schild». «https://dbpedia.org/resource/_Basel» «http://dbpedia.org/_property/municipalityName» "Bâle" (in French); «http://dbpedia.org/_ontology/country» «http://dbpedia.org/_resource/_Switzerland». «http://dbpedia.org/resource/_André_Schild» «http://schema.org/_honorificPrefix» "Phil." (in French); «http://xmlns.org/_foaf/0.1/givenName» "André"; «http://xmlns.org/foaf/0.1/_surname» "Schild".

It might look odd, but I have almost completed the transformation into Turtle,[9] one of the ways we can represent information using the Resource Description Framework (RDF),[10] a set of recommendations and file formats that allow us to share any information that we can model using the methods I've shown in this chapter, namely subjects with properties taking on particular values or pointing to other subjects. RDF calls these *subjects*, *predicates*, and *objects*. A particular subject, predicate, and object together are a *triple*. We always write subjects and predicates as universal resource locaters (URLs)[11] and objects as either URLs (if referencing a subject) or as a literal (e.g. a string or a number).

Some tweaks to the way I write out the parts result in the following Turtle representation. I use prefixes as shorthand for collections of properties that go together. These tend to be collected as vocabularies. For example, the "dc" prefix (`<http://purl.org/dc/elements/1.1/>`) represents the Dublin Core metadata vocabulary commonly used to indicate titles and authorship of creative works:

```
@prefix dbr: <http://dbpedia.org/resource/> .
@prefix dbp: <http://dbpedia.org/property/> .
@prefix dbo: <http://dbpedia.org/ontology/> .
```

```
@prefix dc: <http://purl.org/dc/elements/1.1/> .
@prefix foaf: <http://xmlns.org/foaf/0.1/> .
@prefix lccn: <http://lccn.loc.gov/> .
@prefix schema: <http://schema.org/> .
<lccn:58045006> <dc:title> "COURS D'INTERLINGUA EN
VINGT LEÇONS";
  <cd:date> 1954;
  <dc:publisher> <dbr:Basel>;
  <schema:author> <dbr:André_Schild>.
<dbr:Basel> <dbp:municipalityName> "Bâle"@fr;
  <dbo:country> <dbr:Switzerland>.
<dbr:André_Schild> <schema:honorificPrefix>
"Phil."@fr;
  <foaf:givenName> "André";
  <foaf:surname> "Schild".
```

Note that I slipped in a few changes. Rather than referencing the name of the country of publication, I'm linking to a resource representing that country. I've also changed the "(in French)" annotation to "@fr". The language tags are defined by the Internet Engineering Task Force (IETF).[12]

We might be tempted to link to documents to indicate a topic, but this is bad practice. We might want to say something about the document that doesn't concern the document's topic. For example, we might get away with using the Wikipedia page about whales to indicate a topic present in *Moby Dick* or as a way to tag articles about whales, but if we wanted to tag an article about the Wikipedia page on whales, we would not have a way to say that the article was about the Wikipedia page and not about the topic represented by the Wikipedia page unless we could reference a Wikipedia page that was about the Wikipedia page about whales. Therein lies madness.

We could work around this by using the document URL with another URL that together indicate that we are referencing the primary topic of the document. This is not a common practice. Rather, we develop vocabularies for which the URLs serve only as signifiers of subjects or predicates and not topics in their own right.

VOCABULARIES

Vocabularies are collections of URLs that are designed to work together. Schemas are documents that define how the URLs in a vocabulary relate to each other and the semantics that we should assume apply when we see those URLs used in datasets. For example, the list of property URLs that share the `<http://dbpedia.org/properties/>` prefix is a vocabulary of properties. These URLs have well-defined semantics. That is, each URL in the vocabulary has a specific, particular meaning that allows two independent projects to use that URL to refer to the same concept, thing, or property without prior agreement or knowledge of each other and without having to worry about being misunderstood. Good vocabularies are not ambiguous. Good vocabularies are designed for use in many different contexts. You might see reference to ontologies or taxonomies in linked data literature, but for our purposes, we can consider vocabularies, taxonomies, and ontologies to be synonymous.

Unlike XML schemas in which it is difficult, but not impossible, to allow for mixing of different XML namespaces, linked data vocabularies can be mixed without any prior planning on the part of the vocabulary authors.[13] If a vocabulary we're working with doesn't have what we need, then we look for one that does and include it in the list of vocabularies we are using. The Shared Canvas and International Image Interoperability Framework (IIIF) data models[14] are good examples of this. They use the Exchangeable image file format (Exif) vocabulary[15] to define the size of an image or canvas and the Open Annotation vocabulary to describe the relationships between images, canvases, and transcriptions. Exif contains terms that carry the same meanings as much of the metadata you might encounter in digital photography, such as the height and width of an image in pixels. By using a well-known vocabulary, IIIF allows interoperability with tools that aren't aware of IIIF as a data model. The interaction won't be as rich as might be found in an IIIF-aware tool, but basic queries, such as finding subjects with a particular proportionality, can be answered without knowing anything beyond the Exif terms.

The Open Annotation data model builds on some of the provenance vocabularies,[16] the content in RDF vocabulary,[17] and the Dublin core vocabulary[18] among others. Just as the reader would understand more of the nuances and far-flung threads that might come together in Moretti's sentence if they knew *Trauerspiel*, *Gorboduc*, *Lear*, or *La Vida es Sueno*, the more vocabularies a software application understands, the richer its ability to work with a dataset using Open Annotation or any other set of vocabularies.

A dataset that represents the same information repeatedly but using a different vocabulary each time also does what Moretti did by listing several references. As long as the consuming application understands at least one of the vocabularies used in the dataset, then the information has been communicated successfully.

Additionally, by using the Shared Canvas and IIIF vocabularies as part of our project, we signal that we are aware of the work already done in defining those vocabularies and that the work done informs our own work. Whether we choose to use a vocabulary in full or in part is itself a critique of that vocabulary. The choices we make as to which terms from which vocabulary we use, especially when multiple terms could be nearly synonymous, indicate how much we might agree or disagree with the reasoning behind the semantics assigned to each term.

RELATIONSHIPS

I opened the section on information structuring by quoting strings found on the front page of a book. This material is the bottom of Bloom's taxonomy: knowledge. When exploring a research topic, we climb that hierarchy and learn new ways to approach the data. We set aside the gathering of facts and enter the realm of relationships, of analysis and synthesis.

Knowing only what the strings represent isn't very useful.

The magic is in the relationships between the strings and what they represent, especially in the context of other resources. The value of a linked dataset grows as the number of connections grows, just like the value of a social network. The more links we have, the more ways we can relate two otherwise disparate things. Having a single diary encoded in TEI with linked data references for people and places is nice, but having a trove of documents encoded in TEI with linked data references using the same vocabularies enables relational research that would otherwise be difficult and time consuming.

The sciences use mathematics to represent these relationships, governed by the assumption that the world we inhabit is self-consistent. These mathematical equations aren't about how to get the speed of an apple given how long it's been since it fell from its tree, but rather how the apple and the Earth relate to each other through time. That is, the equations are not concerned with cause and effect, but rather how all of the pieces fit together into a harmonious whole that allows us to make predictions. The digital part of "digital humanities" bears witness to the success of this assumption.

In computation around linked data, mathematics plays a less obvious role. At the end of the day, all of the mathematics used in science comes to naught if it can't make predictions, and predictions must be measurable. Measurements are numbers. But with linked data, and in the humanities, it's not all about the numbers. Rather, the relationships we work with in linked data revolve around inference.

We call a subject, predicate, object triple an *assertion*. That is, a triple represents some piece of knowledge that we are asserting to be true. RDF and linked data work in an "open world" assumption. Rather than assume that a given dataset is complete, we must assume that we can always find more information. We can start with a dataset and add more data by following the links that we find.

If we had to represent every possible assertion as an explicit triple, like I hinted above that I could in order to support multiple vocabularies in the same dataset, then we would have very large datasets. Instead, we use inference engines[19] to derive new assertions based on the assertions we have and the inference rules we have at hand, either as part of schemas or by our own design. With inference rules, we can understand an assertion that two resources are the same entity, or that one resource (e.g. lion) represents a subclass of a larger concept (e.g. cat).

If two resources are the same, then everything we assert about one holds true for the other without us having to repeat everything. If one resource represents a subclass of a larger concept, then all of the expectations that apply to the larger concept should also apply to the subclass. These have parallels in programming and relational databases, but they are designed to work in the open world assumption in which we can encounter new assertions or inference rules at any time that might require us to reconsider how we understand a particular dataset.

USING LINKED DATA

A dataset is like a database. It's a published collection of data in a particular format. An RDF dataset would contain many subject–object–predicate triples in any of several formats: XML, Turtle, and JavaScript Object Notation-Linked Data (JSON-LD) are just three of many options. Most software libraries that we might use to work with RDF can read almost all of the common formats we might encounter.

The defining characteristic of linked data is that it uses URLs (links) to reference things rather than short strings, numbers, or other methods only meaningful within the context of a project. For example, if we have a relational database, then linked data would replace foreign keys (internal references in a relational database) with URLs.[20] Unlike relational databases, linked data can reference things anywhere on the web. One of the goals of linked data is to allow discovery of these resources outside of a dataset without requiring human intervention. A computer should be able to follow a link just as we might follow a link on a web page.

To use a dataset, we need to load it into a database designed to work with linked data graphs, such as a triple-store[21] or a graph database.[22] After all of our data are loaded, we can make queries against the data using query languages such as SPARQL. We won't go into the details of using SPARQL, but for those accustomed to relational databases such as MySQL or Postgresql, SPARQL will look familiar because it has similar patterns to SQL.

Linked data allow maximal agency for each participant in a project, be they primary source holders, researchers, teachers, or students, while still producing a cohesive and coherent whole. Unlike a self-contained dataset that must be loaded into a relational database, linked data can link to web resources outside of the dataset. This allows a fundamental shift in computational scholarly work. No longer must a facsimile, as an example of a linked data application, contain all of the data (e.g. page scan images and transcriptions) in one location. The Shelley–Godwin Archive (Fraistat *et al.*, for example, is the result of several libraries, primarily the Bodleian Library, New York Public Library, and Huntington Library, working with the Maryland Institute for Technology in the Humanities (MITH) to bring together page scans of Mary Shelley's notebooks in which she composed *Frankenstein* with transcriptions in an online facsimile. MITH does not house the page scans on its servers. Instead, the libraries retain ownership and control over the page scans by holding those scans on their own servers. MITH hosts the transcription data and the Shared Canvas (IIIF) dataset that brings all of the material together.

The power of linked data is more than allowing partners to share resources without surrendering ownership. It allows others to make use of what we publish without requiring that we also publish tools or foresee all possible scholarly uses. For example, by referencing a common vocabulary of people when annotating a document with characters, someone else can mix together documents from a wide range of projects and produce a prosopography that couldn't have been done by any project alone without having to go through a laborious normalization process to make sure each reference in each document referenced the correct characters across all of the projects. We can focus on publishing what we know and let others focus on creating data mashups to find new relationships and explore new questions.

PUBLISHING LINKED DATA

Linked data are about community. It's about making available what we have now rather than waiting until we have everything. It's about publishing the article rather than the entire encyclopedia. As with the open-source community, the number of consumers outnumbers the producers. Long before we are ready to contribute linked data, we are consuming them. For the purposes of this section, I look at how we might publish linked data in a textual scholarship context. The general approach is based on a progressive, tiered approach that lets us ease data into a fully open and linked form. It is applicable to a wide range of research methodologies.

The first step towards publishing linked data is getting something published. Rather than wait until we have scanned, transcribed, cross-checked, and linked everything, we should publish what we have when we have it. If this means publishing the scans of documents while we build the transcriptions, then those scans are the first step towards sharing with our community. By publishing the documents, other people can point to them with URLs, starting the process of bringing them into the linked data world.

If we are publishing scans of a set of documents, such as might happen in textual scholarship, then I recommend using IIIF or Shared Canvas to describe how the documents relate to each other. This also provides us with a framework to add transcriptions and commentary as we further develop our project.

The second step is to provide the content of the documents in a machine-readable format. This could be as simple as a cleaned-up OCR transcription of the published scan. If we are working with a text, then we have an opportunity to relate the transcription to the scans using annotations. If our transcriptions are in a proprietary format, such as Microsoft Word^{TM}, then the best we might be able to do is assert that the text in a file is associated with a range of canvases acting as surrogates for the pages from which the images were scanned. If our transcription is a plain-text file, then associating sections of text with particular pages is much easier.

Regardless of the file format for our transcription, the next step is to semantically structure our data. For example, if we are working with a text transcription, we should mark up our text with HTML or the Text Encoding Initiative (TEI) schema. If we are working with a music transcription, we should consider the Music Encoding Initiative (MEI) schema, the music equivalent of TEI. If we are working with tabular data, we will want to convert from a comma-separated value (CSV) or Excel file to something like JavaScript Object Notation (JSON). Each of these file formats allows us to label our information in a way that hints at what the piece of data means or how it fits into the dataset.

We should make sure that we use URLs for everything that we reference, and that each URL is used to mean the same thing every time it is used, and that only one URL is used for each meaning. If we are working with TEI, then all of the references to people, places, things, handwriting styles, and so on should be URLs, and each person, place, thing, and so on should have one and only one URL. If we are working with JSON, we should make sure we are consistent in how we use the properties. Each property should always have the same type of value and should always indicate the same semantic meaning.

Finally, we should make sure that all of our URLs point to resources on the Web. With TEI, all of the references to people, places, things, handwriting styles and so on should be full URLs and not internally defined fragments. We shouldn't use #smith3 to indicate the third Smith encountered by our project but rather use a URL pointing to the entry for the Smith in a shared list.

If we are working with JSON, then we have the opportunity to create a context file describing each of the properties we use by mapping them to URLs. This allows someone else using our JSON to know what we meant without requiring us to use full URLs through our entire file.

SUMMARY

Over the course of this chapter, I've explored the Semantic Web and linked open data showing how similar linked data are to traditional scholarly methods: referencing vocabularies, denoting intended semantics and meanings, and expressing how our work meshes with that of others. In both scholarly writing and in scholarly data, we want to provide the reader or consumer with as much actionable context as we can. We are involved in a human and computational discourse that flows on multiple levels. It is by bringing to our computational work the practices of our scholarly work that we elevate the digital side of digital humanities to be equal with the traditional humanities scholarship practices. Linked data are scholarly data participating in the ongoing exploratory conversation of the field.

FURTHER READING

As you explore how linked data might inform your own work, feel free to browse resources on the web. As much as it is maligned in the scholarly community, Wikipedia is a reasonable source for becoming familiar with the broad outline of the Semantic Web and linked data. The W3C is a good resource for more technical documents as the primary forum for web recommendations.

Many of the commonly used and useful linked data vocabularies can be found at http://lov.okfn.org/dataset/lov/. The DataHub (http://datahub.io/) is an interesting source of open data in various stages of becoming linked data. In many ways, looking through vocabularies and datasets is the digital equivalent of visiting the archives looking for just the right manuscript. There's a lot you won't want to use, but every so often, you find the gem that makes the search worth doing.

If you are interested in getting into more of the technical details of working with RDF, then you won't go wrong with Shelley Powers's *Practical RDF* from O'Reilly. Powers provides an introduction to RDF and some of the basic tools and software libraries with which you can work with RDF. The sample code tends to be oriented towards Java because that was the primary language of the intended audience around 2003 when the book was published. However, you should be able to translate the concepts and algorithmic approaches to your favorite language.

Finally, take a look at linked data projects already available in the digital humanities space: Linked Jazz (https://linkedjazz.org), Out of the Trenches (www.canadiana.ca/en/pcdhn-lod), and the Muninn Project (http://blog.muninn-project.org/) are all excellent examples of projects. The *Semantic Web for the Working Ontologist* website (http://workingontologist.org/) is a good resource for down-to-earth information about the Semantic Web. *The Shelley–Godwin Archive* (http://shelleygodwinarchive.org/) remains a good example of emerging Shared Canvas use in digital facsimile.

NOTES

1 See www.w3c.org/ for information on current efforts and technical reference documents for the various recommendations used on the World Wide Web.
2 Giles (2005).
3 Location 137 of 3665 in "Modern European Literature: A Geographical Sketch" in the Kindle edition.
4 Croxton (1999).
5 Two examples are the HCPCS codes defined by the Centers for Medicare & Medicaid Services (CMS) in the United States available from the CMS website at www.cms.gov/Medicare/Coding/HCPCSReleaseCodeSets/ and

the Oxford Scholarly Editions Online title list available as a spreadsheet download from www.oxfordscholarlyeditions.com/page/18/title-lists (links visited on 4 September 2015).

6 DBPedia is a widely known set of linked data derived from Wikipedia. It is useful for making links that indicate your particular topic.

7 Dublin Core is widely used in online library catalogs. See http://dublincore.org/documents/dces/ for more information about the Dublin Core metadata elements.

8 See http://schema.org/ for details on the available URLs.

9 Turtle (Terse RDF Triple Language) is defined by the W3C. The most recent version of the recommendation at the time of writing is from 25 February 2014 available at www.w3.org/TR/turtle/.

10 RDF is a set of recommendations from the W3C.The most recent version of the W3C RDF overview is from 25 February 2014 available at www.w3.org/RDF/. This page has links to various recommendations and tools known to the W3C.

11 RDF actually makes use of Universal Resource Identifiers (URIs) rather than Universal Resource Locaters (URLs). All URLs are URIs, but not all URIs are URLs. This distinction is not significant for most of this chapter. When working with linked data, the distinction is encountered less often because the names of things (their URIs) are supposed to point to resources on the web. All the resources that you can load in your web browser are named with URLs.

12 Phillips and Davis (2009).

13 For more information about XML and schemas, please see this volume's chapter on TEI.

14 The Shared Canvas data model came out of work related to the Archimedes Palimpsest (see www.archimedespalimpsest.org/ for its online presence) and built on the Open Annotation data model that came from the Mellon-funded Open Annotation Collaboration and Annotation Ontology, now an emerging W3C recommendation. For more information, see http://iiif.io/, www.w3.org/annotation/, and http://shelleygodwinarchive.org/.

15 See www.w3.org/2003/12/exif/.

16 See www.w3.org/TR/prov-o/.

17 See www.w3.org/TR/Content-in-RDF/.

18 See http://purl.org/dc/terms/ for an example of how a schema can be documented as a set of web pages.

19 Examples of inference engines include programming languages such as Prolog and query languages such as SPARQL. Inference engines come out of the artificial intelligence community.

20 For more information about relational databases and foreign keys, please see this volume's chapter on databases.

21 The Apache Jena open-source project (http://jena.apache.org/) provides a suite of tools including a triple-store and query capability.

22 Neo4j, http://neo4j.com/, is an example of an open-source graph database.

REFERENCES

Croxton, D. "The Peace of Westphalia of 1648 and the Origins of Sovereignty." *The International History Review* XXI:3 (September 1999): 569–591.

DBPedia Homepage. http://wiki.dbpedia.org/

Dublin Core Metadata Elements. http://dublincore.org/documents/dces/.

Fraistat, N., Denlinger, E., and Viglianti, R. *The Shelley–Godwin Archive*. http://shelleygodwinarchive.org/.

Giles, J. (2005). "Internet Encyclopaedias Go Head to Head: Jimmy Wales' Wikipedia comes Close to Britannica in Terms of the Accuracy of its Science Entries". *Nature* 438 (7070): 900–901.

International Image Interoperability Framework (IIIF). http://iiif.io/

Moretti, F. *Distant Reading*. "Modern European Literature: A Geographical Sketch." Kindle edn. loc 137 of 3665.

Phillips, A., and Davis, M. *Tags for Identifying Languages*. September 2009. IETF Best Current Practice. http://tools.ietf.org/html/bcp47

W3C. *Resource Description Framework*. www.w3.org/RDF/

W3C. *RDF 1.1 Turtle*. www.w3.org/TR/turtle/

World Wide Web Consortium (W3C) Homepage. www.w3c.org/

CHAPTER 16

Drupal and other content management systems

Quinn Dombrowski

OVERVIEW

Almost any digital humanities project is an amalgamation of the unique and the commonplace. Given limited grant funding, as well as the costs and challenges of project sustainability, it behooves a project director to carefully assess the degree to which a project's novelty lies in its content versus its technology. Adopting widely used technology that is supported and maintained by an entity other than the project itself in order to meet a project's common technical requirements (e.g. providing the project with a web presence) allows a team to devote more of their resources to the intellectual substance of the project. Many digital humanities projects are underpinned by web-based content management systems (CMSes), which are forms of open-source software that allow users to add and organize content in different ways, depending on the scope and nature of a particular platform. This chapter describes previous approaches that have increasingly fallen into disuse in favor of content management systems, before describing some of the major content management systems from two points of view: audience and functionality. It then provides a more detailed description of the Drupal content management system, which demands extensive configuration but enables scholars to build their own highly customized environment, while exclusively using code that is written and maintained by an open-source community of developers. The chapter concludes with links and resources for learning more about all of the major digital humanities content management systems.

EVOLVING APPROACHES TO PROJECT IMPLEMENTATION

Gathering, curating, and presenting collections of primary and secondary sources in a way that facilitates humanistic research has been a major goal of many digital humanities projects for decades. Previously, doing so necessitated a sizable budget to support a large team of programmers who would develop both the technical underpinnings and the user interface from scratch, and package everything in a form compatible with the selected dissemination medium (CD-ROM, Java application, website, etc.). This approach had considerable drawbacks: programmers would often duplicate work that had been done for earlier projects but was never shared in a reusable form (e.g. the many implementations of the once-ubiquitous "turning book page" effect), the fact that only a small number of relatively mainstream projects could secure the amount of money necessary to undertake this work, and the fact that when funding ran out, projects could not afford the ongoing programmer time needed to maintain, support, and update an expansive custom code base.

Partly in response to the shortcomings of earlier approaches that relied heavily on custom programming, over the past decade there has been a shift towards adopting open-source tools, code libraries, and platforms. Even projects that primarily focus on building new tools are likely to incorporate open-source components. The ratio of code reuse to new code generation varies tremendously between projects. Projects that do most of their work using offline tools (for example, topic modeling or doing other computational text analysis on large literary corpora), but also need to present their findings and ongoing work through a compelling web presence, can benefit from using a CMS for their web development. Likewise, for projects that focus on displaying a virtual exhibit, providing a group annotation environment for text, fostering communities of practice, or showcasing non-linear multimedia-rich narratives, modern open-source content management systems can address all these common needs, requiring only minimal, non-programming configuration.

CONTENT MANAGEMENT SYSTEMS

A web-based content management system is software that allows users to easily create and update websites using an interface that allows them to author content, embed multimedia assets, and control how that content will be displayed, without requiring the user to manually write HTML or otherwise intervene in the code that produces the final output.

The most commonly used CMSes for digital humanities projects – Drupal, Omeka, Scalar, and WordPress – are written in the programming language PHP, and store their data in a MySQL database. The databases created by CMSes are typically not structured as transparently as those created by humans (see Chapter 9); a user looking directly at the MySQL database for his CMS-powered website might have a very difficult time finding the content he or she has added, as it may be spread out across tables in unexpected ways. These databases are optimized for use by the CMS itself, and any changes the user wishes to make to the database should be done through the CMS interface, though CMSes vary in the kinds of database operations they support.

Extensibility is a key feature of all widely used CMSes. While the terminology differs between platforms[1] (one can find references to *extensions*, *plugins*, *add-ons*, and *modules*, depending on the CMS), the idea is the same: packaging up pieces of functionality that can be added to a site to give it new features that are not present in the CMS itself. Functionality that is provided as part of one core CMS may be available as an extension for another CMS. Some extensions are available for multiple CMSes, and there may also be multiple extensions for a given CMS that provide essentially the same functionality. The extent to which adding and configuring extensions is a necessary part of creating a site varies among different CMSes; general-purpose CMSes typically require more extensions to be usable by scholarly projects.

It may be useful to compare individual content management systems from the perspectives of audience and functionality.

Scholar-oriented CMSes vs. general-purpose CMSes

Scholars played an active role in the development of both Omeka (http://omeka.org/) and Scalar (http://scalar.usc.edu/). Omeka was built by the Roy Rosenzweig Center for History and New Media (http://chnm.gmu.edu/) at George Mason University, and describes itself as a "free, flexible, and open-source web-publishing platform for the display of library, museum, archives, and scholarly collections and exhibitions" (Omeka: About). Scalar, developed by the Alliance for Networking Visual Culture at the University of Southern California, positions itself as:

> a free, open source authoring and publishing platform that's designed to make it easy for authors to write long-form, born-digital scholarship online. Scalar enables users to assemble media from multiple sources and juxtapose them with their own writing in a variety of ways, with minimal technical expertise required. (Scalar)

The involvement of scholars in the development of these CMSes gives them a sense of legitimacy. For a scholar faced with the decision of which CMS to adopt for her project, it is reassuring to know that the developers focused on use cases that were at least broadly similar to her own (in contrast to, for example, e-commerce use cases.) The uptake of scholar-oriented CMSes contributes to the common perception that the products of digital humanities scholarship are inherently unique, both in their content and in their form. While it is true that specific combinations of features – such as using Dublin Core metadata and an Open Archives Initiative Protocol for Metadata Harvesting (OAI-PMH) repository/harvester as the underpinnings of an out-of-the-box exhibit builder – would most likely only emerge from a community of scholars, librarians, and archivists, there is tremendous overlap between the technical needs of many digital humanities projects and the functionality provided by general-purpose CMSes and their extensions.

The two most widely used general-purpose CMSes for digital humanities projects are Drupal (www.drupal.org/) and WordPress (https://wordpress.org/). Unlike Omeka and Scalar, the vast majority of Drupal and WordPress users and developers are outside the academy. Drupal and WordPress each power hundreds of thousands of sites in a wide variety of industries, including government, journalism, the non-profit sector, and small and large businesses, in addition to primary, secondary, and higher education. Each community of users builds on a common foundation, and develops extensions that accommodate their unique needs. Drupal, Omeka, and WordPress all use the open-source GNU General Public License,[2] which requires that derivative works (interpreted to include all extensions written for the CMS) be released under the same licenses, if they are publicly distributed. This ensures that any extension that is developed and distributed by one community of users will be available for any other community not only to use, but also to modify and adapt to their own needs. While it may be hard to imagine ever needing an extension for running a web-based storefront, a project may include an artistic team member inspired to sell hand-painted t-shirts based on the project's theme, and using a general-purpose CMS would enable the possibility of doing so directly from the project's existing website. While far-fetched "what-if" scenarios should not be a major decision-making criterion in choosing a CMS, the existing support for a wide range of non-scholarly but potentially relevant activities is one factor in favor of a general-purpose CMS.

The significantly larger user bases of general-purpose CMSes can be advantageous in other ways as well. By using any CMS, one can take advantage of one-time and ongoing development and maintenance work that the research project itself does not have to fund. Every new release of the core code of a CMS or a CMS extension represents tens, hundreds, or even thousands of hours of programmers' time that one can simply use, at no cost to their digital humanities project. Not all sites that use a content management system dedicate time and resources to fixing bugs and contributing to the ongoing development of the CMS, but the user base for these general-purpose CMSes is substantial enough to include many large corporations and organizations that do contribute to the production, review, and patching of CMS code. The larger the user base for a CMS, the more likely that security vulnerabilities will be identified and remedied, in ways that benefit all projects that share the same CMS.

The widespread adoption of WordPress in particular has led to the development of scholar-oriented extensions, which provide out-of-the-box functionality geared towards scholarly use cases, while still allowing users to take advantage of the larger ecosystem of extensions and support that comes with a general-purpose content management system. CommentPress (http://futureofthebook.org/commentpress/), developed by the Institute for the Future of the Book (http://futureofthebook.org/), enables granular textual annotation and discussion. Commons In A Box (CBOX, http://commonsinabox.org/), developed by the Graduate Center of the City University of New York, provides pre-configured infrastructure for scholarly networking, allowing users to create and join groups that include a member directory, the ability to jointly edit a group wiki, collaborative document editing and file sharing, and discussion fora. CBOX also takes advantage of WordPress's robust multi-site blogging system. CBOX is an example of a scholarly extension that builds upon a general-purpose extension – in this case, BuddyPress (https://buddypress.org/), which adds social networking features to WordPress sites.

For users who cannot, or do not wish to, install and manage the content management system themselves, each of the CMSes listed here is also available as a hosted service. Scholar-oriented CMSes fare well here, as their hosted services tend to be better calibrated for scholars' expectations and budgets. Both Omeka and Scalar have a functional "free" tier that does not require making compromises that would be unacceptable to many scholars, such as allowing algorithmically selected ads to appear on the site (as is the case with the free tier on WordPress.com). In contrast, of the hosting options offered by WordPress (ranging from a fairly modest $99/year to a staggering $5,000/month), none provide unlimited access to plugins, and the expansive list of supported plugins does not include prominent scholar-oriented ones.

While the origin of a CMS and its intended audience do have implications for projects developed using the platform, functionality is a more significant factor conditioning the choice of a CMS than its origins and the kinds of organization that support its ongoing development.

Dollhouses vs. Lego™

A key question to ask about any content management system is, "What can it do as soon as you install it, or with minimal configuration?" An analogy with children's toys may be instructive here. Most commonly used CMSes can be compared to dollhouses. A dollhouse allows children to promptly engage in simulated domestic play by providing them with a comprehensive set of spaces and furnishings suited to the task. This play may be enhanced by additional objects (plates and cups for the kitchen, or clothes for the closet), or ways of expanding the space (an add-on porch, a basketball hoop for the yard), but the dollhouse by itself is sufficient, and such extensions do not fundamentally alter the nature of the toy. Similarly, while Omeka, Scalar, and WordPress each specialize in providing infrastructure for a different kind of site, all provide a comprehensive suite of functionality to accomplish the given task, either out-of-the-box or with the installation of one or two stand-alone extensions. For example, Neatline (http://neatline.org/), developed by Scholars'

Lab (http://scholarslab.org/) at the University of Virginia, enhances Omeka's exhibit functionality through the incorporation of timelines and maps. If a scholar can find a CMS that provides out-of-the-box functionality that is well matched to his project's scope, nature, and goals, adopting that CMS is the obvious choice, as it will allow him to immediately begin work on the unique scholarly substance of the project without having to divert time towards technical configuration.

Drupal works somewhat differently from the other commonly used CMSes. Installed with no extensions, Drupal 7 resembles a much less functional variant of WordPress, without many of the key features that contribute to WordPress's ease of use, such as a built-in WYSIWYG (what-you-see-is-what-you-get) text editor or an intuitive media upload and embedding interface. Drupal, however, is not meant to be used as a dollhouse, but is more like a set of plastic Lego building blocks, in which Drupal core is only the most minimal starter kit. Drupal core itself is designed to contain only the essential functionality that all or nearly all sites need[3]; to do anything interesting or meaningful with Drupal requires adding and configuring extensions.

On one hand, using Drupal requires dedicating a significantly larger amount of time to a project's technical configuration. On the other, the payoff is an environment that can be tailored to a project's specific needs and the nuances of its data. This level of customization has historically been associated with unsustainable and expensive custom programming, but the expansive scope and diverse nature of the extensions available for Drupal mean that many projects can rely exclusively on pre-built components that are maintained by Drupal's large international development community. Just as assembling an imaginary spaceship out of Lego requires no familiarity with plastics manufacturing, building an environment designed around an individual project's specific requirements can be done without resorting to any custom programming, or even interacting directly with code at all. For projects whose scope or nature is a poor fit for other CMSes, Drupal and its robust ecosystem of extensions provide a compelling alternative that can be undertaken by scholars themselves, even those without programming or database development skills.

OVERVIEW OF DRUPAL

The two features of Drupal that differentiate it from other content management systems are the ability to define *content types*, and to use the *Views* extension (a user interface for configuring database queries) to display the content stored in content types in various ways.

Content types

Most CMSes pre-define the web-based forms used to enter and store content. WordPress posts have a title field, a body field, and tags; Omeka's metadata for items is based on Dublin Core. While a standard Drupal installation comes with minimalist "Article" and "Basic Page" content types that resemble WordPress's "Post" and "Page," respectively, users can delete these content types and create an unlimited number of new ones, and/or transform the functionality of the "Article" and "Basic Page" by adding new fields to them.

To add a new content type, users fill out a web-based form, making decisions such as whether to enable comments, or to display author and date information for each piece of content created using a given content type. Users can add an unlimited number of fields to each content type; Drupal provides a small set of simple field types by default (short text, long text, file upload, multiple fields for different types of numerals), but there are hundreds of extensions available that provide additional field types, including URLs, geospatial coordinates, dates, computed fields (based on values stored in other fields), and Twitter usernames. Additional extensions can be configured to make some fields public, and other fields only editable or viewable by certain groups of users, or to turn fields on or off based on the values of other fields (e.g. making a "Major" field visible only if a user has selected the status "Undergraduate"). Reference fields allow users to store a pointer to another piece of content on the site. These fields allow the user to construct the equivalent of primary key–foreign key relationships between content types (which function much like database tables from the perspective of data modeling, though the mapping between content types and actual tables stored in Drupal's MySQL database is much more complex).

Figure 16.1 shows the content types and fields used by the project Bulgarian Dialectology as Living Tradition (http://bulgariandialectology.org). Each box represents a content type, and each item within a box represents a field. An arrow from a field to a content type indicates a reference to a piece of content with that content type. This site provides transcriptions and audio of field recordings made in Bulgaria since the 1980s. Each word (token) that appears in the recording is annotated with linguistic metadata and linked to the standard Bulgarian dictionary form of the word (lexeme), making it possible to easily view and compare all forms of a given word.

Because Drupal provides its users with complete freedom in defining content types, there is no technical impediment to "needless and heedless divergence," in the memorable phrasing of Martin Mueller (Unsworth 10). While users are free to ignore standards and best practices, an important part of developing a data model for a Drupal site involves researching and identifying applicable standards. Diverging from these standards may be necessary given a project's particular goals and data set, but it is better for divergence to be conscious than to be by chance.

Adding data

Once a user has created a set of content types, some of which may be connected using reference fields, multiple options exist for adding data to the site. Users can enter data manually using Drupal's web-based forms, which present all the fields

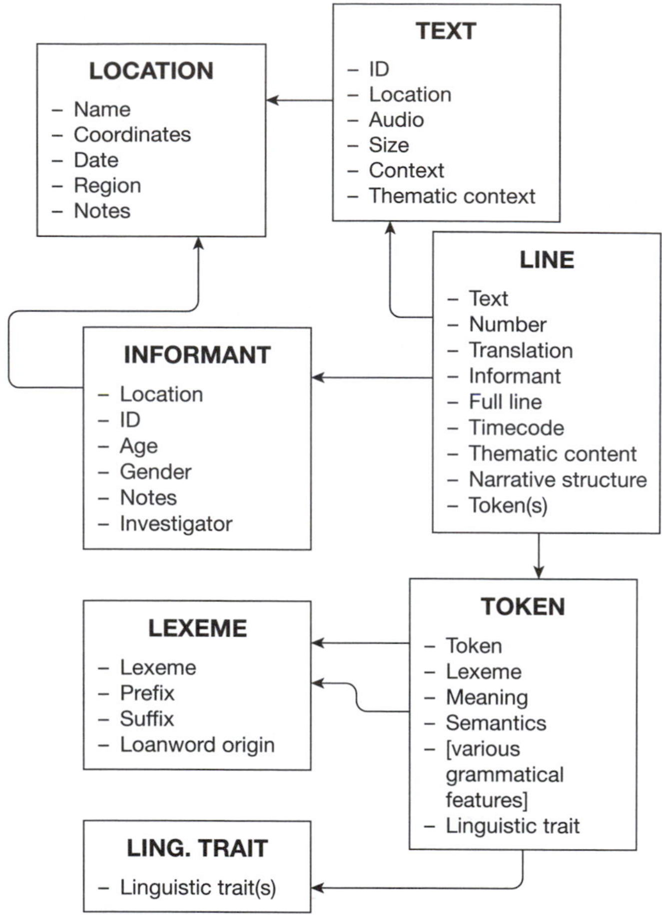

Figure 16.1
Content types and fields used by the project Bulgarian Dialectology as Living Tradition

that a particular content type contains. Other extensions enable a spreadsheet-like interface for adding or editing data.

If a project's data already exist in some other structured form (such as a spreadsheet or an XML file), Drupal's Feeds extension allows users to bulk-import content, mapping data from spreadsheet cells or XML fields to the fields of a particular content type. Imports can be carried out once, or on an ongoing basis, in order to pull in new content periodically added to an external server or provided via an RSS feed.

Generating displays

Out-of-the-box, the only format Drupal provides for displaying content is a teaser-display of all content, from all content types, in reverse-chronological order by post date – much like the default display for WordPress posts. This is not a very useful display format, and it is quickly and necessarily replaced on all sites that are designed to take advantage of Drupal's defining features.

The Views extension provides an interface for building database queries, and styling the results of those queries, without requiring the user to learn any SQL or HTML. It allows users to generate pages, RSS feeds, or blocks (pieces of content or functionality that can appear anywhere on any page, such as a sidebar or footer) that contain the styled output of database queries. The Views interface exposes enough configuration settings that it can seem daunting for beginners, but going through the sections one by one reveals a fairly intuitive set of options: defining which fields to display and how, filtering which pieces of content those fields should come from (by content type, by date posted, or any other piece of metadata), selecting a sort order, configuring the equivalent of database table joins to pull in fields from a related piece of content, and setting up contextual filters, or arguments, that change the content of the display based on, for instance, what piece of content the display appears with. Filters and sort orders can also be made visible, so that visitors to the site can modify the display to only show content that interests them.

Views allows users to define not only the style and formatting of individual fields, but also the style of the display as a whole. Views comes with a handful of default styles, including bulleted and unbulleted lists, grids (commonly used for image galleries), and tables. Moreover, numerous extensions to Views provide additional styles, including slideshows, timelines, and maps.

Figures 16.2 and 16.3 show two displays from the Bulgarian Dialectology as Living Tradition site, both created using Views. Figure 16.2 groups together all the lines of a text, displaying the Bulgarian and English translations, along with linguistic annotations. Figure 16.3 is a map showing all locations where texts were recorded.

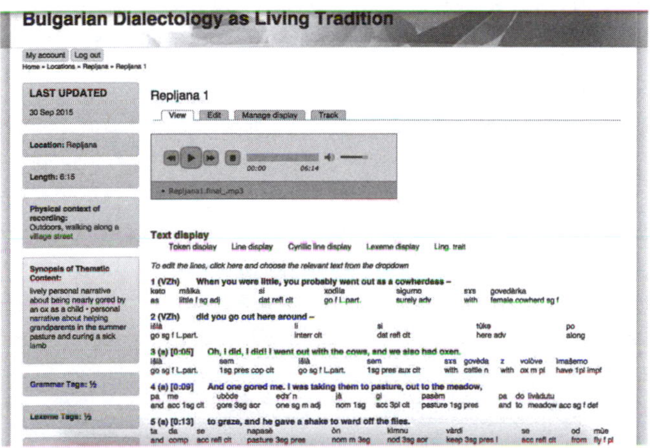

Figure 16.2
Text display on Bulgarian Dialectology as Living Tradition

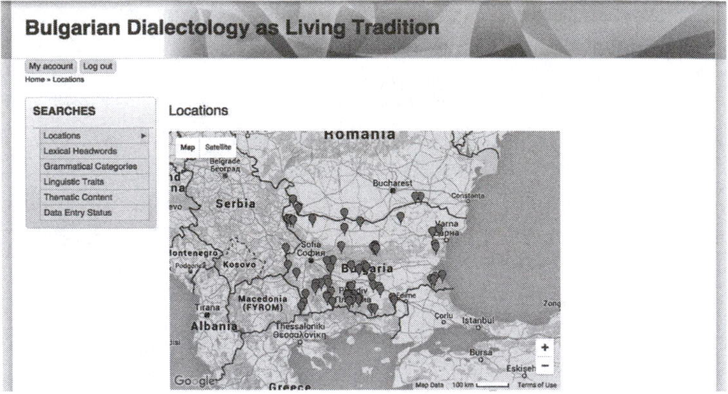

Figure 16.3
Map display on Bulgarian Dialectology as Living Tradition

Exporting and sharing data

The Views Data Export extension allows site builders to attach an export button to any existing view, offering the choice of CSV, Word document, Excel spreadsheet, or XML (using an *ad hoc* schema based on the names of the fields displayed in the view). If the granularity of the fields used in Drupal aligns well with the granularity of elements and attributes that would occur in the corresponding TEI (see Chapter 6), it would be a fairly trivial task to write XSLT to transform Drupal's output into reasonable TEI (see Chapter 12). Other extensions for Views provide JSON and XHTML exports. JSON is a text-based format that is widely used to feed data to visualization code written in Javascript, and XHTML – a variant of HTML that conforms to XML conventions – can be used for stand-alone webpages, or as a code and content snippet that can be incorporated into another content management system.

Drupal core includes RDF support, but additional extensions are needed for mapping custom properties to fields, indexing RDF data, or supporting SPARQL queries. RDF (Resource Description Framework) is one of the standards used to publish linked open data, and SPARQL is a language that allows users to search, retrieve, and manipulate RDF data – for instance, in order to show all person nodes that share a common property, such as place of residence. The Services extension creates a REST API for a Drupal site, which a site builder can configure through the Drupal user interface. Supplemental extensions provide API key authentication and support for API queries using the values of individual fields. A REST API enables programmatic access to data, allowing them to be accessed and used directly by other software, such as a custom-built website or mobile app. For instance, a mobile app might use a REST API from a Drupal site to display a short biography of a historical figure whose birth date coincided with the current date when the user opens the app.

PROJECTS THAT USE DRUPAL

Many projects have adopted Drupal in different ways. While the set of content types and displays implemented by each of these sites is unique, all of them share much of the same code, through their use of Drupal core and common extensions.

Romantic Circles (www.rc.umd.edu/)

Romantic Circles is a complex refereed website with multiple kinds of publications, including critical editions of texts, original essays, pedagogical material, and multimedia galleries. Exhibits that were originally created in Omeka have been incorporated directly into the site. All peer-reviewed materials are encoded in TEI, then transformed to HTML for storage in the Drupal database. The TEI documents also serve as masters from which site metadata is derived.

World Shakespeare Bibliography Online (www.worldshakesbib.org/)

This project uses infrastructure from the publisher (Johns Hopkins University Press) and the editorial team in the English Department at Texas A&M University to provide access to the database itself, but Drupal powers the project's submission system and offers contributors an intuitive web form to upload information. Views is also used to generate an exportable version of the submission data using the project's pre-digital formatting system, which was difficult for contributors to use accurately when they had to format their submissions themselves.

George Washington Financial Papers (http://financial.gwpapers.org)

The George Washington Financial Papers project has transcribed George Washington's detailed ledgers, and enriched each entry by providing the sum in a standardized numerical format, assigning it one or more categories using a controlled vocabulary. The Drupal site provides a web interface for searching and browsing the entries, which was not part of the FileMaker-based DocTracker system the project previously used.

DiRT Directory (http://dirtdirectory.org) and DHCommons (http://dhcommons.org)

The DiRT (Digital Research Tools) directory is a database of tools, focusing primarily on those applicable to humanities research. DHCommons is a directory of digital humanities projects, as well as individuals who are interested in collaborating on a project. They share a similar structure of tool or project profiles, displayed using a Views-generated interface that users can independently sort and filter. Both use the Services extension to provide an API that enables data exchange between the two: DHCommons projects that use a tool appear on the tool's DiRT profile, and DiRT tool descriptions appear on a project's DHCommons profile. The DHCommons site also includes a peer-reviewed journal, and both the journal publication and the peer-review systems are also implemented in Drupal.

SUMMARY

Using a content management system allows a project to use common, rather than custom, code as the foundation for web-based projects. This can save a project money with respect to both development and maintenance of the project. Multiple CMSes are widely used for digital humanities projects, including platforms developed specifically by and for scholars, as well as general-purpose platforms that have been put to scholarly use, sometimes by incorporating scholar-oriented extensions. Most of these CMSes support specific kinds of projects out-of-the-box or with minimal configuration; these systems can simply be adopted and used when a project's goals align well with the CMS's functionality. For projects with needs or data sets that are a poor fit for other content management systems, Drupal allows even non-technical users to develop a robust and highly customized environment for a project by installing and configuring extensions that are written and maintained by a distributed worldwide network of developers. While site builders have complete freedom in shaping their project's content types, looking to established standards before developing completely *ad hoc* data models is better for interoperability and sustainability.

RESOURCES

Drupal

Good for databases and directories that need to capture specific kinds of data that may not be supported by typical CMS fields. Includes support for bibliographic management, along with numerous user-defined ways to filter, sort, display, and visualize whatever data structures the user creates. Steeper learning curve than other CMS options.

- Website: https://drupal.org
- Download: http://drupal.org/download
- Extensions: http://drupal.org/project/project_module
- *Drupal for Humanists* book and resource guide: http://drupal.forhumanists.org
- Projects that use Drupal: http://dhcommons.org/tools/drupal

Omeka

Good for curating digital collections of items using standard metadata and creating online exhibitions. The Neatline extension provides mapping and timeline functionality.

- Website: http://omeka.org/
- Hosted Omeka: http://omeka.net/
- Download: http://omeka.org/download/
- Extensions: http://omeka.org/add-ons/
- Neatline extension: http://neatline.org/
- Documentation: http://omeka.org/codex/Documentation
- *Up and Running with Omeka.net* by Miriam Posner: http://programminghistorian.org/lessons/up-and-running-with-omeka
- Projects that use Omeka: http://dhcommons.org/tools/omeka

Scalar

Good for multimedia-rich publishing. Has particularly strong support for video and audio annotation.

- Website: http://scalar.usc.edu/
- Hosted Scalar: http://scalar.usc.edu/works/system/register
- Download: https://github.com/anvc/scalar
- Documentation: http://scalar.usc.edu/works/guide/index
- Extensions: http://scalar.usc.edu/works/guide/third-party-plugins-and-platforms
- Projects that use Scalar: http://dhcommons.org/tools/scalar

WordPress

Good for creating informational websites (e.g. for individuals, workshops, or projects where the data collection and analysis is mostly happening offline). Very strong support for blogging, including multi-user blogs. CommentPress makes it possible to publish text (anything from a short blurb to an entire book) in a format that facilitates granular annotation. Commons In A Box supports scholarly networking, or project-team workspaces. DH Press provides structures for adding people, events, and documents to a site, and linking them to places.

- Website: https://wordpress.org/
- Hosted WordPress: https://wordpress.com/
- Download: https://wordpress.org/download/

- Documentation: https://codex.wordpress.org/
- Extensions: https://wordpress.org/plugins/
- CommentPress extension: https://wordpress.org/plugins/commentpress-core/
- Commons In A Box extension: https://wordpress.org/plugins/commons-in-a-box/
- DH Press extension: http://dhpress.org/
- Projects that use WordPress: http://dhcommons.org/tools/wordpress

NOTES

1 The added components for content management systems are referred to as *extensions*, *plugins*, *add-ons*, and *modules*, depending on the CMS. "Extension" will be used here as a generic term, referring to this concept for any CMS, including contexts where an individual CMS would use a different term.

2 Scalar uses the Educational Community License (ECL), an open-source license based on the Apache License with some specific modifications to the section on patents to make it compatible with expectations set by many university patent and intellectual property offices.

3 Including only modules that most sites need is the principle behind Drupal core. In practice, the actual selection of extensions that come bundled with Drupal is in many ways more reflective of the origins and early uses of Drupal, which is why Drupal core includes modules for polling and message boards. Even the ability to create custom content types – a cornerstone of Drupal and a key differentiator from the other commonly used CMSes – was only included in core as of Drupal 7, and the ability to display those content types in various ways appeared in core for the first time in Drupal 8.

REFERENCES

Educational Community License. 2007. http://opensource.org/licenses/ECL-2.0

GNU General Public License. 2007. www.gnu.org/licenses/gpl-3.0.en.html

Omeka: About. http://omeka.org/about/. Retrieved 30 May 2015.

Scalar. http://scalar.usc.edu/. Retrieved 30 May 2015.

Unsworth, John. "Clumps and Runners." 3rd Bamboo Workshop, Tucson, Arizona, 13 January 2009. http://people.brandeis.edu/~unsworth/bamboo.1–13.ppt

CHAPTER 17

Augmented reality

Markus Wust

WHAT IS AUGMENTED REALITY?

When attempting to explain the concept of augmented reality, one could do worse than point to examples taken from popular culture, more specifically James Cameron's classic action/science fiction film *Terminator 2: Judgment Day* (1991). The movie features a scene in which the Terminator enters a bar in order to look for clothing. While he scans the bar's patrons, we briefly see the bar's interior shown from the Terminator's point of view. The display includes textual and image data that are layered over his real environment, thereby augmenting it with additional information. This is the basic definition of augmented reality (AR); according to Carmigniani and Furht, AR is "a real-time direct or indirect view of a physical real-world environment that has been enhanced / *augmented* by adding virtual computer-generated information to it" (3). In his early survey of the field of augmented reality, Azuma (1997) described the following three characteristics of AR systems: (1) they combine the real and the virtual; (2) they are interactive in real time; and (3) they are registered in a three-dimensional space.[1] In 1994, Milgram and Kishino attempted to outline the varying degrees to which the "real" and the "virtual" could be combined by placing them on a "virtuality continuum" that ranged from the purely real to the purely virtual; between the two extrema lies a "Mixed Reality":

> The concept of a "virtuality continuum" relates to the mixture of classes of objects presented in any particular display situation . . . where *real environments*, are shown at one end of the continuum, and *virtual environments*, at the opposite extremum. The former case . . . defines environments consisting solely of real objects . . . and includes for example what is observed via a conventional video

> display of a real world scene. . . . The latter case . . . defines environments consisting solely of virtual objects . . ., an example of which would be a conventional computer graphic simulation. [T]he most straightforward way to view a Mixed Reality environment, therefore, is one in which real world and virtual world objects are presented together within a single display, that is, anywhere between the extrema of the virtuality continuum. (1321–1322)

On this continuum, AR would be placed closer to the real environment extremum and an AR display would primarily display real-world objects. Wellner *et al.* also differentiated between virtual and augmented reality; they emphasized AR's ability to let users interact with the physical world instead of enclosing them in a virtual environment, as would be the case with virtual reality:

> Another view of the future of computing is emerging, taking the opposite approach from VR. Instead of using computers to enclose people in an artificial world, we can use computers to augment objects in the real world. We can make the environment sensitive with infra-red, optical sound, video, heat, motion and light detectors, and we can make the environment react to people's needs by updating displays, activating motors, storing data, driving actuators, controls and valves. With see-through displays and projectors, we can create spaces in which everyday objects gain electronic properties without losing their familiar physical properties. *Computer-augmented environments* merge electronic systems into the physical world instead of attempting to replace them. Our everyday environment is an integral part of these systems; it continues to work as expected, but with new integrated computer functionality. (26)

In 1998, Wendy E. Mackay provided an extended notion of AR. Here, it was not just the user who was "augmented" through head-worn displays. Instead, she allowed for augmented objects where "the physical object is changed by embedding input, output or computational devices on or within it" (Mackay 13), thus turning regular into "smart" objects (Barba *et al.* 930). Also, there are augmentations to the user's and object's environment – as in the case of interactive paper – that allow users to "see and interact with electronic information without wearing special devices or modifying the objects they interact with" (Mackay 15). As Barba *et al.* put it, Mackay's vision of augmented reality "was understood to connote technologies that took everyday objects and activities and enhanced them in some way. Making activities more collaborative or more personalized, and giving objects memory or awareness, were all ways of 'augmenting' user experiences" (930). Mackay herself emphasized the enhanced user experiences that augmented objects could provide: "The future we envision is not a strange world in which we are immersed in 'virtual reality.' Instead, we see our familiar world, enhanced in numerous, often invisible ways" (20).

AUGMENTED REALITY: A BRIEF LONG HISTORY[2]

While viable AR devices and applications have only recently entered the consumer market, research and development work in the area has been going on for several decades. During World War II, the British military built the first aircraft heads-up display for its Mark VIII Airborne Interception Radar that could project data onto a plane's windshield (Vaughan-Nichols 19). The first AR head-mounted display (HMD) system was developed in 1968 by Ivan Sutherland, then a computer scientist at Harvard University. His application "used half-silvered mirrors as optical combiners that allowed the user to see both the computer-generated images reflected from *cathode ray tubes* (CRT) and objects in the room, simultaneously" (Bimber and Raskar 4). Two trackers followed the display's motions; based on this data, a computer drew a simple wireframe of a three-dimensional room. In 1992, two Boeing researchers – Tom Caudell and David Mizell – coined the term "Augmented Reality" for a system they developed to help workers assemble and install complex airplane parts without having to resort to multiple editions of printed manuals. Their goal was to provide "a 'see-thru' virtual reality goggle to the factory worker, and to use this device to augment the worker's visual field of view with useful and dynamically changing information" (Caudell and Mizell 660). One year later, the Global Positioning System (GPS) became operational, thus providing a critical infrastructural component for location-based AR. In 1997, a first mobile AR system was introduced. Unlike later systems, it consisted of several bulky components: "a see-through head-worn display with integral orientation tracker; a backpack holding a computer, differential GPS, and digital radio for wireless web access; and a hand-held computer with stylus and touchpad interface" (Arth *et al.* 7). In 1999, Hirokazu Kato and Mark Billinghurst released ARToolKit, a video tracking library that allows developers to correctly align digital objects with fiducial markers. The library has since been used in a variety of AR projects. A first AR browser was developed in 2001 by Rob Kooper and Blair MacIntyre that would provide a user with contextualized information drawn from what they described as the Real-World Wide Web:

> This work is based on a vision of an enhanced WWW in which each information object (i.e. "Web page," containing two-dimensional [2D] and 3D visual and auditory information) may have contextual meta-data associated with it, such as a location, person, or activity. This meta-data could be used to decide when and where to present the information objects to users. We refer to such a space as the *Real-World Wide Web* (RWWW) and interfaces to it as *RWWW browsers*. In an RWWW browser, Web pages would be registered with real-world locations and presented to the user at the appropriate place and time. (Kooper and MacIntyre 427)

The RWWW browser was still dependent on cumbersome hardware; although mobile phone-based AR applications were first demonstrated in 2004, they were limited by the devices on which they ran.[3] Mobile phones at that time "were difficult to develop for, had slow processing and graphics power, and limited sensors" (Billinghurst *et al.* 28). It was not until 2007 that Apple released the first version of its iPhone and thus offered a technology platform that provided the necessary processing capabilities and development environment for a satisfying AR experience in a single device. A year later, HTC released the first smartphone running the Android operating system. Unlike the original iPhone, the device also had GPS and inertial compass sensors and thus could be used as a platform for outdoor AR applications. That same year, Wikitude, an AR browser for Android devices, became available. The application overlayed location-based data on real-time video captured by a phone's camera. In 2009, SPRXmobile published Layar, another AR browser that organized data into separate "layers" that users could select and then serendipitously discover content based on their current location.

Initially, applications such as Wikitude and Layar relied on a device's screen to display content to their users. Head-mounted displays, which had been a staple of AR research projects, were not as successful in the consumer market. This began to change with the announcement of Google Glass, "an optical [head mounted display] that can be controlled with an integrated touch-sensitive sensor or natural language commands" (Arth *et al.* 27). The product became commercially available in 2014, but Google halted production a year later; at the time of this writing, the future of Google Glass remains uncertain. Although the project also generated negative press, primarily around privacy issues,[4] it raised the public's awareness of the affordances of AR.

TECHNOLOGIES

(Visual) AR applications function by overlaying virtual elements on physical objects or video images thereof. In order to accomplish this, the application needs to know where to place these elements on the display and how to size and orient them; this process is also referred to as registration. One can classify such applications into two groups based on how they select and register virtual content: location-based and image-based AR. In the first case, each virtual element is associated with a physical location. If the application's user is in the vicinity of this location, one or more elements are selected. Based on the relative position of the device running the application, its orientation and tilt, the program calculates the correct placement of the virtual element on the display. Image-based AR, on the other hand:

> requires specific labels to register the position of 3D objects on the real-world image. [An] AR book with basic equipment such as a webcam and marker labels is one of the typical marker-based applications and has been employed in several studies . . . A marker label in typical marker-based applications is commonly presented as an iconic coded image . . . By detecting a marker

> label on a book through a webcam capture, a virtual element is then generated by the AR software. This virtual element would be shown upon the book and recovered on the computer screen that can be manipulated by tilting or rotating the book. Moreover, setting with a projector in a traditional classroom, students can operate the card with an AR marker to control the 3D objects on a projected screen . . . or a whiteboard . . . (Cheng and Tsai 451–452)

While the marker labels mentioned by Cheng and Tsai initially had to be very distinctive graphical elements, such as Quick Response codes (QR codes for short), advances in image recognition algorithms as well as improving performance of mobile platforms made it possible to augment any sufficiently distinctive image. Although images without specialized markers allow for greater flexibility as they can be retroactively augmented, they need to somehow indicate to users that augmented content is available, whereas QR codes have become common and users generally know how to use them (see Vogt and Shingles). Commercial AR browsers, such as Wikitude or Layar, initially only provided location-based AR. Later versions added image recognition capabilities to offer powerful print augmentation capabilities.

Another way of differentiating AR systems is based on the type of display that is used. The first kind, head-mounted displays (HMDs), have been used primarily in AR research since Ivan Sutherland's first prototype and can be subdivided into video see-through and optical see-through displays. Video see-through displays capture the user's point of view through two head-mounted cameras and then merge it with virtual elements; the whole scene is then shown on one or two small displays located in front of the user's eyes. Optical see-through displays do not require cameras; the user sees the physical world through a half-mirror while the virtual scene is projected via the mirror onto the user's eyes. As Billinghurst *et al.* discuss, both approaches have clear advantages and disadvantages. Optical see-through systems can provide a real-life, real-time image of the physical environment. Also, since there is no computing required to merge real and virtual elements, they require less processing power. Their main drawback compared to their video see-through counterparts is a less accurate and delayed registration:

> In many cases, optical see-through displays require [a] manual calibration process which ends up with relatively poor quality of registration compared to automated computer vision based approach in video based AR displays. Since the calibration parameters are dependent on the spatial relationship between the user's eyes and the display's image plane, there is a higher chance of parameters changing over time (e.g. wearable displays sliding off from the original position) and eventually causing misalignment between the real and virtual view images. Hence, accurate 3D eye tracking (relative to the display) becomes more important to visualize a correctly aligned AR scene with optical see-through displays.
>
> Temporal delay between the real world and the virtual views is another challenging problem in optical see-through displays. Even with a spatially

> accurate tracking system, there always would be temporal delay for tracking physical objects. As the virtual view is updated based on the tracking results, unless the physical scene and the user's viewpoint is static, the virtual view will have temporal delay compared to the direct view of the real world in optical see-through displays. (65–66)

A second display category is handhelds such as can be found in Personal Digital Assistants (PDAs), smartphones, and tablets. These devices combine video see-through displays with the required sensor technology, processors, and power supplies into small units. Their size is also their main drawback: as the augmented environment is limited to the relatively small screen, they provide a less immersive user experience while at the same time forcing users to point their device at the augmented object.

Finally, there are spatial displays that employ technologies such as video projectors to display augmentations directly on physical objects. Technology is not tied to any particular user as it is with head-mounted or handheld displays, but rather integrated into the environment and thus can be used simultaneously by multiple users. Another advantage of such systems is lower latency in the registration process as there is less relative motion between the augmented object and the augmenting device (Mine *et al.*). Carmigniani *et al.* point out several different kinds of spatial displays:

> There exist three different approaches to [Spatial Augmented Reality] which mainly differ in the way they augment the environment: video-see-through, optical-see-through and direct augmentation. In [Spatial Augmented Reality], video-see-through displays are screen based; they are a common technique used if the system does not have to be mobile as they are cost efficient since only off-the-shelf hardware components and standard PC equipment is required. Spatial optical-see-through displays generate images that are aligned within the physical environment. Spatial optical combiners, such as planar or curved mirror beam splitters, transparent screens, or optical holograms are essential components of such displays. However, much like screen based video see-through, spatial optical-see-through does not support mobile applications due to spatially aligned optics and display technology. Finally, projector-based spatial displays apply front-projection to seamlessly project images directly onto physical objects' surfaces . . . (348)

AUGMENTED REALITY AND THE DIGITAL HUMANITIES

Augmented reality has in the past been put to a wide variety of uses, such as manufacturing, medical care, promotions, and entertainment. However, there are also numerous ways in which it can enrich digital humanities research and practice.

The following examples were created by students in a series of workshops on AR that the author taught at the Digital Humanities Summer Institute from 2012 to 2014. While some were conceptual, others were realized as functioning prototypes implemented in a variety of AR browsers.

One potential contribution that AR can make to a digital humanities project is to provide users with alternative access modes to content that has already been made available through more traditional means. Such was the case with a group project that drew on a set of beer reviews created by the "Digital Humanities Databases" class that was taught during the same summer institute. Students imported parts of the data into a content management system for the Layar AR browser and georeferenced all pub locations. Users of the project could then walk through Victoria and – if they were running Layar on their mobile device and had selected that particular layer – the browser would indicate nearby pubs for which beer reviews existed. The reviews were made available on basic web pages that were linked to each location and became viewable in Layar. In this case, AR not only provided another venue for existing content, but also an alternative way of discovering it: targeted searching in a database was replaced by serendipitous discovery where, by walking through a space, one comes across information associated with that space which one may not have discovered otherwise.

Another project's goal was to promote photographic materials from the University of Victoria's Archives and highlight the donors and benefactors who had university buildings and other landmarks named after them. The student uploaded and georeferenced a selection of images and also provided some biographical information that would be displayed together with the images in Layar. By using AR to make these materials available, the student not only helped to promote university history to a wider community, including potential future donors, but also created new ways of accessing unique materials that might have remained hidden in the archives.

Other projects made use of Layar's image recognition capabilities to augment various types of print materials. One group decided to augment several corporate logos; they scanned the logos and, using Layar's Creator tool, added links to blog entries about products, their ingredients, and politics associated with their creation. The students' goal was to show:

> AR working as not only an activist platform but also a pedagogical model of exposure, discussion and reflection (i.e. critical thinking) as juxtaposed to the pedagogical model of advertising which teaches us what to think and replaces how to think (the antithesis of critical thinking). (Herrera and Dutta)

Augmented reality also lends itself to the print augmentation of historical materials. This was demonstrated by a group who enhanced a booklet entitled *Picturesque Victoria* that was originally published in 1910. Again using Layar Creator, they overlayed the historical images in the booklet with current photographs they had taken from the same location and angle as the originals. While the combination of new and old images would normally have required a republication of the booklet, AR made it possible to achieve the same effect without modifying the physical object.

Augmented reality can not only augment physical objects with additional information, but also reveal information that is hidden within those objects. One student wanted to make watermarks visible that were incorporated into paper commonly employed in the book-making process. Talking about their value, she writes:

> Watermarks are found in laid paper produced between 1500–1850 and convey valuable historical information about book production. They are also beautiful visual artifacts in their own right. As pedagogical tools, they can illustrate changes in economic trading patterns, book history, and iconography. Rarely curated, an exhibition of watermarks would make these important visual resources accessible and understandable to the public. (Wegner)

She retraced watermarks from Alexander Gilchrist's 1880 edition of *Life of William Blake* and linked them to page images from the book. Thus, when a user views the respective pages through the Layar browser, the watermarks become visible on the screen.

Besides displaying images and videos, AR browsers can also display three-dimensional models. This capability was put to good use by a student who wanted to enable users to experience several indigenous military defensive sites in the Victoria area. After he uploaded existing models to the course's content management system and aligned them according to the position of the original structures, users of his layer would be able to move across the augmented locations and experience the building models *in situ*, thus further improving the visitor's experience.

CONCLUSION

Augmented reality has been a relatively recent addition to the toolbox of digital humanists; however, it has great potential to enrich their research, teaching, and outreach. It can be used to augment existing projects with new capabilities or it may inspire new work that takes advantage of what AR in all its forms has to offer. At this point, the tools are available to allow digital humanists to start experimenting with the technology; it is up to them to find new and innovative ways of augmenting the humanities.

NOTES

1 The last requirement relates only to visual augmentations. As Azuma *et al.* point out, other senses, such as hearing and smell, can also be augmented.
2 Unless noted otherwise, this section draws on Arth *et al.*
3 For a discussion of various mobile AR hardware platforms see Papagiannakis *et al.*, pp. 5–6.
4 Several authors point out that besides technical issues, there may also be social reasons that could hinder a wider adoption of AR systems (Azuma *et al.*; Billinghurst *et al.*).

REFERENCES

Arth, Clemens, Lukas Gruber, Raphael Grasset, Tobias Langlotz, Alessandro Mulloni, Dieter Schmalstieg, and Daniel Wagner. "The History of Mobile Augmented Reality. Developments in Mobile AR Over the Last Almost 50 Years." *Technical Report ICG-TR-2015-001*. Graz: Institute for Computer Graphics and Vision, 2015. www.icg.tugraz.at/publications/pdf/the-history-of-mobile-augmented-reality/at_download/file. Accessed 24 July 2015.

Azuma, Ronald T. "A Survey of Augmented Reality." *Presence: Teleoperators and Virtual Environments* 6:4 (August 1997): 355–385. www.cs.unc.edu/~azuma/ARpresence.pdf. Accessed 24 July 2015.

Azuma, Ronald T., Yohan Baillot, Reinhold Behringer, Steven Feiner, Simon Julier, and Blair MacIntyre. "Recent Advances in Augmented Reality." *IEEE* (November/December 2001): 34–47. www.cs.unc.edu/~azuma/cga2001.pdf. Accessed 24 July 2015.

Barba, Evan, Blair MacIntyre, and Elizabeth D. Mynatt. "Here We Are! Where Are We? Locating Mixed Reality in the Age of the Smartphone." *Proceedings of the IEEE* 100.4 (2012): 929–936.

Billinghurst, Mark, Adrian Clark, and Gun Lee. *A Survey of Augmented Reality*. Hanover, MA: Now Publishers, 2015.

Bimber, Oliver and Ramesh Raskar. *Spatial Augmented Reality. Merging Real and Virtual Worlds*. Wellesley, MA: Peters, 2005.

Carmigniani, Julie and Borko Furht. "Augmented Reality: An Overview." *Handbook of Augmented Reality*. Ed. Borko Furht. New York: Springer, 2011. 3–46.

Carmigniani, Julie, Borko Furht, Marco Anisetti, Paolo Ceravolo, Ernesto Damiani and Misa Ivkovic. "Augmented Reality Technologies, Systems and Applications." *Multimedia Tools and Applications* 51:1 (2011): 341–377.

Caudell, Thomas P. and David W. Mizell. "Augmented Reality: An Application of Heads-Up Display Technology to Manual Manufacturing Processes." *Proceedings of the Twenty-Fifth Hawaii International Conference on System Sciences* 2 (January 1992): 659–669.

Cheng, Kun-Hung and Chin-Chung Tsai. "Affordances of Augmented Reality in Science Learning: Suggestions for Future Research." *Journal of Science Education and Technology* 22:4 (August 2013): 449–462.

Herrera, Joseph H. and Nandita Dutta. http://markuswust.com/wordpress/?p=121. Accessed 16 August 2015.

Kooper, Rob and Blair MacIntyre. "Browsing the Real-World Wide Web: Maintaining Awareness of Virtual Information in an AR Information Space." *International Journal of Human-Computer Interaction* 16:3 (2003): 425–446.

Mackay, Wendy E. "Augmented Reality: Linking Real and Virtual Worlds. A New Paradigm for Interacting with Computers." *Proceedings of the Workshop on Advanced Visual Interfaces AVI* (1998): 13–21. www.lri.fr/~mackay/pdffiles/AVI98.AugmentedReality.pdf. Accessed 24 July 2015.

Milgram, Paul and Fumio Kishino. "A Taxonomy of Mixed Reality Visual Displays." *IEICE Transactions on Information and Systems* E77-D.12 (1994): 1321–1329.

Mine, Mark, David Rose, Bei Yang, Jeroen van Baar, and Anselm Grundhoefer. "Projection-Based Augmented Reality in Disney Theme Parks." *Computer* 45:7 (July 2012): 32–40.

Papagiannakis, George, Gurminder Singh, and Nadia Magnenat-Thalmann. "A Survey of Mobile and Wireless Technologies for Augmented Reality Systems." *Computer Animation and Virtual Worlds* 19 (2008): 3–22.

Vaughan-Nichols, Steven J. "Augmented Reality: No Longer a Novelty?" *Computer* 42:1 (2009): 19–22.

Vogt, Frederic P.A. and Luke J. Shingles. "Augmented Reality in Astrophysics." *Astrophysics and Space Science* 347:1 (2013): 47–60.

Wegner, Alia. http://markuswust.com/wordpress/?p=234. Accessed 16 August 2015.

Wellner, Pierre, Wendy E. Mackay, and Rich Gold. "Computer-Augmented Environments: Back to the Real World." *Communications of the ACM* 36:7 (July 1993): 24–26.

CHAPTER 18

Fabrication and research-creation in the arts and humanities

Nicole Clouston and Jentery Sayers

A quick scan of digital fabrication research across the academy suggests that computer-aided manufacturing (CAM) is most common in mechanical engineering, architecture, design, and urban planning departments (Goertz and Morgan 2014: n. pag.). For two examples among many, consider Taubman College's Digital Fab Lab at the University of Michigan and the John H. Daniels Faculty Fab Lab at the University of Toronto. Inspired by Neil Gershenfeld's groundbreaking work at MIT (2005), digital fabrication – or the creation of digital models in tactile form using additive or subtractive computer numerical control (CNC) techniques – appeals to practitioners in these fields because it tightens the loop between screen and prototype, code and material, idea and object. It also allows those practitioners to better anticipate surprises, reduce error in the manufacturing process, and rapidly test their ideas before projects are delivered for small- or large-batch production. But, aside from a few recent publications (e.g. Elliott *et al.* 2012 and Kee 2014), very little attention has been paid to the relevance of CAM techniques to arts and humanities research. In response to such a lack, below we walk readers through the particulars of digital fabrication, with an emphasis on materials design, digital/analog convergence, and manufacturing techniques such as 3-D printing, cutting, etching, routing, and milling. Ultimately, our aim is to demystify digital fabrication for researchers who are new to it, giving them a granular sense of computer-aided manufacturing before they start a lab, acquire equipment and materials, commit to a specific technique, or even write about it from a critical perspective.

Given the rather nascent state of digital fabrication in the arts and humanities, we draw from projects that are experimental in character, adopting Chapman and

Sawchuk's four types of research-creation – "research-for-creation," "research-from-creation," "creative presentations of research," and "creation-as-research" (2012: 15) – to describe work across contexts. One benefit of stressing research-creation as a paradigm for these experimental projects is that fabrication becomes a material intervention in how research happens; it expands what fields such as digital humanities imply by research in the first place. Another benefit is that fabrication may be positioned as a way to conjecture with technologies as core components of the research process. For now, we will echo Chapman and Sawchuk and define research-creation projects broadly as research "projects [that] typically integrate a creative process, experimental aesthetic component, or an artistic work as an integral part of the study" (2012: 6). Through the four types referenced above as well as the examples unpacked below, we add some texture to this definition.

ADDITIVE MANUFACTURING: 3-D PRINTING

One of the most popular computer-aided manufacturing techniques, 3-D printing is an additive process in which successive layers of material are laid down in order to create a form. Three-dimensional printers are often used for rapid prototyping as they can quickly and inexpensively fabricate objects for testing. They are also being used to manufacture finished objects in small runs, although most desktop printers are not ideal for batch manufacturing. Some 3-D printers are capable of printing materials as diverse as gold, clay, and sugar. However, the majority of them use either resin or thermoplastic. Resin 3-D printers use an optical power source to cure liquid resin into a solid form. They are more accurate and create more durable objects than thermoplastic 3-D printers, and are accordingly more expensive. Additionally, resin 3-D printers typically require more maintenance, and the liquid resin necessitates extra care when handling. Printers that use thermoplastics – plastics that become liquid when heated and return to a solid when cooled – are the most common and affordable. Typically, *acrylonitrile butadiene styrene* (ABS) and *polylactide* (PLA) are used. ABS is a petroleum-based plastic with a high degree of flexibility and temperature resistance (Griffey 2014: 13). This flexibility makes it ideal for interlocking parts that are subject to friction. PLA is plant-based and available in a wide range of colours and opacities. It yields sharper edges and is less likely to detach from the printing bed than ABS. However, it has a low melting point that makes it likely to warp in warm environments (Griffey 2014: 14).

Dutch artist Theo Jansen uses thermoplastic 3-D printing to make his sculptural works more accessible. Jansen's *Strandbeests* are massive kinetic sculptures constructed out of PVC tubing and other plastics that move along the landscape powered by the wind. He describes this work as a new species that lives independently on beaches (Azzarello 2015: n. pag.). He reconstructed *Strandbeests* digitally and then uploaded the files to the online 3-D printing service, Shapeways, where they can be printed in thermoplastic for $55.68 to $396.02 CAD (Jansen

2015). This project takes his full-scale sculptures, whose length ranges from 20 to 42 feet, and recreates them at 10 to 21 inches as open editions (Figure 18.1). His decision to 3-D-print thermoplastics links his large and small sculptures through a consistent use of materials and an interest in their properties and connotations, particularly their capacity to survive the elements without degrading. Jansen describes this capacity as a "new way to multiply, by injecting their digital DNA directly into the Shapeways system" (qtd in Azzarello 2015: n. pag).

In addition to prototyping and producing finished objects, 3-D printing can be one step in a larger process. Monika Horčicová, a Czech sculptor, uses 3-D printing in conjunction with mould-making to create highly detailed sculptures that employ repeated forms of human skeletons on a miniature scale. Her 2014 work, *Wheel of Life*, is a wheel of anatomically correct human leg bones connected to each other at the pelvis that measures 55 × 59 × 15 cm (Horčicová 2015: n. pag.). To produce these pieces, Horčicová prints miniature bones using a 3-D printer that extrudes a plaster composite. Rather than printing each bone that comprises the final piece, Horčicová creates a mould of the 3-D printed bones from which she casts multiples in polyurethane resin. 3-D printing enables Horčicová's work to maintain human proportions at a scale that, otherwise, would be incredibly laborious to achieve.

With *Factum Arte* – "a team of artists, technicians and conservators dedicated to digital mediation" – artist Anish Kapoor developed a 3-D printer that extrudes cement.

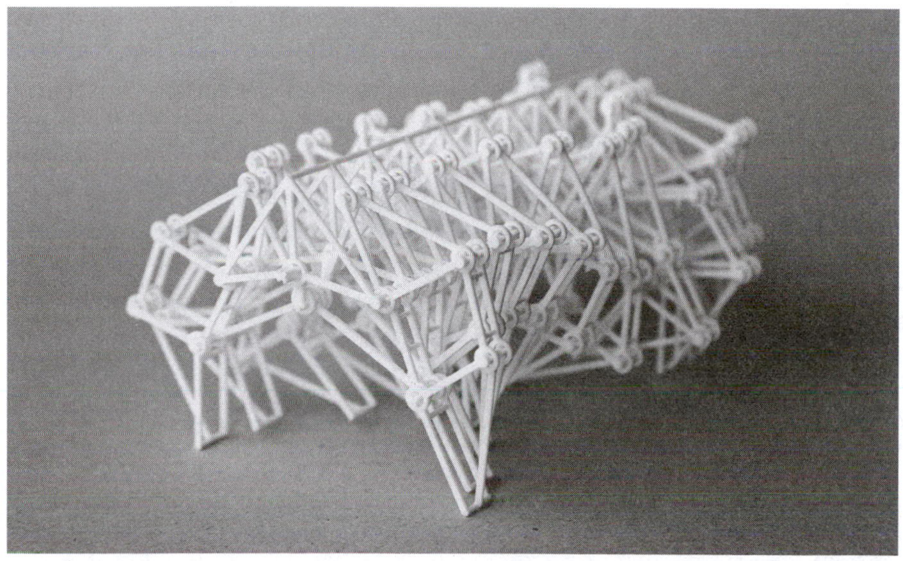

Figure 18.1
Theo Jansen, *Animaris Geneticus Ondularis*, 2014

Photographer Tim van Bentum. Used with kind permission of Theo Jansen and Tim van Bentum.

Kapoor uses the machine to create monumental abstract sculptures that are printed and exhibited on wooden pallets, such as Spittle (2012), which measures 233 × 152 × 143 cm (*Factum Arte* 2015: n. pag.). Unlike Jansen and Horčicová, Kapoor is not interested in precision or detail so much as material qualities and inaccuracies accompanying experimental fabrication processes. His printed cement sculptures tend to be most interesting when the process "fails": when the cement stacks too high, begins to sag, and eventually crumbles (Kapoor 2015: n. pag.). The work can be seen as a valuable investigation into the possibilities and limitations of 3-D printing as a process. Like work by Jansen and Horčicová, it is also a form of creation-as-research, or – returning to Chapman and Sawchuk for a moment – a process "about investigating the relationship between technology, gathering and revealing through creation . . . while also seeking to extract knowledge from the process" (2012: 19). Fabrication technologies are pushed in novel or non-instrumental directions, with process operating as the primary area of inquiry.

Elsewhere in additive manufacturing, historians Devon Elliott, Robert MacDougall, and William J. Turkel use 3-D printing to fabricate components of historical experiments, such as magical effects performed on stage over one hundred years ago. For their work, additive manufacturing prompts questions and facilitates answers difficult to come by through text or images alone. They write: "Fabrication and physical experimentation will not transcend the impossibility of directly accessing the past, but they do offer another route toward apprehending what was happening and how events such as magical performances were constructed and experienced" (Elliott *et al.* 2012: 123). Articulated as such, manufacturing the past implies entering into dialogue with it. From the perspective of materials design, this particular approach to additive manufacturing is more about prototyping history through available materials than about the quality of those materials or even their connotation. As Elliott *et al.* assert, "Exact reproduction of the past is not our goal" (2012: 127). In Chapman and Sawchuk's terms, this resistance to exact reproduction may be understood as a creative presentation of research (Chapman and Sawchuk 2012: 18): the results are presented not only in article form but also as 3-D objects for testing, experimentation, and even role-playing. These objects do not replicate history; they are scenarios for speculation. They creatively recontextualize the stuff of the past in the present, with technologies at hand.

SUBTRACTIVE MANUFACTURING: CUTTING AND ETCHING

A laser cutter functions by directing a laser beam under computer numerical control (CNC) at a precise focal length onto a material. The laser can either cut or etch depending on the chosen settings. The laser cutters commonly used in non-industrial workspaces use a carbon dioxide laser that ranges in power from 30 to 120 watts (Schuocker 1989: 315). These machines can cut wood, cardboard, acrylic, plastic, leather, fabric, mylar, paper, rubber, cork, and more depending on the model of machine. They can etch all of these materials in addition to glass, ceramic, pressboard, and bare metal when coated with a metal marking solution.

As demonstrated in the work of artist, Eric Standley, laser cutters are capable of incredible intricacy. Influenced by the geometry of medieval and Islamic architecture, Standley marries the two to create stained-glass-like paper motifs that range in size from 8.5 × 11 inches to 23 × 19 inches (Standley 2015: n. pag.). Each piece requires laser cutting hundreds of digitally designed layers out of separate sheets of paper. Once these sheets are stacked, the resulting positive and negative cutouts create an ecclesiastical space. Standley is able to achieve this ecclesiasticism through the geometric precision of the laser cutter. He remarks on this machined aspect to the work, stating that he is trying "to project something that is not even human" (2015: n. pag.). By stacking the cut sheets of paper, he is using the laser cutter – which works best with flat, level materials, as the focal length of the laser needs to remain consistent – to create both form and volume.

Working in a similar manner, Oakland-based artist, Gabriel Schama, creates layered wood relief sculptures. Schama draws out each layer in a vector illustration and cuts them out of 1/8-inch mahogany plywood (Schama 2015: n. pag.). When cutting with a laser, a distinctly burnt edge is often left on materials. Schama translates this effect into an aesthetic element, which highlights the abstract, mandala-like shapes in his pieces. When working with plywood it is important to keep in mind thickness as well as the kind of core. The 1/8-inch mahogany plywood that Schama uses is an ideal thickness, although with multiple passes many laser cutters could cut up to a 1/4 inch. Also, he is using high-quality plywood with a solid veneer core, in contrast to a medium density fiber (MDF) core, particleboard core, or combination core used in many other kinds of plywood. This high-quality core type means the plywood will not have any voids (sections where chunks of the core are missing), giving the laser a more consistent surface to cut through and a more aesthetically appealing edge.

Michael Hansmeyer also employs this strategy of stacking flat materials to create volume. Hansmeyer is a computational architect in Zurich who uses algorithms to generate architectural forms. In his project, *Subdivided Columns: A New Order* (Figure 18.2), he used an iterating subdivision algorithm to generate a 3-D model of a column, which he then created in cardboard (Hansmeyer 2015: n. pag.). The columns have millions of facets and would be impossible to draft by hand. But through a series of steps they are translated from a 3-D model into a toolpath understood by the laser cutter (2015: n. pag.). Similar to Standley, Hansmeyer investigates forms that would be impossible without CNC techniques. In all three of his projects the laser cutter has been used to cut various planes, which are then brought together to create a larger whole. Another strategy for using the laser cutter is to etch into a material. When etching, the laser cutter functions like a printer, engraving an image onto the surface.

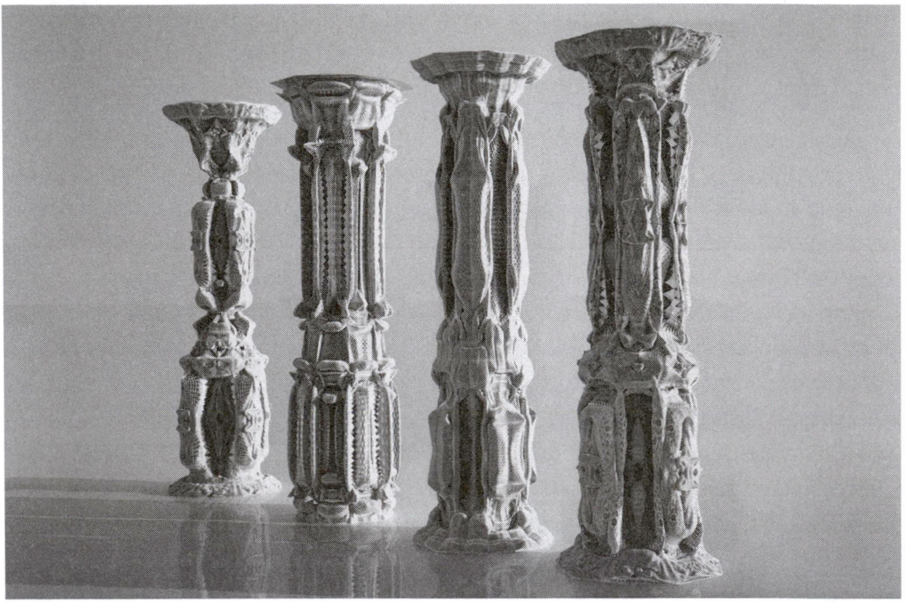

Figure 18.2
Michael Hansmeyer, *Subdivided Columns – A New Order*, 2010

Used with kind permission of Michael Hansmeyer.

In her series, *Surface*, Toronto-based artist, Nicole Clouston, used a scanning electron microscope (SEM) to take images of steel, Baltic birch plywood, and cardboard between 50- and 100-micrometers wide (Figure 18.3). She then enlarged the images and etched them onto a 24 × 17-inch sheet of the material imaged (wood if the image was of wood, etc.). The process of etching allowed the creation of an engraved image composed only of the material, in contrast to additive methods of image making. In particular, the laser cutter makes it possible to etch these images on such diverse materials. The cardboard and wood etch easily while the laser only subtly affects the surface of the bare steel, rendering physical the resistances and fragilities of these materials through the harsh but focused force of CNC techniques. Comparable to the work of Standley, Schama, and Hansmeyer, Clouston's research-creation is creation-as-research, with an emphasis on innovating through materials and techniques (Clouston 2015).

A slightly different approach is taken by the Maker Lab in the Humanities' "Kits for Cultural History" project at the University of Victoria. There, the Lab uses CNC cutting and etching to produce physical boxes – not unlike Fluxkits from the 1960s and 1970s (Sayers 2015a) – containing components of historical mechanisms that are no longer accessible or existed only as 2-D media (Belojevic 2013: n. pag.). Comparable to work by Standley and Hansmeyer, the boxes integrate laser cutting

Figure 18.3
Nicole Clouston, *Surface*, 2015

into their aesthetic. The edges of the boxes' interiors and exteriors are burnt, and their general appearance is quite simple. However, etching adds distinct flourishes, including remediated signatures by the designers and engineers of the inaccessible mechanisms now at hand. Found in digitized drawings from the Victorian and Edwardian periods, these signatures are fed into a CNC machine, which burns them with an accuracy very difficult, if not impossible, to achieve by hand. Here, subtractive manufacturing serves the purposes of what Chapman and Sawchuk call research-from-creation (2012: 16). It generates prototypes that prompt the Lab's research team to pursue archival investigations, including questions about how attribution happens in histories of science, technology, and engineering as well as studies of how and under what assumptions new media are packaged both now and in the past (Sayers 2015b).

SUBTRACTIVE MANUFACTURING: MILLING AND ROUTING

Both millers and routers use a rotary device to remove material, traveling along multiple axes. Due to these common traits, the two terms are often used interchangeably; however, CNC millers are most often used for large-scale work and harder materials (e.g. metal and hardwood), whereas CNC routers are typically used for small-scale work and softer materials (e.g. foam and wax).

The ability of CNC millers to cut large materials can be seen in the work of Italian sculptor, Aron Demetz. In his *Advanced Minorities* series from 2012, Demetz uses a combination of hand-carving techniques and CNC milling to sculpt life-size human figures. Each figure is milled out of a single log of basswood, linden, cherry, spruce, poplar, maple, or cedar (Demetz 2015: n. pag.). He leaves large sections of his sculptures unfinished after milling. These tufts of raw wood show how the path of the bit contrasts with the smooth surfaces that are hand-finished, drawing attention to the processes creating each. This metamorphosis of the material – a persistent theme in Demetz's work – is one that CNC techniques are particularly apt for addressing, in part because of their capability to radically transform materials with precision and persistence.

Milling and routing are also commonly used to create moulds. For his 2013 project, *hommomculus agora (h.a) & alpha (h.a)*, Toronto-based artist, Mark-David Hosale, created moulds out of high-density foam using a CNC miller. From these moulds, he cast multiple 1.25-meter-long hourglass forms in epoxy. Pairs of casts were then joined at the middle with more epoxy and suspended in an architectonic installation. Through CNC milling, Hosale was able to guarantee the pairs would fit together precisely. The choice to use a CNC miller or router to create a mould rather than to sculpt the final piece can be made for many reasons. In the case of *hommomculus agora (h.a) & alpha (h.a)*, the desired material – epoxy – could not be milled due to its density and brittleness. Another factor is time. Foam can be cut quite rapidly, in contrast to plastic, making it more efficient to pour plastic into a foam mould.

Although CNC millers can remove vast amounts of material quickly and are thus the most efficient tools to use when building large works, some practitioners have used smaller routers in order to create highly detailed pieces that can be assembled into something larger. Architect and designer, Ferruccio Laviani, does this precision work in his furniture series, *Good Vibrations*. One piece in the series is a Neo-Renaissance cabinet that appears warped. Laviani was inspired by images taken from fast-forwarded analog videos, where the objects are twisted in a zigzag pattern by digital static (Laviani 2015: n. pag.). Laviani created a 3-D model of the cabinet, added the digital distortion, and then broke it down into smaller sections that could – at least in principle – be routed at very high detail (2015: n. pag.). Although we are unsure whether Laviani ever manufactured the cabinet, it would consume far more time than low-detail milling because the router must move slowly to maintain intricate detail without burning the wood. Due in part to CNC precision, Laviani's piece manifests, or could manifest, a digital glitch in tactile form. As with Demetz and Hosale, this work is anchored in creation-as-research.

MATERIALS DESIGN, OR CHOICES THAT MATTER FOR RESEARCH-CREATION

The techniques and materials employed by a given project typically correspond with its intended uses and audiences as well as its aesthetic and desired shelf life. Below, then, are various factors to consider at the intersection of research-creation with digital fabrication. To be sure, they are not exhaustive. They are simply stress points for starting a fabrication project with research-creation in mind.

Prototyping

Three-dimensional printing is a common technique for prototyping arts and humanities projects. Most desktop 3-D printers afford high-resolution output while also keeping manufacturing costs down. They produce objects with precision even if materials such as PLA and ABS are not resilient over time. Yet laser cutting is also an appealing prototyping technique. It can be used to rapidly generate paper, cardboard, wood, and fabric models that give researchers not only a sense of what an object may look like in 3-D space but also a feel for how it may be handled and afford certain actions or behaviors. When understood this way, prototyping through CAM techniques is neatly aligned with what – following Viviane Folcher (2003), among others – many researchers call "design-in-use," or the "ways in which users take over existing products according to personal needs, and practices beyond product design" (Nelson *et al.* 2009: 3). With design-in-use, the impulse is to avoid pursuing a perfect form, which is only manufactured, without much (if any) feedback, during the final stage of production. Against monolithic forms or decontextualized use, projects are iterated and tested for and by people with various needs and investments. Over time, this procedure "involves [the] emergence of unanticipated uses, and transformations in the structure and characteristics of the product" (2009: 3). Of course, for many researchers, the ultimate goal of this iteration may not be a user-friendly product. For instance, artists may prototype objects not intended for handling, or they may resist notions of intuitive consumption and material legibility. Meanwhile, historians may wish to fabricate objects for interactive exhibits or classroom workshops. Whatever the aim, prototyping can be an informative process for experimentation and development, and the materials used influence how interpretation happens.

Importantly, prototyping may not be a step toward batch or even one-off manufacturing. Recalling Elliott *et al.*'s creative expression of research (2012), historians can reconstruct an experiment from the past in order to better understand how this became that. This process may facilitate writing and argumentation – or research-from-creation – without any investment in circulating a product for acquisition or review. But for designers and artists, prototyping a project may be a middle state between ideation and exhibition. The prototype may thus be smaller, cheaper, rougher, or less durable than the final piece.

Depending on researcher preferences, factors such as texture and setting may also be significant. Should a prototype's texture resemble the desired texture of the final piece? Will a paper prototype suffice for testing an object to be made of wood? Similarly, should the conditions of testing resemble those where the piece will eventually be exhibited or used? Will a prototype in a lab afford the same interactions as the final piece in a gallery or classroom? Questions such as these are fundamental to prototyping critically, with an awareness of choices and decisions across a spectrum of materials design.

Archiving

For projects involving batch manufacturing beyond prototyping, archiving the final piece is neatly intertwined with its composition. Researchers may wish to consider whether the piece will be integrated into an existing collection and how materials in that collection are typically exhibited and preserved. Perhaps obviously, high-quality materials are generally more conducive to durability. Yet, for pieces consisting of component parts, documentation of assembly is often necessary, too. This way, the piece can be more easily repaired, refabricated (in part or in whole), or even repurposed in the future.

In fact, one of the most interesting aspects of digital fabrication is the availability of component parts as digital files and code. Materials intended for computer-aided manufacturing may be archived in productively redundant ways, stored as an object file (OBJ) containing code and metadata, a stereolithography file (STL) describing the surface geometry, G-code with toolpath instructions for fabrication, and a tactile object. Across formats and materials, these different versions of a single project prompt researchers to think between bits and atoms (Sayers *et al.* 2016), without neatly dividing digital from analog from print from screen from whatever is held in hand. These formats must be understood relationally, through their contingencies (e.g. the software, hardware, and settings at hand), as researchers anticipate their shelf lives. At the same time, following legacies of site-specific work by artists such as Robert Smithson, the desire to archive all the things might be balanced with an acknowledgment that materials necessarily degrade – and that degradation is often interesting. Also, interactions with any material cannot be fully captured or somehow frozen. Following Maurice Blanchot (2008: 37), something always escapes.

The ephemerality of interactions, as well as the changing states of atoms and bits, can be some of the most intriguing dimensions of materials design for digital fabrication. Here, a compelling example is the *Transient Materialization* project by SINLAB and the Media and Design Lab at École polytechnique fédérale de Lausanne (Visnjic 2015: n. pag.), where an algorithm generates foam structures that gradually disappear from view, especially when touched. Such a project is impossible to archive or recover completely. With respect to archiving strategies, it reminds researchers that video, audio, and image documentation may supplement the digital files and tactile objects for a particular project. Such documentation gives future audiences a sense of the project in context. It is also crucial for many creation-as-research projects, where processes and design choices are always changing or short-lived.

Distribution and maintenance

As with archiving, distributing digital fabrication projects is a matter between bits and atoms. Returning for a moment to Jansen's *Strandbeests*, online repositories such as Shapeways, Thingiverse, and GitHub are now popular mechanisms for licensing, sharing, describing, and even archiving object files (e.g. see the "Early Wearables" Kit for Cultural History at github.com/uvicmakerlab/earlyWearablesKit). While researchers may wish to manufacture their own objects and then – where necessary – circulate them via the post, they can also use one of the above online networks, their own webspace, or an institutional webspace to distribute materials as code and metadata, via what – for better or worse – is called the "Internet of Things" (Sterling 2005). One appeal of this approach is that people can print, cut, etch, or mill objects they download, with whatever materials and machines they have. Another is that manufacturing can happen off-site, and the printed files can be delivered (e.g. by Shapeways). This option is ideal for people who do not want to invest in or maintain CAM technologies. Finally, with fabrication projects available online, objects are not only rendered as open editions, conducive to crowdsourced sculpture projects such as "Linked" by Jeff de Boer and PrintToPeer (Neal 2013: n. pag.); under particular licenses (e.g. Creative Commons licenses), they can also be modified for particular settings and needs. Their sizes, textures, surfaces, infills, and resolutions can be edited with computer-aided design (CAD) software such as Rhinoceros or SketchUp. From a materials design perspective, this plasticity implies more than manipulating an object's form, surface, content, and metadata. Its physical substance is no longer stable, either. A piece intended for wood can be manufactured elsewhere in acrylic. A project meant for paper can later be cut into fabric.

While it may be tempting to claim that, with digital fabrication, all materials and their distribution are reduced to code – available in their entirety as abstractions or symbolic expressions – practitioners should note that code is physical, too: stored somewhere, impressed on a drive, transmitted through wires. Accordingly, the distribution of objects via an Internet of Things is best understood as a material expansion and diversification of manufacturing, not its flattening into whatever appears on a screen. After all, once an object file is downloaded on the other end, the CAM process still requires hardware, software, and raw materials. What is more, after it is fabricated, the object file now in hand may have textures and affordances distinct from its instantiation elsewhere.

Indeed, across settings, computer-aided manufacturing is hardly uniform; it demands what Chapman and Sawchuk call research-for-creation: "an initial gathering together of material, ideas, concepts, collaborators, technologies, et cetera, in order to begin" (2012:15). This gathering is not only essential to establishing the infrastructures of distribution and perseveration; it is also important for manufacturing and assembly. Before practitioners build infrastructures for fabrication, they may wish to treat infrastructure as a research area unto itself, with considerations of how materials will be made, maintained, exhibited, broken, repaired, reused, repurposed, dissembled, and discarded over time. Such research-for-creation can start small: surveys of metadata vocabularies and preservation strategies, education about sourcing and preservation, site visits (including visits to like-minded labs and studios), environmental scans of protocols for savvy reuse or repurposing, the development of procedures for extending the shelf lives of residual media (Acland 2007), and designing infrastructures for repair instead of replacement (Rosner and Ames 2014). Collectively, these practices afford a long-term approach to research-creation by way of fabrication.

Aesthetics and assembly

With respect to the aesthetics of digital fabrication, one issue in particular persists across arts and humanities projects, namely whether the object is standalone or assembled. This distinction affects how audiences are involved in the interpretation process. Is the object meant to be looked at? Observed? Is it meant to be articulated? Handled? Something in between? Answers to these questions will likely depend on discipline and researcher preference. However, matters of cohesion and relation are central to fabrication research. "Standalone" and "assembled" are entangled states. This entanglement is persuasively exhibited in exploded view sculptures by Cornelia Parker (1995) and Damián Ortega (2002, 2009), among other artists. An exploded view – or a visualization that implies either relationships between parts or their order of assembly into a coherent object – highlights how space, movement, time, and instructions are integral to materials design. With digital fabrication, an assembled object often invites its deconstruction, and component parts frequently gesture toward their cohesion. However a given research-creation project is ultimately exhibited or distributed to audiences (as a collection of parts, as a standalone object, or both), researchers should account for differences between screen-based media and tactile media. Even if digital files assemble easily on screen, they may not do so as tangible objects. Also, the materials used for manufacturing will play a role in the neatness or difficulty of assembly.

Another common issue with respect to aesthetics and assembly is material connotation. Does the fabricated material correspond with history in some way? Does it create an indexical relationship? Does it point to something or someone? Is it intended to evoke a particular feeling, thought, or interaction? In what value systems is it embedded? Again, answers to these questions will likely depend on discipline and researcher preference. Still, researchers should consider how materials make arguments, or how they assert themselves in arts and humanities projects. For instance, while the box for a Kit for Cultural History may announce its affordability or status as a multiple, Demetz's tufts of raw wood declare their material purposiveness and imperfection in relation to automation and CNC precision. These decisions matter all the more for researchers who wish to transition from prototyping into batch manufacturing, or to move across methods involving creation-as-research, creative expressions of research, and research-from-creation.

NOT EXACTLY NEW

Scholars of sculpture, book history, media history, and design are likely familiar with many of the issues raised above. These issues are not somehow detached from the material cultures of writing, print, casting, phonography, photography, and film, and thus we should avoid representing them deterministically as revolutions or ruptures in research-creation. At the same time, digital fabrication is in many ways unique. Not only does it tighten the loop between bits and atoms; it increases the precision, speed, and accessibility of manufacturing. For most researchers in the arts and humanities, appeals to the efficiency of fabrication will matter less than the aesthetics and lines of inquiry it prompts – how it entangles manual and automated production in curious ways, redefines the limits of vision and inscription, or manipulates content, form, and substance across materials. To be sure, these are not lines reserved for science, engineering, and mathematics. Together, the arts and humanities have much to contribute, too.

ACKNOWLEDGMENTS

The Social Sciences and Humanities Research Council, the Canada Foundation for Innovation, and the British Columbia Knowledge Development Fund have supported this research. We would also like to thank Nina Belojevic, Devon Elliott, Katherine Goertz, Kari Kraus, Shaun Macpherson, Kaitlynn McQueston, Danielle Morgan, and William J. Turkel for their feedback and perspectives.

REFERENCES

Acland, Charles R. *Residual Media*. Minneapolis: University of Minnesota Press, 2007.

Azzarello, Nina. "Theo Jansen's Strandbeest Interpreted by 3D Printing at Art Basel Miami." *Designboom*. 8 December 2014. Web. 28 May 2015. www.designboom.com.

Belojevic, Nina. "Kits for Cultural History." *Maker Lab in the Humanities*. 9 September 2013. Web. 30 May 2015. http://maker.uvic.ca/kch/.

Blanchot, Maurice. "Everyday Speech." *The Everyday*. Ed. Stephen Johnstone, 34–42. Cambridge, MA: MIT Press, 2008.

Chapman, Owen and Kim Sawchuk. "Research-Creation: Intervention, Analysis and 'Family Resemblances.'" *Canadian Journal of Communication* 37 (2012): 5–26.

Clouston, Nicole. "Surface." 2015. Web. 28 May 2015. www.nicoleclouston.com/About.

Demetz, Aron. "Advanced Minorities." Web. 28 May 2015. www.arondemetz.it/works.php?lang_id=1.

Elliott, Devon, Robert MacDougall, and William J. Turkel. "New Old Things: Fabrication, Physical Computing, and Experiment in Historical Practice." *Canadian Journal of Communication* 37 (2012): 121–128.

Factum Arte. Web. 30 May 2015. www.factum-arte.com/.

Folcher, Viviane. "Appropriating Artifacts as Instruments: When Design-For-Use Meets Design-In-Use." *Interacting with Computers* 15.5 (2003): 647–663.

Gershenfeld, Neil. *Fab: The Coming Revolution on Your Desktop*. New York: Basic, 2005.

Goertz, Katherine and Danielle Morgan. "Dear Academy: Where's the Fab?" *Maker Lab in the Humanities*. 10 November 2014. Web. 30 May 2015. http://maker.uvic.ca/scan/.

Griffey, Jason. "3D Printers for Libraries: Types of Plastics." *Library Technology Reports* 50.5 (2014): 13–15.

Hansmeyer, Michael. "Subdivided Columns." Web. 21 May 2015. www.michael-hansmeyer.com/projects.

Horčicová, Monika. "Works." Web. 22 May 2015. http://monikahorcicova.wordpress.com.

Hosale, Mark-David. "hommomculus agora (h.a) & alpha (h.a)." Web. 22 May 2015. www.mdhosale.com/.

Jansen, Theo. "Creations." Web. 30 May 2015. www.shapeways.com/designer/TheoJansen.

Jansen, Theo. "Strandbeests." Web. 22 May 2015. www.strandbeest.com/.

Kapoor, Anish. "Cement Printing." Web. 27 May 2015. http://anishkapoor.com/951/Cement-printing.html.

Kee, Kevin, ed. *Pastplay: Teaching and Learning History with Technology*. Ann Arbor: University of Michigan Press, 2014.

Laviani, Ferruccio. "Good Vibrations." Web. 23 May 2015. www.laviani.com/.

Neal, Meghan. "Crowdsourced, 3D-Printed Sculptures Are the Knitting Circles of the Future." *Motherboard*. 4 September 2013. http://motherboard.vice.com/blog/crowdsourced-3d-printed-sculptures-are-the-knitting-circle-of-the-future.

Nelson, J., S. Buisine, and A. Aoussat. "Design in Use: Some Methodological Considerations." *42nd CIRP Conference on Manufacturing Systems* (2009): 3–5.

Rosner, Daniela K. and Morgan Ames. "Designing for Repair? Infrastructures and Materialities of Breakdown." In *Proceedings of the 17th ACM Conference on Computer Supported Cooperative Work & Social Computing*, pp. 319–331. ACM, 2014.

Sayers, Jentery. "Kits for Cultural History, or Fluxkits for Scholarly Communication". *Hyperrhiz* 13 (2015a): n. pag.

——. "Prototyping the Past." *Visible Language* 49.3 (2015b): 157–177.

Sayers, Jentery, Devon Elliott, Kari Kraus, Bethany Nowviskie, and William J. Turkel. "Between Bits and Atoms: Physical Computing and Desktop

Fabrication in the Humanities." *The New Blackwell Companion to Digital Humanities*. Eds. Susan Schreibman, Ray Siemens, and John Unsworth. Oxford: Wiley Blackwell, 2016.

Schama, Gabriel. "About the Work." Web. 27 May 2015. www.gabrielschama.com/.

Schuocker, D. "Laser Cutting." *Materials and Manufacturing Processes* 4.3 (1989): 311–330.

Standley, Eric. "About." Web. 23 May 2015. www.eric-standley.com/about/.

Sterling, Bruce. *Shaping Things*. Cambridge: MIT Press, 2005.

Visnjic, Filip. "Transient Materialization: Ephemeral Material-Oriented Digital Fabrication." *Creative Applications Network*. 27 January 2015. Web. 30 May 2015. www.creativeapplications.net/processing/transient-materialization-ephemeral-material-oriented-digital-fabrication/.

CHAPTER 19

From theory to experience to making to breaking

Iterative game design for digital humanists

Matt Bouchard and Andy Keenan

INTRODUCTION

The great challenge with teaching game design is the balance between theory and design. Like other digital humanities disciplines, learning about games requires active engagement with the object. This includes both games as sites of play and games as sites of design. Participants must play games and make games as much as possible. Through active inquiry with the object, a participant begins to engage with the theory behind games. To facilitate this process, we created a card game called Root of Play that guides participants through the game design process. Root of Play is different from other game-design games because it specifically emphasizes playable prototypes and design iterations. We found this focus on prototyping and playtesting allows participants to enter an agile process, moving between game theory and game building. We can summarize this agile design process as the negotiation between making and breaking. In this chapter, we explore the card game Root of Play as a case study for teaching games to digital humanists.

CONCEPTUAL FOUNDATIONS OF GAMES FOR DIGITAL HUMANISTS

The balance between theory and design draws from the tradition of "knowing in practice" (Lave; Orlikowski) – "knowledge is not primarily a factual commodity or a compendium of facts, nor is an expert knower an encyclopedia. Instead knowledge takes on the character of a process of knowing" (Lave 175). In this approach, knowledge and practice are dialectically related, and the influence of one over the other is difficult to determine. Rather than "knowledge in practice", Orlikowski emphasizes "knowing in practice". Knowledge functions as a noun, connoting things, facts, and processes. Knowing functions as a verb, connoting action, doing, and practice (Orlikowski 250–251). Orlikowski asserts that knowing-in-practice is:

> continually enacted through people's everyday activity; it does not exist "out there" (incorporated in external objects, routines, or systems) or "in here" (inscribed in human brains, bodies, or communities). Rather, knowing is an ongoing social accomplishment, constituted and reconstituted in everyday practice. As such knowing cannot be understood as stable or enduring. (Orlikowski 252)

Using the example of bike riding, Orlikowski argues that as we ride a bike we assume that we "know how" to ride and lose sight of the way in which "knowing how" is an ongoing and recurrent accomplishment. Games for digital humanists embraces this knowing in practice, emphasizing the action and doing of game making as the crucial site for learning.

Orlikowski's work parallels neatly with the everyday practice of the digital humanities, and it explains a tension inherent in DH that informed our approach to teaching game design and the creation of Root of Play, a card game for iterative game design. This tension between theory and practice is in the role and importance of programming in DH. Stephen Ramsay created quite a kerfuffle at the MLA conference in 2011 by suggesting that one must be making/building/programming to be "doing DH" ("On Building"). Geoffrey Rockwell added to the discussion the notion of the knowledge of making or poesis, and the idea that DH (and other craft-based disciplines) is under-theorized because its truths can be difficult to express in traditional, academic writing ("Inclusion in the Digital Humanities"). Both Ramsay and Rockwell are critiquing the dominant notion that DH can be done at arm's reach where service providers do the actual making. In this debate, we come down on the side of Orlikowski; DH programming and DH theory are reciprocally constituted and should therefore be balanced and present in most work. This same approach is applied for teaching games and game design. A combination of theoretical frameworks for games and play, the practice of play, and the making of games are necessary for teaching game critique and game design. Games are complex systems and understanding them requires an understanding of theory and practice, and the interaction between them.

GAME STUDIES AND PLAY STUDIES

We draw from game studies and play studies as core conceptual foundations. In particular, the concepts of procedural rhetoric, ambiguity of play, and lusory attitude.

Procedural rhetoric

Procedural rhetoric is "the practice of using processes persuasively" (Bogost 28). Bogost argues that video games present arguments through their processes. Video games are made up of two broad components: (1) code; (2) rules. The two are closely related – the code places the parameters for what the computer will run and the rules place the parameters for what the player can do. These parameters create what Bogost calls the possibility space, or the ability for a player to take actions within a game:

> the possibility space refers to the myriad configurations the player might construct to see the ways the processes inscribed in the system work. This is really what we do when we play video games: we explore the possibility space its rules afford by manipulating the game's controls. (Bogost 42–43)

This possibility space is explored through play. The player cannot take actions outside of the code and the rules. This places a limitation on what the player can experience in a video game. The procedural rhetoric, or the arguments in the game's processes, is expressed through play inside the limitations of the design.

Bogost argues that video games present a new form of argument. Embedded in the code and the rules is the intention and the bias of the developer. Games present a unique opportunity to present arguments through processes. For our participants, we invite players to consider their argument as a central component of their game design process.

Ambiguity of play

Play is ambiguous; after studying play deeply and writing an important book on the subject, Sutton-Smith still admits that it is quite difficult to even define play: "Any earnest definition of play has to be haunted by the possibility that playful enjoinders will render it invalid" (213). In that book, Sutton-Smith's argument is largely about what play is not, or to at least trouble the dominant notions of what play is and what purpose it serves. He divides the dominant views on play into rhetorics or persuasive narratives (16). Sutton-Smith examines seven of these rhetorics, which include many common answers to the questions of why do we play and what purpose do games serve. Briefly, the rhetorics are progress, fate, power, identity, imagination, the self, and frivolity; each rhetoric is taken in turn and broken down using a variety of studies and arguments. His purpose is not to suggest that play is never about identity, for instance, but that play is not only identity and that it is very difficult to make definitive claims about play, except perhaps that it is ambiguous.

The ambiguity of play is a core feature of this approach to game design. Participants come with a range of notions about what play and games are all about, and Sutton-Smith's work allows us to push back against those notions and encourage participants to break down their own ideas. Sutton-Smith also encourages us to expose and explore the inherent tension between the boundless, difficult-to-define play and the bounded structure of games.

Lusory attitude and the act of playing

Suits provides an elegant definition of games by focusing on the act of playing: "playing a game is the voluntary attempt to overcome unnecessary obstacles" (Suits 55). The voluntary attempt of playing is known as the lusory attitude, the peculiar state of mind of players in games. Players willingly submit to the unnecessary obstacles preventing them from achieving the end-goal in a game. Suits calls this "a sacrifice of efficiency" (Suits 38).

Suits presents a strong case with the example of golf. In golf, the purpose is getting a small round object into a hole in the ground. The most efficient means of achieving this purpose is placing the small round object in the hole with your hand – "But surely I would not take a stick with a piece of metal on one end of it, walk three or four hundred yards away from the hole, and then attempt to propel the ball into the hole with the stick" (Suits 34). Players accept this sacrifice of efficiency in order to make the game possible. This is the lusory attitude, the peculiar state of mind of players in games.

In game design, our participants are reminded of this concept – players willingly sacrifice efficiency when playing a game. This means a game should have an intrinsically compelling reason to play. If designers do not make interesting games, they should not expect their players to enter into this lusory attitude. This also captures our emphasis for participants to make simple games. The more complex a game, or the more difficult it is to understand the rules, the harder it will be for players to accept the premise of the game. Without the players, there is no game. Players must be willing participants, embarking on a journey with the game developers.

PEDAGOGY

We use a scaffolded approach for teaching games to digital humanists, from theory to experience to making to breaking. Each step is outlined in this section.

Theory

The foundation of this design approach is the theory of games and play. This creates the basis for critical engagement with games. Definitions of games and play capture the fluid and often-contradictory nature of games. By comparing and contrasting key theories on games, we encourage participants to explore the messiness inherent to these theoretical foundations.

In particular, we focus on the contradictory relationship between games and play. Games are highly structured activities consisting of rules and boundaries. Without rules, there are no games. Rules limit what is possible by imposing structures, boundaries, limits, and unambiguous consequences. If you disobey the rules, you are cheating. Play is diametrically opposed to rules. Play is free form, creative, improvisational, and unpredictable.

The strange combination of rules and play is one of the inherent paradoxes of games:

> Play is the free space of movement within a more rigid structure. Play exists both because of and also despite the more rigid structures of a system. Rules might not seem like much fun. But once players set the system of a game into motion, play emerges. And play is the opposite of rules. Rules are fixed, rigid, closed, and unambiguous. Play, on the other hand, is uncertain, creative, improvisational, and open-ended. The strange coupling of rules and play is one of the fascinating paradoxes of games. (Zimmerman n.p.)

We play games, and yet games put limitations on the free movement of play. This is a feature of all games. We constantly remind our participants that this paradox is central to their experience of gameplay and game design. Designers must remember that players are submitting to rules, to structures, and to limits when they play a game. Returning to Suits' lusory attitude, players enter a peculiar state of mind when encountering this paradox between games and play.

Experience

Applying Orlikowski's notion of unifying knowledge and practice, we came to the conclusion that prospective game scholars must play games while discussing them so as to reveal/reinforce that gameplay and game theory are reciprocally constituted.

We emphasize play and active engagement with games before starting the design process. We play and discuss several carefully selected games that ensure our participants have broad game experience. We select these experience-games such that they fulfill three objectives. First, our experience-games represent a genre or at least help us begin a genre discussion. Second, since the theory challenges and disrupts the notion of "game", the selected games emphasize that lesson. We select games that do not fit with standard conventions and trouble the boundaries of what is and what is not a game. Third, these games are selected for their ability to encourage critical examination and discussion. This portion of the design process often causes strong reactions from the participants, from dissatisfaction to insight. Participants are often initially frustrated with these boundary-challenging games, which serve as sites of inquiry and discussion around what we consider to be games, how games are created, and potential directions for their upcoming design process. Once players have connected knowledge and practice as players, we introduce the new role of game designer.

Making

After the theoretical lectures and experiential gameplay sessions, we make games. The emphasis is on simplicity. We use the concept of the core mechanic – the action the player performs most often in the game (Salen and Zimmerman 327). In a platform game such as *Super Mario Brothers* (Nintendo; Miyamoto and Tezuka), the core mechanic is precise jumping. In a puzzle game such as *Candy Crush Saga* (King), the core mechanic is creating color patterns. In a card game such as *Go Fish*, the core mechanic is drawing cards and making pairs.

We emphasize one core mechanic for each design team. Our focus is creating simple, playable prototypes in less than two hours. We provide paper, markers, scissors, glue, dice, and other simple objects used in most standard games. Core mechanics for this first prototype include drawing, bluffing, telling stories, dancing, or memorizing, among others. Using this core mechanic, teams design a game in a short time period.

Participants find that this making process combines the previous theoretical and experiential learning. Game design as an activity raises fundamental questions. Participants consider many challenging questions concerning the player, the rules, the social and cultural factors of their game, the intention, and the paradox between play and games. We find that participants begin to ask these questions without specific prompts. The design process itself, the making of the games, encourages this conversation within the small groups.

Making presents design teams with the question of procedural rhetoric – what is my game trying to argue? What are the biases in my rules? What worldview or ideology is represented in my game's procedures? Participants begin to think simultaneously as players and as designers. They consider the consequences and intentions of their rule choices within the context of their core mechanic.

Breaking

Once participants have gone through the act of creation, we immediately encourage them to destroy what they have made. Many of our participants have highly structured views about how play and games function in society, and they are largely informed by their home disciplines. Further, participants often begin game design practice with a strong sense that games can be used to control play and create outcomes, and these preconceived notions strongly affect that first attempt at making a game. Sutton-Smith is employed to remind participants of two things. First, that play experiences are only loosely connected to play theories and that disciplinary views on play are subject to common rhetorics of play, which do not express the entire possibility space of play. Second, games are more like a structural suggestion to indicate how play might happen and outcomes can be planned for but never guaranteed. Certainly, we can verbally intervene as student groups are designing their games, and we can quote Sutton-Smith or repeat "play is subversive" mantras, but the most effective way of learning the difficulties of creating games is to follow your making with some breaking.

Breaking happens fairly naturally, but the right situation has to be created. Simply playing the game within the group that created it is usually not enough. We have found that groups have to get non-group members to play the game. Co-creators of the game will generally play it with the "spirit" they intended whereas others will generally engage with the game more directly. This direct engagement causes the most breaking. For instance, certain players seek maximal/efficient strategies in any game. They are only concerned with the most efficient path to victory. Many fledgling games are immediately broken by this style of play, and game designers are forced to consider if that is an audience that must be dealt with, catered to, or ignored. Less esoteric aspects of game creation are immediately revealed by non-creator play as well. Other players immediately reveal if the instructions are confusing, if the game is too complicated, or if they just could not find the play. As instructors, we are also very active in the breaking process, encouraging creators to consider project scope, existing games, audience tendencies, etc.

ROOT OF PLAY - OVERVIEW

Root of Play is a simple card game to help participants create game design ideas in a short amount of time. The game is designed for participants at various levels of previous game experience, from novices to experts. Participants have ranged from librarians to faculty members to academic administrators to graduate and undergraduate students in the humanities. The goal of Root of Play is based on Orlikowski's concept of knowing in practice. We combine the action of game playing and game making into a structured activity. Root of Play helps participants realize the complex theoretical components of games and gameplay through an active design and playtesting process.

The game consists of five phases – brainstorming, pitch, design, playtest, iterate. We use three decks of cards. Each deck consists of cards that describe different elements of game design. These are: (1) player cards – the audience for the game, or personas for game characters (e.g. teenagers; first date; lions); (2) place cards – the location for play, or fictional worlds where the game takes place (e.g. end of capitalism; kids run the world; under water); (3) constraint cards – in-game actions, or core mechanic (e.g. bluffing; drawing; memorizing).

Participants get twenty minutes to generate two game ideas based on their cards. Participants then pitch those two ideas to the larger group, and the group votes on which game they want to see developed. Participants have thirty minutes to make a playable prototype, and then thirty minutes to playtest the game. This process of revising the prototype and playtesting continues until the participants are satisfied with the game they've created.

Root of Play is structured around the concept of *creativity through constraint*. We provide participants with specific and clear parameters for game design and ask them to develop prototype games based on these constraints. These operate in two ways: (1) limited number of cards for idea generation; (2) limited amount of time.

Iterative design and evidence-based approaches

Root of Play is structured around rapid prototyping – the quick creation of a playable object. We ask participants to have a playable prototype as quickly as possible. To facilitate this process, we provide paper, scissors, markers, dice, and other paraphernalia commonly associated with card games and board games. We encourage participants to have a fully playable prototype within a short time frame, normally forty-five minutes to one hour. If participants have conceived of a more complex game, we ask them to have some component of the game, usually the core mechanic, ready for testing at this first stage.

Once these playable prototypes are ready, participants from other groups are encouraged to try these initial prototypes. In these playing sessions, the breaking points of a game are quickly revealed. This can range from something simple, such as a rule needs clarification, to something complex, such as the logic of the game's economy is unclear. These instances of playtesting generate significant "a-ha!" moments for game designers, who often realize that their vision for the game and the player's actual gameplay are difficult to align.

The Root of Play exercise requires groups to repeatedly challenge and improve the games they are developing, much like when editing scholarly writing for a journal article or book chapter. Many participants are inclined to create a game and begin theorizing its impact or formulating methods for testing its efficacy. We have often encountered fully realized games that have not yet been playtested. Because the nature of play is so elusive, it is especially important to play the games during the act of creation. This process always reveals the edges of the rules and quickly determines whether those edges encourage a lusory attitude in players. When the designers see (and feel) what players experience and see how their game triumphs and breaks down, they can re-enter the design process armed with first-hand data on how to improve their games.

This is an evidence-based design approach. We ask participants to test their ideas as quickly as possible so they can comprehend the slippage between design concept and gameplay. These processes often lead participants to simplify their ideas, and ultimately question their design objectives. Playtesting provides evidence for how a game works, where a game is broken, and how a game may be reconceived. We believe this is the crucial step to teaching people not only about game design but about complex project development.

Outcomes from Root of Play

We have been fortunate to see several successful game prototypes developed using the Root of Play approach. Two exemplar game projects have been developed, one for a commercial game and another for a pedagogical meaningful play activity. The commercial game, called *The Reunion: A Storytelling Card Game*, was successfully funded on Kickstarter with over 500 supporters and over $6,000 in funding. *The Reunion* centers on a family reunion gone wrong and asks players to tell stories about their fictional or lived experiences with uncomfortable family events.

The pedagogical meaningful play activity, called *Digital Zombies*, is a research literacy tool developed by Dr Juliette Levy for her campus-wide classes at the University of California. *Digital Zombies* is part information literacy, part research training, and part library familiarization for first-year students entering the University of California system. The game blends a narrative experience of digital zombies taking over the campus, spending too much time on their mobile devices and relying on Wikipedia for their work. Dr Levy invites students to cure themselves of zombism by understanding how the library can help students in the research process.

Reflections from participants

In the same way that games cannot exist without players, games for digital humanists cannot exist without participants. This is an example of participant feedback:

> It was casual which allowed there to be an amazing amount of flow between participants coming from different backgrounds. We were able to laugh about our differences as well as collaborate on shared experiences. Even as someone with no experience with games, I was able to learn an incredible amount, both from Matt and Andy and from the other group members.

We try to create a situation where participants enter into a dynamic learning environment. They learn from the instructors and from their peers simultaneously, both formally and informally. Ideally, we try and find a way to accommodate all levels of participants, particularly relating to their previous experience with games:

> Lastly, everyone was very pleasantly surprised by the effectiveness of the game design activity portion of the class, which yielded interesting results that gave us all an excellent opportunity to put into practice the theoretical portions of the course material.

This participant captures the major goal of the course – to have the theory come to life in the game design activities. This also aligns well with the making and doing approaches to digital humanities:

> The most amazing thing – and I can only say that in hindsight, is that the course is modeled on the topic of the workshop: their class is a perfect game!

> The incentives are right, the learning happens intuitively, we are given the opportunity to explore, fail, learn, improve. And at the end of the class/game, everyone wins!

The course may be a game, after all it is voluntary and there are unnecessary obstacles, but the most important thing is that the message came through: making and breaking result in learning (and winning).

CONCLUSION

Digital humanities present a unique opportunity to learn through active engagement with the object. Games for digital humanists was created to provide that inquiry for our participants. We emphasize the study of games as sites of play and games as sites of design. By playing and making games, we encourage participants to explore the object, and critically engage with play and with design. We created a card game called Root of Play to help facilitate that process (Keenan and Bouchard). With an emphasis on iteration and playtesting, we encourage players to rapidly prototype their game design concepts and see where they break. This making and breaking relationship provides moments for participants to move into an agile process and ultimately design engaging experiences in a short period of time. We believe this provides a rich learning environment for participants and also satisfies a founding principle of digital humanities – learning through making.

REFERENCES

Bogost, Ian. "Gamification Is Bullshit." N. p., 2011. Web. 1 May 2015.
Bogost, Ian. *Persuasive Games: The Expressive Power of Videogames*. Cambridge, MA: MIT Press, 2007. Print.
Keenan, Andy, and Matt Bouchard. "Root of Play – Game Design for Digital Humanists." *Syllabus* 4.1 (2015): n. pag.
King. "Candy Crush Saga." 2012: n. pag. Video Game.
Lave, J. *Cognition in Practice: Mind, Mathematics and Culture in Everyday Life*. Cambridge: Cambridge University Press, 1988. Print.
Miyamoto, Shigeru, and Takashi Tezuka. "Super Mario Bros." 1985: n. pag. Video Game. Nintendo.
Orlikowski, Wanda J. "Knowing in Practice: Enacting a Collective Capability in Distributed Organizing." *Organization Science* 13.3 (2002): 249–273. Print.
Ramsay, Stephen. "On Building." N. p., 2011. Web. 1 May 2015.
Rockwell, Geoffrey. "Inclusion in the Digital Humanities." N. p., 2011. Web. 1 May 2015.
Salen, Katie, and Eric Zimmerman. *Rules of play: Game Design Fundamentals*. Cambridge, MA: MIT press, 2004. Print.

Suits, Bernard. *The Grasshopper: Games, Life and Utopia*. Toronto: University of Toronto Press, 1978. Print.

Sutton-Smith, Brian. *The Ambiguity of Play*. Cambridge, MA: Harvard University Press, 1997. Print.

Zimmerman, Eric. "Narrative, Interactivity, Play and Games: Four Naughty Concepts in Need of Discipline." N. p., 2004. Web. 1 May 2015.

FURTHER READING

Bartle, Richard. "Hearts, Clubs, Diamonds, Spades: Players Who Suit MUDs." *Journal of MUD Research* 1.1 (1996): 1–19. Print.

Consalvo, Mia. *Cheating: Gaining Advantage in Videogames*. The MIT Press, 2007. Print.

Consalvo, Mia, and Nathan Dutton. "Game Analysis: Developing a Methodological Toolkit for the Qualitative Study of Games." *Game Studies* 6.1 (2006): 1–17. Print.

Gee, James Paul. *What Video Games Have to Teach Us about Literacy and Learning*. New York: Palgrave Macmillan, 2003. Print.

Grimes, Sara M., and Andrew Feenberg. "Rationalizing Play: A Critical Theory of Digital Gaming." *The Information Society* 25.2 (2009): 105–118. Print.

Huizinga, Johan. *Homo Ludens: A Study of the Play Element in Culture*. Taylor & Francis, 1949. Print.

Jenson, Jennifer, Stephanie Fisher, and Suzanne De Castell. "Disrupting the Gender Order: Leveling up and Claiming Space in an After-School Video Game Club." *International Journal of Gender, Science and Technology* 3.1 (2011): n. pag. Print.

Juul, Jesper. "Fear of Failing? The Many Meanings of Difficulty in Video Games." *The Video Game Theory Reader* 2 (2009): 237–252. Print.

Juul, Jesper. *Half-Real: Video Games between Real Rules and Fictional Worlds*. The MIT Press, 2005. Print.

Juul, Jesper, and Marleigh Norton. "Easy to Use and Incredibly Difficult: On the Mythical Border between Interface and Gameplay." *Proceedings of the 4th International Conference on Foundations of Digital Games*. ACM, 2009. 107–112. Print.

Pearce, Celia. *Communities of Play: Emergent Cultures in Multiplayer Games and Virtual Worlds*. MIT Press, 2009. Print.

Squire, Kurt. "From Content to Context: Videogames as Designed Experience." *Educational Researcher* 35.8 (2006): 19–29. Print.

Steinkuehler, Constance. "Massively Multiplayer Online Gaming as a Constellation of Literacy Practices." *E-learning* 4.3 (2007): 297–318. Print.

Taylor, Tina L. *Play between Worlds: Exploring Online Game Culture*. MIT Press, 2006. Print.

FURTHER PLAYING

Bejeweled – http://bejeweled.popcap.com/html5/0.9.12.9490/html5/Bejeweled.html
Browser Quest – http://browserquest.mozilla.org/
Continuity – http://continuitygame.com/playcontinuity.html
Geo Guessr – https://geoguessr.com/world/play/
Progress Wars – http://progresswars.com/
Quake 3 Fortress – www.quakejs.com
The Red Square – http://members.iinet.net.au/~pontipak/redsquare.html
Zork – http://textadventures.co.uk/games/view/5zyoqrsugeopel3ffhz_vq/zork

Serious games

Airport Security – www.shockwave.com/gamelanding/airportsecurity.jsp
Darfur is Dying – www.darfurisdying.com/
dys4ia – www.newgrounds.com/portal/view/591565
HUGPUNX – http://mkopas.net/files/HUGPUNX/
Kabul Kaboom – http://ludology.typepad.com/games/kabulkaboom.html
Lim – http://mkopas.net/files/Lim/
Spent – http://playspent.org/
The Migrant Trail – http://theundocumented.com/
Third World Farmer – www.3rdworldfarmer.com/index.html
Unmanned – http://unmanned.molleindustria.org/

Part 4

Administration, dissemination and teaching

CHAPTER 20

Project management and the digital humanist

Lynne Siemens

INTRODUCTION

Along with those in the social sciences, humanities researchers, librarians, content experts, students and others are turning to collaborations to explore increasingly complex questions and implement new types of methodologies and tools, such as those in the digital humanities (DH). Granting agencies are encouraging this trend with targeted programs such as Digging into Data (Office of Digital Humanities 2010) and Partnership Grants (Social Sciences and Humanities Research Council 2013), among others, and requiring project plans, reporting structures, knowledge mobilization plans, training, and post-project reporting, all of which work to ensure close alignment between the grant application and actual outcomes (National Endowment for the Humanities Office of Digital Humanities 2010; Siemens and INKE Research Group 2014b; SSHRC 2015). As a result, teams need to understand ways to coordinate efforts among tasks, resources and members in order to accomplish project objectives and satisfy stakeholders (Siemens and INKE Research Group 2014b; Siemens 2009; Boyd and Siemens 2014; Williford and Henry 2012). Project management, with its associated methods, tools and techniques, provides a way to do this (Siemens 2012). It can help manage common issues such as project risks, unanticipated obstacles and tasks, team member turnover, and timelines, limit scope creep and budget overspending. Ultimately, project management can "protect and enhance one's professional reputation and networks (with collaborators, funding agencies, and others)" and accomplish successful project completion (Boyd and Siemens 2014). But what is the most appropriate way to translate a series of business-oriented tools and techniques and teach the associated skills to those within the DH community of practice? This chapter will explore these questions through an examination of the Digital Humanities Summer Institute (DHSI) project management workshop developed and delivered for over ten years. It will first consider the factors associated with the implementation of project management within the Humanities component of DH, important definitions, project management workshop outline and agenda, topics related to collaboration and teamwork, and additional resources. By the end, the reader will have gained a start towards a solid foundation in project management and its application to their own projects.

FACTORS ASSOCIATED WITH IMPLEMENTING PROJECT MANAGEMENT WITHIN THE HUMANITIES

While many teams are finding project management to be a beneficial tool, some factors may present barriers to its application to DH, particularly for those coming from the humanities. Drawing on my experiences leading project management workshops in various contexts, these factors tend to cluster around typical humanities work patterns as sole authors and the nature and content of graduate training within the humanities.

Perhaps most importantly, while changing in practice, the single author/researcher is still the typical work pattern for many humanists, which has several implications for those who join the DH community of practice. First, given this emphasis on the individual, a premium is placed on sole author outputs such as articles and the monograph in comparison to those with co-authors and digital projects. Further, the humanities do not have authorship conventions that recognize the collective effort of the team, a practice that is common in other parts of the campus. By way of example, some conferences do not even recognize co-authors within the program, as Siemens, Smith and Liu highlight in their reflection of a collaboration between a humanist and a computer scientist (Siemens, Smith and Liu 2014). Related to this, authorship is assumed to be that person(s) who "held the pen" when writing the article, rather than including other project contributions such as designing an interface, conducting and analyzing interviews, and coding texts, to name but a few intellectually oriented tasks within typical DH projects.

All this is to say that humanists do not necessarily come to DH with the necessary skills and mindset for collaboration. This trend is reinforced through graduate training, which does not generally include skill development in teamwork, collaboration and project management (Leon 2011; Siemens 2013). Further, like many disciplines, graduate training in the humanities tends to focus on training within a single (and often narrow) discipline, rather than in multiple disciplines or across disciplines. This is not to downplay the importance of disciplines, which provide guidance on appropriate research questions, methodologies, vocabulary, funding levels and authorship conventions (Bruhn 2000; Gold and Gold 1985; Cech and Rubin 2004);

but rather to suggest that many humanists may not be "collaborative ready" (Olson and Olson 2000), in that they may not have the required skills needed to value different perspectives and project contributions and may not be able to "play well with others," necessary when working with team members from other disciplines (Bracken and Oughton 2006; Bruhn 1995; Murnighan and Conlon 1991).

However, not all is lost. Many humanists are learning these skills, either through workshops, DH courses or through the school of hard learned experience, and collaborating successfully with others on digital projects (Siemens and Burr 2013; Siemens and INKE Research Group 2014b; 2014a; Leon 2011). Project management is one set of tools, techniques and methods that facilitates the learning of skills as well as successful project completion.

DEFINITIONS

Before outlining the various tools, techniques and methods associated with project management, it is important to outline some definitions and philosophy behind its use.

First, project management is a "set of principles, methods, tools, and techniques for the effective management of objectives-oriented work in the context of a specific and unique organizational environment" (Knutson and Bitz 1991). This means that a plan outlines more than just scheduling, but also references the reasons for the project and specific outcomes as well as stakeholders' needs, which include those both internal and external to the university. For example, stakeholders might be university administration, funding agencies, archives, the public, among others. Second, the digital humanist must account for opportunity costs. If they choose to do a particular project, it will mean that they may not be able to do another one at the same time. Ultimately, the digital humanist and their team work to ensure that the project is completed on schedule, within budget and meets specified performance objectives. As an outcome from the project management process, the work plan then frees resources for other priorities by ensuring that the project is actually achievable.

Second, a project shares several characteristics that separate it from a digital humanist's regular work. Generally, projects are undertaken for a specific purpose or goal and not regularly repeated. They also involve the coordination of skills, tasks, people, budgets and other resources and cross organizational boundaries. They have also a definite life cycle with specific start and end dates. Finally, projects involve relatively new or unknown undertakings, thus requiring skills such as innovation, flexibility, collaboration, communication, negotiation, planning and risk management (Frame 2003; Siemens 2012). Given elements of this definition, the digital humanist must accept that problems will happen during project plan implementation. The key to the project planning process then is to plan carefully in order to minimize disruptions from any potential problems.

OUTLINE OF A PROJECT MANAGEMENT WORKSHOP

Building from these definitions, and mirroring the stages of a project, a typical project management workshop is divided into three primary topic areas: defining the project, planning the project and then working the plan.[1] To aid participant engagement with the material, these topics are often delivered through a combination of lecture, hands-on activities and discussion. Each stage will be examined in turn.

Stage 1: project definition

The first step in the project management process is defining the project to ensure that everyone who is involved agrees to the project's scope and the associated outcomes before full-scale planning and implementation occurs. This sets the project off on the proverbial "right foot". It is helpful to write down as much as possible and ensure written agreement and commitment to minimize the potential for future misunderstandings and manage the inevitable requests for change that can occur later in the planning process.

The key components of project start documentation include:

- Problem and/or opportunity statement: What is the problem or opportunity that this project will address? What is the relevant background and/or context necessary to understand this project?
- Scope: What are the end results? What will the project not accomplish? What will the project explore? What will it not explore?
- Completion Criteria: How will the end results be measured? How will the project team know when the project is finished?
- Assumptions: What has been assumed about the project? Is everyone aware of and in agreement with these assumptions?
- Impact Statement: Upon whom or what will this project have an impact? Are these beneficial or detrimental impacts?
- Risks: What are the risks of doing the project? What are the risks of not doing the project? What are the risks of starting the project and not being able to finish?
- Resource Requirements: What is the proposed budget? How many staff hours are needed? What computing power is needed?
- Constraints: Are there any special constraints imposed on the project, such as technology, copyright and other laws, proprietary software, and others?

Stage 2: project planning

Once the project start documentation is approved, then a team can fully plan the project. At this point, they are modeling and simulating the effort, time and resources required to achieve the project's desired outcomes. This stage's objective is to reduce the amount of uncertainty involved in the project while realizing that uncertainty cannot be fully eliminated, given the definition of a project, as outlined above. Those projects with lower uncertainty will be able to outline greater detail in the plan.

As seen in Figure 20.1, the first planning tool is the work breakdown structure (WBS), which determines all the work effort required to bring the project to a successful completion. It becomes a checklist of every activity that must be performed to achieve the end objectives. Further, all tasks are broken down to a sufficient level of detail where it becomes easy to assign responsibility for tasks, thus making project reporting smoother once the team enacts the plan. In other words, each task has an assigned individual, for whom it is their responsibility to carry it out.

Building from the WBS, the next tool is the network, which shows the relationship between the various tasks and begins to highlight the interdependencies between them. As seen in Figure 20.2, the network maps all tasks between the project start and end, and shows which tasks come first, which are dependent on others and which can be done in parallel.

From the network, one can begin to identify the critical path, that sequence of tasks where a delay can threaten to slow down the entire project. This becomes the path where a project team needs to develop "plan b" scenarios so that they are prepared if problems are encountered.

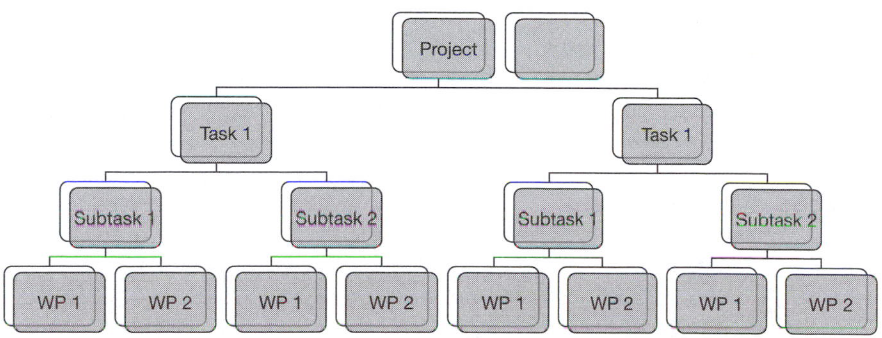

Figure 20.1
Work breakdown structure

Adapted from Lewis 1991

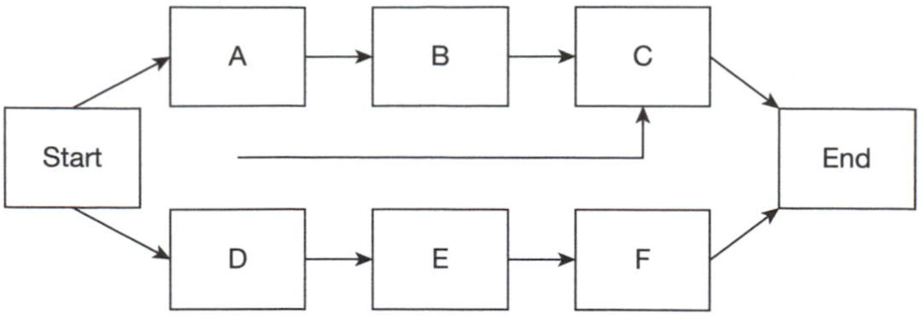

Figure 20.2
Network

Up to this point, the element of time has not yet been considered. As seen in Table 20.1, the Gantt chart is one tool that allows for this. Each task is plotted against a time period, which is specific to the project, ranging from days, weeks, months and even years. Further, the team can also mark those important milestone and deadline points, that time by which certain tasks must be done.

As a collective, these tools serve to facilitate the necessary risk assessment and contingency planning to ensure that a project can be completed on time, on budget and to the specified outcomes. One almost needs to take a practical approach and accept that problems will happen and then plan for their eventuality. Good planning then minimizes problems and their scope and allows for corrective action in a timely and measured manner. By way of advice, teams need to identify those tasks that are along the critical path, have many people responsible, and/or have underskilled or unqualified people assigned. They must also anticipate illness and turnover among team members. With this knowledge, teams can prepare backup plans and/or use more conservative scheduling of tasks and budget and other resources, and assign strong staff and backups to high-risk tasks and those along on the critical path.

The next step involves balancing the plan and limited resources within the project against other project efforts and nonproject efforts, such as teaching schedules,

Table 20.1 Gantt chart

		Time Period									
		1	2	3	4	5	6	7	8	9	10
Task	Duration										
1	2 time period										
2	3 time period										
3	2 time period										
4	3 time period										
5	4 time period										
6	2 time period										

statutory holidays, vacations and other similar events. In other words, can a project be achieved given everything else going on?

The final step is then project approval by the team and those who are committing staff, time, budget and/or other resources. As with the project start documentation, it is useful and beneficial to ensure the approval is in writing to reduce future misunderstandings and tensions.

Stage 3: project implementation

In this final stage, the focus becomes implementing the plan, tracking progress against it and managing the inevitable requests for change, and finally communicating progress. Here several points are important to emphasize. First, within progress tracking, the focus becomes evaluating progress against the plan to determine if there are any differences and the potential causes for these. The answers to these questions can guide decision-making around the necessity (or not) of changes to the plan and associated outcomes. Within this stage, the tools that aided in planning become important for tracking and reporting progress. For example, the WBS becomes a checklist of activity that guides progress tracking and reporting. Did the person assigned to a task do it within the time allocated and with the assigned resources? If not, why not? How does that impact related tasks and the overall timeline? As seen in Table 20.2, this information can be supplemented with a Gantt chart which tracks progress against the plan and can quickly provide a visualization of that progress, thus reducing the need for narrative reporting.

Second, the plan becomes the basis for negotiating the inevitable requests for changes to the expected outcomes, tasks, budget and resources, and timelines. And it is important to remember that the answer to these can always be "no". By understanding where a project is relative to the plan, a team can make measured decisions about a need for change, if any. For in some cases, the request for

Table 20.2 Gantt chart with actual progress charted

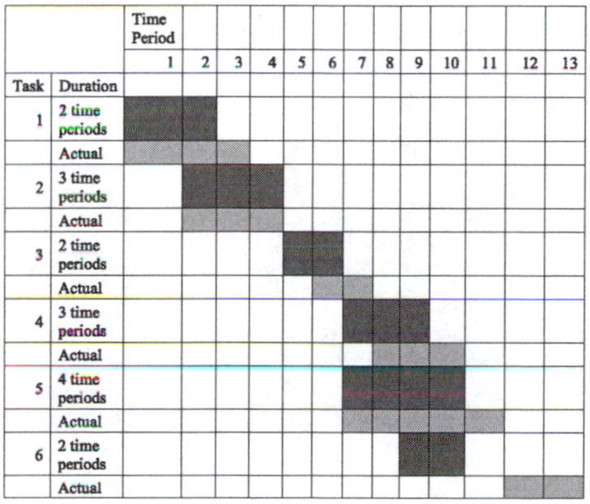

		Time Period												
		1	2	3	4	5	6	7	8	9	10	11	12	13
Task	Duration													
1	2 time periods													
	Actual													
2	3 time periods													
	Actual													
3	2 time periods													
	Actual													
4	3 time periods													
	Actual													
5	4 time periods													
	Actual													
6	2 time periods													
	Actual													

changes to the project will result in a new one that will then need to be planned anew, which may not be feasible. In others, the fact that the project is not proceeding as planned is not reason enough to make changes.

Planning tools

In terms of the mechanics of creating WBS, networks, Gantt charts and others, no ideal method exists (for a comparison of PM software, see "Comparison of Project Management Software" 2015). It is very much dependent on the project, team members' needs, geographical distribution and other factors. For some projects where all team members are co-located in the same lab and the project is relatively straightforward, "low"-tech tools such as a whiteboard, flipcharts, markers, and sticky notes can be sufficient, as seen in Figure 20.3.

In other cases, where team members might be geographically distributed and the project relatively more complex, "higher"-tech tools might be more appropriate. By no means an exhaustive list, these might include the use of:

- Online calendars
  - Outlook
  - Google Calendar (www.google.com/calendar/)
  - iCalendar
- Online Gantt charts
  - Google Docs templates (https://drive.google.com/templates?q=gantt&sort=hottest&view=public&ddrp=1#)
  - dotProject (www.dotproject.net)
  - OmniPlan (www.omnigroup.com/omniplan)

Figure 20.3
"Low"-tech planning tools

- Online project spaces
  - Basecamp (https://basecamp.com) and its associated app
  - Asana (https://asana.com) and its associated app
- File sharing
  - Dropbox (https://www.dropbox.com) and its associated app
  - Evernote (https://evernote.com) and its associated app.

Project reflection

Though often neglected, an important final step for any project should be review and reflection (Lewis 1991). This evaluation considers whether the project was successful in attaining its objectives, the effectiveness of the project plan and the organization and management systems, any deficiencies and problems experienced and the identification of lessons learned and suggested improvements. Some projects undergo this review as part of requirements from funding agencies (National Endowment for the Humanities Office of Digital Humanities 2010). Others write blog posts (The Praxis Program at the Scholars' Lab nd; Guiliano 2012), conference papers (Ramsay 2008; Ruecker and Radzikowska 2007; Hjartarson *et al.* 2011; Ruecker *et al.* 2008) and peer-reviewed articles (Causer *et al.* 2012; Quan-Haase *et al.* 2014; Simeone *et al.* 2011; Siemens *et al.* 2014) as part of that reflection and review.

SPECIAL TOPICS IN COLLABORATION

As outlined in the definition, a project involves the coordination of interdependent tasks and skills, which means that almost all projects involve teamwork and collaboration. Working together can create benefits, such as more diverse and higher-quality ideas, work and responsibility distribution, an opportunity to learn new skills and perspectives and might even be potentially fun and social. However, challenges also exist. Collaboration can be time consuming, with associated communication, conflict management, coordination and accountability structures needed (Siemens and Burr 2013; Siemens *et al.* 2011; Siemens *et al.* 2014). Individuals may also need new skills, which can include the willingness and ability to work with others (Olson and Olson 2000; Spiller *et al.* 2014). Finally, academic teams have particular challenges, including the need for models to recognize member contributions. All of these challenges can be more difficult when a team is geographically distributed. Responses to each of these challenges will be addressed in turn.

Project charters

Project charters can be one way to make explicit the principles that guide the working and accountability relationships between team members. They tend to cover topics such as:

- Meeting norms:
  - When, where and how often to have meetings?
  - What is expected in terms of attendance, timeliness and preparation?
- Working norms:
  - What are expectations with regards to quality standards and deadlines?
  - What is the expected timeframe for reply to emails and/or voice mail messages?
  - How will work and effort be distributed?
  - Where will data, documents and/or research be stored?
  - What to do if people do not follow through?
- Communication norms:
  - How should communication take place? By phone, email, in person, etc?
  - When are messages sent to the whole team?
  - Who is responsible for communication?
  - How to discuss feelings about the team and/or members?
- Leadership norms:
  - Where and when is a leader needed?
  - What are their responsibilities?
  - How to keep the leader from doing all the work?
- Consideration norms:
  - What are expectations around smoking, swearing, jokes, and other considerations? (Siemens 2012; Duarte and Tennant Snyder 2006)

These charters can be relatively short with just a page or two (Ruecker and Radzikowska 2007; Hjartarson *et al.* 2011; The Praxis Program at the Scholars' Lab 2011) or a more formal document which is longer in length (Siemens and INKE Research Group 2012b). In all cases, it is beneficial to have team members sign the charter as an indication of their commitment to work collaboratively.

Authorship conventions

As outlined above, the humanities lack clear models for recognizing team member contributions due to the historical emphasis on the single author. As a result, several groups have been developing recognition conventions that are broader than just authorship by a sole individual. As one example, the participants of the "Off the Tracks – Laying New Lines for Digital Humanities Scholars" workshop developed the collaborators' bill of rights with the fundamental principle that "all kinds of work on a project are equally deserving of credit . . ." (Off the Tracks 2011). Credit may be represented in authorship, drawing upon conventions from the sciences and arts, and/or on project webpages (Off the Tracks 2011). Nowviskie (2011) echoes this and argues for more multiple authorship on papers and DH projects that reflect contributions in the areas of content, analysis, design, and others. The Implementing New Knowledge Environments (INKE) project has developed an authorship convention, "and the INKE Research Group", which is grounded in the collaborative nature of the endeavour (Siemens and INKE Research Group 2012b).

Virtual teams

Given the variety of skills and expertise needed for DH projects, teams often comprise content experts, librarians, programmers and developers, research assistants, and others who may be locally, nationally and even internationally based. A priority for these teams is finding methods to ensure effective communication and collaboration (Siemens 2010; Siemens and Burr 2013). Obvious choices for this are email, online project spaces such as Basecamp, and conference calls. However, as comfortable as we have all become in virtual space, the importance of formal and informal face-to-face meetings has not diminished. These gatherings create a sense of personal obligation to each other and social capital that is not easily created online. Further, they are also time to plan work and resolve "thorny" issues that cannot be easily addressed by email or on conference calls (Siemens 2010; Siemens and INKE Research Group 2014a). And these meetings are not just spent around the conference table in formal discussions. The time over dinner, drinks and even walking together can be important planning time along with building social cohesion (Siemens 2010; Siemens and INKE Research Group 2012a; 2013).

CONCLUSION AND GOOD LUCK WITH YOUR PROJECTS

This chapter has served as an introduction to, and grounding in, project management and related topics within the DH context. We outlined the definitions of project management and project, introduced the three stages of project planning and implementation along with tools to model the associated tasks, project timelines, resources and people, and explored special topics such as virtual teams, authorship conventions, and project charters. At this point, the logical next step is the application of these tools, methods and techniques as outlined above within one's own projects, knowing, of course, that good planning will not eliminate problems but rather hopefully minimize their disruption and allow one to complete a project on time, on budget and to the desired outcomes. Good luck with your projects!

FURTHER RESOURCES

If you are interested in learning more about project management, some important resources include:

- DevDH is a repository of training materials, recorded lectures, exemplars and links about project management within DH. It covers topics such as team development, budgeting, publicity campaigns, data management, and others (Appleford and Guiliano 2013).
- Digital Project Planning and Management Basics is a workshop manual for a two-day workshop on digital project management, developed on behalf of the Library of Congress and the Association for Library Collections and Technical Services. Topics include team building and planning, business plan development, planning and grant writing, project management, and outcome evaluation and assessment. It includes slides, instructor notes and classroom activities and exercises (Woodley 2008).
- The Praxis Program at the Scholar's Lab is a training program in which graduate students at the University of Virginia are funded to work as a team to develop a DH project or tool. To prepare them for this work, the program has developed a series of modules, including "toward a project charter", "intro to project management" and "grants, budgets and sustainability". The participants also regularly blog about their experiences (Scholars' Lab 2011).

Additional training opportunities also exist at:

- Digital Humanities Summer Institute at the University of Victoria (dhsi.org);
- European Summer University in Digital Humanities at the University of Leipzig (www.culingtec.uni-leipzig.de/ESU_C_T/node/97);
- Humanities Intensive Learning and Teaching (HILT) at Indiana University – Purdue University Indianapolis (www.dhtraining.org/hilt2015/).

NOTE

1 The full PM workshop course materials can be found at http://dhsi.org/content/2012Curriculum/12.ProjectPlanning.pdf

REFERENCES

Appleford, Simon, and Jennifer Guiliano. "Devdh: Development for the Digital Humanities". 2013. 5 March 2015. http://devdh.org

Boyd, Jason, and Lynne Siemens. "Project Management." *DHSI@Congress 2014*. 2014.

Bracken, Louise J., and Elizabeth A. Oughton. "'What Do You Mean?' The Importance of Language in Developing Interdisciplinary Research." *Transactions of the Institute of British Geographers* 31.3 (2006): 371–382.

Bruhn, John G. "Beyond Discipline: Creating a Culture for Interdisciplinary Research." *Integrative Physiological & Behavioral Science* 30.4 (1995): 331–342.

Bruhn, John G. "Interdisciplinary Research: A Philosophy, Art Form, Artifact or Antidote?" *Integrative Physiological & Behavioral Science* 35.1 (2000): 58–66.

Causer, Tim, Justin Tonra, and Valerie Wallace. "Transcription Maximized; Expense Minimized? Crowdsourcing and Editing the Collected Works of Jeremy Bentham." *Literary & Linguistic Computing* 27.2 (2012): 119–137.

Cech, Thomas R., and Gerald M. Rubin. "Nurturing Interdisciplinary Research." *Nature Structural & Molecular Biology* 11.12 (2004): 1166–1169.

"Comparison of Project Management Software." 2015. Ed. The Free Encyclopedia. Wikimedia Foundation Wikipedia, Inc.: 5 March 2015. http://en.wikipedia.org/wiki/Comparison_of_project_management_software

Duarte, Deborah L., and Nancy Tennant Snyder. *Mastering Virtual Teams: Strategies, Tools and Techniques That Succeed*. 3rd edition. San Francisco, CA: John Wiley & Sons, 2006.

Frame, J. Davidson. *Managing Projects in Organizations: How to Make the Best Use of Time, Techniques and People*. Vol. 3rd edition. San Francisco, CA: Jossey-Bass, 2003.

Gold, Harvey, and Shirley E. Gold. "Implementation of a Model to Improve Productivity of Interdisciplinary Groups." *Managing High Technology: An Interdisciplinary Perspective*. Eds. Brian W. Mar, William T. Newell, and Borje O. Saxberg. Amsterdam: Elsevier, 1985. 255–267.

Guiliano, J. "Neh Project Director's Meeting: Lessons for Promoting Your Project." *MITH Blog 2012*. 3 October 2012.

Hjartarson, Paul, Kirstin Fast, and Andrea Hasenbank. "Modelling Collaboration in Digital Humanities Scholarship: Foundational Concepts of an EMIC UA Project Charter." *Space/Place/Play*. 2011.

Knutson, Joan, and Ira Bitz. *Project Management: How to Plan and Manage Successful Projects*. New York, NY: AMACOM, 1991.

Leon, Sharon M. "Project Management for Humanists: Preparing Future Primary Investigators". 2011. 24 June 2011. http://mediacommons.futureofthebook.org/alt-ac/pieces/project-management-humanists

Lewis, James P. *Project Planning, Scheduling and Control: A Hands-on Guide to Bringing Projects in on Time and on Budget*. Chicago: Probus, 1991.

Murnighan, J. Keith, and Donald E. Conlon. "The Dynamics of Intense Work Groups: A Study of British String Quartets." *Administrative Science Quarterly* 36.2 (1991): 165–186.

National Endowment for the Humanities Office of Digital Humanities. *Summary Findings of NEH Digital Humanities Start-up Grants (2007–2010)*. Washington, DC: National Endowment for the Humanities, 2010.

Nowviskie, Bethany. "Where Credit Is Due: Preconditions for the Evaluation of Collaborative Digital Scholarship." *Profession* 13 (2011): 169–181.

Off the Tracks. "Collaborators' Bill of Rights." 2011. 5 March 2015. *Project Management and the Digital Humanist 8.docx*.

Office of Digital Humanities. "Digging into Data Challenge." 2010. 26 September 2010. www.diggingintodata.org/

Olson, Gary M., and Judith S. Olson. "Distance Matters." *Human–Computer Interaction* 15.2/3 (2000): 139–178.

Quan-Haase, Anabel, Juan Luis Suarez, and David M. Brown. "Collaborating, Connecting, and Clustering in the Humanities: A Case Study of Networked Scholarship in an Interdisciplinary, Dispersed Team." *American Behavioral Scientist* 59.4 (2014): 443–456.

Ramsay, Stephen. "Rules of the Order: The Sociology of Large, Multi-Institutional Software Development Projects." *Digital Humanities 2008*. 2008.

Ruecker, Stan, and Milena Radzikowska. "The Iterative Design of a Project Charter for Interdisciplinary Research." *DIS 2007*. 2007.

Ruecker, Stan, Milena Radzikowska, and Stéfan Sinclair. "Hackfests, Designfests, and Writingfests: The Role of Intense Periods of Face-to-Face Collaboration in International Research Teams." *Digital Humanities 2008*. 2008.

Scholars' Lab. "The Praxis Program at the Scholars' Lab." 2011. 12 September 2011. http://praxis.scholarslab.org/

Siemens, Lynne. "DHSI Project Planning Course Pack." 2012. 5 March 2015. http://dhsi.org/content/2012Curriculum/12.ProjectPlanning.pdf

Siemens, Lynne. "'It's a Team If You Use "Reply All"': An Exploration of Research Teams in Digital Humanities Environments." *Literary & Linguistic Computing* 24.2 (2009): 225–233.

Siemens, Lynne. "Meta-Methodologies and the DH Methodological Commons: Potential Contribution of Management and Entrepreneurship to DH Skill Development." *DH 2013*. 2013.

Siemens, Lynne. "Time, Place and Cyberspace: Foundations for Successful E-Research Collaboration." *E-Research Collaboration: Theory, Techniques and Challenges*. Eds. Murugan Anandarajan and Asokan Anandarajan. Berlin, Germany: Springer-Verlag, 2010. 35–48.

Siemens, Lynne, and Elisabeth Burr. "A Trip Around the World: Accommodating Geographical, Linguistic and Cultural Diversity in Academic Research Teams." *Linguistic and Literary Computing* 28.2 (2013): 331–343.

Siemens, Lynne, *et al.* "A Tale of Two Cities: Implications of the Similarities and Differences in Collaborative Approaches within the Digital Libraries and Digital Humanities Communities." *Literary & Linguistic Computing* 26.3 (2011): 335–348.

Siemens, Lynne, and INKE Research Group. "Firing on All Cylinders: Progress and Transition in INKE's Year 2." *Scholarly and Research Communication* 3.4 (2012a): 1–16.

Siemens, Lynne, and INKE Research Group. "INKE Administrative Structure: Omnibus Document." *Scholarly and Research Communication* 3.1 (2012b).

Siemens, Lynne, and INKE Research Group. "'NKE-Cubating' Research Networks and Projects: Reflections on INKE's Fifth Year." *Research Foundations for Understanding Books and Reading in the Digital Age: Emerging Reading, Writing, and Research Practices*. 2014a.

Siemens, Lynne, and INKE Research Group. "Research Collaboration as 'Layers of Engagement': INKE in Year Four." *Scholarly and Research Communication* 5.4 (2014b): 1–12.

Siemens, Lynne, and INKE Research Group. "Responding to Change and Transition in INKE's Year Three." *Scholarly and Research Communication* 4.3 (2013): 12 pp.

Siemens, Lynne, Jeff Smith, and Yin Liu. "Mapping Disciplinary Differences and Equity of Academic Control to Create a Space for Collaboration." *Canadian Journal of Higher Education* 44.2 (2014): 49–67.

Simeone, M., *et al.* "Digging into Data Using New Collaborative Infrastructures Supporting Humanities-Based Computer Science Research." *First Monday* 16.5 (2011).

Social Sciences and Humanities Research Council. "Partnership Grants: An Overview." 2013. 9 December 2013. www.sshrc-crsh.gc.ca/about-au_sujet/partnerships-partenariats/partnership_grants-bourses_partenariats-eng.aspx

Spiller, Keith, *et al.* "Carnivalesque Collaborations: Reflections on 'Doing' Multi-Disciplinary Research." *Qualitative Research* (2014): 1–17.

SSHRC. "Insight Grants." 2015. 13 April 2015. www.sshrc-crsh.gc.ca/funding-financement/programs-programmes/insight_grants-subventions_savoir-eng.aspx

The Praxis Program at the Scholars' Lab. "2011–12 Praxis Program Charter." 2011. 19 September 2012. http://praxis.scholarslab.org/charter.html

The Praxis Program at the Scholars' Lab. "What We're Working On." nd. 14 April 2015. http://praxis.scholarslab.org

Williford, Christa, and Charles Henry. *One Culture: Computationally Intensive Research in the Humanities and Social Sciences: A Report on the Experiences of First Respondents to the Digging into Data Challenge*. Council on Library and Information Resources, 2012.

Woodley, Mary S. *Digital Project Planning & Management Basics: Instructor Manual*, 2008.

CHAPTER 21

Doing DH in the classroom

Transforming the humanities curriculum through digital engagement

Diane Jakacki and Katherine Faull

In this chapter, the authors reproduce the theory/praxis model we employ when teaching digital humanities pedagogy workshops at DHSI and other institutions. By first situating each aspect of the process in a broader pedagogical framework, we present sound practices for the integration of DH methods and tools into humanities courses. We then present a case study that demonstrates how these practices can be employed effectively in the classroom. At the end of the chapter we offer a "Further Reading" section that offers course websites, sample syllabi and additional readings on DH pedagogy. In the chapter we focus on courses rooted in research-based or experiential learning, which we believe offers the teacher an opportunity to involve students in the kind of humanistic enquiry that we as DH scholars engage in as we undertake our own scholarship. We believe that this approach is most effective when helping other instructors adapt and adopt these models for their own use.

In the summer 2014 issue of *The CEA Critic*, authors Lindsay Thomas and Dana Solomon remarked on the notable lack of discussions of pedagogy in the development of the digital humanities in undergraduate institutions. Arguing that DH pedagogy should be something far more than an afterthought, Thomas and Solomon outlined how their undergraduate project "RoSE" at the University of California, Santa Barbara developed students to be active users and researchers of DH. In the same issue of *The CEA Critic*, E. Leigh Bonds drew on the discussions of Melissa Terras, Stephen Ramsey, Alan Liu, and others about the fundamental difference between the learning goals of DH courses and those of traditional courses in the humanities. How do we teach students to be critical makers and doers together? Or, in Liu's terms, how do we develop a pedagogical hermeneutic of "practice, discovery, community"?[1]

The term "digital pedagogy" has gained traction in the wake of the digital humanities' move from margin to center in the academy.[2] But there is no one definition for digital pedagogy: the term is used to identify everything from massive open online courses (MOOCs) and clickers, to flipped classrooms and hybrid courses, to blog and wiki assignments, to scaffolded projects in which the digital is intrinsic to course design and learning outcomes. Experimentation at the assignment level gives "digi-curious" instructors the opportunity to test digital tools and methods. However, this is very different from the design and execution of an intentionally designed course in DH. When we overhaul our syllabi and our teaching methods to transform the classroom and course structure with specifically DH-inflected learning goals and outcomes, it may seem alien and unsettling to our students and even to our departmental colleagues; but it is progressive and truly distinctive in ways that reflect the changing nature of humanities programs and curricula. This radical shift in design and execution is both exciting and necessary, and challenges us, as digital humanists, to become more effective teachers by incorporating our own DH research and interests into the classroom.

One of the fundamental differences between digital *humanities* pedagogy and a more general integration of technology into the classroom lies in the intentionality of course learning goals; in other words, how we lead students to new forms of understanding through the methods of the digital humanities. Integration of technology into the classroom is predicated upon the development of fundamental forms of discrete digital literacies to encourage students to think critically about media engagement so that they can become better digital citizens. Often, these entry-level approaches focus on forms of collaborative writing and introductory multimodal assignments. This foundation establishes a trajectory for both students and instructors in which they develop digital skills and the vocabulary to assess particular types of assignments. Courses that are designed as *sui generis* DH courses occupy the other end of a trajectory of digital learning. Here, digital humanities scholar-practitioners shape their syllabi to teach DH-specific learning goals that are deeply embedded within digital ways of knowing, a specifically DH hermeneutic. To achieve these learning goals, such courses focus on intermediate-to-advanced integration of methodologies – such as text encoding analysis and topic modeling, data visualization, and geospatial analysis – into humanities-based critical enquiry that creates even more compelling DH learning environments. Often, in such courses, digital humanists teach research-based learning that is tied to their own DH projects.

This chapter focuses on the far end of the spectrum, modeling what we believe is best practice in digital humanities pedagogy by means of an extended case study: our experience of planning and implementing a new DH project-based course at Bucknell University. This course introduced undergraduate students to the world of digital humanities through the use of selected digital tools and methods of analysis. We believe that in the context of this volume, *Doing Digital Humanities*, it will serve to demonstrate the importance of planning, assessment, training, support, and evaluation to do DH in the classroom.

COURSE DESIGN AND GOALS

The integration of digital humanities at the core of a course – whether when designing a new course or restructuring an existing one – requires that the teacher pays particular attention to course goals and learning objectives. This form of pedagogical intentionality may surprise instructors who have taught a particular subject using more traditional methods in the past, but is crucial to the implementation of a course that establishes a sound learning framework and ensures the successful pedagogical coalescence of DH into a humanities context. In this section we will model ways in which the creation of a new course requires the teacher to question and re-address accustomed approaches to teaching, and to identify specific digital learning goals while still meeting departmental curricular requirements.

In the case of Humanities 100 – a course without precedent at Bucknell and with few guiding models at other undergraduate institutions – the development and implementation of the syllabus and learning goals was challenging and required a high level of commitment from both instructors. While we had both co-taught courses before, neither of us had developed what both agreed was a high-risk, high-profile course that could have significant impact on our colleagues as well as on students. We believed from the outset that the course clearly had the potential to establish a foundation that could scale to a much broader presence for the digital humanities across the Bucknell University curriculum.

This course, taught within the Comparative Humanities program,[3] was designed specifically for first- and second-year undergraduate students with no background in digital humanities, in order to encourage the development of digital habits of mind at the earliest phases of their liberal arts curricular experience. The Comparative Humanities program at Bucknell University provides an ideal curricular environment in which to teach such classes with its explicit learning goals of comparativity (historical period, cultures, genres, modality). This program context is important for the success of such explicitly DH-focused courses, in that the process of practice and discovery happens within a curricular community where that is the norm. For these program-based goals, course-specific learning goals that pertain to DH were developed. These goals speak to the specificity of digital humanities pedagogy as a mode of learning: namely, students learn to identify, use, and discuss the advantages and disadvantages of different DH methodologies and tools; they develop sound research questions that can be answered with DH methodologies and tools; they create projects using the tools taught in the course; they learn to articulate and assess success (or failure) of a humanities research project involving DH methods; finally, they work individually and collaboratively to create projects that relate to specific interests. This multi-section course not only provided the instructors the opportunity to expose students to methodologies related to distant and close reading, network and spatial visualization, but also required that they learn to think critically about what each of these methods, and the tools that they used within the course, reveal in the texts with which they worked.[4]

One of the crucial decisions that must be made when undertaking such a course is what kind of data students will develop and use in the execution of these course goals. We realized early in the design process that student success was contingent upon their understanding of how DH data are developed. We therefore decided to make archival material the core source of data for the course. Further, the size of the corpus should be small enough that students could gain an oversight over the material even without needing to implement techniques of distant reading. Therefore, the decision to root the course in a multifaceted analysis of archival materials provided the rare chance for undergraduate students to also engage in the research process typical for a humanities scholar: namely, the discovery of artifacts, the formulation of research questions, followed by the analysis and synthesis of findings culminating in the publication of initial findings in a digital medium. In the process, we introduced students to the basic structure of how to develop a DH research project.

The first time the course was taught we decided to run it in two sections, anticipating an opportunity to reflect different perspectives of our expertise with DH methods and tools, and therefore to cross-teach while learning from each other: Jakacki's focus until then had been on text encoding and analysis, while Faull's had been on mapping and data visualization. We also worked with discrete data sets of archival materials. Faull's course focused on the Colonial mission diaries of the Moravians from Shamokin, Pennsylvania (today Sunbury) and situated near the university on the Susquehanna River. Written in English, the diary sections selected dealt with interactions between some of the first Europeans to the area and the Native peoples they met and worked among. Faull has spent the past five years working with this subject matter, and is considered an expert in the field of Moravian studies. Jakacki's course concentrated on a subset of the diaries of James Merrill Linn, one of the first graduates of the university and a soldier in the American Civil War. Linn's family left his life papers to the Bucknell Archives, and these were accessible to students. The choice of this material was based on Jakacki's interest in finding a subject with another connection to Bucknell's location, and offered an opportunity for students to consider first-hand the differences between material and digital archives. In the second iteration of the course in spring 2015, Faull selected a different set of Moravian archival materials that took the students slightly further afield, but still kept them within the Susquehanna River watershed and the Chesapeake Bay. In fall 2015 Jakacki shifted the archival emphasis in her section to sixteenth-century English theatre studies using a collection of anecdotes and performance records as core text and dataset. The instructors' choices reflect and extend Bucknell's interest in digital/spatial thinking in terms of place in the larger historical and cultural narrative. This was particularly important for Faull's decision to root her courses in regional history; students responded well to the investigation of places familiar to them, with several students having family connections to specific locales mentioned in the archival materials. In all cases, we taught material that (to our knowledge) had not been incorporated previously into learning environments and that was unpublished, either in traditional print form or in digital format.

In the design of the course, we decided to implement a scaffolding of assignments to accommodate both the selected core archival texts while reinforcing the importance of considering how different DH-based methods strengthen students' understanding of that subject matter. This approach allowed both instructors to develop more sophisticated and complex course modules while assisting one another through complementary strengths and skills. This transparency challenged us to consider whether we were co-teaching two sections of one course or two courses in collaboration. This simultaneous or parallel mode of teaching also allowed us to identify moments that offered a richer learning environment for both sections, supporting each other in the separate sections when individual DH expertise and pedagogical approaches needed to be supplemented. In essence, the instructors learned how to teach one another while teaching the subject matter to students. Early on in the course development process, we realized that in order for students to understand the evolving nature of DH research, we would have to reveal our own status as learners. Teaching unfamiliar material – not only across sections but within a particular class – required an at times uncomfortable degree of transparency. It must be said that such honesty can have varying effects on students. Some recognize that learning from each other happens to everyone, and respect that mode of collaboration and camaraderie. Others, perhaps more used to the "one way" pedagogy of the lecture hall, are definitely uncomfortable with the non-hierarchical class structure.

Another challenge to the class design was the high number of L2 students (students for whom English is a second language) who were enrolled in the course. In Faull's fall 2014 section over 20 per cent were from mainland China; in her spring section that ratio increased to 60 per cent. In the fall 2014 there was also one student from Australia and one from Vietnam (neither L2s but international students); one student in the spring course was from South Africa – her first language was Afrikaans. Although the students admitted to being challenged by the readings and also the public-facing writing in the course website, a means for adjusting for student errors and allowing for corrections was developed that would allow the students to post their blog reflections in a way that did not impede their openness to reflection, knowing that they would have an opportunity to correct their English.

Some institutions may already have a culture of digital engagement that focuses on one or another facet of engagement. At Bucknell, the focus in digital humanities scholarship and learning to date has been primarily on spatial thinking, until recently rooted in working with ArcMap-type geospatial analysis and thinking about humanities in "place." It was important to both instructors to emphasize and extend that objective in the development of the course and its learning outcomes; and so the focus moved to using more DH approaches that would be of interest to students so that they could relate to the historical context more directly. Therefore, in addition to a mapping module, we added close and distant reading and data visualization, relying on an array of platforms: ArcGIS Online (mapping); Juxta Editions (text markup using the Text Encoding Initiative guidelines); Voyant and Gephi (text analysis and visualization); and Omeka (digital curation of archival materials). To tie it together, a WordPress site was created as a course management system and a platform for student reflection.[5] Students wrote public-facing posts on the site, embedded screenshots of their work, and commented on each other's work. Students were also able to point to the website when explaining to curious family and friends what their course was about.

INTEGRATING CRITICAL REFLECTION

One of the distinguishing features of a Digital Humanities course is the foregrounding of critique. Unlike more CS-based classes, students in DH classes are required to reflect on the process they have undertaken in developing their projects to be able to place their praxis within the broader scholarly discourse of DH. Therefore, carefully selected readings that are directly linked to development of each of the student's competencies should be embedded within the class schedule. Teaching students to use these digital platforms requires the conscious placement of the course within a curricular context; in our case, within the context of the program in Comparative Humanities.

To this end, each module required students to read key secondary texts and reflect upon the theoretical as well as practical aspects of DH. For example, students had to reflect on what Johanna Drucker says about the visual rhetoric of visualization. They had to account for Elena Pierazzo's argument for the epistemic difference of diplomatic editions. They considered Daniel Rosenberg and Anthony Grafton's essay on the development of timelines and the conceptualization of history. The interdisciplinary humanistic approach was thus clearly and directly linked to the learning goals of the course and reinforced departmental learning goals of analyzing intellectual materials of different and opposing types and theorizing the difference between textual and material artifacts. Students also learned to identify, use, and discuss the advantages and disadvantages of different DH methodologies and tools and were encouraged to identify and use key terms and concepts. As a result, students learned to develop research questions that could be answered with DH tools and methodologies, and work collaboratively in groups to create projects that related to their own research interests.

SCAFFOLDING ASSIGNMENTS

One benefit of DH-focused course design that distinguishes it from many more traditional approaches is the ability to build assignments across the semester, expanding and enhancing student engagement with source material and emphasizing how DH scholars must focus on process rather than product. By scaffolding digital assignments, teachers can also encourage students to gain confidence in their own particular learning strengths – visual and textual learners alike can find moments of connection with the same source materials.

As outlined above, the pedagogical hermeneutics of Humanities 100 were intentionally designed to encourage student examination, experimentation and discovery with a range of digital humanities approaches. To this end, the sequencing of the modules was carefully designed so that the "product" of each module then became the "data" of the next module. This established an environment in which learning was both iterative and generative.

For example, we modeled professional archival (DH) research practice by having students transcribe and produce a clean digital text. In the first iteration of the course, students transcribed the assigned pages of the facsimile into a shared Google doc. This digital text was then color-coded in terms of "proto" tags to ease the way into close reading with TEI tags in the oXygen XML editor. At the beginning of the second semester, we obtained an institutional subscription to the online platform Juxta Editions which established a "transcription desk" work process in which students did their transcriptions and the first pass at TEI tagging, helping us to better prepare them to think about tagging schema and standardized markup. As one student noted:

> For us it was important to tag dates, events, and places because it is a journal that we are transcribing and we want to keep track of a journey. Sometimes we had to face even tougher decisions than just whether or not to tag a word. For example, it required some more thinking to determine whether a word was a place vs. an object. We had to just all agree on the same tag so we could be as consistent as possible.

Once a reliable text had been established, we then introduced students to the concept of "distant reading" through the Voyant platform.[6] At the same time as students were encouraged to "play," we also pointed out the circular motion of discovery and confirmation that is inherent in any research experience. The students had just read these archival texts very carefully in order to transcribe them, so we asked them the usual kinds of questions one asks when approaching any kind of new text. What is it about? What are the major themes? Who are the most important characters? Then, having read Edward Whitley's text on distant reading, we asked the students to think about what reading a text distantly does to that hermeneutic. Describing her process, one student in Faull's class wrote, "We put the Travel Diary and the Powell Diary – two documents which are similar – together in DocuBurst. [We were] able to show connections between words related to 'justice'. This is really cool to use digital tools to connect 2 old documents." (Figure 21.1)

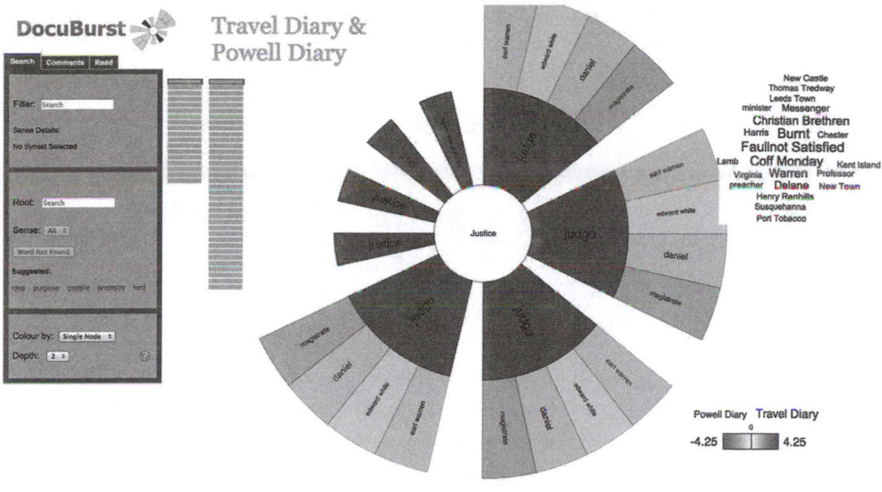

Figure 21.1
Student-generated Docuburst visualization comparing two Moravian mission diaries

From the transcription came the lightly marked-up digital text which was then imported into oXygen for more complex tagging. Students began tagging in earnest and were introduced to the discoveries of close reading involved in marking up a text. Names, places, and dates were easy (they had already been tagged in Juxta Edition). However, the hermeneutical fun started with trickier distinctions; for example, was a boat a place or an object; is God a person; or just what was balsam, an object? an emotion? During these classes, the historical remoteness of the texts was reduced by the act of tagging and the lively discussions that accompanied it. A student remarked how:

> As a class, we have had multiple discussions on whether certain things are objects or places and event versus time . . . each side would have to give an appealing argument to support their claim. This kind of action in class made for a very productive work environment, and helped bring about discussion that benefitted everyone.

These data, the TEI tags, crucial to the success of the students' markup assignment and the production of a final digital document, needed some restructuring as we moved on to the next module. To manage this, we developed a prosopography for each core text – a database of people, places, and connections that grew organically out of the focus of each specific section and provided the data for entry into Gephi, and was then built out in adding geospatial data for GIS.

For example, one group of students wanted to use Gephi to interrogate the assumption that relationships between the missionaries and the Native Americans in the area around the mission remained constant. Importing the words they had tagged in TEI as `<persName>` and importing them into Gephi node/edge tables, the students in Faull's classes were able to show how relations between the Native leaders and the Moravian missionaries changed over a five-year period of the mission (Figure 21.2). Network analysis was less helpful in the first iteration of Jakacki's section, as the Linn diary offered a very small data set of related people. It became clear from all iterations of the class that the hermeneutics of social networks was the hardest for the students to analyze and manipulate (which is surprising, given how most of them are well plugged into social media).

The last module in each section of the course focused explicitly on place, with students effectively writing map-based essays. The nature of the travel journals in the first three course iterations provided us with a valuable opportunity to challenge students to rethink their conceptions of space and journey. We prepared georectified historical maps and pertinent cultural, environmental, and historical GIS data layers, and urged students to use them to think about how a traveler in the eighteenth or nineteenth century would conceptualize space. They analyzed the contemporary maps and associated data to consider how a traveler might have to rely on a manuscript map, or was faced with travel conditions that would affect chosen routes: terrain, weather, rudimentary pathways, etc.

In all cases, the students incorporated contemporary accounts and records as direct evidence within the context of ArcGIS Online story map templates, added map notes, paths and shapes to propose theses about locations and sequence of events, and framed the map interface with textual and visual arguments and conclusions (Figure 21.3). This dynamic and creative approach to GIS analysis provided those students who had sometimes struggled with negotiating their archival materials through textual means with a more visual way to understand the role their subjects played in historical events. As one such student noted:

> When I started this project, I knew I wanted to talk about Linn's naval travel, but I was unsure about what specific aspect would be most interesting. My research question was how did naval warfare affect the way that the Civil War was fought, and how did the weather, tides, wind, and other nautical issues affect the way that the war played out. The answer, however, was hidden deeper than I expected.

Both the composition of the class (in terms of student personalities) and also the nature of the material determined to some extent the kind of final project students chose. For example, in Faull's section there were some natural groupings of students and there were a variety of final projects (one involving Gephi; two TEI markup; one hybrid ArcMap and TEI; and one story map). In Jakacki's class all but two students chose to work independently. In the second iteration of Faull's course, students decided that they would produce one final group project all together – a course website that highlighted the best of their DH work.[7]

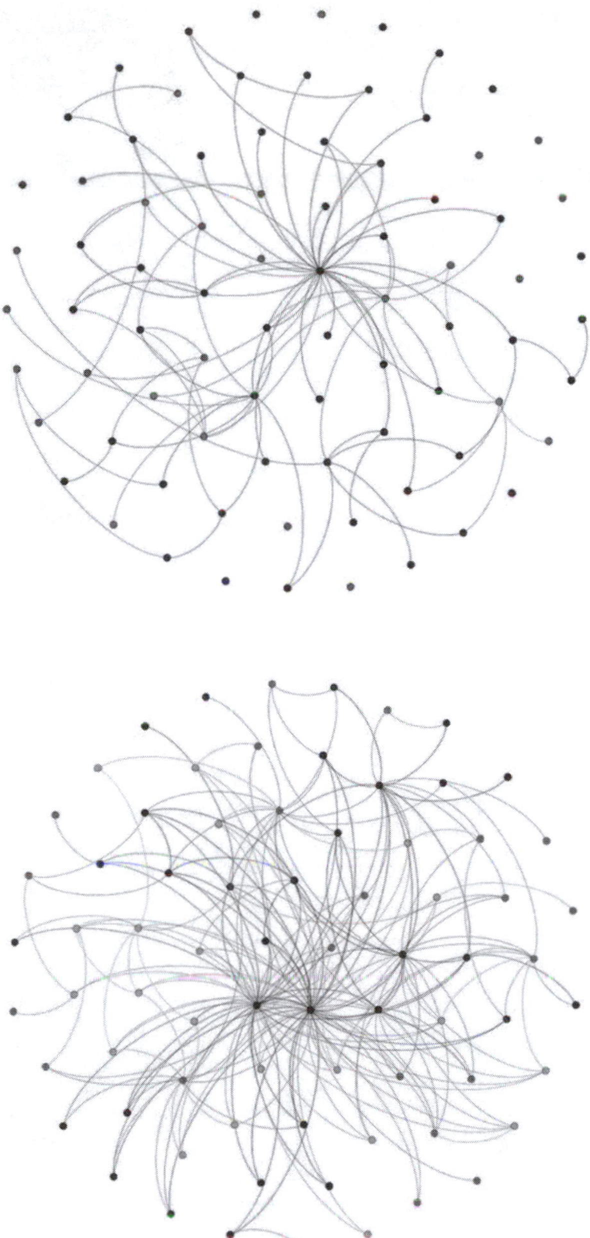

Figure 21.2
A Gephi network visualization of two sections of a historical diary, revealing a change in social relations in two distinct time periods

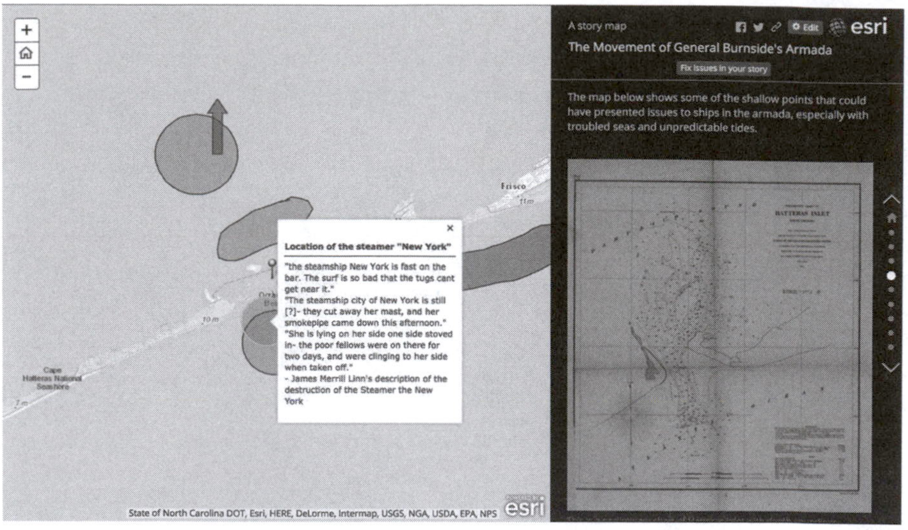

Figure 21.3
A segment of a student's ArcGIS Online story map

Thus, by scaffolding the assignments to build one on another in an iterative process, both students and faculty are able to engage in the building of complex digital artifacts that are manageably scaled and that reveal in their construction the importance of understanding the abstraction, structuring and retrieval of DH data.

For all the challenges involved in teaching the class, there were moments of glory. Disengaged students became engaged; solitary learners recognized the essential need to collaborate in order to succeed; participants recognized the transformative nature of the course to their own concepts of the humanities. Students were eager to participate in crowdsourced data collection; they were intrigued to visualize ego-networks as they learned the concepts of network theory; they were excited to see their marked-up transcriptions published in an online digital edition. Through these discoveries, they realized that they were creating a community of young DH-ers and expressed eagerness to take part in more of these learning experiences.

All iterations of the course proved to be successful for a number of reasons. Our students showed facility engaging both with unfamiliar materials and with new approaches that constituted rhetorical engagements – textually, visually, spatially – in ways that surprised them and gave them a confidence and ownership in their work that they would not have experienced in a more traditional first- or second-year humanities survey course. For the teachers, we had to be ready to course-correct when students wanted more time to work with a particular module; we had to learn to accommodate one another's distinctive teaching styles; we had to be honest with our students about course material in ways that we hadn't really expected. For Jakacki, that meant the experiment working with "found" local materials left her feeling self-conscious about teaching subject matter so outside of her field of scholarship, and resulted in the change in subject matter for fall 2015. For Faull, that meant continuing to scour the Moravian Archives for appropriate English language materials that will spark the interest of students and lend themselves to the hermeneutical lens of DH.

RUBRICS AND ASSESSMENT

When DH is built into humanities-focused assignments, specific rubrics can help students to better meet expectations and understand degrees of competency. Through clear articulation of rubrics, teachers also help themselves as they give feedback to students. In addition, it is helpful to build formal and informal reflection and assessment across the course so as to gauge when things are working and when more time needs to be taken to ensure that students can meet expectations. In this section, we will reflect upon how we met challenges and adjusted our expectations for the course as we continued to develop it across iterations.

How well did our students meet our learning goals? For Faull's fall semester class, 80 per cent of students met the learning goals at grade B or above. There were challenges, especially in meeting some of the Comparative Humanities departmental learning goals for this group of students. For example, in order to meet the learning goal that requires students to gain the ability to compare historical periods, students had to grapple with the differences between the present-day world and early American culture. Some of the students were challenged in understanding the Colonial American world of the 1740s. Similarly, most students had very little knowledge of Native American history in the Contact period and their analyses of Iroquois culture, movement and contact were less than satisfactory. In Jakacki's section, similar difficulties were encountered. In order to understand the perspective and relevance of Linn's field observations, it was necessary for students to understand the broader context of the Civil War, national and global events and trends in the 1860s. For all sections, we devised an assignment that required students to collaborate on a multimedia TimeMapper timeline. This helped them to question to what degree, for example, Linn internalized his role as a combatant. For Faull's section, TimeMapper allowed students to contextualize the events of Colonial America in terms of European imperialism, exploration and invention. In the spring semester, helped by a smaller class size and a very different group of students, 100 per cent of the students met the learning goals. The collaborative exercises were far better integrated and the process of discovery was equally shared and mutually beneficial.

How well did we do in the students' eyes? They realized they were doing something really new and very transportable to other courses. Furthermore, despite the highly structured nature of the syllabus, students did not feel as though they were being forced through a machine. Rather, they experienced a growing sense of agency as DH practitioners.

CONCLUSION

Taking this class as a case study for how to incorporate a DH course into the Humanities curriculum and designing it to model the very core of DH's pedagogical hermeneutics, we have aimed to help our colleagues in the field who would like to develop their own courses. We hope that our experience provides a model for how digital humanities can and should be taught at the earliest stage of an undergraduate's university experience, and that this type of learning experience is transformative in terms of demonstrating the interdisciplinarity within the humanities. If such courses are well planned, modestly ambitious, truly collaborative in both conceptualization and execution, they can promote radically new ways of understanding the goals of humanistic enquiry; a new pedagogical hermeneutic for both teachers and students.

NOTES

1 Alan Liu has published many essays on the way in which digital humanities has the potential to engage students and researchers alike in hermeneutical and critical acts that deeply reflect and inflect the humanities. Most recently, Liu has delivered the talk "Key Trends in Digital Humanities – How the Digital Humanities Challenge the Idea of the Humanities" in the US, New Zealand, and Siberia. These are key terms from that as yet unpublished talk, which was also delivered at Bucknell on 30 April 2015.

2 See in particular Liu's "The Meaning of the Digital Humanities," the collective issue in the Spring 2014 issue of *Differences* that came out of the "Dark Side of Digital Humanities" panel at MLA 2013, and the edited volume *Digital Humanities Pedagogy: Practices, Principles and Politics*.

3 www.bucknell.edu/ComparativeHumanities

4 All sections of the Humanities 100 course taught by Faull and Jakacki are licensed under Creative Commons Attribution-NonCommercial ShareAlike licenses. Course websites with goals, outlines, and assignments can be viewed at http://dhpedagogy.blogs.bucknell.edu/

5 Bucknell University has an educational site license for ESRI's ArcMap suite, and provides all Bucknell students, faculty, and staff with ArcGIS Online accounts. Bucknell also hosts WordPress and Omeka installations on its servers.

6 In 2014–15 sections we used the Voyant 1.0 web version. In Fall 2015 we introduced the Voyant 2.0 VoyantServer, then still in beta and hosted locally.

7 http://paynefroehlich.blogs.bucknell.edu/

REFERENCES

Bonds, E. Leigh. "Listening in on the Conversations: An Overview of Digital Humanities Pedagogy." *CEA Critic* 76.2 (2014): 147–157.

Drucker, Johanna. *Graphesis: Visual Forms of Knowledge Production*. Harvard University Press. Cambridge, MA. 2014. 56–137.

Liu, Alan. "The Meaning of the Digital Humanities." *PMLA* 128 (2013): 409–423.

Pierazzo, Elena. "A Rationale of Digital Documentary Editions." *Literary and Linguistic Computing* 26.4 (2011): 463–477.

Rosenberg, Daniel and Anthony Grafton. "Time in Print." *Cartographies of Time: A History of the Timeline*. Princeton Academic Press. New York. 2000. 10–15.

Thomas, Lindsay and Dana Solomon. "Active Users: Project Development and Digital Humanities Pedagogy." *CEA Critic* 76.2 (2014): 211–220.

Whitley, Edward. "Visualizing the Archive." *The American Literature Scholar in the Digital Age*. Amy E. Earhart and Andrew Jewell, eds. University of Michigan Press. Ann Arbor, MI. 2011. 185–205.

FURTHER READING

Course websites, sample syllabi, and an annotated bibliography of articles and essays pertaining to digital humanities pedagogy can be accessed at: http://dhpedagogy.blogs.bucknell.edu/

Bodenhamer, David J. "The Potential of Spatial Humanities." *The Spatial Humanities: GIS and the Future of Humanities Scholarship*. Bloomington, IN: Indiana University Press 2010. 14–30.

Clement, Tanya. "Text Analysis, Data Mining, and Visualization in Literary Scholarship." *Literary Studies in the Digital Age: An Evolving Anthology*. Kenneth M. Price and Ray Siemens, eds. MLA Commons. Modern Language Association of America. 2013. Web. https://dlsanthology.commons.mla.org/text-analysis-data-mining-and-visualizations-in-literary-scholarship/

Faull, Katherine and Diane Jakacki. "Pedagogical Hermeneutics and Teaching DH in a Liberal Arts Context." Digital Humanities 2015 Annual Meeting.

Faull, Katherine and Diane Jakacki . "Digital Learning in an Undergraduate Context: Promoting Long Term Student-Faculty Collaboration." *Digital Scholarship in the Humanities*. DOI: http://dx.doi.org/10.1093/llc/fqv050 Web. http://dhpedagogy.blogs.bucknell.edu/select-readings/

Grusin, Richard, ed. The Dark Side of Digital Humanities issue of *Differences: A Journal of Feminist Culture*. 25.1(2014). Durham, NC: Duke University Press. www.c21uwm.com/2013/01/09/the-dark-side-of-the-digital-humanities-part-1/

Hirsch, Brett, ed. *Digital Humanities Pedagogy: Practices, Principles and Politics*. Cambridge: Open Book Publishers 2012.

Kretzchmar, William A., Jr. "GIS for Language and Literary Study." *Literary Studies in the Digital Age: An Evolving Anthology*. Kenneth M. Price and Ray

Siemens, eds. MLA Commons. Modern Language Association of America. 2013. Web. https://dlsanthology.commons.mla.org/gis-for-language-and-literary-study/

Liu, Alan . "The State of the Digital Humanities: A Report and a Critique." *Arts & Humanities in Higher Education* II (2011): 8–41.

Schreibman, Susan. "Digital Scholarly Editing." *Literary Studies in the Digital Age: An Evolving Anthology*. Kenneth M. Price and Ray Siemens, eds. MLA Commons. Modern Language Association of America. 2013. Web. https://dlsanthology.commons.mla.org/digital-scholarly-editing/

Sinclair, Stéfan, Stan Ruecker, and Milena Radzikowska. "Information Visualization for Humanities Scholars." *Literary Studies in the Digital Age: An Evolving Anthology*. Kenneth M. Price and Ray Siemens, eds. MLA Commons. Modern Language Association of America. 2013. Web. https://dlsanthology.commons.mla.org/information-visualization-for-humanities-scholars/

Southall, Humphrey R. "Applying Historical GIS beyond the Academy: Four Use Cases for the Great Britain HGIS." *Toward Spatial Humanities*. Bloomington, IN: Indiana University Press 2010.

Underwood, Ted. "Digital Humanities Might Never Be Evenly Distributed." *The Stone and the Shell*. 7 September 2015. http://tedunderwood.com/2015/09/07/digital-humanities-might-never-be-evenly-distributed/

CHAPTER 22

Digital liberal arts and project-based pedagogies

Aaron Mauro

> Can we not devise a system of liberal education which shall find its foundations in the best things of the here and now? Literature and art are all about us; science and faith offer their daily contributions; history is in the making to-day; industry pours forth its wares; and children, no less than adults, are sharing in the dynamic activities of contemporary social life. Not in the things of the past, but in those of the present, should liberal education find its beginnings as well as its results. (David Snedden, "What Of Liberal Education?" *The Atlantic Monthly*, 1912. Quoted in *New Liberal Arts*, edited by Tim Carmody and Robin Sloan)

In 2009, Tim Carmody and Robin Sloan published a collection of blog posts and eclectic writings called *New Liberal Arts*. Their goal was to reopen a conversation about the need for liberal education with a contemporary focus. As explained in their introduction, they sought "to collectively identify and explore twenty-first-century ways of doing the liberal arts." Their epigraph, which I have borrowed for this chapter, is evidence of the ongoing need to combat a perception of a musty and old-fashioned liberal arts education. Their inspiration came not from the past but from the present. Carmody and Sloan's project was generated by a community of bloggers who were reflecting on their place in a post-2008 recessionary period and on the new forms of scholarly debate they were sharing through blogs. Jason Kottke, who authors and edits an influential and long-running blog bearing his name – kottke.org, first coined the term "Liberal Arts 2.0" which was then remixed by Carmody and Sloan as simply *new*. The project failed to attain its goal of publishing a book in the traditional sense, but it still exists in the "simple HTML" I am now citing. In some ways, this early attempt to define a twenty-first-century liberal arts set the stage for conversations that are only now finding root in digital humanities

(DH). As open access publishing and community engagement are increasingly celebrated, it is appropriate that Carmody and Sloan are not full-time academics nor are they engaged in current debates in digital humanities. Sloan is a former Twitter employee who went on to author *Mr. Penumbra's 24-Hour Book Store* in 2012, which Matthew Kirschenbaum christened as "the first novel of the digital humanities" on Twitter. Carmody is a self-proclaimed "recovering academic" and freelance writer, publishing in venues such as *Wired*, *The Verge*, and *The Atlantic*. Cues for the next steps in humanities education are coming, in part, from outside the academy and are representative of an increasingly responsive curriculum design process. In the best tradition of the liberal arts, this new curriculum balances *ars* and *techne* without forsaking the critical and theoretical basis of a twentieth-century humanities education.

It is really no surprise that an outward-facing humanities, which leverages digital tools to ask new questions and reach new audiences, must also be receptive to outside influence. After all, DH has long been a discipline existing on the margins of traditional academic institutions and curricular structures. Training graduate students and faculty in computational methods has been made possible by a broad network of extracurricular settings, such as the humanities research labs, centers, and institutes, and many of these institutions are now catalogued on centerNet (www.dhcenternet.org). For example, Bethany Nowviskie's 2012 keynote lecture delivered to the Japanese Association for Digital Humanities, "Too Small to Fail," recounts the history of the University of Virginia's Scholars' Lab and how its evolution helped sustain "extracurricular" opportunities for graduate students through its Praxis Program. Graduate student participation in particular has been exceedingly successful in such contexts. However, in his 18 March 2014 blog post entitled "How much DH can we fit in a literature department," Ted Underwood warns that "the marriage between disciplinary and extradisciplinary institutions may not be so easy," particularly at the undergraduate level. It is in such a context that this chapter will describe how the traditional disciplinary and institutional boundaries actually serve to animate the new undergraduate major in Digital Media, Arts, and Technology at Penn State Behrend by incorporating collaboration and community engagement at the core of a broad set of pedagogical practices. By taking hints from graduate student training, the marriage between curricular and research goals is now anchoring a broadly conceived undergraduate digital humanities education.

BIG TENT, SMALL CAMPUS

In the words of Kirschenbaum's now canonical "What is Digital Humanities and What's It Doing in English Departments?" published in the *ADE Bulletin* in 2010, the digital humanities is about "a scholarship and pedagogy that are collaborative and depend on networks of people that live an active 24//7 life online" (6). There is certainly a vibrant discussion about teaching and learning in the humanities with digital tools on many blogs, most visibly on the *ProfHacker* blog hosted by *The Chronicle of Higher Education*. There is a growing awareness about the need to balance in-person discussions and those occurring online ("The Balance"). The Digital Humanities Summer Institute (DHSI) has been a cornerstone for the DH community and has been a highly successful pedagogical experiment in its own right since its founding at the University of Victoria in 2001. The Humanities, Arts, Science and Technology Alliance and Collaboratory (HASTAC) is a virtual organization with a broad mandate to improve education at all ages and is now developing a "Pedagogy Project" that collects suggestions from faculty on digital or collaborative projects. The various iterations of The Humanities and Technology Camp (THATCamp) have also shown how invested the DH community is in professionalization and teaching, with multiple pedagogically themed meetings occurring around the world in recent years. The responsiveness of DH practitioners to new teaching methods can be seen in the community participation at DHSI, the vibrant online community of HASTAC scholars, and the sheer diversity of THATCamps occurring throughout the year.

This chapter is an extension of a conversation that began at the 2015 Modern Language Association (MLA) meeting in Vancouver, British Columbia on a panel called "Big Tent, Small Campus: Digital Humanities, Digital Liberal Arts, and Undergraduate Education." The panel, organized by Jacob Heil, was focused on an emerging trend towards aligning undergraduate digital humanities training with a liberal arts tradition that is common in smaller teaching-focused colleges. William Pannapacker's article in *The Chronicle of Higher Education*, "Stop Calling it 'Digital Humanities'" (2013), first coined the term Digital Liberal Arts (DLA) as a "more inclusive" alternative to the sense of elitism and research emphasis of DH being taught at the graduate level. Rafael Alvarado responded in another post shortly after, "Start Calling it Digital Liberal Arts" (2013), by saying that "DLA is as concerned with pedagogy as it is with research." Regardless of such naming conventions, there has been a push to match teaching and research in an explicit way for some time now. Because of the affordances of being a small college within a big university, faculty tasked with teaching DH at Behrend are encouraged to work across disciplines and explore affinities with both computer science and the social sciences. By blending a liberal-style education with project-based undergraduate research opportunities that directly complement curriculum, we have sought to emulate the collaborative environment of a technology incubator with an outward-facing humanities education.

With that said, Underwood's warning about such disciplinary marriages is borne out by experience. At Behrend, we are already learning that many of our students come to humanities classes with hardened opinions about technology. Consumer-level digital technologies have formed the basis of their socialization from their earliest years and many students have developed sophisticated opinions in both personal and educational contexts. Students have often internalized Marc Prensky's myth of "the digital native" with a skewed sense of competency with digital tools.

One of my students recently described their experiences in a "Writing for the Web" class with a great deal of clarity and self-awareness:

> This "digital native" status, however, implies that current scholars are uniquely qualified to interact and communicate online purely because they are "already" digitally literate. Yet, my own experience with blogging reflects that there is a weak correlation between one's status as a digital native and one's ability to write digital content.

Matt Ratto, in his article "Ethics of Seamless Infrastructures" (2007), offers the language necessary to describe how this weak correlation between perception and ability is masked by such "seamless infrastructures" (24). Users develop, says Ratto, a false sense of proficiency, while not yet possessing the critical vocabulary to describe the technology that supports contemporary culture. To begin this critical exchange with "seamful" infrastructures (23), students must first glimpse the dependent systems that support their daily experiences with technology and witness them fail.

As education becomes more social and more public, we must also be aware of how many students have been raised on standardized testing and have a habituated respect for strict numerical measures of teaching and learning; they may be dubious about a new discipline's embrace of experimentation and, as Lisa Spiro describes it, "failure in the pursuit of innovation" (29). Stephen Ramsay's "hermeneutics of screwing around" may even, despite the validity of his broader reworking of critical methods, have the potential to cause students to underestimate the rigor and value of a potential major feature in many DH classes. When their primary experience of software comes in the form of sleek and seamless mobile apps, some students are simply unimpressed by "the digital" as such. Digital technology is an everyday reality and is not a debate; digital technology is productive when it works and is not productive when it fails. The main hindrance for digital humanities in an undergraduate context may well be the term *digital humanities*. Ryan Cordell describes in "How Not to Teach Digital Humanities" a highly suspicious and resistant student body that does not share the sense of growing optimism that digital humanities promises: "Undergraduate students do not care about digital humanities. And their disinterest is right and even salutary because what I really mean is that undergraduates don't care about DH qua DH." When discovering the metadiscourse on digital humanities in their university classrooms, students are confronted with a range of seemingly esoteric debates that are simply too far removed from the common concerns facing undergraduates. A collection of the most influential examples of this genre of DH scholarship has been assembled by Melissa Terras, Julianne Nyhan, and Edward Vanhoutte in *Defining Digital Humanities* (2013). The breadth of these essays demonstrates how digital humanities has taken on much larger discussions about disciplinarity, institutional reform, and tenure alongside strictly literary, historical, or philosophical issues. Undergraduates are only beginning to learn how to participate in scholarly dialogue and are often unwilling to petition for new methods or institutions until they experience the problems with the established norms. If the ubiquitous "digital" adjective is to be jettisoned, as some have argued (Pannapacker; Hall; Liu), I suspect the final inspiration will come from the healthy skepticism of undergraduates.

ALOOF TO DIGITAL HUMANITIES

Digital humanities practitioners are very forthcoming about the need to bridge successes in research with an effective pedagogy. Luke Walter remarks that "current work in the digital humanities . . . values research and scholarship far more than teaching, learning, and curriculum development" (338). Stephen Brier adds that "teaching and learning are something of an afterthought for many DHers" (390–391). Alvarado even goes so far as to say that "the hard core of DH has always been aloof to teaching." Is it any surprise that students would be aloof to digital humanities? Social media represents a particularly contentious site. Digital humanists have long shown a preference for Twitter for social academic sharing and networking. Dan Cohen has continued to maintain a "Comprehensive list of scholars in digital humanities" on Twitter, which allows the community to self-identify and coalesce around the term "digital humanities." The journal *Hybrid Pedagogy* has reflected at length on this preference for Twitter in scholarly communication and teaching (Kim; Rorabaugh; Strommel). There is an existential connection between Twitter and DH. However, student preferences for social media platforms are often confirmed by hundreds or thousands of hours of direct experience. We can expect our students to have an expert-level knowledge of social media before entering the classroom, and we often expect students to be enthusiastic to use this knowledge for credit. However, platform-specific understanding of usability does not always transfer, which can be frustrating for students accustomed to seamlessness (DeAndrea *et al.*). Recently, the Educause report "Study of Undergraduate Students and Information Technology, 2014" found that 73 per cent of students want to keep their academic and social lives separate online, and half of those students have had a poor experience of social media in an educational context (Dahlstrom and Bichsel 11). "Platform studies" has emerged as a sub-genre within new media studies as a way to articulate the "connection between technical specifics and culture" (Bogost and Montfort 12). This connection has become strained for a generation pestered with messages of digital literacy throughout grade school and chastised for being dependent on smartphones. Students associate their experience of social media, in the form of blogging or message board discussion, as a direct extension of their highly cultivated social media identity. To link this emotional and social investment to a new kind of "social scholarship" (Greenhow and Gleason) requires participation and involvement on a similarly personal level. Students must be knowledge stakeholders and feel that their participation has tangible benefits to their academic performance. Without this emotional and professional involvement, DH might be misinterpreted as just another departure from the rigorous education based on thoughtful insights and close reading that our students are so earnestly seeking. The problem then becomes scaling this deep sense of involvement across an entire undergraduate degree.

Many students are all too aware that our twenty-first-century media environment is increasingly dominated by digital technology and that technological literacy is now necessary to live a full and well-connected life. The humanities have long been tasked with finding new ways to understand and interpret the human condition. The means by which humanists continue this work are being shaped by our rapidly evolving technological context. When literary scholars make decisions about teaching a literary period or a national literature – or when historians make decisions about social and political movements that have shaped decades and centuries – they too are taking a bet on the ideas and skills that will matter in the future. The problem educators face in the twenty-first century is the problem of speed. Computational development has simply outstripped the speed of institutional and curricular renewal. The durability of DH will require that students become comfortable with what Julia Flanders calls "the productive unease" of constantly learning and applying new technologies (12).

Writing is, of course, the prime example of such a technology. Students in the humanities have become very comfortable struggling to perfect their writing, and humanities disciplines have become synonymous with the claim that the academic essay is a genre worthy of years of practice. If writing remains the core technology of humanists, as Geoffrey Rockwell and Stephen Ramsey argue in *Debates in the Digital Humanities*, educators must be careful not to lose sight of the *trivium* of the liberal arts: namely grammar, rhetoric, and logic. It is necessary to strike a balance between technical training with computers, while still reifying writing as the primary humanistic art. Alan Galey and Stan Ruecker's foundational essay, "How a Prototype Argues" (2010), describes DH scholarly inquiry as being grounded in an ethos of "thinking through making" (407). When this ethos is applied in an undergraduate teaching context, students become engaged in experiential and process-based learning. When a student is learning through making, doing is believing. However, all this tinkering is useful only when equally balanced with the critical faculties needed to describe and make humanistic arguments. Jerome McGann's words in *Radiant Textuality* (2001) remain prescient to this day: "The next generation of literary and aesthetic theorists who will most matter are people who will be at least as involved with making things as with writing texts" (19).

PROJECT-BASED PEDAGOGY

The need for collaborative and interdisciplinary methods requires a similar shift in the basic form of scholarly practice for students. As Christopher Blackwell and Thomas R. Martin remind us, the humanities have long relied on the academic essay as a form of scholarly training and skill development. The scholarly article is, they argue, a poor medium to mobilize undergraduate research because achieving originality is so often unattainable and the result is "a 'diluted' version of professional scholarship" (5). The digital humanities project must emerge as an additional unit of meaning in undergraduate scholarly practice. Tanya Clement's excellent history of digital humanities undergraduate curriculum, published in *Digital Humanities Pedagogy* (2012), identifies the need for "project based learning" in an environment in which "undergraduate students can learn to become 'builders'" ("Multiliteracies" 372). In *Digital_Humanities* (2014), Johanna Drucker *et al.* go so far as to declare "the project as a basic unit" of digital humanities scholarship (124). It is well known that large digital projects are reshaping the scale of research by requiring multidisciplinary and team-based approaches that require graduate student support (Reid), but this same model has not yet scaled well with undergraduate education. The evaluation of course-based projects that may become part of a larger public project will require layers of assessment and several rounds of student participation. Clement has also shown how evaluation remains a thorny issue for faculty and graduate students ("Half-baked" 876), but digital projects require that students can also "approximate equivalencies" to the academic essay (Drucker *et al.* 128). This emphasis on community outreach, collaboration, and creative problem-solving can be achieved by students participating directly in larger faculty-led projects.

The undergraduate digital humanities project must emphasize iterability, openness, and extensibility. These projects must be large enough to accommodate an entire class or even generations of cohorts. Research goals must be tokenized into assignment-like tasks that can be repeated and integrated into an aggregated whole, while also fulfilling curricular goals and maintaining appropriate attribution. The "recipe" model described by Stéfan Sinclair and Geoffrey Rockwell allows students to use technical tools to follow an established research method, while also becoming proficient with a new skill. The contribution structure must be flexible enough to accommodate a range of media and broad enough to link a wide range of issues. If the goal is to solve a particular problem with an algorithm or refine a particular program, the project must allow for a scaffolding of attempts across many students while attributing individual contributions. If the goal is to digitize a portion of a text in XML/TEI, the project schema would need to become part of the class syllabus, and students would then be graded against their ability to generate validated documents. For both interoperability and extensibility to occur between research and teaching contexts, projects must be founded and maintained on a premise of openness and transparency that allows for individual contributions to be accounted for within a larger collective endeavor. Provided they meet the evaluation criteria necessary in the project documents, students would then have the option to enter rounds of faculty-led and student-conducted peer review and copyediting.

The benefits of such a process are abundant: students are given the opportunity to build a professional portfolio of work and showcase meaningful team-based contributions to employers. Students are able to make their course work more meaningful by imagining the potential to reach outside of the isolated scholarly tradition of honing their individual talent. These undergraduate research opportunities (UROs) must be offered regularly throughout a degree to shape an overall educational experience. There is some anecdotal evidence about the importance of UROs in DH projects already. Lindsey Thomas and Dana Solomon explain that, in the development of the NEH-funded Research Oriented Social Environment (RoSE), "We learned, quite simply, that the involvement of students in this iterative development process was integral to the project itself" (218). Science, Technology, Engineering, and Mathematics (STEM) fields have been studying the value of UROs for much longer and have a proven track record of success. In a study published in *Science*, the study's authors demonstrated a 68 per cent increase in STEM careers after participating in a URO for a year or more. Eighty-three percent of study participants described an increasing confidence in their research abilities while 29 per cent claimed to have developed a new interest in pursuing a PhD in a STEM field (Russell *et al.* 548–549). For reasons like these, faculty teaching within the Digital Media, Arts, and Technology undergraduate major have the option to align their course content and media-specific requirements to the contribution guidelines of Lab projects. The DH UROs must link course-specific skills and project methods in explicit ways that respect the needs of the project and the course objectives.

The Penn State Digital Humanities Lab at Behrend hosts several ongoing projects directed by faculty and sees a constant influx of content from classes as well as paid research assistants. The Lab has determined the following requirements for integrating UROs into undergraduate coursework: a project charter, a physical space, a virtual collaboration toolset, a flexible means of dissemination, an evaluation and peer mentorship mechanism, and a project sustainability and archiving plan. A clearly conceived project charter delineates the terms of collaboration and the relationship between faculty and student contributions. Requirements for participation are defined with regard to the role of faculty mentors as they assist students to author rigorous and scholarly contributions. The Implementing New Knowledge Environments project charter, published under a Creative Commons Attribution Non-Commercial License, has served as the basis for the collaboration statement of the projects in the Lab at Behrend ("INKE Administrative Structure" 20). The responsibilities of faculty and students are clearly defined along with authorship and licensing of contributions. *The 12th Street Project* is an example of a large-scale collaborative project that accepts submissions from students in a variety of formats. The "About" page for the project says the following:

> 12th Street collects the history, culture, and contemporary voices of those living in Erie, PA. The project takes its name from a major street in Erie that has been lined with factories and businesses throughout the region's history. We take 12th Street as a microcosm of the social, cultural, and economic forces that have shaped the region since the mid-19th century. Together we are charting the history of the region in an effort to imagine its potential futures.

The project accepts critical and historical essays in addition to creative submissions with an emphasis on sound, image, or text. Digital-humanities-based projects must be able to accept multimedia content generated from a range of courses, including those from our technically demanding course offerings in digital animation, game studies, and electronic music composition. For example, WordPress, Omeka, and Scalar are all suitable platforms for this kind of linked and open means of dissemination of digitized or born-digital content. *12th Street* uses Omeka to organize a range of content according to a growing metadata schema and presents nodes of content using the Neatline add-on. Participating classes are required to tokenize their assignments to reflect the medium-specific requirements of making a contribution. Professional Writing work-study students are then tasked with copyediting and compiling the submissions. The growth and evolution of the project are guided by the medium and content of submissions, which are determined by initial faculty direction in class and the final editing process.

There are many moving parts in an integrated teaching and research paradigm, and the faculty and student responsibilities become fluid between course and research goals. Students must see themselves as active participants in an engaged community, while also being responsible for their own academic success. Faculty must see their students as potential collaborators, while also instructing and mentoring their students through the rigors of course work. The "artful integration" of researchers with differing backgrounds and levels of experience, as Stan Ruecker and Milena Radzikowska describe, requires a detailed assessment of each cohort's skills and attitudes. However, artfully integrating these diverse skills and roles into a broader research and teaching culture allows for a responsive curriculum that shifts with the interests and abilities of students and faculty alike. Because it will be visible online, faculty will be better able to communicate a clear message to students and employers about the robust technical and cultural training available. The success of a community will be tied to an increasingly deep emotional connection to their education through direct participation in scholarly and cultural production. The so-called "soft skills" associated with a liberal education – superior oral and written communication alongside a rigorous critical and analytical sensibility – will now be supplemented with an ongoing imperative to embrace technological innovation and renewal. There has never been a contradiction between innovative methods and scholarly rigor, but new programs will be mindful to assert both in equal measure.

REFERENCES

Alvarado, Rafael. “Start Calling it Digital Liberal Arts.” *The Transducer*. 19 February 2013. Web. 26 May 2015.

Blackwell, Christopher and Thomas R. Martin. “Technology, Collaboration, and Undergraduate Research.” *Digital Humanities Quarterly* 3.1 (2009): 1–56. Web. 26 May 2015.

Bogost, Ian and Nick Montfort. “Platform Studies: Frequently Questioned Answers.” *Digital Arts and Culture Conference Proceedings* (12–15 December 2009): 12–15. Web. 26 May 2015.

Brier, Stephen. “Where’s the Pedagogy? The Role of Teaching and Learning in the Digital Humanities.” *Debates in the Digital Humanities*. Ed. Matthew K. Gold. Minneapolis: University of Minnesota Press, Print. 390–401.

Carmody, Tim and Robin Sloan. *The New Liberal Arts in Simple HTML*. Snarkmarket/Revelator Press. 2009. Web. 26 May 2015.

Clement, Tanya. “Half-baked: The State of Evaluation in the Digital Humanities.” *American Literary History* 24.4 (2012): 876–890. EBSCOhost.

Clement, Tanya. “Multiliteracies in the Undergraduate Digital Humanities Curriculum: Skills, Principles, and Habits of Mind.” *Digital Humanities Pedagogy: Practice, Principles, and Politics*. UK: Open Book Publishers, Print. 365–388.

Cordell, Ryan. “How Not to Teach Digital Humanities.” Case Western Reserve University: Fredman Center YouTube. 7 November 2014. YouTube. 26 May 2015.

Dahlstrom, Eden and Jacqueline Bichsel. “ECAR Study of Undergraduate Students and Information Technology, 2014.” Research report. Louisville, CO: ECAR (October 2014). Web. 26 May 2015.

DeAndrea, David C. *et al.* “Serious Social Media: On the Use of Social Media for Improving Students’ Adjustments to College.” *The Internet and Higher Education* 15.1 (January 2012): 15–23. Science Direct.

Drucker, Johanna *et al. Digital_Humanities*. Cambridge: MIT University Press, 2012. Print.

Flanders, Julia. “The Productive Unease of 21st-Century Digital Scholarship.” *Digital Humanities Quarterly* 3.3 (2009): 1–27. Web.

Galey, Alan and Stan Ruecker. “How a Prototype Argues.” *Literary and Linguistic Computing* 25.4 (2010): 405–424. EBSCOhost.

Greenhow, Christine, and Benjamin Gleason. “Social Scholarship: Reconsidering Scholarly Practices in the Age of Social Media.” *British Journal of Educational Technology* 45.3 (2014): 392–402

Hall, Gary. “There are No Digital Humanities.” *Debates in the Digital Humanities*. Ed. Matthew K. Gold. Minneapolis: University of Minnesota Press, Print. 133–136.

Kim, Dorothy. “The Rules of Twitter.” *Hybrid Pedagogy* (December 2014). Web. 26 May 2015.

Kirschenbaum, Matthew. “Robin Sloan’s Mr. Penumbra’s 24 Hour Bookstore is Quite Likely the First Novel of the Digital Humanities.” 26 Nov 2012, 6:56 a.m. Tweet.

Kirschenbaum, Matthew. “What Is Digital Humanities and What’s It Doing in English Departments?” *ADE Bulletin* 150 (2010): 1–7. Web.

Liu, Alan. "The State of the Digital Humanities: A Report and a Critique." *Arts and Humanities in Higher Education*. (December 2011): 1–34. Sage.

McGann, Jerome. *Radiant Textuality: Literature After the World Wide Web*. New York: Palgrave, 2001. Print.

Nowviskie, Bethany. "Too Small to Fail." nowviskie.org Web. 26 May 2015. http://nowviskie.org/2012/too-small-to-fail/

Pannapacker, William. "Stop Calling It 'Digital Humanities': And 9 Other Strategies to Help Liberal-arts Colleges Join the Movement." *The Chronicle of Higher Education*. 18 February 2013. Web. 26 May 2015.

Ramsay, Stephen. "The Hermeneutics of Screwing Around; or What You Do with a Million Books." *Pastplay: Teaching and Learning History with Technology*. Ed. Kevin Kee. Ann Arbor: University of Michigan Libraries, Web: 111–172. 26 May 2015.

Ratto, Matt. "Ethics of Seamless infrastructures: Resources and Future Directions." *International Review of Information Ethics* 8 (December 2007): 20–27. Web.

Reid, Alexander. "Graduate Education and the Ethics of the Digital Humanities." *Debates in the Digital Humanities*. Ed. Matthew K. Gold. Minneapolis: University of Minnesota Press, Print. 350–367.

Rorabaugh, Pete. "Twitter Theory and the Public Scholar." *Hybrid Pedagogy*. March 2012. Web. 26 May 2015.

Ruecker, Stan and Milena Radzikowska. "The Iterative Design of a Project Charter for Interdisciplinary Research." *Proceedings of the 7th ACM conference on Designing interactive systems (DIS '08)*. ACM, New York, Web. 26 May 2015.

Russell, Susan H., Mary P. Hancock, and James McCullough. "Benefits of Undergraduate Research Experiences." *Science* 316 (2007): 548–549.

Siemens, Lynnes, Raymond G. Siemens, Richard Cunningham, Teresa Dobson, Alan Galey, Stan Ruecker and Claire Warwick. "INKE Administrative Structure, Omnibus Document." *Scholarly and Research Communication* 3.1 (2012): 1–21. Web.

Sinclair, Stéfan and Geoffrey Rockwell. "Teaching Computer-Assisted Text Analysis: Approaches to Learning New Methodologies." *Digital Humanities Pedagogy: Practice, Principles, and Politics*. UK: Open Book Publishers, Print.

Snedden, David. "What of Liberal Education?" *The Atlantic Monthly* (January 1912): 111–117. Web. 26 May 2015.

Spiro, Lisa. "'This Is Why We Fight': Defining the Values of the Digital Humanities." *Debates in the Digital Humanities*. Ed. Matthew K. Gold. Minneapolis: University of Minnesota Press, Print. 16–340.

Strommel, Jesse. "The Twitter Essay." *Hybrid Pedagogy* (January 2012). Web. 26 May 2015.

Terras, Melissa, Julianne Nyhan, and Edward Vanhoutte. *Defining Digital Humanities: A Reader*. Burlington: Ashgate, 2013. Print.

Thomas, Lindsay and Dana Solomon. "Active Users: Project Development and Digital Humanities Pedagogy." *CEA Critic* 76.2 (July 2014): 211–220. Project Muse.

Underwood, Ted. "How Much DH can you Fit in a Literature Department?" *The Stone and the Shell*. Web. 26 May 2015.

CHAPTER 23

Dissemination as cultivation

Scholarly communications in a digital age

James O'Sullivan, Christopher P. Long and Mark A. Mattson

INDIVIDUAL VOICES IN PARTICIPATORY SPACES

Participatory web platforms have greatly enhanced the means by which students, scholars, and practitioners engage in arts and humanities research. Intuitive interfaces and content delivery systems have brought about paradigm shifts in the ways in which scholars connect and communicate, removing the need for advanced technical expertise when conducting a range of scholarly activities. Collaborative networks of both research and communications are now facilitated across ubiquitous systems that interact to form a transdisciplinary and dynamic interconnection of thought and practice. This chapter introduces readers to the underlying principles of scholarly communications and publishing in the digital age, uncovering the affordances and limitations of online public scholarship. The relationship between form and content is discussed, drawing upon relevant case studies to demonstrate how scholars should consider cultivating the habits and practices of thick collegiality. From here, an overview of relevant platforms is offered, before strategies for social media are detailed, all of which are supplemented by this chapter's corresponding electronic materials.

At the heart of scholarly communication in the digital age is the notion of "open access," which as Martin Paul Eve notes, began as "little more than a quiet murmur in the niche scientific sub-disciplines," but is now something of a "globally mandated revolution" (1). Scholars now have a platform through which they can disseminate their work across a broad public audience, harnessing participatory models so as to enhance both their process and product with a variety of social components. Openness is fast becoming the defining trait of scholarly transmission, but as the humanities become increasingly public, we must be mindful of the need to protect the core principles of our discipline.

The revolution of which Eve speaks is just that – this is not merely an evolution, for a tension still exists between scholars who wish to see the status quo maintained and those who wish to explode pre-existing academic structures. That is not to say that digital advocates do not cherish the codex, but a willingness to adopt more varied forms and content is not as pervasive as one might think. The network of asymmetric knowledge exchange afforded by platforms such as Twitter is being harnessed by the digital humanities, but as Matthew Kirschenbaum outlines – drawing from Amanda French and Jennifer Howard – the centrality of the tweet to the DH community far surpasses that of the broader arts and humanities. Social media are not just venues for promotion; they are the instruments that have allowed a community to emerge from what Matthew K. Gold has aptly termed the "DH moment," the mechanisms through which our disciplinarily has evolved into a cohort:

> Twitter, along with blogs and other online outlets, has inscribed the digital humanities as a network topology, that is to say lines drawn by aggregates of affinities, formally and functionally manifest in who follows whom, who friends whom, who tweets whom, and who links to what. (Kirschenbaum)

Where the aforementioned have argued the importance of social media to scholarly communities, the emergence of such is effectively an offshoot of openness, which is, as already noted, the central tenant of digital dissemination.

When we speak of openness, it is not just a case of liberating publications of economic barriers, it is about sharing, in the broadest sense: social media present scholars with an opportunity to share knowledge, in all of its various forms, be that a 140-character epiphany, or a 6,000-word peer-reviewed research article on an esoteric subject matter. Be it tweeting, blogging, or otherwise, the Web provides a home for ideas that, while not quite developed to the point where they are suitable for peer-reviewed venues, deserve more than a place in the graveyard of one's filesystem:

> Blogging has brought new vitality to a folder full of work that otherwise would have remained stagnant on my computer, in a folder that by all rights I should have titled "Phantom Zone" (after *Superman II*) – given the hours of research and academic labour that I'd cast in there never to see the light of day again. (Gaertner)

Melissa Terras goes further and demonstrates the direct impact of such platforms on the dissemination of peer-reviewed scholarship. For Terras, discovery can be achieved through adherence to a simple formula: "If (social media interaction is often) then (open access + social media = increased downloads)."

Yet, harnessing the digital for the purposes of scholarly communications must be critical and robust, and conscious of the many constraints that one encounters – often covertly – when interacting with a particular technology. Kathleen Fitzpatrick, referencing Jay David Bolter, aptly states: "Social and institutional structures develop new technologies to serve their purposes, but the design of those technologies can have effects that are often unforeseen" (54). Academics, as educators and public servants, have a duty to explore the scholarly potential offered through the many new publishing mechanisms presented by contemporaneity's obsession with mass communications, but remain responsible for ensuring that, where the process might change, the product, even when re-envisioned, retains its scholarly value. Value is essential, and the retention of that value is the responsibility of scholars, and we use "scholars" in the broadest sense of the term. Publishing is an inherent part of our identity as academics, in that it is the mechanism through which we give voice to ideas, and ideas are the currency of our field. A transformation in distribution means a transformation in reception (see Davidson, for example), so we must be conscious of any repercussions that might accompany shifts in disseminative and communicative trends.

The need for possessing an awareness of the consequences of any such shift goes beyond the inherent issues in the reinvention of those processes by which we facilitate the transfer of knowledge – even the criteria by which we select new mechanisms can be problematic. Typically, platforms achieve disciplinary adoption through barometers such as intuitiveness and sustainability, but we must also account for the inherent biases in any product. One such issue is raised by Dorothy Kim in her timely piece, "Social Media and Academic Surveillance," who accepts that Twitter is "a multivalent, rhizomatic platform with voices that form communities," but warns against the potential for this "panopticon"-like structure becoming a source of data. The excuse that "Twitter is public," she argues, is insufficient justification for academics using the "digital bodies" that constitute this space as "data points or experimental cells in a petri dish." As a community of scholars, we encourage, and indeed, at gatherings such as the Digital Humanites Summer Institute, even teach, the use of social media for the purposes of scholarly communications and dissemination. If we are to continue this trend, we must be as mindful of the dangers as we are of the opportunities, being as critical of the screen as we have been of the page, so that the repercussions of any transformation in the transaction between creator and receiver are fully comprehended and expressed.

FORM MATTERS AS MATTER INFORMS

The question of the relationship between form and content lies at the most ancient roots of the humanities. The dactylic hexameter through which ancient rhapsodies told and developed what has been handed down as Homer's *Iliad* and *Odyssey* determined the content of the stories and provided the structure by which finite human memory could preserve them. The aphorisms of Heraclitus were not empty obscurantism, but an attempt to give voice to the enigmatic nature of human existence. The dialogues of Plato were not simply ways to dress up dry pedantic arguments, but a recognition that the attempt to seek wisdom and justice is always bound up with lived relationships within a community.

Despite all of this, of course, there is a tendency, as ancient as the examples just mentioned, to prioritize form over matter, structure over content. This tendency can already be heard in book two of Aristotle's *Physics* where form, *eidos*, the look of a thing, is identified with its nature, and the four causes are reduced to two, with "form" encompassing the "first," "formal," and "final" causes.[1] Even in a text as seminal and influential as Aristotle's *Physics*, form does not reign supreme; for matter does not succumb to its authority. And there is good reason for this: form matters, and matter informs. The one cannot be reduced to the other, nor can a privileging of one be permitted to eclipse the power of the other – meaning itself is the dynamic interplay of the two.

The great affordance of the digital humanities as an endeavor is the opportunity to engage this dynamic relationship between form and matter in sophisticated ways that open new insights into their capacity to make meaning. Every attempt to craft a meaningful life, be it through art or science, engineering or agriculture, is caught up in the complex relationship between form and matter, so the opportunity to engage it in a substantive way is not the exclusive purview of this field. And yet, the emergence of new, more dynamic and public modes of digital communication requires us to think critically about and reflect imaginatively on the manner in which form matters, and matter informs.

One area of digital humanities scholarship that has taken up this issue in substantive and potentially transformative ways is that of digital scholarly communications. This makes sense, of course, because the dynamics of scholarship and communication have been substantively altered by the emergence of digital technology that enables academic content to be easily and widely shared. This has brought to the forefront an area of scholarship focused on the affordances and limitations of the technologies of scholarship and scholarly communication. This field is not new – it can arguably be traced back to the debates between Plato and Isocrates about the value of rhetoric and its relationship to philosophy, and it certainly was at the root of the rich explosion of scholarly communication in the Middle Ages. Still, scholars such as Fitzpatrick and N. Katherine Hayles have brought new energy to the question, raising important concerns about and suggesting the transformative possibilities of what Clay Shirky has termed the "publish then filter" model (98).

Indeed, at its root, the emerging emphasis on design in the digital humanities indicates that scholars are increasingly concerned with and interested in the dynamic and complex relationship between form and matter as it is recast in a digital age. For example, Cheryl Ball and Douglas Eyman rightly understand design as rhetoric, reminding us that style "is an integral element of all rhetorical communication, and the question is not whether we want style or substantive but what kind of style we want to deploy as a component of substance" (68). The ancient emphasis on the rhetorical importance of *tropos*, the manner in which something is expressed, is rooted in the recognition that style is rhetoric. However, when Ball and Eyman insist that design is an "enactment of rhetorical practice" (68), they are highlighting the performative dimension of all communication.

Scholarship has always been performance. From the earliest conversations in which an idea germinates, to the conference presentations through which professional scholarship has, for the past few hundred years, been developed, to the genres through which new work is published, scholarship is performative. What has changed is that the advent of the web marked a qualitative leap in the nature of performative scholarship. No longer are ideas limited by space and accessibility; rather, they are, in principle at least, public in a wider sense than has heretofore been possible and at a scale that is difficult to comprehend.

New affordances in dynamic modes of digital scholarly communications have enabled authors to tailor the content of their texts to the forms in which they appear in public. The diversity of ways it is now possible to perform the argument for a text in its mode of digital publication is one of the most exciting dimensions of digital scholarship. This is not least because of the manner in which it blurs the traditional boundary between theory and practice in order to more explicitly allow practice to be animated by theory, and theory embodied by practice. The rigid distinction between theory and practice has long permitted authors to write one thing and live another. The boundary has in this way opened a space for hypocrisy that scholars have too often been tempted to exploit for their own expedience. Performative publishing requires authors to reflect upon how their arguments and ideas are best set into action. If publication is the manner in which ideas become effective in the world, publishing has always been a kind of performance.

Whatever else the emergence of digital modes of communication inhibits or enables, it opens unforeseen new opportunities for scholars to collaborate and to engage a wide public. Publication here becomes more explicitly what it has always been: a way of creating publics (Joy 13). If, however, we take the community-creating capacity of publishing seriously, we need to cultivate habits and practices that enable us to establish and nourish scholarly publics that enrich the relationships and expand the scholarship at its root. As a practice of community building, the practices of digital publishing need to attend to the cultivating of certain habits, what the ancients called virtues: excellences. These are ways of relating to one another that enrich the world and open new possibilities of connection.

As part of their Mellon-funded project to create the *Public Philosophy Journal* as an ecosystem of scholarly community and communication, Mark Fisher and Christopher P. Long have sought to articulate a thick conception of collegiality capable of creating a rich and enriching community of scholarship online. As one would expect, there has been no end to appeals to collegiality in discussions of online communication and behavior. Such appeals, often in the name of increased "civility," amount to little more than an attempt to police what is and is not legitimate to say and, more significantly, which voices are and are not legitimately to be included in the conversation. Often this insistence is couched in terms of "tone" and invoked to exclude or undermine the authority of a particular position. The "collegiality" to which such rhetoric appeals is thin: it is neither rooted in a relation of mutual respect nor animated by a shared endeavor.

The thick spirit of collegiality that the *Public Philosophy Journal* ecosystem of scholarly communication seeks to cultivate takes its cue from the etymology of the word itself. "Collegiality" comes from the Latin *collēga*, one chosen along with another, a partner in office, etc. It derives from the prefix, "*col-*," together and "*legĕre*," to choose. In the context of DH performative publishing, what is together chosen is the shared attempt to develop and improve the scholarly artifacts under consideration, be they written articles, video documentaries, podcasts, or other modes of scholarly expression.

To paraphrase Aristotle, one comment or one review does not thick collegiality make. Collegiality thickens over time as partners choose one another again and again in their shared endeavor to create something rich in meaning. The challenge, of course, is how to cultivate the thickening of collegiality in a digital environment that often seems to reward the snarky witticism over the thoughtful, well-formulated critique that pushes the work to new, more interesting, and richer depths. Thick collegiality might best be rooted in three dimensions of scholarly encounter:

1. hermeneutic empathy: the ability to accurately describe what animates the scholarship under review;
2. hermeneutic generosity: the willingness to invest expertise, experience, insight, and ideas to improving the scholarship under review;
3. hermeneutic transformation: the ability to engage the community in ways that enrich the scholarship we are producing together.

Drawing on the important work done by the team at ELI Review to create a helpfulness score in peer assessment at the undergraduate level, the *Public Philosophy Journal* is developing ways to computationally identify phrases and formulations that signal that one or another of these dimensions of thick collegiality is at play in a given review or comment. When the machines identify moments of possible collegiality, human members of the community can focus their attention on those sites of exchange, bringing their own judgment to bear on the dynamics of the interaction.

Cultivating the habits and practices of thick collegiality is made more difficult when the institutional context in which DH scholars are evaluated and rewarded do not adequately consider or recognize the significance of the scholarship that unfolds in the dynamic online interactions described here. Traditional humanities scholarship has long been willing to turn a blind eye to the important scholarship that unfolds in the blind peer-review process.[2] By making that work more public and by cultivating the habits and practices that enable us to do it well, DH publishing should be able both to document effectively the quality of the work being done, but also, to enrich the community of scholars doing the work.

INNOVATIVE FORMATS WITH A FAMILIAR FEEL

The emerging frameworks for knowledge sharing that inform humanistic modes of dissemination in the digital age may, upon initial examination, appear foreign, but once users become acclimated to the new formats, the traditional pillars of scholarly communication at the foundation of these frameworks provide a sense of the familiar. The traditional facets of scholarly communication – publishing, peer-review, discovery, and professional networks – have all moved, in their own ways, into the digital sphere and have been expanded upon and shaped by new digital modes; still, the virtues and principles of these constants remain intact. Scholars in the digital world continue to seek the most relevant resources, the effective dissemination of knowledge, the most strategic avenues for building and maintaining scholarly prestige, and the most advantageous methods for connecting and collaborating with their colleagues. With this in mind, then, the consideration of several of the most prevalent new platforms, networks, and organizations which enable the emerging knowledge-sharing frameworks becomes more accessible.

Perhaps the most intuitive transition into the digital world of scholarly communications is in the transformation of the proven mechanisms of scholarly publishing; journals, monographs, and published conference proceedings. A 2013 study by the University of Tennessee and the CIBER Research Group found that "peer reviewed journals were the most trusted source [of scholarly material] by a huge margin" (Tenopir *et al.*); this, when coupled with the fact that access to journals has largely moved into the digital realm, suggests that the shift in the mode of transmission from "traditional" to digital has not diminished their utility. In their digital form, these publishing tools have both the familiar look and feel that mimics the pre-digital world, while also enabling previously unimaginable possibilities. The ability to embed accompanying media and data into a digital text, along with the ability to link out to other relevant additional resources, while allowing the reader's active participation, has led to exciting and innovative scholarly publishing projects.

There exist myriad platforms and systems for the creation and dissemination of traditional scholarly communication tools in the digital space; far more than can be mentioned in a single chapter. Accordingly, it is important that the needs of any project are fully considered when choosing a digital solution. Some of the more common tools for online journal and conference proceedings publishing are Open Journal Systems, Bepress, WordPress, and Open Conference Systems. All of these platforms provide a system on which to digitally publish the cumulative work of multiple contributors and manage the editorial workflow, which are hallmarks of the academic journal. Each platform allows for embedded media, linked supplemental material, and audience engagement through open or moderated commenting. These systems provide both the editorial back-end system and the user-facing "performance" side of the publication.

Monograph publications in the electronic world provide a much broader spectrum of creative possibilities including, but not limited to, multi-linear constructions, multimedia-infused narratives, and interactive-collaborative creations of text. Consequently, the digital-solutions environment provided by both the commercial and free open-source markets is considerably more varied and complex. Each digital tool provides a host of potential benefits and drawbacks, and once again, no single tool can be applied as the solution for every project. Representative of this type of digital solution is The Alliance for Networking Visual Culture's Scalar platform ("About Scalar"). Scalar is billed as:

> a free, open-source authoring and publishing platform that [is] designed to make it easy for authors to write long-form, born-digital scholarship online . . . [and] gives authors tools to structure essay- and book-length works in ways that take advantage of the unique capabilities of digital writing, including nested, recursive, and non-linear formats.

The platform showcases the innovative and creative possibilities that digital publishing can facilitate when traditional publishing tools are re-imagined and reconfigured.

Moving down the spectrum from the well-established and relatively secure positioning of traditional peer-reviewed scholarly communication tools in their digital form, digital self-publishing is undergoing its own redefinition. The anathema of any serious scholar in the pre-digital age, self-publishing has become a prolific, if not respected, form of scholarly communication in the digital era in the form of blogs, whatever form that practice might take. Thanks to the collaborative and interactive nature of digital publishing, the peer-review process, once the key distinction between academic publishing and disdainful self-publishing, has found its place within the self-publishing infrastructure. If appropriately implemented, commenting and other facilities for interaction can now allow for a robust and public peer-review process, and in many cases, even facilitate productive public debate. In a sense, it is scholarship 2.0.

Blogging, vlogging, and microblogging platforms share a common purpose in allowing users to communicate ideas to their targeted audience and to engage readers in public dialogue. While not dedicated exclusively to scholarly communication, popular web tools such as WordPress, Blogger, and Twitter have become important scholarly tools not only in the dissemination of knowledge but also in the creation of digital spaces for fruitful discussion, which may lead to new insights and conclusions. Unlike traditional dissemination formats such as journals, digital self-publishing benefits from expediency and, by its very nature, a more transparent peer-review process. Most of the self-publishing platforms and services available today are developed to be user-friendly and convenient; however, as mentioned, in order to realize the full potential of digital self-publishing, it is important to understand how the careful selection and/or construction of a platform can shape and influence the resulting discourse.

Another recent digital innovation related to self-publishing is the proliferation of online digital repositories. Often sponsored by an institution or group of institutions, online digital repositories provide scholars with an additional venue for self-publishing scholarly works and offer the possibility of making open access versions of traditionally published works available. Institutional repositories, such as Penn State's ScholarSphere, and subject-specific repositories such as ArXiv, provide both a venue for self-publication and a point of discovery for researchers. By allowing for sufficient public peer-oversight through feedback and commenting mechanisms, online repositories can be of critical importance to research communities in that they facilitate the sharing of large complex data sets, a facet of the publishing process which was often more unwieldy or less timely with traditional publishing tools. The development of these repositories may be, in part, a response to the proliferation of mandates issued by funding bodies which require open access to resulting publications as well as its associated data. Some examples of these types of mandates and policies are those of the National Institute of Health in the United States, the Indian Council of Agriculture, the Research Council of Norway, the Canadian Cancer Society, the National Natural Science Foundation of China, the European Research Council, UNESCO, the Australian Research Council, and the Bill and Melinda Gates Foundation.[3]

Similar to the significant shift in modes and dissemination in self-publishing, the introduction of digital instruments into academia has had an unprecedented impact on the degree to which scholars are able to network and collaborate. The larger trend of digital technology's impact on the interpersonal interactions within society is mirrored in academic circles in that it easily accommodates inter-institutional, international, and interdisciplinary networking. It is worth remembering, however, that "ease" is a relative term, and that we must be mindful of cultural contexts where such technical affordances are not so readily available. Most of the traditional scholarly networks such as scholarly societies, institutional networks, annual conferences, and discourses facilitated through print publications have, at least in some aspects, considered the creation of a digital presence; consequently, new scholarly infrastructural frameworks have been developed as a result of employing digital tools in publishing.

New scholarly digital networking tools such as ORCID, LinkedIN, Academia.edu, Zotero, and ResearchGate are competing with non-specialized tools such as Facebook, Google+, and Twitter to become the digital "home" of scholars and those interested in their scholarly output. In reality, a dynamic mix of digital solutions is being used by modern scholars to supplement traditional scholarly networking infrastructure. The main difference between new digital structures and traditional constructs is to be found in their scope and rate of dissemination. In the digital network, the scope becomes global and the rate of dissemination accelerates exponentially. This is not to say that the organizations and establishments which make up the traditional infrastructure are now obsolete; rather, many such institutions have taken advantage of recent networking technologies and incorporated them into their culture, utilizing tools from listservs and Twitter to web conferencing and podcasts.

Having reviewed some of the most prevalent new platforms, networks, and organizations which enable emerging frameworks for knowledge sharing, it is clear that the virtues and essences of the traditional facets of scholarly communication – publishing, peer-review, discovery, and professional networks – remain intact in the digital era. Likewise, the institutions and organizations which have long supported the infrastructure that supports scholarly communications – libraries, presses, researchers, funding agencies, and scholarly societies – have not been replaced by digital technologies and tools, but have instead adapted to the new reality of scholarly communication and continue to play their crucial cultural, pragmatic, and economic roles. In today's digitally oriented environment, scholars are not entering into a strange new territory devoid of familiar landmarks, but instead moving through a well-worn and familiar landscape which happens to be rapidly evolving. As the traditional blends with the technical in the publishing world, academia continues to evolve as it questions and explores the benefits that digital technologies bring, and the scholarly process and its associated ecosystem.

SCHOLARLY STRATEGIES FOR SOCIAL MEDIA

It is strange to think that almost a decade has passed since Aimée Morrison defined the blog as "a relatively new genre in digital literary studies." Even stranger is the fact that there was a time when blogging was considered "a relatively new" practice. Morrison's remarks from 2008 have never been more cogent. She notes that the "landscape of blogging is changing rapidly as new users come to write and read in this medium," pre-empting much of the commentary that has been offered in recent years:

> Academic bloggers face . . . personal and professional pressures when they blog, but are drawn to the form for compelling reasons, among them the opportunities to network with scholars they might not otherwise meet, to avoid academic isolation if theirs is an arcane subspecialty, to test new ideas on a willing expert audience in an informal manner, to ask for help from this same audience, and to keep abreast of colleagues and research.

The pressures to which Morrison refers are sometimes institutional in origin, with the merits of public scholarship often dismissed by promotion boards; but they can also be personal, as for many academics, the idea of making public a treatise or thought process that has not undergone the validation of peer-review can be a frightening experience. But if scholars are to avail of digital scholarly communications for the benefit of their work – be that in blogging or otherwise – then they must face up to this fear by familiarizing themselves with the technologies and strategies necessary to accomplish the potentialities outlined by Morrison.

As discussed earlier, dissemination as cultivation, in essence, is a matter of striking the right balance between form and content. Typically, the content is something with which most scholars will be more familiar, as that rarely undergoes much by way of evolution, though digital materials should strive to be media-rich if they are to be compelling. As content creators – and this can be difficult for people who have written on a paper surface throughout the entirety of their careers – scholars must not seek to impose the restrictions of the pre-digital upon the screen. Digital scholarly communications should adhere to the same values as any critical argument. The very nature of the form is such that the readership will most likely be broader, so there is a case to present information in as compelling and intuitive a manner as possible. Doing so is not about aspiring to popular acclaim, but rather, about ensuring that voices have clarity in an environment where there is often more noise than there is knowledge. Clarity does not necessarily mean readership, but for scholars, market saturation is not the objective – the aim is to penetrate a community of like-minded scholars, practitioners, and enthusiasts, whatever the size of that community.

Everything you disseminate should be a reflection of your identity as an academic – if anything else, digital platforms are an opportunity to tell your own research story. In this respect, content is not just about clicks, it is about taking control of your scholarly profile. By failing to do so, as Kelli Marshall warns, "you are allowing Google, Yahoo, and Bing to create your identity for you." In this respect, Marshall offers a sound framework for cultivation:

1 Take control.
2 Build a network.
3 Practice uniformity.
4 Monitor yourself.

Scholars should seek to direct search engines to relevant and compelling content that is frequently maintained; visible to their students and peers; ideologically, biographically, and professionally consistent; and conscious of the public space in which it resides.

There are also rules which, while not enforced, should be respected. Oftentimes, the academic context will be pedagogical, and when such is the case, the stakes are only higher (see Kim, "The Rules of Twitter"). But rules are not only concerned with ethics; there are conventions with which one must conform, and scholars should familiarize themselves with these conventions before adopting a platform. This is not just about ensuring the appropriate citation of fellow tweeters; it is about ensuring the use of hashtags to disseminate and propagate content; using handles in a manner that will allow the community to efficiently begin, enter, and expand conversations.

Form can present more of a barrier to users looking to bring those trends found across the digital humanities to bear upon their own research and scholarly communications. The issue one is faced with is the same issue that was present when consolidation of our field was still very much in its infancy: "Different media serve different content types more or less effectively; it's important to recognize what a medium is best suited for" (Jensen). Overcoming this challenge involves gaining familiarity with multiple technologies, but most tools are now sufficiently intuitive so as to allow non-technical individuals to develop the necessary competencies. Identifying a form appropriate to the content in question is a matter of recognizing the implementation potential of any platform. Blogging, for example, is a practice, not a platform, and offerings such as WordPress are not simply blogging software, but rather, content management systems which can be adapted to a range of purposes, whether that be hosting blog posts, or developing a fully fledged scholarly profile or digital project. The flexibility that one finds in open-source platforms is such that the chief concern is no longer functionality, but rather, usability and support. Adopters need to account for system requirements and institutional restrictions, and in the case of open-source software, the size of the community from which they can draw support.

In essence, bringing scholarship into the public realm via digital means is about awareness – awareness of the affordances, limitations, and repercussions of juxtaposing technology with those critical and creative practices so crucial to the arts and humanities. The importance of the latter should not be diluted by the former, in that technology should always be harnessed *in support* of the human; it should enable rather than dictate our purpose as scholars and practitioners of disciplines which are conscious of the cultural, the critical and creative. Potential always comes at a cost, so we must be conscious of that cost, but also, willing to seek the benefits. We do not need to change what it is that we are saying; technology merely presents an opportunity to say it in new ways, to new people, drawing new responses and insights, which, in turn, create new knowledge. The transaction between reader and writer is no less significant; it has simply undergone a transformation of sorts, and it is our responsibility to oversee this transformation so that it continues to benefit those scholarly values which we have for centuries held so dear.

NOTES

1 In the *Physics*, Aristotle is concerned to articulate and identify the principles of things capable of moving and changing themselves – *ta physika*. This is the context in which the priority of form begins to emerge (see Aristotle 193b19 and 198a24–8). The more complicated and interesting story about the emergence of the priority of form is told by Long in "The Hegemony of Form and the Resistance of Matter," Graduate Faculty Philosophy Journal 21.2 (1999): 21–46.

2 For a good articulation of the importance of review as a scholarly activity and, indeed, as a teachable and learnable one, see Hart-Davidson, William, Michael McLeod, Christopher Klerkx, and Michael Wojcik, "A Method for Measuring Helpfulness in Online Peer Review" in *Proceedings of the 28th ACM International Conference on Design of Communication*, 115–121.

3 For more information about open access mandates and policies, see the Registry of Open Access Repository Mandates and Policies (ROARMAP) at roarmap.eprints.org.

REFERENCES

"About Scalar." *The Alliance for Networking Visual Culture*. N.p., n.d. Web. 8 August 2015.

Ball, Cheryl, and Douglas Eyman. "Digital Humanities Scholarship and Electronic Publication." *Rhetoric and the Digital Humanities*. Ed. William Hart-Davidson and Jim Rodolfo. Chicago: University Of Chicago Press, 2015. 65–79. Print.

Davidson, Cathy. *Now You See It: How the Brain Science of Attention Will Transform the Way We Live, Work, and Learn*. New York: Viking, 2011. Print.

Eve, Martin Paul. *Open Access and the Humanities: Contexts, Controversies and the Future*. Cambridge: Cambridge University Press, 2014. CrossRef. Web. 5 March 2015.

Fitzpatrick, Kathleen. *Planned Obsolescence: Publishing, Technology, and the Future of the Academy*. New York: NYU Press, 2011. Print.

Gaertner, David. "To Blog, or Not to Blog?: Social Media as Academic Practice." *Novel Alliances*. N.p., n.d. Web. 3 March 2015.

Jensen, Michael. "Intermediation and Its Malcontents: Validating Professionalism in the Age of Raw Dissemination." *A Companion to Digital Humanities*. Ed. Susan Schreibman, Ray Siemens, and John Unsworth. Oxford: Blackwell, 2004. Web.

Joy, Eileen. "A Time for Radical Hope." *Chiasma: A Site for Thought* 1.1 (2014): 10–23. Print.

Kim, Dorothy. "Social Media and Academic Surveillance: The Ethics of Digital Bodies." *Model View Culture*. N.p., 7 October 2014. Web. 26 August 2015.

Kim, Dorothy . "The Rules of Twitter." *Hybrid Pedagogy*. N.p., 4 December 2014. Web. 3 March 2015.

Kirschenbaum, Matthew. "What Is Digital Humanities and What's It Doing in English Departments?" *Debates in the Digital Humanities*. Ed. Matthew K. Gold. Minneapolis: University of Minnesota Press, 2012. Web.

Marshall, Kelli. "How to Curate Your Digital Identity as an Academic." *The Chronicle of Higher Education*. N.p., n.d. Web. 3 March 2015.

Morrison, Aimée. "Blogs and Blogging: Text and Practice." *A Companion to Digital Literary Studies*. Ed. Susan Schreibman and Ray Siemens. Oxford: Blackwell, 2008. Web.

Shirky, Clay. *Here Comes Everybody: The Power of Organizing Without Organizations*. New York: Penguin Press, 2008. Print.

Tenopir, Carol *et al. Trust and Authority in Scholarly Communications in the Light of the Digital Transition: Final Report*. University of Tennessee and CIBER Research Ltd, 2013. Web. 8 August 2015.

Terras, Melissa. "The Impact of Social Media on the Dissemination of Research: Results of an Experiment." *Journal of Digital Humanities* 1.3 (2012): n. pag. Web. 3 March 2015.

Index